Understanding Antitrust and Its Economic Implications

CAROLINA ACADEMIC PRESS

Understanding Series

UNDERSTANDING ADMINISTRATIVE LAW
Seventh Edition
Kristin E. Hickman

UNDERSTANDING ALTERNATIVE DISPUTE RESOLUTION,
Second Edition
Kristen M. Blankley and Maureen A. Weston

UNDERSTANDING ANIMAL LAW
Adam Karp

UNDERSTANDING ANTITRUST AND ITS ECONOMIC IMPLICATIONS
Eighth Edition
Christopher R. Leslie, E. Thomas Sullivan, and Jeffrey L. Harrison

UNDERSTANDING BANKRUPTCY
Fifth Edition
Jeffrey Ferriell and Edward J. Janger

UNDERSTANDING CALIFORNIA COMMUNITY PROPERTY LAW
Second Edition
Jo Carrillo

UNDERSTANDING CAPITAL PUNISHMENT LAW
Fifth Edition
Linda E. Carter, Ellen S. Kreitzberg, Scott W. Howe, and Celestine Richards McConville

UNDERSTANDING CIVIL PROCEDURE
Seventh Edition
Gene R. Shreve, Peter Raven-Hansen, and Charles Gardner Geyh

UNDERSTANDING CIVIL PROCEDURE
The California Edition
Walter W. Heiser, Gene R. Shreve, Peter Raven-Hansen, and Charles Gardner Geyh

UNDERSTANDING CIVIL RIGHTS LITIGATION
Third Edition
Howard M. Wasserman

UNDERSTANDING CONFLICT OF LAWS
Fourth Edition
William M. Richman, William L. Reynolds, and Chris A. Whytock

UNDERSTANDING CONSTITUTIONAL LAW
Sixth Edition
William D. Araiza

UNDERSTANDING CONTRACTS
Fifth Edition
Jeffrey Ferriell

UNDERSTANDING COPYRIGHT LAW
Eighth Edition
Marshall A. Leaffer

UNDERSTANDING CORPORATE LAW
Sixth Edition
Arthur R. Pinto and James A. Fanto

UNDERSTANDING CORPORATE TAXATION
Fifth Edition
Leandra Lederman and Emily Cauble

UNDERSTANDING CRIMINAL LAW
Ninth Edition
Joshua Dressler

UNDERSTANDING CRIMINAL PROCEDURE VOL. 1: INVESTIGATION
Eighth Edition
Joshua Dressler, Alan C. Michaels, and Ric Simmons

UNDERSTANDING CRIMINAL PROCEDURE VOL. 2: ADJUDICATION
Fifth Edition
Joshua Dressler, Alan C. Michaels. and Ric Simmons

UNDERSTANDING DISABILITY LAW
Fourth Edition
Mark C. Weber

UNDERSTANDING
ELECTION LAW AND VOTING RIGHTS
Second Edition
Michael R. Dimino, Bradley A. Smith, and Michael E. Solimine

UNDERSTANDING
EMPLOYEE BENEFITS LAW
Second Edition
Kathryn L. Moore

UNDERSTANDING
EMPLOYMENT DISCRIMINATION LAW
Fourth Edition
Thomas R. Haggard and Bruce N. Cameron

UNDERSTANDING
EMPLOYMENT LAW
Fourth Edition
Richard A. Bales, Jeffrey M. Hirsch, and Paul M. Secunda

UNDERSTANDING
ENVIRONMENTAL LAW
Fourth Edition
Kevin A. Reilly and Philip Weinberg

UNDERSTANDING
ESTATE AND GIFT TAXATION
Third Edition
Brant J. Hellwig and Robert T. Danforth

UNDERSTANDING EVIDENCE
Sixth Edition
Paul C. Giannelli and Jules Epstein

UNDERSTANDING FAMILY LAW
Fourth Edition
John Gregory, Peter N. Swisher, and Robin Wilson

UNDERSTANDING
FEDERAL AND CALIFORNIA EVIDENCE
Paul C. Giannelli

UNDERSTANDING
FEDERAL COURTS AND JURISDICTION
Second Edition
Linda Mullenix, Martin H. Redish, and Georgene Vairo

UNDERSTANDING
FEDERAL INCOME TAXATION
Seventh Edition
J. Martin Burke and Michael K. Friel

UNDERSTANDING
THE FIRST AMENDMENT
Ninth Edition
Russell L. Weaver

UNDERSTANDING
IMMIGRATION LAW
Fourth Edition
Kevin R. Johnson, Raquel Aldana, Bill Ong Hing, Leticia M. Saucedo, and Enid Trucios-Haynes

UNDERSTANDING
INSURANCE LAW
Seventh Edition
Robert H. Jerry, II and Douglas Richmond

UNDERSTANDING
INTELLECTUAL PROPERTY LAW
Fourth Edition
Tyler T. Ochoa, Shubha Ghosh, and Mary LaFrance

UNDERSTANDING
INTERNATIONAL BUSINESS AND FINANCIAL TRANSACTIONS
Fourth Edition
Jerold A. Friedland

UNDERSTANDING
INTERNATIONAL CRIMINAL LAW
Fourth Edition
Ellen S. Podgor, Roger S. Clark, and Lucian E. Dervan

UNDERSTANDING
INTERNATIONAL LAW
Third Edition
Stephen C. McCaffrey

UNDERSTANDING JEWISH LAW
Second Edition
Steven H. Resnicoff

UNDERSTANDING JUVENILE LAW
Fifth Edition
Martin Gardner

UNDERSTANDING LABOR LAW
Sixth Edition
Douglas E. Ray, Robert N. Strassfeld, and Ariana Levinson

UNDERSTANDING
THE LAW OF TERRORISM
Second Edition
Erik Luna and Wayne McCormack

UNDERSTANDING THE LAW OF ZONING AND LAND USE CONTROLS
Fourth Edition
Barlow Burke

UNDERSTANDING LAWYERS' ETHICS
Sixth Edition
Monroe H. Freedman and Abbe Smith

UNDERSTANDING LOCAL GOVERNMENT
Second Edition
Sandra Stevenson

UNDERSTANDING MODERN REAL ESTATE TRANSACTIONS
Fourth Edition
Alex M. Johnson, Jr.

UNDERSTANDING NEGOTIABLE INSTRUMENTS AND PAYMENT SYSTEMS
Second Edition
William H. Lawrence

UNDERSTANDING NONPROFIT AND TAX EXEMPT ORGANIZATIONS
Third Edition
Nicholas P. Cafardi and Jaclyn Fabean Cherry

UNDERSTANDING PARTNERSHIP AND LLC TAXATION
Fifth Edition
Jerold A. Friedland

UNDERSTANDING PATENT LAW
Fourth Edition
Amy L. Landers

UNDERSTANDING PRODUCTS LIABILITY LAW
Second Edition
Bruce L. Ottley, Rogelio A. Lasso, and Terrence F. Kiely

UNDERSTANDING PROPERTY LAW
Fifth Edition
John G. Sprankling

UNDERSTANDING REMEDIES
Fourth Edition
James M. Fischer

UNDERSTANDING SALES AND LEASES OF GOODS
Third Edition
William H. Henning, William H. Lawrence, and Henry Deeb Gabriel

UNDERSTANDING SECURED TRANSACTIONS
Sixth Edition
William H. Henning, R. Wilson Freyermuth, and Brook E. Gotberg

UNDERSTANDING SECURITIES LAW
Eighth Edition
Marc I. Steinberg

UNDERSTANDING SPORTS LAW
Timothy Davis and N. Jeremi Duru

UNDERSTANDING TAXATION OF BUSINESS ENTITIES
Second Edition
Walter D. Schwidetzky and Fred B. Brown

UNDERSTANDING TORTS
Seventh Edition
John L. Diamond, Lawrence C. Levine, and Anita Bernstein

UNDERSTANDING TRADE SECRET LAW
John G. Sprankling and Thomas G. Sprankling

UNDERSTANDING TRADEMARK LAW
Fourth Edition
Mary LaFrance

UNDERSTANDING TRUSTS AND ESTATES
Seventh Edition
Roger W. Andersen and Susan N. Gary

UNDERSTANDING WHITE COLLAR CRIME
Fifth Edition
J. Kelly Strader and Todd Haugh

Understanding Antitrust and Its Economic Implications

EIGHTH EDITION

Christopher R. Leslie
CHANCELLOR'S PROFESSOR OF LAW
UC IRVINE SCHOOL OF LAW

E. Thomas Sullivan
PRESIDENT EMERITUS
UNIVERSITY OF VERMONT
DEAN EMERITUS
UNIVERSITY OF MINNESOTA LAW SCHOOL AND
UNIVERSITY OF ARIZONA ROGERS COLLEGE OF LAW

Jeffrey L. Harrison
EMERITUS HUBER C. HURST EMINENT SCHOLAR
UNIVERSITY OF FLORIDA COLLEGE OF LAW

CAROLINA ACADEMIC PRESS
Durham, North Carolina

ISBN 978-1-5310-3126-8
eISBN 978-1-5310-3127-5

Library of Congress cataloging-in-publication data
is available at catalog.loc.gov

Carolina Academic Press
700 Kent Street
Durham, NC 27701
(919) 489-7486
www.caplaw.com

Printed in the United States of America

For Leslie and Sarah and Tony.

Contents

Preface to the Eighth Edition

For over thirty-five years and seven editions, *Understanding Antitrust and Its Economic Implications* has been the product of a collaboration between Tom Sullivan and Jeffrey Harrison. They shepherded the treatise through major changes in antitrust doctrine and philosophy. Since the publication of the Seventh Edition, both men have retired, Tom from the presidency of Vermont Law School and Jeff from his chaired professorship at the University of Florida College of Law. I am honored that they have entrusted me to take over this project.

This Eighth Edition continues the original authors' vision of providing an accurate explanation of current antitrust doctrine, while providing relevant historical and economic context, where appropriate. In particular, this new edition updates legal developments relating to refusals to deal, price squeezes, anticompetitive product design, and abuse of patents and other intellectual property rights, as well as procompetitive justifications for anticompetitive conduct. This edition also addresses important procedural and evidentiary issues relating to summary judgment standards and applications and how to prove horizontal agreements with circumstantial evidence. The most significant recent development in merger law has been the announcement of new merger guidelines by the Department of Justice and the Federal Trade Commission in December 2023. This new edition presents and details those 2023 Merger Guidelines, including how they differ from earlier merger guidelines.

This new edition is based on the structure and substance of the first seven editions, which provided a solid foundation for explaining the continued evolution of antitrust law. The new caretaker of this volume appreciates the hard work of the original authors and the confidence they have placed in him.

CHRISTOPHER R. LESLIE
Chancellor's Professor of Law
University of California Irvine School of Law

Preface to the Seventh Edition

Thirty years ago, the First Edition of *Understanding Antitrust and Its Economic Implications* appeared. At that time, a major transformation in antitrust law was well under way. Those changes included movement away from per se rules toward the rule of reason, tightening of the standards with respect to private plaintiffs eligible to bring antitrust actions, and greater emphasis on economic analysis generally, including with respect to merger standards. Since the First Edition, the trend toward narrowing the reach of the antitrust laws has continued. This narrowing has both a substantive and procedural component. It may or may not be consistent with legislative history, and it may or may not be consistent with overall welfare. That is for the reader to decide.

As in the past, this Seventh Edition attempts to offer an accurate and balanced description of the current state of antitrust law, as well as its historical foundations and the evolution of the law. Although the state of the law has remained much the same since the last edition, applications of it continue to evolve. For example, this edition discusses reverse payments, product hopping, the Supreme Court's recent assessment of two-sided platforms, and activity with respect to mergers. The effective end of Robinson-Patman Act enforcement and lower court developments also are addressed.

As with prior editions, this represents a joint and equal effort. The authors express their appreciation to each other and to commentators, including students, who have taken the time to offer suggestions for improving the book. Tom Sullivan would like to extend his appreciation to Worth Allen, law student at Vermont Law School, and Logan Hovie, law student at Boston College Law School, for their able research assistance.

E. THOMAS SULLIVAN
Burlington, Vermont

JEFFREY L. HARRISON
Gainesville, Florida

Preface to the Sixth Edition

This is the Sixth Edition of *Understanding Antitrust and its Economic Implications* and thirty years since the initial edition appeared. The changes in this thirty year period have been vast and marked by a level of judicial activism that is probably unmatched by any other area of law. The impact of this procedural and substantive activism has been mostly to disadvantage private plaintiffs as well as public enforcement agencies. Whether this is or is not beneficial to the public generally is up to the reader.

Each edition of this book has been an effort to track this development and to offer an accurate and balanced description of critical decisions and the implications of those decisions. In addition, each has been designed to provide a historical perspective in order for the reader to understand how and to what extent this area of law has been reshaped, sometimes in manners that may seem to be inconsistent with legislative history.

This edition carries forth this effort. Since the last edition, the implications of the Supreme Court's decisions with respect to summary judgment have taken hold. Cases that would have gone forward ten years ago are now often dismissed at an early stage. On the substantive side, the Supreme Court has been decisive in rejecting the so called "leverage" theory of monopolization. The Court was far less decisive, however, in the case of reverse payments—instances in which competitor pays a potential competitor to delay its entry into the market. The importance of the Robison-Patman Act has continued its decline. Further, the Court has addressed the broad pressing issue of whether the goal of the antitrust laws is to increase efficiency or consumer welfare—two goals that are not always consistent. Finally, once again the Merger Guidelines issued by the Justice Department and Federal Trade Commission have been adjusted and refined.

As with prior editions, this represents a joint and equal effort. The authors express their appreciation to each other and to commentators who have taken the time to offer suggestions on improving the book.

August 2013

E. THOMAS SULLIVAN
Burlington, Vermont

JEFFREY L. HARRISON
Gainesville, Florida

Preface to the Fifth Edition

It has been twenty-one years since Understanding Antitrust and Its Economic Implications first appeared and six years since the last edition. When the first edition was written, the United States Supreme Court was in the midst of reshaping antitrust law to reflect its philosophy that it should adhere to the teachings of economics. During the last six years, this process continued as the Court sought to achieve greater consistency. For example, the Court removed resale price maintenance (RPM) from the list of *per se* unlawful activities. To many, this change was a necessary, albeit belated, response to the Court's *Sylvania* decision over 30 years ago. The Court has also made it clear that it would treat secondary line price discrimination—perhaps the last remaining element of the populous antitrust philosophy of the 1960s—in a matter consistent with its emphasis on efficiency. In addition, the Court made one of its first forays into the theory of monopsony and addressed the question of how antitrust law applies to market power on the buying side of the market.

The process of rationalizing antitrust law is far from complete. For example, the Court's newly announced position on RPM raises a number of issues. Specifically, many past decisions by the Supreme Court and lower courts reflect either approval or disapproval of the *per se* status of RPM. Now that the rule has been changed, the relevance of that law is in question. In addition, a truly consistent antitrust policy requires close attention to various exemptions. Exemptions based on non economic considerations are hard to reconcile with the path the Court has chosen. Finally, in a global economy, matters of market power and the competitive impact of various agreements must be viewed from an international perspective.

This edition of Understanding Antitrust and Its Economic Implications examines all these matters. Like all books on law, however, it only captures the moment in an ever changing, challenging, and fascinating area of law. As noted in every previous edition, this effort is a shared one, with each author contributing equal amounts of effort and each author responsible for any omissions or errors. The authors thank those who have communicated their suggestions for improvements. Professor

Harrison would like to thank Sarah Harrison for her editorial assistance. Professor Sullivan would like to thank Calvin Hoffman, Charles Dickinson, Mark Creer, and Sarah Gillstom.

November 2008

E. THOMAS SULLIVAN
University of Minnesota Law School

JEFFREY L. HARRISON
University of Florida College of Law

Preface to the Fourth Edition

Fifteen years ago the first edition of this book appeared. At that time, lower courts were still in the process of recognizing the importance of two important shifts in antitrust law. The first was an increased emphasis on economic analysis as signaled by *Continental T.V. Inc. v. Sylvania*. The second was the application of the doctrines of antitrust standing and antitrust injury to narrow the scope of potential antitrust plaintiffs.

Subsequent editions of this book have treated further refinements with respect to these two crucial antitrust concerns. In addition, the intervening years witnessed progress toward a predictable standard for predatory prices, an effort by the Supreme Court to describe what a "quick look" analysis means, and much greater sophistication with respect to the analysis of market power. This fourth edition tracks further developments with respect to all of these traditional areas of analysis.

As with most areas of law, there always are new challenges as the world changes. In the case of antitrust, the new challenges stem from continued economic globalization and technological advances. Globalization requires consideration of the international reach of the United States' antitrust law. Technological change requires one to consider the intersection of antitrust law and intellectual property. This fourth edition includes greatly expanded treatment of these two important areas of analysis.

Since the last edition, clearly the most public display of antitrust came in the *Microsoft* case. The long-run impact of that case on antitrust law may not be felt for some time. In this volume we examine the possible implications of *Microsoft* for a variety of areas including monopolization, market power analysis, and tying doctrine.

As always this has been a joint undertaking. We have enjoyed our collaboration in producing what we hope will be a useful hornbook to students, practitioners and judges. Professor Harrison would like to thank Margie Tyler for her help in preparing the manuscript. Professor Sullivan would like to thank David James and Matt Scheidt. Both of us greatly appreciate the work of Ally VonHockman whose diligence at LexisNexis made our work easier.

February 2003

E. THOMAS SULLIVAN
University of Minnesota Law School

JEFFREY L. HARRISON
University of Florida College of Law

Preface to the Third Edition

Ten years have now passed since the first edition of this book. It has been a period during which antitrust law continues to be shaped by the judicial philosophy found in *Continental T.V. v. GTE Sylvania.* This perspective was played out most recently in *State Oil v. Khan*, in which the Supreme Court (finally, some would say) overruled *Albrecht v. Herald Co.*

More noteworthy, perhaps, has been lower court reaction to two Supreme Court decisions made just prior to the publication of our second edition. Thus, over the past five years, courts have begun applying the teachings of both *Eastman Kodak Co. v. Image Technical Services* and *Brooke Group Ltd. v. Brown & Williamson Tobacco Co.* This volume addresses *Khan* as well as judicial reaction to *Image Tech.* and *Brown & Williamson* and other antitrust "events" like the 1997 Merger Guidelines.

At the heart of the book, however, is a more expansive treatment of traditional antitrust matters. The theory of market power is considered in a more focused manner as is the continuing efforts by courts to make sense of the complexities of market power analysis. In addition, substantial new treatment of antitrust standing, of domestic and international "commerce" issues, and of conspiracy and its multiple permutations has been added.

In preparing this edition, the authors once again thank each other and report that the book is the result of a joint effort. Dean Sullivan would also like to thank Deidre McGrath and David Schlutz for their research assistance. Professor Harrison would like to thank Danny Payne for his secretarial efforts and Bill Shilling for his research assistance. Finally, the authors thank Kent Hanson, their editor at Matthew Bender, whose tireless work on the manuscript was of inestimable value.

May 1998

E. THOMAS SULLIVAN
University of Minnesota Law School

JEFFREY L. HARRISON
University of Florida College of Law

Preface to the Second Edition

Six years have passed since the publication of the first edition of this book. The Sherman Act has closed its first 100 years and began its second. It would be misleading to suggest that the 100th anniversary was marked by landmark decisions or even by a significant change in emphasis. It is clear that the economic approach to antitrust announced in *Continental T.V., Inc. v. GTE Sylvania* and the judicial philosophy compatible with that approach remain dominant.

When the first edition was published, the teachings of *Sylvania* had already influenced the law of both vertical and horizontal restraints. In the past six years, those teachings have been applied even further afield. In its latest term, the Supreme Court announced tough standards for plaintiffs relying on a theory of predatory pricing. Additional hurdles have been erected for private parties attempting to enforce the Robinson-Patman Act. Recent decisions concerning such threshold issues of summary judgment, antitrust standing, and antitrust injury are also generally consistent with the view that antitrust should play a smaller role in modern society.

Antitrust law is, however, nothing if not complex. While its influence may be withering, there continue to be decisions that cannot be easily reconciled with a reduced role. In the past six years, the Supreme Court has indicated that there is a lasting and important role for *per se* rules in appropriate cases. It has given new hope to plaintiffs in tying cases. It has narrowed, or at least refined, the antitrust exemption for "the business of insurance." More importantly, the Court has, on more than one occasion, been critical of the use of economic theory in the absence of supporting empirical data. It is this complexity that makes antitrust an exciting and challenging field.

In preparing this edition, the authors would once again like to thank each other and report that this book is the result of a joint effort throughout. In addition to those acknowledged in the first edition, Dean Sullivan would like to thank Craig Marquiz for his able research assistance. Professor Harrison would like to thank Danny Payne and Gwen Reynolds.

E. THOMAS SULLIVAN
University of Arizona Law School

JEFFREY L. HARRISON
University of Florida College of Law

Preface to the First Edition

This volume on federal antitrust laws is both timely and overdue. It is merely because we are on the eve of celebrating the 100th anniversary of the Sherman Act and the 75th anniversary of the Clayton Act and Federal Trade Commission Act. Accordingly, it is an appropriate time to reflect on the state of antitrust law and to consider its future. These two objectives informed the direction and content of this text. The effort is overdue, as we believe this is the most comprehensive and balanced treatment of antitrust law in a single volume since the United States Court's 1977 landmark decision in *Continental T.V., Inc. v. GTE Sylvania*, which signaled a new era of antitrust law.

As every antitrust practitioner and scholar knows, the changes in the wake of *Sylvania* have made antitrust one of the most challenging and exciting fields of contemporary law. At times, it is also bewildering. Business activities that were once subject to "bright line" tests of legality are increasingly judged under the elusive "rule of reason" standard. For example, it can no longer be stated with confidence that pricing agreements among competitors are *per se* violations of § 1 of the Sherman Act. Similarly, mergers that were readily condemned 15 years ago are now commonplace. Pervading these changes is an increased reliance by the courts and by public enforcement agencies on the sophisticated economic analysis.

We approached our task with several goals in mind. First, we have attempted to highlight and restate those areas of antitrust law where the law is relatively clear. At the same time, where the issues are especially difficult and the law remains unclear, we have endeavored to provide the reader with an appropriate analytical approach. Second, we have discussed fully the latest cases as well as their landmark forerunners. Third, we have identified what appear to be the trends and competing points of view which are likely to dictate the direction of antitrust law in the years to come. This treatise is specifically designed not to become obsolete with the release of the latest Supreme Court decision. Fourth, the book offers full coverage, including horizontal and vertical conduct, monopolies, mergers, price discrimination, private and public enforcement issues, and antitrust economics.

Finally, our intent is to present a balanced presentation which does not put forth the "Chicago School" approach or any doctrine as providing the "right" answers to the complex economic, political, and social issues that are woven throughout this area of law. We have made an effort to present a wide spectrum of ideas and opinions regarding the goals and economic underpinnings of antitrust law.

A number of individuals assisted in this project and deserve recognition. Professor Sullivan would like to acknowledge the able research assistance of Winston Smart, Gail Israelievitch, Tom Glassberg, and Gerald Bassett. He also would like to give special recognition to Jane Bettlach for her indispensable secretarial skills. Professor Harrison would like to thank Warren Braums, Charles Carlson, Laurel Judd, and Tony Smith. In addition, we would like to thank each other and report that the book is, in every sense, a joint effort and the product of a rewarding collaboration.

We offer this treatise as a restatement and critical assessment of antitrust law in anticipation of the first of many anniversaries celebrating the antitrust laws. We hope it will stimulate discussion about the role antitrust has played in the twentieth century and, as we approach the twenty-first century, the role it should play in our society and economy in the next century.

January 1988

E. THOMAS SULLIVAN
Washington University School of Law

JEFFREY L. HARRISON
University of Florida College of Law

Understanding Antitrust and Its Economic Implications

Chapter 1

Antitrust Policy: An Introduction

§ 1.01 The Focus of Antitrust

Antitrust law establishes the rules of competition in the marketplace. This body of law seeks to assure competitive markets by identifying and condemning various types of anticompetitive conduct. In competitive markets, consumers and sellers each pursue their own interests. For example, as a consumer, you are motivated by a desire to purchase products at the highest quality and lowest price, maximizing your satisfaction. Sellers of products seek to maximize their profits by responding to consumer demand while expending the least amount of resources. In pursuing their own individual interests in a competitive market, consumers and sellers engage in exchanges that make both parties better off.

The single most important feature of this competitive interaction is that buyers and sellers act independently, not in concert. For sellers this means that each searches for opportunities to respond to the demands of consumers. The search is intensified by knowledge that, if sellers do not respond to the needs of consumers with the desired product at a fair price, a competitor is likely to fill the void by offering the product and earning a profit by doing so. Competition among sellers gives consumers an opportunity to pick and choose among alternatives in order to maximize your satisfaction from each dollar spent.

Contrast this independent action by sellers with a case in which they have agreed to act in concert. For example, suppose the presidents of all the textbook publishing companies gathered in the proverbial "smoke-filled room" and agreed that only one publisher would produce antitrust books or that no textbooks would be sold for less than a set price. This agreement not to compete would mean that each producer would be far less concerned about responding to your needs. As a result, the range of choices available to you would be severely restricted. It is very likely that the satisfaction derived by you per dollar spent would decline.

Antitrust law centers on the principle that society is better off if markets behave competitively. Thus, antitrust law focuses on the relationship between buyers and sellers in individual markets, how products and resources are allocated, and how quantities and prices are determined within those markets. Because we are all consumers, antitrust law affects everyone.

As we study antitrust, we see that it attempts to constrain producers and suppliers of products and services from engaging in anticompetitive conduct. As a matter of policy, Congress has decided that markets should be competitive. When the market—the interaction of buyers and sellers—deviates from the competitive ideal, antitrust law has a role to play. Private parties and federal and state governments may invoke the antitrust laws to proscribe anticompetitive conduct and remedy associated harms. Antitrust violations are essentially market failures, and antitrust enforcement seeks to restore competitive markets. We must be cautious, however, that the cost of antitrust intervention does not exceed the cost associated with the identified anticompetitive conduct. If the cost of antitrust enforcement is greater than the costs of the breakdown of the market forces, another kind of failure exists; it too can result in higher prices and injury to consumers. The cost of excessive intervention, as in the case of market failure, is ultimately borne by each of us as consumers.

The development of antitrust law has been evolutionary, changing over time as we gain new knowledge about how exchanges occur between buyers and sellers. In studying antitrust, we are drawn into a lively debate not only on what the law is but what it ought to be. This implicates ideology and philosophy, as well as history, economics, and public policy. In short, the study of antitrust, as told in this text, is about an evolution of assumptions about production and exchange functions in society and how those activities are ordered and regulated by society when there is a breakdown of market forces. While the reader may be introduced to new terminology in this book, the conduct described here is familiar to all of us. We experience it each day as consumers. This book gives each of us an opportunity to reflect on the dynamics of the marketplace and the kinds of laws that ought to govern it.

Each chapter of this book addresses separate problems that affect competition. Chapter 2 reviews the economic assumptions and implications of antitrust conduct. Chapter 3 introduces the reader to jurisdiction and enforcement requirements under each antitrust law. It also sets forth certain exceptions and defenses to antitrust coverage. Chapter 4 discusses the problems involved when competitors enter into agreements that have the effect of restraining competition. Agreements among competitors are called horizontal restraints. In contrast, Chapter 5 concerns competition issues raised by agreements between firms at different levels in the production or distribution of a product, firms that are not in competition with each other. These are called vertical restraints. For example, if a manufacturer of a product attempts to establish the price at which the product is sold by the retailer to the consumer, antitrust law is implicated. Chapter 6 analyzes monopolies and when their conduct violates antitrust law. Mergers and acquisitions, which have been frequent topics in the popular press, are discussed in Chapter 7. Finally, Chapter 8 analyzes the law that prohibits sellers from discriminating in price when they sell a product.

What you are about to discover is that antitrust law has a rich, diverse, and interesting history, and a critical role to play in contemporary society. Its rich fabric surrounds all of our lives, whether consumers or producers, and especially as students studying the marketplace, where mergers, monopolies, and contracts that rig public bids and agreements that restrict competition seem pervasive. Knowledge of antitrust is relevant whether we work on Wall Street or shop on Main Street.

§ 1.02 Legislative History and Antitrust Goals

Antitrust is the study of competition. But disagreement exists over what competition means and what the goals of antitrust law should be. The answers may vary depending on one's ideology and views of the legislative history and development of the antitrust laws and their underlying values. Policy choices confront the antitrust student at every turn. This is true whether one seeks a contemporary interpretation of antitrust or whether one starts by reviewing the legislative history of the antitrust laws.

Contemporary debates about antitrust laws have a certain *déjà vu* quality. The central arguments heard today in antitrust policy discussions are similar to those echoed in the early, formative years of this country. The genesis of antitrust law predates the first antitrust statute, the Sherman Act in 1890. The debate is as old as Thomas Jefferson's and Alexander Hamilton's view of government.[1]

Jefferson urged a deconcentrated society and government, one that valued independent decision-making and equality-enhancing opportunities for small, local businesses. Minimizing economic concentrations of industrial power was central to Jeffersonian populism. Hamilton, on the other hand, feared that decentralization might interfere with the goal of efficiency. He advocated a strong national government, particularly central control over financial and economic issues and institutions.[2] The tension between these two themes was fundamental to the formation and shape of our government. As we will see in this text, they are evident in the study of antitrust today.

Antitrust scholars have debated whether Jefferson or Hamilton predominantly influenced the 1890 Congress that passed the Sherman Act. Jeffersonianism was evident in the legislative history of the Sherman Act, as senators and representatives expressed concern with business concentration, acquisition of monopoly power, and

1. *See generally* A.D. Neale & D.G. Goyder, *The Antitrust Laws of the U.S.A.* 439–43, 470 (3d ed. 1980); *The Political Economy of the Sherman Act: The First One Hundred Years* (E. Thomas Sullivan ed., 1991); Arthur M. Schlesinger, Jr., *The Cycles of American History* 220–23, 242 (1986); Donald I. Baker & William Blumenthal, *Ideological Cycles and Unstable Antitrust Rules*, 31 Antitrust Bull. 323, 324–25 (1986); Daniel A. Crane & Herbert Hovenkamp, *The Making of Competition Policy* 41 (2013).

2. *The Federalist* Nos. 9, 11, 16 (Alexander Hamilton) (Clinton Rossiter ed., 1961).

cartels that might lead to increased prices to consumers. Some legislators speaking in favor of the Sherman Act championed entrepreneurial individualism, independent decision-making and contracting in the market, and dispersing economic power and stimulating access to free markets. Other legislators also recognized distributional effects and equity concerns, as well as the need to protect consumers from a redistribution of wealth from consumers to monopolists and toward protecting competitors from predatory practices.[3] Generally speaking, these goals are unrelated to the Hamiltonian goal of efficiency.

On the other hand, some antitrust scholars have invoked Hamiltonianism to assert that the main, if not the sole, purpose behind the Sherman Act was the promotion of economic efficiency.[4] Grounded in a Hamiltonian approach, this theory argues that antitrust policy should sanction business conduct that promotes efficient allocations of resources. For many students of antitrust, the ultimate question is whether the challenged practice produces a net gain or loss to consumers. This is often referred to as the consumer welfare standard.

An objective, balanced reading of the legislative history of the Sherman Act reveals that multiple goals and values were expressed by supporters as the legislation was debated.[5] There is agreement today, however, that Congress enacted the antitrust laws primarily to encourage competition.[6] Although disagreeing as to the primacy or hierarchy of the various goals and policies expressed in the congressional debates, most antitrust commentators agree that, ultimately, Congress was most concerned with

---

3. S. 1, 51st Cong. (1st Sess. 1889), *reprinted in* 1 *The Legislative History of the Federal Antitrust Laws and Related Statutes* 89 (Earl W. Kintner ed., 1978); 21 Cong. Rec. 2460, 2457, 3146, 3152 (1890); *see also* Harlan M. Blake & William K. Jones, *In Defense of Antitrust*, 65 Colum. L. Rev. 377 (1965); John J. Flynn, *Antitrust Jurisprudence: A Symposium on the Economic, Political and Social Goals of Antitrust Policy*, 125 U. Pa. L. Rev. 1182 (1977); Eleanor M. Fox, *The Modernization of Antitrust: A New Equilibrium*, 66 Cornell L. Rev. 1140 (1981); Robert H. Lande, *Wealth Transfers as the Original and Primary Concern of Antitrust: The Efficiency Interpretation Challenged*, 34 Hastings L.J. 65, 68–70 (1982); Stephen F. Ross, *Principles of Antitrust Law* 6–11 (1993); Louis B. Schwartz, *"Justice" and Other Non-Economic Goals of Antitrust*, 127 U. Pa. L. Rev. 1076 (1979); E. Thomas Sullivan, *The Economic Jurisprudence of the Burger Court's Antitrust Policy: The First Thirteen Years*, 58 Notre Dame L. Rev. 1 (1982).

4. Richard A. Posner, *Economic Analysis of Law* 10 (2d ed. 1977); Richard A. Posner, *Antitrust Law: An Economic Perspective* 4, ch. 2 (1976); Robert H. Bork, *Legislative Intent and the Policy of the Sherman Act*, 9 J.L. & Econ. 7 (1966); Herbert Hovenkamp, *Distributive Justice and the Antitrust Laws*, 51 Geo. Wash. L. Rev. 1, 1–4 (1982).

5. Richard Hofstadter, *What Happened to the Antitrust Movement?*, *in The Paranoid Style in American Politics and Other Essays* 199–200, 205, 209 (1965); *see also* William H. Page, *Ideological Conflict and the Origins of Antitrust Policy*, 66 Tul. L. Rev. 1 (1991).

6. Lande, *supra* note 3; *see also Standard Oil Co. v. FTC*, 340 U.S. 231, 248–49 (1951); Walter Adams & James W. Brock, *The Bigness Complex: Industry, Labor and Government in the American Economy* 87–117 (1986).

cartel and monopoly conduct[7] that restrict output, increase prices to consumers,[8] and reduce quality of products and services.[9]

Although the historic record seems clear that Congress cared primarily about protecting consumers, farmers, and workers from anticompetitive conduct,[10] some scholars continue to argue that the Sherman Act was rooted in concern over allocative efficiency.[11] Notwithstanding the academic debate over congressional intent, scholars and judges agree that antitrust law is designed to promote competition in the marketplace. Contemporary disagreement centers on how competition is best achieved.

The Sherman Act has two primary provisions. Section One condemns agreements that unreasonably restrain trade. And Section Two condemns monopolization, attempted monopolization, and conspiracies to monopolize. None of these terms are defined in the statute.

---

7. *See* Chapters 4 and 6 for definitions of these terms.

8. *See, e.g.*, Hovenkamp, *supra* note 4, at 16–17; Thomas C. Arthur, *Farewell to the Sea of Doubt: Jettisoning the Constitutional Sherman Act*, 74 Cal. L. Rev. 263, 286–87 (1986).

9. *See generally* Robert H. Bork, *The Antitrust Paradox* 20–21 (1978); Posner, *supra* note 4, at 23; Bork, *supra* note 4, at 16–21; Hovenkamp, *supra* note 4, at 27–31; E. Thomas Sullivan, *On Nonprice Competition: An Economic and Marketing Analysis*, 45 U. Pitt. L. Rev. 771 (1984).

10. *See, e.g.*, Robert M. Lande, *Consumer Choice as the Ultimate Goal of Antitrust*, 62 U. Pitt. L. Rev. 503, 525 (2001) (suggesting that the focus of antitrust should shift from price to consumer choice).

11. The legislative intent regarding the other antitrust statutes discussed in this book is clearer. For example, the dominant underpinning of the Robinson-Patman Act in 1936, 15 U.S.C. § 13, was the protection of small businesses from leveraged buying practices of larger businesses; the legislation plainly was designed to promote small business over larger firms. *See infra* Chapter 8. *See generally* Philip Elman, *The Robinson-Patman Act and Antitrust Policy: A Time for Reappraisal*, 42 Wash. L. Rev. 1 (1966); Hugh C. Hansen, *Robinson-Patman Law: A Review and Analysis*, 51 Fordham L. Rev. 1113 (1983).

The same is true for the Clayton Act in 1914, particularly with regard to the 1950 Celler-Kefauver Amendments. *See* Derek C. Bok, *Section 7 of the Clayton Act and the Merging of Law and Economics*, 74 Harv. L. Rev. 226, 233 (1960); Fox, *supra* note 3, at 1144 n.12; Hovenkamp, *supra* note 4, at 24–26 ("Bork's description of the legislative history of the Celler-Kefauver amendment is so inconsistent with the legislative history itself that it is difficult to believe Bork had the correct book in his hands when he described its contents."); Lande, *supra* note 3, at 126–40; *infra* chs. 5 & 7; *see also* 51 Cong. Rec. 9088 (1914) (statement of Rep. Mitchell); 96 Cong. Rec. 11,506 (1950) (statement of Sen. Kefauver).

The Federal Trade Commission Act in 1914 had efficiency, as well as wealth distribution, concerns. "Monopoly is the evil we wish to control. Competition is the thing we wish to maintain." 51 Cong. Rec. 8855 (1914) (statement of Rep. Morgan). Most antitrust observers agree that the purpose of the FTC Act was the same as the Sherman Act but that expanded powers were needed. As Congressman Stevens, a sponsor of the bill, observed: the purpose of the FTC Act was to serve as "a method of enforcing [the Sherman Act] and making it more effective and preventing its misuse." 51 Cong. Rec. 14,934 (1914); *see also* Neil W. Averitt, *The Meaning of "Unfair Acts or Practices" in Section 5 of the Federal Trade Commission Act*, 70 Geo. L.J. 225 (1981). Here, too, the debate continues whether allocative efficiency or wealth distribution was the primary objective of the statute. See Lande, *supra* note 3, at 106–26; *see also* Bork, *supra* note 9, at 20–21, 51; Crane & Hovenkamp, *supra* note 1, at 392.

The legislative history of the Sherman Act shows that Congress intended to incorporate and federalize the common law antitrust precedents.[12] Prior to the Sherman Act, several states had their own common law precedents that condemned certain anticompetitive acts as illegal restraints on trade. A problem of interpretation arose, however, because no unified common law of trade restraints existed. The common law in 1890 included English as well as American judge-made decisions and statutes,[13] espousing the contemporary economic philosophies.[14] As one authority explained:

> The congressmen who drafted and passed the Sherman Antitrust Law thought they were merely declaring the illegality of offenses that the common law had always prohibited. [Like others, they have too easily] accepted the mistaken view that the attitude of the common law towards freedom of trade was essentially the same throughout its history.[15]

Congress delegated to federal courts the authority to develop and expand a new federal common law of antitrust.

§ 1.03 Early Interpretation

The initial interpretation of the Sherman Act by courts was difficult because, in the words of Senator Sherman, the sponsor of the legislation:

> [I]t is difficult to define in legal language the precise line between lawful and unlawful combinations. This must be left for the courts to determine in each particular case. All that we, as lawmakers, can do is to declare general principles, and we can be assured that the courts will apply them as to carry out the meaning of the law, as the courts of England and the United States have done for centuries. This bill is only an honest effort to declare a rule of action. . . .[16]

Congress, therefore, delegated broadly to the courts the role of applying general principles and filling in the large gaps left by the open-ended text of the statute. Common

---

12. 21 Cong. Rec. 2456, 3146, 3151–52 (1890); *see* Arthur, *supra* note 8, at 277, 279–80, 284.

13. Hans B. Thorelli, *The Federal Antitrust Policy: Origination of an American Tradition* 10 (1954); Donald Dewey, *The Common-Law Background of Antitrust Policy*, 41 Va. L. Rev. 759 (1955); *see also* James May, *Historical Analysis in Antitrust Law*, 35 N.Y.L. Sch. L. Rev. 857 (1990).

14. William Letwin, *Law and Economic Policy in America: The Evolution of the Sherman Antitrust Act* 18–32 (1965). *See generally* Herbert Hovenkamp, *The Sherman Act and the Classical Theory of Competition*, 74 Iowa L. Rev. 1019 (1989).

15. Letwin, *supra* note 14, at 18. *See generally* James May, *Antitrust Practice and Procedure in the Formative Era: The Constitutional and Conceptual Reach of State Antitrust Law, 1880–1918*, 135 U. Pa. L. Rev. 495 (1987).

16. 21 Cong. Rec. 2460 (1890).

law was to serve as the background for the "meaning of the law."[17] But, as noted above, this was no easy task. Operational standards and underpinnings eluded early courts.

Early decisions saw the Supreme Court rapidly change the course of its interpretation, showing an evolutionary decision-making process. In the first Sherman Act case, *United States v. E.C. Knight Co.*,[18] decided in 1895, the Court held that restraints affecting merely the manufacturing of commodities did not come within the jurisdictional reach of the Act because manufacturing was not commerce. This narrow definition of commerce, however, did not last. When the Court decided its first Sherman Act case on the merits in *United States v. Trans-Missouri Freight Ass'n*,[19] it adopted an over-inclusive interpretation of § 1 of the Sherman Act, declaring every restraint illegal.

The next year, the Court rejected its reasoning in *Trans-Missouri* by distinguishing common law restraints from those condemned by the Sherman Act. In *United States v. Joint-Traffic Assoc.*,[20] the Court clarified that market practices directly affecting competition are illegal without inquiry into their reasonableness. Indirect or incidental restraints, under the so-called common law "ancillary restraint" doctrine,[21] however, are not condemned under § 1. Thus, the *Trans-Missouri* rule that *all* restraints were unlawful under the new Sherman Act was rejected. From *Joint-Traffic* to the present, courts and the antitrust academic community have debated the original intentions of the antitrust laws and this "characterization" process of determining whether the restraint is a direct or indirect interference with commerce.

As we shall see throughout this text, the arguments on original intent of the Sherman Act have varied from a general welfare test, a consumer welfare approach, or a total welfare consideration. Chapter 2 that follows underscores some of these principles and descriptions as does the discussion in each chapter. Notably, in *F.T.C. v. Actavis, Inc.*,[22] eight Justices of the Court arguably agreed that antitrust's goal is "consumer welfare," asking whether consumers were injured by an output restriction or higher prices caused by the exercise of market power, and whether net efficiencies offset the consumers' loss.[23]

---

17. *See also* James May, *The Role of the States in the First Century of the Sherman Act and the Larger Picture of Antitrust History*, 59 Antitrust L.J. 93 (1990). *Compare* Arthur, *supra* note 8, at 290–300, *with* William F. Baxter, *Separation of Powers, Prosecutorial Discretion, and the "Common Law" Nature of Antitrust Law*, 60 Tex. L. Rev. 661 (1982).

18. 156 U.S. 1 (1895).

19. 166 U.S. 290 (1897).

20. 171 U.S. 505 (1898).

21. *See infra* § 4.05.

22. 570 U.S. 136 (2013).

23. *See* E. Thomas Sullivan, Herbert Hovenkamp, Howard Shelanski & Christopher Leslie, *Antitrust, Law, Policy, and Procedure* (7th ed. 2014); Herbert Hovenkamp, *Implementing Antitrust's Welfare Goals*, 81 Fordham L. Rev. 2471 (2013). Some confusion exists because Robert Bork incorrectly defined consumer welfare to include producer welfare. *See* Christopher R. Leslie, *Antitrust Made (Too) Simple*, 79 Antitrust L.J. 917 (2014).

Chapter 2
Antitrust Economics

§ 2.01 Introduction

Since the origins of antitrust, economic theory has become increasingly important in shaping antitrust law and policy.[1] Economists originally shunned or were indifferent towards antitrust development; they did not play a central role in the legislative debates of the Sherman Act. Only later did economists join the discussion about the economic implications of antitrust. Now, courts routinely use economic concepts and theories. Economic theory often informs and shapes antitrust doctrine. Judges weave these concepts into decisions to support their results.

Congress founded antitrust law on the premise that some industries contribute best to overall social welfare if they are competitive. In a competitive market, consumers attempt to maximize their satisfaction by allocating their spending among various goods and services. Producers, on the other hand, direct their resources into developing goods and services that consumers value the most (allocative efficiency), and they try to produce these products at the lowest per unit cost (productive efficiency). The economic theory underlying antitrust centers on price theory or microeconomics: the study of individual markets, including how prices and quantities are determined, and how products and resources are allocated.

In a market driven economic system, individual firms[2] decide what and how much to produce, and what prices to charge; individual consumers decide how much to buy based on the available price. Individual decisions determine market prices. In order

1. The discussion in this chapter is based on the following sources: Armen A. Alchian & William R. Allen, *Exchange and Production* (1983); R. Blair & D. Kaserman, *Antitrust Economics* (1985); Jack Hirshleifer, *Price Theory and Applications* (3d ed. 1984); Herbert. Hovenkamp, *Federal Antitrust Policy: The Law of Competition and its Practice* (2d ed. 1999); Frederick M. Sherer & D. Ross, *Industrial Market Structure and Economic Performance* (3d ed. 1991); George Stigler, *The Theory of Price* (3d ed. 1966). *See also* Ernest Gellhorn, *An Introduction to Antitrust Economics*, 1975 Duke L.J. 1.

2. The firm is the principal target of antitrust scrutiny. In economics terminology, the firm is a unit of production that converts input factors (capital, labor, raw materials, etc.) into goods and services which in turn are traded with consumers or other firms. In short, firms are "productive agents of society, engaged in the conversion of resources into final goods. [They] constitute the supply side of the product market and individuals the demand side." Hirshleifer, *supra* note 1, at 173. When several independent firms are engaged in the production of the same commodity, they comprise the "industry." A "market" is made up of the buyers and sellers in a given industry "who communicate and

to analyze and predict market behavior, economists generalize about individual economic behavior from two basic assumptions: (1) the individual makes market decisions based upon self-interest; one buys and sells[3] to maximize one's own personal wealth, utility, or satisfaction; and (2) the aggregates of these individual decisions serve to maximize the wealth of society. Throughout this book, the various topics discussed are introduced with an examination of economic considerations.

Here, however, some fundamental definitions are set out and central theories examined. First, the economic consequences of competition are compared with those of monopoly. This discussion provides the background for an understanding of the most common justification for the existence of the antitrust laws. Second, the concept of market power is examined in some detail. In recent years, in particular, the determination of the degree of market power has become a central focus of many antitrust cases ranging from agreements among competitors to behavior by single firms to mergers. For this reason, the market power material is critical to a full understanding of the materials that follow in Chapters 4–8.

§ 2.02 Perfect Competition

Levels of competition can be described along a continuum, extending from what is called "perfect competition" to "pure monopoly." In order for a market to be perfectly competitive, several conditions must hold: (1) there are many buyers and sellers; (2) no individual firm is large enough to affect price by its individual action; (3) products in the market are homogeneous, with (4) each product capable of serving as a substitute for another; (5) barriers to entry do not exist; and (6) firms have the ability to increase production without restriction. In addition, producers and consumers have complete information of all relevant market factors. Perfect competition is characterized by uncoordinated individual decision making by each producer and consumer.

[A] Demand and Supply

In order to understand how a perfectly competitive market functions, it is necessary to understand the concepts of demand and supply. Demand is a schedule of prices and the quantities individuals are willing and able to purchase at each price. One might determine demand by asking individuals how many units of a good they would buy at one price. The amounts would be added to get the total amount demanded at that price. Then the same question could be asked about a series of higher and lower prices.[4] We would have a list of prices and the amounts that would be demanded at each price.

---

3. The price of a good is the rate at which one unit can be exchanged for money or for other goods.

4. The process involves "horizontally summing" the demand curves of individual consumers. The summation is horizontal because quantity demanded is typically plotted along the X or horizontal axis of a graph.

Note that a consumer must be both willing and able to buy in order to be counted in the economist's definition of demand. A person who lacks money to buy a particular product is not, according to the economist, included in the demand for that product.

Customarily, demand is depicted on a graph. In Figure 2-1, the X or horizontal axis represents quantity. The Y or vertical axis represents price. The demand curve displays the amount of goods consumers are willing to purchase at any given price. At $10 per unit, consumers will demand 10 units. At $5 per unit, consumers will demand 50 units. At $1 per unit, consumers will demand 100 units. Demand curves almost always slope downward and to the right. As the price declines, consumers find the good increasingly attractive compared to other goods and that they are able to buy more of the good.[5]

Figure 2-1. Demand

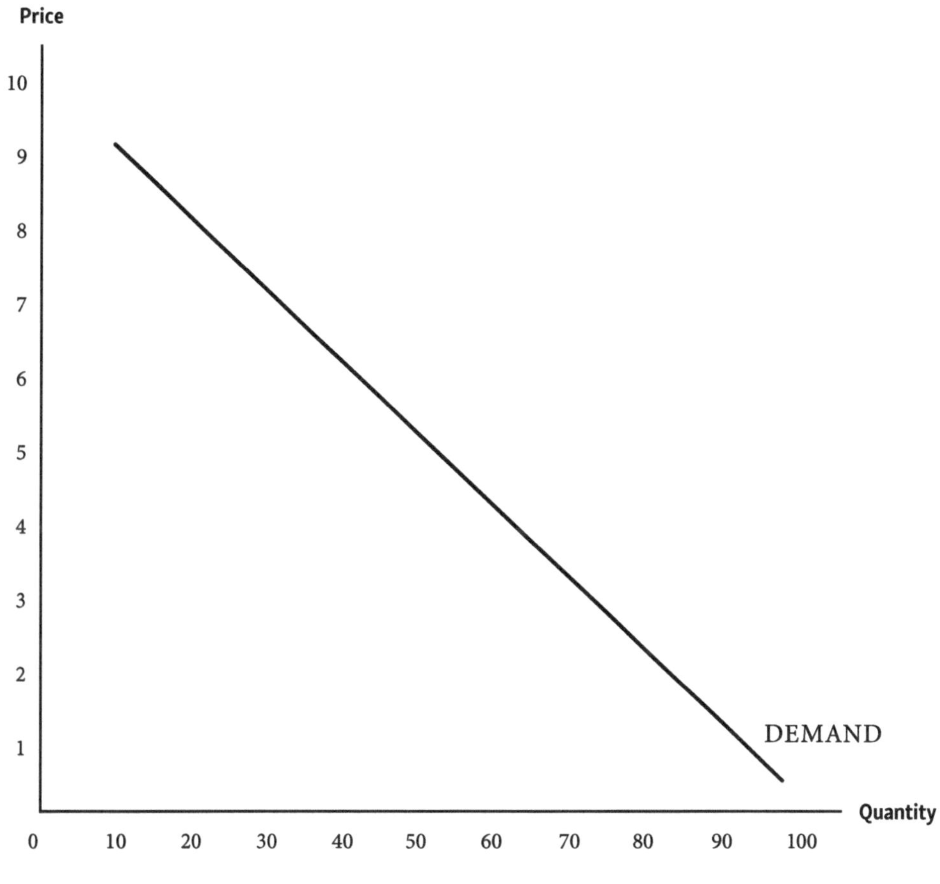

transact for a given good." William G. Shepard, *The Economics of Industrial Organization* 5 (1979). As explained in Chapter 6, this market is defined further by cross-elasticity of demand.

5. There is both a "substitution" and an "income" effect. As price decreases, consumers substitute the good with the decreased price for other goods used for the same purpose. For example, if the price of champagne decreases, they might drink more champagne and less grape soda. In addition, as the price of any good decreases, the real income or "buying power" of consumers increases. This increase in "income" results in increased consumption of some goods and services.

Supply is the converse of demand. It is a schedule of prices and the amounts sellers are willing to make available to consumers at each price. To derive it one could ask all sellers how much they would make available at each price. By summing the amounts each would make available at that price, one would determine the total supply at that price. By repeating the process for a series of prices, one would get a total amount offered for sale at each price.

Obviously higher prices mean a greater opportunity for profit, and one would expect suppliers to offer more as prices increase. As shown in Figure 2-2, this results in an upward sloping supply curve. For example, at $10 per unit, producers will attempt to sell 100 units. At $5 per unit, producers will offer 50 units for sale. At $1 per unit, producers will offer only 10 units for sale.

Figure 2-2. Supply

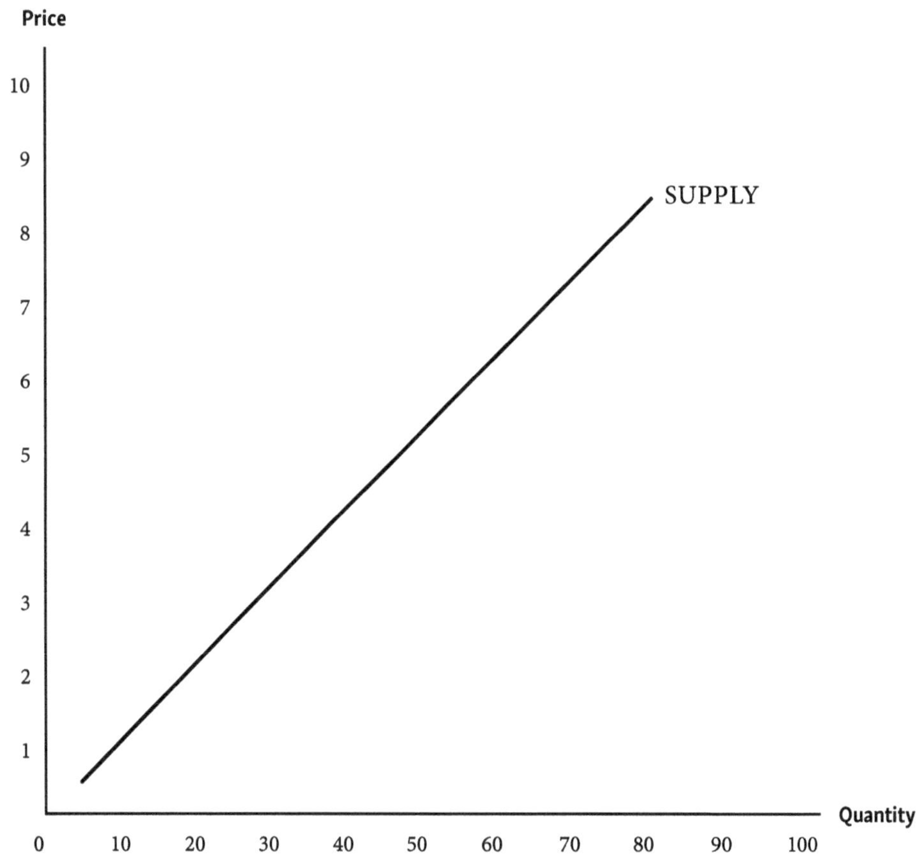

[B] Elasticity

The "laws" of demand and supply tell us that quantity demanded is inversely related to price, and quantity supplied is directly related to price. In other words, as price increases, demand decreases but supply increases. The measure of how sensitive buyers and sellers are to price changes is called "elasticity." Technically, it is the ratio of the percentage change in quantity to the percentage change in price leading to the quantity change. Or, stated differently, it is the percentage change in quantity divided by the percentage change in price (% change in quantity / % change in price).

In the case of demand, when the percentage change in quantity exceeds the percentage change in price—elasticity is greater than 1—the demand is elastic and amounts purchased will be greatly affected by a change in price. Buyers are quite responsive to changes in price. When the percentage change in quantity is less than the percentage change in price, demand is said to be inelastic. In this case, buyers are not very responsive to price changes and purchases will not be drastically affected.

As will be discussed in greater detail below, elasticity of demand or "price elasticity" is critical in determining whether a firm possesses market power—that is, the ability to raise prices above what they would be in a competitive market. As a general matter, a firm facing an inelastic demand curve has greater market power than one facing an elastic demand because a firm can raise price without losing sales when demand is inelastic.[6] The most important determinate of demand elasticity is the availability of substitute goods. If a firm raises price and its customers respond by turning to sellers of substitutes, there is a cross-elasticity of demand between the seller's product and the substitute goods. On the other hand, if the seller is the sole seller of a necessary item without substitutes, demand is likely to be relatively inelastic.

Supply elasticity measures how suppliers respond to changes in price. For example, supply is elastic if firms respond to price increases by increasing output. Supply is more likely to be elastic if firms are able to increase output at a relatively low additional cost. This might be the case if the firm's plant is not operating at full capacity or if the good is produced with inexpensive inputs. Supply will also be elastic if new producers can readily enter the industry.[7] On the other hand, if it is quite costly to produce an additional unit, the firm will not respond to price increases by greatly increasing the quantity offered for sale.

The term which is used to describe the way in which a firm's costs behave as it increases output is "marginal cost." Marginal cost is the additional cost to a firm of producing one more unit of output. In Figure 2-3, the marginal cost of unit 3 is $3. The marginal cost of unit 4 is $4, and so on.[8] When the marginal cost of each unit is displayed on the graph, we have the firm's "marginal cost curve." The steeper the curve,

---

6. As a technical matter, all demand curves include an elastic and inelastic range. Sellers generally set prices in the elastic range.

7. The reader who has a background in economics will note that the authors have studiously avoided making the distinction between "short run" and "long run" adjustments. We feel that the basic logic of microeconomics relevant to the study of antitrust can be understood without reference to this distinction. As a technical matter, though, the entrance of new producers is a "long run" phenomenon.

8. The complete marginal cost curve would be U-shaped with the curve first sloping downward at low levels of output and then back up. The relevant portion of the curve, however, is the upward sloping segment.

the lower is the elasticity of supply for the firm. In other words, when costs increase rapidly as output increases, producers tend not to be very responsive to price changes.

Figure 2-3. The Firm's Marginal Cost Curve

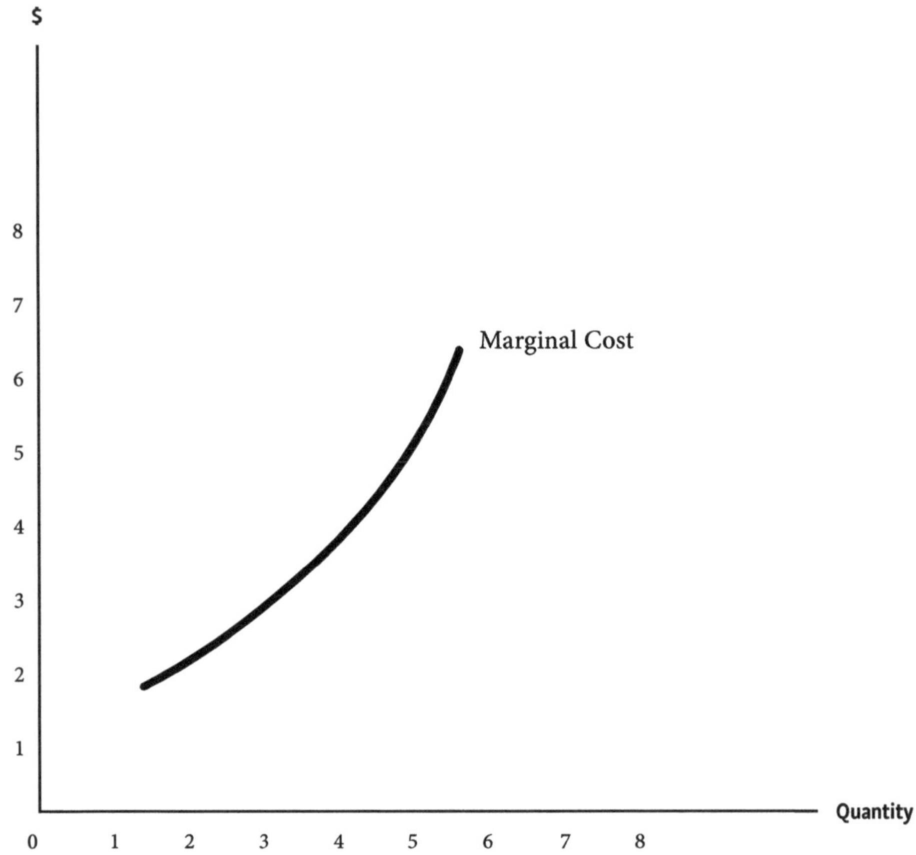

[C] Market Equilibrium

In a competitive market, the market price of a good or service and the quantity sold are determined by the interaction of demand and supply. In Figure 2-4, the demand curve from Figure 2-1 is superimposed over the supply curve from Figure 2-2. The price in the market will gravitate towards $5—the equilibrium price—and the quantity bought and sold with gravitate towards 50—the equilibrium quantity.[9] At any price other than $5 there will be a "surplus" or "shortage" in the market, and forces will be set in motion to bring the price back to $5.

For example, at a price of $3, consumers will seek to purchase 70 units, but suppliers will offer only 30 units for sale. The shortage of 40 units will mean that consumers will

9. This is not to say that the price will be $5 or the quantity 50 units all the time. These are equilibrium points that the market will gravitate toward.

bid the price up, and that suppliers will offer more for sale as price increases. The price will increase until the quantity supplied is equal to the quantity demanded. At a price of $7, producers will offer 70 units for sale, but consumers will be willing to buy only 30 units. There will be a surplus of 40 units and prices will tend to fall. Only at a price of $5 and a quantity of 50—where the demand and supply curves intersect—will quantity demanded equal quantity supplied. This is the point of competitive equilibrium.

Figure 2-4. Supply and Demand

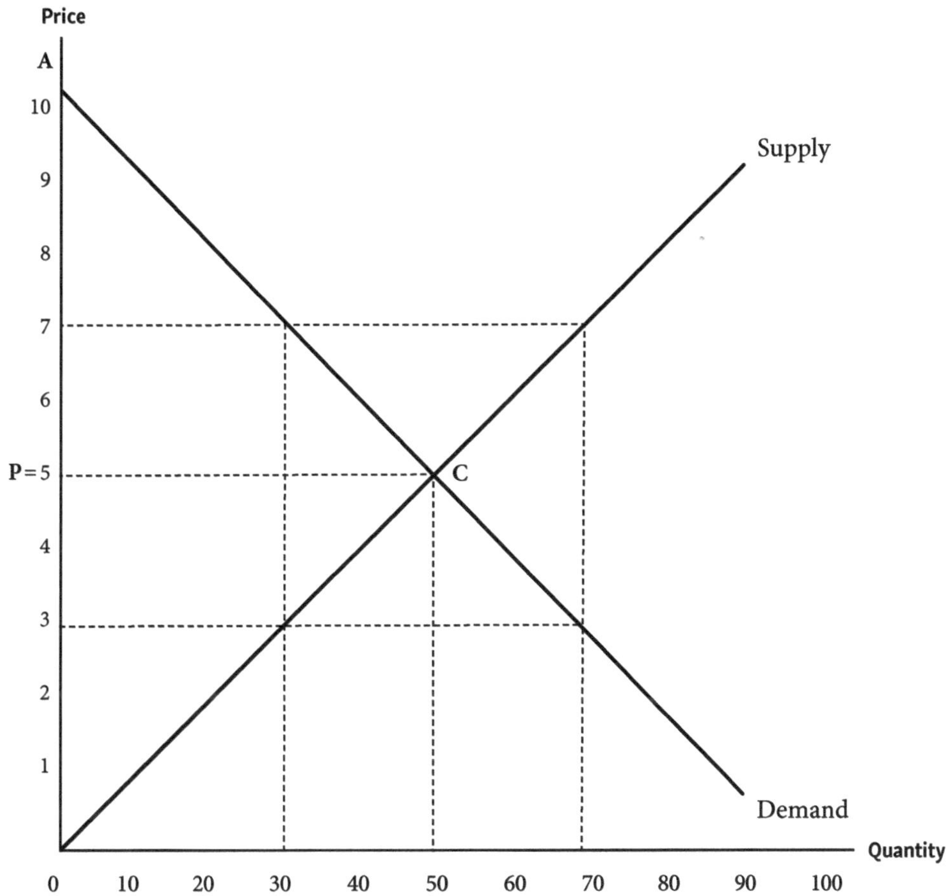

Figure 2-4 illustrates two additional important concepts in antitrust economics: consumer surplus, and producer surplus. Although the price determined in the market is $5, the demand curve indicates that there were some consumers willing and able to pay more than $5 for the product. In other words, they placed a higher value on the good than the amount they were required to pay. The difference between the amount paid and the maximum a buyer would have been willing to pay is consumer surplus. There is consumer surplus associated with every unit sold.[10] This is because rational

10. The 50th unit is sold for exactly the maximum price the consumer is willing to pay. Thus, as a technical matter, the consumer is actually indifferent with respect to the purchase of this unit.

consumers will not buy items that are not at least as valuable to them as the price they are required to pay.[11] The total consumer surplus in the market is the area of triangle PAC. It is the summation of all the consumer surplus accruing to buyers in the market.

From the supply curve, we know that some sellers were willing to offer units for sale at prices less than $5. When a producer sells an item for more than the least that would have been acceptable, it receives producer's surplus. There is producer's surplus associated with every unit sold out to unit 50. This is because, at every level of production out to 50 units, producers would have been willing to sell the unit for less than $5. The triangle PCO approximates the total producer's surplus in the market.[12] It is the sum of all of the producer surplus accruing to sellers.

The total surplus created by the exchanges in this market is equal to the area of triangle OAC—the sum of consumer and producers' surplus. The market, by establishing a price and quantity, determines the size of this total surplus and how it is to be divided between consumers and producers.

[D] The Individual Firm Under Perfect Competition: The Marginal Revenue = Marginal Cost Rule

So far, the discussion has focused on the perfectly competitive industry. It is important, however, to examine the behavior of the individual firm under perfectly competitive conditions. Remember that under perfect competition, no single firm is large enough to affect the market price. In other words, no firm can cause prices to rise by withholding its output from the market or cause prices to fall by offering all of its output for sale. In effect, the market price is set by the interaction of market supply and demand, and the individual firm simply responds to this impersonally determined price. The firm is a "price taker."

The individual firm faces a horizontal demand curve at the market price as shown in Figure 2-5. A horizontal demand curve is perfectly elastic; the firm can sell all it wishes at the market price, but if it raises price above the market price its sales will drop to zero. The horizontal demand curve also indicates what is called "marginal revenue." Marginal revenue is the amount of increase in a firm's total revenue resulting from the sale of an additional unit. In this case, the firm receives an additional $5 each time it sells a unit. Thus, the price it charges and its marginal revenue are $5. As we will see in the examination of monopoly,[13] price and marginal revenue are the same only when the demand curve is horizontal.

---

11. The price they are "required to pay" is in reality the goods and services that cannot be purchased if this item is purchased.

12. It is unlikely that a supply curve would extend to the origin in the manner depicted in the graph. Instead, it will intersect the Y axis at a price above 0. Thus, PCO overstates producer's surplus.

13. *See* Chapter 6.

Figure 2-5. Supply and Demand for the Perfectly Competitive Firm

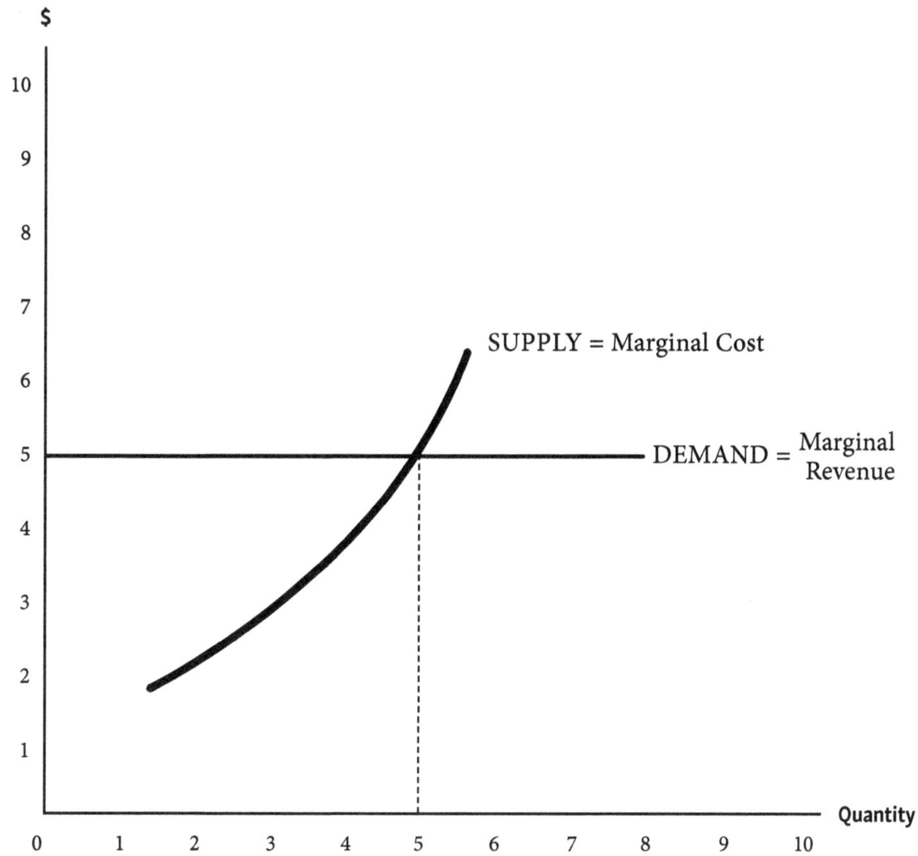

On the supply side of the analysis, the firm's supply curve is the same as its marginal cost curve. The reasoning is that the number of units a firm offers at a particular price depends on a comparison of the price offered with the marginal cost of producing an additional item. It will offer a particular unit as long as the addition to total cost (marginal cost) does not exceed the price offered. Thus, the firm's marginal cost curve also indicates the number of units that will be offered for sale at each price.

The firm's output is determined in the same manner as output was determined for the industry as a whole; it settles on the quantity where demand and supply intersect. In Figure 2-5 the firm's demand curve—set at the market price—intersects its supply curve at 5 units. But something even more fundamental is illustrated in the graph. Remember, in the case of a horizontal demand curve, price and marginal revenue are the same. The firm has, therefore, decided on the output where marginal cost and marginal revenue intersect. This is its profit maximizing output. As long as the marginal revenue—the addition to total revenue from selling a unit—exceeds the marginal cost of its production, the sale of that unit adds to the firm's profits. In Figure 2-5, this is true out to unit 5. Beyond unit 5, marginal cost exceeds marginal revenue and the firm will not offer additional units for sale. Profit maximization occurs where marginal cost and marginal revenue intersect. Although explained here in the context of monopoly, this fundamental rule holds true regardless of how competitive the market is.

[E] Equilibrium Under Perfect Competition

Further understanding of competitive equilibrium requires the introduction of a few additional economic concepts. Costs of production are generally classified as being fixed or variable. Fixed costs do not vary with the level of output. Examples are rent on a parcel of land or executives' salaries. Variable costs do change as output changes—increasing as output increases and decreasing as it falls. Labor and raw materials are good examples. Total cost is the sum of fixed and variable costs. To economists, a "normal" or fair return to investors is regarded as a cost of production like any other. Thus, total cost includes a profit for shareholders.

A better indication of the firm's efficiency can be had by calculating the average per unit cost of production. The most relevant calculations are average variable cost (variable cost divided by the number of units produced) and average total cost (total cost divided by the number of units produced). Less useful is average fixed cost, which is the fixed cost divided by the number of units produced.

The way in which these three measures of average cost behave is illustrated in Figure 2-6. The horizontal axis is quantity of output; the vertical axis is dollars. Average fixed cost (AFC) steadily declines as output increases; it is the same amount divided by higher and higher levels of output. Average total cost (ATC) and average variable cost (AVC) tend to be U-shaped. This is because a firm generally operates more efficiently as output increases, thereby lowering the average cost per unit of production. After some point though, a firm begins to strain against its designed capacity and average cost is likely to begin increasing. The optimal level of output is where average total cost reaches its minimum point—quantity 5 in the graph. Average total cost and average variable cost converge because the difference between them is average fixed cost, which steadily declines as output increases.

The graph also includes the firm's marginal cost curve (MC). Note that it intersects average variable cost (AVC) and average total cost (ATC) at their lowest points. The reason for this can be understood by considering the relationship of marginal to average cost. Marginal cost is the additional cost of producing another unit. As long as it is less than average cost—either variable or total—one would expect those curves to decline. It would be like calculating the average height of a basketball team and then recalculating after a player is added who is shorter than the previous average. The new team member is the marginal member and he or she lowers the team's average height.

On the other hand, if the marginal unit of output is more expensive to produce than the average, one would expect it to cause the average to increase. Thus, as long as marginal cost is above average cost, the average cost curve is upward sloping. Technically, at their minimum points, average variable cost and average total cost are sloping

Figure 2-6. The Individual Firm's Cost Curves

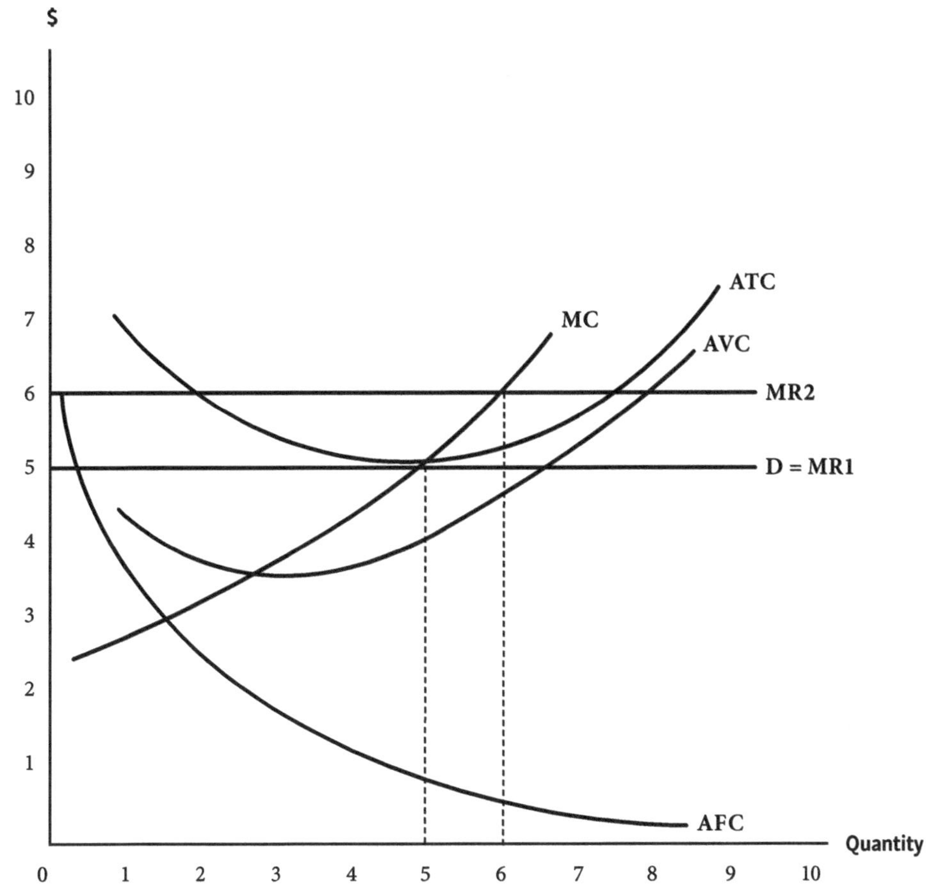

neither upward nor downward; they are flat for a very short interval. At this point, marginal cost equals average cost.

Figure 2-6 also includes the demand curve faced by the firm under competitive conditions. Remember that this is a flat or perfectly elastic demand curve, as the individual firm in perfect competition is a "price taker." In the graph, the firm will sell the quantity where marginal revenue (MRl) equals marginal cost—5 units—at the market price of $5. (Ignore for the moment the line drawn at the price of $6.) The graph has been drawn so that this also happens to be the level of output where the firm produces at its lowest average total cost. Thus, the firm is selling for a price equal to its marginal cost and is producing at its lowest possible average total cost. From the consumers' standpoint, this is ideal. And, since average total cost includes a fair return on investment, this outcome is satisfactory to investors as well. Of course, any firm that is unable to produce the good at a minimum average cost of $5 will not earn a satisfactory profit and eventually will exit the industry.[14]

---

14. This is another "long run" adjustment. *See* note 7, *supra.*

How likely is this ideal outcome? Under the assumptions set forth at the beginning of this discussion of perfect competition, market forces will work to produce exactly this result. For example, if industry demand and supply interacted to produce a higher price of $6 (MR2 in the graph), the firm would expand output to 6 units and its price would exceed its average total cost. It would receive above normal or supracompetitive profits. Under the assumptions about perfect competition, however, entry into the market is easy and information readily available. Thus, the supracompetitive profits will attract new entrants into the market. Their competition will drive prices back down to minimum average total cost.

In sum, under conditions of perfect competition, price is set by large numbers of buyers and sellers interacting in impersonal markets. Perhaps the closest real life examples are the stock market and markets for some agricultural commodities. Individual firms operate where this price—which is also marginal revenue—is equal to marginal cost. Because of the competitive pressure caused by the large number of firms in the industry, each firm will tend to produce at a level where average total cost is minimized. They earn "normal" but not supracompetitive profits. If the market changes to enable existing firms to charge prices in excess of average total cost, new firms will enter the market, driving the price back to average total cost.[15]

§ 2.03 Monopoly

Perfect competition forms one end of a continuum which describes the level of competition. At the other end of that continuum is monopoly. In reality, just as perfect competition is a theoretical construct, pure monopolies rarely exist. The discussion that follows, however, is true of any firm that, although not a true monopolist, possesses some degree of monopoly power. Monopoly power is a single firm's ability to control market price. If it has a high enough market share, a firm can exercise monopoly power even if it is not truly a monopolist in the sense of having no rival firms in the market. Under conditions of pure monopoly, there is one seller of a good for which there is an absence of acceptable substitutes. Although the basic process of determining price and output under conditions of monopoly are the same as they are in perfect competition, the result is significantly different.

Since the monopolist is the only producer in the market, the industry demand is the demand faced by the monopolist. Thus, unlike the firm in perfect competition, the monopolist faces a downward sloping demand curve because when it raises price, consumers will purchase less of the product. Because of this, the marginal revenue curve is also downward sloping. However, it does not coincide with the demand curve. For example, suppose on the demand curve faced by the monopolist, 20 units would be demanded at a price of $8. If the monopolist wished to sell one more unit, it

15. After this adjustment, the average total cost may not be the same as it was prior to entry by the new firms. Their entry could cause some of the resources used in the industry to become more or less costly and, consequently, the new average total cost to be higher or lower.

might have to lower the price to $7.90. Before the price change, the total revenue was $160 ($8 x 20). After the price change and sale of 21 units, total revenue is $165.90 ($7.90 x 21). The increase in total revenue from selling one more unit—marginal revenue—is $5.90. Marginal revenue is less than the price charged for the additional unit because, in order to increase sales to 21 units, the monopolist had to lower the price for all units sold from $8 to $7.90. Thus, as depicted in Figure 2-7, the marginal revenue curve for the monopolist lies below the demand curve.

Figure 2-7. Price and Output Determination by a Monopolist

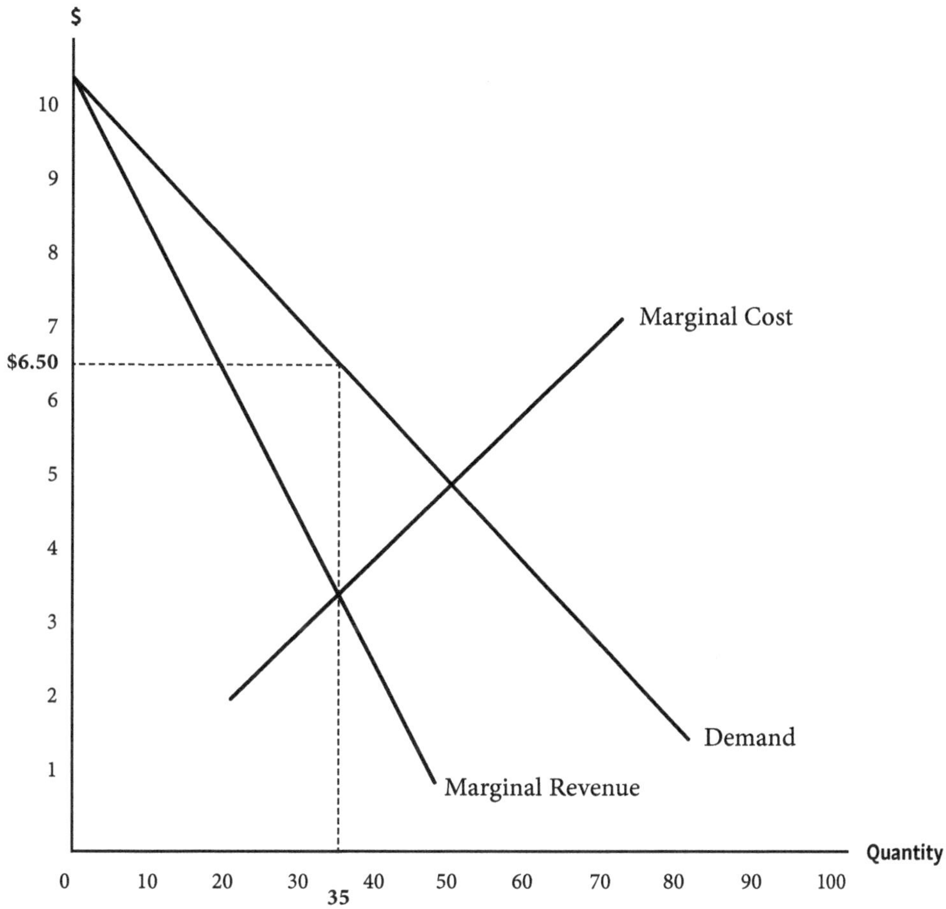

In order to ascertain its profit maximizing level of output, the monopolist applies the marginal revenue equals marginal cost rule. It will sell each unit where the increase in total revenue from selling that unit exceeds the addition to total cost resulting from its production. In the graph, this means it will produce 35 units. It will then set the price at the highest level consistent with selling 35 units. In the graph this is $6.50. Note that under conditions of monopoly, there is no supply curve or series of prices and quantities that would be offered for sale at each price. Instead, the monopolist simply sets a price that is consistent with its profit maximizing level of output.

§ 2.04 Monopoly vs. Competition: A Synthesis

One way of comparing perfect competition and pure monopoly is to assume that a once perfectly competitive industry becomes a monopoly when all the individual producers merge. The comparison is depicted in Figure 2-8. D and S are the demand and supply curves under competitive conditions. The competitive price is Pc, and Qc units would be sold. When the firms are united, the single firm now faces a downward sloping demand curve and a corresponding marginal revenue curve (MR). Since the supply curve was once the sum of all the individual firms' marginal cost curves, it is now the monopolist's marginal cost curve.[16] The monopolist's profit maximizing level of output is Qm and its profit maximizing price is Pm.

Figure 2-8. Perfect Competition and Monopoly Prepared

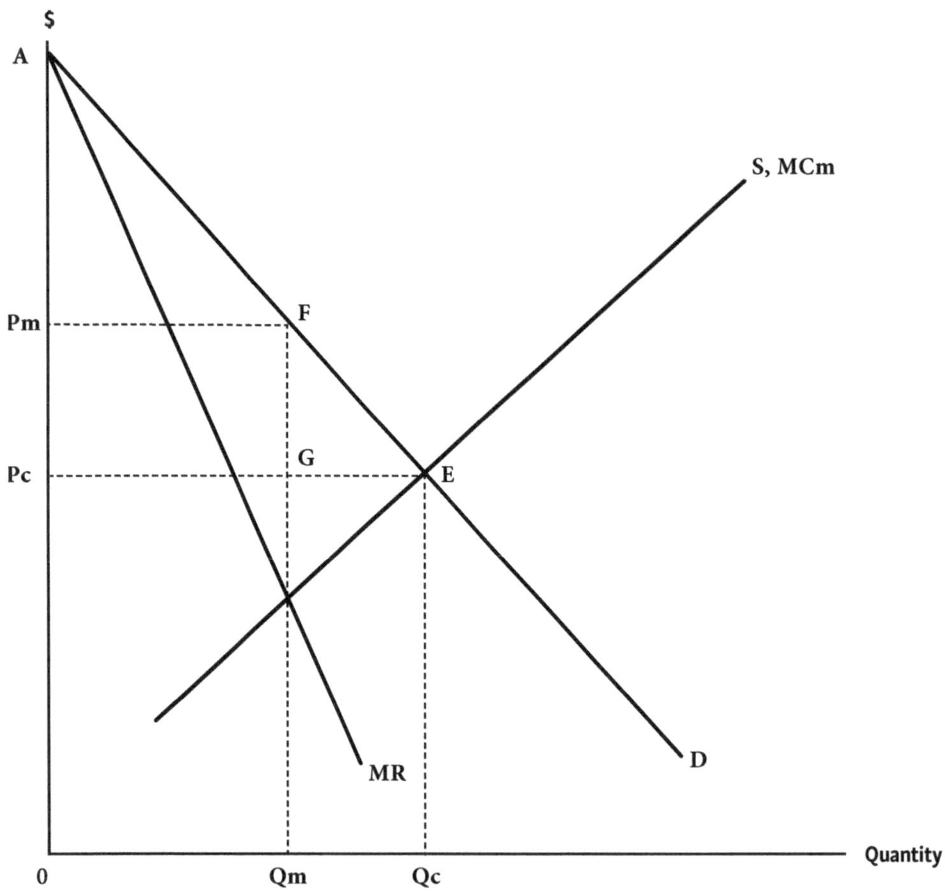

16. This assumes that the monopolist is unable to increase efficiency.

The monopolist produces less than is the case under competitive conditions. In addition, it charges a higher price. It may not charge a price equal to marginal cost nor are there competitive forces at work in the market that would force its price down to average total cost.[17] Thus, it may "earn" indefinitely a supracompetitive profit. In addition, consumer surplus, which was triangle PcAE, has been reduced to triangle PmAF under monopoly. Some of the consumer surplus has been transferred from consumers to the monopolistic producer. Some of it—triangle GFE—has been eliminated. This "deadweight" loss is a decrease in consumer surplus or welfare that is not offset by a gain to anyone else.

The deadweight loss actually flows from a misallocation of resources caused by the monopolist. The price individuals are willing and able to pay for a commodity is a measure of how much they value it. The marginal cost of producing a commodity is the measure of the value society attributes to the resources that must be used to produce an additional unit of the commodity.[18] Society's resources are allocated most efficiently when used to produce units of output that consumers say—through the prices they offer—are more valuable than the resources used in their production.

If resources were allocated efficiently in the market illustrated in Figure 2-8, Qc units would be produced. There would not be a deadweight loss. The monopolist's profit maximizing level of output, however, is lower than the allocatively efficient level. Unlike the competitive market, resources are not automatically funneled into the production of goods consumers find most valuable.

Another loss associated with monopoly flows from the lure of supracompetitive profits. From a cost/benefit point of view, if monopoly status results in $1,000,000 in supracompetitive profit, it would make sense for a firm to invest up to that amount to maintain its monopoly position or to achieve monopoly status. Thus, it may invest money in entry deterring practices designed to exclude potential competitors, or predatory practices aimed at injuring present competitors. Expenditures devoted solely to these purposes can hardly be regarded as producing anything that enhances social welfare.[19]

Another cost associated with monopoly cannot be depicted on a graph nor is it readily quantifiable. It lies in the political clout that may flow from concentrated economic power. Certainly, large firms have disproportionate access to media and can make their self-serving messages heard more readily than small firms or individuals. Greater resources are also available for lobbying activities and appearances before regulatory agencies. In many instances, the efforts that serve the interests of the monopolist are inconsistent with overall social welfare.

---

17. Ultimately it may charge a price equal to average total cost, but this would be the result of the relative levels of demand and cost, not the result of competition with other firms.

18. Resources are demanded for other uses, and their value in those uses is reflected in their price. Thus, the marginal cost—the price paid to attract those resources—indicates their value in the production of other goods or services.

19. The expenditures do not "create" income or welfare, they merely redistribute it.

The discussion so far has noted the clear advantages of competitive markets over monopolistic ones. The reasons for favoring an antitrust policy designed to promote markets characterized by large numbers of competitors have been highlighted. This does not necessarily mean, however, that every market with monopolistic tendencies should be divided into firms so small that they all would be price takers. To do so could mean sacrificing "productive efficiency."

Productive efficiency concerns the production of goods or services at the lowest cost per unit. Economies associated with large scale production can result in lower per unit costs as a firm expands. These "economies of scale" can flow from factors ranging from the specialization of labor to the use of highly advanced (and typically expensive) equipment.[20] Breaking large firms up into smaller firms could mean that these sources of efficient production would no longer be usable. For example, if the automobile industry were broken up into 100,000 small producers, it is unlikely that the smaller producers would be able to take advantage of robotics and assembly techniques to the extent current producers do. This would mean higher costs of production and higher prices.

The existence of economies of scale does not mean that every market must be dominated by a few large producers. Certainly, there are instances in which many firms can take full advantage of all available economies of scale. That is, they can all operate at the "minimum efficient scale." In these industries, allocative efficiency caused by intense competition can be achieved along with productive efficiency resulting from use of the best production techniques.

In other instances, in order to achieve productive efficiency, a firm must serve a large share of the market. The most extreme example of this is a "natural monopoly"—a condition under which a single firm can serve the entire market at the lowest per unit cost. When this is the case, policy makers typically forego antitrust altogether and directly regulate the firm's prices.

An unregulated natural monopoly creates a dilemma for antitrust policy. On the one hand, the firm can be expected to charge a profit maximizing price which exceeds its marginal cost, thereby deviating from the allocatively efficient level of output. On the other hand, by producing the good at the lowest possible average total cost, productive efficiency is achieved. One might consider breaking the industry up into 100 firms. They might be intensely competitive and force price down to a level approaching their marginal and average total costs, which could be lower than that charged by the monopolist. At the same time, though, the firms will produce the good in an inefficient manner.

In short, when the minimum efficient scale of a firm requires serving a substantial portion of a market, there is a trade-off between productive efficiency and allocative efficiency; seeking one means losing some of the other. One solution is to attempt to maximize the total of allocative and productive efficiency. That is, one might give up allocative efficiency and permit industrial concentration as long as it is offset by gains

20. *See* Paul A. Samuelson & William D. Nordhaus, *Economics* 323 (15th ed. 1995).

in productive efficiency.[21] Of course, this requires one to accept the view that efficiency is the sole concern of antitrust—a notion that is far from unanimous. Clearly, though, concern with productive efficiency means that antitrust policy is a much more complicated matter than it once was. Moreover, scholarly and judicial attention to productive efficiency underlies much of the change antitrust law has undergone in recent years.

§ 2.05 Oligopoly

Oligopoly is a market structure characterized by few producers. It is very common in the American economy. Because there are few firms, sellers in an oligopoly perceive that their interdependent actions will be more profitable than independent actions. Interdependence refers to each seller taking into account the actual or potential market reactions of competitors when making output or price decisions. Interdependent decision-making is not collusion because the firms are not agreeing with each other; rather, they are making independent decisions based on the expected reactions of other firms in the market.

If one seller were to increase output and reduce price in order to capture more sales, other producers in the oligopoly would follow suit and, if the first price change is not concealed, the reaction would be swift. A price cutter would gain little. Accordingly, the incentive to price compete is reduced. Likewise, unless an oligopolist were confident that its rivals would follow its lead, a firm in a concentrated market would be unlikely to raise price unilaterally because consumers would buy from the sellers that did not increase price. However, if a firm in an oligopoly market believed its rivals would follow its lead, it would raise its price above the competitive level. If rivals didn't raise their prices, the initial firm could reduce its price back to the competitive price. But if its rivals matched the price increase, all firms could increase their profits through this interdependent pricing. Reaction, anticipation, and strategic behavior are, therefore, important elements of oligopoly behavior.

Even if interdependence results in price rigidity in oligopoly markets, nonprice competition in the form of advertising, quality improvements or pre- or post-point of sale service may take place. Each form of nonprice competition, however, may be subject to the same limits as price competition. For example, quality improvements may be quickly duplicated, giving the innovator only a temporary advantage. Moreover, each form of nonprice competition has a cost which will be a restraining force on its use or on the minimum price of the product.

From an antitrust perspective, oligopolies are problematic because they may increase price without conspiring in a way that violates § 1 of the Sherman Act, which requires an agreement among rival firms. As a consequence, a great deal of oligopoly

---

21. *See generally* Robert H. Bork, *The Antitrust Paradox* 107–10 (1978).

behavior, even though anticompetitive, falls through the cracks. The more interdependence that exists among firms in an oligopoly, the more the market may result in higher prices without violating the law.

§ 2.06 Market Power

The question of market power is pervasive in antitrust; it arises in the analysis of agreements between and among firms under § 1 of the Sherman Act, of monopolization and attempted monopolization cases under § 2 of the Sherman Act, of tying and exclusive dealing claims under § 3 of the Clayton Act, and in merger cases under § 7 of the Clayton Act. The Supreme Court has defined market power as "the power to control prices or exclude competition."[22] The logical interpretation of the Court's language is that market power is a measure of a firm's ability to raise prices above competitive levels without incurring a loss in sales that more than outweighs the benefits of the higher price.

This section begins with an examination of the economic theory of market power. Most important is consideration of the limitations of market share—the proxy courts have historically used for market power. Next, market power analysis in practice is discussed.

[A] The Economic Theory of Market Power

Theoretically, a firm's market power can be measured by the Lerner Index, which is expressed mathematically as follows:

$$L = (P - C)/P$$

L is the Lerner Index, P is the firm's profit maximizing price and C is the marginal cost at the profit maximizing output.[23] Since the price charged under competitive conditions is equal to marginal cost, the formula measures the difference between the firm's profit maximizing price and the competitive price divided by the profit maximizing price.[24] The higher the index, the greater the firm's market power.

Obviously, a firm's ability to charge a price above competitive levels is related to the elasticity of demand it faces. Thus, the Lerner Index also is equal to the reciprocal of

---

22. *United States v. E.I. Du Pont de Nemours & Co.*, 351 U.S. 377, 391–92 (1956).

23. The original discussion of the Lerner Index can be found in Abba Lerner, *The Concept of Monopoly and the Measurement of Monopoly Power*, 1 Rev. Econ. Stud. 157 (1934). *See also* Robert M. Landes & Richard A. Posner, *Market Power in Antitrust Cases* 94 Harv. L. Rev. 937 (1981).

24. The monopolist's cost at its profit maximizing level of output may differ from the costs that would exist under conditions of perfect competition. Thus, it may not be entirely accurate to say that the ratio is based on the difference between the monopolist's price and costs under competitive conditions. Still, the Index stands as a measure of the monopolist's power to raise prices above its own costs. Landes & Posner, *supra* note 23, at 941.

the elasticity of the firm's demand curve, 1/Ed.[25] Predictably, a lower elasticity means a higher index and greater market power, and a higher elasticity means a lower index and less market power.

Although the Lerner Index makes a great deal of theoretical sense, the data required to make the actual calculation are often unavailable. Consequently, courts rarely use this measure of market power. Instead courts have traditionally started from the premise that market share—the firm's sales in the market divided by total sales (or industry capacity)—is typically used as a proxy for market power. Strict reliance on market share as a measure of market power is problematic, however, for two reasons. First, market share is only one of the determinants of power. Second, the determination of market share requires defining the relevant product and geographic market, a far from exact process.

One obvious implication from the Lerner Index is that market power can be determined by examining a firm's profits. The existence of economic profits in a market is a strong indicator that substitutes are not readily available. In fact, the entire market definition/market share analysis can be seen as an indirect and imperfect way of approaching the question of whether a firm has market power.[26]

[1] Market Share and Market Power

The problem of relying too heavily on market share as a measure of market power can be illustrated by expanding on the mathematical relationships in the Lerner Index. There, the ability to raise price above competitive levels was shown to be related to the elasticity of the demand curve faced by the individual firm. The elasticity of the firm's demand is in turn a function of the elasticity of demand for the industry, the firm's market share, and the elasticity of supply of competing firms. Combining these elements, the Lerner Index can be formally expressed as:

$$L = S / (Em + Es(1 - S))$$

where S is the firm's market share, Em is the elasticity of the demand faced by the industry collectively, and Es is the elasticity of supply of competing firms. The formula reveals that market power is positively related to market share. After all, one would hardly expect a firm with only 10% of the market to increases prices without a rapid decline in sales. In contrast, a firm with 90% of the market may be able to successfully raise price because consumers have insufficient alternative suppliers to turn to. In addition, market power is inversely related to the industry demand elasticity. Again, this is what one would expect. If the product sold is one that consumers regard as interchangeable with others, the individual firm is likely to find that its customers are responsive to its own price changes. The elasticity of supply measures how readily competing firms can increase their supply if the individual firm raises price. Again,

25. *Id.* at 940.

26. *See generally* Louis Kaplow, *Why (Ever) Define Markets* 124 Harv. L. Rev. 437 (2010); Micheal A. Williams et al., *Estimating Market Power with Economic Profits*, 10 U.C. Davis. Bus. L.J. 125 (2010).

the more responsive competitors can be, the less power the individual firm has to raise price above competitive levels. In general, if everything else remains constant, three general propositions can be stated:

(1) Market power varies directly with market share;

(2) Market power varies inversely with the elasticity of the industry demand; and

(3) Market power varies inversely with supply elasticity.

As an example of the potentially misleading consequences of relying on market share alone as a proxy for market power and as an illustration of how the three variables interact, consider two hypothetical firms, each with a market share of 75%. Firm A is part of an industry that faces, collectively, a generally elastic demand. In short, consumers buy less when prices increase. In addition, suppose that firm A's competitors have excess capacity and that the costs of entering the industry are relatively modest.

On the other hand, suppose firm B's industry faces a demand curve that is relatively inelastic—consumers are likely to continue purchasing the product regardless of price. Here the principal question is from whom. Further suppose that all firms are operating near capacity and that the industry is relatively costly to enter. Obviously, the two firms, although having identical market shares, do not have the same degree of market power. Firm A is, in fact, relatively powerless and unlikely to be able to raise prices without suffering a great loss in sales. Conversely, Firm B is in a good position to raise price without suffering as great a loss in sales.[27]

The above propositions are important reminders of the dangers of relying solely on market share as the determinant of market power. On the other hand, the fact that some fairly convincing mathematical relationships can be stated should not create the impression that the determination of market power is a matter of simply adding a few numbers. From a practical standpoint, one is unlikely to find sufficiently reliable market share, industry elasticity, and supply elasticity data to permit a precise estimate of market power. Indeed, if these data were available, it seems likely that a direct computation of the Lerner Index would be possible from the individual firm's elasticity.

The equations presented thus far to some extent beg the issue. Certainly, market share data should be qualified by examination of the elasticity of demand for the industry and the elasticity of supply. The problem is that these two measures themselves depend on estimates of the relevant market. For example, to derive the demand elasticity for the industry one must initially decide what is to be included in the industry. Similarly, the calculation of supply elasticity requires one to determine which firms are included in the group of suppliers or potential suppliers.

---

27. To some extent, the full equation has a self-correcting character. For example, a high market share as a consequence of not including all of the possible substitutes in the market will be off-set by high elasticities of demand for the industry and high supply elasticities. *See* Landes & Posner, *supra* note 23, at 962–63.

Examination of the factors influencing firm elasticity and the Lerner Index is an important step in market power analysis. Insights about market power can shield courts from the hazards that have plagued their efforts to determine a firm's market power from market share. In recent years, although market share remains the starting point for a market power analysis, courts have shown an increased receptivity to a more refined analysis. This usually takes the form of examining data that tend to qualify the accuracy of market share as a proxy for market power.

[2] Market Definition and Cross-Elasticity of Demand

A defendant's market share is its sales divided by total sales in the relevant market, including items that consumers regard as reasonable substitutes. The economic tool most commonly referred to in determining what should be included in the market from which one then determines the defendant's market share is cross-elasticity of demand. Cross-elasticity of demand is a measure of the substitutability of products from the point of view of buyers. More technically, it measures the responsiveness of the demand for one product to changes in the price of a different product. It can be expressed as:

% change Qx / % change in Py

where Qx is the quantity of product X and Py is the price of product Y. A high cross-elasticity indicates that the products are good substitutes and should be included in the same market.

Cross-elasticity of demand is probably more useful in theory than in practice. There can be a number of problems that limit its utility, one of which is illustrated by *United States v. E.I. Du Pont de Nemours & Co.*,[28] a leading Supreme Court monopolization decision. The defendant's market share was critical and hinged on whether the market was defined as cellophane, in which case DuPont's market share would have been 75%, or flexible wrapping paper, in which case its share would have been 20%.[29] The Court described the question as whether flexible wrappings were reasonably interchangeable. It asserted that the high cross-elasticity between cellophane and other flexible wrapping materials meant that they competed in the same market.[30]

In defining the relevant product market, however, the *DuPont* Court committed a fundamental error. The Court concluded the cellophane competes against other flexible wrapping materials because if DuPont raised the price of cellophane any more, it would lose sales to those other products. But that's the wrong issue. The proper question is whether the defendant can raise prices above the competitive level profitably without losing too many sales to other products. If a firm is already charging a monopoly price, it would not be able to profitably raise prices. Evidence suggested that DuPont was already charging a monopoly price for cellophane, which meant

28. 351 U.S. 377 (1956).

29. *Id.* at 394–404.

30. *Id.* at 400.

that other flexible wrapping materials were not price disciplining cellophane and, therefore, should not have been included in the relevant product market. The *DuPont* Court used the wrong starting point for analyzing DuPont's price increase, a mistake so infamous that subsequent courts and scholars call this error the Cellophane Trap or the Cellophane Fallacy. To avoid the Cellophane Fallacy, one must ask what consumers do when the defendant raises price above a competitive level; products that consumers switch to should be included in the definition of the relevant product market.

Another distortion in cross-elasticity can occur if the products involved are sold in greatly differing quantities. For example, the producer of product Y may raise price substantially and discover that all or most of its relatively modest number of customers switch to product X. Product X, however, can be used for a number of purposes, including those product Y was used for, and its total sales are so large that the addition of former product Y users results in a very small percentage increase in sales. Clearly, product X is a good substitute for product Y. On the other hand, the actual measure of cross-elasticity—% change in Qx / % change in Py—may indicate that they are poor substitutes.

Further caution is in order in understanding the limitations of cross-elasticity: the actual numerical cross-elasticity may differ depending on the time period examined. For example, if the price of a home heating fuel increases, one may not, in the short run, find a significant increase in the demand for other fuels. The reasons are fairly clear; most home or business owners are committed to a particular method of heating and cannot easily convert to one requiring a different fuel. Over a longer period of time, however, conversion is more likely and cross-elasticity higher.

[3] Elasticity of Supply

The measure of the responsiveness of producers to price increases is called supply elasticity. Supply is elastic if an increase in market prices leads to new sellers entering the market and/or current sellers expanding their output. Here, the primary focus is on the behavior of competitors and potential competitors and the costs of production. If costs increase slowly with increases in production, competitors are in position to add their output relatively easily to that already in the market. The best example is firms with existing excess capacity that could be used to produce the same good as the defendant or one that is regarded as an acceptable substitute. The elasticity of supply of these firms may be high enough to warrant including their capacity in the defendant's market.

If the denominator of the market share fraction is limited to the productive capacity of all manufacturers who currently produce the good sold by the defendant and the capacity of all manufacturers selling a reasonable substitute, it may understate the size of the market and, consequently, overstate the market power of the defendant. In particular, there may be firms that produce goods that are not reasonable substitutes but employ labor and capital that are easily adaptable to the production of the defendant's good. If so, the elasticity of supply with respect to these firms may be high enough for them to be regarded as competitors and their potential output should be added to the denominator of the market share equation. Similar reasoning may be applied to firms that sell in different geographic regions. If slight increases in the defendant's price make it worthwhile for outsiders to ship into the defendant's market, their responsiveness may be high enough to warrant including their productive capacity in that market. Indeed, if entry costs are low, it may make sense to include the output of even nonexistent firms. After all, the possibility of entry by others limits the defendant's pricing discretion.

Obviously, the analysis of potential supply for the purpose of determining what is to be included in the denominator of the market share fraction is far from a simple matter. Two complications arise. First, there are data problems that preclude accurate assessment of the responsiveness of competitors or potential competitors to price increases by the defendant. Second, one must make a judgment about how elastic the supply of a particular competitor must be in order to be included in the market. In a sense, every self-interested entrepreneur in the world is a potential competitor. The key is to include those firms that may actually have an influence of reasonable magnitude on the defendant's decision-making.

[4] Geographic Markets

Typically, the process of determining market share includes defining the relevant product and geographic markets.[31] The emphasis courts have placed on this distinction obscures the point that a full definition of "product market" includes a geographic component. Thus, cement in San Diego from the point of view of building contractors in San Diego is not reasonably interchangeable with cement in Chicago.

For the most part, a definition of the geographic market requires the same general analysis described above. From the point of view of demand, the issue is whether buyers of the defendant's output have a tendency to increase purchases from more distant suppliers as the defendant's price increases. If this tendency is great—the cross-elasticity is high—the distant suppliers should be counted as part of the defendant's market. On the supply side, if distant sellers already make sales in competition with the defendant and can relatively easily expand their sales to these customers, their capacity should be included as part of the defendant's market. Just how responsive distant suppliers are, and whether their entire capacity should be counted, are the primary points of dispute in geographic market definition considerations.[32]

As one would expect, the most important factor influencing the scope of a geographic market is transportation costs.[33] Transportation costs shelter local producers and allow them a range within which prices can be raised without suffering unacceptable losses in sales. If transportation costs are low absolutely, or low relative to the

31. *See, e.g.*, *United States v. Grinnell Corp.*, 384 U.S. 563 (1966).

32. *Compare* Landes & Posner, *supra* note 23, at 966–67, *with* Timothy J. Brennan, *Mistaken Elasticities and Misleading Rules*, 95 Harv. L. Rev. 1849 (1982).

33. *See generally* Kenneth G. Elzinga & Thomas F. Hogarty, *The Problem of Geographic Market Delineation in Antimerger Suits*, 18 Antitrust Bull. 45 (1973).

total price of the product, the sheltering effect is not as great and the market power enjoyed by the defendant is less. Other factors affecting the definition of the relevant geographic market include tariffs and the nature of the product, such as, whether it is durable, fragile, or perishable.

[5] Further Refining the Importance of Market Share

A further word of caution is in order for the purpose of putting the role of market analysis in perspective. As already noted, market power is an important part of a case under § 1 or § 2 of the Sherman Act and §§ 3 and 7 of the Clayton Act. In § 2 cases, the plaintiff will generally be required to show that a single firm either possesses monopoly power or that there is a dangerous probability that the firm will acquire it. In other cases, and especially those in which the charge is that firms have conspired to reduce competition, a showing of monopoly is not required. Furthermore, the Supreme Court has noted that in these cases, the purpose of the market definition is to assess whether the agreement will have anticompetitive effects. In other words, market analysis is a means to an end of determining the likely impact. If the impact can be assessed without a complete market analysis, a court may not require the plaintiff to go through the market analysis.[34] As the Court reasoned, proof of detrimental effect "can obviate the need for an inquiry into market power."[35] One possible detrimental effect may not be reflected by price at all, or at least not directly. For example, if a firm's customers are dissatisfied with its service and are unable to turn to alternate suppliers, this would be suggestive of market power.[36]

[B] Market Power in the Courts

The application of sound economic principles to market power analysis has had an uneven history in the courts. Courts sometimes approach the market power issue with a methodology that is consistent with economic theory, and sometimes not. The classic example of this is the Supreme Court's reasoning in *DuPont*, in which the Court held that DuPont must not have monopoly power because it could not raise its price above current levels without losing too many sales. The Court failed to appreciate that DuPont could not profitably raise its price because it was already charging the monopoly price. No monopolist can profitably raise price above the monopoly power, but that does not mean the firm is not a monopolist.

As the following cases and guidelines indicate, the analysis of power frequently involves three questions. First, what is the relevant market for ascertaining the defendant's market share? Second, what is the defendant's market share within that market? Finally, what does that market share indicate about market power when all relevant

---

34. *FTC v. Indiana Federation of Dentists*, 476 U.S. 447 (1986).

35. *Id.* at 461. *See also National Athletic Ass'n v. Board of Regents of the University of Oklahoma*, 468 U.S. 85 (1984).

36. *See Byars v. Bluff City News Company*, 609 F.2d 843, 853 n.26 (6th Cir. 1980).

factors are considered? This analysis begins with an examination of two important and older cases, *United States v. Aluminum Company of American (Alcoa)*[37] and *United States v. Grinnell Corp.*,[38] in which the courts did not apply the current understanding of the variety of factors influencing market power. The remainder of the cases illustrate more recent interpretations.

[1] United States v. Aluminum Company of America (Alcoa)

In *Alcoa*, Judge Learned Hand penned one of the earliest, best known and most frequently discussed efforts to define markets and calculate market share. Several facts complicated Hand's analysis of Alcoa's market share in the virgin aluminum ingot market. First, some ingot was imported. Second, some ingot was manufactured by Alcoa and then fabricated by Alcoa into shapes that were sold. Third, to some extent, ingot could be made from aluminum that was recaptured. This is secondary ingot that could be reused or recycled. In determining that Alcoa's market share was 90%, Judge Hand took a number of steps. First, he excluded from the market, or the denominator of the market share fraction, all foreign produced ingot except that sold within the United States. He implicitly recognized the concept of supply elasticity and the impact foreign production could have on Alcoa's pricing decisions. Although he observed that foreign producers could "immediately . . . divert to the American market what they have been selling elsewhere,"[39] foreign producers were unlikely to ship their aluminum to the United States market due to barriers created from "the tariff and the cost of transportation."[40]

Second, Judge Hand also excluded from the market all secondary ingot. He reasoned that Alcoa was ultimately in control of the secondary market. In addition, there were users who found secondary ingot unacceptable regardless of the price of virgin ingot. In all likelihood, the cost of recycling may have been high enough to result in a low elasticity of supply. Still, Judge Hand's reasoning on this point was questionable because it is unlikely that Alcoa's pricing of virgin ingot was unaffected by the availability of secondary aluminum. The fact that Alcoa was ultimately in control of the amount of "secondary" available does not mean that it could control the amount recycled in any one year. Complete exclusion of the secondary market may have resulted in an inappropriately narrow market.[41]

Alcoa illustrates how critical market definition is in determining market share. Because Judge Hand excluded foreign production and scrap while including Alcoa's

---

37. 148 F.2d 416, 426 (2d Cir. 1945).

38. 384 U.S. 563, 566–67 (1966).

39. 148 F.2d at 426.

40. *Id.*

41. Professor Landes and Judge Posner suggest that the narrow market definition may have influenced Judge Hand's decision to require high market shares in order for Alcoa to be characterized as a monopoly. Landes & Posner, *supra* note 23, at 978–79.

internal fabrication, he calculated Alcoa's market share to be 90%, which he characterized as "enough to constitute a monopoly."[42] If the market had included scrap aluminum, Alcoa's market share would have been around 64%, which the court labeled "doubtful" that that would be enough to constitute a monopoly. And, if scrap were included while Alcoa's internal fabrication was excluded, Alcoa's market share would have been 33%, which the court stated would not be enough to be a monopoly. Courts have often used these numbers from *Alcoa* when discussing whether a defendant's market share is high enough to be considered a monopoly. These numbers are just a starting point because a high market share alone does not indicate monopoly power; one must also consider whether that high market share is protected by barriers to entry.

When additional products are included in the denominator of the market share calculation, the defendant's market share is smaller and the inference of market power weaker. When products are excluded, the denominator is smaller and the defendant's market share increases as does the strength of the market power inference. Thus, plaintiffs generally want to define the market narrowly around the defendant's product. And defendants want to define the market broadly to include as many products (that they do not sell) as possible.

[2] United States v. Grinnell Corp.

The Supreme Court's market power analysis in *Grinnell* is typically noted because of its geographic market designation. Both the product and geographic market analyses are, however, worthy of review. Grinnell owned controlling interest of three firms which in combination provided 87% of accredited central station protective services. Accredited central station services include the installation of detection devices on the premises that transmit an electronic signal to a central location in the event of a break-in or fire. From the central station, the proper officials are notified. Accreditation is a result of approval by insurance underwriters; it means lower insurance premiums for subscribers.[43]

The relevant market in *Grinnell* is an example of a cluster market, which is a product (or services) market that combines individual products (or services) that do not directly compete against each other.[44] For example, fire protection services are not substitutes for burglary protection services. Even though the central station service could be designed to provide burglary protection or fire protection separately, the Court designated the market as all central services. It reasoned that the market was actually the central service protection of property.[45] To compete effectively, according to the Court, a seller had to offer all central services. Moreover, it found that other

---

42. 148 F.2d at 424.

43. 384 U.S. at 566–67.

44. *Fed. Trade Comm'n v. Staples, Inc.*, 190 F. Supp. 3d 100, 117 (D.D.C. 2016) ("Cluster markets allow items that are not substitutes for each other to be clustered together in one antitrust market for analytical convenience.").

45. 384 U.S. at 572.

forms of property protection were not reasonably interchangeable under the standards of *DuPont*.[46] Although the Court recognized that the firms did not have "unfettered power to control the price of their services," it explained that many customers would "be unwilling to consider anything but central station protection."[47]

In *Grinnell*, the Court defined the relevant geographic market as national. Although each individual central station was able to serve an area within a 25-mile radius and was literally useless to residents outside of that local area, the Court reasoned that the business was "operated on a national schedule of prices, rates, and terms."[48] Justices Fortas and Stewart dissented, noting the lack of a connection between the scope of the seller's planning and its power to raise prices and restrict output.[49] It has been suggested that the geographic market definition in *Grinnell* can be understood by reference to supply elasticity and the possibility of national firms entering local markets with relative ease.[50] This may have been the case, but it is not an explanation that can be gleaned easily from the Court's opinion.

Since *Grinnell*, courts have gained a firmer understanding of what constitutes a geographic market. In *Heerwagen v. Clear Channel Communications*,[51] the Second Circuit distinguished *Grinnell*. The case concerned the promotion and production of live entertainment and the sales of tickets. The specific allegation was that Clear Channel used its dominance in the radio market to increase its market share in the market for ticket sales. Plaintiff claimed that Clear Channel operated and set prices nationally and, thus, relied on *Grinnell*. The court rejected that analysis. Instead, it correctly noted that the geographic market is determined by "the area in which the seller operates and where consumers can turn, as a practical matter, for supply of the relevant product."[52] In the context of the case, it noted that there was little cross elasticity between tickets in different local markets. It added that "*Grinnell* involved the formation of nationwide procurement contracts, horizontal agreements between multistate competitors and an interstate manufacturing business."[53] This may distinguish *Grinnell* as a factual matter but does not reconcile it with the modern and more accurate approach to geographic market definition.

In *Gulf States Reorganization Group v. Nucor Corporation*,[54] the court addressed a claim that a steel producer's funding of an equipment dealer's purchase of a failed producer's equipment was an attempt to monopolize by keeping the equipment away from competing steel producers. In denying the claim, the court noted the failure of the plaintiff to define an appropriate geographic market. The court correctly observed that a geographic market existed only when it was shown that "consumers in the

---

46. *Id.* at 574.
47. *Id.* (citation omitted).
48. *Id.* at 575.
49. *Id.* at 588–89 (Fortas, J., dissenting).
50. *See* Hovenkamp, *supra* note 1, at 116.
51. 435 F.3d 219 (2d Cir. 2006).
52. *Id.* at 227.
53. *Id.* at 230.
54. 822 F. Supp. 2d 1201 (N.D. Ala. 2011).

geographic area cannot realistically turn to outside sellers should prices arise in the defined area."[55] In this case, it was clear that suppliers outside the proposed geographic market had consistently shipped to buyers within that market.

[3] *Cross-Elasticity of Supply:* Telex Corp. v. IBM Corp. *and* Rebel Oil Co. v. Atlantic Richfield Co.

In *Telex Corp. v. IBM Corp.*,[56] the Tenth Circuit addressed the supply-side factors relevant to the market definition issue. The case arose as a challenge by producers wishing to sell peripheral equipment for IBM computers. In the early era of personal computers, disk drives and memory storage were physically separate products (called peripheral devices) that plugged into the central processing unit (CPU). For a peripheral device to work with a particular CPU, it had to be plug compatible. In other words, the peripheral device had to have a plug that fit into the CPU's socket. Plaintiffs charged that IBM had monopolized the market of equipment that was "plug compatible" with its central processing units. The plaintiffs argued that the relevant product market was IBM-plug-compatible peripheral devices, while IBM argued that the market comprised all peripheral equipment including some that was not "plug compatible" with IBM central units.

The trial court judge settled on the narrower definition, reasoning that for owners of IBM central units, non-plug compatible peripheral equipment was not reasonably interchangeable with "plug compatible" equipment. In other words, the cross-elasticity between types of peripherals was low. The Court of Appeals reversed, focusing on the supply rather than demand side of the market. It noted the lower court's finding that "suppliers of peripherals plug compatible with non-IBM systems could in various instances shift to the production of IBM plug compatible peripherals, . . . should the economic rewards in the realities of the market become sufficiently attractive."[57] In other words, the Tenth Circuit reasoned that if IBM raised the price of IBM-plug-compatible peripheral devices, firms making incompatible devices could shift their production and start making compatible ones that competed against IBM's. Because the court found that cross-elasticity of supply existed, the court defined the market broadly.

In *Rebel Oil Co. v. ARCO*,[58] plaintiffs claimed defendant (ARCO) attempted to monopolize the market in retail gasoline in Las Vegas, Nevada. They defined the relevant market as self-serve retail gasoline stations in Las Vegas. ARCO argued that the market was all sales of retail gasoline in Las Vegas, including full-serve gas. From the consumer standpoint, there is no cross-elasticity of demand because full-serve consumers who value services won't switch to self-serve gas, and self-serve consumers who value low prices won't pay more for full-service gas. The Ninth Circuit, however,

---

55. *Id.* at 1236.
56. 510 F.2d 894 (10th Cir. 1975).
57. *Id.* at 916.
58. 51 F.3d 1421 (9th Cir. 1995).

defined the market to include both self-serve and full-service gas based on supply elasticity, reasoning that sellers of full-serve gasoline could easily convert their full-serve pumps, at virtually no cost, into self-serve pumps, expanding output and thus constraining any attempt by ARCO to charge supracompetitive prices for self-serve gasoline.

[4] Qualifying Market Share: United Parcel Service *and* Dimmit Agri Industries

In theory, a firm can possess monopoly power despite controlling less than 50% of the market. In *Broadway Delivery Corp. v. United Parcel Service* (*UPS*),[59] UPS was charged with monopolizing and attempting to monopolize the pickup and delivery of small packages sent by wholesalers in the New York City garment district. The trial court instructed the jury that a finding that plaintiff possessed less than a 50% share of the relevant market was sufficient to establish an absence of the required market power for a monopolization claim. The Second Circuit Court of Appeals found the instruction erroneous and emphasized that an instruction on market power should not "deflect the jury's attention from the indicia of monopoly power other than market share."[60] The court implied, however, that market shares in the range of 50% would require additional direct evidence of market power to provide a basis for a finding that § 2 had been violated.[61]

In *Dimmitt Agri Industries Inc. v. CPC International Inc.*,[62] the defendant's market shares were 25% and 17% in the national cornstarch and national corn syrup markets, respectively. The jury found for the plaintiff; the Fifth Circuit Court of Appeals reversed the lower court denial of judgment *non obstante verdicto*. The defendant's basis for requesting a j.n.o.v. was the claim that "as a matter of law" the low market share controlled could not establish the market power required for a monopolization offense. The Fifth Circuit found that market shares in the range of the defendant's "are insufficient—at least absent other compelling structural evidence—as a matter of law to support monopolization."[63] The court held that the evidence of the defendant's ability to control price was, in this instance, insufficient to overcome the strong presumption that it did not possess sufficient market power. In particular, the court noted the ease with which the remainder of the industry could meet the demand of disaffected buyers if the defendant attempted to lower its output and raise prices. It stopped short, if ever so slightly, of ruling that market shares in the 25% range always would be indicative of insufficient market power.

---

59. 651 F.2d 122 (2d Cir. 1981).

60. *Id.* at 130.

61. *Id.*

62. 679 F.2d 516 (5th Cir. 1982). *See also Ball Memorial Hospital Inc. v. Mutual Hospital Insurance*, 784 F.2d 1325 (7th Cir. 1986); *United States v. Waste Water Management Inc.*, 743 F.2d 976 (2d Cir. 1984).

63. 679 F.2d at 529.

[5] Eastman Kodak v. Image Technical Services *and the Lock-in Issue*

More recently, courts have been concerned with the issue of market power when buyers are arguably locked into a market by virtue of a prior purchase in a market in which the defendant did not have market power. The Supreme Court addressed the issue in *Eastman Kodak v. Image Technical Services.*[64] Kodak sold photocopiers and office equipment for which it also sold parts and service. Parts manufactured for non-Kodak machinery were not interchangeable with Kodak replacement parts. In essence, buyers of Kodak equipment were dependent on Kodak for replacement parts. When their Kodak machines broke down, many customers preferred that repairs be performed by independent service organizations (ISOs), not Kodak's own repair service. But ISOs needed Kodak parts to perform many repairs. And Kodak refused to sell its spare parts to ISOs. Kodak directly sold replacement parts only to owners of Kodak equipment who repaired their own machines or used Kodak service. ISOs claimed that Kodak's tying of parts and service precluded ISOs from being able to compete effectively with Kodak for the business of repairing Kodak equipment. ISOs claimed that Kodak had monopolized or attempted to monopolize the markets for Kodak replacement parts and service. There was evidence that Kodak controlled nearly 100% of the replacement parts market and 80% to 95% of the service market. But Kodak argued it faced competition in the market for photocopiers and office equipment (the upstream market) and consequently could not have market power over parts (the downstream market, or aftermarket) because if it raised prices over parts, consumers would stop buying Kodak's equipment in the upstream market. The Court considered whether Kodak's lack of market power in the market for the original equipment foreclosed, as a matter of law, the possibility of violating § 2 with respect to the markets of parts and service.

The Court first noted that a single brand of a product can be a relevant market for antitrust purposes. It reasoned that, for owners of Kodak equipment, the only relevant choices were suppliers of Kodak replacement parts and Kodak service. The Court then responded to the theory, put forth by the defendants, the dissenting Justices, and the Department of Justice, that any effort by Kodak to exercise monopoly power in the aftermarket would undermine Kodak's position in the market for original equipment. In effect, the defendants argued that aftermarket consumers could not be treated as though they were part of a "captive market" as long as there were readily available substitutes for the original equipment. The theory was that potential buyers of original equipment would not buy from manufacturers who charged supracompetitive prices in the aftermarket and those who already had purchased Kodak equipment would purchase substitutes when the opportunity arose. In economic terms, the argument was that Kodak's high market share in the replacement parts and service markets overstated Kodak's actual market power due to the high cross elasticity of demand in the market for original equipment.

64. 504 U.S. 451 (1992).

The Court held that Kodak could have market power in the aftermarket for parts even if it lacked market power in the upstream market for original equipment. First, because of information costs, consumers may not be aware of Kodak's supracompetitive prices for repairs when they were deciding which office equipment to purchase. For supracompetitive pricing in the aftermarket to have an impact on the original equipment markets, potential buyers would have to have accurate and possibly expensive to obtain information about the cost of the product over its entire lifecycle. Second, those buyers who already had purchased original equipment could not switch costlessly even if aftermarket prices were supracompetitive. Thus, depending on information and switching costs, it was, according to the majority, possible to have monopoly power in the aftermarket without market power in the original equipment market.[65]

Despite the *Kodak* opinion recognizing the possibility of market power in aftermarkets, some lower courts have not been receptive to claims by those who have agreed contractually to be "locked in." For example, in *Queen City Pizza, Inc. v. Domino's Pizza, Inc.*,[66] plaintiffs sought to describe the relevant market as "the $500 million aftermarket for sale of supplies to Domino's franchisees." This was based on a requirement, under the franchise agreement, that franchisees buy these aftermarket supplies from Domino's or approved suppliers. The plaintiffs relied on the contract for the proposition that they were locked into the purchases of Domino's aftermarket supplies. The Third Circuit Court of Appeal rejected this argument. First, it noted that there were aftermarket supplies that were reasonably interchangeable with those offered by Domino's. The fact that the plaintiffs had agreed contractually to buy only from Domino's did not warrant creating a market of buyers who had opted to deal with a single supplier. In addition, the court noted that *Kodak* concerned an instance in which there were unilateral changes in conditions of sale after the purchase was made of the original equipment. In the case of these franchisees, however, the terms of the exchange, including aftermarket purchases, was known at the time of the original contract. In short, one is not locked in, at least for market definition and antitrust purposes, if one voluntarily consents to the arrangement.[67]

Much the same reasoning is found in *SMS Systems Maintenance Services, Inc. v. Digital Equipment Corp.*,[68] which dealt with the sales of computer systems that included warranties. Plaintiff claimed that by locking in computer buyers to the manufacturer's warranty, independent service organizations were kept out of the market. At one level, the court applied the same reasoning as the court in *Queen City Pizza*, observing that the warranty was known about at the outset of the transaction and that any consumer aversion to the warranty would be felt in the market for computers—a market in which the defendant did not possess power.[69] The court also responded to an argument that

65. *Id.* at 472–79.

66. 124 F.3d 430 (3d Cir. 1997).

67. The issue of what it means to "consent" can arise in these cases. *See Little Caesars Enterprises v. Smith*, 34 F. Supp. 2d 459 (E.D. Mich. 1998).

68. 188 F.3d 11 (1st Cir. 1999).

69. *Id.* at 19.

buyers were locked-in by virtue of having invested in software and personnel training consistent with using defendant's equipment. Plaintiff's reasoning appeared to be that switching costs were high and, as a consequence, defendant did have market power with respect to those who had devoted significant resources to defendant's computers. The court rejected this argument and distinguished the switching costs in *Kodak* from those at hand. In *Kodak*, attempting to use independent service organizations would have meant actually buying new equipment. In the case at hand, plaintiffs were free to use independent service organization if they were willing to write off that portion of the selling price that represented the warranty.[70]

A more nuanced analysis is found in *NewCal Industries, Inc. v. Ikon Office Solution: General Electric Corp.*[71] which, like *Kodak*, dealt with aftermarket sales in the copier industry. The plaintiff claimed that Ikon was attempting to monopolize this market by amending the leases and service contracts of its customers to extend the period of service without disclosing that effect to the customers. This extension meant that competing sellers of after-market providers of services could not effectively compete for these customers. Defendants argued that they were like the defendants in *Queen City Pizza* and that whatever market power existed was the result of contractual agreements. The Ninth Circuit Court of Appeals described the distinction that needed to be made:

> ... [I]n determining whether the defendant's market power falls in the *Queens City Pizza* category of contractually-created market power or in the *Eastman Kodak* category of economic market power, the law permits an inquiry into whether a consumer's selection of a particular brand in the competitive market is the functional equivalent of a contractual commitment, giving that brand an agreed-upon right to monopolize its consumers in an aftermarket. The law permits an inquiry into whether consumers entered into such "contracts" knowing that they were agreeing to such a commitment.[72]

The court held that the case at hand was more like *Eastman Kodak* than *Queen City Pizza*. It reasoned that, like *Kodak*, the allegation here was that the defendant was exploiting a unique relationship with its customers. In *Kodak*, that relationship was established by the fact that replacement parts were only obtainable from *Kodak*. Here, the unique relationship was established by virtue of service provided by Ikon under its original contracts with its customers. Second, the extensions or "flex contracts" were not part of the initial lease. In addition, there was evidence that Ikon customers did not make a "knowing choice" to limit their aftermarket suppliers.[73]

---

70. *Id.* at 21.
71. 513 F.3d 1038 (9th Cir. 2008).
72. *Id.* at 1048–49.
73. *Id.* at 1050.

[6] Market Definition and Methods of Distribution

Market definition is not a function of products alone. In *FTC v. Staples*,[74] the Federal Trade Commission challenged the merger of Staples and Office Depot, two retailers of office supplies. Office supply retailers sell a multitude of products that were available from multiple sources, such as local stationers. The defendants, therefore, sought to have the market defined as "office products,"[75] which would give the merging firms a 5.5% market share. The Commission defined the relevant market as "the sale of consumable office supplies through office superstores." The Commission argued that, although office supplies purchased from a superstore were functionally interchangeable with those purchased from other retailers, this was a different matter than whether there was high cross elasticity.

The court noted that within markets, submarkets could exist. In this instance, it was faced with evidence that there was a low cross elasticity of demand between consumable office supplies sold by superstores and those same items when offered by other retailers. In particular, the FTC was able to demonstrate that in the market in which the three office supply superstores—Staples, OfficeMax and Office Depot—competed, Staples' prices were 13% lower than in markets in which it faced no superstore competition.[76] In effect, this and other data tended to support the position that the cross elasticity between an item sold by a superstore and the very same item sold elsewhere was low because consumers did not switch to regular retailers when superstores raised their prices. Thus, the court upheld the market definition based on the type of retailer.

A similar case involved the acquisition of Wild Oats Markets by Whole Foods.[77] Again, both parties sold individual products for which there were substitutes. Nevertheless, as outlets, they were viewed by the Commission as "premium, natural, and organic supermarkets." The FTC took the position that the newly merged entity could profitably raise prices because conventional supermarkets were not viewed by core customers of the merging firms as reasonable substitutes. Those customers were, in effect, purchasing a "lifestyle."[78] The case resulted in an extended battle of the experts who disagreed on the impact of the availability of conventional stores as substitute sellers. A settlement was eventually reached.

[7] Submarkets

A submarket is an "economically distinct" market that is smaller than the general relevant product market.[79] The court in *Biddle v. Walt Disney Co.* explained that "[w]hether a submarket is economically distinct is determined by 'examining such practical indicia,' including: (1) industry or public recognition of the submarket,

---

74. 970 F. Supp. 1066 (D.C. 1997).
75. *Id.* at 1073.
76. *Id.* at 1075–76.
77. *See FTC v. Whole Foods Market, Inc.*, 548 F.3d 1028 (D.C. Cir. 2008).
78. *Id.* at 1039.
79. *Biddle v. Walt Disney Co.*, 696 F. Supp. 3d 865, 881 (N.D. Cal. 2023).

(2) peculiar characteristics and uses of the product, (3) unique production facilities, (4) distinct customers, (5) distinct prices, (6) sensitivity to price changes, and (7) specialized vendors."[80] The analysis of submarkets can be traced generally to *Brown Shoe Co. v. United States*,[81] a merger case that is discussed at length in Chapter Seven. In most instances, the notion of a submarket refers to the fact that one or more sellers of a functionally interchangeable product are deemed to be preferable, by some segment of consumers, to other sellers.[82] The labeling of something as a submarket is arguably an unnecessary step, since there is little indication that the requirements for identifying a submarket are any different from those for identifying a market.[83] The issue does lead to an interesting and so far unanswered question. Since submarket analysis seems to focus on specific groups of customers within a market, how does one decide that the group is economically significant? For example, in the *Whole Foods* case discussed above, much of the economic analysis concerned the importance of "core customers"—those who would not switch to lower priced conventional super markets in response to price increases—and "marginal" customers—those who would switch.[84]

[8] Microsoft *and the Relevance of Network Effects*

In *United States v. Microsoft*,[85] the D.C. Circuit held that Microsoft had illegally monopolized the market for Intel-compatible personal computer (PC) operating systems. The court rejected Microsoft's arguments that the relevant product market should include Apple's operating system Mac OS, operating systems for non-PC devices like handheld units, and middleware, such as internet browsers.[86] The D.C. Circuit agreed with the district court's finding that none of these options were currently reasonably interchangeable.

Microsoft next argued that its high market share—over 95%—was not indicative of monopoly power because there were low entry barriers to the market. The court rejected this argument based on a form of network effects, which the court described as "the 'applications barrier to entry.'"[87] Microsoft's operating system had the largest installed base of users and the largest number of applications written for it. Thus, consumers deciding which operating system to buy would favor Microsoft's operating system because the most applications could run on it, and program developers would choose to write their applications for Microsoft's operating system because the largest

80. *Id.* at 881 (citing *Brown Shoe Co. v. United States*, 370 U.S. 294, 325 (1962)).

81. 370 U.S. 294 (1962).

82. For a recent discussion, see *Hanover 3201 Realty LLC v. Village Supermarkets, Inc.*, 806 F.3d 162 (3d Cir. 2015).

83. *See Flovac v. Airvac, Inc.*, 817 F.3d 849 (1st Cir. 2016); *Geneva Pharm. Tech. Corp. v. Barr Labs., Inc.*, 386 F.3d 485, 496 (2d Cir. 2004).

84. 548 F.3d at 1038–1040.

85. 253 F.3d 34 (D.C. Cir. 2002). An expansive treatment is found at William H. Page & John Lopatka, *The Microsoft Case: Antitrust, Technology and Consumer Welfare* (2007).

86. Middleware is software that contains some of the general protocols (application programming interfaces) found in an operating system.

87. *Id.* at 55.

number of consumers were likely to buy and use their applications. Consumers would not purchase a new and different operating system unless there were sufficient applications written that could run on that new operating system. But program developers would not write applications for a new operating system unless a sufficient number of consumers were using that operating system. This created a chicken-and-egg problem within the market.

In effect, high "entry barriers" owing to consumer preference for a highly "networked" product might be consistent with higher consumer surplus. The court expressly addressed the concept of network effects but generally avoided suggesting that their existence would affect its analysis.[88] First, it noted that there appeared to be no consensus on the importance of network effects to antitrust policy. Second, the existence of network effects would seem to be irrelevant in the analysis of the conduct of a firm that already had achieved market dominance.

[9] Two-Sided Platforms

Market definition and the measurement of market power is more difficult in markets with two-sided platforms.[89] Two-sided platforms exist when a firm contracts with two different groups on opposite sides of a transaction. The platform brings these two groups together to facilitate their transaction. For example, people needing rides use Uber (or Lyft or another ride-sharing service) to find drivers, and drivers use Uber to find paying passengers. Other firms operating two-sided platforms include Ebay, Open Table, Scholastica, real estate listing services, and credit card companies. Uber brings drivers and passengers together and sets a price for their transaction. But the platform operator need not necessarily set a price; it can simply charge one or both parties a fee for facilitating the transaction.

Consider credit cards. Merchants who rely on them pay a small percentage of a sale to the credit card company. Purchasers who use them are typically assessed a yearly fee. A card is more attractive to purchasers if more merchants accept the cards. On the other hand, the cards are more attractive to merchants if many customers possess the card. In effect, the demand in market A will depend not just on the price charged in market A but on the demand in market B. And demand in market B will depend on price in market B and the demand in market A.

The problem arises when a firm takes what is arguably anticompetitive action in market A that causes demand to increase in market B. Market A's customers may be worse off and, examined alone, the practice might be condemned. On the other hand, the practice could make customers in market B better off. Now the issue arises of how to define the market, a process that is now required in all but a few categories of antitrust cases. Should the relevant market be the one directly affected or should there

---

88. *Id.* at 49.

89. *See generally* Patrick Ward, *Testing for Multisided Platform Effect in Antitrust Market Definition,* 84 U. Chi. L. Rev. 2059 (2017); David Evans & Michael Noel, *Defining Antitrust Markets When Firms Operate Two-Sided Platforms,* 2005 Colum. Bus. L. Rev. 667 (2005).

be an effort to define the market so that it includes consideration of the net pro- or anticompetitive effects?

This issue was addressed by the Supreme Court in *U.S. v. American Express Co.*[90] American Express (Amex) had imposed a set of rules for merchants who accepted its cards. Amex imposed an anti-steering rule to prevent merchants from encouraging customers to use non-Amex credit cards that were less expensive to the merchant.[91] The government challenged this vertical restraint as violating § 1 of the Sherman Act. The district court defined the market as "core enabling functions provided by networks, which allow merchants to capture, authorize, and settle transactions for customers who elect to pay with their credit or charge card."[92] In other words, the lower court concentrated on the market populated by merchants. The Second Circuit held this was in error, and that the market had to consider both consumer groups. According to the court:

> This was error because the price charged to merchants necessarily affects cardholder demand, which in turn has a feedback effect on merchant demand (and thus influences the price charged to merchants). In order to retain cardholders, a network may need to increase cardholder benefits—or, viewed another way, "decrease prices" to cardholders. This may call for an increase in merchant fees to fund the increased cardholder rewards. If an increase in merchant fees leads to merchant attrition high enough to render the increased merchant fees unprofitable for the network, then the network will not raise merchant fees and consequently will not increase cardholder rewards. This, in turn, may cause the network to lose cardholders.[93]

In 2018, a sharply divided Supreme Court affirmed the decision of the Second Circuit.[94] Justice Thomas wrote the majority opinion in which he reasoned that the actual market was neither that composed of merchants alone nor card holders alone. Instead, Justice Thomas defined a two-sided platform market as the market centered around transactions. According to Justice Thomas, "[f]or credit cards the network can only sell its services if a merchant and a cardholder both simultaneously choose to use the network."[95] Justice Thomas argued that in two-sided platform markets, antitrust plaintiffs must show anticompetitive effects on both sides of the market. Thus, although merchants were injured by Amex's anti-steering rule, Justice Thomas asserted that consumers benefitted through Amex's cardholder rewards program. Justice Thomas seemed to ignore the fact that only a fraction of Amex's merchant fees were funneled into cardholder rewards, and thus, merchants were injured more

---

90. 838 F.2d 179 (2d Cir. 2017).
91. *Id.* at 191.
92. *Id.* at 197.
93. *Id.* at 200 (notes omitted).
94. *Ohio v. American Express Co.*, 138 S. Ct. 2274 (2018).
95. *Id.* at 2286.

than consumers were benefitted. This definition of the market did not explain how to reconcile this imbalance.

Given the imprecision of Justice Thomas' opinion and the 5-4 split on the court, it is useful to examine Justice Breyer's dissent. Justice Breyer took a practical view and asked how the decision to treat a two-sided market as a single market was useful with respect to the purpose of market definitions in antitrust cases.[96] He noted that two-sided platforms had four characteristics: "(1) they offer different products or services, (2) to different groups of customers, (3) whom the 'platform' connects, (4) in simultaneous transactions."[97]

Justice Thomas himself distinguished the case of credit cards from that of newspapers. Newspapers are in a sense two-sided platforms in that they sell to readers and to advertisers. Advertisers will pay more depending on the number of likely readers. On the other hand, he reasoned that readers were largely unconcerned with the quantity of advertising. In short, the demand for newspapers is independent of the amount of advertising contained.[98] This indicates that a critical element in determining whether the market definition must encompass the platform as a whole is the interdependence of the two products. Just how strong that interdependence must be is undetermined.

Justice Breyer went on to note that the first two characteristics hardly called for a special market definition given that many firms sell two or more products to two or more groups of customers. He also argued that firms connecting two groups of customers who make simultaneous transactions are commonplace and gave the examples of farmers' markets and travel agents.[99] He concluded, "Nothing in antitrust law ... suggests that a court, when presented with an agreement that restricts competition in any one of the markets my examples suggest, should abandon traditional market definition approaches. . . ."[100] In fact, it is correct that Justice Thomas offered no rationale in terms of advancing the goals of antitrust for including complementary products into a single market.

Because Justice Thomas' opinion makes it harder for antitrust claims to prevail in a two-sided platform market, antitrust defendants have asserted that they operate in two-sided markets, hoping to take advantage of the *Amex* opinion.

[10] Market Definition in the Context of Monopsony

Most antitrust discussions of market power involve sellers having power over buyers, either through monopolies or seller-based collusion. But antitrust also cares about market power on the buyers' side, such as monopsonies (markets with a single

96. *Id.* at 2297.

97. *Id.* at 2298.

98. This may be true in the traditional sense of newspapers, but there exists a wide variety of newspaper-like publications in which the relationship between the two products—advertising and access to advertisements—is similar to that of credit card holders and merchants.

99. *Id.* at 2299.

100. *Id.*

dominant buyer) or buyer-based cartels, such as when employers conspire to reduce workers' wages, or buyers combine to set prices or the terms of exchange.[101] Like illegal monopolies, a monopsony violates § 2 when it is acquired or maintained through anticompetitive conduct. Also, an agreement among buyers violates § 1 of the Sherman Act when it unreasonably restrains trade.

Antitrust claims against monopsonists and buyer cartels generally require the plaintiffs to define the relevant market. The key to market definition in the context of monopsony is to assess the market from the point of view of sellers attempting to sell their goods or services. This is similar to the demand and supply substitutability analysis used to define markets in more traditional antitrust claims. For example, when the focus is on sellers, we ask whether buyers can find substitute products or whether new suppliers might enter the market to lower the ability of sellers to raise prices above competitive levels. In the case of monopsony, we ask whether sellers could find alternative buyers for their goods or services or whether prices might be forced so low by the monopsonist that new buyers would enter the market.

Although producers paying lower prices for inputs would seem to benefit consumers, antitrust law condemns illegal monopsonies and buyer-side cartels for several reasons. First, it should be noted that the antitrust laws are designed to encourage competitive markets in the interest of allocative efficiency. The use of monopsony power, much like the use of monopoly power, prevents the market from working to allocate resources to their most valued uses. Second, the fact that a firm may pay less for an input does not mean that savings will be passed on to consumers. Lower input prices may mean that producers of the inputs supply less, and the output of the final product is lower, and prices actually increase. Third, antitrust law cares about employees. When employers conspire to reduce wages or to not poach each other's workers, this necessarily implicates antitrust principles.

In *Todd v. Exxon Corporation*,[102] in which professional workers claimed that several employers had, in effect, conspired to suppress wages, the Second Circuit correctly noted that the market power of buyers was the "mirror image" of that involved in the case of sellers.[103] Thus, the issue in terms of the relevant market was whether there were substitute buyers for the employee services that would have an impact on the ability of the defendants to lower wages. If so, these buyers would be included in the relevant market.

Buying power has played a role in a number of recent cases. For example, in *NCAA v. Alston*,[104] the Supreme Court noted that the National Collegiate Athletic Association (NCAA) possessed monopsony power in the relevant market of athletic services in men's and women's Division I basketball and Football Bowl Subdivision football.

---

101. *See, e.g., Fraser v. Major League Soccer*, 284 F.3d 47 (1st Cir. 2002); *Todd v. Exxon Corp.*, 275 F.3d 191 (2d Cir. 2001); *Kartell v. Blue Shield of Mass.*, 749 F.2d 922 (1st Cir. 1984). *See generally* Roger D. Blair & Jeffrey L. Harrison, *Monopsony in Law and Economics* (2010).

102. 275 F.3d 191 (2d Cir. 2001).

103. *Id.* at 202 (citations omitted).

104. 594 U.S. 69 (2021).

The NCAA used its monopsony power to depress wages below competitive levels for student-athletes. The Court upheld the district court's finding of antitrust liability, as well as a permanent injunction against the NCAA.

In *West Allegheny Health Services, Inc. v. UPMC,*[105] the complaint was that a competing hospital and an insurance company had conspired to reduce the reimbursement rates paid to the plaintiff hospital. The court noted that the insurance company had a 60–80% share of the insurance market in the relevant geographic market and that rival insurers would face high entry barriers. In short, the defendant possessed monopsony power in the market for the purchase of hospital services.[106] In the course of its decision, the court addressed the issue of whether lower reimbursement rates would mean lower premiums for customers. It noted that there is no necessary connection between consumer welfare and the use of monopsony power to lower payments to suppliers.[107]

105. 627 F.3d 85 (3d Cir. 2010).
106. *Id.* at 105.
107. *Id.* at 104–06.

Chapter 3

Antitrust Coverage: Jurisdiction, Enforcement, and Exceptions

§ 3.01 Introduction

Several independent actors can enforce antitrust law.[1] The Department of Justice Antitrust Division and the Federal Trade Commission (FTC) are the primary federal agencies enforcing antitrust law. The two agencies have concurrent jurisdiction over several sections of the Clayton Act and the Robinson-Patman Act. Only the Department of Justice has criminal jurisdiction, however. The Department also has authority over the Sherman Act, while the FTC exercises authority over the Federal Trade Commission Act. On the state level, state attorneys general have authority to file Sherman Act suits for damages or equitable relief as *parens patriae* on behalf of individuals (consumers) residing within the state.[2] Private civil enforcement can be commenced by "any person who [is] injured in his business or property" by reason of a violation of "anything forbidden in the antitrust laws."[3] The action can be for either treble damages[4] or injunctive relief.[5] Reasonable attorney's fees and costs are awarded under either a damage award or injunctive relief.

1. 15 U.S.C. § 15 (2012). Subject matter jurisdiction rests exclusively in the federal district court. No minimum amount in controversy is required. For a Sherman Act violation, the conduct need only have a substantial "effect" on commerce. *Summit Health, Ltd. v. Pinhas*, 500 U.S. 322 (1991); *McLain v. Real Estate Bd. of New Orleans Inc.*, 444 U.S. 232 (1980). The Clayton Act, however, is only triggered if the alleged practices are "in" interstate commerce. An exception is made for § 7 of the Act (mergers): jurisdiction is present if the "effects" test is met. The Robinson-Patman Act's jurisdictional reach requires antitrust conduct "in" interstate commerce. The FTC's jurisdiction extends to practices which affect interstate commerce. Both the Sherman Act and the FTC Act also have an extraterritorial reach extending to foreign commerce. But the "effects" on foreign commerce must be direct, foreseeable, and substantial.
2. 15 U.S.C. §§ 15, 15h.
3. 15 U.S.C. § 15 (2012).
4. *Id.*
5. 15 U.S.C. § 26 (2012).

§ 3.02 Private Enforcement

The Court interprets § 4 of the Clayton Act[6] to require that a plaintiff bringing a civil action for damages demonstrate that she has suffered an actual injury to her property or business and that the injury was caused by defendant's conduct that violated the antitrust law.[7] Section 4 provides that successful private plaintiffs shall automatically receive treble damages, meaning that compensatory damages are tripled.[8] Congress intended treble damages to deter anticompetitive conduct, penalize antitrust defendants, compensate victims, disgorge illicit gains, create an incentive for private suits, and supplement public enforcement.

The treble damage remedy, however, has not been without challenge or controversy.[9] First, some economists and antitrust commentators have criticized treble damages as inefficient and unfair. Others argue that they produce over-deterrence and encourage nuisance or strike suits.[10] Section 4 is inefficient, the argument goes, because it gives consumers an incentive to purchase from overcharging sellers "in order to benefit . . . threefold the amount of damages actually sustained."[11] The statute does not encourage consumers to mitigate damages. On the other hand, single damages would not be much of a deterrent, since the probability of detection and liability is less than one.

Second, because the proscribed antitrust conduct is sometimes vague, treble damages may create a disincentive for competitors to compete aggressively for fear that their conduct may overstep the bounds of legality. Thus, the competitor avoids the risk of illegality and forgoes the conduct. This argument does not apply to naked

6. 15 U.S.C. § 15.

7. *Brunswick Corp. v. Pueblo Bowl-O-Mat, Inc.*, 429 U.S. 477 (1977). *See infra* § 3.02[B] for a discussion of *Brunswick*. The antitrust laws incorporated by reference into § 4 include the Sherman and Clayton Acts and certain portions of the Wilson Tariff Act, but not § 5 of the FTC Act or § 3 of the Robinson-Patman Act.

8. A couple statutory exceptions to trebling exist. For example, the National Cooperative Research and Production Act and the Standards Development Organization Advancement Act of 2004 reduce antitrust damages to single damages for members of qualifying and appropriately registered joint ventures and standard setting organizations. And, under the government's antitrust leniency program, the Antitrust Criminal Penalty Enhancement and Reform Act of 2004 limits the first confessing cartel member to single damages in follow-on litigation.

Courts sometimes undermine trebling by approving class action settlements based on single damages. Christopher R. Leslie, *De Facto Detrebling: The Rush to Settlement in Antitrust Class Action Litigation*, 50 Ariz. L. Rev. 1009, 1042 (2008).

9. *See, e.g.*, *Blue Shield of Va. v. McCready*, 457 U.S. 465, 472 (1982); *Am. Soc'y of Mech. Eng'rs, Inc. v. Hydrolevel Corp.*, 456 U.S. 556, 572 (1982); George Garvey, *Report of the Comm. on the Judiciary, U.S. House of Representatives—Study of the Antitrust Treble Damage Remedy*, 98th Cong., 2d Sess. (1984); Kenneth G. Elzinga & William Breit, *The Antitrust Penalties: A Study in Law and Economics* 65 (1976); Edward D. Cavanagh, *Detrebling Antitrust Damages: An Idea Whose Time Has Come?*, 61 Tul. L. Rev. 777 (1987); Frank H. Easterbrook, *Detrebling Antitrust Damages*, 28 J.L. & Econ. 445 (1985); Robert H. Lande, *Are Antitrust "Treble" Damages Really Single Damages?*, 54 Ohio St. L.J. 115 (1993).

10. *See* Cavanagh, *supra* note 9, at 781–820, where the author sets out an excellent review of the competing theories.

11. Elzinga & Breit, *supra* note 9, at 430. *Contra* Easterbrook, *supra* note 9, at 451.

restraints that are clearly anticompetitive, like horizontal price fixing.[12] Some commentators argue that an optimal sanction might be somewhere between actual damages and treble damages, but this remains only a theoretical proposition.[13]

Third, treble damages could encourage meritless suits[14] if defendants are unwilling to risk an outcome that may award damages three times actual injury; hence, the antitrust defendant is more likely to settle with a plaintiff. The antitrust suit also may be used as a predatory, strategic tactic against a rival for the purpose of either extracting a commercial concession or discouraging vigorous competition.[15] It can serve as a form of protectionism for the antitrust plaintiff.[16] Given how difficult it is for antitrust plaintiffs to survive summary judgment,[17] let alone win a verdict on the merits, it remains unclear whether the prospect of treble damages actually results in frivolous antitrust lawsuits.

Finally, treble damages have been called unfair because the amount awarded compensates a plaintiff in excess of the losses from actual injury ("windfall") and penalizes a defendant (or the stockholders of the corporate defendant rather than management) in excess of the gains from actual misconduct. This argument is undermined by other aspects of antitrust law that reduce damages.[18] Moreover, most antitrust litigation settles, and courts approve proposed class action settlements based on single damages, not treble damages.[19]

Because antitrust law provides for joint and several liability with no right to contribution, a single conspirator could be responsible for treble damages for all of the conspiracy's damages, even on sales it did not make.[20] Antitrust defendants may try to create a right to contribution through a judgment-sharing agreement, a private contract that provides that each defendant will pay an agreed-upon percentage of

---

12. *See* Christopher R. Leslie, *False Analogies to Predatory Pricing*, 172 U. Pa. L. Rev. 329 (2024).

13. *See generally* William Breit & Kenneth G. Elzinga, *Private Antitrust Enforcement: The New Learning*, 28 J.L. & Econ. 405 (1985); Easterbrook, *supra* note 9; William M. Landes, *Optimal Sanctions for Antitrust Violations*, 50 U. Chi. L. Rev. 652, 678 (1983).

14. *See* Fed. R. Civ. P. 11, 16.

15. *See, e.g.*, Thomas G. Krattenmaker & Steven C. Salop, *Anticompetitive Exclusion: Raising Rivals' Costs to Achieve Power over Price*, 96 Yale L.J. 209 (1986); Arthur D. Austin, *Negative Effects of Treble Damage Actions: Reflections on the New Antitrust Strategy*, 1978 Duke L.J. 1353.

16. William J. Baumol & Janusz A. Ordover, *Use of Antitrust Laws to Subvert Competition*, 28 J.L. & Econ. 247 (1985).

17. *See* Christopher R. Leslie, *The Decline and Fall of Circumstantial Evidence in Antitrust Law*, 69 Am. U. L. Rev. 1713 (2020).

18. See Lande, *supra* note 9.

19. See Leslie, *supra* note 8.

20. *See generally* Donald J. Polden & E. Thomas Sullivan, *Contribution and Claim Reduction in Antitrust Litigation: A Legislative Analysis*, 20 Harv. J. on Legis. 397 (1983); E. Thomas Sullivan, *New Perspectives in Antitrust Litigation: Towards a Right of Comparative Contribution*, 1980 U. Ill. L.F. 389. For an excellent review and analysis, see Edward D. Cavanagh, *Contribution, Claim Reduction, and Individual Treble Damage Responsibility: Which Path to Reform of Antitrust Remedies?*, 40 Vand. L. Rev. 1277 (1987).

any antitrust damages.[21] Because judgment-sharing agreements can help conceal and stabilize price-fixing conspiracies, they may themselves violate antitrust law.[22]

The debate continues on each of these challenges to treble damages. Some commentators urge a discretionary use of treble damages. This has the advantage of reducing the inherent unfairness of treble damages, but it also decreases deterrence, reduces incentives for private causes of action, reduces business predictability, and increases litigation complexity and costs. Others suggest a modified trebling rule which would reserve trebling for *per se* offenses or when anticompetitive intent is demonstrated, leaving actual damages recoverable for rule of reason cases.[23]

[A] Standing

Civil damage actions under § 4 of the Clayton Act require an allegation of injury to plaintiff's "business or property." In *Hawaii v. Standard Oil Co.*,[24] the Supreme Court invoked standing doctrine to deny a state the right to sue under the antitrust laws for injuries to the state's general economy. Distinguishing between the "business or property" requirement of § 4, the Court held that personal injuries alone were not sufficient to grant standing. The Court observed that the language of § 4 refers to "commercial interests or enterprise."

In contrast, the Court cautioned that the pleading rules governing § 4 differ from those under § 16. Because the "business or property" requirement is lacking in § 16, pleading and proof requirements are less severe. One need not establish that an injury already has been sustained but rather that there is a threatened loss or damage. Further, injunctive relief has not been limited to injuries to business or property under § 16; non-commercial interests also have been protected.[25]

In *Reiter v. Sonotone Corp.*,[26] the Court gave a more liberal interpretation to the "business or property" requirement of § 4 for damage suits. In referring to its decision in *Hawaii*, the *Reiter* Court said "[u]se of the phrase 'commercial interests or enterprise,' read in context, in no sense suggests that only injuries to a business entity are within the ambit of § 4."[27] The Court held that a consumer can maintain a treble damage action, although no commercial or profit interest is at stake, as long as a monetary injury is alleged, such as an overcharge paid by consumers to price fixers or an

---

21. Christopher R. Leslie, *Judgment-Sharing Agreements*, 58 Duke L.J. 747 (2009).

22. *Id.*

23. *See generally* Cavanagh, *supra* note 9, at 820–48. As the *per se* categories are narrowed and the rule of reason classification expanded (*see* Chapters 4 and 5 on horizontal and vertical restraints), the application of treble damages is significantly decreased.

24. 405 U.S. 251 (1972).

25. *See, e.g., Mid-West Paper Prods. Co. v. Cont'l Group, Inc.*, 596 F.2d 573 (3d Cir. 1979). *See generally Cargill, Inc. v. Monfort of Colo., Inc.*, 479 U.S. 104 (1986).

26. 442 U.S. 330 (1979).

27. *Id.* at 341. "The phrase 'commercial interest' was used there as a generic reference to the interests of the State of Hawaii as a party to a commercial transaction."

illegal monopolist. By giving the words "any person" and "property" in § 4 broad and inclusive meaning, *Reiter* encouraged antitrust enforcement through private causes of action by consumer suits.

This judicially created antitrust standing doctrine significantly reduces the class of persons capable of filing an antitrust damage action. In *Blue Shield of Virginia v. McCready*,[28] the Supreme Court considered whether a policyholder of a group insurance plan, who employed a particular psychologist, had standing to sue the insurance company that had engaged in a concerted refusal to deal with that psychologist for payment of treatment. The defendant's policy limited reimbursement to treatment by psychiatrists. Plaintiff alleged that she was injured when the group health plan refused to reimburse her for the costs of psychologist's services.

Holding that plaintiff had standing to sue Blue Shield, the Supreme Court reasoned that plaintiff's injury was directly integral to the conduct of the insurance company because psychologists were the target of a boycott and the patients were the means through which defendant achieved the boycott. McCready was "within that area of the economy ... endangered by the breakdown of competitive conditions, resulting from Blue Shield's selective refusal to reimburse,"[29] because she was a "consumer of psychotherapy services entitled to financial benefits under the ... plan."[30] Her injury "was inextricably intertwined with the injury the conspirators sought to inflict on [the] market."[31]

From an economic viewpoint, the refusal to reimburse psychologists reduced the demand for their services, and resulted in a decrease in competition and increased prices for the services of psychiatrists. The overcharge would be passed on to the users of the services of psychiatrists.

Setting forth the test of standing, the Court said: "It is reasonable to assume that Congress did not intend to allow every person tangentially affected by an antitrust violation to maintain an action to recover threefold damages for the injury to his business or property;"[32] a court should look "to the physical and economic nexus between the alleged violation and the harm to the plaintiff,"[33] and whether the injury is the type

28. 457 U.S. 465 (1982).

29. *Id.* at 480–81, (quoting *In re Multidistrict Vehicle Air Pollution M.D.L. No. 31*, 481 F.2d 122, 129 (9th Cir. 1973)).

30. *Id.*

31. *Id.* at 484.

32. *Id.* at 477.

33. *Id.* at 478. For instance, the inquiry might be how fortuitous or incidental is the harm to the plaintiff from the actual challenged conduct.

See also *id.* at 476–77, where the *McCready* Court readily admitted to the difficulty of setting out a concrete test for the abstract concept of "standing." The Court stated that, without Congressional guidance, "courts are thus forced to resort to an analysis no less elusive than that employed traditionally by courts at common law with respect to the matter of 'proximate cause.'" The Court suggested that much of this elusiveness can be attributed to the broad language and remedial objectives of § 4. Clearly, the potential problems associated with determining standing and defining its parameters have been apparent from the beginning.

that Congress was concerned with when it made the alleged conduct unlawful. This latter inquiry generally is referred to as the "antitrust injury" test, while the former standard is the standing rationale. Standing focuses on the relationship or closeness (or remoteness) of the injury to the antitrust conduct.

In the term after *McCready*, the Court heightened the requirement for antitrust standing in *Associated General Contractors of California, Inc. v. California State Council of Carpenters*.[34] In an opinion written by Justice Stevens, who had dissented in *McCready*, the Court held that a union lacked standing to sue a multiemployer association which allegedly coerced certain third parties not to enter business relationships with union firms. As a matter of law, the union was not injured within the meaning of § 4 because it was not a consumer or competitor in the market in which trade was restrained. It was unclear whether the union's "interests would be served or disserved by enhanced competition in the market."[35] With regard to "antitrust injury," the Court noted:

> [A] union's primary goal is to enhance the earnings and improve the working conditions of its membership; that goal is not necessarily served, and indeed may actually be harmed, by uninhibited competition among employers striving to reduce costs in order to obtain a competitive advantage over their rivals. Set against this background, a union, in its capacity as bargaining representative, will frequently not be part of the class the Sherman Act was designed to protect, especially in disputes with employers with whom it bargains. In this case, particularly in light of the longstanding collective bargaining relationship between the parties, the Union's labor-market interests seem to predominate.[36]

With regard to "standing," the Court observed that the chain of causation between the union and the restraint on construction subcontracts was vague, indirect, and speculative. The union failed to allege (1) that any collective bargaining agreement was terminated as a result of the coercion; (2) that the aggregate share of the contracting market controlled by union firms had diminished; (3) that the number of employed union members had declined; (4) that union revenues in the form of dues or initiation fees had decreased; or (5) that any firm was prevented from doing business with a union.[37] In short, the plaintiff union did not satisfy the standing require-

---

34. 459 U.S. 519 (1983). *See generally* Note, *More Trouble with Treble: The Effects of McCready and Associated General Contractors on Antitrust Standing Opinions of the Federal Courts of Appeals*, 10 J. Corp. L. 463 (1985); Kevin D. Gordon, Note, *Private Antitrust Standing: A Survey and Analysis of the Law After Associated General*, 61 Wash. U. L.Q. 1069 (1984); Daniel C. Richman, Note, *Antitrust Standing, Antitrust Injury, and the Per Se Standard*, 93 Yale L.J. 1309 (1984); Charles N. Charnas, Comment, *Segregation of Antitrust Damages: An Excessive Burden on Private Plaintiffs*, 72 Cal. L. Rev. 403 (1984); Clare Deffense, Comment, *A Farewell to Arms: The Implementation of a Policy-Based Standing Analysis in Antitrust Treble Damage Action*, 72 Cal. L. Rev. 437 (1984).

35. 459 U.S. at 539.

36. *Id.* at 539–40.

37. *Id.* at 542. Lower federal courts subsequent to *Associated General* have required that a plaintiff demonstrate that it was a "participant in the same market as the alleged malefactors." *See, e.g.*, *Bhan v. NME Hosps., Inc.*, 772 F.2d 1467, 1470 (9th Cir. 1985).

ment because it did not demonstrate a *direct* link between the alleged injury and a decrease in competition.

One interpretation of *Associated General* is that only consumers or competitors have standing under § 4. That conclusion may distinguish the results of *McCready* and *Associated General*. Both cases, in addition to standing, address the "antitrust injury" test and seem to incorporate it into the standing inquiry. Consequently, under modern antitrust analysis, the plaintiff must satisfy the antitrust injury requirement *and* otherwise be an "appropriate" party to bring the action.

[B] Antitrust Injury

In order to establish antitrust standing, a private plaintiff needs to show that it has suffered antitrust injury, which is an injury caused by a reduction of competition. In *Brunswick Corp. v. Pueblo Bowl-O-Mat*,[38] plaintiffs, owners of bowling centers, challenged Brunswick's acquisition of a competitor as violating § 7 of the Clayton Act, which proscribes anticompetitive mergers and acquisitions. Plaintiffs alleged that Brunswick's acquisition of the plaintiffs' failing rival injured them because, if Brunswick did not acquire this competing bowling center, it would have gone out of business, and plaintiffs would have received greater profits and increased market share.

Although Brunswick's acquisition "injured" plaintiffs by reducing their expected profits, the Court explained that this was not an antitrust injury because the injury flowed from increased competition, which is not "the type that the statute was intended to forestall."[39] Mere injury to a competitor is not necessarily antitrust injury because the antitrust laws were enacted for the "protection of *competition* not competitors."[40] The Court held that private plaintiffs seeking treble damages "must prove *antitrust* injury, which is to say injury of the type the antitrust laws were intended to prevent and that flows from that which makes defendants' acts unlawful."[41]

Brunswick, therefore, requires that an antitrust plaintiff seeking damages under § 4 of the Clayton Act plead and prove that its injury was caused by illegal conduct that reduced competition.[42] Lost profits or reduced market share by reason of an *increase* in competition is not actionable under the *Brunswick* doctrine. The antitrust loss must occur "by reason of" that which makes the conduct unlawful.

38. 429 U.S. 477 (1977). *See generally* Roger D. Blair & Jeffrey L. Harrison, *Rethinking Antitrust Injury*, 42 Vand. L. Rev. 1539 (1989).

39. *Id.* at 487–88 (quoting *Wyandotte Co. v. United States*, 389 U.S. 191, 202 (1967)).

40. *Id.* at 488 (quoting *Brown Shoe Co. v. United States*, 370 U.S. 294, 320 (1962) (emphasis added)).

41. *Id.* at 489 (emphasis added) (citation omitted).

42. *See Daniel v. Am. Bd. of Emergency Med.*, 428 F.3d 408, 440 (2d Cir. 2005) (holding that the harm allegedly suffered by the plaintiffs, namely exclusion from the anticompetitive scheme, was not an injury to competition); *Spanish Broad. Sys. of Fla. Inc. v. Clear Channel Commc'ns Inc.*, 376 F.3d 1065, 1072–74 (11th Cir. 2004) (finding that rival's advertising pricing strategy was only an injury to plaintiff and not an injury to competition); *Nat'l Ass'n of Review Appraisers & Mortgage Underwriters, Inc. v. Appraisal Found.*, 64 F.3d 1130, 1134–35 (8th Cir. 1995) (holding plaintiff responsible for own injuries through incidents evidencing poor management and development of reputation as a "diploma mill").

The Third Circuit's pronouncement in *Philadelphia Taxi Ass'n v. Uber Technologies*[43] illustrates this requirement. The court dismissed a claim that Uber's allegedly illegal entry into the market absent approval from the Philadelphia Parking Authority caused an antitrust injury to members of the taxicab association. Emphasizing that antitrust law compensates plaintiffs for injuries that occur as a result of anticompetitive conduct, not conduct that merely harms competitors, the court determined that Uber's entry into the market, whether legal or illegal under Philadelphia law, increased the number of vehicles-for-hire available and lowered prices for consumers. Therefore, the plaintiffs lacked an antitrust injury, because Uber's entry made the market more competitive.

Unlike ordinary standing principles, which look to the directness or remoteness of the injury from the antitrust violation, the doctrine of "antitrust injury" centers on the nature of plaintiff's injury.[44] Each requirement is a separate pleading and proof burden on the plaintiff; the Court must be sure each is satisfied. In *Associated General*, the Court joined the two tests—standing and antitrust injury—into a single broad-based inquiry.

Courts also have applied the antitrust injury standard to substantive provisions of the Sherman Act as well as the Clayton Act, and to injunction requirements under § 16 of the Clayton Act.[45] In *Cargill, Inc. v. Monfort of Colorado, Inc.*,[46] the Court applied *Brunswick's* antitrust injury test to a private action for equitable relief. Holding that a plaintiff who seeks injunctive relief must show more than a casual connection between the injury and the antitrust violation, the Court held that even under § 16 of the Clayton Act the plaintiff must demonstrate a *threat* of antitrust injury.

---

43. 886 F.3d 332 (3d Cir. 2018).

44. *See generally* William H. Page, *Antitrust Damages and Economic Efficiency: An Approach to Antitrust Injury*, 47 U. Chi. L. Rev. 467 (1980). The standing inquiry also will consider, secondarily, the risk of multiple liability, damage allocation complexity, and the presence of other more directly affected plaintiffs. *See* Blair & Harrison, *supra* note 37, at 1551.

45. *See, e.g.*, *J. Truett Payne Co. v. Chrysler Motors Corp.*, 451 U.S. 557 (1981); *B-S Steel of Kan., Inc. v. Tex. Indus., Inc.*, 439 F.3d 653 (10th Cir. 2006); *Schoenkopf v. Brown & Williamson Tobacco Corp.*, 637 F.2d 205, 210–11 (3d Cir. 1980); *Berkey Photo, Inc. v. Eastman Kodak Co.*, 603 F.2d 263 (2d Cir. 1979); *see also* Phillip E. Areeda & Herbert Hovenkamp, *Antitrust Law* § 334.2 (1993 Supp.).

In *Atlantic Richfield Co. v. USA Petroleum Co.*, 495 U.S. 328 (1990), the Court applied the antitrust injury test to the substantive antitrust law governing a vertical, maximum price-fixing scheme. The Court held that a plaintiff who loses sales to a competitor charging nonpredatory prices within a vertical, maximum price-fixing scheme did not suffer antitrust injury and thus was precluded from bringing a claim under § 4 of the Clayton Act. As long as the competitor's prices were not predatory—below marginal cost—the plaintiff was not injured by reason of the defendant's conduct because the pricing was not anticompetitive, but rather procompetitive, reasoned the Court. "[U]ntil a private party is adversely affected by an *anticompetitive* aspect of the defendant's conduct . . . in the context of pricing practices, only predatory pricing has the requisite anticompetitive effect." *Id.* at 339. Plainly, then, before a plaintiff can recover from a federal antitrust violation, it must first demonstrate that it was the kind of person sought to be protected by the antitrust laws and one who suffered by reason of a decrease in competition brought about by defendants' behavior. *See* further discussion of *Atlantic Richfield* in § 5.01[B](2).

46. 479 U.S. 104 (1986).

The Court in *Cargill* explained that standing may take on different meanings under § 16 or § 4, and the remedy sought may dictate the analysis. Because § 4 provides for damage recovery, the Court, under the standing rubric, is concerned also with multiple lawsuits, duplicative recoveries and complexity of damage apportionment. These concerns are not present, however, if the remedy sought is an injunction under § 16. Thus, standing under § 16 may be easier to prove than under § 4. To satisfy the antitrust injury test, a plaintiff, under either section, must plead and prove that the injury (or threat of injury under § 16) was in fact caused by a decrease in competition through defendant's conduct, and not merely that plaintiff's injury (or the threat of injury) was caused by procompetitive conduct of the defendant. A casual connection between plaintiff's injury and defendant's conduct is insufficient: the injury or threat of injury must be by reason of defendant's violation of antitrust law, the result of which is a decrease in market competition.

The Court, in *Atlantic Richfield Co. v. USA Petroleum Co.*, found that an independent gas merchant was not unduly injured by an alleged vertical conspiracy between Atlantic Richfield and its dealers which fixed maximum resale prices for Atlantic Richfield gas. Although maximum resale price maintenance was per se illegal at the time of the opinion,[47] the plaintiff's ability to compete as an independent dealer was not affected by the activity, nor was the plaintiff a consumer directly affected by the activity. The purpose of the antitrust injury requirement is to make sure the plaintiff is injured by competition-reducing activity. Merely because the activity is *per se* unlawful doesn't mean the plaintiff is injured by it. The Court in *Atlantic Richfield* held "proof of a *per se* violation and of antitrust injury are distinct matters that must be shown independently."[48]

There is uncertainty among the circuits with respect to how the standing and antitrust injury requirements affect plaintiffs who are neither customers nor competitors of defendants. In *Sullivan v. Tagliabue*,[49] the First Circuit said *McCready* extended recovery rights to some plaintiffs who were neither competitors nor direct victims of the violation, but instead stood in a "vertical relation" to the direct victim.[50] The plaintiff was denied relief in that case, however, because he was not a "'necessary' instrument[] to effectuate the alleged conspiracy."[51] In contrast, the First Circuit held, one year later, that "presumptively proper" plaintiffs are consumers or competitors, and the "inextricable intertwin[ing]" of injury and antitrust violation may not be enough if the plaintiff does not fit into one of the two proper categories.[52]

---

47. *Id.* at 335. Resale price maintenance is no longer per se illegal. In *State Oil Co. v. Khan*, 522 U.S. 3 (1997), the Court held that maximum vertical price-fixing agreements are not *per se* illegal (discussed, *infra* § 5.01[B](2)). And in *Leegin Creative Leather Prods., Inc. v. PSKS, Inc.*, 551 U.S. 877 (2007), the Supreme Court held that all vertical price fixing is evaluated under the rule of reason.

48. *Id.* at 344 (quoting Phillip E. Areeda & Herbert Hovenkamp, *Antitrust Law* ¶ 334.20, p. 330 (1989 Supp.) (emphasis added)).

49. 25 F.3d 43 (1st Cir. 1994).

50. *Id.* at 48.

51. *Id.* at 50.

52. *SAS of P.R., Inc. v. P.R. Tel. Co.*, 48 F.3d 39, 44, 46 (1st Cir. 1995).

There is a fair amount of controversy and disagreement surrounding whether noncompetitors and nonconsumers can actually suffer "antitrust injury" as traditionally understood and whether the courts can accord such plaintiffs standing without completely disregarding *Brunswick*. There does not seem to be a strong trend in either direction.

[C] Direct Purchaser Requirement

Even an antitrust plaintiff who suffers an injury caused by a reduction in competition may not have standing to seek recovery for an antitrust violation if the plaintiff is not a direct purchaser from the defendant. In *Illinois Brick Co. v. Illinois*,[53] the Court ruled that a plaintiff cannot recover for an illegal overcharge due to a price-fixing agreement if the plaintiff did not purchase directly from a member of the price-fixing conspiracy. Indirect purchasers, in other words, are not "persons" injured in their "business or property" under § 4 of the Clayton Act. In order to bring a treble damage claim under a price-fixing theory, the plaintiff must have been a direct purchaser from an alleged wrongdoer. The fact that the direct purchaser "passed on" the overcharge to the ultimate consumer is not enough.

The Court feared, as a matter of policy, that if indirect purchasers were permitted to sue under the pass-on theory: (1) the process costs of litigation would increase because of the tracing complexities and uncertainty; (2) defendants would be exposed to multiple liability from direct purchasers to middlemen, as well as from the ultimate consumer; (3) that plaintiffs as a class would recover duplicative recoveries; and (4) that inconsistent judgments would result. Antitrust policy, the Court opined, is better served by permitting the direct purchaser to recover the full amount of the overcharge than apportionment of damages among all parties in the distribution process.[54]

Nonetheless, the Court suggested some exceptions to the rule that only direct purchasers state a claim for relief under § 4. First, the rule does not apply if there is a preexisting, fixed quantity, cost-plus contract between the first purchaser and the indirect buyer which automatically passes on the overcharge to the indirect buyer who is committed to buying the fixed quantity regardless of price.[55] But the pass-on cannot be discretionary. If these conditions are met, the problems of tracing and duplicative recovery are minimized.

---

53. 431 U.S. 720 (1977).

54. *Id.* at 730. The Court reasoned that deterrence is greater because the magnitude of the loss to the direct purchaser is greater than multiple suits by indirect purchasers. *Id.* at 745. But deterrence may be reduced if direct purchasers are precluded from litigating against the price fixer because the antitrust violator has forced its direct purchasers to submit to mandatory arbitration. Mark A. Lemley & Christopher R. Leslie, *Antitrust Arbitration and Illinois Brick*, 100 Iowa L. Rev. 2115 (2015).

The Court also reaffirmed the *Hanover Shoe, Inc. v. United Shoe Machinery Corp.*, 392 U.S. 481 (1968), doctrine that prohibited defensive use of pass-on: defendant is not permitted to show that the plaintiff passed the overcharge on down the distribution chain and thus was not injured by the overcharge. *Illinois Brick*, 431 U.S. at 736.

55. 431 U.S. at 726 n.2 (citing *Hanover Shoe*, 392 U.S. at 494).

Second, where the first purchaser is "controlled or owned" by the wrongdoer, an indirect buyer may state a claim for relief and show that the overcharge was passed-on. The relevant inquiry is whether defendants may suffer multiple liability[56] and whether more than one transaction occurred.

Third, if a vertical price-fixing conspiracy is alleged, *Illinois Brick* does not apply because the plaintiff (consumer) becomes a direct purchaser from a co-conspirator.[57] However, in order to foreclose the possibility of multiple liability, the co-conspirator middleman may have to be joined in the suit.[58] Indeed, the Third Circuit adopted a limited co-conspirator exception in *Howard Hess Dental Labs., Inc. v. Dentsply Int'l, Inc.*[59] The *Dentsply* court denied standing under the *Illinois Brick* rule, because the plaintiffs failed to join intermediary dealers in an alleged vertical price-fixing conspiracy. The court reasoned that joinder was needed to fulfill the policy justifications of *Illinois Brick*—specifically to eliminate duplicative recovery and to avoid evidentiary complexities in apportioning harm.[60]

Finally, lower courts have held that indirect purchasers are not barred from filing injunction actions, as long as they establish "that equity principles entitle them to injunctive relief."[61] The specter of windfall recovery, speculative damages, multiple litigation, and intricate tracing problems is avoided when injunctive relief is sought, unlike in damages actions. Like the standing requirement, courts have liberalized the "direct purchaser" rule for injunction actions under § 16.[62]

In *Apple Inc. v. Pepper*,[63] the Supreme Court found consumers who bought applications from manufacturer Apple's electronic retail store to be "direct purchasers" who could sue the manufacturer for alleged monopolization. Owners of Apple iPhones could only lawfully purchase applications directly through Apple's App Store, which primarily sold apps created by independent developers. Plaintiff iPhone owners sued Apple for unlawfully monopolizing the aftermarket for iPhone apps. Apple argued that *Illinois Brick* prevented the lawsuit because the iPhone owners were not direct purchasers from Apple. Instead, according to Apple, iPhone owners were directly purchasing their apps from the developers, who set the price of their apps. The Supreme Court disagreed, concluding that the rationale underlying *Illinois Brick* did not apply

56. *Illinois Brick*, 431 U.S. at 730.

57. *See, e.g.*, *Arizona v. Shamrock Foods Co.*, 729 F.2d 1208 (9th Cir. 1984); *Jewish Hosp. Ass'n. v. Stewart Mech. Enters., Inc.*, 628 F.2d 971, 975 (6th Cir. 1980). *But see In re ATM Fee Antitrust Litig.*, 686 F.3d 741 (9th Cir. 2012) (denying the co-conspirator exception to plaintiff ATM cardholders who did not pay a price directly fixed by the alleged conspiracy.) Under the *In re ATM Fee Antitrust Litig* holding, an ATM cardholder, perhaps an impoverished law student traveling outside of her bank's region, who withdraws money from another bank's ATM is not able to maintain suit against ATM networks for the setting of interchange fees among the banks. *Id.*

58. *See, e.g.*, *In re Beef Indus. Antitrust Litig.*, 600 F.2d 1148 (5th Cir. 1979).

59. 424 F.3d 363 (3d Cir. 2005).

60. *Id.* at 379–80.

61. *Mid-West Paper Prods. Co. v. Cont'l Group, Inc.*, 596 F.2d 573, 594 (3d Cir. 1979).

62. See also *infra* § 3.05 for discussion on *in pari delicto* and the impact of that doctrine on cases such as these.

63. 587 U.S. 273 (2019).

because allowing iPhone owners to sue Apple would facilitate more effective enforcement of antitrust laws, would not complicate damages calculations, and would not risk duplicative damages against antitrust defendants.

Courts divide on the application of *Illinois Brick* to direct purchases made from nonconspirators whose prices have increased as a result of the conspiracy. An early influential case is *Mid-West Paper Products Co. v. Continental Group, Inc.*,[64] where the Third Circuit Court held that *Illinois Brick* would prevent suit in cases where the plaintiff has purchased goods or services from a nonconspirator. The court based its decision on the belief that applying *Illinois Brick* to such cases would lead inevitably to "speculative" evidence surrounding damages and complex economic inquiries that *Illinois Brick* forbids. It would be unduly difficult to determine whether direct purchases actually led to injury, and, if so, how much.[65] The court also noted that it would be "at the very least highly conjectural" to determine what the price would have been had no conspiracy existed, especially given the various and subjective considerations that go into setting product price.[66] Finally, the court feared that if such suits were permitted under *Illinois Brick*, it could lead to those who directly purchased from nonconspirators recovering even though they may not have been injured, while indirect purchasers who actually were injured would be denied recovery.

The Third Circuit later adopted a narrower interpretation of *Mid-West Paper*. In *In re Lower Lake Erie Iron Ore Antitrust Litigation*,[67] a suit was brought against railroad companies by steel producers, private docking companies, and trucking companies. The plaintiffs alleged a conspiracy to block the implementation of new vessels intended to increase efficiency and decrease the need for manpower in hauling iron ore. The docking and trucking companies were found to have been directly injured by the railroads' activities and, hence, to have met the requirements for standing and antitrust injury.[68] The claim by the steel companies, however, was a bit more questionable. Nonetheless, the court found them to have standing on two separate theories. First, the steel companies claimed that they were forced to pay more to haul ore to nonconspiring companies. The court accepted the argument that this "directly impacted the steel companies" even though the claim basically revolved around nonconspiring third parties, which was held to be insufficient for standing in *Mid-West Paper*.[69] The court stated that just because other victims also suffered directly from the activity, that did not mean the steel companies did not have standing. The injuries of the third parties were "tangential" to those of the steel companies, not the duplicative type that *Illinois Brick* sought to prevent.[70] However, to avoid duplicative recovery issues, as mandated by *Illinois Brick and Mid-West Paper*, the steel companies had to

64. 596 F.2d 573 (3d Cir. 1979).
65. *Id.* at 585.
66. *Id.* at 584.
67. 998 F.2d 1144 (3d Cir. 1993).
68. *Id.* at 1164 n.14, 1171.
69. *Id.* at 1168.
70. *Id.* at 1168–69.

show "meticulously" that their damages would not overlap with those claimed by the trucking and docking companies.[71]

The second theory on which the court found the steel companies to have standing was the company's claims for damages from the increased dock handling charges paid to the railroads. Standing existed here, the court reasoned, because the steel companies were acting as direct purchasers.[72]

Hence, the court in *Iron Ore* seemed to disregard the "speculative damages" argument of *Mid-West Paper* out of a belief that duplicative damages could be avoided through careful proof of damages by all parties involved.[73] While this may be advantageous for those sincerely injured but more than one step removed from the alleged conspiracy, it could also lead courts to become mired in subjective analysis when ruling on standing issues, further confusing an already ambiguous concept.[74]

The Supreme Court has stated that when the purchase is made from an intermediary in a vertical situation who is a nonconspirator, the indirect purchaser does not have standing to sue. This is true even if one hundred percent of the price overcharge was passed on to the indirect purchaser.[75] In *Kansas v. Utilicorp United, Inc.*,[76] the defendant originally brought suit against a pipeline company and five natural gas companies under a price inflation conspiracy theory. The states of Missouri and Kansas brought separate suits against the defendant as *parens partriae* for all citizens of the respective states who actually had paid the increased prices after the defendant passed them on. After consolidating the actions, the district court rejected the states' claims for lack of standing, stating that the utility company, and not the citizens at large, suffered direct injury from the conspiracy. The Court of Appeals affirmed, as did the Supreme Court. The plaintiffs attempted to formulate an exception to *Illinois* by suggesting that, since the pass-on was one hundred percent of the price inflation, the problems associated with apportioning damages between direct and indirect purchasers did not exist.[77] The Court rejected this line of reasoning and found that, in order for the indirect purchaser to prove that the utility company was not at all damaged by

71. *Id.* at 1169. See also *supra* § 3.05 for further discussion on *in pari delicto* as applied to antitrust suits between conspirators and their former co-conspirators.

72. 998 F.2d at 1169–70.

73. *But see Steamfitters Local Union No. 420 Welfare Fund v. Phillip Morris, Inc.*, 171 F.3d 912, 932 (3d Cir. 1999) (distinguishing *Iron Ore* and rejecting its application to union health and welfare funds that sought to recover damages for the funds 'costs of treating their participants' smoking-related illnesses because the injuries they "allegedly suffered are simply too remote from that wrongdoing to be cognizable under the antitrust laws"); *see also Campos v. Ticketmaster Corp.*, 140 F.3d 1166, 1169 (8th Cir. 1998) (ticket purchasers are indirect purchasers "by virtue of an antecedent transaction between the monopolist and another, independent producer").

74. *See generally* Roger D. Blair & Jeffrey L. Harrison, *Reexamining the Rule of Illinois Brick in Modern Antitrust Standing Analysis,* 68 Geo. Wash. L. Rev. 1 (1999).

75. *See, e.g., Kloth v. Microsoft Corp.*, 444 F.3d 312, 320–21 (4th Cir. 2006) (holding *Illinois Brick* prohibited a suit against Microsoft by plaintiffs who had purchased Microsoft software from retailers rather than Microsoft directly).

76. 497 U.S. 199 (1990).

77. *Id.* at 208.

the overcharge, "the indirect purchaser would have to prove, among other things, that the direct purchaser could not have raised its rates prior to the overcharge."[78] Thus, courts would have to find that "the State's regulatory schemes would have barred any rate increase except for the amount reflected by cost increases."[79] This is exactly the speculative sort of proof the Court sought to avoid. The Court also voiced concerns about issues of timing related to the various factors which might delay the passing-on of a price increase and lead to damages for the utility.[80]

Second, the plaintiffs asserted an exception would be proper in this case because the states and the utility company would be seeking different, rather than multiple, damages. The Court rebutted this argument with the simple assertion that this case was complicated enough, with the states representing indirectly affected citizens and directly affected agencies. Trying to guarantee no damages overlapped would add an unnecessary level of complexity to the analysis.[81] Finally, the Court refused to apply an industry-wide exception for indirect purchasers where utility companies are involved, stating that "[t]he possibility of allowing an exception, even in rather meritorious circumstances, would undermine the rule."[82] The Court also held that the "cost-plus contract" exception to *Illinois Brick* was inapplicable because "[t]he respondent did not sell the gas to its customers under a pre-existing cost-plus contract."[83] Clearly, the Supreme Court is serious about evenly applying the direct purchaser rule, even in cases where the indirect purchaser is bearing what appears to be all the costs of the price-fixing scheme.

A possible exception to the direct purchaser rule deals with an assignment of the antitrust claim. In *Gulfstream III Associates, Inc. v. Gulfstream Aerospace Corp.*,[84] Judge Greenberg noted in his concurring opinion that an antitrust claim can be assigned, and, thus, an exception can be made to the direct purchaser rule, but only if the assignment is express. A general assignment that includes a potential antitrust claim "would be disfavored under the direct purchaser rule."[85] Therefore, "general assignments, without specific reference to antitrust claims, cannot validly transfer the right to pursue those claims."[86] Express assignments, on the other hand, are not victim to the problem of duplicative recovery.[87]

The policy implications are sweeping for *Illinois Brick*'s direct purchaser requirement. For example, although the plaintiff in *Reiter* was declared a "party" within the meaning of § 4 and one injured in her "property" by reason of a manufacturers' vertical price-fixing scheme, she was not a "direct purchaser" and could not state an antitrust

78. *Id.* at 209.
79. *Id.* at 210.
80. *Id.* at 210–11.
81. *Id.* at 213.
82. *Id.* at 216.
83. *Id.* at 218.
84. 995 F.2d 425 (3d Cir. 1993) (Greenberg, J., concurring).
85. *Id.* at 438–39.
86. *Id.* at 440.
87. *Id.*

claim unless one of the exceptions applied.[88] Thus, while *Reiter* grants consumers standing to bring an antitrust claim, *Illinois Brick* limits that rule, in price-fixing damage suits, to consumers that are direct purchasers. Similarly, if the consumer lacks a claim for relief under § 4, the attorney general of the consumer's state cannot bring a *parens patriae* action (on behalf of consumers) under § 4c of the Clayton Act.[89]

The holding in *Illinois Brick* raises the question whether states could permit, under state antitrust law, damage actions for indirect purchasers.[90] The question implicates the preemption doctrine under the federal constitution: Does the federal antitrust law, as interpreted by *Illinois Brick*, preempt states from creating an antitrust claim for relief on behalf of indirect purchasers? The Supreme Court in *California v. ARC America Corp.*,[91] held that state antitrust laws permitting indirect purchasers to sue to recover illegal overcharges were not preempted by the federal statute.

Under *ARC America*, downstream antitrust victims retain a remedy, if provided by state law, even though such damage recovery is precluded in federal court. The Court concluded that the two decisions are not in conflict because: (1) such state statutes will not affect unnecessarily federal proceedings since there is no federal remedy provided for the indirect purchasers, (2) the state remedy will not decrease the direct purchaser's incentives to bring a federal suit because the state action might exhaust defendant's assets, and (3) by permitting an indirect purchaser's suit in state court, no federal policy condemning multiple liability is contravened because *Illinois Brick* construed only federal policy under § 4 of the Clayton Act, not state law or state policy.

The Court observed that this dual enforcement approach might have an effect on reducing the direct purchaser's recovery in federal court but that this is a "function of the fact and form of settlement rather than the impermissible operation of state indirect purchaser statutes."[92] Moreover, the Court was not persuaded that dual enforcement would expose antitrust defendants to multiple liability, contrary to the dictates of *Illinois Brick*, *McCready*, and *Associated General*. The policy of preventing multiple

---

88. *Reiter v. Sonotone Corp.*, 442 U.S. 330 (1979). It should be noted that on remand, the lower court in *Reiter* found that the direct purchaser rule did not apply because of the allegations of vertical price fixing and because injunctive relief also was requested under other theories.

89. *Illinois Brick*, 431 U.S. at 735 n.14.

90. George J. Benston, *Indirect Purchasers' Standing to Claim Damages in Price Fixing Antitrust Actions: A Benefit Cost Analysis of Proposals to Change the* Illinois Brick *Rule*, 55 Antitrust L.J. 213 (1986); Edward A. Snyder, *Efficient Assignment of Rights to Sue for Antitrust Damages*, 28 J.L. & Econ. 469 (1985).

91. 490 U.S. 93 (1989). Sixteen states had enacted such laws in response to the *Illinois Brick* decision when *California v. ARC America Corp.* was heard. *Id.* at 98. The number of states with legislation "to exclude the prohibition against indirect purchasers' claims is now around thirty." Johan Ysewyn, *Private Enforcement of Competition Law in the EU: Trials and Tribulations*, 19 Int'l L. Practicum 14, 15 (2006). *Illinois Brick* had not addressed the issue of federal preemption. *See* 490 U.S. at 102. *But see* William H. Page, *The Limits of State Indirect Purchaser Suits: Class Certification in the Shadow of Illinois Brick*, 67 Antitrust L.J. 1 (1999) (discussing that in practice *ARC America* has not led to successful indirect purchaser suits under the so-called repealer laws in state courts because class certification often acts as a barrier).

92. 490 U.S. at 105.

liability is one limited to multiple liability *in the federal courts*, the Court reasoned, since state claims are not generally preempted by federal law merely because a defendant may be exposed to additional liability. "Ordinarily, state causes of action are not preempted solely because they impose liability over and above that authorized by federal law. . . ."[93]

In short, the Court held that *Illinois Brick* "was a [narrower] decision construing [only] the federal antitrust laws," unlike *ARC America*, which rests on important federalism grounds "defining the interrelationship between the federal and state antitrust laws."[94]

In sum, in order to plead and establish a private antitrust damage action, plaintiffs must demonstrate that the injury suffered is directly related to the proscribed antitrust conduct and that the injury is of the kind intended by Congress to be redressed. But when a price-fixing overcharge is alleged, indirect purchasers are generally without a claim for relief in federal court for treble damages.

§ 3.03 Domestic and International Antitrust 'Commerce' Jurisdiction

[A] Sherman Act Requirements

The basis for Sherman Act or Clayton Act jurisdiction is the Commerce Clause of the United States Constitution, which gives Congress the ability to "regulate commerce with foreign nations, and among the several states."[95] Practices which are "in" interstate commerce or which have an "effect" on interstate commerce are included under the purview of either the Sherman or Clayton Act.

The Supreme Court addressed the jurisdictional reach of the Sherman Act in *Mandeville Island Farms, Inc. v. American Crystal Sugar Co.*,[96] in which the Court

93. *Id.* Consider what effect this dual enforcement approach might have on a defendants' incentive to enter pretrial settlements, and whether the twin claims for relief might create over-deterrence of the underlying legal policies. *See Paper Sys. Inc. v. Nippon Paper Indus. Co.*, 281 F.3d 629 (7th Cir. 2002) (noting that *Illinois Brick* does not preclude application of joint and several liability); *Free v. Abbott Labs., Inc.*, 176 F.3d 298, 301 n.7 (5th Cir. 1999), *aff'd by an equally divided court*, 529 U.S. 333 (2000) (listing state appellate decisions that follow *Illinois Brick*).

94. 490 U.S. at 105; *see* Blair & Harrison, *supra* note 74, at 2 (arguing that the Court or Congress needs to revisit *Illinois Brick* to reconcile it with "more general principles of antitrust standing" in part because state statutes that allow indirect purchasers to recover antitrust damages expose defendants to liability based on geography, not the level of anticompetitive conduct); *see also Kansas v. Utilicorp United, Inc.*, 497 U.S. 199 (1990) (holding that, subsequent to *ARC America*, only a utility has a claim for relief under § 4 when a supplier overcharges a public utility for natural gas and the utility passes the overcharge on to its customers. *See generally* Herbert Hovenkamp, *The Indirect Purchaser Rule and Cost-Plus Sales*, 103 Harv. L. Rev. 1717 (1990); Stephen Breyer, Regulation and Its Reform (1982).

95. U.S. Const. art. III, § 2.

96. 334 U.S. 219 (1948).

found certain sugar refiners to have conspired to restrain trade. Because the refiners' activities had an effect on interstate commerce, the Sherman Act applied.[97] This holding was affirmed later in *McLain v. Real Estate Bd. of New Orleans, Inc.*,[98] where the Court held that the Sherman Act applied to activities "in commerce" or having an "effect on commerce."[99] The jurisdictional element was easily fulfilled by showing the defendant's activities had a substantial effect on interstate commerce.

In *Summit Health, Ltd. v. Pinhas*,[100] the Court clarified *Mandeville* and *McLain*. The Court rejected the defense that there did not exist a natural connection between the alleged trade-restricting activity, which was a conspiracy to drive the plaintiff ophthalmologist out business, and interstate commerce. Instead, the Court found that one need not prove an *actual* effect on interstate commerce in order to prove Sherman Act jurisdiction.[101] Rather, the judiciary is to concentrate on "the potential harm that would ensue if the conspiracy were successful," and the plaintiff need only allege an anticompetitive effect on the market (defined in the case as the ophthalmologist market), suggesting an effect on interstate commerce.[102]

Most lower courts have followed the *Summit Health* Court's "effects test."[103] Subsequently, in *Hammes v. AAMCO Transmissions, Inc.*,[104] the Seventh Circuit held that allegations of a "restraint on commerce" would be sufficient for fulfilling the Sherman Act jurisdictional requirement.[105] The court added that the allegation does not have to be that the restraint is "substantial."[106] At issue was the refusal of the members in a call-forwarding network for a transmission repair center to include the plaintiffs in their group, leading to a marked decrease in business for the plaintiffs and eventual bankruptcy. The court decided that the jurisdictional requirement would be fulfilled as long as "the complaint alleges that the plaintiff was engaged in interstate commerce and was injured by the alleged antitrust violation."[107]

Hammes leaves unanswered, however, the question of the necessity of a "substantial" effect on interstate commerce in proving jurisdictional requirements. Although the Seventh Circuit found that no such requirement existed under the *Hammes* facts,

---

97. *Id.* at 234.

98. 444 U.S. 232 (1980).

99. *Id.* at 242.

100. 500 U.S. 322 (1991).

101. *Id.* at 331.

102. *Id.* By definition federal antitrust laws apply to interstate commerce and a plaintiff must prove that a defendant's conduct had or would have the requisite anticompetitive effect. The Court's narrowing of the commerce clause in *United States v. Lopez*, 514 U.S. 549 (1995), *United States v. Morrison*, 529 U.S. 598 (2000), and other cases is unlikely to affect antitrust enforcement. *See* E. Thomas Sullivan, *Judicial Sovereignty, The Legacy of the Rehnquist Court*, 20 Const. Comment 171 (2003).

103. *See generally Fuentes v. S. Hills Cardiology*, 946 F.2d 196 (3d Cir. 1991) (finding jurisdiction to be legitimate in plaintiff's allegations that a hospital that revoked certain of its staff privileges had entered a conspiracy with five doctors in order to restrain interstate commerce).

104. 33 F.3d 774 (7th Cir. 1994).

105. *Id.* at 779.

106. *Id.*

107. *Id.* at 782.

the same court decided to the contrary in *BCB Anesthesia Care, Ltd. v. Passavant Memorial Area Hospital Ass'n*,[108] the same year.

[B] Clayton Act Requirements

The jurisdictional reach of the Clayton Act is not, for the most part, as extensive as that of the Sherman Act. This fact was set out in *Gulf Oil Corp. v. Copp Paving Co.*,[109] in which the Court found the Clayton Act to apply only to those activities constituting a part of the flow of commerce between states.[110] Hence, the "effects" test does not apply to Clayton Act claims, with the exception of § 7, which governs mergers.[111]

Section 7 of the Clayton Act, which deals with mergers and acquisitions, is considered to have the same jurisdictional requirements as the Sherman Act.[112] The text of § 7 suggests the similarities between it and the Sherman Act. It prohibits any corporation acting within the realm of commerce or engaging in an activity affecting commerce from merging with or acquiring another firm when the merger or acquisition will have the *effect* of lessening competition or creating a monopoly.[113]

[C] International Application of U.S. Antitrust Laws

Gains in technology and trade interdependence between countries have increased international antitrust enforcement's importance. Although the reach and application of the Sherman and Clayton Acts to anticompetitive conduct abroad is controversial, it is clear that American antitrust laws apply equally to activities in interstate and foreign commerce.[114] Since the Clayton Act has a more limited reach than the Sherman Act, its extra-territorial scope is correspondingly more limited. In general, three situations have necessitated application of domestic antitrust law to activity in foreign markets. "(1) activities of foreign firms within the United States which have an effect in this country, (2) activities of foreign firms outside United States boundaries which have an adverse effect on the United States economy, and (3) activities of United States firms located outside of the country which have adverse effects on

---

108. 36 F.3d 664 (7th Cir. 1994).

109. 419 U.S. 186 (1974).

110. *Id.* at 195.

111. *Id.*; *see also Able Sales Co. v. Compania de Azucar de Puerto Rico*, 406 F.3d 56 (1st Cir. 2005) (applying the "in commerce" language to § 2(a) of the Robinson-Patman Act.

112. C. Douglas Floyd & E. Thomas Sullivan, *Private Antitrust Actions: The Structure and Process of Civil Antitrust Litigation* § 1.1.3, at 13 (1996 and supp.) (1996).

113. 15 U.S.C. 18 (2012).

114. Areeda & Hovenkamp, *supra* note 45, ¶ 2706. Both civil and criminal actions may be brought against defendants who intend that their foreign activities have a substantial effect on United Sates commerce. *United States v. Nippon Paper*, 109 F.3d 1 (1st Cir. 1997).

the economy of the United States."[115] When a foreign plaintiffs' claim, however, rests solely on independently-caused foreign injury, a purchaser may not bring a Sherman Act claim.[116]

Traditionally, courts have utilized two approaches to define the proper extraterritorial scope of the Sherman Act. The first is the "effects" test, which was established in *United States v. Aluminum Co. of America (Alcoa)*.[117] At issue was Alcoa's alleged monopoly, both domestically and internationally, of aluminum ingot. The government suggested that the defendant had become a part of a foreign aluminum cartel which lent itself to artificial price increases.[118] The Second Circuit upheld the application of the Sherman Act to the foreign activity because the extraterritorial conduct was intended to and, in fact, did effect the United States market for aluminum.[119] The effects test has since been described as having its basis in "the notion that if a regulating nation or its citizens are hurt, and hurt rather directly, the nation has a stake in regulating the conduct and ought to be able to do so."[120]

This approach was criticized and transformed into a balancing test in *Timberlane Lumber Co. v. Bank of America Nat'l Trust & Saving Ass'n*.[121] The Ninth Circuit determined that the *Alcoa* test neglected to consider the interests of foreign parties when considering antitrust claims. Hence, the court set out various elements which every court should weigh in deciding to apply the Sherman Act abroad:

> [1] the degree of conflict with foreign law or policy, [2] the nationality or allegiance of the parties and the locations or principal places of business or corporations, [3] the extent to which enforcement by either state can be expected to achieve compliance, [4] the relative significance of effects on the United States as compared with those elsewhere, [5] the extent to which there is explicit purpose to harm or affect American commerce, [6] the foreseeability of such effect, and [7] the relative importance to the violations charged of conduct within the United States as compared with conduct abroad.[122]

---

115. Floyd & Sullivan, *supra* note 112, § 1.1.4, at 14; *see also* Areeda & Hovenkamp, *supra* note 45, ¶ 2706. Both civil and criminal actions may be brought against defendants who intend that their foreign activities have a substantial effect on United States commerce.

116. *F. Hoffmann-LaRoche Ltd v. Empagran S.A.*, 542 U.S. 155, 173 (2004). On remand, plaintiffs were unable to prove that anticompetitive activities in the United States were the direct causal link between the defendants' conduct in the United States and the plaintiff's foreign injury. 417 F.3d 1267, 1271.

117. 148 F.2d 416 (2d Cir. 1945) (the Second Circuit heard what was essentially a Supreme Court case, because four Justices had removed themselves from the decision). The Supreme Court subsequently validated Judge Hand's test in *Steele v. Bulova Watch Co.*, 344 U.S. 280 (1952).

118. 148 F.2d at 422.

119. *Id.* at 443–44.

120. Eleanor M. Fox, *U.S. Law and Global Competition and Trade—Jurisdiction and Comity*, Antitrust Report 3, 4 (Oct. 1993).

121. 549 F.2d 597 (9th Cir. 1976).

122. *Id.* at 614.

The Ninth Circuit remanded the case. The district court determined that the extension of the Sherman Act abroad was inappropriate, since subject matter jurisdiction did not exist.[123]

Timberlane suggests a one-step analysis, in which comity and subject matter jurisdiction are considered simultaneously. This approach was split into a two-step inquiry in *Mannington Mills, Inc. v. Congoleum Corp.*,[124] where the Third Circuit listed a new set of comity considerations while incorporating those suggested by the Ninth Circuit:

(1) Degree of conflict with foreign law or policy;

(2) Nationality of the parties;

(3) Relative importance of the alleged violation of conduct within the United States compared to that abroad;

(4) Availability of a remedy abroad and the pendancy of litigation there;

(5) Existence of intent to harm or affect American commerce and its foreseeability;

(6) Possible effect upon foreign relations if the court exercises jurisdiction and grants relief;

(7) If relief is granted, whether a party will be placed in the position of being forced to perform an act illegal in either country or be under conflicting requirements by both countries;

(8) Whether the court can make its order effective;

(9) Whether an order for relief would be acceptable in this country if made by the foreign nation under similar circumstances, and;

(10) Whether a treaty with the affected nations has addressed the issue.[125]

Once a negative effect on commerce has been determined, one must then turn to these ten factors in deciding whether to extend the existing jurisdiction.[126]

These two approaches to international application of the domestic antitrust laws have been codified several times in various federal legislation and agency actions. For instance, in 1982, Congress passed the Foreign Trade Antitrust Improvement Act (FTAIA),[127] which prohibited Sherman Act claims dealing with export or nonimport foreign commerce without a "direct, substantial and reasonably foreseeable effect" on commerce.[128]

---

123. *Timberlane Lumber Co. v. Bank of Am. Nat'l Trust & Sav. Ass'n*, 574 F. Supp. 1453, 1465 (N.D. Cal. 1983).

124. 595 F.2d 1287, 1297–98 (3d Cir. 1979).

125. *Id.*

126. Floyd & Sullivan, *supra* note 112, § 1.14, at 22–23.

127. 15 U.S.C. § 6a (2006).

128. *Id.; see United Phosphorus Ltd. v. Angus Chem. Co.*, 322 F.3d 942, 952 (7th Cir. 2003) (holding that the plaintiff, an Indian drug company, lacked standing because the anticompetitive conduct by an American drug company did not cause the requisite effect in the United States); *Den Norske Stats v. HeereMac V.O.F*, 241 F.3d 420 (5th Cir. 2001) (holding that the plaintiff's claim must arise directly out

The Department of Justice officially adopted the FTAIA in 1988 with the issuance of the Antitrust Enforcement Guidelines for International Operations. The Department enunciated that the Sherman Act should be applied only to conduct that presented a "direct anticompetitive harm to users *in the United States*."[129] The Department eliminated this requirement in 1992, however, making claims actionable under the Sherman Act in which no domestic entities have been harmed.[130] The Guidelines adopted the *Mannington Mills* approach to international comity, as well.

The first suit to be brought and settled under the revised 1988 Guidelines was *United States v. Pilkington PLC*,[131] which had been brought against a British manufacturer of flat glass, charging the company with closing off the flat glass production market from all foreign competition in violation of the Sherman Act. The suit was settled in favor of the plaintiff, enabling the United States to compete for business in newly developed flat glass plants and leading to potentially hundreds of millions of dollars in increased export revenue.[132]

The *Mannington Mills* two-part approach was implicitly called into question by *Hartford Fire Ins. Co. v. California*, when the Supreme Court affirmed the Ninth Circuit's contention that international comity did not act as a restraint on the extension of Sherman Act subject matter jurisdiction to a complaint against London-based reinsurers.[133] Instead of undertaking a two-part analysis, the Court assumed that the defendant's activities had an adverse effect on interstate commerce. Working from that assumption, the Court could not find a legitimate conflict between the foreign and domestic laws at issue.[134] As such, international comity was not a concern. The decision suggests a new doctrine in international antitrust that requires a finding of subject matter jurisdiction and an application of the Sherman Act unless a conflict exists.[135]

---

of the domestic effect of the challenged conduct in order for § 1 to apply to foreign conduct); *Caribbean Broad. Sys., Ltd. v. Cable & Wireless PLC*, 148 F.3d 1080, 1087 (D.C. Cir. 1998) (holding that alleged monopolization of foreign companies, their fraudulent misrepresentations about their broadcast capabilities, and their sham opposition to plaintiff's broadcast application, constitute a direct, substantial, and reasonably foreseeable effect on United States commerce).

129. Floyd & Sullivan, *supra* note 112, at 25 (citing E. Thomas Sullivan & Herbert Hovenkamp, *Antitrust Law, Policy and Procedure* 13 (3d ed. 1994) (emphasis added)). This view is referred to as "Footnote 159." *British Glass Manufacturer Settles Case Attacking Restrictions on U.S. Exporters*, 66 Antitrust & Trade Reg. Rep. (BNA) No. 1666, at 617 (June 2, 1994).

130. Floyd & Sullivan, *supra* note 112, at 25 (citing E. Thomas Sullivan & Herbert Hovenkamp, *Antitrust Law, Policy, and Procedure* 13 (3d ed. 1994) (emphasis added)).

131. 1994 U.S. Dist. LEXIS 21648 (D. Ariz. Dec. 22, 1994).

132. *British Glass Manufacturer Settles Case Attacking Restrictions on U.S. Exporters, supra* note 129, at 618.

133. 509 U.S. 764 (1993); *see infra* § 3.06[D][2].

134. *Id.* at 799.

135. Accord *Metro Indus., Inc. v. Sammi Corp.*, 82 F.3d 839, 843 (9th Cir. 1996) (that "[W]hen alleged illegal conduct occurred in a foreign country, we must first examine the impact on commerce in the United States before we can determine we have subject matter jurisdiction over the claim."). *But see Filetech S.A.R.L. v. France Telecom*, 978 F. Supp. 464, 476 (S.D.N.Y. 1997), *vacated on other grounds*, *Filetech v. France Telecom S.A.*, 157 F.3d 922 (2d Cir. 1998) (asserting that *Hartford* requires threshold inquiry of conflict with foreign law before other factors of *Timberlane* test apply and that

This approach was explicitly adopted by the Department of Justice in the Antitrust Enforcement Guidelines for International Operations of 1995,[136] which were updated by the Antitrust Guidelines for International Enforcement and Cooperation (2017). In addition to adopting a strict effects doctrine, the Department also adopted the "substantial" test in assessing the required effect on commerce, adding fire to the recurring debate about how substantial is substantial enough.

The Supreme Court clarified the "substantial" test in 2004 with its opinion in *F. Hoffmann-LaRoche Ltd. v. Empagran, S.A.*[137] Here, foreign plaintiffs, who purchased vitamins outside the United States from foreign sellers, sought to sue under the Sherman Act in the United States to recover treble damages for price overcharges caused by a worldwide cartel.

The *Empagran* Court first ruled that the price fixing alleged in the complaint fell within the FTAIA's exclusion clause that "conduct involving trade or commerce with foreign nations" is not covered by the Sherman Act. Given this holding, the Court then considered whether this conduct came within the "exception" to the exclusion: whether the conduct had a "direct, substantial, and reasonably foreseeable effect" on domestic commerce, and that "such effect gives rise to a [Sherman Act] claim."[138]

Ultimately, the Court held that this exception did not apply "where the plaintiff's claim rests solely on the independent foreign harm." In short, while a purchaser in the United States could bring a Sherman Act claim under FTAIA because of a domestic injury, a purchaser in a foreign country could not bring an action based on foreign harm.[139]

The Court remanded to the lower courts to determine if the alleged anticompetitive behavior "independently caused foreign injury; that is, [whether] the conduct's domestic effects did not help to bring about the foreign injury."[140] The Court thus held open the possibility that a foreign plaintiff could maintain an action if it could show that its injury was closely linked to the injuries suffered in the United States.

On remand from the Supreme Court decision, the D.C. Circuit held that "[t]he statutory language—'gives rise to'—indicates a direct causal relationship, that is, proximate causation, and is not satisfied by the mere but-for 'nexus.'"[141] Concerned that a broad interpretation of the FTAIA would "open the door to [undesirable]

---

comity considerations govern regardless of lack of conflict).Academic commentary on *Hartford* has varied. *See, e.g.*, Eleanor M. Fox, *National Law, Global Markets, and Hartford: Eyes Wide Shut*, 68 Antitrust L.J. 73 (2000); Varun Gupta, Note, *After* Hartford Fire: *Antitrust & Comity*, 84 Geo. L.J. 2287 (1996); James P. Rhatican, Comment, *Hartford Fire Insurance Co. v. California: A Mixed Blessing for Insurance Antitrust Defendants*, 47 Rutgers L. Rev. 905 (1995).

136. U.S. Dep't of Justice & FTC, Antitrust Enforcement Guidelines for International Operations (1995) [hereinafter 1995 Guidelines]. In addition to adopting the *Hartford Fire* test, the Department of Justice noted that the FTAIA continues to apply to foreign commerce other than imports.

137. 542 U.S. 155 (2004).

138. *Id.* at 155.

139. *Id.* at 159.

140. *Id.* at 175.

141. *Empagran, S.A. v. F. Hoffmann-LaRoche, Ltd.*, 417 F.3d 1267, 1271 (D.C. Cir. 2005).

interference with other nations' prerogative to safeguard their own citizens from anticompetitive activity within their own borders," the court held that the causation link asserted did not rise to the level of proximate cause.[142]

The D.C. Circuit also indicated the requisite causation under the "gives rise to" language of the FTAIA was well demonstrated in *Caribbean Broad. Sys. v. Cable and Wireless PLC.*[143] The Eighth Circuit followed *Empagran II* in affirming dismissal for lack of subject matter jurisdiction of foreign purchasers claims under the FTAIA.[144]

In 2011, The Third Circuit overturned its own precedent and held in *Animal Science Products Inc. v. China Minmetals Corp.*[145] that FTAIA added only statutory elements for defining the "merits" of an antitrust claim alleging foreign conduct but did not restrict the federal subject matter jurisdiction of the federal courts. Subsequent to the Third Circuit's decision, the Seventh Circuit changed its position and agreed.[146] Finding that FTAIA relates to the scope of antitrust coverage, the court explained that "limitations on the extraterritorial reach of a statute describe what conduct the law purports to regulate and what lies outside its reach."[147]

The practical consequence of this shifting view is that the defense challenge to a FTAIA claim is a motion to dismiss under Rule 12(b)6, not Rule 12(b)(1) of the Federal Rules of Civil Procedure. Under Rule 12(b)(6), the judge must accept factual allegation in a complaint. By contrast, the court can make its own jurisdictional fact finding when assessing a 12(b)(1) motion. Further, because jurisdiction cannot be waived the judge can decide the jurisdictional issue at any time, even on its own motion.

As the United States' policies of international antitrust enforcement have developed, so have its efforts to enter into cooperative agreements with other nations.[148] The Guidelines do recognize, however, that substantiality will vary with the facts of each case.[149] Similarly, the relative weight of the comity factors will depend on the individual circumstances involved in each claim.[150] In short, under the 1995

---

142. *Id.*

143. 148 F.3d 1080 (D.C. Cir. 1998) (defendant's eastern Caribbean radio station's monopolizing conduct caused the plaintiff to lose revenue because it was unable to sell advertising to the same U.S. businesses).

144. *In re Monosodium Glutamate Antitrust Litig.*, 477 F.3d 535 (8th Cir. 2007).

145. 654 F.3d. 462 (3d. Cir. 2011)

146. *See Minn-Chem v. Agrium Juc.*, 683 F.3d. 845 (7th Cir. 2012).

147. *Id.* at 852.

148. The United States has entered into formal bilateral agreements with Australia, Canada, Germany, and Japan, as well as "positive comity" agreements with the European Union. *See* Agreement Between the Government of Canada on the Application of Positive Comity Principles to the Enforcement of Their Competition Laws, Trade Regulation Reports ¶ 13,503; 1995 Guidelines, *supra* note 136, § 2.91; U.S. and European Union Sign Antitrust Cooperation Agreement, 74 Antitrust Trade and Reg. Rep. (BNA) No. 1864, at 592 (July 11, 1998).

149. *Justice and FTC Draft Guidelines on International Antitrust Enforcement*, 67 Antitrust & Trade Reg. Rep. 488 (Oct. 20, 1995).

150. *Id.*; *see* Christopher Sprigman, *Fix Prices Globally, Get Sued Locally? U.S. Jurisdiction Over International Cartels*, 72 U. Chi. L. Rev. 265 (2005); Diane Wood, *Antitrust at the Global Level*, 72 U. Chi. L. Rev. 309 (2005).

Guidelines, "jurisdiction exists when conduct has a direct, substantial, and reasonably foreseeable effect on U.S. domestic commerce, U.S. import commerce, or the commerce of U.S. exporters."[151] Although the Ninth Circuit and the Department of Justice have made clear their preference for the effects test, the debate over the doctrines is still very much alive.

The 1995 Guidelines also set out the four exceptions in which a foreign country can escape United States jurisdiction over antitrust matters. The first is foreign sovereign immunity, which is governed by the Foreign Sovereign Immunities Act of 1976 (FSIA).[152] Some activities are "the type that only sovereign government can perform" and, as such, are immune from the Sherman Act.[153] Second, conduct which is compelled by the foreign sovereign because of an inherent conflict of laws between the two countries may be immune.[154] Nonetheless, if the compelled activity takes place within United States borders, the exception does not apply.[155] Third, acts of state on "matters pertaining to its governmental sovereignty" are immune.[156] Finally, foreign lobbying of the United States government is protected from Sherman Act jurisdiction, even if it is done with the intent of restraining trade within the United States.[157]

Also in 1995, Congress passed the International Antitrust Enforcement Assistance Act (IAEAA). This law calls for the creation of assistance treaties which mandate the sharing of evidence of antitrust violations between countries.[158] Under the Act, the FTC or the Attorney General will provide foreign antitrust enforcement agencies with information to be used in determining whether an antitrust violation has occurred or is about to occur, and vice versa.[159] Confidential information, however, is still protected in the usual manner.[160] The evidence will prove useful for a number of reasons, especially for generating enforcement effectiveness and magnifying the need for countries to form cooperative alliances to prevent illegal infringements on interstate commerce.[161]

---

151. Diane P. Wood, Address to Business Development Associates, Inc. in Washington D.C. (March 15, 1995) (transcript available with authors).

152. 28 U.S.C. § 1602–1611 (2012).

153. 1995 Guidelines, *supra* note 136, at 24.

154. *Id.* at 25.

155. *Id.* at 26.

156. *Id.* at 27.

157. *Id.* at 28. This exemption is based on the Noerr-Pennington doctrine, which is covered more fully *infra* § 3.04[A].

158. Floyd & Sullivan, *supra* note 112, at 30.

159. *Id.*

160. Wood, *supra* note 151.

161. *See International Antitrust Enforcement Assistance Act of 1994: Hearings on H.R. 4781 Before the Subcomm. on Economic and Commercial Law of the House of Representatives Comm. on the Judiciary*, 103d Cong. 4 (1994) (statement of Anne K. Bingaman, Assistant Attorney General, Antitrust Division, Department of Justice) ("In some of these cases, only the U.S. is targeted and only U.S. antitrust laws are involved. Others of these cartels are aimed at both U.S. and foreign markets, and could be far more effectively investigated and prosecuted by joint action between U.S. and foreign antitrust authorities.").

Another similar agreement is the Mutual Legal Assistance Treaty (MLAT) between Canada and the United States. In place since 1990, this treaty has allowed the countries to gain evidence from each other to be used in criminal antitrust cases.[162] The act was put to the test in 1994, when the United States and Canada "broke up a $120 million dollar [sic] a year international cartel in the fax paper market" whose members included "a Japanese corporation, two American subsidiaries of Japanese companies, and the former president of one of the U.S. subsidiaries. . . ."[163] The defendants pleaded guilty to criminal charges in both countries, culminating in fines of approximately $7 million dollars.[164]

An important development in the extraterritorial enforcement of United States antitrust law in a criminal context occurred in 1997, when the First Circuit affirmed that the Sherman Act applies to anticompetitive conduct that takes place entirely in another country, but which is intended to have, and does have, substantial effects on the United States economy. In *United States v. Nippon Paper*,[165] the Department of Justice brought a criminal action against a Japanese manufacturer of facsimile paper, alleging that defendants had colluded to fix the price of thermal fax paper throughout North America. The Japanese manufacturer moved to dismiss, stating that United States antitrust laws do not reach conduct that occurs wholly outside the United States. The district court agreed and dismissed the indictment.[166]

The First Circuit reversed, stating that the extraterritorial application of the Sherman Act was well established in the civil context. "Common sense" dictated that the same statute should be read the same way in both civil and criminal actions.[167] Although its decision appeared unprecedented, the court stated that "absence of earlier criminal actions is probably more a demonstration of the increasingly global nature of our economy than proof that Section One cannot cover wholly foreign conduct in the criminal milieu."[168] The court rejected the defendant's comity-based argument, which would have defeated the court's jurisdiction, because the charged conduct was illegal under Japanese and American laws. Furthermore, to dismiss on the basis of lack of subject matter jurisdiction would create a safe harbor for future cartels or price-fixers, who could simply erect territorial barriers between them and the United States, even while targeting the United States economy.[169]

In the aftermath of *Nippon Paper*, aggressive international enforcement of criminal antitrust laws became a high priority for the Antitrust Division, with corporate

---

162. Anne K. Bingaman & Joel I. Klein, *Cooperating on Antitrust*, Legal Times (Wash., D.C.), Jan. 1, 1996, at 27.

163. *Hearing on S2297 Before the Subcommittee on Antitrust, Monopolies and Business Rights of the Senate Committee on the Judiciary*, 103d Cong. 5 (1994) (statement of Anne K. Bingaman, Assistant Attorney General, Antitrust Division, Department of Justice).

164. *Id.*

165. 109 F.3d 1 (1st Cir. 1997).

166. *United States v. Nippon Paper Indus. Co.*, 944 F. Supp. 55 (D. Mass. 1996).

167. 109 F.3d at 4.

168. *Id.*

169. *Id.* at 8–9.

defendants based in foreign countries comprising over fifty percent of defendants in criminal cases in 2002 compared to less than one percent in 1991.[170] In more recent years, of the 157 Sherman Act violation fines of $10 million or more that the Division obtained, 142 were collected from foreign-based corporations.[171] In short, international enforcement and cooperative measures have gained great importance in the antitrust arena over the past years. As the market becomes more globally integrated, internationally acceptable antitrust policies will become even more crucial for adequately protecting the flow of commerce.[172]

§ 3.04 First Amendment Defenses

[A] *Noerr-Pennington* Doctrine

If competitors join in combination for the purpose of influencing government decision making, their action is protected from antitrust challenge. This is true even if their underlying intention is to restrain competition or gain an advantage over competitors. This defense, called the Noerr-Pennington Doctrine, is grounded in the First Amendment constitutional theory of the right to petition government. The doctrine is named after two leading Supreme Court decisions.

In the first case, *Eastern R.R. Presidents Conference v. Noerr Motor Freight, Inc.*,[173] the Supreme Court held that antitrust law does not apply to restraints which are the result of valid government actions. Only private restraints are regulated under the antitrust laws. In *Noerr*, railroads influenced legislation restricting competition from the trucking industry. The Court found this activity protected.[174] Similarly, in *UMW v. Pennington*,[175] where mine operators and workers lobbied the executive branch to induce the Tennessee Valley Authority, a government agency, to curtail spot market purchases and to increase minimum wages. The Court remarked that "[j]oint efforts

170. Wendy Wineholt, Lauren Inge & Joseph Albano, *Antitrust Violations*, 52 Am. Crim. L. Rev. 753, 788–89 (2015).

171. William Chang, Aasha Rajani, Natalie George & Mark Tucker, *Antitrust Violations*, 60 Am. Crim. L. Rev. 531, 574 (2023).

172. *See* Spencer Weber Waller, *Can U.S. Antitrust Laws Open International Markets?*, 20 Nw. J. Int'l L. & Bus. 207 (2000), for a discussion of the positive role that U.S. antitrust law plays in ensuring an open market globally. *But see* Andrew T. Guzman, *Is International Antitrust Possible?*, 73 N.Y.U. L. Rev. 1501 (1998) (arguing that as efforts begin to focus on substantive, and not procedural, agreement on antitrust policy the more difficult agreement becomes, resulting in "losers" whose specific antitrust policies are trumped).

173. 365 U.S. 127 (1961).

174. *See generally* Earl W. Kintner & Joseph P. Bauer, *Antitrust Exemptions for Private Requests for Government Action: A Critical Analysis of the Noerr-Pennington Doctrine*, 17 U.C. Davis L. Rev. 549 (1984); Milton Handler & Richard A. De Sevo, *The Noerr Doctrine and Its Sham Exception*, 6 Cardozo L. Rev. 1 (1984).

175. 381 U.S. 657 (1965).

to influence public officials do not violate the antitrust laws even though intended to eliminate competition. Such conduct is not illegal, either standing alone or as a part of a broader scheme itself violative of the Sherman Act."[176] Later, the Court extended its protection for lobbying activities to include judicial and adjudicatory agencies. It made clear that the defense was grounded on the First Amendment right to petition for government action.[177] *Noerr-Pennington* protection also has been extended to include activities not necessarily a part of the petitioning process, but reasonably incident or "normally attendant" to it.[178] However, the defense is not absolute.

If efforts by competitors to influence government are a "sham,"[179] the defense is inapplicable. In *California Motor Transport v. Trucking Unlimited*,[180] the Court held that concerted activities resulting in a "pattern of baseless repetitive claims"[181] which attempted to bar a party from government access were, in reality, a "sham" to conceal an attempt to interfere with the commercial interest of the competition. Trucking companies through administrative and judicial harassment had attempted to prevent competitors from obtaining operating privileges. The Court also commented that the defense would be unavailable if there were evidence of perjury, bribery, fraud, or a conspiracy where a government official participated.[182]

The Supreme Court clarified the sham and conspiracy exception in *City of Columbia v. Omni Outdoor Advert., Inc.*,[183] holding that the sham exception only "encompass[es] situations in which persons use the governmental *process*—as opposed to the *outcome*—as an anticompetitive weapon."[184] The Court distinguished *Cal. Motor Transport* as "a classic example [of] the filing of frivolous objections" for the sole purpose of using the government process "simply in order to impose expense and delay."[185] On the other hand, legitimate or genuine attempts to achieve a *result* which is anticompetitive, through the governmental process, is protected behavior.

Omni broadens *Noerr-Pennington's* protection to apply whenever the defendant genuinely seeks favorable government action and blocks that defense from being

---

176. *Id.* at 670.

177. *Cal. Motor Transp. Co. v. Trucking Unlimited*, 404 U.S. 508 (1972). But see *Sessions Tank Liners, Inc. v. Joor Mfg. Inc.*, 53 Antitrust Trade Reg. Rep. (BNA) 449 (9th Cir. Sept. 17, 1987), where the Ninth Circuit held that a manufacturer is protected under *Noerr-Pennington* in efforts to persuade a private code-setting organization. Said the court, the *Noerr-Pennington* doctrine covers "appeals to some who are not government actors but who are nevertheless in the political process." However, in *Allied Tube & Conduit Corp. v. Indian Head, Inc.*, 486 U.S. 492 (1988), the Court held that no immunity existed for private standard-setting.

178. *McGuire Oil Co. v. Mapco, Inc.*, 958 F.2d 1552, 1560 (11th Cir. 1992).

179. 365 U.S. at 144.

180. 404 U.S. 508 (1972).

181. *Id.* at 513.

182. *Compare Affiliated Capital Corp. v. City of Houston*, 735 F.2d 1555 (5th Cir. 1984), *with Metro Cable Co. v. CATV of Rockford, Inc.*, 516 F.2d 220, 229 (7th Cir. 1975).

183. 499 U.S. 365 (1991).

184. *Id.* at 380.

185. *Id.*

accepted if the defendant only attempts to delay or abuse the *process* of government decision making. The sham test focuses on whether there is a genuine attempt to gain a favorable result as opposed to merely an attempt to misuse the government process. By drawing the distinction between a genuine attempt to influence the *process* or to affect the *result* of government decision making, the Court created an issue of how "intent" should be interpreted in applying the sham exception. This question was answered in *Prof. Real Estate Inv'r Inc. v. Columbia Pictures Indus., Inc.*,[186] where the Court considered whether a copyright infringement action was a sham, and thus without *Noerr-Pennington* protection. *Prof. Real Estate* established a two-prong test for determining whether litigation is a sham and thus unprotected by the *Noerr Pennington* doctrine. First, "the lawsuit must be objectively baseless in the sense that no reasonable litigant could realistically expect success on the merits."[187] Second, after the antitrust plaintiff has shown objective baselessness, the court should then examine the defendant's subjective intent: "the court should focus on whether the baseless lawsuit conceals an attempt to interfere directly with the business relationships of a competitor through the use of governmental *process*—as opposed to the *outcome* of that process—as an anticompetitive weapon."[188]

In short, the Court's reformulation of the sham exception will protect a petition for government action if there is evidence of an objectively reasonable effort to affect the government's decision making, regardless of the subjective intent of the petitioner. Only if the Court finds an objectively meritless petition *and* anticompetitive intent to injure a competitor will it conclude that the petition was a sham and, consequently, unworthy of *Noerr-Pennington* protection.

The majority holding in *Prof. Real Estate* indicates that any claim that has some reasonable possibility of success on the merits falls under *Noerr* protection, even if it is clear that the plaintiff is manipulating the process of litigation. Justice Steven's concurrence in *Prof. Real Estate*, however, suggests that this should not be the case in some complex situations. Justice Stevens opined that the plaintiff in some cases might harbor a collateral purpose for the litigation, such as imposing burdensome costs on the defendant in an attempt to weaken his financial position. Such would most likely be the case in instances where litigation needlessly has become repetitive or drawn out. In these cases, Justice Stevens believes that even those arguments should not be given *Noerr* protection.

The Ninth Circuit adopted this position in *USS-Posco Indus. v. Contra Costa County Bldg. Trades Council.*[189] The Court of Appeals found the two-tier *Prof. Real Estate* test did not apply to a pattern of claims which had been undertaken without prior consideration of merit, regardless of whether some of them showed promise of success. This is clearly contrary to the position taken in *Prof. Real Estate*, and it is too early to forecast whether other courts will adopt the approach of the Ninth Circuit.

---

186. 508 U.S. 49 (1993).
187. *Id.* at 60.
188. *Id.* at 60–61 (emphasis in original).
189. 31 F.3d 800 (9th Cir. 1994).

Nevertheless, a suit that is ultimately adjudicated as successful will *never* be found to be a sham, because, by definition, the claim had "probable cause."[190]

Taken together, *Omni* and *Prof. Real Estate* expand *Noerr-Pennington's* First Amendment protections and limit significantly the application of the sham exception. In addition, the Court has broadened *Noerr-Pennington's* immunity also by narrowing the conspiracy exception.

In *Omni*, the Court rejected earlier case precedent that created an exception to *Noerr-Pennington* immunity when government officials participated in the antitrust conspiracy with private parties seeking government action. The conspiracy exception fell because

> it is both inevitable and desirable that public officials often agree to do what one or another group of private citizens urges upon them, such an exception would virtually swallow up the [purpose underlying the immunity]: All anticompetitive regulation would be vulnerable to a 'conspiracy' charge.[191]

The Court observed, in addition, that [f]ew government actions are immune from the charge that they are "not in the public interest" or in some sense "corrupt."[192] Moreover, "virtually all regulation benefits some segments of society and harms others."[193] Thus, the Court concluded, it would be impractical "to allow plaintiffs to look behind the actions of state sovereigns to base their claims on 'perceived conspiracies to restrain trade.'"[194]

Finally, several courts have refused to apply *Noerr-Pennington* protection when the attempt to influence was not directed at the government's sovereign authority but rather at a purely commercial or proprietary venture of the government.[195] Governments frequently act in commercial capacities, such as a purchaser of goods in a commercial market, and when they do they are not acting as a deliberative political body.[196] The circuit courts, however, are split on whether there should be a "commercial enterprise" exception to the *Noerr-Pennington* doctrine. The Ninth Circuit, for example, has reasoned that "the nature of the government activity is [but] one factor in determining the type of public input acceptable to the particular decision making process."[197] It has rejected the "commercial enterprise" exception as an airtight defense. But in *Omni* the Supreme Court implied that it might entertain a commercial dealing or market participant exception.[198]

---

190. 508 U.S. at 49.

191. 499 U.S. at 375; *see also United Airlines, Inc. v. U.S. Bank N.A.*, 406 F.3d 918 (7th Cir. 2005); *Knology, Inc. v. Insight Commc'ns, Inc.*, 393 F.3d 656 (6th Cir. 2004).

192. *Id.* at 377.

193. *Id.*

194. *Id.* at 379 (quoting *Hoover v. Ronwin*, 466 U.S. 558, 580 (1984)).

195. *See, e.g., Fed. Prescription Serv. v. Am. Pharm. Ass'n.*, 663 F.2d 253 (D.C. Cir. 1981).

196. *George R. Whitten Jr., Inc. v. Paddock Pool Builders, Inc.*, 424 F.2d 25 (1st Cir. 1970).

197. *See In re Airport Car Rental Antitrust Litig.*, 693 F.2d 84 (9th Cir. 1982); *see also Greenwood Utils. Comm'n v. Miss. Power Co.*, 751 F.2d 1484 (5th Cir. 1985).

198. 499 U.S. 365, 379 (1991).

Other courts have confronted the issue whether conduct which goes beyond mere lobbying and includes an economic boycott directed at private parties in order to achieve political ends, such as new legislation, ought to be protected by the *Noerr-Pennington* immunity. Although the courts are split on this issue, the weight of authority seems to protect "an economic boycott, politically motivated, to achieve a legislative goal."[199] Courts have been willing to examine the purpose behind the means, and if the overriding purpose, in fact, is to influence government action, the fact that economic rather than political means were employed has not destroyed the defense.[200]

The Supreme Court addressed this question directly in *FTC v. Superior Court Trial Lawyers Ass'n*,[201] where criminal defense lawyers engaged in a collective boycott by refusing to take more court-appointed indigent clients in an attempt to influence the city government to raise the lawyers' compensation. The economic boycott was used as the means, together with lobbying the city council, to achieve an economic advantage for the lawyers.

In distinguishing the *Noerr* case, the Court said, "in the *Noerr* case the alleged restraint of trade was the intended consequence of legislation; in this case the boycott was the *means* by which [the lawyers] sought to obtain favorable legislation."[202] The Court observed that "the undenied objective of the boycott was an economic advantage for those who agreed to participate," the result of which would be an increase in the price of lawyers services.

Thus, in finding that the lawyers' boycott was not protected under the First Amendment, even though there was a component of political petitioning to the local government, the Court held that when the immediate and ultimate objective of the restraint is economic, as is the principal means through a boycott, the conduct is not protected under *Noerr* or under broader First Amendment principles.

Noerr's protection, after *Trial Lawyers*, therefore turns on motivation and means employed. It matters whether the economic boycott was the means by which the challenged party petitioned the government or rather the consequence of the petitioning conduct.[203] Because the lawyers who had an economic motive used principally economic means to achieve an economic objective, even though they sought to influence the local government, their antitrust conduct was not protected from challenge.[204]

---

199. *See, e.g., NAACP v. Claiborne Hardware Co.*, 458 U.S. 886 (1982); *Mo. v. Nat'l Org. for Women, Inc.*, 620 F.2d 1301 (8th Cir. 1980).

200. *See, e.g., Borough of Lansdale v. Phila. Elec. Co.*, 692 F.2d 307 (3d Cir. 1982); *Feminist Women's Health Ctr. v. Mohammed*, 586 F.2d 530, 543 n.7 (5th Cir. 1978); *see also* Daniel R. Mandelker, Jules B. Gerard & E. Thomas Sullivan, *Federal Land Use Law* § 13.06[2] (2001).

201. 493 U.S. 411 (1990).

202. *Id.* at 424–25.

203. *Id.* at 425. The Court found the unprotected conduct to be a *per se* violation of the antitrust laws.

204. In *Sandy River Nursing Care v. Aetna Casualty*, 985 F.2d 1138 (1st Cir. 1993), the court rejected the argument that *Trial Lawyers* is limited to cases where the government is a purchaser or market participant. "What was significant about the concerted activity in *Trial Lawyers* was that the

The Third Circuit granted *Noerr* immunity to the American Bar Association (ABA) in *Massachusetts School of Law at Andover v. American Bar Assoc.*,[205] where the plaintiff brought a challenge to the defendant's accreditation requirements after being denied ABA accredited status. The court held that the ABA was protected from liability because, among other things, it had lobbied the states to convince them to adopt ABA accreditation decisions as their own.[206] Since there was no proof of a sham and the ABA had not directly attempted to dissuade others from dealing with the plaintiff, no exceptions to Noerr applied.[207] Thus, the injury complained of by the plaintiff was the indirect product of state lobbying and, as such, constituted protected activity.

Finally, *Noerr* protection has been questioned in settlement agreements. The Second Circuit in *Freedom Holdings, Inc. v. Spitzer*[208] held that *Noerr* does not immunize settlement legislation once it has been passed. The court reasoned that *Noerr* protects those engaged in a petitioning process during the creation of legislation, but does not protect legislation once passed, except under state action immunity, from antitrust scrutiny.

[B] Overbroad Remedial Orders

The First Amendment is also implicated when antitrust remedial orders regulate conduct. Behavior-oriented administrative or judicial decrees can infringe on the commercial speech rights of the defendant. First recognized by the Supreme Court in *Virginia State Bd. of Pharmacy v. Virginia Citizens Consumer Council, Inc.*,[209] the commercial speech doctrine now is analyzed under a four-tiered evaluation established in *Central Hudson Gas & Elec. Corp. v. Public Serv. Comm'n.*[210] To be protected, the speech must involve a lawful activity and not be related to illegal conduct. To be constitutional, the regulation must serve a substantial government interest, directly advance the asserted government interest, and be no more extensive than necessary to serve that interest. Thus, if the challenged conduct violates the antitrust laws, or is integral to or facilitates part of the antitrust conduct, it can be prohibited as long as the order prohibiting it does not deter other, competitive conduct.[211] If the decree extends beyond the interests it serves, it may be held to be impermissibly broad and offensive to constitutional sensitivities.

---

defendants sought to influence the government through an economic boycott that directly affected the marketplace.

205. 107 F.3d 1026 (3d Cir. 1997).

206. *Id.* at 1038.

207. *Id. But see* Marina Lao, *Discrediting Accreditation?: Antitrust and Legal Education*, 79 Wash. U. L.Q. 1035 (2001).

208. 357 F.3d 205 (2d Cir. 2004).

209. 425 U.S. 748 (1976).

210. 447 U.S. 557, 566 (1980).

211. E. Thomas Sullivan, *First Amendment Defenses in Antitrust Litigation*, 46 Mo. L. Rev. 517 (1981); *see also* E. Thomas Sullivan, *Comparing Antitrust Remedies in the U.S. and E.U.: Advancing a Standard of Proportionality*, 48 Antitrust Bull. 377 (2003).

§ 3.05 Common Law Defenses

In equity, the unclean hands doctrine is recognized as a defense. In essence, this defense blocks a plaintiff from recovery if the plaintiff has violated some other antitrust provision unrelated to the alleged violation in plaintiff's complaint. In antitrust litigation, it has lost much of its force and application.[212] In *Kiefer-Stewart Co. v. Joseph E. Seagram & Sons, Inc.*,[213] the Court said:

> If [plaintiff] and others were guilty of [violations] of the antitrust laws, they could be held responsible in appropriate proceedings brought against them by the Government or by injured private persons. The alleged illegal conduct of [plaintiff], however, could not legalize the unlawful combination by respondents nor immunize them against liability to those they injured.[214]

Kiefer-Stewart, however, was a treble damage action. Lower federal courts are divided on the doctrine's application in antitrust injunction suits.[215] To the extent the doctrine finds application in antitrust actions for equitable relief, the incentive to sue and the deterrent effect of the laws are reduced.[216]

At common law, a related defense, *in pari delicto*, was recognized when the plaintiff was involved in the alleged illegality set forth in the complaint.[217] The term literally means that if the plaintiff is "of equal fault," the action is barred. In *Perma Life Mufflers, Inc. v. Int'l Parts Corp.*,[218] the Court required a showing that plaintiff was truly of equal fault before it recognized the defense and barred the action. As a matter of policy, the Court rejected the defense, absent clear evidence of equal fault.

---

212. Conversely, in the patent or copyright infringement suit context, patent and copyright misuse defenses, which also have their origin in the unclean hands doctrine, have gained currency. The misuse defense overlaps proscribed monopoly conduct that comes under the scrutiny of the antitrust laws. *See Morton Salt Co. v. Suppiger Co.*, 313 U.S. 555 (1942); *Alcatel USA, Inc. v. DGI Techs., Inc.*, 166 F.3d 772, 793 (5th Cir. 1999); *Lasercomb Am., Inc. v. Reynolds*, 911 F.2d 970 (4th Cir. 1990); *see also* David McGowan, *Innovation, Uncertainty, and Stability in Antitrust Law*, 16 Berkeley Tech. L.J. 729, 811 (2001); E. Thomas Sullivan, *The Confluence of Antitrust and Intellectual Property at the New Century*, 1 Minn. Intell. Prop. Rev. 1 (2000); Note, *Clarifying the Copyright Misuse Defense: The Role of Antitrust Standards and First Amendment Values*, 104 Harv. L. Rev. 1289 (1991).

213. 340 U.S. 211 (1951).

214. *Id.* at 214.

215. *See, e.g., Memorex Corp. v. IBM*, 555 F.2d 1379 (9th Cir. 1977); *Singer v. A. Hollander & Son*, 202 F.2d 55 (3d Cir. 1953).

216. *Chrysler Corp. v. Gen. Motors Corp.*, 596 F. Supp. 416, 419 (D.D.C. 1984) (where the court, striking the unclean hands defense by General Motors, said "lower courts have almost uniformly declined to permit the unclean hands defense in antitrust suits where injunctive relief is sought"); *see also Polk Bros. v. Forest City Enters., Inc.*, 776 F.2d 185 (7th Cir. 1985) (rejecting the unclean hands defense).

217. The doctrine had its early origins, as applied in antitrust actions, in *Eastman Kodak Co. v. Blackmore*, 277 F. 694 (2d Cir. 1921). *See also Simpson v. Union Oil Co.*, 377 U.S. 13 (1964). See also *supra* § 3.05 for further discussion *pari dilecto* as applied to antitrust suits between conspirators and their former co-conspirators.

218. 392 U.S. 134 (1968), *overruled on other grounds, Copperweld Corp. v. Independence Tube Corp.*, 467 U.S. 752 (1984).

> The plaintiff who reaps the reward of treble damages may be no less morally reprehensible than the defendant, but the law encourages his suit to further the overriding public policy in favor of competition. A more fastidious regard for the relative moral worth of the parties would only result in seriously undermining the usefulness of the private action as a bulwark of antitrust enforcement. And permitting the plaintiff to recover a windfall gain does not encourage continued violations by those in his position since they remain fully subject to civil and criminal penalties for their own illegal conduct.[219]

In *Perma Life* the Court found that although plaintiffs sought the franchises with defendant, they did not seek each provision of the agreement. Some were in fact detrimental to their interests. Moreover, the Court found that plaintiffs lacked relative bargaining power and had unequal economic leverage. Acquiescence seemed necessary to achieve the business opportunity. The Court observed:

> The possible beneficial byproducts of a restriction from a plaintiff's point of view can of course be taken into consideration in computing damages, but once it is shown that the plaintiff did not aggressively support and further the monopolistic scheme as a necessary part and parcel of it, [plaintiff's] understandable attempts to make the best of a bad situation should not be a ground for completely denying [plaintiff] the right to recover which the antitrust acts give him.[220]

And in a broad sweep, the Court concluded that "the doctrine of *in pari delicto* ... is not to be recognized as a defense to an antitrust action."[221]

The lower federal courts largely have ignored the sweeping admonition of the Court; they have attempted to weigh the relative degrees of fault among the antitrust violators.[222] The defense, under these decisions, turns on the nature and degree of involvement. Before applying the defense, courts have required that the plaintiff be a co-initiator, possess equal bargaining strength, or be a perpetrator. They also have inquired whether an arm's length transaction was involved. In concurring opinions in *Perma Life*, Justices White and Fortas noted that, even if the doctrine is not applicable, a plaintiff may have difficulty establishing causation of the injury when its conduct is equal or greater than defendant's.

After *Perma Life*, the Court seemed to recede from its absolute ban on the use of the *in pari delicto* defense. In *Eichler v. Berner*, a securities case, the Court concluded

219. *Id.* at 139.

220. *Id.* at 140.

221. *Id.*

222. *Moecker v. Honeywell Int'l, Inc.*, 144 F. Supp. 2d 1291, 1312–14 (M.D. Fla. 2001) (asserting that the defense is available but that "application of the defense is to be made on a case by case basis and is limited to the situation where the plaintiff's responsibility is 'essentially indistinguishable' from or 'clearly greater' than the responsibility of the defendant."). *See, e.g., THI-Hawaii, Inc. v. First Commerce Fin. Corp.*, 627 F.2d 991, 995–96 (9th Cir. 1980).

that "a private action for damages . . . may be barred on the grounds of the plaintiff's own culpability only where: (1) as a direct result of his own actions, the plaintiff bears at least substantially equal responsibility for the violations he seeks to redress, and (2) preclusion of suit would not significantly interfere with the effective enforcement of the . . . laws. . . ."[223]

§ 3.06 Antitrust Enforcement in Regulated Industries

[A] Introduction

The antitrust laws seek to ensure that firms compete under free market conditions. Markets may not operate efficiently when externalities or other market failures are present. Antitrust is supposed to assure competitive markets and to make corrections for market failures, such as externalities, that artificially interfere with efficient market forces. Cartel behavior and monopolies are examples of market failures.

There are many industries, however, where government officials have replaced competition with regulation. Federal and state agencies regulate some or all of the market behavior within a given industry, including market entry, price, output, or exit.[224] Regulation or government intervention can take many forms, such as direct price controls or licensing requirements. Because regulation displaces market forces, it is generally considered, on a continuum, as the opposite of antitrust enforcement, which seeks to restore the conditions for a free market to flourish.

According to the First Circuit in *Town of Concord v. Boston Edison Co.*,[225] "regulation and antitrust typically aim at similar goals—i.e., low and economically efficient prices, innovation, and efficient production methods—but they seek to achieve these goals in very different ways."[226]

> Economic regulators seek to achieve them *directly* by controlling prices through rules and regulation; antitrust seeks to achieve them *indirectly* by promoting and preserving a process that tends to bring them about. An antitrust rule that seeks to promote competition but nonetheless interferes with regulatory controls could undercut the very objectives the antitrust laws are designed to serve.[227]

---

223. 472 U.S. 299, 311–12 (1985); *see also Gen. Leaseways, Inc. v. Nat'l Truck Leasing Assn*, 830 F.2d 716, at 721 (7th Cir. 1987) (denying antitrust damages because plaintiff initially supported challenged restraints).

224. Breyer, *supra* note 94.

225. 915 F.2d 17 (1st Cir. 1990).

226. *Id.* at 22.

227. *Id.*

Therefore, the question in any regulatory scheme should be whether the intent of Congress was to repeal the antitrust laws through enacting the regulation.[228]

In fact, the Supreme Court has clearly stated

> [e]ven when an industry is regulated substantially, this does not necessarily evidence an intent to repeal the antitrust laws with respect to every action taken within the industry ... Intent to repeal the antitrust laws is much clearer when a regulatory agency has been empowered to authorize or require the type of conduct under antitrust challenge.[229]

Industry behavior may be controlled by an agency or commission through statutory or rulemaking directives, rather than free market forces.[230] Economic or other policy reasons drive the decision whether to formally regulate an industry through agency action or to permit regulation through antitrust enforcement and market forces. Economic justifications for regulation include (1) market failures that suggest noncompetitive conditions or that competition is not workable; (2) inadequate or scarce resources; (3) inadequate market information; or (4) the existence of a natural monopoly. Noneconomic justifications include political reasons that attempt to *protect* certain industries from competition.[231]

[B] Regulation of Natural Monopoly

Natural monopolies best illustrate the economic justification for regulation rather than market competition. A natural monopoly is a market that can be served at the lowest per unit cost by one firm satisfying the entire market demand.[232] In theory, a natural monopoly market is most efficient and can be run more cheaply when there is only one seller. But we know a monopolist does not price at marginal costs, as one would expect if there were perfect competition. Rather a profit-maximizing monopoly will price where marginal cost equals marginal revenue.[233] We can expect the monopolist "to capture much of the extra value that would otherwise accrue to consumers,"[234] the so-called consumer surplus, thus facilitating a redistribution of income from the consumer to the monopolist. Introducing more competitors into this market would raise production costs and may not make consumers better off. Price regulation, however, could lower prices for consumers while allowing the natural

---

228. *Nat'l Gerimedical Hosp. & Gerontology Ctr. v. Blue Cross*, 452 U.S. 378, 389 (1981).

229. *Id.* at 379.

230. Jeffrey L. Harrison, Thomas D. Morgan & Paul R. Verkuil, *Regulation and Deregulation* (1995). If an industry is exempt from antitrust coverage, there may or may not be a regulatory agency that controls it.

231. *See* John Shepard Wiley, Jr., *A Capture Theory of Antitrust Federalism*, 99 Harv. L. Rev. 713 (1986).

232. Alfred E. Kahn, *The Economics of Regulation: Principles and Institutions* 65–70 (1970); Richard A. Posner, *Natural Monopoly and Its Regulation*, 21 Stan. L. Rev. 548, 550–53 (1969).

233. *See* Chapter 2 on antitrust economics and Chapter 6 on monopolization.

234. Posner, *supra* note 232, at 550.

monopolist a reasonable profit without undermining market efficiency. Regulation, by an agency charged with monitoring price and restricting monopoly pricing, is a means to recapture the consumer surplus that otherwise would be lost. The regulator optimally wants to restrict the natural monopolist so that price is set at the most efficient level—at average cost. In this way, supracompetitive profits are minimized.

Regulation over a natural monopoly results in a single producer subject to government control occupying the entire market. Numerous industries, including many utilities, are regulated in this way by federal, state, and local agencies. But not all economists agree that natural monopolies lack competition and therefore should be regulated in this manner. For instance, the theory of "contestable markets" argues that the appropriate economic model for viewing a natural monopoly is one which recognizes that, while competitors will not compete *in* the market because it is inefficient to do so, they will compete *for* the market.[235] The theory asserts that the effect that potential competitors might have on the market has been ignored under the traditional theory of natural monopoly. The theory of contestable market views pricing in the market as dependent on potential as well as actual competition; potential competition can create a restraining influence on the incumbent's pricing[236] and can inhibit monopoly pricing. But contestable market theory may not lead to lower prices in natural monopolies that are entrenched or have high fixed costs, especially if those costs are sunk, in other words, expended and not recoverable. Low sunk costs decrease barriers to entry and increase the level of potential competition.

[C] Antitrust or Regulation?

Not all formal regulation displaces competition. Regulation and competition sometimes co-exist.[237] Some regulated industries face scrutiny under both agency review and traditional antitrust. Numerous legal and policy issues may be in conflict when antitrust and regulation interact.

A frequent inquiry is: When is antitrust displaced by regulation? Explicit and implicit exemptions from antitrust coverage occur. The "pervasiveness" of the regulatory scheme may dictate whether antitrust enforcement has any role to play. Exemptions can be absolute or qualified.[238] If only qualified, the industry may be subject to

235. *See, e.g.*, Elizabeth E. Bailey & William J. Baumol, *Deregulation and the Theory of Contestable Markets*, 1 Yale J. on Reg. 111 (1984); Elizabeth E. Bailey, *Contestability and the Design of Regulatory and Antitrust Policy*, 71 Am. Econ. Rev. 178 (1981); William J. Baumol, John C. Panzar & Robert D. Willig, *Contestable Markets and the Theory of Industry Structure* (1982); Harold Demsetz, *Why Regulate Utilities?*, 11 J.L. & Econ. 55 (1968); Steven A. Morrison & Clifford Winston, *Empirical Implications and Tests of the Contestability Hypothesis*, 30 J.L. & Econ. 53 (1987).

236. *See* Chapter 7 on mergers.

237. Harrison, Morgan & Verkuil, *supra* note 230.

238. *See generally United States v. AT&T*, 461 F. Supp. 1314 (D.D.C. 1978).

both "regimes of government control."[239] This may raise tensions between antitrust enforcement and traditional regulation.

Questions of primary jurisdiction arise whether the antitrust court or the regulatory agency should determine the exemption issue in the first instance. In turn, when should an antitrust court defer to the agency on antitrust issues?[240] Generally, if the antitrust resolution would frustrate a specific regulatory provision or frustrate agency approval, the federal regulatory scheme will control over antitrust,[241] and that agency initially will review the issues. But if primary jurisdiction is invoked, the antitrust court, where the issue was first brought, will refer the issue but retain ultimate authority to decide.

Federal regulation, either explicitly or implicitly, may preempt the antitrust law's application.[242] The intent of Congress and specific language of the regulatory scheme will have to be consulted. The more pervasive the regulation, the more likely antitrust principles may have been displaced. But regulated industries are not necessarily exempt from antitrust. Where the enabling legislation does not confer express immunity nor indicate a "plain repugnancy" or inconsistency between antitrust enforcement and the administration of the regulatory system, courts are reluctant to immunize an industry from antitrust liability.[243] In fact, the Supreme Court has stated that "[e]ven when an industry is regulated substantially, this does not necessarily evidence an intent to repeal the antitrust laws with respect to every action taken within the industry.... Intent to repeal the antitrust laws is much clearer when a regulatory agency has been empowered to authorize or require the type of conduct under antitrust challenge."[244] Thus, we must consider explicit statutory exemptions, where the expressed intent was to displace competition, and implied exemptions allowed by the courts. Implied exemptions require two conditions:

(1) When a regulatory agency has, with Congressional approval, exercised explicit authority over the challenged practice itself (as distinguished from the general subject matter) in such a way that antitrust enforcement would interfere with regulation ... and

---

239. Harrison, Morgan & Verkuil, *supra* note 230, at 527.

240. *See Far E. Conference v. United States*, 342 U.S. 570 (1952); *Pan Am. World Airways v. United States*, 371 U.S. 296 (1963); *Keogh v. Chi. & Nw.Ry. Co.*, 260 U.S. 156 (1922); *MCI Commc'ns Corp. v. Am. Tel. & Tel. Co.*, 708 F.2d 1081 (7th Cir. 1983).

241. *See, e.g., U.S. Postal Serv. v. Flamingo Indus. (USA) Ltd.*, 540 U.S. 736 (2004); *Keogh*, 260 U.S. 156; *see also Hughes Tool Co. v. Trans World Airlines*, 409 U.S. 363 (1973); Israel Convissor, *Primary Jurisdiction: The Rule and Its Rationalization*, 65 Yale L.J. 315 (1956).

242. *See, e.g., United States v. Phila. Nat'l Bank*, 374 U.S. 321, 350 (1963); *Pan Am. World Airways v. United States*, 371 U.S. 296 (1962); *Gordon v. New York Stock Exchange*, 422 U.S. 659 (1975); *California v. Federal Power Comm'n*, 369 U.S. 482 (1962).

243. *Otter Tail Power Co. v. United States*, 410 U.S. 366, 372 (1973) (quoting *United States v. Phila. Nat'l Bank*, 374 U.S. 321 (1963); *see also Georgia v. Pa. R.R. Co.*, 324 U.S. 439 (1945)).

244. *Nat'l Gerimedical Hosp. & Gerontology Ctr. v. Blue Cross*, 452 U.S. 378, 389 (1981).

(2) when regulation by an agency over an industry or some of its components or practices is so pervasive that Congress is assumed to have determined competition to be an inadequate means of vindicating the public interest.[245]

This second requirement is somewhat elusive, however. In *Gordon v. New York Stock Exchange*,[246] the Court plainly rejected the argument that *only* a pervasive regulatory scheme can trump the antitrust laws.[247] The Court found that, although the SEC's authority over the stock exchange was not all-encompassing, the agency did have some power to approve or prohibit behavior, and, in that situation, there was an implicit preclusion, thus protecting the exchange members from antitrust liability.[248] But *Gordon* reasoned that an "implied repeal" is present only "when there is a 'plain repugnancy between the antitrust and regulatory provisions.'"[249] More recently, in *Credit Swiss Securities LLC v. Billing*,[250] the Court, in 2007, focused on three factors, present in *Gordon*, in deciding whether there is "clear repugnancy":

> (1) the existence of regulatory authority under the securities laws to supervise the activities in question; (2) evidence that the responsible regulatory entities exercise that authority; and (3) a resulting risk that the securities and antitrust laws, if both applicable, would produce conflicting guidance, requirements, duties, privileges, or standards of conduct.[251]

[D] Express Federal Exceptions

On numerous occasions Congress explicitly has granted antitrust exemptions to certain industries.[252] Several reasons suggest why enforcement of the antitrust laws may not be ideal in every instance. First, the promotion of competition may produce some undesirable results which we may wish to minimize from a policy perspective. Second, there may be other policy objectives which are equal to, or more important than, the promotion of competition through market forces. Regulation assumes that the "judgment of expert agencies may produce results superior to those of the marketplace, and that for this reason competition . . . will necessarily not serve the public interest."[253]

Conscious choices are made to relax or minimize enforcement in certain industries where market competition would lead to diminished social welfare. The express exemptions are of two kinds: (1) those that further broad national policy, and,

---

245. *United States v. AT&T*, 461 F. Supp. 1314, 1322 (D.D.C. 1978).

246. 422 U.S. 659 (1975).

247. *Id.* at 688.

248. *Id.* at 667, 672, 679, 684.

249. *Id.* at 682.

250. 127 S. Ct. 2383 (2007).

251. *Id.* at 2385.

252. States, cities, and other political subdivisions have done so also. The question of preemption, whether a state or local regulation is in conflict with the federal antitrust law, will be discussed later in § 3.07[B].

253. *United States v. AT&T*, 461 F. Supp. 1314, 1321 (D.D.C. 1978).

(2) those that apply to specific industries. Among the former are the promotion of the right of workers to organize, combine, and bargain collectively; the promotion of export activity; the encouragement and promotion of research, development, and technological change; the need to minimize restrictions on national defense capabilities in times of emergency; and the need to promote small business development. Industries' specific exemptions include insurance, railroads, agriculture, fisheries, and professional baseball.

[1] Exemptions Furthering National Policy

Two examples are illustrative of specific exceptions that further national policy.

[a] Labor Organizations

Section 6 of the Clayton Act states that the antitrust laws do not apply to union organizations or to union members acting within the legitimate objective of the union.[254] This exemption was designed to further the Congressional policy favoring collective bargaining. In order to qualify for the exemption, the union must act in its own self-interest and not in combination with non-labor groups or third parties. As the Supreme Court said in *United States v. Hutcheson*,[255] "[s]o long as a union acts in its self-interest and does not combine with non-labor groups, the licit and illicit under § 20 [of the Clayton Act] are not to be distinguished by any judgment regarding the wisdom or unwisdom, the rightness or wrongness, the selfishness or unselfishness of the end of which the particular union activities are the means."[256]

The Ninth Circuit has held that both of the *Hutcheson* requirements must be met in order for the exemption to apply.[257] The Court applied stringent meaning to the words "legitimate union purpose," broadly stating that whether the ends are legitimate depends on whether the "ends to be achieved are among the traditional objectives of labor organizations" *and* whether the means adopted are "activities normally associated with labor disputes."[258] The court remanded the case, suggesting that activities like pressing baseless lawsuits and mechanically objecting to the plaintiff's application for assorted permits are "troublesome" due to their "nontraditional" nature.[259] This opinion is considerably more constricting for unions than is *Hutchenson*; however, it is not without some textual support.[260] Section 20 of the Clayton Act provides that

---

254. 15 U.S.C. § 17 (2006). *See generally* Gary R. Roberts, *Reconciling Federal Labor and Antitrust Policy: The Special Case of Sports League Labor Market Restraints*, 75 Geo. L.J. 19 (1986).

255. 312 U.S. 219 (1941).

256. *Id.* at 232.

257. *USS POSCO Indus. v. Contra Costa County Bldge. & Constr. Trades Council*, 31 F.3d 800 (9th Cir. 1994).

258. *Id.* at 808–09.

259. *Id.* at 809.

260. The Norris-LaGuardia Act 29 U.S.C. §§ 101–115, which was passed by Congress in 1932 to largely prohibit the issuance of injunctions in labor dispute cases, contains broad language which can be read to support *USS-Posco*'s holding.

specified labor activities are not to be considered "violations of any law of the United States."[261] The statutory exemption on its face, however, protects conduct by a union or its members; it does not speak to a union agreement with an employer,[262] which normally would be outside the statutory exemption. For employer-union agreements, the Court has created a further exemption.[263]

The nonstatutory exemption for employer-union agreements was first set out in *United Mine Workers v. Pennington*.[264] Pennington claimed that the union engaged in unfair trade and labor practices by entering assorted agreements with larger coal operations for the purpose of eliminating competition from smaller mining companies. These agreements had the effect of increasing wages in the larger companies, necessitating that the smaller companies do the same, despite their lack of funds, in order to remain competitive. The defendant used this argument in his cross-claim and cited other steps that had been undertaken by the union to "exclude the marketing, production, and sale of nonunion coal."[265]

The Supreme Court found that "[n]either the Clayton nor the Norris-LaGuardia Acts deal with arrangements between employers and unions" nor do they "tell us whether such agreements are barred or permitted by antitrust laws."[266] The Court also clearly found that the alleged activity did not constitute a direct restraint on the product market, which would deny the union the protections of the labor exemption.[267] Therefore, the Court was faced with the formidable task of determining whether this type of wage bargaining fell under the nonstatutory labor exemption.

Although the Court admitted that the determination of wage levels is an integral part of the bargaining process, it refused to hold that *any* agreement dealing with or impacting wages is immediately exempt from the antitrust laws.[268] Rather, the Court held that not all labor market restraints integrated in collective bargaining agreements are covered by the exemption. As such, wage bargaining was said to have its limitations. The dissent, however, did not share in this point of view. Instead, Justices Goldberg, Harlan, and Stewart felt that wage bargaining should be exempt throughout. Justice Goldberg opined that "[t]he Court should hold that, in order to effectuate congressional intent, collective bargaining activity concerning mandatory subjects of bargaining under the Labor Act is not subject to the antitrust laws."[269]

The Eighth Circuit extended *Pennington* in *Powell v. NFL*.[270] The plaintiffs challenged the NFL's "Right of First Refusal/Compensation" system, which had been

---

261. 29 U.S.C. § 52 (2012).
262. *United Mine Workers v. Pennington*, 381 U.S. 657, 662 (1965).
263. *Connell Const. Co. v. Plumbers Local 100*, 421 U.S. 616, 622 (1975).
264. 381 U.S. 657 (1965).
265. *Id.* at 660.
266. *Id.* at 662.
267. *Id.* at 663.
268. *Id.* at 665.
269. *Id.* at 710. The reference is to the National Labor Relations Act, which required unions and employers to engage in wage bargaining, among other types.
270. 930 F.2d 1293 (1989).

adopted into the collective bargaining agreement between the league and the players' union and which put restrictions on the rights of players to sign with other teams once their contract was up. After the agreement between the union and NFL expired, the union attempted to revise the provision to no avail. An impasse followed, and the players attempted unsuccessfully to strike. The Court of Appeals found that, even though an impasse had occurred, the exemption still applied. The court stated that the point of impasse could not be the point of expiration of the exemption, given the fact that impasses were often temporary in nature, leading to a final agreement between the bargaining parties.[271] The court also suggested that making an impasse the endpoint for the exemption would lead to problems with employers intentionally driving impossible bargains in order to gain access to antitrust protections. Impasse is a "lawful stage of the collective bargaining process" and, as such, should not be treated as "misconduct by the defendants."[272]

The Eighth Circuit suggested that the exemption would terminate only when the parties no longer share an "ongoing collective bargaining relationship."[273] The court concluded that "[a]s long as there is a possibility that proceedings may be commenced before the Board, or until final resolution of Board proceedings and appeals therefrom, the labor relation continues and the labor exemption applies."[274]

The Second Circuit faced a similar question in *National Basketball Ass'n v. Williams*,[275] where the NBA sought to continue the terms of an expired collective bargaining agreement. The court found that the NBA could not be prevented from doing so, as the activity was consistent with hard bargaining and the use of economic force in the employment arena.

The Supreme Court addressed the issue of collective bargaining and the nonstatutory exemption in *Brown v. Pro Football, Inc.*[276] Professional football players challenged the NFL's implementation of a salary cap and requirement of $1000 for all members of the developmental squads which scrimmaged with players during practices and substituted for them in cases of injury. This cap had been the subject of much controversy between the union and the NFL, and, eventually, the parties had bargained to an impasse on the issue, with the union feeling that all players should have the ability to bargain individually for salary. Despite the impasse, the NFL implemented the fixed salary requirement.

The Supreme Court found the NFL exempt from antitrust liability. In adhering to the limited power accorded the judiciary under the nonstatutory exemption, the Court held that the collective bargaining engaged in by the NFL was a reasonable practice deserving antitrust exemption. The Court tersely rejected the three arguments

---

271. *Id.* at 1299. (citation omitted).

272. *Id.* at 1302.

273. *Id.* at 1303.

274. *Id.* at 1303–04.

275. 45 F.3d 684 (2d Cir. 1995).

276. 518 U.S. 231 (1996); *see also Clarett v. NFL*, 369 F.3d 124 (2d Cir. 2004) (holding an NFL agreement regarding the eligibility of entry draft players qualified for the nonstatutory exemption).

offered by the plaintiffs. The first theory suggested that the exemption applies only to labor-management agreements, as opposed to labor-management negotiations.[277] The Court said this argument simply reflects the fact that agreements usually have been the focus of previous similar cases, and the argument says nothing about the rationale behind the exemption.[278] The purpose behind the exemption is a policy favoring the association of employees to prevent excess competition for jobs, leading to wage depression and poor working conditions.[279] As such, the process of the bargaining arrangement is just as important as the agreement eventually reached. This was a new stretch in terms of the nonstatutory exemption because now the entire process of collective bargaining is exempt from antitrust law, unless the agreement eventually decided upon is "sufficiently distant in time and circumstances from the bargaining process."[280]

This finding doomed the plaintiff's second theory, as well. The Solicitor General attempted to argue, once again, that the exemption should terminate at the point of impasse. The *Brown* Court adopted the same point of view as the *Powell* court, saying that impasses are often temporary, with effective collective bargaining continuing afterwards.[281] The Court found that "[i]mpasse and an accompanying implementation of proposals constitute an integral part of the bargaining process," necessitating exemption.[282] The Court also rejected the Solicitor General's alternate suggestion that the exemption should only be "reasonably extended" in such cases, stating that "even so modified, the impasse-related rule creates an exemption that can evaporate in the middle of the bargaining process, leaving later antitrust courts free to second-guess the parties' bargaining decisions and consequently forcing them to choose their collective-bargaining responses in light of what they predict or fear that antitrust courts will eventually decide."[283]

Finally, the Court dismissed the suggestion that the exemption for post-impasse agreements should only apply to bargaining tactics, but not to substantive terms. The Court found this unacceptable, as it would require courts to look into employers' purposes and motives, which is both "amorphous" and outside the regular concerns of the labor exemption.[284] In sum, the Court applied the nonstatutory exemption in this case because

> [the] conduct took place during and immediately after a collective-bargaining negotiation. It grew out of, and was directly related to, the lawful operation of the bargaining process. It involved a matter that the parties

277. *Id.* at 243.

278. *Id.*

279. *See Richards v. Neilson Freight Lines*, 810 F.2d 898, 905 (9th Cir. 1987) (explaining *Connell Constr. Co. v. Plumbers & Steamfitters Local Union No. 100* in terms of the policy driving the decision).

280. *Brown*, 518 U.S. at 250.

281. *Id.* at 244–46.

282. *Id.* at 239.

283. *Id.* at 246–47.

284. *Id.* at 247.

> were required to negotiate collectively. And it concerned only the parties to the collective-bargaining relationship.[285]

The Court, however, was adamant in its position that the decision did not insulate completely from antitrust law every multi-employer imposition of terms couched in a collective bargaining agreement.[286]

Justice Stevens' dissent strongly discouraged the majority's broad application of legality to any activity implemented during the collective bargaining process. He feared that the majority opinion would effectively allow employers to be protected in denying employees the opportunity to negotiate their salaries individually through an exemption designed to protect collective action by employees.[287] Nonetheless, it cannot be denied that the *Brown* decision, while broad, does clarify the nonstatutory labor exemption and is certainly in accord with current trends in interpreting the exemption, as demonstrated in *Powell* and *Williams*.

The only issue the *Brown* Court left untouched is whether a labor law violation should immediately invalidate the exemption. The lower courts are largely split on this issue.[288] Some critics feel that this is a moot point in the case of *Brown*, since "[a]s long as the collective bargaining relationship remains intact and the negotiations do not substantially affect outside parties, violations of labor laws should not extinguish the antitrust exemption."[289]

Four points are worth noting regarding the modern interpretation of the labor exemption. First, in order for it to apply, the union must act in its own self-interest.[290] Second, the union can only use means that are the least restrictive necessary to achieve the goals.[291] Third, there must be a specific employer-employee relationship, as opposed to, for example, an independent contractor relationship.[292] Fourth, the exemption applies only when the union is acting in its official capacity as a representative

285. *Id.* at 250.

286. *Id.* ("Distance in time and circumstances from the collective-bargaining process" may overcome the exemption.).

287. 518 U.S. at 251–66.

288. *Compare Consol. Express v. N.Y. Shipping Ass'n (Conex)*, 602 F.2d 494 (3d Cir. 1979) (holding that a labor law violation can destroy the nonstatutory labor exemption), *with Richards v. Neilson Freight Lines*, 810 F.2d 898 (9th Cir. 1987) (finding that a possibly illegal bargaining agreement is still exempt from antitrust enforcement).

289. *The Supreme Court, 1995 Term-Leading Case*, 110 Harv. L. Rev. 327, 337 (1996).

290. *United Mine Workers v. Pennington*, 381 U.S. 657, 665–66 (1965) (noting that wages are included, but not an agreement between a union and an employer to impose a certain wage on another employer).

291. *H.A. Artists & Assocs. v. Actors' Equity Ass'n*, 451 U.S. 704, 722 (1981); *Allen Bradley Co. v. Local Union No. 3*, 325 U.S. 797, 809 (1945) (stating that agreements that bar entry of new employers not exempt).

292. *Columbia River Packers Ass'n v. Hinton*, 315 U.S. 143 (1942) (question of fact in determining whether relationship is with employee or independent contractor); *Burlington N. Santa Fe Ry. Co. v. Int'l Bhd. of Teamsters, Local 174*, 203 F.3d 703 (9th Cir. 2000) (union members who are subcontractors are employees).

of workers.[293] If the union engages in its own commercial or productive activity, its activity is covered under the Sherman Act and is not exempt.

[b] Export Associations

Historically, most foreign countries, including advanced capitalist economies, did not proscribe and punish cartel organizations as did the United States. As a result, American firms selling in export markets faced severe competition from foreign cartels. Congress attempted to reduce the disadvantages to United States exporting companies through the adoption of two statutes: the Webb-Pomerene Act and the Export Trading Company Act.

Congress first enacted the Webb-Pomerene Act in 1918 to encourage American exports through joint export associations. Export associations are exempt from the antitrust laws if their "sole purpose" is to engage in export trade and if their actions (1) do not interfere with or restrain trade in the United States or (2) restrain the export trade of domestic competitors.[294] Congress passed the Webb-Pomerene Act largely as an attempt to remedy the competitive disadvantage that firms in the United States suffered due to their inability to form joint associations.[295]

To qualify for an antitrust exemption, associations must file reports on their export activities with the Federal Trade Commission, which investigates export associations. If conduct outside the exemption occurs, the FTC may refer the matter to the Department of Justice for prosecution.[296] Nonexempt conduct includes the export association (1) joining with a foreign cartel,[297] (2) establishing a foreign subsidiary,[298] or (3) joining with non-members to restrict competition.[299]

The Third Circuit further clarified the reach of Webb-Pomerene protections in *Int'l Raw Materials v. Stauffer Chemical Co.*[300] One of the defendants was the American National Soda Ash Corporation (ANSAC), an association of soda ash producers. All association members were domestic corporations, with their principal place of business in the United States, and all but one were owned by or affiliated with a major foreign corporation. ANSAC reached an agreement with International Raw Materials (IRM) for terminal services. After the contract expired, however, ANSAC took its business to Hall-Buck Marine, a competitor of IRM, because Hall-Buck offered ANSAC a better price. ANSAC was to have a 50% ownership interest in the operation of the terminal. IRM sued ANSAC, among others, under a price-fixing theory,

---

293. *Streiffer v. Seafarers Sea Chest Corp.*, 162 F. Supp. 602 (E.D. La. 1958) (holding that a business subsidiary owned by union not exempt).

294. 15 U.S.C. § 62 (2012).

295. *Horizons Int'l, Inc. v. Baldrige*, 811 F.2d 154, 163 (3d Cir. 1987).

296. *See generally United States Alkali Exp. Ass'n v. United States*, 325 U.S. 196 (1945); *United States v. Concentrated Phosphate Exp. Ass'n*, 393 U.S. 199 (1968).

297. *United States v. United States Alkali Exp. Ass'n*, 86 F. Supp. 59 (S.D.N.Y. 1949).

298. *United States v. Minn. Mining & Mfg. Co.*, 92 F. Supp. 947 (D. Mass. 1950).

299. *Exp. Screw Ass'n*, 43 F.T.C. 980 (1947).

300. 978 F.2d 1318 (3d Cir. 1992).

stating that ANSAC did not qualify for Webb-Pomerene protection because (1) many members of ANSAC were foreign owned and (2) ANSAC had acted outside its "sole purpose" requirement by engaging in terminalling.

The court rejected both arguments and found ANSAC's actions fully protected by the Act. As for the IRM's first theory, the court stated that "[n]othing in the language of the statute or its legislative history explicitly restricts membership in Webb-Pomerene associations to American-owned firms."[301] In fact, the legislative history suggests otherwise, as the House of Representatives firmly rejected the suggested addition of such limiting language.[302] The court found that a Congressional intent to so limit the Act could not be inferred from individual statements or debates either.[303]

IRM's second theory was based on ANSAC's part ownership and somewhat integrated business activity with Hall-Buck Marine. The plaintiff suggested that this association brought ANSAC outside the "sole purpose" requirement because ANSAC was effectively in the business of terminalling, as well as soda ash producing. The court found that, in order for this assertion to hold true, Hall-Buck and ANSAC would have to be in either a joint venture or partnership arrangement, which they were not. The court held that, even though ANSAC may receive some economic benefit from Hall-Buck's dealings with other customers, as the terminal could not be built without that extra revenue, this did not constitute a joint venture.[304] Additionally, there was no agreement between Hall-Buck and ANSAC to apportion losses, further proving that no partnership or joint venture existed.[305] As such, both arguments failed.

In 1982 Congress passed another statute to encourage export activity and to reduce trade deficits. The Export Trading Company Act[306] provides for a "certification" issued by the Department of Commerce with the concurrence of the Department of Justice. When it is issued, the certification immunizes an export trading company from federal and state antitrust enforcement. Several conditions must first exist, however, before the certification will issue. The export activity (1) cannot result in a "substantial lessening of competition" in the United States or with an export competitor; (2) cannot "unreasonably" affect prices in the United States; (3) cannot amount to an "unfair method[] of competition" against competitors in the export market; and (4) cannot engage in the sale or resale of goods in the domestic market.[307] Once the certificate is issued, there is a presumption of legality that attaches to the export activity.[308] But a private right of action for injunctive relief and actual (not treble) damages exists if the exporter goes outside the conditions stated in the certificate.[309]

---

301. *Id.* at 1323.
302. *Id.*
303. *Id.* at 1324.
304. *Id.* at 1332.
305. *Id.*
306. 15 U.S.C. §§ 4001–4021 (2012). *See generally* Areeda & Hovenkamp, *supra* note 45, ¶ 251a.
307. 15 U.S.C. § 4013(a) (2012).
308. Areeda & Hovenkamp, *supra* note 45, ¶ 251a.
309. *Id.*

A further restriction was added in 1982. Before a court has jurisdiction to entertain an enforcement action against exporting companies, the plaintiff must show that the conduct had a "direct, substantial, and reasonably foreseeable effect" on commerce in the United States, or on the export commerce of a United States resident.[310]

[2] Exemptions for Specific Industries

[a] Insurance

Although there are several congressional exemptions which are industry specific, this discussion is limited to one central exemption—the insurance industry. Prior to 1944, insurance was regulated exclusively by the states because it was believed that it was not "commerce" within the meaning of Congress' regulatory powers. In *United States v. South-Eastern Underwriters Ass'n*,[311] the Supreme Court held that insurance was within the regulatory ambit of the commerce clause and thus subject to the antitrust laws.

Several challenges were addressed to this expanded antitrust coverage. First, there was fear that this would restrict the power of the states to regulate the business of insurance; second, a preemption issue was raised when there was tension between the state regulation and the Sherman Act; and third, there was fear of loss of "efficiency-enhancing joint insurer activities."[312]

In response, Congress, in 1945, enacted the McCarran-Ferguson Act.[313] Section 2(b) of the Act provides that that the federal antitrust laws shall not cover "the business of insurance" as long as it is "regulated by state law." If the conduct engaged in by the insurance company is not regulated and authorized by state law, or is not a part of the business of insurance, it is not exempt from the federal antitrust laws.[314]

Several definitions have been advanced for what is meant by the "business of insurance." Certainly underwriting and the spreading of risk are the core of the insurance business. A broader definition also includes the relationship between the insurer and

---

310. 15 U.S.C. § 6a (2012). *See* discussion of the Foreign Trade Antitrust Improvement Act, § 3.03[C], *supra*.

311. 322 U.S. 533 (1944). *See generally* Earl W. Kinter, Joseph P. Bauer & Michael J. Allen, *Application of the Antitrust Laws to the Activities of Insurance Companies: Heavier Risks, Expanded Coverage, and Greater Liability*, 63 N.C. L. Rev. 431 (1985).

312. Statement of Charles Rule, Acting Asst. Atty. Gen. before the Committee on Small Business, House of Representatives (Apr. 29, 1987). Note also that the "state action doctrine," discussed *infra* § 3.07[A], is a basis for a state to regulate and immunize conduct subject to the federal antitrust laws. *See Southern Motor Carriers Rate Conference, Inc. v. United States*, 471 U.S. 48 (1985). In light of the developments of this doctrine, perhaps no other exemption is warranted. Apparently, the recent trend in state regulation is to permit freer competition among insurers. *See* 133 Cong. Rec. S. 342–44 (daily ed. Jan. 6, 1987) (statement of Sen. Metzenbaum).

313. 15 U.S.C. §§ 1011–1015 (2012).

314. *See, e.g., Group Life & Health Ins. Co. v. Royal Drug Co.*, 440 U.S. 205 (1979).

the insured. In *Union Labor Life Ins. Co. v. Pireno*,[315] the Supreme Court set forth the test for determining whether the antitrust insurance exemption applies to a challenged practice: "First, whether the practice has the effect of transferring or spreading a policyholder's risk; second, whether the practice is an integral part of the policy relationship between the insurer and the insured; and third, whether the practice is limited to entities within the insurance industry."[316]

The Supreme Court revisited the *Pireno* three-part test for the "business of insurance" in *U.S. Dep't of Treasury v. Fabe*.[317] The Court was faced with a challenge to an Ohio statute that gave the federal government fifth priority in liquidation proceedings for insolvent companies. The United States argued that it should be given first priority under the corresponding federal statute and that the McCaran-Ferguson Act did not apply to this situation because the state statute did not regulate the "business of insurance."[318] The Supreme Court held that the Ohio statute fell under the first clause of § 2(b) and, hence, was protected from federal preemption.

The Court relied largely on its previous decision in *Securities & Exchange Comm'n v. Nat'l Securities, Inc.*,[319] which stated that a state law intended to protect policyholders and their interests would be related to the business of insurance.[320] As such, the Ohio statute's purpose was to ensure the performance of insurance agreements, thereby protecting policyholders and regulating the "business of insurance." The Court stated that *Pireno* should not be read to say that the "business of insurance" deals only with the writing, as opposed to the performance, of contracts, as both activities are integral to the business.[321] In fact, "without performance of the terms of the insurance policy, there is no risk transfer at all."[322] The Court expanded *Pireno* to include protection of activities that are directly related to the performance of an insurance contract, even if the activities do not necessarily spread risk by themselves. The Court also found that the fact that only part of the statute was enacted for the purpose of regulating the business of insurance did not prevent it from enjoying at least partial protection under the McCarran Act.

The unusual aspect of *Fabe* lies in the Court's comment that *Pireno* does not apply as precedent for the case. The Court supported this suggestion by differentiating between the first and second clauses of § 2(b). The second clause, upon which *Pireno* was decided, states that antitrust law "shall be applicable to the business of insurance

---

315. 458 U.S. 119 (1982).

316. *Id.* at 129 (summarizing factors identified by the Court in *Group Life & Health Ins. Co. v. Royal Drug Co.*, 440 U.S. 205 (1979)).

317. 508 U.S. 491 (1993).

318. The first clause of section 2(b) of the McCarran-Ferguson Act provides that no federal statute shall preempt a state statute enacted for the purpose of regulating the business of insurance.

319. 393 U.S. 453 (1969).

320. *Id.* at 460.

321. 508 U.S. at 504.

322. *Id.*

to the extent that such business is not regulated by State law."[323] The first clause, upon which the *Fabe* holding rests, states that "[n]o Act of Congress shall be construed to invalidate, impair, or supersede any law enacted by any State for the purpose of regulating the business of insurance, . . . unless such Act specifically relates to the business of insurance."[324] The Court read the first clause more broadly as dealing with "laws that possess the end, intention, or aim of adjusting, managing, or controlling the business of insurance" and making up the Act's "primary objectives."[325] Thus, the performance of a contract becomes the "business of insurance." This unprecedented step in the interpretation of the McCarran-Ferguson Act was criticized by the dissent.

Courts define certain activities as part of the "business of insurance" and certain others as outside the realm of the McCarran-Ferguson Act. The Third Circuit in *Ticor Title Ins. Co. v. FTC*[326] held that fixing fees for title search and examination services is not within the "business of insurance" contemplated by § 2(b). The court found that rate fixing of this sort does not spread risk for the policyholder, and the activity was better characterized as "ancillary" to insurance contracting and performance,[327] effectively overruling prior Third Circuit decisions which had held otherwise.[328] However, this view about title search and examination and price fixing is not held by all circuits. The Tenth Circuit in *Commander Leasing Co. v. Transamerica Title Ins. Co.*[329] held that, in deciding what is in the business of title insurance, one cannot fragment insurance from searches and examinations.[330]

Notwithstanding the broad exemptions, Congress provided for specific limitations on the scope of the exemption. If the insurance company engages in agreements to boycott, coerce, or intimidate, the exemption does not apply.[331] For example, a refusal to deal except at a fixed price is a boycott and subject to antitrust challenge.[332] According to the Supreme Court in *St. Paul Fire & Marine v. Barry*,[333] the victim of the boycott does not have to be a competitor of the boycotting parties in order for the exception to apply.[334] "Boycott," as used in the McCarran-Ferguson Act, should be defined in its usual way. Plainly, it is "a method of pressuring a party with whom one has a dispute by withholding or enlisting others to withhold, patronage or services

323. 15 U.S.C. § 1012(b) (2012).

324. *Id.*

325. 508 U.S. at 504–05.

326. 998 F.2d 1129 (3d Cir. 1993).

327. *Id.* at 1134, 1136.

328. *See, e.g., In re Real Estate Title & Settlement Serv. Antitrust Litig.* 1686-1 Trade Cas. (CCH) Paragraph 67, 149, 62,933 (E.D. Pa. 1986), *aff'd*, 815 F.2d 695 (3d Cir. 1987) (holding such activities to be protected by the McCarran-Ferguson Act because of their close relation to the issuance of title insurance and the fact that they had been historically performed by title insurance companies).

329. 477 F.2d 77 (10th Cir. 1973).

330. *Id.* at 82.

331. 15 U.S.C. §§ 1013(b), 1014 (2012).

332. *Cal. League of Indep. Ins. Procedures v. Aetna Cas. & Sur. Co.*, 179 F. Supp. 65 (N.D. Cal. 1959).

333. 438 U.S. 531 (1978).

334. *Id.* at 543, 550.

from the target."[335] In addition, where transactions are so interstate in nature that the state cannot effectively regulate the activity, the exemption is not "regulated by state law," hence the exemption may not apply.[336]

In *Hartford Fire Insurance Co. v. California*,[337] nineteen states and various private plaintiffs alleged that the defendants, both domestic and foreign insurance carriers, conspired to restrict the terms of coverage for commercial general liability (CGL) insurance within the United States. In their complaint, the plaintiffs alleged that the purpose behind the conspiracy was to force certain primary insurers (those insurers who sell insurance directly to consumers) to change the terms of their standard CGL insurance policies to conform with the policies the defendant insurers wanted to sell. While the foreign defendants raised international comity as a bar to extension of extraterritorial jurisdiction, the domestic defendants argued that the alleged conduct fell within the grant of antitrust immunity for insurance contained in § 2(b) of the McCarran-Ferguson Act[338] because it amounted to "the business of insurance" and was "regulated by State law."

After all the actions were consolidated, the district court granted defendants' motions to dismiss believing the alleged conduct fell within the grant of antitrust immunity contained in § 2(b) of the McCarran-Ferguson Act, and that the conduct did not constitute an unprotected "boycott" within § 3(b) of the Act.[339] On appeal, however, the Ninth Circuit Court of Appeals reversed and held that although the conduct involved the "business of insurance," the domestic defendants could not claim antitrust immunity since (1) they forfeited their § 2(b) exemption when they conspired with the nonexempt foreign reinsurers, and (2) the conduct fell within the § 3(b) exclusion for "acts of boycott, coercion, or intimidation."[340]

The Supreme Court affirmed the Ninth Circuit's holding regarding the inapplicability of antitrust immunity for the alleged conduct in question and observed four propositions concerning "boycotts" under § 3(b) of the McCarran-Ferguson Act: "First, . . . only those refusals to deal involving the coordinated action of multiple actors constitute § 3(b) boycotts. . . . Second, a § 3(b) boycott need not involve an absolute refusal to deal. . . . Third, . . . a § 3(b) boycott need not entail unequal treatment of the targets of the boycott and its instigators. . . . Fourth, although a necessary element, 'concerted activity' is not, by itself, sufficient for a finding of 'boycott' under § 3(b)."[341]

---

335. *Id.* at 541.
336. *See FTC v. Travelers Health Ass'n*, 362 U.S. 293 (1960).
337. 509 U.S. 764 (1993).
338. 15 U.S.C. §§ 1011–1015 (2012).
339. *In re Ins. Antitrust Litig.*, 723 F. Supp. 464 (N.D. Calif. 1989).
340. *In re Ins. Antitrust Litig.*, 938 F.2d 919 (9th Cir. 1991).
341. Hartford Fire Ins. Co. v. California, 509 U.S. 764, 785–87 (1993) (Souter, J., concurring in judgment as to Part II.B).

§ 3.07 Federalism

[A] The State Action Doctrine

The antitrust laws regulate private agreements and conduct that restrain trade; they are not directed at regulating "state action or official action directed by the state."[342] State action immunity was first expressed by the Supreme Court in the seminal case of *Parker v. Brown*,[343] where the Court applied the concept of federalism to uphold a state statute that created a commission to set prices and restrict output among raisin growers. Federalism is a policy that emphasizes leaving certain decision-making functions to state and local governments. Noting that "[i]n a dual system of government in which, under the Constitution, the states are sovereign, save only as Congress may constitutionally subtract from their authority,"[344] the Supreme Court reasoned that as long as there is no direct conflict with federal policy, the two schemes of regulation, federal and state, may co-exist.

The Court did mention, however, that this immunity does not apply when a state pardons "those who violate the Sherman Act by authorizing them to violate it, or by declaring that their action is lawful."[345] In other words, the state cannot simply authorize a party to break the law under the Sherman Act. In *Goldfarb v. Virginia State Bar*,[346] the Supreme Court struck down a state bar association's creation of a minimum fee schedule for lawyer services. The fee schedule established by the state bar association had not been mandated, compelled, or supervised by the state supreme court, although it was implicitly sanctioned. *Goldfarb* implied that antitrust conduct is only immunized when the state through its sovereign power *requires* the practice under question and actually supervises it.[347] Not every act of the state or its subdivisions therefore automatically comes within the state action immunity.[348] In *Goldfarb*, the price-fixing agreement was not immunized because the state did not require the practice. Soon the focus turned to the degree of the initial authorization and on the degree of supervision by the state.

In *Cantor v. Detroit Edison Co.*,[349] plaintiff challenged as anticompetitive the utility company's practice of tying the sale of light bulbs to electricity sales. The state utility

342. *Parker v. Brown*, 317 U.S. 341 (1943). For a discussion of how antitrust regulation has fostered a theme of federalism over competition the last 50 years in local government issues, see E. Thomas Sullivan, *Antitrust Regulation of Land Use: Federalism's Triumph Over Competition, The Last Fifty Years*, 3 Wash. U. J. L. & Pol'y 473 (2000).

343. 317 U.S. 341.

344. *Id.* at 351.

345. *Id.* at 351 (citations omitted).

346. 421 U.S. 773 (1975).

347. *Id.* at 791.

348. *See Cal. Retail Liquor Dealers Ass'n v. Midcal Aluminum, Inc.*, 445 U.S. 97 (1980) (state failed to establish or review prices required to be filed under state statute); *Cantor v. Detroit Edison*, 428 U.S. 579 (1976) (in absence of state requirement, state utility commission approved light bulb sale by utility).

349. 428 U.S. 579 (1976).

commission had approved a tariff which included the costs of the bulbs. Cantor alleged that through this tying defendant utility used its monopoly power in one market (electricity) to suppress competition in another market (light bulbs). The Court declined to apply the state action doctrine once it concluded that passive approval by the state was not enough to trigger the immunity. A policy of "state neutrality" regarding the challenged practice was insufficient as a matter of law.[350] Beyond mere tolerance of the practice, the Court required both a clear articulation of state policy and state supervision to displace competition with the challenged anticompetitive conduct.[351]

Those two conditions were satisfied the following year in *Bates v. State Bar of Arizona*,[352] in which the Court applied the immunity once it found that the restrictions on lawyer advertising were compelled by the state supreme court and actively supervised by it. Thus the Court extended *Parker's* federalism rationale, with its deference to state regulation, to private parties regulated by the state.

In *California Retail Liquor Dealers Association v. Midcal Aluminum, Inc.*,[353] the Supreme Court established a two-element test for a challenged restraint to be protected by the state action doctrine. First, it must be "clearly articulated and affirmatively expressed as state policy."[354] Second, "the policy must be 'actively supervised' by the state itself."[355] This is generally referred to as the *Midcal* test. Subsequent decisions have discussed how to apply the two elements.

The Supreme Court clarified the "active supervision" requirement in *FTC v. Ticor Title Ins. Co.*[356] In *Ticor Title*, the Federal Trade Commission filed an administrative complaint against six of the nation's largest title insurance companies alleging a horizontal price-fixing agreement in their fees for title searches and examinations.[357] Within each state, "uniform rates were established by a rating bureau licensed by the State and authorized to establish joint rates for its members. Rate filings were made to the state insurance office and became effective unless the State rejected them within a specified period."[358] In each of these states, however, a "negative option" system was used to approve rate filings by the bureaus. Under this system, "the rating bureau filed rates with the state insurance office which became effective unless the state rejected

350. *Id.* at 585.

351. *See* Phillip Areeda, *Antitrust Immunity for "State Action" After Lafayette*, 95 Harv. L. Rev. 435, 438 (1981).

352. 433 U.S. 350 (1977).

353. 445 U.S. 97 (1980).

354. *Id.* at 105.

355. *Id.*

356. 504 U.S. 621 (1992).

357. "Title insurance is the business of insuring the record title of real property for persons with some interest in the estate, including owners, occupiers, and lenders. A title insurance policy insures against certain losses or damages sustained by reason of a defect in title not shown on the policy or title report to which it refers. Before issuing a title insurance policy, the insurance company or one of its agents performs a title search and examination. The search produces a chronological list of the public documents in the chain of title to the real property. The examination is a critical analysis or interpretation of the condition of title revealed by the documents disclosed through this search." *Id.* at 625–26.

358. *Id.* at 621.

them within a specified period of time, such as 30 days."[359] In their defense, the defendants claimed that the insurance practices in question were actively supervised by state officials and thereby warranted state-action immunity.[360]

In addressing whether the states "actively supervised" the fee setting practices in question, the Supreme Court commented:

> [O]ur decisions make clear that the purpose of the active supervision inquiry is not to determine whether the State has some normative standard, such as efficiency, in its regulatory practices. Its purpose is to determine whether the State has exercised sufficient independent judgment and control so that the details of the rates or prices have been established as a product of deliberate state intervention, not simply by agreement among private parties.[361]

Consequently, the Court held that in the absence of *active* supervision, the negative option procedure was inadequate to trigger the state action immunity.[362]

Regarding the active supervision requirement, courts have considered who can legally supervise private conduct. *Parker* suggested that a state agency can practice active supervision over anticompetitive activities in order to immunize them, as the supervising body in that case was a state agricultural commission. In *N.C. State Bd. of Dental Examiners v. FTC*,[363] however, the Court determined that the North Carolina State Board of Dental Examiners (Board), an agency of the state that regulates the practice of dentistry, needed to show active supervision by the state because active market participants controlled the board. The case arose after the Board of eight members, including six practicing dentists, sent forty-seven cease-and-desist letters to nondentists charging lower prices than dentists for teeth whitening services. The Court rejected the Board's assertion of *Parker* immunity, noting, "State agencies are not simply by their governmental character sovereign actors for the purposes of state-action-immunity. ... Limits on state-action immunity are most essential when the State seeks to delegate its regulatory power to active market participants for established ethical standards may blend with private anticompetitive motives. ..."[364]

Because cities are not sovereigns in our constitutional structure, the state action doctrine does not apply the same to local regulation. In *City of Lafayette v. Louisiana Power and Light Co.*,[365] the Court curtailed, at the local government level, the concept of federalism. Drawing the boundaries of federalism and local authority to regulate commerce, the Court held that cities are not automatically treated the same as states:

---

359. *Id.* at 629.

360. *Id.* at 634–35.

361. *Id.*

362. *Cf. Snake River Valley Elec. Ass'n. v. Pacificorp*, 228 F.3d 972 (9th Cir. 2000) (finding that state and regulatory scheme gave authorization for, but not adequate supervision of, utility's refusal to wheel power for plaintiff).

363. 135 S. Ct. 1101 (2015).

364. *Id.* at 1111.

365. 435 U.S. 389 (1978).

> Cities are not themselves sovereign; they do not receive all the federal deference of the States that create them.... *Parker's* limitation of the exemption to "official action directed by a state," ... is consistent with the fact that the States' subdivisions generally have not been treated as equivalents of the States themselves. In light of the serious economic dislocation which could result if cities were free to place their own parochial interests above the Nation's economic goals reflected in the antitrust laws, ... we are especially unwilling to presume that Congress intended to exclude anticompetitive municipal action from their reach.[366]

The question was whether a city-owned utility enjoyed state action immunity. It is not enough, the Court reasoned, that the city is an agent of the state. There must be a clear, intentional displacement of competition by regulation on the part of the state before the local regulation will be covered under the doctrine. Two requirements remain: first, there must be evidence that "the legislature contemplated the kind of action complained of" and second, the challenged practice must be rationally necessary to carry out the legislative intent.[367] The first condition called for a "clearly articulated and affirmatively expressed" state policy, although explicit authorization was not required.[368]

Two years later, the Court again suggested, as it had in *Goldfarb* and *Bates*, that active state supervision of the challenged practice was required.[369] Before later calling this requirement into question, the Court directed its attention again to local government regulation, this time in the context of home-rule charters.

Plaintiffs in *Community Communications Co. v. City of Boulder*[370] challenged a city ordinance that temporarily restricted its local cable television operation from extending service while the city surveyed the market in order to enact a systematic cable television ordinance. The city of Boulder argued that it was immune from suit under the state action doctrine because of Colorado's home-rule charter, which conferred and guaranteed local autonomy. It asserted that the home-rule provision constituted a "clearly articulated and affirmatively expressed" approval.

The Supreme Court disagreed. It ruled that home-rule charters which merely express a "neutral" state policy on the challenged practice are insufficient to warrant the state action immunity: "A state that allows its municipalities to do as they please can hardly be said to have 'contemplated' the specific anticompetitive actions for which municipal liability is sought. . . ."[371] Colorado's provision entitled each city to independently choose competition or monopoly service. Given this open-ended discretion, the state could not have "clearly articulated and affirmatively expressed" a policy in favor of regulation over competition. Federalism, the sharing of government

366. *Id.* at 412–13.
367. Areeda, *supra* note 351, at 446.
368. 435 U.S. at 410.
369. *Cal. Retail Liquor Dealers Ass'n v. Midcal Aluminum, Inc.*, 445 U.S. 97 (1980).
370. 455 U.S. 40 (1982).
371. *Id.* at 55.

power and responsibility between the states and the federal government, "has no place for sovereign cities,"[372] the Court remarked.

Boulder created many tensions between states and their cities and at least one irony. Larger cities generally enjoy home-rule authority to govern, while smaller cities regulate under specific grants of authority from the state such as local zoning authorizations. Under *Boulder*, the smaller city, with its subject-matter specific authority, may enjoy state-action immunity from antitrust challenge, while the larger city, with its general home-rule charter, would be subject to antitrust scrutiny.[373] *Boulder* and *Lafayette* seemed to retreat significantly from *Parker's* drive to return market regulation from the federal level to a more decentralized control. *Boulder* did not reach, however, the question whether there must be "active state supervision" over the local regulation. That issue was answered by the Court in 1985.

In *Town of Hallie v. City of Eau Claire*,[374] a city's monopoly in sewage treatment services was challenged by four unincorporated townships. The townships alleged that they were potential competitors of the city in the collection and transportation of sewage and that the city had engaged in tying arrangements and refusals to deal in order "to gain an unlawful monopoly."[375] The Court, however, extended state action immunity for the alleged conduct.

Clarifying the immunity standard applied to local regulations, the Court said that local governments "need not 'be able to point to a specific, detailed legislative authorization' in order to assert a successful *Parker* defense to an antitrust suit."[376] Wisconsin's home-rule statute met the "clearly expressed policy . . . to displace competition" standard because it granted cities authority to "construct, add to, alter, and repair sewage systems [including the power to] describe with reasonable particularity the district to be [served]."[377] The Court found that this language "clearly contemplat[ed] that a city may engage in anticompetitive conduct," since it is a "foreseeable result of empowering the city to refuse to serve unannexed areas."[378] The Court was able to easily distinguish its earlier holding in *Boulder*:

> [In *Boulder*] . . . the municipality was . . . free to decide every aspect of policy relating to cable television, as well as policy relating to any other field of regulation of local concern. Here, in contrast, the State has specifically authorized Wisconsin cities to provide sewage services and has delegated to the cities the express authority to take action that foreseeably will result in anticompetitive effects.[379]

---

372. *Id.* at 53.

373. Victoria Mikesell Mather, *Antitrust Implications of Municipal Land Use Planning*, 33 Wayne L. Rev. 965, 986–88 (1987).

374. 471 U.S. 34 (1985).

375. *Id.* at 38.

376. *Id.* at 39.

377. *Id.* at 40.

378. *Id.* at 41.

379. *Id.* at 43.

In short, as long as the state has specifically authorized local government to occupy or regulate a particular field and the challenged conduct is "foreseeable," state authorization is established. All specific conduct that may be subject to challenge need not be mentioned in the state authorization for immunity to attach.[380] It is important to remember, however, that it is the *specific conduct* engaged in by the defendant that must be foreseeable, not anticompetitive conduct in general.

Moreover, the *Hallie* court disclaimed the requirements, set forth in *Cantor* and *Goldfarb*, that state compulsion and state supervision were preconditions to immunity when the antitrust defendant is a local government. In a companion case, *Southern Motor Carriers Rate Conference, Inc. v. United States*,[381] the Court held that the "active state supervision" requirement was a precondition to immunize a private party engaged in conduct regulated by a state or local law. Compulsion by the state, however, is not a requirement. Addressing the rationale for this distinction, the earlier *Hallie* Court had observed:

> Where a private party is engaged in anticompetitive activity, there is a real danger that he is acting to further his own interests, rather than the governmental interests of the state. Where the actor is a municipality there is little or no danger that it is involved in a *private* price-fixing arrangement. The only real danger is that it will seek to further purely parochial public interests at the expense of more overriding state goals. This danger is minimal, however, because of the requirement that the municipality act pursuant to a clearly articulated state policy. Once it is clear that state authorization exists,

380. Floyd & Sullivan, *supra* note 112, § 4.1.7.7 n.135; Mandelker, Gerard & Sullivan, *supra* note 200, § 11.06 (2001); *see, e.g., Jackson, Tennessee Hosp. Co., LLC v. West Tennessee Healthcare, Inc.*, 414 F.3d 608 (6th Cir. 2005) (legislature authorized hospital authority to act without regard to competitive consequences, so state action doctrine protects authority from antitrust liability); *Columbia Steel Casting Co. v. Portland Gen. Elec. Co.*, 60 F.3d 1390 (9th Cir. 1995); *Askew v. DCH Reg'l Health Care Auth.*, 995 F.2d 1033 (11th Cir. 1993) (anticompetitve acquisition of private hospital immune due to authority of health care entity to acquire health care facilities); *Porter Testing Lab. v. Bd. of Regents for the Okla. Agric. & Mech. Colls.*, 993 F.2d 768 (10th Cir.) (authority of educational institution to conduct agriculture extension services led to foreseeability of displaced competition).

381. 471 U.S. 48 (1985). Defendants were private rate bureaus of motor common carriers which submitted *joint* rate proposals to state public service commissions. State laws permitted but did not require a joint submission. The Department of Justice alleged that the rate bureaus were engaged in price fixing when joint proposals were submitted. It argued that "collective ratemaking [was] not compelled by any of the states." 471 U.S. at 51. *See also 324 Liquor Corp. v. Duffy*, 479 U.S. 335 (1987), where the Supreme Court held that New York's Alcoholic Beverage Control Law, which required retailers to charge at least 112% of the "posted" wholesale price, but permitted wholesalers to sell to retailers at less than the "posted" price, was "clearly articulated and affirmatively expressed as state policy," but was not "actively supervised," because the statute did not provide for a system of state regulation nor did it monitor market conditions. Thus, the state statute did not cloak the wholesalers and retailers with state action immunity. Said the Court, "[t]he national policy in favor of competition cannot be thwarted by casting such a gauzy cloak of state involvement over what is essentially a private price-fixing arrangement." *Id.* at 345 (*citing Midcal*, 445 U.S. 97, 106 (1980).

> there is no need to require the State to supervise actively the municipality's execution of what is a properly delegated function.[382]

Likewise, in *Southern Motors*, the Court concluded that the compulsion requirement would be inconsistent with the "principles of federalism and the goal of the antitrust laws"[383] because it "reduces the range of regulatory alternatives available to the state."[384] On the other hand, evidence of compulsion directed to the private party is strong evidence that the state has clearly articulated a policy to displace competition. Although such evidence is relevant, it is not a requirement for invoking the state action doctrine.

In *City of Columbia & Columbia Outdoor Advert., Inc., v. Omni Outdoor Advertising, Inc.*,[385] the Supreme Court reaffirmed *Hallie's* and *Midcal's* two-tier test to determine the existence of state action immunity. For the *Parker* defense to apply, "authority to regulate" and a "clear articulation of a state policy to authorize anticompetitive conduct" must exist.[386] In *Omni*, an outdoor advertising company sued its principal competitor[387] and the City of Columbia for an alleged conspiracy to maintain Columbia's monopoly position through billboard advertising zoning restrictions.[388] Following a jury verdict in favor of Omni, Columbia successfully moved the trial court for a judgment notwithstanding the verdict. On appeal, however, the U.S. Court of Appeals for the Fourth Circuit reversed the judgment and reinstated the jury verdict. Specifically, the Fourth Circuit invoked a "conspiracy" exception and declared that "*Parker* [immunity] does not apply ... where 'politicians or political entities are involved as conspirators' with private actors in the restraint of trade."[389] The Supreme Court reversed.

Commenting that South Carolina's zoning statutes authorized the City of Columbia to regulate the size, location, and spacing of billboards,[390] the Court held that the city council possessed the "authority to regulate" for purposes of state action immunity.[391] It rejected the idea, again, that the statute must explicitly authorize displacement of competition. The Court, though, specifically overruled the "conspiracy" exception to

382. 471 U.S. at 47.

383. 471 U.S. 48.

384. *Id.*

385. 499 U.S. 365 (1991).

386. *Id.* at 372.

387. Columbia Outdoor Advertising controlled over 95 percent of the relevant market. The company also had close relations with city officials and lobbied them to enact zoning ordinances restricting billboard construction. *Id.* at 367.

388. The ordinance restricted the "size, location, and spacing of billboards" within downtown Columbia. *Id.* at 368. Since Columbia already had its billboards in place, its monopoly power was significantly strengthened by the ordinance, whereas Omni, as a new competitor to the market, was unable to freely construct new billboards.

389. *Id.* at 374 (*citing Omni Outdoor Advert., Inc. v. Columbia Outdoor Advert. Inc.*, 891 F.2d 1127, 1134 (4th Cir. 1990)).

390. *Id.* at 371.

391. "[T]he city's restriction of billboard construction was *prima facie* entitled to *Parker* immunity." *Id.* at 374.

state action immunity. In particular, the Court commented that "the general language of the Sherman Act should not be interpreted to prohibit anticompetitive actions by the States in their governmental capacities as sovereign regulators."[392] Rather, it is enough if the supervision of competition is a "foreseeable result" of the state authorization. [T]his immunity, [however, may] not obtain where the State acts as a commercial participant in a given market."[393]

Consequently, "with the possible market exception, *any* action that qualifies as state action is '*ipso facto* . . . exempt from the operation of the antitrust laws.'"[394]

In 2013, the Supreme Court tightened the legal standard for state action immunity's "clearly articulated and affirmatively expressed" prong. In *F.T.C. v. Phoebe Putney Health Sys., Inc.*,[395] the FTC challenged an attempt by the Hospital Authority of Albany-Dougherty County, created under Georgia's Hospital Authorities Law, to merge two hospitals accounting for 86% of the acute-care hospital services provided in the relevant six-county market. The Eleventh Circuit concluded that the Authority was entitled to state action immunity because the challenged conduct was a foreseeable result of the Georgia law's delegated power to acquire and lease hospitals. However, because Georgia had not clearly articulated and affirmatively expressed a policy permitting hospital acquisitions that substantially lessen competition, the Supreme Court found that state-action immunity did not apply. Justice Sotomayor delivered the unanimous opinion of the Court finding that state-action immunity did not attach because the harm to competition was not sufficiently "foreseeable" when the powers exercised by the substate entity "mirror general powers routinely conferred by state law upon private corporations."[396] A "substate governmental entity must also show that it has been delegated authority to act or regulate anticompetitively" in order for the immunity to apply.[397]

Although the Court did not expressly alter its "foreseeable result" standard from *Hallie*, it did find that the Court of Appeals had applied the concept of "foreseeability" too loosely. Furthering the principle that "state-action immunity is disfavored," the Court clarified that, unless the authorization to act or regulate was inherently anticompetitive, a State's grant of general power to act is done "against the backdrop of federal antitrust law." In short, the Court is requiring more specificity from the legislature as to what it contemplates before the foreseeability requirement will be satisfied and hence the immunity will apply. The Court found that nothing in the state law clearly articulated a policy to exercise general corporate powers without regard to negative effects on competition and that the State's objective of improving access to affordable health care did not logically suggest the intended use of mergers that create monopolies.

---

392. *Id.* at 374.
393. *Id.* at 374–75.
394. *Id.* at 379 (quoting *Hoover v. Ronwin*, 466 U.S. 558, 580 (1984)).
395. 568 U.S. 216 (2013).
396. *Id.* at 227.
397. *Id.* at 228.

Because the Court found that Georgia had not clearly articulated and affirmatively expressed a state policy to displace competition, the case was remanded without consideration of the Authority's minimal participation in negotiating the terms of the sale and limited supervision of the two hospitals' operations.

[1] Local Government Antitrust Act

Before *Hallie* and *Southern Motor Carriers* were decided, Congress passed a statute in response to *Boulder* to ease the tension created between the federal antitrust policy of promoting competition and potential municipal antitrust liability. Many believed that judgments rendered against cities could bankrupt local governments, given the provisions for treble damages and attorney's fees.

The Local Government Act of 1984[398] precludes damage actions under the federal antitrust laws against local governments or officials of local governments. Congress broadly defined "local government" to include any "city, county, parish, town, township, village, or any other general function governmental unit, established by state law,"[399] and any "school district, sanitary district, or any other special function governmental unit established by State law in one or more States."[400] Injunctive actions[401] are still permitted, however, and attorney's fees[402] for equitable relief are retained. Immunity from damage suits also is extended to third parties who are "expressly required" by local governments to engage in anticompetitive conduct.[403]

In *Tarabishi v. McAlester Regional Hospital*,[404] the Tenth Circuit narrowed the Act's broad definition of "local government," where it broke with tradition and held that a hospital district did not fall under the Act's immunity. The hospital was a "public trust" hospital, and even though it was formed to further public functions, had public officers as trustees, and was created for the benefit of the city of McAlester, the court denied it immunity. Behind the court's unusual decision was the fact that, under Oklahoma law, public trust hospitals are considered separate from their beneficiary cities for legal purposes. Thus, the city could not be held liable for any judgment

---

398. 15 U.S.C. §§ 34–36 (2012). Ordinarily when we think of potential antitrust violations by a local government, we consider violations of § 1 (price fixing, market division, concerted refusal to deal, or exclusive dealing arrangements) or § 2 (monopolization). But in *Cine 42nd Street Theater Corp. v. Nederlander Org.*, 790 F.2d 1032 (2d Cir. 1986), the Second Circuit held that the state action doctrine applied to § 7 of the Clayton Act (mergers). New York City had acquired several independent theaters for a rehabilitation project which eventually were leased back to the same firm.

399. 15 U.S.C. § 34(1)(A).

400. *Id.* § 34(1)(B).

401. Section 16 of the Clayton Act, 15 U.S.C. § 26 (2012).

402. *Id.*

403. *See Commc'ns, Inc. v. City of Detroit*, 650 F. Supp. 1570, 1578–79 (E.D. Mich. 1987) (once it is determined that the municipality is entitled to immunity from the antitrust laws, the private parties who are regulated by the municipality are also entitled to immunity as long as the effective decision maker is the municipality rather than the private parties).

404. 951 F.2d 1558 (10th Cir. 1991).

rendered against the hospital.[405] Because determining whether an entity has the necessary characteristics to fall under the federal definition of "local government" is "a question of state law,"[406] the court acted within its realm of authority in denying the hospital an immune status.

Explicit in the Act is the congressional intention, expressed for the first time, that local governments come within the jurisdiction of the federal antitrust law, although the scope of the Act is limited to injunctive relief. To this extent, the federal antitrust goal of promoting competition is emphasized, but the burden of treble damages is eased. Thus, if the state action doctrine does not completely immunize the local conduct, an antitrust plaintiff may sue a local government or its officials, when acting in their official capacity, for injunctive relief for conduct which is anticompetitive. If *Hallie* applies, however, the "official action directed by the local government" is immune from all antitrust suits, since the intent of the Act was to codify the state action doctrine.

[B] The Doctrine of Preemption

Under the Supremacy Clause of the Constitution, federal laws preempt contradictory state laws (and local laws).[407] This means that the Sherman Act can theoretically preempt certain state and local laws. In *Fisher v. City of Berkeley*,[408] landlords challenged a city's rent control ordinance, arguing that it was preempted by § 1 of the Sherman Act. The *Fisher* Court held that preemption was not present because the local ordinance did not necessarily violate § 1 "in all cases," nor did it force private parties to violate the Sherman Act. An antitrust violation did not "necessarily" flow from the ordinance because concerted action was not present; the ordinance was unilaterally imposed by the city, and thus there was no agreement.[409]

---

405. *Id.* at 1565, n.6.

406. *Id.* at 1565–66.

407. *Cmty. Commc'ns Co. v. City of Boulder*, 455 U.S. 40, 61 (1982) (Rehnquist, J., dissenting) (quoting Milton Handler, *Antitrust—1978*, 78 Colum. L. Rev. 1363, 1379 (1978)). Article VI, Section 2 of the United States Constitution mandates that federal statutes and treaties are the supreme law of the land and supersede any state law or rule to the contrary. *See also Cal. Liquor Dealers v. Midcal Aluminum, Inc.*, 445 U.S. 97 (1980); Robert Eisig Bienstock, Comment, *Municipal Antitrust Liability: Beyond Immunity*, 73 Cal. L. Rev. 1829 (1985); Anders Laren, Note, *Preemption and Anticompetitive State Statutes by Section 1 of the Sherman Act: Is an Agreement Required?*, 54 Ford. L. Rev. 247 (1985).

408. 475 U.S. 260 (1980). *See generally* Daniel J. Gifford, *The Antitrust State-Action Doctrine After Fisher v. Berkeley*, 39 Vand. L. Rev. 1257 (1986).

409. Compare *Hertz v. City of New York*, 1 F.3d 121, 126–27 (2d Cir. 1993), where the court distinguished a New York City ordinance regulating prices for car rentals from the statute in *Fisher* by finding there to be no "unilateral restraint" in the ordinance at bar. The court stated that the ordinance failed the *Fisher* test because "the law [was] not a 'pure regulatory scheme . . .'; [it lacked] the independent, quasi-judicial board that in *Berkeley* could adjust rates and provide relief in individual circumstances," and the City of New York was not "operating in an area vital to its municipal authority" like the City of Berkeley.

In *Rice v. Norman Williams Co.*,[410] the Court decided an antitrust challenge to a state statute by invoking the preemption analysis. In *Rice*, a California statute provided that a liquor importer could purchase liquor from outside the state "*only* if the beverages [were] consigned to a licensed importer."[411] In a suit that sought injunctive relief against the enforcement of the statute, the Supreme Court held that the proper inquiry was whether there was an irreconcilable conflict between the federal antitrust law and the state regulatory scheme. A mere hypothetical or potential conflict was not enough to trigger the preemption analysis. The state statute on its face must irreconcilably conflict with the federal antitrust policy before there is preemption.[412] Only if the state statute or regulation "necessarily constitutes a violation of the antitrust laws *in all cases*, or if it places irresistible pressure on a private party to violate the antitrust laws in order to comply with the [state] statute"[413] is it preempted by the federal antitrust laws.

This condition is satisfied if the challenged conduct is a *per se* violation of the antitrust laws. Conversely, if the conduct is analyzed under the rule of reason standard, preemption is not applicable—a facial inconsistency is lacking. Since the state statute at issue did not fall under the *per se* ban of conduct proscribed by the Sherman Act, a preemption analysis was inappropriate. The state statute could co-exist with the antitrust law.

How then are we to reconcile, analyze, and apply the doctrines of preemption and state action? *Fisher* teaches that the following tests should be applied to the interaction of these doctrines. First, determine whether there is, on the face of the state or local regulation, a direct conflict with the federal antitrust law so that action under the regulation conflicts with the federal policy. If so, there is federal preemption. Second, if preemption exists, inquire if the state or local regulation is protected under the state action doctrine.[414] Third, if state action immunity is lacking, turn to the challenged conduct and determine whether there is a substantive violation under the antitrust law. This was the analysis employed by the Court in *324 Liquor Co. v. Duffy*[415] where it found preemption but not state action because there was no active supervision by the state over the private wholesalers' and retailers' resale price maintenance system.

If federal preemption does not exist because there is no irreconcilable conflict in each case, two approaches are evident from *Fisher* and *Rice*. First, if the challenge to the state or local regulation is to the face of the regulation, then the court's antitrust inquiry is ended. Both the federal and state regulatory schemes can co-exist. This was

---

410. 458 U.S. 654 (1982).

411. *Id.* at 656.

412. *Id.* at 659.

413. *Id.* at 661 (emphasis added).

414. "Legislation that would otherwise be preempted under *Rice* may nonetheless survive if it is found to be state action immune from antitrust scrutiny under *Parker*." *Fisher*, 475 U.S. at 265–66. Even if the action is protected under the state action immunity, the state's regulation cannot burden interstate commerce or offend First Amendment rights of commercial speech. *See* E. Thomas Sullivan, *First Amendment Defenses in Antitrust Litigation*, 46 Mo. L. Rev. 517 (1981).

415. 479 U.S. 335 (1987).

the result in both *Fisher* and *Rice*. Second, if the challenge is not to the face of the local regulation but rather how it is applied,[416] the Court, after finding no preemption, should determine whether the challenged conduct is immune by reason of the "state action" doctrine, and if not, whether it violates the antitrust law. These analyses are set forth in the following chart.

Preemption-Exemption Analysis

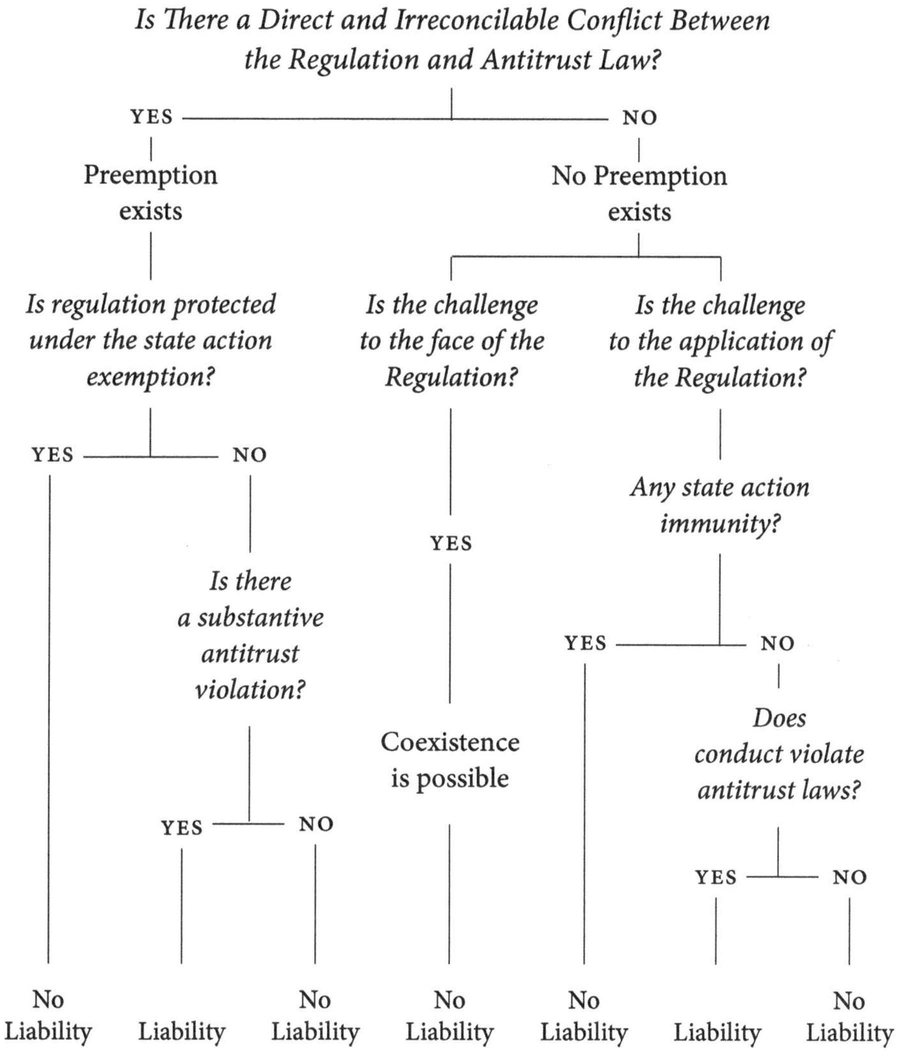

416. For example, a city may lawfully have *authority* to establish zoning restrictions, but *how* it exercises that authority (the manner in which the restriction is applied)—by granting one competitor an exclusive commercial zone but not another—may be challenged as anticompetitive. Likewise, Boulder's *authority* to grant a cable television franchise may not have been challenged; the challenge may have been to the conditions under which it was *exercised*—an exclusive franchise was given to one firm, but all others were denied access.

Chapter 4
Horizontal Restraints and Cartel Behavior

§ 4.01 Introduction

Section 1 of the Sherman Act condemns concerted activity that unreasonably restrains trade or commerce. When competitors enter into an agreement which interferes with interstate commerce, the conduct is classified as a horizontal restraint. Such conduct takes many forms, including price fixing, market divisions, or concerted refusals to deal. The concern of § 1 is cartel behavior: agreements among competitors that restrict output, increase price, and otherwise exclude competition. If the concerted action restricts "consumer choice by impeding the 'ordinary give and take of the market place,'"[1] § 1 is implicated. A cartel cannot "pre-empt the working of the market by deciding for itself that its customers do not need that which they demand."[2]

§ 4.02 Policy Introduction

From the early days of the Sherman Act to the present, Supreme Court antitrust jurisprudence has undergone several distinct changes. Over the years, the Court has generally focused on one of two major themes underlying its antitrust policy: (1) controlling economic concentrations of industrial power and (2) enhancing efficiency. The first emphasizes protection of the small competitor; the second is regarded as protecting competition rather than competitors. Because large firms are sometimes more efficient than small businesses, those goals can be in tension. At times the Court has had difficulty reconciling these two often conflicting antitrust policies. A brief overview of the Court's changing antitrust theories is helpful in understanding how prior case law affects the Court's current interpretation. The Court's analytical shifts are particularly evident in the context of horizontal price-fixing cases.

---

1. *FTC v. Ind. Fed'n of Dentists*, 476 U.S. 447, 459 (1986) *(citing Nat'l Soc'y of Prof'l Eng'rs v. United States*, 435 U.S. 679, 692 (1978)).

2. 476 U.S. at 462.

[A] Populism

A populist theme focusing on concern for small business was evident in the first Sherman Act cases. In *United States v. Trans-Missouri Freight Ass'n*,[3] the Court focused on the effects of defendants' conduct on "worthy men whose lives have been spent [in trade or commerce], and who might be unable to readjust themselves to their altered surroundings. Mere reduction in the price of the commodity dealt in might be dearly paid for by the ruin of such a class and the absorption of control over one commodity by an all-powerful combination of capital."[4] In *Chicago Bd. of Trade v. United States*,[5] the Court considered the legality of an agreement by members of the Board of Trade that fixed the price that any member could pay for grain purchased after the Board's normal closing hour. The Court announced the test of legality as "whether the restraint imposed is such as merely regulates and perhaps thereby promotes competition or whether it is such as may suppress or even destroy competition."[6] This balancing approach was necessarily broad enough to weigh the various competing interests. In applying this test, the Court upheld the challenged conduct because it "helped to improve market conditions."[7] *Chicago Bd. of Trade*, like *Trans-Missouri*, reflected the Court's populist concern over the fate of small competitors as they faced increasing competition from larger, perhaps more efficient firms.

[B] Structuralism, Effects and Efficiency

The Warren Court rejected the earlier balancing approach in favor of a structuralist approach. It focused on the structure of markets, reasoning that normal market structures will yield competitive environments, at least in the absence of explicit horizontal price fixing. This approach enabled the Warren Court to avoid balancing social and economic policy concerns. Market structure was viewed as a means to predict market behavior.

---

3. 166 U.S. 290 (1897).
4. *Id.* at 323.
5. 246 U.S. 231 (1918).
6. *Id.* at 238.
7. *Id.* at 240; *see also* Peter C. Carstensen, *The Content of the Hollow Core of Antitrust: The Chicago Board of Trade Case and the Meaning of the "Rule of Reason" in Restraint of Trade Analysis*, 1992 Res. L. & Econ. 1 (1992). Some judges have explicitly espoused this populist viewpoint. *See, e.g., MCI Commc'n Corp. v. Am. Tel. & Tel. Co.*, 708 F.2d 1081 (7th Cir. 1983) (Wood, J., concurring and dissenting). Judge Harlington Wood, Jr. observed,

> There is a persistent strain running through creation and political endurance of the antitrust laws which reveals them to be instruments to ensure the disaggregation of concerted economic power and to assure fairness among competitors and not just instruments to assure neoclassical economic efficiency, as worthy and beneficial a goal as that may be.

Id. at 1177–78. After quoting Senator Sherman as suggesting that large, aggregate economic powers should be subject to "strong resistance of the state and national authorities," *id.* at 1178 (*quoting Trans-Missouri* as proof of the Supreme Court adoption of this point of view), Judge Wood closed by questioning the "enthusiasm with which many embrace the theory that these laws stand only for economic efficiency." *Id.* at 1179.

For example, in *United States v. Container Corp.*,[8] the Warren Court held that the exchange of current price information among competitors selling a fungible product in an oligopolistic market—one that is highly concentrated—is a violation of § 1 of the Sherman Act, even when the price exchange yields lower, rather than higher, prices. The Court focused on the price stabilizing effect of defendants' conduct, which, it found, resulted from horizontal price exchanges. The *Container* Court's principal concerns were to assure that the natural market structure would not be interfered with by cooperation among market participants and that independent decision-making by competitors would not be compromised. The limited focus on preserving natural market structure eliminated the need to balance competing social and economic policy concerns or to deal with economic efficiency arguments.

Numerous Burger Court decisions rejected the Warren Court's *per se* antitrust analysis in favor of more rule of reason analysis, where plaintiffs have to prove anticompetitive effects and defendants could argue efficiency justifications for their challenged conduct. The Burger Court was more persuaded by the Chicago school's reliance on price theory and its aversion to per se illegality. The rule of reason permits weighing competitive harm against economic benefit even when the allegedly unlawful conduct directly affects price competition.[9]

In *United States v. United States Gypsum Co.*,[10] a criminal case, the Burger Court flatly rejected *Container*'s limited analysis. The Court reviewed the legality of price exchanges among wallboard manufacturers competing in an oligopolistic market.[11] The Court held that exchange of price information is not *per se* unlawful but that the antitrust plaintiff must prove general intent by showing that defendants acted with knowledge of the consequences. The Court reasoned that exchange of price information does not necessarily have anticompetitive effects and "can in certain circumstances increase economic efficiency and render markets more, rather than less, competitive."[12] In effect, the Court discarded *Container*'s structural approach in favor of reversion to the broad-based *Chicago Board of Trade* rule of reason where the Court determines the effect of the exchange within the given structure of the industry.

The Burger Court's predisposition for economic efficiency underlies many of its decisions. For example, in *Nat'l Soc'y of Prof'l Engineers v. United States*,[13] the Court stated that the competitive effect of certain agreements "can only be evaluated by analyzing the facts peculiar to the business, the history of the restraint, and the reasons

---

8. 393 U.S. 333 (1969).

9. *See generally* E. Thomas Sullivan, *The Political Economy of the Sherman Act: The First One Hundred Years* (1991); E. Thomas Sullivan, *The Economic Jurisprudence of the Burger Court's Antitrust Policy: The First Thirteen Years*, 58 Notre Dame L. Rev. 1, 20 (1982) (*citing Broad. Music, Inc. v. Columbia Broad. Sys.*, 441 U.S. 1 (1979)).

10. 438 U.S. 422 (1978).

11. The gypsum board industry was highly concentrated, with only 9 to 15 competitors, the eight largest of which accounted for 94% of national gypsum board sales. *Id.* at 426.

12. *Id.* at 441 n.16.

13. 435 U.S. 679 (1978).

why it was imposed."[14] Similarly, in *Broadcast Music, Inc. v. Columbia Broadcasting System, Inc. (BMI)*,[15] the Court, in rejecting a *per se* unlawful label for defendants' conduct, reasoned that the search for "redeeming competitive virtues [of the challenged practice] ... is not almost sure to be in vain."[16] And in *NCAA v. Bd. of Regents*,[17] the Court applied a rule of reason analysis for a joint venture in the face of both a price-fixing agreement and an output restriction. All of these cases are discussed in this Chapter.

[C] Guidelines for Collaborations Among Competitors

On April 7, 2000, the Federal Trade Commission and the Department of Justice issued Guidelines for Collaborations Among Competitors. These set forth an enforcement framework that allows businesses to understand the current governmental view of horizontal agreement, enabling them to determine the likelihood of an antitrust action.

The Guidelines distinguish between *per se* and rule of reason analysis, treating conduct that raises prices or reduces output as illegal *per se*. Agreements that do not fall into this category will be analyzed under rule of reason, and market factors will be considered. Moreover, the Guidelines establish "safe zones" for specified collaborations that are unlikely to have anticompetitive effects.[18]

§4.03 Modes of Antitrust Analysis

Many of the Supreme Court opinions discussed in the next sections contain an analysis of the economic ramifications of the challenged conduct. However, when a challenged restraint is *per se* illegal, courts generally assume anticompetitive effects as a matter of law, and thus courts eschew economic analysis in these cases. The economic models discussed in Chapter 2 inform our understanding of the cases considered in this Chapter.

The open-ended text of §1 of the Sherman Act gives courts broad discretion in interpretation. The statute sets forth only general principles, giving reviewing courts authority to engage in diverse interpretation, if not expansion. The pre-Sherman Act common law precedents served as benchmarks throughout the development of the law.

---

14. *Id.* at 692.

15. 441 U.S. 1 (1979).

16. *Id.* at 13.

17. 468 U.S. 85 (1984).

18. *But see* John J. Flynn, *The Role of Rules in Antitrust Analysis*, 3 Utah L. Rev. 605 (2006) (economic theory behind the *per se* rule had led to "rule rigidity and concept calcification").

Early cases struggled with the breadth of the statutory language. In *Standard Oil Co. v. United States*,[19] the Supreme Court began to chart the range of discretion available to courts in interpreting § 1. The Court advanced the rule of reason standard, permitting courts to weigh competitive factors and determine whether the restraint is reasonable: whether there has been a significant interference with or impact on competition.

Under this standard, only *unreasonable* restraints are illegal. But *Standard Oil* also recognized that certain conduct is, by its very nature or character, inherently anticompetitive and thus unreasonable.[20] Such conduct, therefore, does not need to be evaluated under the broad rule of reason standard to determine the actual effects of the challenged conduct. This observation foreshadowed the development of the competing *per se* rule of illegality and its application to price-fixing agreements.

The distinction is not always clear when the rule of reason or the *per se* standard should be employed. Not all restrictive conduct is inherently anticompetitive. Courts are called upon to draw fine line distinctions on a case by case basis. At times it is difficult to reconcile all the precedents. Inconsistencies frequently result because antitrust laws are largely judge-made, derived from statutory interpretations.

As the following discussion reveals, the case law trend is away from a cursory analysis under the *per se* approach, especially if the court has had little experience with the challenged practice. A more detailed factual inquiry, which scrutinizes the purpose and effect of the challenged conduct, is used more frequently today. As we will see, the characterization process, whether rule of reason or *per se*, is critical to the court's analysis and in many respects determinative of the result.

The *per se* rule of illegality, as a policy matter, furthers the goals of clarifying the law, promoting certainty for business planning and promoting judicial economy. As the Supreme Court noted in *Northern Pacific Ry. v. United States*:[21]

> [T]here are certain agreements or practices which because of their pernicious effect on competition and lack of any redeeming virtue are conclusively presumed to be unreasonable and therefore illegal without elaborate inquiry as to the precise harm they have caused or the business excuse for their use. This principle of *per se* unreasonableness not only makes the type of restraints which are proscribed by the Sherman Act more certain to the benefit of everyone concerned, but it also avoids the necessity for an incredibly complicated and prolonged economic investigation into the entire history of the industry involved, as well as related industries,

---

19. 221 U.S. 1 (1911).

20. In *United States v. Joint Traffic Ass'n*, 171 U.S. 505, 568 (1898), the Court held that price fixing was such an illegal agreement because its effects are "direct and immediate."

21. 356 U.S. 1, 5 (1958).

> in an effort to determine at large whether a particular restraint has been unreasonable—an inquiry so often wholly fruitless when undertaken.[22]

In *National Society of Professional Engineers v. United States*,[23] the Court noted:

> There are ... two complementary categories of antitrust analysis. In the first category are agreements whose nature and necessary effect are so plainly anticompetitive that no elaborate study of the industry is needed to establish their illegality—they are "illegal *per se*." In the second category are agreements whose competitive effect can only be evaluated by analyzing the facts peculiar to the business, the history of the restraint, and the reasons why it was imposed. In either event, the purpose of the analysis is to form a judgment about the competitive significance of the restraint; it is not to decide whether a policy favoring competition is in the public interest, or in the interest of the members of an industry.[24]

§ 4.04 Horizontal Price Fixing

[A] Early Supreme Court Cases

In *Chicago Bd. of Trade v. United States*,[25] members of the Board of Trade entered an agreement requiring all members who purchased grain after closing hours to purchase at a price set at the close of the day's business. Even though this agreement could be characterized as one that foreclosed price competition during the nonregular trading hours, thus subject to a *per se* condemnation, Justice Brandeis, writing for the court, outlined instead a broad rule of reason test:

> The true test of legality is whether the restraint imposed is such as merely regulates and perhaps promotes competition or whether it is such as may suppress or even destroy competition. To determine that question the court must ordinarily consider the facts peculiar to the business ...; its conditions before and after the restraint was imposed; the nature of the restraint and its effect, actual or probable. The history of the restraint, the evil believed to exist, the reason for adopting the particular remedy, the purpose or end sought to be attained are all relevant facts.[26]

This standard was then used to determine the reasonableness of the restraint. The Court upheld the challenged conduct on the theory that this price restraint actually promoted competition by "perfecting market conditions," by regulating the

---

22. *See* Ian Ayres, *How Cartels Punish: A Structural Theory of Self-Enforcement Collusion*, 87 Colum. L. Rev. 295 (1987); *see also* F.M. Scherer & David Ross, *Industrial Market Structure and Economic Performance* 509–13 (3d ed. 1990).
23. 435 U.S. 679 (1978).
24. *Id.*
25. 246 U.S. 231 (1918).
26. *Id.* at 238.

Exchange's business hours, by breaking up a monopoly previously held by a limited number of warehouses that purchased grain during nonregular hours, and by increasing the number of possible transactions.[27] In using a wide-open rule of reason analysis, Justice Brandeis was able to further those values he perceived essential under § 1—the protection of small business in a pluralistic society increasingly dominated by large business.[28]

In 1927, in *United States v. Trenton Potteries Co.*,[29] the Court reviewed the conduct of members of a trade association that controlled 82% of the domestic vitreous bathroom fixture production (e.g., sinks and toilets). Members of the association were charged with combining to fix and maintain uniform prices. In ruling defendants' conduct to be illegal, the Court limited its holding to "those controlling in any substantial manner a trade or business in interstate commerce."[30] This language suggests that *per se* treatment is applicable only when price fixing is effective; it is also the forerunner of the Court's later full-blown market analysis. The Court subsequently rejected, in *United States v. Socony-Vacuum Oil Co.*,[31] the requisite that a price fix is only *per se* unlawful if it is effective, stating that "a conspiracy to fix prices violates § 1 of the [Sherman] Act . . . though it is not established that the conspirators had the means available for the accomplishment of their objective. . . ."[32] Indeed, the Court found, "Any combination which tampers with price structures is engaged in an unlawful activity."[33]

Although the *Standard Oil* decision introduced the distinction between the rule of reason and *per se* illegality, the summary analysis implicit in the *per se* conclusive presumption was not developed in any detail until *United States v. Trenton Potteries Co.*[34] Twenty-three corporations and twenty individuals were indicted and charged with fixing the price of pottery for bathrooms. The trial court instructed the jury that if it found "the agreements or combination complained of, it might return a verdict of guilty without regard to the reasonableness of the price fixed, or the good intentions of the combining units. Defendants argued that the instruction was erroneous on the theory that the established prices were reasonable and noninjurious to the public. The Supreme Court upheld the jury instruction, rejecting the defense that fixed prices may nevertheless be reasonable.

> The aim and result of every price-fixing agreement, if effective, is the elimination of one form of competition. The power to fix prices, whether reasonably exercised or not, involves power to control the market and to fix

27. *Id.* at 240–41; *see also* E. Thomas Sullivan, *The Economic Jurisprudence of the Burger Court's Antitrust Policy: The First Thirteen Years*, 58 Notre Dame L. Rev. 1, 12–13 (1982).

28. Sullivan, *supra* note 27, at 13.

29. 273 U.S. 392 (1927).

30. *Id.* at 398.

31. 310 U.S. 150 (1940).

32. *Id.* at 224 n.59.

33. *Id.* at 225 n.59.

34. 273 U.S. 392 (1927).

> arbitrary and unreasonable prices. The reasonable price fixed today may through economic and business changes become the unreasonable price of tomorrow.... Agreements which create such potential power may well be held to be in themselves unreasonable or unlawful restraints, without the necessity of minute inquiry whether a particular price is reasonable or unreasonable as fixed and without placing on the government in enforcing the Sherman Law the burden of ascertaining from day to day whether it has become unreasonable through the mere variation of economic conditions.[35]

Implicit in *Trenton Potteries* is the idea that the range of judicial discretion is narrower in price-fixing cases. One conclusion that follows is that in price-fixing cases the only inquiry is whether an agreement to fix the price can be established. If found, the agreement is illegal and further inquiry (including the reasonableness of the price) is irrelevant. Illegal purpose will be inferred from the agreement.

Trenton Potteries implies that by definition a price-fixing agreement is *per se* unlawful. But the Court used the limited terms, "if effective," to couch its reasoning. This raised the additional question whether price fixing was *per se* illegal only if the conspirators had market power to achieve the object of the conspiracy. The issue was decided 13 years later in *United States v. Socony-Vacuum Oil Co.*[36] It was clear, however, in *Trenton Potteries* that the Court believed that price competition was at the core of § 1.

Like *Chicago Bd. of Trade*, the Supreme Court, in *Appalachian Coals, Inc. v. United States*,[37] sanctioned a rule of reason standard in another case characterized by a price-fixing cartel. Producers of bituminous coal in the Appalachian area entered into an agreement to establish an exclusive selling agent. Appalachian Coals, Inc., the selling agent, was to sell at the highest prices the entire production for all 137 producers. The producers held 12% of the bituminous production east of the Mississippi and 74% of the Appalachian territory.

Upholding the exclusive selling agreement, the Court reasoned that the arrangement was justified because of the realities of "deplorable economic conditions in the industry." The opinion was issued during the depression, which perhaps explains the Court's broadly-based weighing analysis:

> The question of the application of the statute is one of intent and effect, and is not to be determined by arbitrary assumptions. It is therefore necessary in this instance to consider the economic conditions peculiar to the coal industry, the practices which obtained, the nature of defendant's plan of making sales, the reasons which led to its adoption, and the probable consequences of the carrying out of that plan in relation to market prices and other matters affecting the public interest in interstate commerce in bituminous coal.[38]

---

35. *Id.* at 397–98.
36. 310 U.S. 150 (1940).
37. 288 U.S. 344 (1933).
38. *Id.* at 361.

Appalachian Coals advances a rule of broad discretion in favor of courts weighing competitive market factors before reaching antitrust conclusions. These cases also are important for introducing the role of efficiency and integration of productive capacity as acceptable antitrust inquiries and defenses. As the subsequent discussion indicates, agreements designed to facilitate the operation of a market and efficiency within markets are increasingly being evaluated under the rule of reason standard.[39]

In 1936, in *Sugar Institute, Inc. v. United States*,[40] the Court considered the legality of an agreement among competitors to make advance announcements of price changes and to not change their announced prices. Defendants were sugar refiners with a self-imposed code of ethics that prohibited secret price concessions and discriminatory rebates. The Court held that an agreement to make advance announcements of price changes is lawful but that agreeing to abide by previously announced prices, coupled with an enforcement mechanism among competitors, is illegal.

In reaching this conclusion, the Court focused on the defendants' role in the sugar market. Fifteen members of the Sugar Institute refined practically all the imported raw sugar processed domestically; they supplied 70 to 80 percent of the sugar consumed. Sugar was a fungible product sold in a market where the only competition was on price. The Court was concerned that defendants' conduct occurred in an oligopolistic market for a fungible product. Although defendants had not literally agreed to fix prices, because of the nature of the sugar market, their agreement was found to affect prices.

In *Socony*, the Court was confronted with whether an agreement among competitors to reduce the supply of petroleum products from the market was a *per se* price-fixing agreement. The Court held unequivocally that a conspiracy that "tampers with price structures" is *per se* unlawful, thereby foreclosing possible defenses that attempt to weigh competing interests or policies. The *per se* classification was applied, with its conclusive presumption of illegality, even though the agreement did not set or peg the exact price of gasoline. Conduct that directly *affects* price, said the Court, has by its nature and necessary effect no social utility and should be condemned without further consideration.[41] The Court's conclusion was grounded in the theory that an agreement which interferes with independent market decisions is contrary to § 1 of the Sherman Act.

---

39. The trend is obvious in a number of cases, but the Eleventh Circuit may have best embodied this general affinity for the rule of reason when it said, "We apply the *per se* rule 'only when history and analysis have shown that in sufficient similar circumstances the rule of reason unequivocally results in a finding of liability,' i.e. when the conduct involved 'always or almost always tend[s] to restrict competition and decrease output.'" *Levine v. Central Fla. Med. Affiliates, Inc.*, 72 F.3d 1538, 1549 (11th Cir. 1996) (citations omitted); *see also* Thomas C. Arthur, *A Workable Rule of Reason: A Less Ambitious Antitrust Role for the Federal Courts*, 68 Antitrust L.J. 337, 389 (2000) (suggesting that "the Supreme Court get out of the competition regulation business," leaving that to the FTC and instead focusing on the Sherman Act's prescription of "cartels, monopolistic mergers, and nakedly predatory practices").

40. 297 U.S. 553 (1936).

41. *Id.* at 224.

In its now famous footnote 59, the *Socony* Court made clear that market power is not a precondition to finding a *per se* violation:

> [I]t is well established that a person "may be guilty of conspiring although incapable of committing the objective offense." ... It is the "contract, combination ... or conspiracy in restraint of trade or commerce" which § 1 of the Act strikes down, whether the concerted activity be wholly nascent or abortive on the one hand, or successful on the other....
>
> ....
>
> ... Only a confusion between the nature of the offenses [under § 1 and § 2] ... would lead to the conclusion that power to fix prices was necessary for proof of a price-fixing conspiracy under § 1.[42]

Socony is perhaps the strongest Supreme Court decision in support of a *per se* condemnation for price-fixing agreements. Its classic definition of price fixing, "tampering with the price structure" is a broad standard capable of sweeping in various market conduct, some of which may not *directly* affect price. The conduct challenged in *Socony*, however, was clearly pernicious and the most effective method of affecting price—an agreement to reduce output or supply in the market. Under *Socony*'s *per se* characterization process, the judicial inquiry is limited to whether the challenged agreement, once established, comes within the price-fixing category.[43]

[B] Developing the Modern Per Se Rule Against Price Fixing

Questions also arose after *Socony* whether agreements that were attenuated from direct price fixing, or those that only had indirect effects on price should be treated under the narrow *Socony* approach. The Court has been far from clear on this issue, but in *Catalano, Inc. v. Target Sales, Inc.*[44] it addressed the subject.

In *Catalano*, the Court held that a horizontal agreement among competitors to eliminate credit was the equivalent of a discount and thus an inseparable part of the price. The agreement was condemned as *per se* unlawful. The Court noted, "[W]e have held agreements to be unlawful *per se* that had substantially less direct impact on price than the agreement alleged in this case."[45] The Court concluded that if the challenged conduct has an effect on an inseparable component of the price, the only question open for consideration is whether the conduct occurred. In doing so, the Court rejected the Ninth Circuit's approach that weighed the procompetitive benefits of lowered entry barriers and increased price visibility against the increase in price. The

42. *Id.* at 224 n.59.
43. *See, e.g., United States v. Alston*, 974 F.2d 1206, 1208 (9th Cir. 1992) (vigorously upholding *Socony*'s characterization of price fixing as per se illegal).
44. 446 U.S. 643 (1980).
45. *Id.* at 647.

court reasoned that once the agreement to eliminate credit was established, the judicial inquiry ended. "It is no excuse that the prices fixed are themselves reasonable."[46]

In *Arizona v. Maricopa County Medical Society*,[47] the Court struck down a maximum fee schedule agreed upon by doctors for reimbursement for health services provided to policyholders of certain insurance plans. Concluding that a maximum price was just as anticompetitive as a minimum price, the Court observed that:

> The *per se* rule "is grounded on faith in price competition as a market force [and not] on a policy of low selling prices at the price of eliminating competition." In this case, the rule is violated by a price restraint that tends to provide the same economic rewards to all practitioners regardless of their skill, their experience, their training, or their willingness to employ innovative and different procedures in individual cases. Such a restraint also may discourage entry into the market and may deter experimentation and new developments by individual entrepreneurs. It may be a masquerade for an agreement to fix uniform prices, or it may in the future take on that character.[48]

At bottom, the *Maricopa* Court held that maximum fees as well as minimum fees are illegal *per se* regardless of their potential procompetitive features. In addition, the Court did not hesitate to apply, although for the first time, the *per se* rule to professionals.[49] Despite the clear resolution in Maricopa, the Court failed to articulate any systematic criteria for reviewing horizontal price-affecting cases.

Perhaps it was critical to the Court's holding that the competing doctors were the source of and participated in the pricing scheme, when the insurance company could have implemented the cost containment efficiencies. The result seems to turn on whether the agreement among the doctors was necessary to achieve the desired efficiencies or whether less restrictive means were available. The Court seemed to conclude that the doctors' participation was not necessary for this arrangement to be effective, that the doctors' agreement was "not a 'necessary consequence' of [the] arrangement with the insurer,"[50] and that a less restrictive alternative was available.

Also, because the challenged conduct directly fixed the price of the medical reimbursement, the ancillary restraint doctrine, at least as traditionally formulated, was

---

46. *Id.*

47. 457 U.S. 332 (1982).

48. *Id.* at 348 (citation omitted).

49. See *Goldfarb v. Va. State Bar*, 421 U.S. 773 (1975), and *Nat'l Soc'y of Prof'l Eng'rs v. United States*, 435 U.S. 679 (1978), where the Court implied that a rule of reason balancing analysis would be employed if the restraint were premised on noncommercial objectives such as public service or ethical norms or if the restraint enhanced professional services. But to weigh noncommercial objectives against competitive harms would conflict directly with the central holding of *Professional Engineers* and *Broadcast Music, Inc. v. Columbia Broadcasting System, Inc. (BMI)*, 441 U.S. 1 (1979). *See also* Jeffrey L. Harrison, *Price Fixing, the Professions, and Ancillary Restraints: Coping with Maricopa County*, 1982 U. Ill. L. Rev. 925.

50. 457 U.S. at 356–57, 356 n.33.

inapplicable as a defense. Interestingly, if the Court had applied an output restriction analysis, it would have found that this plan did not restrict physicians from charging a competitive price to patients not insured under the approved plan. Hence, although a maximum fee may have been established, it did not restrict the doctors' ability to recoup any loss by charging higher prices to others.

In the 1978 case *National Society of Professional Engineers v. United States*,[51] the government charged that the professional association's canon of ethics prohibiting competitive bidding by its members violated § 1 of the Sherman Act. The issue was "whether the canon [was] justified under the Sherman Act, . . . because it was adopted by members of a learned profession for the purpose of minimizing the risk that competition would produce inferior engineering work endangering the public safety."[52] Defendant urged the Court to apply a rule of reason in order to weigh the public safety against the restraint imposed by the canon.

The test of "competitive significance" was limited to an economic analysis of the agreement's competitive impact. The safety or "quality product" defense was excluded from the balancing process because defendants did not argue that it would increase efficiency or promote competition. The underlying assumption of the Sherman Act, the Court reasoned, was that "competition will produce not only lower prices, but also better goods and services."[53] To weigh public interest, including public safety, would be beyond the discretion of the Court.

Specifically, the analysis employed by Justice Stevens, writing for the Court, was to examine the business justification for the canon. Once he found that it actually restricted competition, he rejected the practice as illegal. In short, *Prof'l Eng'rs* teaches that the rule of reason in price-affecting cases is focused on an examination whether the challenged practice promotes or suppresses competition. Here, the Court found that the ban on bidding, which resulted in an output restriction, would, by definition, increase price with no offsetting procompetitive feature. By its nature, the ban on competitive bidding resulted in maintenance of price levels; it also prevented customers from making price comparisons. As *Socony* instructed, an agreement to maintain price levels is illegal.

Prof'l Eng'rs also made clear that the Sherman Act does not permit competitors to agree on one form of competition over another. To do so would interfere with free and open markets. Consumers, the Court noted, should be able to decide whether they want higher quality or lower priced buildings:

> "The heart of our national economic policy long has been faith in the value of competition." . . . The assumption that competition is the best method of allocating resources in a free market recognizes that all elements of a bargain—quality, service, safety, and durability—and not just the immediate

51. 435 U.S. 679 (1978).

52. *Id.*

53. *Id.* at 695.

cost, are favorably affected by the free opportunity to select among alternative offers.[54]

Thus, under *Prof'l Eng'rs*, a structured or focused rule of reason is adopted. It is, however, far narrower than that recognized in *Chicago Bd. of Trade*. The parameters of the antitrust analysis are defined by the nature of the competition. The range of decisional options includes only whether the challenged agreement promotes or restrains competition. No room is left for an evaluation of noneconomic factors such as social or political benefits.[55] But certainly the Court was more willing to permit an examination that went beyond a quick *per se* classification to the extent that it weighed the net economic, competitive consequences of the challenged practice. A retreat from the high point of *per se* analysis, illustrated in *Socony* and *Container*, was evident.

Prof'l Eng'rs analytical style raised numerous questions: whether the Court would apply a focused rule of reason to commercial conduct outside a profession and whether the defenses would be limited to economic justifications. A partial answer came in the next Supreme Court term.

The following year in 1979, in *Broadcast Music, Inc. v. Columbia Broadcasting System (BMI)*,[56] CBS, a licensee, challenged the arrangement as a price-fixing agreement. Invoking the *Prof'l Eng'rs* balancing test, defendants urged that the blanket license agreement was procompetitive because it facilitated the orderly and efficient operation of the market by reducing the transaction costs between players in the market. By providing a blanket license covering all members of the defendants' association, a purchaser of musical or artistic works would only have to negotiate and contract with one entity for the right to use all products represented by the licensor rather than individual contracting. The cost of transacting would be reduced accordingly.

Because the Court lacked substantial experience with blanket licensing arrangements, it rejected the quick characterization process of the *per se* rule, even though it conceded that a price-fixing agreement was "literally" at stake.[57] The Court stressed that the review standard was limited to whether the conduct was "designed to 'increase economic efficiency and render markets more, rather than less, competitive.'"[58]

Applying the efficiency test, the Court concluded that the blanket license arrangement produced cost efficiencies in the monitoring and integration of sales and in enforcement against unauthorized copyright use that could not have been achieved by individual composers. Even though the arrangement foreclosed "competitive pricing

---

54. *Id.* (citation omitted).

55. See also *Reiter v. Sonotone Corp.*, 442 U.S. 330, 344–45 (1979), where the Court refused to weigh under the Clayton Act, the interests and policies involved in the issue whether "the cost of defending consumer class actions will have a potentially ruinous effect on small businesses ... and will ultimately be paid by consumers."

56. 441 U.S. 1 (1979). Membership in BMI included composers, authors, and publishing houses. The association issued blanket licenses of copyrighted musical composition for fees set by the individual member competitors. *Id.*

57. *Id.* at 19.

58. *Id.* at 20 (citing *United States v. United States Gypsum Co.*, 438 U.S. 422, 441 (1978)).

as a free market's means of allocating resources," the Court remanded the issue to the Second Circuit for determination, under the rule of reason standard, whether individual transaction costs were too high for individual licensing to work competitively. The lower court found that they were and the license arrangement was upheld.[59]

Another factor important to the analysis in *BMI* was the finding that the individual copyright owners were free to sell compositions separately from the blanket license.[60] Thus, supply and output were not restricted by the license. Moreover, unlike the doctors in *Maricopa*, participation of the individual composers in *BMI* was essential to the plan.[61] With this distinction in mind, *BMI's* admonition established a turning point in price-fixing cases: "[n]ot all arrangements among ... competitors that have an impact on price are *per se* violations of the Sherman Act or even unreasonable restraints."[62] *BMI* takes *Professional Engineers*' "competitive significance" standard and defines it in the context of an efficiency analysis: (1) whether the challenged conduct (the market integration) is reasonably necessary to achieve the cost-reducing efficiencies; (2) whether the restraint that follows is actually necessary to the integration; and (3) whether the efficiency achieved by integration outweighs the adverse effect of the restraint.[63] The net effect determines the outcome under the new rule of reason.

BMI also suggests that the price-fixing label is applied or rejected after the Court makes this harm-benefit analysis. At this point, the Court is able to reach a conclusion whether the conduct is a naked restraint or whether it has redeeming virtues. When the *per se* classification is accepted, it now seems more like a substantive law conclusion at the end of the balancing analysis that the net effect of the practice is not procompetitive. Thus, the initial summary analysis under the *per se* rule is on the decline, although at times the Court vacillates on where the line should be drawn in classifying price fixing.

[C] Evading Per Se Condemnation

[1] The Learned Profession Doctrine

On several occasions, the Supreme Court has ruled on the legality of concerted conduct by professionals. The analysis employed by the Court has varied between a rule of reason and *per se* illegality.

In *Goldfarb v. Va. State Bar*,[64] a minimum fee schedule for lawyers enforced by the state bar association was challenged as a price-fixing agreement in violation of

---

59. *CBS v. Am. Soc'y of Composers & Publishers*, 620 F.2d 930 (2d Cir. 1980).

60. 441 U.S. at 29 (Stevens, J., dissenting).

61. This "essentialness" aspect has been the basis for distinguishing other horizontal market arrangements subjected to *per se* analysis. *See United States v. Alston*, 974 F.2d 1206 (9th Cir. 1992).

62. 441 U.S. at 23.

63. *See* Peter M. Gerhart, *The Supreme Court and Antitrust Analysis: The (Near) Triumph of the Chicago School*, 1982 Sup. Ct. Rev. 319.

64. 421 U.S. 773 (1975).

§ 1. Chief Justice Burger, writing for the Court, held that professional services come within the Sherman Act and that the minimum fee schedule was an illegal price-fixing scheme:

> The nature of an occupation, standing alone, does not provide sanctuary from the Sherman Act, nor is the public service aspect of professional practice controlling in determining whether § 1 includes professions. . . . Congress intended to strike as broadly as it could in § 1 of the Sherman Act, and to read into it so wide an exception as that urged on us would be at odds with that purpose.[65]

But the Court added a statement that foreshadowed a rule of reason analysis for professional organizations when the restraint was in the public interest:

> [T]he fact that a restraint operates upon a profession as distinguished from a business is, of course, relevant in determining whether that particular restraint violates the Sherman Act. It would be unrealistic to view the practice of professions as interchangeable with other business activities, and automatically to apply to the professions antitrust concepts which originated in other areas. The public service aspect, and other features of the professions, may require that a particular practice, which could properly be viewed as a violation of the Sherman Act in another context, be treated differently.[66]

Implicitly, the Court seemed to say that it would balance and perhaps accommodate noneconomic interests and policies when professional conduct was under scrutiny. But the Court also concluded that the minimum fee schedule was a "naked agreement," language generally used to connote *per se* illegality.

The next case to address the issue was *Nat'l Soc'y of Prof'l Eng'rs v. United States*,[67] in which the Court rejected a broad reading of the *Goldfarb* dictum. While sharing *Goldfarb's* deferential tone for professional conduct, including a statement that "professional services may differ significantly from other business services, and, accordingly the nature of the competition in such services may vary,"[68] the Court nevertheless found the ban-on-bidding practice by engineers to be anticompetitive. The Court, however, observed that "[e]thical norms may serve to regulate and promote . . . competition and thus fall within the Rule of Reason."[69] But because the ban on competitive bidding reduced competition and increased price, the Court was unwilling to accept the defense that the competition itself was unreasonable. Thus, the Court applied a focused rule of reason that balanced market factors as means to determine

---

65. *Id.* at 787.

66. *Id.* at 788 n.17.

67. 435 U.S. 679 (1978).

68. *Id.* at 696.

69. *Id.* See also *Tripoli Co. v. Wella Corp.*, 425 F.2d 932 (3d Cir. 1970) (en banc), where the court upheld restraints on marketing related to product safety, provided they were ancillary to the seller's main purpose of protecting the public from harm or itself from product liability.

the competitive consequences. But the Court found no offsetting competitive features since the canon of ethics actually suppressed competition rather than promoted it. Hence, the practice was declared illegal.

Prof'l Eng'rs portended a more willing acceptance of the rule of reason approach when professional conduct is challenged. However, judicial discretion is limited to weighing the competitive effects; the net consequences must be procompetitive before the practice will be declared legal.

Prof'l Eng'rs raised the question whether *per se* condemnations might ever be applied to professional conduct. The answer was forthcoming in *Arizona v. Maricopa Cty. Med. Soc'y*,[70] in which doctors were charged with establishing a maximum fee schedule on insurance reimbursement plans. In applying a *per se* test, the Supreme Court reasoned that the doctors did not argue that the quality of the public service they provided would be enhanced by reason of the price restraint, or that the restraint was necessary because of ethical considerations. Thus, the conduct fell out of rule of reason protection. The economic investigation of weighing the competitive benefits and harms, which was central to *Prof'l Eng'rs*, ends once inferences are drawn that the challenged practice is a price-fixing agreement.

In *FTC v. Indiana Federation of Dentists*, the Court, under §5 of the FTC Act, held that a concerted refusal by dentists to provide x-rays to insurance companies for reimbursement approval should be examined under the rule of reason because the dentists had argued that the refusal to deal (group boycott) was based on an ethical and moral policy designed to enhance the patients' welfare through quality dental care.[71] But once the Court began to weigh the competitive factors, it concluded that the boycott was no more than a scheme to protect the price the dentists charged to the patient—precisely the justification rejected in *Professional Engineers*. The insurance requirement of submitting x-rays was designed to reduce the marginal costs of providing insurance in the dental services market. The effect of the boycott was to impair this mechanism.[72]

Similarly, in *Superior Court Trial Lawyers Ass'n v. FTC*,[73] the Court held that a horizontal arrangement among lawyers to withhold the supply of legal services and thereby increase hourly wage rates represented a "naked restraint" on price and output. In *Superior Court Trial Lawyers*, a group of private-practice lawyers, pursuant to a well-publicized plan, agreed not to represent indigent criminal defendants in the District of Columbia Superior Court until the city government increased the lawyers' hourly compensation.[74]

---

70. 457 U.S. 332 (1982).

71. 476 U.S. 447, 458–59 (1986).

72. *Id.* at 457.

73. 493 U.S. 411 (1990).

74. *Id.* at 413. "Although over 1,200 lawyers [were] registered for District of Columbia Criminal Justice Act Appointments, relatively few applied for such work on a regular basis. In 1982, most appointments went to approximately 100 lawyers who derive almost all of their income from representing indigents." *Id.* at 415.

The lawyers' refusal to accept new appointments until their hourly wages increased had dramatic effects on the criminal justice system. Convinced that the system was on the brink of collapse, key figures within the District of Columbia's criminal justice system advocated a temporary increase in hourly wages—an increase that was subsequently authorized by the city council. The FTC, however, filed suit against the lawyers, alleging that the boycott constituted an unfair method of competition in violation of § 5 of the Federal Trade Commission Act.

In evaluating the requisite conduct, the Court commented that although there was a political impact, the means employed (the boycott) to obtain the more favorable legislation was economic, rather than political in nature. In the end, it was clear that the goal of the lawyers was to raise the price of legal services to indigent clients. Thus, the means employed, as well as the objective of the agreement, was economic in nature. Said the Court:

> The effectiveness of price-fixing agreements is dependent upon many factors, such as competitive tactics, position in the industry, the formula underlying pricing policies. Whatever economic justification particular price-fixing agreements may be thought to have, the law does not permit an inquiry into their reasonableness.[75]

Because the lawyers' only goal was a salary increase, and they failed to also advance an ethical norm or compelling public interest, the Court found the boycott conduct illegal on its face.

Finally, in *Massachusetts School of Law at Andover v. American Bar Ass'n*,[76] the Third Circuit quickly rejected the plaintiff's argument for a *per se* analysis. At issue were certain provisions in the ABA's standards for accreditation, particularly the provision calling for a consideration of faculty salaries before granting accreditation. The court felt that, although the practice somewhat resembled price-affecting conduct, a rule of reason analysis was still appropriate. Citing *Indiana Federation of Dentists*, the court explained that the Supreme Court is "'slow to condemn rules adopted by professional societies as unreasonable *per se*,' even when the behavior resembles conduct usually subject to a *per se* approach."[77] Thus, the Third Circuit chose to follow the Supreme Court's lead in this regard and apply a rule of reason analysis.

An attempt to reconcile the six professional conduct cases leads to the following rules. If a defense is asserted that the challenged practice promotes a public interest (quality) or an ethical norm, the Court will apply a structured rule of reason.[78] The

75. *Id.* at 435 (citing *United States v. Socony-Vacuum Oil Co.*, 310 U.S. 150 (1940)).

76. 107 F.3d 1026 (3d Cir. 1997).

77. *Id.* at 1033 (citing *Ind. Fed'n.*, 476 U.S. 447, 458 (1986)).

78. For an example of a circuit court applying the rule of reason to a case in which the "quality control" defense was implicit, see *Sanjuan v. American Board of Psychiatry & Neurology, Inc.*, 40 F.3d 247 (7th Cir. 1995). *See also Nat'l Ass'n of Review Appraisers & Mortgage Underwriters, Inc. v. Appraisal Found.*, 64 F.3d 1130, 1134 n.2 (8th Cir. 1995) (holding that the defendant's behavior should be examined under a rule of reason analysis after the court considered "relevant economic structures and market forces").

second step is to determine whether it also promotes competition. If the result is procompetitive, the conduct is legal. But if the conduct interferes directly with price and no public interest or ethical norm is asserted in its defense the practice may be condemned unlawful under the *per se* classification. Of course, even in the absence of a public interest or ethical justification, the conduct can be legal if its net result enhances the competitive forces in the market.

Note also that if the Court now employs the *per se* terminology it is usually a conclusion at the end of the analysis rather than an initial presumption. Only if it is clear from the record that the agreement among professionals is "so plainly anticompetitive that no elaborate study of [its effects] is needed to establish [its] illegality" may a court properly make a *per se* judgment. The *per se* label should not be assigned without carefully considering substantial benefits and procompetitive justifications.[79]

[2] BMI *and Agreements that Create New Products*

Broadcast Music, Inc. v. Columbia Broadcasting System, Inc. (BMI)[80] declined to apply the *per se* rule to an agreement among copyright owners (through the performing rights organizations, BMI and ASCAP, which managed their copyrighted musical works) to offer a blanket license even though the arrangement was "literally" price fixing. The Court reasoned that the blanket license was a valuable new product that increased the efficiency of the music licensing market and that "a necessary consequence of an aggregate license is that its price must be established."[81] The Court concluded that "cooperative arrangements are . . . not usually unlawful, at least not as price-fixing schemes, where the agreement on price is necessary to market the product at all."[82] This effectively creates an exception to the *per se* rule for horizontal price agreements that are necessary for a new and beneficial product to exist.

Although on remand, the blanket license was upheld under the rule of reason, it is possible for an agreement to escape *per se* condemnation but to nonetheless violate the rule of reason. For example, the Court in *NCAA v. Bd. of Regents*[83] declined to apply the *per se* rule to an output agreement that would otherwise be condemned *per se*. Echoing *BMI*, the Court stated that "this case involves an industry in which horizontal restraints on competition are essential if the product is to be available at all."[84]

---

79. *Prof'l Eng'rs*, 435 U.S. at 692. In *Palmer v. BRG of Georgia, Inc.*, 498 U.S. 46 (1990), however, a case involving the professional training of lawyers, the Supreme Court reaffirmed a rule of *per se* illegality for horizontal market divisions between competitors irrespective of whether the competitors had previously competed in the same market. In addition, the Court reaffirmed that a combination formed for the purpose and with the effect of raising, depressing, fixing, pegging, or stabilizing the price of a commodity in interstate or foreign commerce is illegal per se.

80. 441 U.S. 1 (1979).

81. *Id.* at 21.

82. *Id.* at 23.

83. 468 U.S. 85 (1984).

84. *Id.* at 101.

Consequently, their horizontal cooperation was not *per se* unlawful; rather, a rule of reason analysis was applied. The Court, however, distinguishing *BMI* when it reached the merits and held that the NCAA's output restriction violated § 1 of the Sherman Act even though some "cooperation is necessary if the type of competition that [defendant] and its member institutions seek to market is to be preserved."[85]

[D] Hub and Spoke Conspiracies

The *per se* rule is generally used to evaluate horizontal agreements, while vertical agreements are evaluated using the rule of reason. However, in 2015, the Second Circuit ruled that a vertical price-fixing conspiracy could be so flagrantly in violation of antitrust law as to be *per se* illegal. In *U.S. v. Apple, Inc.*, the federal government alleged that Apple, as a retail seller of iPads and online operator of the iBookstore, conspired with the six largest publishing companies in the United States to set prices for ebooks.[86] Apple characterized the evidence, which included emails, phone records, contracts, and the resulting prices, as ambiguous, but the district court and the Second Circuit disagreed, finding the evidence "overwhelming."[87]

Apple attempted to advance alternate arguments that the contracts at issue could not be violations of the Sherman Act as the company had different motivations for setting prices than did the publishers or that the publishers' price setting was merely the result of parallel decision-making.[88] The court declared that each of these arguments failed "and dramatically so."[89] The Second Circuit had no trouble finding that, despite the vertical nature of Apple's participation, "Apple had orchestrated a conspiracy among the Publisher Defendants to raise the price of ebooks" and that the conspiracy was blatant enough to "constitute a *per se* violation of the Sherman Act and, in the alternative, unreasonably restrained trade under the rule of reason."[90]

---

85. *Id.* at 117. In a later Ninth Circuit opinion, the court noted that form of cooperation will not be permitted if there is a substantially less restrictive alternative. *O'Bannon v. National Collegiate Athletic Association*, 802 F.3d 1049, 1074 (9th Cir. 2015). *See generally* Martin B. Louis, *Restraints Ancillary to Joint Ventures and Licensing Agreements: Do Sealy and Topco Logically Survive Sylvania and Broadcast Music?*, 66 Va. L. Rev. 879 (1980).

86. *United States v. Apple Inc.*, 791 F.3d 290, 296 (2d Cir. 2015).

87. *Id.* at 319.

88. *Id.* at 317.

89. *Id.* at 318.

90. *Id.* at 297.

§ 4.05 Ancillary Restraint Doctrine

Congress enacted the Sherman Act in 1890, which on its face made unlawful "[e]very contract, combination . . . or conspiracy in restraint of trade."[91] Five years later, the Supreme Court decided *United States v. E.C. Knight*,[92] its first case under the Act. In *Knight*, the defendant sugar trust was charged with acquiring the stock of four sugar refiners and thereby "acquir[ing] nearly complete control of the manufacture of refined sugar within the United States,"[93] an alleged restraint of trade in violation of the Sherman Act. In holding that the Sherman Act did not apply to restraints of trade affecting only the manufacture of commodities, because "[c]ommerce succeeds to manufacture, and is not a part of it,"[94] the Court bespoke of the early beginnings of the ancillary restraint doctrine:

> [c]ontracts, combinations, or conspiracies to control domestic enterprise in manufacture, agriculture, mining, production in all its forms, or to raise or lower prices or wages, might unquestionably tend to restrain external as well as domestic trade, but the restraint would be an *indirect* result, however inevitable, and whatever its extent, and such result would not necessarily determine the object of the contract, combination or conspiracy.[95]

Thus, the *Knight* Court reasoned that mere manufacturing is not commerce and, is therefore not within the reach of the Sherman Act. This result, however, is unlikely to be reached today.

Although *Knight* severely narrowed the reach of the Sherman Act, the next case considered by the Court concluded that the scope of the Act was not limited to the confines of common law antitrust. In *United States v. Trans-Missouri Freight Ass'n*,[96] defendants were a group of railroad companies controlling rail service west of the Mississippi. They were members of an association that established uniform freight rates in an attempt to eliminate price wars that allegedly were devastating to the railroad industry. Defendants argued that the rates, as fixed, were reasonable in amount and would have been legal under the common law. The Court applied the literal language of the Sherman Act in rejecting an argument that the Act only makes unlawful unreasonable restraints of trade. The Court held that every restraint of trade violates § 1 of the Sherman Act, even those restraints deemed reasonable and lawful under the pre-Sherman Act common law. In dissent, Justice White argued that such a strict statutory interpretation would condemn every contract, however reasonable, would "work an enormous injustice, and operate to the undue restraint of the liberties of the citizen."[97]

91. 15 U.S.C. § 1 (2012).
92. 156 U.S. 1 (1895).
93. *Id.* at 9.
94. *Id.* at 12.
95. *Id.* at 16 (emphasis added).
96. 166 U.S. 290 (1897).
97. *Id.* at 354.

In *United States v. Joint-Traffic Ass'n*,[98] a year later, the Court found no substantial difference between the alleged conduct and the conduct found unlawful in *Trans-Missouri* and refused to overrule the earlier *Trans-Missouri* case. In condemning railroad rate fixing in *Joint-Traffic*, however, the Court suggested that perhaps not every restraint violates § 1, and that those restraints with only an incidental effect on competition may be lawful under the Sherman Act. The Court was concerned that the "natural and *direct* effect [of the rate-fixing agreements in *Trans-Missouri* and *Joint-Traffic*] is . . . to maintain rates at a higher level than would otherwise prevail. . . ."[99] This language suggested permissiveness with respect to indirect restraints of trade; it foreshadowed the establishment of the "ancillary restraint" doctrine announced the same year by the Sixth Circuit in *United States v. Addyston Pipe*.[100]

The Court also suggested, in *Hopkins v. United States*,[101] a difference in applicability of the Sherman Act depending upon whether the restraint imposed was direct or indirect. In *Hopkins*, the Court reasoned that "[t]he contract condemned by the [Sherman Act] is one whose *direct and immediate* effect is a restraint. . . . There must be some *direct and immediate* effect upon interstate commerce, in order to come within the [Sherman] Act."[102]

In *United States v. Addyston Pipe*,[103] defendants were six competing cast-iron pipe producers who allocated territories among themselves and jointly fixed prices in each territory. The apparent purpose of the combination was to create an artificial barrier to entry by establishing prices low enough to discourage new entrants, albeit higher than prices that would have occurred from natural market conditions. Defendants argued that the arrangement had the benign purpose of preventing ruinous competition and that their association would have been valid at common law because the prices they fixed were reasonable.

The Sixth Circuit rejected both arguments. In an opinion by Judge Taft, later Chief Justice of the Supreme Court, the court reasoned that even under the common law all such agreements were unlawful unless they were ancillary. "[N]o conventional restraint of trade can be enforced unless the covenant embodying it is merely ancillary to the main purpose of a lawful contract. . . ."[104] Having found that the defendants' territorial and price-fixing contract was not ancillary to a main lawful purpose, the court rejected defendants' "reasonable" argument by stating that "we do not think that at common law there is any question of reasonableness open to the courts with reference to such a contract."[105]

98. 171 U.S. 505 (1898).

99. *Id.* at 565 (emphasis added).

100. 85 F. 271 (6th Cir. 1898), *aff'd*, 175 U.S. 211 (1899).

101. 171 U.S. 578 (1898).

102. *Id.* at 592 (emphasis added).

103. 85 F. 271.

104. *Id.* at 282.

105. *Id.* at 293.

Addyston Pipe established the ancillary restraint doctrine. It provides that all direct restraints are *ipso facto* unlawful, even when the outcome is reasonable; ancillary restraints which are unreasonable are unlawful; and ancillary restraints that are reasonable are lawful. The Supreme Court affirmed the Sixth Circuit's holding in *Addyston Pipe*.[106] The Court, however, emphasized Judge Taft's finding that the prices fixed were not reasonable, thus, at least temporarily, diluting the importance of Judge Taft's ancillary restraint doctrine. The doctrine is depicted graphically as follows:

	Direct Restraint	Ancillary Restraint
Restraint Reasonable	Unlawful	Lawful
Restraint Unreasonable	Unlawful	Unlawful

In *Standard Oil Co. v. United States*,[107] the Supreme Court modified a portion of the *Addyston Pipe* ancillary restraint doctrine. *Addyston Pipe* had concluded that a direct restraint is *per se* unlawful and that no inquiry into reasonableness of the restraint is justified. The *Standard Oil* defendants, a group of thirty-seven oil companies managed by a single holding company, were charged with predatory conduct—conduct designed to destroy a competitor—and anticompetitive abuses. Although the Court found Sherman Act violations and ordered dissolution of the holding company, it softened the impact of the ancillary restraint doctrine by ruling that even direct restraints of trade may be lawful if reasonable. Thus, a rule of reason analysis may apply to both direct and ancillary restraints. Once applied, the rule examines the context and nature of the entire agreement to decide if it is reasonable, and, under *Standard Oil*, the Court will assess reasonableness whether the restraint is direct or ancillary.[108] If, however, the agreement encompasses rate fixing among competitors, then the restraint will be characterized as a presumptively illegal "naked" restraint and reasonableness will not be a defense.

The origins of the ancillary restraint doctrine discussed above still maintain validity today and indeed the doctrine is being expanded. In *Polk Bros., Inc. v. Forest City Enterprises, Inc.*,[109] the Seventh Circuit reviewed a challenge to a horizontal agreement not to compete on both a territorial and a product line basis. Plaintiff and defendant entered into an agreement requiring the plaintiff to erect a building in which plaintiff and defendant would operate retail stores within a single building but separated by a partition. Each party agreed not to stock or sell certain products which the other would have the exclusive right to sell within the building. Due to declining profits and a change in management, defendant sought to be relieved of its covenant not to

106. 175 U.S. 211 (1899).

107. 221 U.S. 1 (1911).

108. *See infra* § 4.04[A] for a more in-depth explanation and development of the rule of reason analysis.

109. 776 F.2d 185 (7th Cir. 1985).

compete with the plaintiff. When the defendant informed the plaintiff that it considered the noncompete covenant to be invalid, plaintiff sued for an injunction.

The core of the Seventh Circuit's inquiry in *Polk Bros.* was to determine whether the allegedly unlawful covenant was a naked or an ancillary restraint. In an opinion by Judge Easterbrook, the court observed that an ancillary restraint would be evaluated under a rule of reason analysis, but that "the *per se* rule is designed for 'naked' restraints."[110]

The court ruled that to determine if a restraint should be characterized as ancillary or naked it is appropriate to "ask whether an agreement promoted enterprise and productivity *at the time it was adopted*."[111] By this, the court meant whether "it may contribute to the success of a cooperative venture that promises greater productivity and output. . . . Only when a quick look reveals that the practice facially appears to be one that would always or almost always tend to restrict competition and decrease output should a court cut off further inquiry."[112] The court concluded that the principal purpose of the agreement between the parties was to embark on a new venture to build a joint facility. The parties "were cooperating to produce, not to curtail output; the cooperation increased the amount of retail space available and was at least potentially beneficial to consumers. . . ."[113] Thus the covenant not to compete within that building was ancillary, even though the covenant was an essential part of the arrangement. The agreement was not *per se* unlawful. Judge Easterbrook's opinion is worth review at least for the broad and expansive interpretation placed on the definition of an ancillary restraint.

In *National Ass'n of Review Appraisers & Mortgage Underwriters, Inc. v. Appraisal Foundation*,[114] the Eighth Circuit found that the defendant's refusal to admit the plaintiff as a member of its association was best characterized as an ancillary restraint on trade. The Foundation was created to promote educational and ethical standards for appraisal services, and its membership criteria appeared to be designed to accomplish those goals by establishing such standards and requiring non-profit status for appraisal organizations. Such requirements generally pose merely incidental market restraints and are necessary to successful industry self-regulation.[115] As such, the activities were not presumptively illegal. In fact, the court affirmed summary judgment in favor of the defendants, holding their actions to be legal and actually procompetitive.[116]

The Seventh Circuit, in *Blackburn v. Sweeney*, refused to apply the ancillary restraint doctrine to a dissolution agreement that divided the market for attorney services geographically by permanently delineating certain areas in which each of the former

110. *Id.* at 188.
111. *Id.* at 189 (emphasis added).
112. *Id.* (quoting *Broad. Music, Inc. v. Columbia Broad. Sys.*, 441 U.S. 1, 19–20 (1979)).
113. *Id.* at 190; *see also SCFC ILC, Inc. v. Visa USA, Inc.*, 36 F.3d 958 (10th Cir. 1994).
114. 64 F.3d 1130 (8th Cir. 1995).
115. *Id.* at 1133.
116. *Id.*

partners could advertise.[117] The agreement was neither necessary to the dissolution of the partnership nor legitimate as a temporary covenant not to compete.[118] Hence, the Seventh Circuit held the agreement to be a *per se* violation of § 1.[119]

One must be careful not to take the protections of the ancillary restraint doctrine too far. In *Sullivan v. NFL*,[120] the First Circuit had to determine whether the NFL's restraints on public ownership of teams was ancillary to its overall purpose of facilitating effective and efficient sports team management. The court readily admitted that the NFL's policy exemplified an ancillary restraint in the form of a joint venture policy restricting membership and that the policy "contributes to the ability of the NFL to function as an effective sports team, and that the NFL's functioning would be impaired if publicly owned teams were permitted."[121] The court refused to find, however, that these factors alone established, "as a matter of law, that the NFL's policy [did] not unreasonably restrain trade."[122] "The holdings in *BMI*, *Rothery Storage*,[123] and *Northwest Stationers*[124] do not foreclose rule of reason out the window merely because one establishes that a given practice among joint venture participants is ancillary to legitimate and efficient activity—the injury to competition must still be weighed against the purported benefits under the rule of reason."[125]

§ 4.06 Horizontal Price Exchanges

Horizontal restraints can be created by exchanges of commercial information among competitors. The clearinghouse for such industry data is generally a trade association, but the exchange also can occur between individual firms within an industry. The mere exchange of data concerning prices, output, inventories, production quotas, and supply levels may have effects on price. The competitive consequences will depend on the structure of industry, the nature of the information exchanged, and how the firms respond to the data exchanged. The mere exchange of price information, however, is not unlawful.[126]

---

117. 53 F.3d 825 (7th Cir. 1995).

118. *Id.* at 828–29.

119. The court maintained its holding without questioning *Polk Bros.* by admitting that, if the partnership dissolution could have been characterized as a temporary covenant not to compete, *Polk Bros.* would have applied.

120. 34 F.3d 1091 (1st Cir. 1994).

121. *Id.* at 1102.

122. *Id.*

123. 792 F.2d 210 (D.C. Cir. 1986).

124. 472 U.S. 284 (1985).

125. *Sullivan*, 34 F.3d at 1102. The case was reversed and remanded in the defendant's favor due to a series of prejudicial errors at the trial court level.

126. *Sugar Inst., Inc. v. United States*, 297 U.S. 553 (1936). *Sugar Institute* indicates that the relationship between the communication and a price-fixing agreement must be more than merely incidental before the price exchange can be enjoined. *See* E. Thomas Sullivan, *First Amendment Defenses in Antitrust Litigation*, 46 Mo. L. Rev. 517 (1981).

In fact, price sharing can be a logical and helpful activity to stimulate competition. In *Wallace v. Bank of Bartlett*,[127] the defendant argued, and the court agreed, that it is natural for banks to survey the rates charged by their competitors for overdrawn accounts "in order to make strategic competitive decisions."[128] Hence, although price sharing can lead to a violation of § 1, plaintiffs must do more than simply present evidence of price evaluation among competitors.

Professor Areeda emphasizes that one must always find a motive to conspire before speculating on the potential § 1 implications of shared information.[129] This helps answer the core question in any price-sharing inquiry—"whether a conspiracy to deal concertedly with the plaintiff can be inferred from the price-exchange."[130]

The forming of a trade association, of course, is a "combination" within the meaning of § 1 of Sherman Act.[131] The remaining question is whether the activities of the trade association unreasonably restrain trade. Trade associations do engage in lawful and productive activities that can enhance competition as, for example: exchange of information on the availability of raw materials, advancement of technology through the sharing of product innovation, promotion of the industry through institutional advertising, and promotion of the standardization of certain products. But when the exchange affects price, even indirectly, antitrust laws are implicated.

Because of the ambiguous or uncertain consequences of an exchange, courts generally apply a rule of reason analysis. They analyze the structure of the industry, including market power of the firms engaged in the exchange, the effect of the exchange, and the purpose underlying the exchange.

In *American Column Lumber Co. v. United States*,[132] the Supreme Court was unsympathetic to a trade association that required its members to make daily reports, subject to audits, on sales, purchases, production, and to require immediate reporting on any price changes. Speeches and memoranda were circulated among the members stressing the danger of overproduction. Discussions followed regarding restrictions on output and price maintenance. Even though the association membership represented only 33% of the industry production, there was evidence of actual increases in price. The Court found that the "purpose and effect were to restrict production and to encourage members to unite in pressing for higher and higher prices."[133] It observed that the extensive interchange of reports, supplemented by monthly meetings,

---

127. 55 F.3d 1166 (6th Cir. 1995).

128. *Id.* at 1169.

129. VI Phillip E. Areeda *Antitrust Law*, ¶ 1423 (1986).

130. *Id.*

131. However, see *Alvord-Polk, Inc. v. F. Schumacher & Co.*, 37 F.3d. 996, 1007–08 (3d Cir. 1994), where the court held that a trade association is capable of conspiring within itself, but only if it acts as an "entity." The court added that a full examination of the facts and circumstances may be necessary in such an instance, since "concerted action does not exist every time a trade association member speaks or acts." *Id.*

132. 257 U.S. 377 (1921).

133. *Id.* at 407.

certainly constituted a combination through which agreements, actual or implied, could readily be arrived at and maintained.

Specifically, the Court in *American Column* disapproved of a trade association soliciting views of members as to future market conditions, including production estimates and analyses which suggested price levels and production limits. But the exchange of past, closed transaction prices was sanctioned.

Several years later, in *Maple Flooring Manufacturing Ass'n v. United States*,[134] the Court upheld a data exchange plan where the exchange of statistical data included only past prices and other data in summary, average, or aggregate form and which did not identify individual customers. The information also was fully available to customers of the trade association members, the public, and all buyers and sellers in the industry. Defendants controlled 70% of total production, but the Court reasoned that it was important that there be a free exchange of ideas and knowledge of the competitive factors. The Court observed that information exchanges increase the likelihood of rational competition, even though this market fell short of perfect competition. No evidence of price stabilization was found, even though the dissemination of market data could lead to this result.

In 1990, in *Stephen Jay Photography, Ltd. v. Olan Mills, Inc.*,[135] the Fourth Circuit rejected the plaintiff photographer's claim of an illegal price sharing agreement between two other high school yearbook photographers who had one hundred percent of the market combined. The court held, "The fact that the price information about one company is found in a competitor's files or an employee reports a competitor's pricing policy to his home office and the two companies charge similar prices for their products, without more, cannot support an inference that the two competitors entered into an agreement to share prices."[136] The court found the plaintiff's price sharing theory meritless because the plaintiff offered no proof that suggested that the defendants had not acted independently.[137] In fact, the evidence showed that one had secured the information without the knowledge of the other.

A review of the important Supreme Court cases on data dissemination indicates that the Court is inclined to approve an exchange of *past* data in summary or aggregate form which do not disclose individual transactions or customers, (1) where there is no disclosure of present or future information, (2) where there are no enforcement or coercive mechanisms that pressure the membership, (3) where the data are available to nonmembers for reasonable fees, or at least to those that have a "commercial need to know" or would be at a competitive disadvantage without the information, and (4) where the market structure of the industry suggests that it is not highly concentrated or tending towards collusion.[138]

---

134. 268 U.S. 563 (1925); *see also United States v. Am. Linseed Oil Co.*, 262 U.S. 371 (1923).

135. 903 F.2d 988 (4th Cir. 1990).

136. *Id.* at 996.

137. *Id.*

138. The Ninth Circuit noted two situations where the exchange of price information would help to establish whether an antitrust violation had occurred. *In re Coordinated Pretrial Proceedings in*

As discussed above, the structure of the industry can inform our thinking about the competitive significance of an exchange among competitors of commercial information. The less concentrated the market, the more the exchange can be procompetitive. The more market information that is available to competitors, the greater the chance that allocative efficiency (sellers producing products desired by consumers in appropriate quantities) will be enhanced. When buyers and sellers have a wide variety of available market information, they buy and sell at the lowest prices, thereby promoting efficiency and competition in the market. Conversely, as *United States v. Container Corp. of America*[139] teaches, the more concentrated a market is, the more predisposed it is toward collusive stabilization of prices when there is a price exchange. In both *Container* and *United States v. U.S. Gypsum Co.*,[140] the Supreme Court's analytical focus shifted from a review of the purpose of the exchange to a prediction of the probable price consequences of the exchange given a certain market structure.

Container was the Court's first explicit recognition that market structure may affect price exchanges. Economic theory suggests that the vigor of competition in a market is related positively to the number of firms in the relevant industry. In a market dominated by a few sellers, with a product which is homogeneous and fungible, price exchanges may tend to stabilize prices.[141] A highly concentrated market, or oligopoly, may exhibit interdependence among the firms in the market—sellers taking into account pricing and output decisions of each competitor before any price changes are undertaken.[142]

Container accepted the theory that coordinated behavior may facilitate anticompetitive consequences, and it inferred anticompetitive conduct from the market structure. Market structure was thus critical to predicting market behavior. In *Container*, there was only a moderate degree of concentration, cross-elasticity of demand existed among products, market entry was easy, and the market was characterized by over-capacity.[143] The Court, nevertheless, found the conclusion "irresistible that the exchange of price information ... had an anticompetitive effect."[144] A *per se* rule of illegality was suggested.

Petroleum Prods. Antitrust Litig., 906 F.2d 432 (9th Cir. 1990). Where "the exchange indicates the existence of an express or tacit agreement to fix or stabilize prices, or the exchange is made pursuant to an express or tacit agreement that is itself a violation of § 1 under a rule of reason analysis," price sharing becomes a more valuable piece of evidence for the plaintiff. *Id.* at 447 n.13.

139. 393 U.S. 333 (1969). *But see Cement Mfrs. Protective Ass'n. v. United States*, 268 U.S. 588 (1925)

140. 438 U.S. 422 (1978).

141. 393 U.S. at 337.

142. Donald F. Turner, *The Definition of Agreement Under the Sherman Act: Conscious Parallelism and Refusal to Deal*, 75 Harv. L. Rev. 655 (1962). As the Court said in *Container*: "Price information exchanged in some markets may have no effect on a truly competitive price.... The exchange of price data tends toward price uniformity" in oligopolistic markets. 393 U.S. at 337.

143. 393 U.S. at 336–37. *See generally* Lawrence Anthony Sullivan, *Handbook of the Law of Antitrust* 272 (1977). Eighteen defendants accounted for 90% of the corrugated container production in the particular geographical region. Defendants agreed to exchange current price information on request; no other conduct was challenged.

144. 393 U.S. at 337.

In two subsequent cases,[145] including *Gypsum*, the Court explicitly rejected a *per se* approach when employing a market structure analysis: "[t]he exchange of price data and other information among competitors does not invariably have anticompetitive effects; indeed such practices can in certain circumstances increase economic efficiency and render markets more, rather than less, competitive."[146] Interseller price communications, therefore, are regulated on a rule of reason basis.

In *United States v. Container Corp. of America.*,[147] the Court employed a full-blown market power and market structure analysis. The Court concluded that the mere exchange of current price information among competitors in an oligopolistic market for a fungible product is unlawful. The *Container* Court first characterized the allegedly unlawful conduct as the exchange of current prices among competitors, inferred an agreement to exchange prices from the fact that price exchanges occurred regularly, and finally reviewed the structure of the market in which this conduct occurred. It found that defendants controlled a 90% market share; the product was non-differentiated and fungible; demand for corrugated containers was inelastic because buyers placed orders for only short run needs; and the market was dominated by relatively few sellers. Based upon these market factors, the Court concluded that the price exchange agreement, even though informal, "had an anticompetitive effect in the industry, chilling the vigor of price competition."[148]

The Court employed a similar analysis, although it reached a different conclusion, in *United States v. United States Gypsum Co.*[149] *Gypsum*, like *Container*, involved defendants selling a fungible product, gypsum wall board, and facing an inelastic demand curve. The industry was highly concentrated, with the eight largest producers accounting for 94% of all sales nationwide. The basis of the government's criminal charge was that defendants fixed prices by regularly exchanging price information among competitors.

The Court focused on the effect of the exchanges on the competitiveness of the industry. In doing so, the Court utilized a modified market structure analysis, stating that "[a] number of factors including most prominently the structure of the industry involved and the nature of the information exchanged are generally considered in divining the procompetitive or anticompetitive effects of this type of interseller communication."[150]

---

145. *United States v. United States Gypsum Co.*, 438 U.S. 422 (1978); *United States v. Citizens & S. Nat'l Bank*, 422 U.S. 86 (1975).

146. 438 U.S. at 441 n.16. Suspiciously, the Court provided no citation or analysis for these supposed efficiency justifications, and the parties did not argue this issue in their briefs or oral arguments. Joseph E. Harrington, Jr. & Christopher R. Leslie, *Horizontal Price Exchanges*, 44 Cardozo L. Rev. 2301, 2319–20 (2023).

147. 393 U.S. 333 (1969).

148. *Id.* at 337.

149. 438 U.S. 422 (1978).

150. *Id.* at 441 n.16 (1978) (citing *United States v. Container Corp. of Am.*, 393 U.S. 333, 338 (Fortas, J., concurring) (1969)); *see also Bhan v. NME Hosps., Inc.*, 929 F.2d 1404, 1413 (9th Cir. 1991).

More recent scholarship has explained how horizontal price exchanges are likely to have anticompetitive consequences and should be treated more harshly by antitrust law.[151]

§ 4.07 Horizontal Agreements to Restrict Output

In *NCAA v. Bd. of Regents*,[152] the Court rejected a *per se* analysis even though it found horizontal price and output restrictions. The rule of reason was again accepted, this time on the belief that in certain markets "horizontal restraints on competition are essential if the product is to be available at all."[153] The context was a joint venture among college sports teams and their conference leagues that entered into contracts with television networks for broadcast rights to football games. The contracts restricted the total number of games that could be broadcast, specified the number of times any one team could appear on a broadcast, required the networks to carry different schools a minimum number of times,[154] and set the price of the telecasts. Two schools sued the NCAA on theories that the restrictions restrained trade and amounted to price fixing.

Agreeing with the plaintiff schools, the Supreme Court found that the contracts did restrict output (the number of times a school could appear on the network) and did fix the price for each telecast by establishing the total compensation paid to member schools.[155] But the Court rejected the *per se* approach because this was a market, the Court reasoned, that required cooperation or interdependence among competitors before a product could be produced. Accordingly, the Court went beyond its findings of price and output restrictions and asked whether, under the *BMI* analysis, there were offsetting procompetitive features that could take this case out of the "naked restraint" category.

The NCAA offered three procompetitive justifications in defense of its contract. First, the television restrictions minimized loss of game attendance; second, they minimized loss of athletic program revenues; and third, they spread the television income among many schools, thus increasing competition among more schools. The Court rejected each defense.

As to the first, the Court found that the restrictions could not minimize game attendance losses because the games were shown on television at the same time the

---

151. See Harrington & Leslie, *supra* note 146; Peter C. Carstensen & Annkathrin Marschall, *Pooling and Exchanging Competitively Sensitive Information Among Rivals: Absolutely Illegal Not Just Unreasonable*, 92 U. Cin. L. Rev. 335 (2023).

152. 468 U.S. 85 (1984).

153. *Id.* at 101.

154. *Id.* at 92–93.

155. *Id.* at 93 n.11.

games were being played, thus potentially drawing viewers out of the stands. Moreover, the Court said competitors could not choose one form of competition over another. Second, the restrictions would not minimize loss of athletic program revenue because, by definition, the restrictions reduced revenue by mandating fewer games. Finally, although the Court found the third defense laudable and legal in purpose, it found that it was flawed in execution because with fewer opportunities to appear on television, schools had less chance to share the proceeds. Concluding that the NCAA plan lacked procompetitive justifications, the Court declared the scheme illegal. Unlike *BMI*, the price and output restrictions remained without offsetting efficiencies. Moreover, in *BMI* there were not output restrictions.

In finding that the NCAA television plan was illegal, the Court rejected a market power analysis as a part of plaintiff's burden of proof.[156] As long as defendant is unable to demonstrate an offsetting procompetitive rationale for the restraint,[157] the conduct is deemed a naked restriction, and therefore illegal, when price and output limitations are established.[158] Hence, plaintiffs need only show price and output restrictions and the lack of procompetitive justification for a conclusion of illegality to follow. If price or output limitations cannot be shown, then plaintiff may need to establish that defendant does have market power[159]—ability to set price above competitive levels without a drop in demand. This condition is evident when price and supply are not responsive to consumer demand.[160] However, "[a]s a matter of law, the absence of proof of market power does not justify a naked restriction on price or output."[161]

---

156. *Id.* at 111. The Court went on to find market power by the NCAA, nevertheless. *See also FTC v. Ind. Fed'n of Dentists*, 476 U.S. 447, 460–61 (1985) ("Proof of actual detrimental effects, such as a reduction of output, can obviate the need for an inquiry into market power.").

157. Courts are in disagreement as to whether the procompetitive effects and the anticompetitive injury must be felt in the same market. Some courts argue that varying effects in different markets lead to factors which cannot be compared because they do not correlate, while others see no problem with using benefits and burdens in separate markets as a reference point. See *Sullivan v. NFL*, 34 F.3d 1091, 1111–12 (1st Cir. 1994), for a listing of cases and circuits that have dealt with this issue and a brief discussion of the implications.

158. *See also Big Apple BMW v. BMW N. Am.*, 974 F.2d 1358, 1375–80 (3d Cir. 1992) (holding that defendant's justifications for stifling competition must be more than "pretextual" to be valid).

159. *Lie v. St. Joseph Hosp.*, 964 F.2d 567, 569 (6th Cir. 1992) (holding that since the plaintiff could not prove "actual detrimental effects," he was obliged to prove market power).

160. See *Levine v. Central Fla. Med. Affiliates, Inc.*, 72 F.3d 1538, 1553, 1555 (11th Cir. 1996), where the court refused to find antitrust violations in either the defendant medical organization's refusal to extend an invitation for membership to the plaintiff doctor or the defendant hospital's temporary suspension of staff privileges for the plaintiff. The court ruled that the plaintiff had failed to establish either anticompetitive effects on the market or market power in both cases.

161. *NCAA v. Bd. of Regents*, 468 U.S. 85, 109 (1984).

§ 4.08 Bid Rigging

Another activity that has been held to be *per se* unlawful is bid rigging between competitors. In *United States v. Reicher*,[162] the defendant convinced a fellow engineering company (Giolas) to submit a bid higher than the defendant's on a contract with Los Alamos National Laboratory in order to secure that the defendant would get the job. The defendant's partner in the bid rigging had neither the financial capacity nor the desire to engage in the project. However, the court still labeled him a "competitor," thereby making the defendant guilty of a *per se* violation of the Sherman Act.

Despite its ultimate inability to perform the contract, Giolas held itself out as a competitor for the purposes of rigging what was supposed to be a competitive bidding process. This is exactly the sort of "threat to the central nervous system of the economy" that the antitrust laws are meant to address.[163]

This opinion is consistent with the holdings of other circuits on bid rigging.[164] In *Denny's Marina, Inc. v. Renfro Productions, Inc.*,[165] the Seventh Circuit reversed the district court's refusal to apply the *per se* rule to a horizontal conspiracy among various defendants engaged in the production of boat shows to exclude the plaintiff from participating in the shows. The lower court based its refusal on the fact that the plaintiff regularly undersold its competitors and that the plaintiff had not shown a "potential market-wide impact" from the defendant's actions.[166] The Court of Appeals readily asserted that the defendant's actions warranted a *per se* analysis, as they constituted illegal price fixing and an unreasonable restraint of trade.[167] Also, because one of the justifications for the *per se* rule is to destroy the need for individualized showings, no potential market impact needed to be proved by the plaintiff.[168]

Bid rigging can be the product of lawful activity in a few limited cases, however. As Professor Areeda has indicated, bids that are based on a "standard and uniform market price" and are, therefore, identical, are not a product of illegal *per se* price fixing.[169] Also, "pricing . . . based upon traditional applications of common cost factors" can serve as exceptions to the per se illegal treatment of bid rigging.

Although *Maricopa*, *Catalano*, and *Palmer* are consistent with *Socony*, except for the output analysis, another standard of review, embracing a focused rule of reason,

---

162. 983 F.2d 168 (10th Cir. 1992); *see also U.S. v. All-Star Indus.*, 962 F.2d 465 (5th Cir. 1992).

163. 983 F.2d at 170 (citation omitted).

164. *See United States v. MMR Corp.*, 907 F.2d 489 (5th Cir. 1990); *United States v. WF Brinkley & Son Constr. Co.*, 783 F.2d 1157 (4th Cir. 1986); *United States v. Finis P. Ernest, Inc.*, 509 F.2d 1256 (7th Cir. 1975).

165. 8 F.3d 1217 (7th Cir. 1993).

166. *Id.* at 1219.

167. *Id.* at 1220–21; *see also ES Dev., Inc. v. RWM Enters., Inc.*, 939 F.2d 547, 556 (8th Cir. 1991) (holding horizontal agreement between car dealerships to prevent plaintiff from building car mall subject to *per se* analysis as an unreasonable restraint of trade).

168. 8 F.3d at 1222.

169. VI Phillip E. Areeda, *Antitrust Law*, ¶ 1420 (1986).

was being advanced simultaneously in the Supreme Court. The clash between these analyses has left us with no easy guide for evaluating horizontal price fixing.[170]

§ 4.09 Quick Look Analysis

In 1999, the Supreme Court decided *California Dental Ass'n v. FTC*, which addressed advertising restrictions that the professional association placed on its members.[171] The Court found that quick-look analysis was inappropriate because "any anticompetitive effects of given restraints [were] far from intuitively obvious."[172] The Court, in an opinion by Justice Souter, explained that quick-look analysis is appropriate when "the great likelihood of anticompetitive effects can easily be ascertained."[173] Because this was not the case here, the Ninth Circuit incorrectly analyzed the restriction under a quick look.[174] Moreover, the Court suggested that there is no bright-line test for the depth of analysis that must be taken, indicating instead that it should be determined case-by-case.[175] Justice Breyer, in dissent, would have affirmed the Ninth Circuit's adjudication, because he determined that even under traditional rule of reason analysis, the restrictions violated the antitrust laws.[176]

The *per se* rule of illegality is applied less and less frequently. Plaintiffs in cases subsequent to *California Dental* have had *per se* arguments rejected in favor of a rule of reason approach.[177] In 2005, the District of Columbia Court of Appeals in *Polygram Holding, Inc. v. FTC*[178] indicated that the Supreme Court had moved away from categorizing conduct as *per se* unlawful or subject to a full-blown rule of reason analysis; rather, the inquiry in each case must be tailored to the nature of the contested

---

170. *See Am. Ad Mgmt., Inc. v. GTE*, 92 F.3d 781, 785 (9th Cir. 1996) (holding the rule of reason to be the proper level of analysis, despite *Socony* and *Catalano*, because the relationship involved was "one of agency, not wholesale retail.").

171. 526 U.S. 756, 759 (1999).

172. *Id.*

173. *Id.* at 770.

174. *Id.* at 769.

175. *Id.* at 779–80.

176. *Id.* at 781 (Breyer, J., dissenting). Several journal articles address the implications of *California Dental Ass'n*. *See, e.g.*, Thomas A. Piraino, Jr., *A Proposed Antitrust Approach to Collaborations Among Competitors*, 86 Iowa L. Rev. 1137, 1207 (2001) (suggesting that *California Dental Ass'n* illustrates the federal judiciary's failure to develop a unified approach to § 1 of the Sherman Act, and proposing a continuum-based approach to resolve the confusion); Sam Stanton, *Burden Shifting and Presumptions Under Section One of the Sherman Act After* California Dental Ass'n v. FTC, 53 Rutgers L. Rev. 247, 275 (2000) (arguing that *California Dental Ass'n* is limited to advertising self-regulation by professional associations).

177. *See Craftsmen Limousine, Inc. v. Ford Motor Co.*, 363 F.3d 761 (8th Cir. 2004) (reversing a $5.9 million group boycott award in which the district court applied a *per se* test and holding that the rule of reason should have been applied); *Int'l Healthcare Mgmt. v. Haw. Coal. for Health*, 332 F.3d 600 (9th Cir. 2003) (rejecting a *per se* approach when physician and consumers attempted to influence managed health care plans).

178. 416 F.3d 29 (2005).

conduct.[179] To determine whether a restraint is unlawful, a court must consider the "circumstances, details, and logic of [the] restraint."[180] The court must determine if the experience of the market is sufficient to provide confidence as to whether the "principle tendency of a restriction will follow from a quick (or at least quicker) look, in place of a more sedulous one."[181] If, based on the economic knowledge and market experience, a restraint of trade is obviously likely to impair competition, it is presumed unlawful. The defendant must then respond with reasons why the restraint is "unlikely to harm consumers or identify some competitive [offsetting] benefit."[182] The rebuttable presumption is based on the similarity of the disputed conduct to conduct that has already been ruled harmful to consumers.

The Court of Appeals affirmed a finding by the trial court that an agreement between Polygram Holding and Warner Communications violated § 1. The two entities agreed to suspend advertising and discounting of two earlier Three Tenor albums, issued independently, to ensure the success of the joint project on the third album, a concert at the 1998 World Soccer Cup. The court found the petitioners' agreement to have a rebuttable presumption of competition impairment. Based on economic knowledge and market experience, a joint venture agreement restricting advertising and marketing of products outside the joint venture was likely a *per se* illegal naked restraint. The court rejected Polygram's proposed procompetitive benefit of profitability of the joint venture as insufficient to offset the restraint to products outside the joint venture. The court did note, however, that possible acceptable justifications could include "increasing output, creating operating efficiencies, making a new product available, enhancing service or quality, and widening consumer choice."[183]

For decades, the quick-look approach represented a method only for condemning restraints as unreasonably anticompetitive. In *National Collegiate Athletic Association v. Alston*,[184] however, the defendant NCAA argued that the lower "courts should have given its restrictions at most an 'abbreviated deferential review,' or a 'quick look,' before approving them."[185] Instead of saying that no such standard exists—because the quick-look rule is a method for condemning challenged restraints, not exonerating them—the Supreme Court stated in dicta that depending on the facts of the case, "a quick look is sufficient for approval or condemnation."[186] This represented a sea change, as the quick look rule had previously only referenced how anticompetitive effects could be recognized with a quick look.[187] The *Alston* Court did not apply "abbreviated deferential review," and it remains to be seen what courts will do with

179. *Id.* at 34.
180. *Id.* at 35 (quoting *California Dental Ass'n v. FTC*, 526 U.S. 756, 781 (1999)).
181. *Id.*
182. *Id.*at 36.
183. *Id.* at 38 (quoting *Law v. NCAA*, 134 F.3d 1010, 1023 (10th Cir. 1998)).
184. 594 U.S. 69 (2021).
185. *Id.* at 87.
186. *Id.* at 88.
187. Christopher R. Leslie, *Disapproval of Quick-Look Approval: Antitrust After NCAA v. Alston*, 100 Wash. U.L. Rev. 1 (2022).

this language, but it creates the potential for creating false negatives in which anticompetitive restraints are improperly absolved.[188]

§ 4.10 Joint Ventures

Similar in many respects to a trade association is a joint venture. The leading cases[189] on point have been discussed above, but at this point a brief overview of the major antitrust issues is in order.

By definition, a joint venture is the formation of a single entity by two or more independent firms for the purpose of engaging in research, production or marketing activities. The joint conduct may be of the type that either firm is capable of carrying out individually or, because of its nature, could not be undertaken if the firms acted separately.

Firms engage in joint ventures for numerous reasons—some lawful, some not. Benefits that may flow from joint ventures include increased productivity and competition. By joining skills, spreading risks, achieving certain economics of scale, and reducing transaction costs, the joint firm may be more efficient and willing to undertake research or production. "The combined capital, assets, or know-how of two companies may facilitate entry into new markets and thereby enhance competition, or may create efficiencies or new productive capacity unachievable by either alone."[190]

However, the costs associated with joint ventures include the potential for price fixing, output restrictions, market divisions, and increased monopoly power.[191] The members of the joint venture may include competitors, potential competitors, or those in a vertical relationship. The potential is substantial that competition may be reduced if such firms are permitted to join as a single entity. But the benefits may be great as well. Thus, we are concerned, from an antitrust perspective, with not only the creation[192] but also with the continuing nature of the venture: Will it reduce competition between the members? To what extent does the venture control the competitive

---

188. *Id.* at 22–46.

189. A joint venture may be challenged under either § 1 of the Sherman Act or § 7 of the Clayton Act. *Nat'l Collegiate Athletic Ass'n v. Bd. of Regents, 468 U.S. 85 (1984); Broad. Music, Inc. v. Columbia Broad. Sys.*, 441 U.S. 1 (1979); *Associated Press v. United States*, 326 U.S. 1 (1945); *Appalachian Coals, Inc. v. United States*, 288 U.S. 344 (1933); *Chi. Bd. of Trade v. United States*, 246 U.S. 231 (1918); *Polk Bros., Inc. v. Forest City Enters., Inc.*, 776 F.2d 185 (7th Cir. 1986); *United States v. Addyston Pipe*, 85 F. 271 (6th Cir. 1898), *aff'd*, 175 U.S. 211 (1899).

190. *In re Brunswick Corp.* 94 F.T.C. 1174, 1265 (1979), *aff'd sub. nom., Yamaha Motor Co. v. FTC*, 657 F.2d 971 (2d Cir. 1981).

191. *See* Robert C. Marshall & Michael J. Meurer, *Bidder Collusion and Antitrust Law: Refining the Analysis of Price Fixing to Account for the Special Features of Auction Markets*, 72 Antitrust L.J. 83 (2004) (arguing that bidder collusion affects the market similarly to horizontal price fixing).

192. *Citizen Publ'g Co. v. United States*, 394 U.S. 131 (1969) (finding formation illegal); *United States v. Sealy, Inc.*, 388 U.S. 350 (1967); *Haw. Newspaper Agency v. Bronster*, 103 F.3d 742 (9th Cir. 1996).

activities of its members? Will they remain significant competitors in the market? The purpose and effect of the venture are the core of our analysis.

Because joint ventures have the potential of producing benefits as well as costs, courts analyze them under the rule of reason. They attempt to weigh the economic efficiencies against the actual costs of the venture. The cases reveal a spectrum of antitrust scrutiny. The more "pure" research oriented the venture, the more likely it is lawful. Research and development are key to productivity and competition, and in most industries, both can be expensive and risky if undertaken individually. As the venture moves toward production, and certainly into marketing, more serious antitrust concerns are implicated. Joint price and output decisions may be undertaken. Collusion and cartel behavior may result. Restraints involving the use of the results may be more than ancillary.

Courts begin their analysis with an inquiry into the nature (whether research, production or marketing) of the joint venture and whether the actual creation was lawful, especially in purpose. They consider, in addition, the joint venturers and the competitive relationship, or lack thereof, of the members of the venture. Direct competitors who join together in a joint venture have a greater potential for anticompetitive conduct than other relationships. The industry is surveyed with a view towards how much market power is held by the members of the venture. Joint ventures within concentrated markets are scrutinized more carefully.

Finally, courts analyze the restraints imposed on the joint venturers in scope and duration, and determine whether they are reasonably necessary to achieve the benefits of the venture or whether they are overbroad. A venture which is broad in scope and lengthy in time is more problematic.[193]

If the collateral restrictions include price agreements, output limitations, market divisions, customer allocations, or refusals to deal, they probably will be declared *per se* unlawful. But if the restraints are merely ancillary to an otherwise lawful agreement[194] and limited in scope and duration to that reasonably necessary to achieve the goals of the project, they will be held lawful. The Department of Justice has stated, as an enforcement policy, that the following collateral restrictions generally are lawful: "the obligation to exchange any results from research undertaken previously in the field of the joint venture, the duty not to disclose results of the joint research to outside parties until patents are obtained, and the division of particular aspects of the research between the venturers."[195]

In short, antitrust is concerned with the joint venture's purpose, effect, restrictions, and access. Specifically, the venture should not eliminate competition, at least to the

193. *See also* Joseph F. Brodley, *Joint Ventures and Antitrust Policy*, 95 Harv. L. Rev. 1521 (1982); Joseph F. Brodley, *The Legal Status of Joint Ventures Under the Antitrust Laws: A Summary Assessment*, 21 Antitrust Bull. 453 (1976). *See generally* U.S. Dep't of Justice & FTC, *Antitrust Guidelines for Collaborations Among Competitors* (2000).

194. *See Polk Bros., Inc. v. Forest City Enters., Inc.*, 776 F.2d 185 (7th Cir. 1986).

195. *U.S. Dep't of Justice, Antitrust Guide Concerning Joint Ventures* 5 (1980).

extent that procompetitive benefits are not realized; the collateral restrictions placed on the members and outsiders must be closely related to the venture's essential purpose, limited in scope and duration; and access to the results of the undertaking must be reasonable so as not to raise questions of a concerted refusal to deal.[196]

The Third Circuit in *Int'l Raw Materials, Ltd. (IRM) v. Stauffer Chemical Co.*,[197] identified four factors which courts generally analyze in determining the existence of a joint venture. Specifically:

> (1) whether there is an express or implied agreement that demonstrates the parties' intent to form a partnership or joint venture; (2) whether the parties share a common interest in the subject matter of the joint venture; (3) whether the parties share profits and losses from the venture; and (4) whether the parties have joint control or the joint right of control over the venture.[198]

In *Int'l Raw Materials*, IRM, a terminal operator who loaded products including soda ash[199] into ocean-going vessels, alleged that an association of soda ash producers (ANSAC)[200] and its members[201] conspired to fix the rates of domestic services for the export of soda ash.[202] In its complaint, IRM alleged that "prior to ANSAC's formation, each soda ash producer bargained separately for terminal services" and after its formation, ANSAC negotiated a common rate for all association members.[203] Shortly thereafter, ANSAC entered into a service agreement with IRM's competitor, Hall-Buck, Inc. The agreement provided for a specified shipping quantity at rates substantially lower than IRM's in exchange for an option to acquire a 50% share of a newly constructed terminal. This arrangement, IRM alleged, "restrained trade and depressed competition in the business of terminal services."[204] In response, ANSAC petitioned the district court for summary judgment claiming antitrust immunity under the Webb-Pomerene Act.[205]

---

196. *United States v. Topco Assoc.*, 405 U.S. 596 (1972). *See generally* Thomas M. Jorde & David J. Teece, *Antitrust, Innovation, and Competitiveness* (1992); Thomas M. Jorde & D. Teece, *Innovation and Cooperation Implications for Competition and Antitrust*, 4 J. Econ. Persp. 75 (1990); Joseph Kattan, *Antitrust Analysis of Technology Joint Ventures: Allocative Efficiency and the Rewards of Innovation*, 61 Antitrust L.J. 937 (1993).

197. 978 F.2d 1318 (3d Cir. 1992).

198. *Id.* at 1332 (citing Harry G. Henn & John R. Alexander, *Laws of Corporations* 106 (3d ed. 1983)).

199. Soda ash is primarily used in making glass. *Id.* at 1320 n.1.

200. All but one of the soda ash producers who comprise the American National Soda Ash Corporation (ANSAC) is either owned, in full or part, or affiliated with a major foreign corporation." *Id.* at 1320.

201. Association members include the Stauffer Chemical Co., TG Soda Ash, Chemical General Partners, Tenneco Minerals, Kerr-McGee, and the FMC Wyoming Corp. *Id.* at 1320 n.2.

202. *Id.* at 1320.

203. *Id.*

204. *Id.* at 1322.

205. "[T]he Webb-Pomerene Act permits associations to form export cartels without fear of suit under the Sherman Act, provided they do not restrain domestic trade in the good or product they

On appeal,[206] the Third Circuit held that the Webb-Pomerene Act did, in fact, authorize such an arrangement. "Even assuming ANSAC [receives] subsidized rates, it [did] not enter into a risk sharing agreement in relation to the losses or potential losses of the terminal." Without an agreement to apportion losses or potential losses, the relationship does not amount to a joint venture" and, therefore, is not beyond the scope of the Webb-Pomerene Act.[207]

The Tenth Circuit reversed a finding of a violation of § 1 by a joint venture in *SCFC ILC, Inc. v. Visa USA, Inc.*[208] The court began by admitting that the line between conduct necessitating *per se* analysis and that requiring rule of reason analysis "especially blur[s]" when joint ventures are involved, because, in those cases, "competitive incentives between independent firms are intentionally restrained and their functions and operations integrated to achieve efficiencies and increase output."[209] Visa USA is a joint venture between Visa and MasterCard. The facts of the case dealt with Visa USA's refusal to accept the plaintiff Sears and its Discover Card's application for membership. The court did not read Supreme Court precedent as requiring anything but the usual application of rule of reason analysis to joint ventures.[210] Hence, upon review of the facts under the rule of reason, the court found the defendants did not violate the Sherman or Clayton Acts.

The court first inquired into whether Visa USA had the requisite level of market power to "facilitate the determination that the practice harms competition and not simply a single competitor."[211] The court divided the relevant market into intra-and intersystem subparts. Discover ranked second in intrasystem competition.[212] It is defined as the market in which individual card issuers, whether they be members of Visa USA or not, compete for customers.[213] The intersystem market, on the other hand, is defined as "the competition among the manufacturers of the same generic product."[214] The court held there to be five relevant competitors in this market, with

---

export, or hinder the export trade of domestic competitors that are not members of the association." *Id.* at 1323 (*citing* 15 U.S.C. § 62 (2006)). For a further discussion of the Webb-Pomerene Act and export association immunity, see *supra* § 3.06.

206. Following the district court's approval of defendants' motion, IRM appealed to the U.S. Court of Appeals for the Third Circuit. Commenting that "a more complete factual record" was required before a determination of Webb-Pomerene immunity could be made, the Third Circuit reversed and remanded. *Id.* at 1321–22. After additional discovery was conducted and IRM filed an amended complaint, the association renewed its motion for summary judgment which was subsequently granted by the trial court.

207. *Id.* at 1332.

208. 36 F.3d 958 (10th Cir. 1994). One of the authors served as counsel in this case.

209. *Id.* at 963.

210. *Id.* at 964–65.

211. *Id.* at 965.

212. Discover Card was found to be the second largest in terms of charge volume or amount owed on cards. "Citicorp's [charge volume] is 21.9% in the relevant market, while that of Sears Discover Card is 5%." *Id.* at 967. These figures are not indicative of market power for either Citicorp or Discover Card in the intra-system/issuer market.

213. *Id.* at 967.

214. *Id.* at 966 (citation omitted).

Visa holding 45.6%, MasterCard (Visa's joint venture partner) at 26.4%, American Express at 20.5%, Discover with 5.5%, and Diner's Club with 2%.[215] Although it appeared that Visa USA had market power in the intersystem market, the relevant market in the case was the issuer or intrasystem market, where Visa USA did not have market power.

The court then rejected the contention that Visa USA's ability to make rules calling for collective activity between Visa and MasterCard suggested market power and the possibility for a § 1 violation. "A joint venture made more efficient by ancillary restraints is a fusion of the productive capabilities of the members of the venture."[216] The court stated that the effect of the rules, not the simple act of making them, was the relevant inquiry when delving into issues of market power.[217] As such, upon reviewing the facts, Visa USA could not be said to possess the requisite market power. The exclusion of Sears, the parent corporation of Discover Card, from the joint venture also "did not alter the character of the general purpose credit card market or change any present pattern of distribution," thus showing that there were no anticompetitive effects on the market.[218]

In *United States v. Visa USA Inc.*,[219] the Second Circuit affirmed the lower court's holding that Visa and MasterCard payment card networks violated § 1 because of their exclusionary rules. Namely, banks choosing to issue either Visa or Master Card were precluded from issuing other types of cards, for example, American Express or Discover. Because there was no allegation of *per se* illegality, the Second Circuit applied a rule of reason analysis. The court noted that the case involved "two interrelated, but separate, product markets: . . . the general purpose card market, consisting of the market for charge cards and credit cards, and (2) the network services market for general purpose cards."[220] The court found the competitive harms caused by the exclusionary rules exceeded the procompetitive effects.

In *Texaco, Inc. v. Dagher*,[221] the Supreme Court, in an opinion by Justice Thomas, held that it was not *per se* unlawful for a joint venture to set the prices at which it sells its products. Petitioners Texaco Inc. and Shell Oil Co. set up a joint venture, Equilon Enterprises, to refine and sell gasoline in the western United States. Respondents, Shell and Texaco station owners, alleged that Texaco and Shell engaged in price fixing through their joint venture when it, Equilon, set a single price for gasoline to be sold by each joint venturer under its respective brand name.

Texaco and Shell formed the joint venture to "pool their resources and share the risks of and profits from Equilon's activities."[222] Respondents initially alleged that

---

215. *Id.* at 967.
216. *Id.* at 968 (quoting *Rothery Storage v. Atlas Van Lines*, 792 F.2d 210, 230 (D.C. Cir. 1986)).
217. *Id.*
218. *Id.* at 971.
219. 344 F.3d 229 (2d Cir. 2003).
220. *Id.* at 238–39.
221. 547 U.S. 1 (2012).
222. *Id.* at 4.

petitioners violated the *per se* rule against price fixing under § 1. The District Court dismissed the petitioners' action because they failed to raise a triable issue of fact, resting their case on the *per se* rule or quick look doctrine, rather than the rule of reason the court determined governed the claim. On appeal, the Ninth Circuit reversed, determining that respondents presented sufficient evidence for a triable issue of fact as to whether the joint venture pricing scheme was *per se* illegal. Thus, the issue before the Court was "to determine the extent to which the *per se* rule against price fixing applies to ... the joint venture."[223] The Court distinguished the joint venture from *per se* illegal price-fixing agreements between two or more competitors because Texaco and Shell did not compete with each other in the sale of gasoline to service stations in the western United States. "The pricing policy challenged here amounts to little more than price setting by a single entity—albeit within the context of a joint venture—and not a pricing agreement between competing entities with respect to their competing products."[224] The Court noted that while the joint venture's pricing policy was price fixing in a literal sense, it was not so in the antitrust sense. The Court also dismissed the Circuit Court's use of the ancillary restraint doctrine in holding the pricing policy as *per se* unlawful, stating that the ancillary doctrine does not apply to the "core activity of the joint venture itself—namely, the pricing of the very goods produced and sold by Equilon."[225] Thus, the Court reemphasized that in the context of joint ventures, price-fixing schemes are usually not per se unlawful.

The common law principles discussed here have their roots in the 1918 *Chicago Bd. of Trade*[226] opinion written by Justice Brandeis. There a broad rule of reason was sanctioned for joint ventures. It was continued through the depression period in *Appalachian Coals*.[227] That same approach continues today, although perhaps more focused or limited, as illustrated in the *BMI*[228] and *NCAA*[229] cases. Even in the face of price restraints and output limitations, the Court has been willing to weigh the anticompetitive costs against the procompetitive benefits in determining whether the net consequences are procompetitive. If procompetitive justifications are outweighed by the restraints imposed, the joint venture will be declared illegal. The ancillary restraint doctrine also has played a major analytical role in determining the legality of joint ventures. From *Addyston Pipe* in 1898[230] to *Polk Brothers* in 1986,[231] courts have been receptive to restraints which are only ancillary to an otherwise lawful objective, as long as they are limited in scope and duration.

In 2004, Congress has carved out an exemption from antitrust coverage for the medical school graduate residency matching program. Graduating medical students

223. *Id.* at 5.
224. *Id.* at 6.
225. *Id.* at 7.
226. 246 U.S. 231 (1918).
227. 288 U.S. 344 (1933).
228. 441 U.S. 1 (1979).
229. 468 U.S. 85 (1984).
230. 85 F. 271 (6th Cir. 1898), *aff'd*, 175 U.S. 211 (1899).
231. 776 F.2d 185 (7th Cir. 1986).

preparing for their medical residency training are traditionally matched to teaching hospitals by a computer database. The match program, coordinated nationally by the Association of American Medical Colleges, severely limits the number of hospitals at which new graduates may seek residency. Under the law, evidence of conduct involving participation in a matching program is inadmissible "to support any claim or action alleging a violation of the antitrust laws."[232] The Act does not exempt agreements that fix the amount of stipends or other benefits that the medical residents may receive.

In 1984, Congress passed the National Cooperative Research Act (NCRA) intending to encourage procompetitive joint research. Among other provisions, the statute detrebles antitrust liability and allows prevailing defendants to recover attorney's fees and costs attributable to frivolous suits. In order to come within the Act, parties must give notification to the Department of Justice and the FTC of the intended venture by identifying the parties and the nature and goals of the undertaking. Moreover, a "reasonableness" standard is incorporated into the Act.[233]

In 1993, the NCRA was significantly expanded with the enactment of the National Cooperative Production Amendments Act (NCPA).[234] Similar to the 1984 Act, the new law limits antitrust damage exposure to actual, single damages for qualifying production joint ventures, requires a voluntary notification procedure, and employs a rule of reason analysis to assess the alleged restraint. Contrary to the 1984 Act, however, the new statute requires that a qualifying production joint venture must locate its principal production facilities in the United States or its territories. Furthermore, except for the product manufactured by the joint venture, marketing and distribution agreements are excluded from the immunity.

§ 4.11 Maximum Horizontal Price Fixing

The Court in *Maricopa*[235] held that the *per se* rule "is grounded on faith in price competition as a market force [and not] on a policy of low selling prices at the price of eliminating competition."[236] The Court found that the evils inherent in maximum price agreements include the fact that such conduct might discourage market entry and deter research and development by entrepreneurs because the maximum price may be too low to create incentives for entry or product development or service. Further, the Court was concerned that a maximum price might masquerade for an agreement to fix uniform or minimum prices.

---

232. *See* Section 207 of the Pension Funding Equity Act of 2004, codified at 15 U.S.C. § 37b.

233. *See* 15 U.S.C. §§ 4301–05 (2012).

234. *See* Pub. L. 103-42, 107 Stat. 117 (1993).

235. 457 U.S. 332 (1982).

236. 457 U.S. at 348 (quoting James A. Rahl, *Price Competition and the Price-Fixing Rule—Preface and Perspective*, 57 Nw. U. L. Rev. 137, 142 (1962)).

The Court in *Maricopa* rejected procompetitive justifications for the restraint. Said the *Maricopa* Court,

> The anticompetitive potential inherent in all price-fixing agreements justifies their facial invalidation even if procompetitive justifications are offered for some. Those claims of enhanced competition are so unlikely to prove significant in any particular case that we adhere to the rule of law that is justified in its general application.[237]

The *Maricopa* Court weighed the purpose and effect of the maximum price fixing agreement (to reduce costs of medical services) before it reached its conclusion that the arrangement lacked offsetting procompetitive effects. It was declared *per se* illegal. The economic learning suggests that the maximum price fixing in *Maricopa* probably was not, as the Court surmised, a disguised agreement "to fix minimum or uniform price."[238] If it were a price (fee) below which the subscribing doctors could not go, why would the insurance company, really the buyer of the services (the proxy for the patient), agree? Insurance companies generally want to reduce transaction costs and prices of services to their customers. An agreement to enter such an arrangement would make little economic or business sense from the standpoint of the insurance company (the buyer of the service). A strict *per se* rule would foreclose this kind of searching analysis.

§ 4.12 Concerted Refusals to Deal

Agreements by firms to refuse to deal with another firm can be anticompetitive. Collusion may be designed to limit competition either by creating entry barriers or facilitating market exits. When the agreement is between competitors, it is a horizontal restraint known as a group boycott or a concerted refusal to deal.

Group boycotts come in many different forms. For example, firms at one level of competition may refuse to deal with a supplier or customer that deals with a competitor of the agreeing firms. The pressure may force the vertical partner to cease doing business with the target in order to retain the business of the target's competitor. Or a firm at one level (retailer) may enter an agreement with a firm at another level (supplier) to refuse to deal with a competitor of the retailer.[239] Alternatively, some group boycotts involve an arrangement is between noncompeting firms in a vertical relationship aimed at a target in competition with at least one of the conspirators; the effect is horizontal, although the agreement is not.

---

237. 457 U.S. at 351.

238. 457 U.S. at 348.

239. For an example of an antitrust claim that was brought under the first theory but decided upon the second, see *Discon, Inc. v. Nynex Corp.* 93 F.3d 1055, (2d Cir. 1996), *vacated by* 525 U.S. 128 (1998). *See also E&L Consulting Ltd. v. Doman Indus. Ltd.*, 472 F.3d 23 (2d Cir. 2006); *Center Video Indus. Co., Inc. v. United Media, Inc.*, 995 F.2d 735, 736–37 (7th Cir. 1993).

The purpose of a boycott may be to punish a maverick price cutter or others not adhering to certain industry standards. It also may be designed to gain market power at the expense of other competitors. Some concerted refusals to deal, however, especially those where the firms are engaged in a joint venture, may enhance efficiency, thus making the market more competitive. Other agreements may be designed to avoid free riders. Once again, the Court's characterization process of the refusal to deal is at the core of the analysis and may preordain the legal conclusion.

The Court's approach to group boycotts has evolved over time. In 1914, in *Eastern State Retail Lumber Dealers' Ass'n v. United States,*[240] the Supreme Court held that a retail lumber trade association violated § 1 of the Sherman Act when it circulated to its members a list of maverick wholesalers who also attempted to sell at retail in competition with the members of the trade association. "The particular thing which this case concerns is the retailers' efforts . . . by the *circulation* of the reports in question, to keep the wholesalers from selling directly to the local trade."[241] The "blacklisting" was a means to insulate the membership from increased price competition at the retail level by new entrants. The aim of the boycott was to affect price and protect the market power of member retailers.

If an individual retailer ceased doing business with a maverick wholesaler, such unilateral conduct would not be violative of § 1, but here the concerted agreement, inferred from the circulation, was unlawful. "An act harmless when done by one may become a public wrong when done by many acting in concert, for it then takes on the form of conspiracy, and may be prohibited or punished, if the result be hurtful to the public or to the individual against whom the concerted action is directed."[242] The natural effect of the circulation would be to cause retailers to boycott the wholesalers engaged in retail businesses. *Eastern States* is an example of an exclusionary, commercial, nonregulatory boycott. It established the rule that an agreement by firms at one level of competition (retail) not to deal with firms at another level (suppliers), that also compete on the first level, is an illegal concerted refusal to deal.

The same conclusion was reached in *Fashion Originators' Guild of Am., Inc. (FOGA) v. FTC*[243] under § 5 of the Federal Trade Commission Act. Members of the trade association that designed and manufactured women's dresses sought to prevent "style piracy" through an agreement to refuse to deal with retailers who had purchased from the targeted manufacturers that sold copies. As a result of the Guild's collective action, 12,000 retailers signed agreements to cooperate with the Guild's boycott.

The Guild's action limited competition, reducing the number of outlets to which the member manufacturers could sell and the sources from which the retailers could buy. Freedom of choice was affected in the market. The Court came close to declaring a *per se* standard for such conduct when it upheld the FTC's refusal to consider

---

240. 234 U.S. 600 (1914).

241. *Id.* at 606.

242. *Id.* at 614 (quoting *Grenada Lumber Co. v. Mississippi*, 217 U.S. 433, 440 (1910)).

243. 312 U.S. 457 (1941).

evidence of the "reasonableness" of the methods pursued. But the Court did evaluate the purpose behind the conduct and the market power (60% for higher priced garments) of the member firms. The Court also noted that less restrictive alternatives were available such as state civil tort actions against the piracy, rather than the creation of an "extra-governmental agency" to punish the price discounters.[244]

FOGA is a model boycott case in which the parties engaged in industry self-regulation by putting pressure on buyers to refuse to deal with competing suppliers in competition with defendants. The Court found no public interest protected by the refusal to deal; only the self-interest and protection from commercial competition was at stake. In a similar case today, defendants would interpose as a defense the theory that the Guild's boycott was an effective method of avoiding "free rider" problems[245] and would ask the court to balance these externalities against the effect of the refusal to deal on price and the protection of market power.

In 1959, in *Klor's Inc. v. Broadway-Hale Stores, Inc.*,[246] the Court explicitly concluded that a concerted refusal to deal by competitors was *per se* unlawful. A retailer, Broadway, entered into an agreement with suppliers of appliances "either not to sell to Klor's or to sell to it only at discriminatory prices and highly unfavorable terms."[247] Broadway was alleged to have monopolistic buying power. Broadway did not dispute the allegation but moved for summary judgment, asserting a failure to state a cause of action because there was no public injury: "there were hundreds of other household appliance retailers, some within a few blocks of Klor's who sold many competing brands of appliances, including those the defendants refused to sell to Klor's."[248] In short, defendant argued that because consumers and other competitors had access to supply, the public was not injured.

Klor's per se finding is implied in the following statement of the Court:

> [g]roup boycotts or concerted refusals by traders to deal with other traders, have long been held to be in the forbidden category. They have not been saved by allegations that they were reasonable in the specific circumstances, nor by a failure to show that they "fixed or regulated prices, parceled out or limited production, or brought about a deterioration in quality."[249]

The Court's phrasing of "forbidden category" implies *per se* illegality because the *per se* rule is categorical: agreements that fall in a *per se* category are deemed unreasonably

---

244. *Id.* at 465.

245. *See infra* §4.13[A][3]. *Contra Phil Tolkan Datsun, Inc. v. Greater Milwaukee Datsun Dealers' Adver. Ass'n, Inc.*, 672 F.2d 1280 (7th Cir. 1982); *United States v. Realty Multi-List*, 629 F.2d 1351 (5th Cir. 1980); *but see United States v. Gen. Motors Corp.*, 384 U.S. 127 (1966) (boycotts are unlawful even when they are effective methods of controlling free riding).

246. 359 U.S. 207 (1959).

247. *Id.* at 209.

248. *Id.* at 209–10.

249. *Id.* at 212 (citing *Fashion Originators' Guild v. FTC*, 312 U.S. 457, 466 (1941)); *see also United States v. Gen. Motors Corp.*, 384 U.S. 127 (1966); *Radiant Burners, Inc. v. People's Gas Light & Coke Co.*, 364 U.S. 656 (1961).

anticompetitive as a matter of law. The competitive harm included Klor's inability to buy in an open, competitive market, its inability to be a dealer in defendants' products, and the manufacturers' inability to sell to Klor's. The conduct had a "monopolistic tendency," the Court concluded. Summary judgment for defendants was reversed.

Unclear from the Court's logic in *Klor's* is how Broadway, a local appliance store with numerous local competitors, could have used monopolistic, i.e., monopsony, buying power to force major suppliers like RCA and General Electric from dealing with Klor's. The Court seemed concerned that if this conduct went unchecked there could be a "tendency toward monopoly," with the result that small competitors, like Klor's, would be driven out of the market only to have prices then increase. This was not the case where a retailer was denied access to one product or brand with other suppliers or brands available. The concerted refusal to deal included numerous major brands. The implication was that the makers of these brands all agreed with Broadway (and perhaps among themselves) to withhold supply from Klor's. This conduct went beyond "a manufacturer and dealer agreeing to an exclusive distributorship [thereby tying up one product]. . . . [A] wide combination consisting of manufacturers, distributors and a retailer" was alleged.[250]

In *Silver v. New York Stock Exchange*,[251] the Court made clear that an agreement by firms at one level of competition to deny a market through a group boycott by themselves or through others to competing firms is illegal *per se* without more. Through the New York Stock Exchange, securities brokers denied access to facilities to nonmember broker-dealers. Although finding that the exchange enjoyed a qualified immunity from antitrust coverage under the federal securities law,[252] the Court observed that, but for this fact, the concerted refusal to deal was *per se* unlawful. The Court concluded that defendants violated the law because they failed to give plaintiff sufficient regulatory notice and hearing as to the grounds for the refusal to deal and the exclusion. The Court rejected an inquiry into the reasons underlying the boycott, implying an unqualified *per se* rule of illegality.

In sum, *Eastern States*, *FOGA*, *Klor's*, and *Silver* teach that concerted refusals to deal aimed at a competitor to deny access or supply at that level of competition, either through vertical or horizontal agreements, are illegal. However, the extent of the analysis varied; at times the focus was on purpose, at other times it was on market power and effect. But, the Court, despite its *per se* predilections and broad language, seemed not to foreclose completely all justifications for a boycott.[253] This became evident in 1985 when the Court receded from its sweeping *per se* language. Only a narrow window remains through which the Court will apply its *per se* presumption of illegality to concerted refusals to deal. Otherwise, the rule of reason is the standard benchmark.

---

250. 359 U.S. at 212–13.
251. 373 U.S. 341 (1963).
252. Securities Exchange Act of 1934, 15 U.S.C. § 78b (2012).
253. *See* Phillip Areeda, *Antitrust Analysis* § 376, at 514 (3d ed. 1981).

In *Northwest Wholesale Stationers v. Pacific Stationary and Printing Co.*,[254] the Court, in a unanimous decision, rejected, except for a narrow category of cases, the *per se* characterization for concerted refusals to deal. A cooperative purchasing agency expelled a member without a *Silver* due process hearing which would have provided an opportunity for a hearing before termination. The cooperative was made up of 100 office supply retailers acting as a wholesaler to member retailers. Nonmember retailers could purchase at the same price as members, but they were not permitted to share in the cooperatives' profits. Members received their profits in the form of a rebate percentage on the purchase price. The cooperative also provided warehousing facilities.

The plaintiff was denied membership after the cooperative changed its policy and began dealing as a wholesaler as well as retailer. Prior to the refusal to deal, plaintiff received $10,000 annually in rebates on purchases as a member of the retail cooperative. The expulsion allegedly created a competitive disadvantage as a nonmember. Defendant cooperative urged that the purpose and effect were to achieve economies of scale and to reduce transaction costs in purchasing and warehousing.

In addressing *Silver*'s due process requirement, the Court held,

> [T]he absence of procedural safeguards can in no sense determine the antitrust analysis. If the challenged concerted activity of Northwest's members would amount to a *per se* violation of § 1 of the Sherman Act, no amount of procedural protection would save it. If the challenged action would not amount to a violation of § 1, no lack of procedural protections would convert it into a *per se* violation because the antitrust laws do not themselves impose on joint ventures a requirement of due process.[255]

In effect, *Silver*'s process requirements apply only when the challenged conduct had a qualified antitrust immunity.

The Court surveyed its prior concerted refusal to deal cases and found that the *per se* approach had been applied when there were "joint efforts by a firm or firms to disadvantage competitors by 'either directly denying or persuading or coercing suppliers or customers to deny relationships the competitors need in the competitive struggle.'"[256] The Court noted that frequently the boycotting firms also had market power or a dominant position and that the challenged practices did not enhance overall efficiency.

Here, however, the Court concluded that Northwest was designed to increase economic efficiency by achieving "economies of scale in both the purchase and warehousing of wholesale supplies, and also [that the plan] ensure[d] ready access to a stock of goods" that otherwise might not be available.[257] Reversing the *per se* approach of the

---

254. 472 U.S. 284 (1985).
255. *Id.* at 293.
256. *Id.* (quoting Sullivan, *supra* note 143, at 261–62).
257. 472 U.S. at 295.

court of appeals, the Supreme Court held that the *per se* standard is only acceptable when the boycotting cooperative possesses market power or has exclusive access to supply or an essential element so that competition is affected. Otherwise, the refusal to deal is to be judged under the rule of reason analysis.

Thus, the Court raised the plaintiff's burden of proof in refusal to deal cases. In reviewing its prior cases, the Court noted that those group boycott cases in which the Court applied the *per se* rule shared three characteristics: (1) "the boycott often cut off access to a supply, facility, or market necessary to enable the boycotted firm to compete"; (2) "frequently the boycotting firms possessed a dominant position in the relevant market"; and (3) "the practices were generally not justified by plausible arguments that they were intended to enhance overall efficiency and make markets more competitive."[258] The Court did not characterize these three considerations as elements.

Once again the Court embraced an economic analysis that focused on reduced transaction costs and enhanced efficiency as a means of promoting competition—an approach entirely consistent with the Court's price-fixing cases in *BMI* and *NCAA*. The benefits of the bright line *per se* test were waning. This was proven even more so the next Supreme Court term.

In 1986, *Indiana Federation of Dentists* evaluated an agreement by competing dentists to deny patient x-rays to insurance companies.[259] Insurers used the x-rays to serve as a peer review check on the appropriateness of the dentists' charges and as a cost containment mechanism. The Court declined to apply the *per se* rule, reasoning that the Court has been "slow to condemn rules adopted by professional associations as unreasonable *per se*. . . ."[260]

Although it claimed to apply the rule of reason, the Court rejected the defendants' argument that the arrangement was not anticompetitive because they lacked market power. The Court gave two separate arguments. First, as a matter of law, the Court held that the defendants' argument was inappropriate because their agreement was "a naked restriction on price or output." This suggests that the Court was applying a *per se* approach, even though it said it wasn't. Second, as a matter of fact, the Court found that the dentists did possess market power.

The Court condemned the defendants' agreement as "concerted and effective effort to withhold (or make more costly) information desired by consumers [that was] likely enough to disrupt the proper functioning of the price-setting mechanism. . . ."[261] Finally, the Court rejected the defendants' "'quality of care' justification" for the group boycott as flawed both legally and factually.

Northwest and *Indiana Federation of Dentists* together suggest, at the least, that *Klor's* announced *per se* treatment of group boycotts is not a true *per se* approach. Antitrust plaintiffs must do more than show that the defendants engaged in a group

---

258. *Id.* at 294.
259. *FTC v. Ind. Fed'n of Dentists*, 476 U.S. 447 (1986).
260. *Id.* at 458.
261. *Id.* at 461.

boycott before the *per se* label attaches. In many respects, *Indiana Fed'n of Dentists* was a better candidate for the *per se* classification than *Klor's*, particularly in light of the market power held by the dentists and the horizontal agreements.

In a case labelled as a group boycott but having an aspect of price fixing, the Court again seemed to treat the arrangement as *per se* illegal. In *Superior Court Trial Lawyers Ass'n v. FTC*,[262] the Court held that a horizontal arrangement among lawyers to withhold the supply of legal services and thereby increase hourly wage rates represented a "naked restraint" on price and output. In *Superior Court Trial Lawyers*, a group of private-practice lawyers, pursuant to a well-publicized plan, agreed not to represent indigent criminal defendants in the District of Columbia Superior Court until the city government increased the lawyers' hourly compensation.[263]

In evaluating the requisite conduct, the Court commented that although there was a political impact, the means employed (the boycott) to obtain the more favorable legislation was economic, rather than political in nature. Therefore, irrespective of "whatever economic justification particular price-fixing agreements may be thought to have, the law does not permit an inquiry into their reasonableness."[264]

Thus, in a concerted refusal to deal context, the facts of the given case will likely dictate whether the Court applies a *per se* or rule of reason approach to assess the alleged restraint.

§ 4.13 Horizontal Market Divisions

Section 1 of the Sherman Act condemns unreasonable restraints of trade. Although the most obvious horizontal restraint of trade is price fixing among competitors, price fixing is not the only anticompetitive behavior condemned under § 1. A horizontal market division is created when competitors agree not to compete in a designated market. Such an agreement may divide a market in various ways.[265]

---

262. 493 U.S. 411 (1990).

263. *Id.* at 413.

264. *Id.* at 435 (*quoting United States v. Socony-Vacuum Oil Co.*, 310 U.S. 150 (1940)). In *Betkerur v. Aultman Hospital Ass'n*, 78 F.3d 1079 (6th Cir. 1996), the Sixth Circuit rejected the plaintiff's claim of *per se* illegality under a group boycott theory. Defendants had terminated a program at the hospital which allowed for blind referrals of neonatologists (like the plaintiff by OB/GYN physicians to their patients). The plaintiff claimed among other things, that this constituted a group boycott. The court quickly disposed of this claim because the plaintiff still practiced at the defendant hospital and received referrals from those allegedly boycotting her. *Id.* at 1090. More importantly, the court found most of the defendants to have no incentive to try to freeze out the plaintiff, meaning that there was no danger of the defendants acting in concert to harm consumers through boycotting the plaintiff's services. *Id.* Finally, the court could not discern any negative economic effect originating out of the defendant's decision to terminate the blind referral program. *Id.* at 1091.

265. It should be noted that market divisions that involve domestic firms but occur in foreign countries are not subject to *per se* analysis under the Sherman Act. *Metro Industries, Inc. v. Sammi Corp.*, 82 F.3d 839, 844–45 (9th Cir. 1996). However, "it is well established . . . that the Sherman Act

(1) Territorial market divisions are created when competitors allocate markets along geographic lines. For example, one conspirator may be assigned the western region and another the eastern region of an area.[266]

(2) Customer market divisions are created when competitors allocate specific customers among themselves, agreeing not to solicit business from customers allocated to designated competitors.

(3) Functional market divisions are created when competitors allocate, for example, the wholesale market to selected members of a conspiracy and the retail market to other members.

(4) Product market divisions are created when competitors agree not to compete along certain product lines. For example, conspirators may agree that one will market only small appliances while the other will market only large appliances in a defined area.

Many horizontal market division agreements constitute a combination of one or more of the above market division arrangements. For example, in *Polk Bros., Inc. v. Forest City Enters., Inc.*,[267] two firms agreed to occupy a physically divided common retail establishment in which the firms would sell only non-competing, yet complementary, products. The agreement thus called for both product and territorial allocations.

Horizontal market division agreements generally have the effect of reducing price competition. When competition is reduced, participants in the market no longer need to compete on price to the extent that price competition would exist in the absence of a horizontal market division. If the market division is sufficiently pervasive, a small number of firms may effectively enjoy a monopoly in a designated territory, for a certain product line, or with a selected group of customers. When this occurs the market division may be as anticompetitive as direct price fixing.[268]

[A] Dividing Territories and Fixing Price

Price-fixing conspirators may also agree to divide markets in order to stabilize their conspiracy. When conspirators agree to fix prices, there is always the possibility that one or more of the conspirators may be tempted to "cheat" on the co-conspirators by lowering selected prices in anticipation that competitors will not detect the price

---

applies to foreign conduct that was meant to produce and . . . produc[ed] some substantial effect in the United States." *Hartford Fire Ins. Co. v. California*, 509 U.S. 764, 795 (1993).

266. Territorial market divisions are often combined with price-fixing agreements, as in *Timken Roller Bearing Co. v. United States*, 341 U.S. 593 (1951), overruled on other grounds by *Copperweld Corp. v. Independence Tube Corp.*, 467 U.S. 752 (1984). Similarly, in *United States v. Sealy*, 388 U.S. 350 (1967), licenses were combined with price fixing. In contrast, the defendants in *United States v. Topco Associates, Inc.*, 405 U.S. 596 (1972), allocated territories but did not fix prices.

267. 776 F.2d 185 (7th Cir. 1985).

268. *See* Christopher R. Leslie, *False Analogies to Predatory Pricing*, 172 U. Pa. L. Rev. 329 (2024).

deviation. When this occurs, detection is difficult, at least in nonretail markets, because wholesale price information is customarily not available to competitors, and customers suspicious of being victimized by an illegal price-fixing scheme are unlikely to report a supplier who "cheats" on the cartel by lowering its price. When, however, competitors agree to divide markets and one member of the conspiracy deviates from the agreement, detection by other members of the conspiracy is much easier than in price fixing because of the greater visibility of sales in markets or to customers allocated to others. Horizontal market divisions, then, may be more easily monitored and enforced by the conspirators, and in this sense, may be even more anticompetitive than price-fixing agreements. Moreover, in an air tight market division no competition exists, but where the only restraint is price fixing, other nonprice competition (on quality, service, or inventory) may exist and even be robust. Consequently, a market division in some circumstances may be more pernicious than price fixing.[269]

[1] Introductory Cases

One of the earliest territorial division cases decided under the Sherman Act was *United States v. Addyston Pipe & Steel Co.*[270] Defendants in *Addyston Pipe* were competing cast iron pipe producers who allocated territories among themselves and jointly fixed prices in each territory. The apparent purpose of the combination was to create an artificial barrier to entry by establishing prices low enough to discourage new entrants, albeit higher than prices that would have resulted from competitive forces. Defendants argued that the arrangement had the benign purpose of preventing ruinous competition and that their association would have been valid at common law because the prices fixed were reasonable.

The Sixth Circuit rejected both arguments. In an opinion by Judge Taft, later Chief Justice of the Supreme Court, the court reasoned that even under the common law all such agreements were unlawful unless they were ancillary. "No conventional restraint of trade can be enforced unless the covenant embodying it is merely ancillary to the main purpose of a lawful contract. . . ."[271] Having found that the defendants' territorial and price-fixing contract was not ancillary to a main lawful purpose, the court rejected defendants' reasonableness argument, stating that "we do not think that at common law there is any question of reasonableness open to the courts with reference

---

269. A claim of *per se* illegality based on a horizontal restraint failed in *Betkerur v. Aultman Hosp. Ass'n*, 78 F.3d 1079 (6th Cir. 1996). The Sixth Circuit refused to find that an agreement between a neonatologist, her employer hospital, and several OB/GYN's to discontinue a blind referral system of neonatologists (including the plaintiff) by OB/GYN's constituted a *per se* illegal horizontal restraint. Because the OB/GYN's were not competitors with the plaintiff neonatologist and because the one defendant who was in direct competition with the plaintiff did not "secure an exclusive referral arrangement in order to increase her prices and undermine a competitor's prices," no *per se* violation of § 1 had occurred. *Id.* at 1092. Hence, the rule of reason analysis applied by the district court did not constitute an error; the judgment was upheld.

270. 85 F. 271 (6th Cir. 1898), *aff'd*, 175 U.S. 211 (1899).

271. *Id.* at 282.

to such a contract."[272] Because the *Addyston Pipe* court focused most of its analysis on defendants' price-fixing conduct, the case does not provide meaningful guidance as to the legality of territorial allocations.

In 1947's *United States v. Nat'l Lead Co.*,[273] the Supreme Court upheld the lower court's finding of a § 1 violation by defendants who pooled their numerous patents and allocated markets for the manufacture and sale of titanium. The pooling of the multiple patents by agreement among defendants resulted in "domination of an entire industry."[274] The territorial division was unlawful even though competition was vigorous between selected plants operated by the defendants.[275]

Four years after it decided *Nat'l Lead*, the Court reviewed the legality of a territorial restriction combined with price fixing. In *Timken Roller Bearing Co. v. United States*,[276] defendants were a corporate parent and its partially owned subsidiaries who were producers of antifriction bearings sold in the international market. Defendants were parties to agreements which licensed the trademark "Timken," allocated territories in which each of the parties would market "Timken" bearings, and established prices to be charged when one defendant sold bearings in a territory assigned to another.

Defendants argued that their agreements were ancillary to the otherwise lawful purposes of protecting the "Timken" trademark and effectuating the relationship among the defendants. They characterized this as a joint venture. The Court rejected defendants' argument, holding that an agreement that divided territorial markets among competitors and fixes prices violates § 1 if the dominant purpose of the market divisions is to avoid competition among the conspirators.

Reasoning that the agreement to divide territories was broader than necessary to protect the "Timken" trademark, the Court found that the market division was the dominant purpose, not trademark protection. This suggests "a least restrictive alternative" test to determine if certain restraints are valid. For example, the restraint in *Timken* affected competition in the interbrand market because the agreements "went far beyond the protection of the name 'Timken,' and provided for control of the manufacture and sale of antifriction bearings whether carrying the ['Timken' trade]mark or not."[277] The court reasoned that because the restraint operated in the interbrand market, it was more likely to be overbroad. If, however, the restraint applied only to products bearing the "Timken" trademark, affecting only the intrabrand market, then defendants might have argued that such effects were less restrictive and accordingly less anticompetitive.

The *Timken* Court did not specifically state whether defendants' conduct was unlawful *per se* or subject to a rule of reason analysis. A *per se* conclusion would seem

272. *Id.* at 293.
273. 332 U.S. 319 (1947).
274. *Id.* at 328.
275. *Id.* at 352.
276. 341 U.S. 593 (1951).
277. 341 U.S. at 598–99.

to be inconsistent with the Court's consideration of defendant's market power. The issue was clarified in *United States v. Sealy, Inc.*,[278] however, when the Court, citing *Timken*, condemned market divisions in combination with price fixing. The Court said that "they are unlawful under § 1 of the Sherman Act without the necessity for an inquiry in each particular case as to their business or economic justification, their impact in the marketplace, or their reasonableness."[279] Clearly, this language rejects a rule of reason analysis in favor of a *per se* conclusion, but subsequent cases call into question such a broad generalization.

[2] Exclusive License for an Assigned Area

Like *Timken, United States v. Sealy, Inc.*[280] involved both territorial allocations and price fixing.[281] Defendants were mattress manufacturers who combined to form Sealy, Inc. Sealy licensed thirty mattress manufacturers who owned substantially all the stock of Sealy, Inc. Each licensee was assigned an exclusive geographic territory in which it alone was licensed to sell mattresses with the Sealy label; however, each licensee was free under the licensing agreement to manufacture and sell mattresses under non-Sealy private labels both within its assigned Sealy territory and anywhere else it chose. The licensing agreements also stipulated the minimum retail prices for the advertising and retail sale of Sealy-labeled mattresses. It provided, in addition, for Sealy, Inc. to police the enforcement of the price minimums.

The defendants first argued that the territorial allocations were merely vertical arrangements between Sealy, Inc. and the various licensees. The Court, however, "look[ing] at substance rather than form, found them to be horizontal restraints."[282] The Court reasoned that the licensees, as shareholders and directors of Sealy, Inc., were in charge of Sealy's operations, and because they were competitors the restraints were horizontal rather than vertical limitations imposed by a separate entity upon independent manufacturers. The Court held that territorial market divisions, in combination with price fixing by competitors in the interbrand market, constituted a *per se* violation. The Court did not clarify whether territorial allocations, standing alone without price-fixing, are similarly condemned; rather, it merely attached the *per se* label to the "aggregation of trade restraints," which, of course, included both market divisions and price-fixing.[283]

In *dictum*, the *Sealy* Court opined that territorial allocations in the intrabrand market may be subject to a rule of reason analysis. It gave as an example a small number of grocers using a common name and sharing advertising, combined with exclusive

---

278. 388 U.S. 350 (1967).
279. *Id.* at 357–58.
280. *Id.* at 351.
281. 388 U.S. 350 (1967).
282. *Id.* at 352.
283. *Id.* at 357 (citing *Timken Roller Bearing Co. v. United States*, 341 U.S. 593, 598 (1951)).

territorial allocations.[284] Five years later the Court reconsidered its hypothetical in *United States v. Topco Assoc., Inc.*[285]

In *Topco*, the Supreme Court finally clarified the ambiguous "aggregation of trade restraints" language of *Sealy* and *Timken*. Topco Associates was comprised of several dozen regional supermarket chains that operated as a purchasing agent for its members. Topco was organized by the regional chains in order to compete with national chains that marketed private-label grocery products. By taking advantage of their combined size and purchasing power, the regional members were able, through Topco, to advertise and purchase in volume their own private-label products. The Topco outlets had low market shares—1.5% to 16% with an average 6% market share—and, thus, it did not have substantial market power.

The alleged unlawful conduct in *Topco* consisted of territorial allocations, together with Topco members' effective veto power over the membership application of competitors. Each Topco member was licensed to sell the private-labeled Topco products only in a designated area. Members were prohibited from selling the products outside the assigned areas. Most licenses were exclusive; no member could sell Topco private label products in another member's assigned territory.

The *Topco* defendants argued that their association actually increased interbrand competition because it enabled its members to increase efficiency in competing with the larger national chains. The Court rejected this argument, however, holding that geographic market divisions among competitors, standing alone, are *per se* violations of § 1. Even though the Court unambiguously attached the *per se* label once it concluded that the territorial allocation was horizontal in nature,[286] Topco's market power discussion[287] indicates at least some limited rule of reason analysis, and it belies a pure *per se* conclusion.

In 1990, in *Palmer v. BRG of Georgia, Inc.*,[288] the Supreme Court declared a price fixing and horizontal market allocation agreement *per se* unlawful.[289] In *Palmer*, a former law student alleged that the price of his bar review course with BRG was raised due to an unlawful market allocation agreement entered into by the defendant and another provider, HBJ.[290] Palmer alleged that prior to 1980, both BRG and HBJ directly competed within Georgia for bar review business. In 1980, however, both parties "entered into an agreement that gave BRG an exclusive license to market HBJ's material in Georgia and to use its tradename 'Bar/Bri.'"[291] Pursuant to this agreement,

284. *Id.* at 357 n.4 (citing *N. Pac. R. Co. v. United States*, 356 U.S. 1, 6–7 (1958)).

285. 405 U.S. 596 (1972).

286. *Id.* at 608.

287. *Id.* at 600.

288. 498 U.S. 46 (1990).

289. *See also Blue Cross & Blue Shield of Wisc. v. Marshfield Clinic*, 65 F.3d 1406, 1415 (7th Cir. 1995) (holding that the defendant had engaged in market dividing by territory, a practice that violates § 1 of the Sherman Act).

290. 498 U.S. at 46–47.

291. *Id.* at 46.

both parties "agreed that HBJ would not compete with BRG in Georgia and that BRG would not compete with HBJ outside of Georgia."[292]

The Supreme Court found the agreement unlawful on its face, commenting that the "agreement was formed for the purpose and with the effect of raising the price of bar review courses"[293] and that "horizontal territorial limitations . . . are naked restraints of trade with no purpose except stifling competition." Both practices, said the Court, "are per se violations of the Sherman Act."[294] *Palmer* clarified that market allocations between competitors are *per se* unlawful even (1) in the absence of an agreement on price or evidence that one party has the right to be consulted about the other's prices, and (2) when the parties had not competed previously in the same market.[295]

[3] Externalities and the Free-Rider Defense

An externality is a cost (or a benefit) generated by a decisionmaker's actions that the decisionmaker does not pay (or receive). Rational decisionmakers may not take account of an externality when deciding which actions to take. The cost of the externality may be borne by society. For example, prior to government regulation of the environment, when an electrical utility generated power by fossil fuel rather than hydroelectric means, the decision may not have accounted for the detrimental downstream thermal effect of the power generating plant's condenser water discharge. Such detrimental effect is a negative externality. Externalities can also be positive, as when homeowners improve their front yard landscaping or paint the exterior of their homes. This may improve the neighborhood—including increasing the value of nearby homes. The original homeowner created value for neighbors, who did not have to contribute.

Expressed in economic terms, "[e]xternalities or spillovers are . . . examples of market failure that may justify government intervention. Externalities are effects on third parties that are not transmitted through the price system and that arise as an

292. *Id.* at 47.

293. *Id.* at 49.

294. This treatment of horizontal market divisions as *per se* violations of § 1 was affirmed by the Seventh Circuit in *Blackburn v. Sweeney*, 53 F.3d 825 (7th Cir. 1995). The issue in this case involved a partnership dissolution agreement which provided that half of the partners would have the exclusive right to advertise within a specific geographical area and half would advertise in a separate area. The Seventh Circuit reversed the district court, holding that the agreement constituted a *per se* illegal horizontal market division. Even though all parties to the agreement could still practice law throughout the state, the court still struck down the agreement, stating that "[t]o fit under the *per se* rule, an agreement need not foreclose all possible avenues of competition." *Id.* at 827.

The court also refused to apply the ancillary restraint doctrine. The agreement "was not necessary for the dissolution of the partnership and the resulting increase in competition." *Id.* at 828. Also, because of its "infinite duration," the agreement could not be characterized as an ancillary covenant not to compete. *Id.*

The court did deny the plaintiff treble damages and attorneys' fees, however, because the parties were deemed to be equally at fault for the materialization of the agreement.

295. E. Thomas Sullivan, Herbert Hovenkamp, Howard Shelanski & Christopher R. Leslie, *Antitrust Law, Policy and Procedure* ch. 2 (9th ed. 2024).

incidental by-product of another person's or firm's activity."[296] Externalities may cause market failure, or market imperfections, which "prevent the allocation of resources in accord with consumer valuations."[297]

A "free-rider" benefits from a positive externality. When an individual builds a levee that protects both his or her property as well as a neighbors' property, the neighbor gets a free-ride on the builder's expenditure. The neighbors of the homeowner whose home is freshly painted or lawn is recently fertilized similarly "ride free" because they made no expenditure, yet gained a benefit from the decision and expenditure of another. Indeed, the benefit may be economic, for when the free-rider sells his or her home, its value may be increased by the enhanced attraction of the neighborhood.

An understanding of externalities and free-riders is important to application of the antitrust laws. A form of government regulation or intervention that may be justified by an externality, market failure, or free-rider is enforcement of the antitrust laws. Parties may have a legitimate interest in eliminating free riders. If the manufacturer of a new product wishes to induce a retailer to advertise and promote the manufacturer's product, the manufacturer must create an incentive for the retailer to do so. If, however, the retailer knows that if it makes advertising and promotion expenditures that its competitors do not make, then its cost of doing business will be higher than those of its competitors. Competitors will be free-riders because they will be able to take advantage of the greater consumer awareness of the new product as a result of the retailer's advertising and promotional expenditures. Thus, the manufacturer and retailer may agree on contractual restrictions to prevent or control this free-rider problem.

The manufacturer may, for example, agree that the retailer will have an exclusive right to sell the manufacturer's product within a designated geographic area. This is known as an output contract which binds the manufacturer. In return, the retailer may agree to sell only the manufacturer's product and no other competing products. This is a requirements contract which binds the retailer. Ultimately one of the parties may attempt to void the contractual restriction on the grounds that it is anticompetitive and violative of the antitrust laws. The legal question then becomes whether avoidance of free-riders is sufficient grounds for upholding the restraint even though it is facially anticompetitive.

The manufacturer-retailer hypothetical is an example of the free-rider defense in the context of a vertical constraint. The free-rider defense also has applicability to horizontal market divisions as the next cases illustrate.[298]

---

296. Steven E. Rhoads, *The Economist's View of the World, Government, Markets, & Public Policy* 67 (1985).

297. *Id.* at 66.

298. In *SCFC ILC, Inc. v. Visa USA, Inc.*, 36 F.3d 958 (10th Cir. 1994), the Tenth Circuit reversed an antitrust violation against Visa USA for denying plaintiff Sears Company membership in its credit card issuer association. Besides finding that no violation could exist because there was no anticompetitive effect on the relevant market and Visa USA did not have market power, the court also accepted Visa USA's argument that the exclusion was based on free-rider concerns. As Sears and Visa USA were

Polk Bros., Inc. v. Forest City Enters., Inc.[299] illustrates the free-rider defense in a horizontal market division case. The plaintiff, Polk Bros., was in the retail appliance and home furnishing business. The defendant, Forest City Enterprises, sold building materials, lumber, tools, and other related products. Because of the complementary nature of their products, the two firms decided to occupy a common building with their respective sales areas divided by a partition. Pursuant to an agreement between them, Polk Brothers built the common building and leased space to Forest City, with an option to buy. In order to maximize the benefits of their joint undertaking and to prevent competition between themselves, the agreement also contained a restrictive covenant that identified specific product lines that each party agreed not to sell in the new building. When Forest City subsequently exercised its option to buy, the restrictive provisions of the lease became covenants running with the land for fifty years.

About seven years after the two stores opened for business, Forest City decided to sell products that were covered by the restrictive covenant. Polk Bros. sought an injunction to enforce the restrictive covenant and to prevent Forest City from selling the prohibited products.[300]

The restraint in *Polk Bros.* contained two kinds of horizontal market divisions. First, the agreement restricted sales of designated products, and was thus a product division. Second, because the agreement limited what each party could sell from a specified location, it also served as a geographic division. Forest City argued that the market division was unenforceable as a *per se* restraint of trade in violation of § 1.

In rejecting Forest City's argument, the Seventh Circuit held that a horizontal agreement not to compete is *per se* unlawful only if it is a "naked" restraint, but if ancillary to an otherwise lawful purpose it is subject to a rule of reason analysis. The court relied on the *Addyston Pipe*[301] ancillary restraint doctrine in distinguishing between naked and ancillary restraints. Reasoning that the restrictive covenant

---

viable competitors in the brand and operating systems market for credit cards, Visa USA sought to avoid the extra costs of taking Sears under its wing and producing for it a new credit card, when Sears had done nothing to contribute to Visa USA and had spent a considerable amount of time competing against it. *Id.* at 970. Visa USA contended, and the Tenth Circuit agreed, that Sears was trying to get a free ride off Visa USA's success as a credit card company when "it [did] not need Visa USA to compete in the relevant market and [could not] demonstrate it [could] only issue a low-cost card with Visa USA's help." *Id.* at 970–71. *See also Alvord-Polk, Inc. v. F. Schumacher Co.*, 37 F.3d 996, 1012 (3d Cir. 1994) (rejecting a summary judgment motion to a horizontal restraint claim based on a free rider defense because it was a possible pretext for the defendant's true motives behind its alleged trade restraining actions).

299. 776 F.2d 185 (7th Cir. 1985).

300. Polk Bros. filed suit for injunctive relief in state court. "Forest City removed the action to the district court under 28 U.S.C. § 1441, where it could have been filed initially under the diversity jurisdiction." *Id.* at 188. Under the *Erie* doctrine, the federal court analyzed the case under the antitrust law of Illinois. Illinois antitrust law, however, "refers courts to federal antitrust law as a guide to questions of interpretation." *Id.* Thus the *Polk* Court held that "[i]n order to find out what Illinois law forbids, we inquire into what federal antitrust law forbids." *Id.*

301. *United States v. Addyston Pipe & Steel Co.*, 85 F. 271, 280–83 (6th Cir. 1898), *aff'd*, 175 U.S. 211 (1899); *see also supra*, § 4.05 (discussing the ancillary restraint doctrine).

facilitated "productive cooperation" between *Polk Bros.* and *Forest City,* the court found that the restraint was ancillary and subject to rule of reason analysis.[302]

The court's rule of reason analysis recognized the free-rider defense as "a legitimate objective of a system of distribution."[303] When it entered into the contract, Polk Bros. was legitimately concerned that it might spend substantial sums advertising appliances to attract customers into its store only to have them lured away by Forest City. As long as Forest City did not advertise and promote appliances to the same extent as did Polk Bros., its costs would be less and, hence, its prices might be lower. The restrictive covenant reflected Polk Bros.' legitimate attempt to eliminate the possibility that Forest City would become a free-rider.

Reasoning that but for the restrictive covenant Polk Bros. would have neither constructed the new building nor permitted Forest City to become its lessee, the court found that "the cooperation increased the amount of retail space available and was at least potentially beneficial to consumers; the restrictive covenant made the cooperation possible."[304] Because Forest City's arguments were directed toward a *per se* condemnation of the restrictive covenant, it had not presented evidence of substantial market power. Due to the lack of market power evidence, and the reasoning that an assessment of market power is the first step of any rule of reason analysis, the court concluded that Forest City could "prevail under the *per se* rule or not at all. 'Not at all' it must be."[305]

Other circuits agree. The District of Columbia Circuit has held that the several Supreme Court cases seem to effectively overrule *Topco* and *Sealy,* at least if those cases stand for the proposition that horizontal restraints are illegal *per se.* Judge Bork, writing for the court, reasoned that horizontal restraints that reduce free-rider problems and promote efficiency are legal, absent market power. The issue was addressed in *Rothery Storage & Van Co. v. Atlas Van Lines, Inc.*[306] in which a van line company adopted, as a result of deregulation, a policy of terminating independent, local agents who competed against the national van line, Atlas, or who dealt with another national carrier while using the Atlas name. The Supreme Court denied without dissent the petition for certiorari.

The question arises whether *Polk Bros.* and *Rothery* are reconcilable with *Topco* or whether they are mere examples of judicial activism by lower federal court judges. None of the defendants in *Topco, Polk Bros.* or *Rothery* had substantial market power, yet *Topco* held that territorial market divisions among competitors are *per se* violations of § 1, while *Polk Bros.* and *Rothery* applied a rule of reason analysis.

---

302. 776 F.2d at 190. Polk Bros. "would not have entered into this arrangement . . . unless it had received assurances that [Forest City] would not compete with it in the sale of products that are the 'foundation of [Polk's] business.' . . . The agreement not to compete was an integral part of the lease and land sale." *Id.* (quoting the district court opinion).

303. 776 F.2d at 190 (citing *Monsanto Co. v. Spray-Rite Serv. Corp.*, 465 U.S. 752, 760–61 (1984)).

304. *Id.*

305. *Id.* at 191.

306. 792 F.2d 210 (D.C. Cir. 1986).

The cornerstone of the Seventh Circuit's analysis in *Polk Bros.* is the ancillary restraint doctrine of *Addyston Pipe.* Judge Easterbrook opined in *Polk Bros.* that

> The reason for distinguishing between "ancillary" and "naked" restraints is to determine whether the agreement is part of a cooperative venture with prospects for increasing output. If it is, it should not be condemned *per se*. . . . The benefits of cooperation may be greatest when launching a new venture.[307]

Because the arrangement to build and lease the new building would not have been consummated without a contractually guaranteed resolution of the potential free-rider problem, the *Polk Bros.* restriction was not a naked restraint. Similarly, in *Topco* it could be argued that the restraint was ancillary to the otherwise lawful purpose of increasing defendants' ability to compete with major supermarket chains in the private label market. Arguably both restraints inured to the benefit of consumers. But the Supreme Court's discussion in *Palmer* suggests a return to the more rigid *per se* approach for market division agreements, even in the absence of a price agreement and even when the parties have not previously competed in the market.

§ 4.14 Reverse Payment Patent Settlements

Reverse payment settlements, also known as "pay for delay" settlements or exclusion payments, are agreements between patent holders and would-be competitors where the patent holder pays to prevent the competitor from entering the market and/or challenging a patent's validity.[308] Unlike typical patent payments that flow from competitors to patent holder for the right to enter a market, reverse payment settlements are so named because money is paid in the opposite direction. Reverse payment settlements are particularly common in the pharmaceutical industry where drug developers use them both to recoup their high drug development and patenting costs and also to extend their exclusive rights by paying would-be competitors to not enter the market.

The Hatch-Waxman Act[309] streamlined the introduction of "bioequivalent" generic drugs. Rather than undergoing the same testing as the pioneer, the Act allows generic

---

307. 776 F.2d at 190. *But see Gen. Leaseways v. Nat'l Truck Leasing Ass'n*, 744 F.2d 588 (7th Cir. 1984) (applying *Topco* after finding that market division was not efficient).

308. Herbert Hovenkamp, *Anticompetitive Patent Settlements and the Supreme Court's Actavis Decision*, 15 Minn. J. L. Sci. & Tech. 3 (2014). Reverse payments can be viewed as horizontal restraints under § 1 of the Sherman Act or as attempts to monopolize under § 2. Section 2 analysis is found in Chapter 6.

309. Drug Price Competition and Patent Term Restoration (Hatch-Waxman) Act of 1984, Pub. L. No. 98-417, 98 Stat. 1585 (codified as amended in sections of 15, 21, 28, and 35 U.S.C.).

manufacturers to gain Food and Drug Administration (FDA) approval by showing bioequivalence.[310] The generic may file an Abbreviated New Drug Application (ANDA) as the pioneer drug nears the end of its patent exclusivity or if it believes the patent is invalid, to which the pioneer may respond with a patent infringement lawsuit. Filing this lawsuit stays FDA approval of the generic for up to thirty months. Once the generic attains a right to produce, however, it has a 180-day exclusivity period, where it functions as a duopoly alongside the pioneer. "Pay for delay" emerges when the pioneers settle the infringement lawsuit, rather than risk the patent being declared invalid. As commentators have noted, "the more questionable the patent—and thus the greater the likelihood that consumer benefits will be lost—the more the pioneer will be willing to pay to save it from challenge."[311] Moreover, "if the value of the patent were zero, because it is clearly invalid, but the courts were not able to examine it, then the profit-maximizing solution for the pioneer and the first generic would still be a pay-for-delay settlement."[312] Because plaintiff's and defendant's interests align in favor of maintaining exclusivity, such payments can work to the detriment of consumers, as they often result in less competition and higher prices.[313]

Because the settlement functions as an agreement between would-be competitors to avoid competition, it seemingly fits within the realm of a horizontal restraint. But what standard is applicable when assessing such a settlement? Nonetheless, the circuit courts split on the applicability of antitrust law to reverse payment schemes.

The Federal, Second, and Eleventh Circuits developed and utilized what came to be known as the "scope-of-the-patent" test, where courts would ask "whether the agreements restrict competition beyond the exclusionary zone of the patent."[314] So long as the settlement covered only the realm of the patent it was considered lawful.[315] The Third Circuit took a different approach, holding such agreements as "prima facie evidence of an unreasonable restraint of trade, which could be rebutted by showing that the payment (1) was for a purpose other than delayed entry or (2) offers some procompetitive benefit".[316]

310. Herbert Hovenkamp, *Anticompetitive Patent Settlements and the Supreme Court's Actavis Decision*, 15 Minn. J. L. Sci. & Tech. 3, 6 (2014).

311. *Id.* at 12.

312. *Id.*

313. *Id.* at 17–18.

314. *In re Ciprofloxacin Hydrochloride Antitrust Litig.*, 544 F.3d 1323, 1337 (Fed. Cir. 2008), abrogated by, *F.T.C. v. Actavis, Inc.*, 570 U.S. 136 (2013).

315. *Id.* "A settlement is not unlawful if it serves to protect that to which the patent holder is legally entitled—a monopoly over the manufacture and distribution of the patented invention." (quoting *In re Tamoxifen*, 466 F.3d 187, 208–09 (2d Cir. 2006)).

316. *In re K-Dur Antitrust Litig.*, 686 F.3d 197, 218 (3d Cir. 2012), *cert. granted, judgment vacated sub nom. Merck & Co. v. Louisiana Wholesale Drug Co.*, 570 U.S. 913 (2013), and *cert. granted, judgment vacated sub nom. Upsher-Smith Lab'ys, Inc. v. Louisiana Wholesale Drug Co.*, 570 U.S. 913 (2013), and *reinstatement granted*, No. 10-2077, 2013 WL 5180857 (3d Cir. Sept. 9, 2013), and *abrogated by F.T.C. v. Actavis, Inc.*, 570 U.S. 136 (2013).

The Supreme Court landed somewhere in the middle in *F.T.C. v. Actavis, Inc.*,[317] where it resolved the circuit split, rejecting the "scope-of-the-patent" test and holding that reverse payment settlement agreements even within the exclusionary zone of a patent were capable of violating antitrust law. In *Actavis*, patent-holder Solvay Pharmaceuticals paid multimillion dollar settlements to Actavis and two other generic producers in exchange for the generics remaining off the market. The FTC sued the settling parties for allegedly violating Section 5 of the FTC Act by unlawfully agreeing to share Solvay's monopoly profits. After the Eleventh Circuit ruled that, barring fraud or sham litigation, reverse payment settlements were immune from antitrust attack under the "scope-of-the-patent" test, the Supreme Court agreed to hear the issue. Justice Breyer rejected the Eleventh Circuit's holding. He reasoned that "it would be incongruous to determine antitrust legality by measuring the settlement's anticompetitive effects solely against patent law policy, rather than by measuring them against procompetitive antitrust policies as well."[318] Unlike the Third Circuit, however, the Court did not accept presumptive illegality of such agreements and advised lower court to employ rule of reason rather than a "quick look" analysis.[319] The dissent in *Actavis* favored adherence to the "scope-of-the-patent" test to determine whether the settlement provides monopoly power beyond what the patent already provided.[320] In dissent, Chief Justice Roberts joined by Justices Scalia and Thomas criticized the Court's new approach for not being grounded in any statute and potentially discouraging the settlement of patent litigation.[321]

Because the patentholder in *Actavis* paid cash in its reverse settlements, some district courts limited *Actavis* to exclusion payments made in cash.[322] Such opinions have largely been reversed because although "*Actavis* does contain references to money[,] . . . the key word used throughout the opinion is 'payment,' which connotes a much broader category of consideration than cash alone."[323] Drug patentees may describe their exclusion payments to generic pharmaceutical firms as legitimate fees for licenses or marketing services, but large pharma firms do not pay smaller generic drug firms for promotional services outside of the reverse-settlement context,[324] which makes these payments suspicious from an antitrust standpoint.[325]

---

317. 570 U.S. 136 (2013).

318. *Id.* at 148.

319. *Id.* at 158–59.

320. *F.T.C. v. Actavis, Inc.*, 570 U.S. 136, 162 (2013) (Roberts, C.J., dissenting).

321. *Id.*

322. *See, e.g.*, *In re Loestrin 24 Fe Antitrust Litig.*, 45 F. Supp. 3d 180 (D.R.I. 2014), *vacated and remanded by* 814 F.3d 538 (1st Cir. 2016).

323. *In re Loestrin 24 Fe Antitrust Litig.*, 814 F.3d 538, 550 (1st Cir. 2016). *See also King Drug v. Smithkline*, 791 F.3d 388 (3d Cir. 2015) (explaining why *Actavis* is not limited to cash payments).

324. Michael A. Carrier, *Payment After Actavis*, 81 Iowa L. Rev. 7 (2014).

325. For more on reverse settlement payments, see Herbert Hovenkamp, Mark D. Janis, Mark A. Lemley, Christopher R. Leslie & Michael A Carrier, *Antitrust and IP: An Analysis of Antitrust Principles Applied to Intellectual Property Law* § 15.3 (3d ed. 2016).

§ 4.15 The Agreement Element

Section 1 of the Sherman Act makes unlawful "[e]very contract, combination . . . or conspiracy in restraint of trade."[326] Courts do not distinguish between "contract," "combination," and "conspiracy."[327] Courts generally refer to them collectively as "agreement" or "concerted action."[328] This is the threshold element of a § 1 claim. Absent an agreement between two or more separate entities, there can be no violation of § 1.

[A] Proof of an Agreement

[1] Direct Evidence of Agreement

Examples of direct evidence include admissions by price-fixing defendants, recordings of price-fixing negotiations or agreements being made, or eyewitness testimony of someone who observed price-fixing activities.[329] Direct evidence of price collusion rarely exists because conspirators undertake significant measures to conceal their price-fixing activities.[330] For example, conspirators conspire using pay phones and untraceable burner phones.[331] Face-to-face negotiations occur in secret meetings or under cover of trade association meetings, some of which are convened explicitly to hold clandestine cartel summits. Price fixers destroy incriminating documents and forge exculpatory documents.

[2] Circumstantial Evidence

Because price fixers destroy direct evidence of their illegal agreements, plaintiffs generally make their price-fixing cases through circumstantial evidence.[332] Federal courts have recognized that "'circumstantial evidence is the lifeblood of antitrust law'

---

326. 15 U.S.C. § 1 (2012). Section 3 of the Clayton Act makes unlawful leases, sales, or contracts "on the condition, agreement, or understanding that the lessee or purchaser thereof shall not use or deal in the goods . . . of . . . competitors of the lessor or seller." 15 U.S.C. § 14 (2012).

327. *Bogosian v. Gulf Oil Corp.*, 561 F.2d 434, 445 (3d Cir. 1977).

328. This "meeting of the minds" requirement does not have to arise out of a fully voluntary relationship. *See MCM Partners, Inc. v. Andrews-Bartlett & Assocs., Inc.*, 62 F.3d 967, 973, 975 (7th Cir. 1995) ("[A]cquiescence in an illegal scheme is as much a violation of the Sherman Act as the creation and promotion of one. . . . So long as defendants knew that they were acquiescing in conduct that was in all likelihood unlawful . . . they thereby joined a combination or conspiracy. . . ." (quoting *United States v. Paramount Pictures, Inc.*, 334 U.S. 131 (1948)).

329. Christopher R. Leslie, *The Decline and Fall of Circumstantial Evidence in Antitrust Law*, 69 Am. U. L. Rev. 1713, 1721–22 (2020).

330. Christopher R. Leslie, *How to Hide a Price-Fixing Conspiracy*, 2021 U. Ill. L. Rev. 1199 (2021).

331. *In re Urethane Antitrust Litig.*, 913 F. Supp. 2d 1145, 1155–56 (D. Kan. 2012) (conspirator used "pay phone at a gas station using a prepaid credit card").

332. *In re Se. Milk Antitrust Litig.*, 801 F. Supp. 2d 705, 714 (E.D. Tenn. 2011) ("In conspiracy cases, '[t]he element of agreement, . . . is nearly always established by circumstantial evidence, as

because direct evidence will rarely be available to prove the existence of a price-fixing conspiracy."[333]

[a] Early Cases

In *Interstate Circuit v. United States*,[334] the Supreme Court faced the question whether a trial court finding of an inference of an agreement could be upheld. The standard of review dictates that the trial court cannot be reversed unless the finding of fact is clearly erroneous.

Interstate Circuit was a movie exhibitor with a complete monopoly of first run theatres and a significant share of the subsequent-run theatre market in several cities. Interstate, together with Consolidated Theatres, Inc., another defendant that was affiliated with Interstate, contributed over 74% of the license fees paid in their areas to certain motion picture distributors, who represented a second group of defendants. The distributor defendants had approximately 75% market share of all first-class feature films exhibited domestically.

The Government alleged that the distributor defendants had violated § 1 of the Sherman Act by combining to control theatre admission prices and exhibition of double-features. The evidence demonstrated that Interstate sent a letter to the distributors naming their representatives and asking them to agree to impose controls over admission prices and double-features as a condition of Interstate's continued patronage of the distributors' films. There was no direct testimony that the distributors agreed with each other to comply with Interstate's demand; however, each distributor did subsequently agree with at least some of Interstate's requested conditions. Thus the government was "compelled to rely on inferences drawn from the course of conduct of the alleged conspirators" in order to prove the requisite § 1 agreement.[335]

The Supreme Court upheld the trial court's inference of an agreement. The Court identified several facts[336] from which such an inference properly could be made.[337]

* Defendants' actions were a *radical departure* from prior practice.

* Defendants were *aware* that their co-defendants had been solicited to conduct themselves similarly.

* Defendants had been *invited* to engage in the alleged conspiracy when it was solicited.

---

conspirators seldom make records of their illegal agreements.' *United States v. Short*, 671 F.2d 178, 182 (6th Cir.1982).").

333. *City of Rockford v. Mallinckrodt ARD, Inc.*, 360 F. Supp. 3d 730, 749 (N.D. Ill. 2019) (quoting *United States v. Falstaff Brewing Corp.*, 410 U.S. 526, 534 n.13 (1973)).

334. 306 U.S. 208 (1939).

335. *Id.* at 221.

336. Subsequent courts would later treat these facts as "plus factors," but that nomenclature did not exist when the Supreme Court issued its opinion in *Interstate Circuit*.

337. *Id.* at 222–23.

* Defendants *actually participated* in the scheme and engaged in substantial *unanimity of action*, or uniform conduct.

* Defendants failed to offer any testimony explaining how they allegedly made their decisions independently.

Interstate Circuit shows that although mere evidence of parallel conduct by competitors is not enough for an antitrust plaintiff to obtain a directed verdict, an agreement is properly inferred from circumstantial evidence.[338] *Interstate Circuit* also held that the plaintiff's showing may be rebutted by defendants' evidence: "When the proof supported . . . the inference of such concert[ed] [action], the burden rested on [defendants] of going forward with the evidence to explain away or contradict it."[339]

Defendants in *Interstate Circuit* failed to carry this burden when they called as witnesses only lower-level local managers, with questionable authority to act, to testify that they had acted independently. Defendants did not "call as witnesses those officers who did have authority to act for [them] and who were in a position to know whether they had acted in pursuance of agreement."[340] From this absence, the Court inferred that testimony of such officers would have been adverse to the defendants, noting that "[t]he production of weak evidence when strong is available can only lead to the conclusion that the strong would have been adverse."[341] *Interstate Circuit* shows that when the burden shifts to the defendant to rebut an inference of collusion, a threshold requirement is the use of the defendant's strongest available evidence.

In *Am. Tobacco Co. v. United States,*[342] the Court stated that "[w]here the circumstances are such as to warrant a jury in finding that the conspirators had a unity of purpose or a common design and understanding, or a meeting of minds in an unlawful arrangement, the conclusion that a conspiracy is established is justified." The Court held that a conspiracy could be inferred from the facts that the defendants at times controlled 90% of the cigarette production, maintained identical list prices and discounts, raised prices in unison even when costs were decreasing, and offered no economic justification for their price hikes.

In *Theatre Enters., Inc. v. Paramount Film Distributing Corp.*,[343] the Supreme Court considered parallel conduct in a different procedural context than it did in *Interstate Circuit*.[344] In a treble damage civil action tried before a jury, the trial judge denied the

338. 306 U.S. at 225–27.

339. 306 U.S. at 225–26.

340. *Id.* at 226.

341. *Id.*

342. 328 U.S. 781, 810 (1946).

343. 346 U.S. 537 (1954).

344. In *Interstate Circuit*, the Supreme Court reviewed the factual finding of the trial court that defendants' agreement could be inferred from their conduct. The applicable standard of review was that the lower court's finding was not reversible unless clearly erroneous. In *Theatre Enterprises*, the jury returned a general verdict for defendants. The Supreme Court reviewed the lower court's denial of plaintiff's motion for a directed verdict. The applicable standard of review of denial of plaintiff's motion was that a directed verdict should issue only if the evidence "raised [no] fact issues requiring the trial judge to submit the issue of conspiracy to the jury." *Id.* at 542.

plaintiff's motion for directed verdict after the jury ruled for the defendants. In affirming, Justice Clark reiterated that "this Court has never held that proof of parallel business behavior conclusively establishes agreement or . . . that such behavior itself" is sufficient to warrant a directed verdict for a plaintiff in a civil antitrust suit.[345] In contrast to the defendants in *Interstate Circuit*, the defendants in *Theatre Enterprises* presented plausible profit-maximizing business justifications why each defendant would independently make their decisions. Additionally, the plaintiff failed to show that all the defendants knew of their co-defendants' conduct, thus negating knowledge. Furthermore, defendants introduced testimony of their responsible corporate officers as strong evidence to rebut the inference of an agreement. The Court affirmed the jury verdict in favor of defendants because their actions made sense as independent decisions arrived at without collusion.

[b] The Modern Approach: Conscious Parallelism and Plus Factors

In general, the process of proving collusion through circumstantial evidence involves a two-step process.[346] First, the plaintiff shows the defendants raised their prices in parallel (or engaged in other parallel conduct), which is called "conscious parallelism." Conscious parallelism alone is insufficient to prove collusion[347] because prices can move concurrently in a competitive market,[348] as when input costs increase or decrease.

Second, antitrust plaintiffs present evidence of plus factors, which suggest that the defendants' parallel conduct is the result of collusion, not independent decision-making.[349] The presence of plus factors, "when viewed in conjunction with the parallel acts, can serve to allow a fact-finder to infer a conspiracy."[350]

Courts are supposed to view the plaintiff's proffered plus factors collectively, not one at a time in isolation.[351] Courts must examine circumstantial evidence of price fixing holistically because, "while each of these factors taken in isolation does not necessarily provide a basis alone for inferring an agreement or conspiracy, in combination, these factors, taken together and 'on the ground,' may support a reasonable inference that an agreement or conspiracy existed."[352] One court explained, "[p]ieces of a puzzle viewed separately form unintelligible, irregular shapes, but considered

345. *Id.* at 541.

346. *In re Flat Glass Antitrust Litig.*, 385 F.3d 350, 378 n. 11 (3d Cir. 2004).

347. *In re Chocolate Confectionary Antitrust Litig.*, 801 F.3d 383, 398 (3d Cir. 2015).

348. *In re Graphics Processing Units Antitrust Litig.*, 527 F. Supp. 2d 1011, 1022 (N.D. Cal. 2007).

349. *In re Musical Instruments & Equip. Antitrust Litig.*, 798 F.3d 1186, 1194 (9th Cir. 2015) (describing plus factors as evidence of "economic actions and outcomes that are largely inconsistent with unilateral conduct but largely consistent with explicitly coordinated action").

350. *Apex Oil Co. v. DiMauro*, 822 F.2d 246, 253–54 (2d Cir. 1987).

351. *Continental Ore Co. v. Union Carbide & Carbon Corp.*, 370 U.S. 690, 699 (1962); *Erie County, Ohio v. Morton Salt, Inc.*, 702 F.3d 860, 870 (6th Cir. 2012); *Jung, M.D. v. Ass'n Am. Med. Colleges*, 300 F. Supp. 2d 119, 155-56 (D.D.C. 2004).

352. *In re Medical X-Ray Film Antitrust Litigation*, 946 F. Supp. 209, 218 (E.D.N.Y.1996).

together reveal a discernible image."[353] Plaintiffs endeavor to present a bundle of plus factors that, viewed holistically, would allow a reasonable jury to infer collusion.

Different plus factors have probative value for different reasons.[354] Some plus factors address whether the defendants' market is more susceptible to cartelization. For example, concentrated markets with few firms are more predisposed to price fixing because a smaller group of competitors is positioned to solve the coordination and trust problems that price-fixing cartels must overcome.[355] Markets with high barriers to entry and products with inelastic demand are plus factors because these characteristics allow price fixers to raise price without losing sales.[356] Additionally, courts treat product homogeneity as a plus factor because it is easier to fix prices when the defendants sell identical products.[357]

Another set of plus factors relates to cartel formation, such as whether one defendant invited the others to collude,[358] whether the defendants had a motive and an opportunity to conspire,[359] such as whether there were numerous inter-competitor communications.[360]

Some plus factors relate to cartel management. Price-fixing conspiracies need to adjust prices in response to changes in consumer demand or foreign exchange rates or other unanticipated circumstances.[361] Thus, many cartels have ongoing communications that can be plus factors. For example, competitors exchanging price information is a plus factor.[362] Because price fixers sometimes exchange their pricing documents, a defendant's possession of its rival's confidential pricing plans is a plus factor.[363]

---

353. *Six West Retail Acquisition, Inc. v. Sony Theatre Management Corp.*, 2000-1 Trade Cas. (CCH) ¶ 72823, 2000 WL 264295 (S.D. N.Y. 2000).

354. Christopher R. Leslie, *The Probative Synergy of Plus Factors in Price-Fixing Litigation*, 115 Nw. U. L. Rev. 1581 (2021).

355. Christopher R. Leslie, *Trust, Distrust, and Antitrust*, 82 Tex. L. Rev. 515, 564–65 (2004).

356. *In re Blood Reagents Antitrust Litig.*, 266 F. Supp. 3d 750, 772 (E.D. Pa. 2017); *Stanislaus Food Prod. Co. v. USS-POSCO Indus.*, 782 F. Supp. 2d 1059, 1076–77 (E.D. Cal. 2011); *In re High Fructose Corn Syrup Antitrust Litig.*, 295 F.3d 651, 657 (7th Cir. 2002).

357. *See, e.g.*, *In re High Fructose Corn Syrup Antitrust Litig.*, 295 F.3d at 656; *In re Titanium Dioxide Antitrust Litig.*, 959 F. Supp. 2d 799, 822 (D. Md. 2013).

358. *See In re Delta/Airtran Baggage Fee Antitrust Litig.*, 245 F. Supp. 3d 1343, 1372 (N.D. Ga. 2017), *aff'd sub nom. Siegel v. Delta Air Lines, Inc.*, 714 F. App'x 986 (11th Cir. 2018).

359. *Burtch v. Milberg Factors, Inc.*, 662 F.3d 212, 227 (3d Cir. 2011); *Mitchael v. Intracorp, Inc.*, 179 F.3d 847, 858–59 (10th Cir.1999); *Re/Max Intern., Inc. v. Realty One, Inc.*, 173 F.3d 995, 1009 (6th Cir.1999); *In re Disposable Contact Lens Antitrust*, 215 F. Supp. 3d 1272, 1297 (M.D. Fla. 2016).

360. *Blomkest Fertilizer, Inc. v. Potash Corp. of Saskatchewan*, 203 F.3d 1028, 1033 (8th Cir. 2000); *In re Polyurethane Foam Antitrust Litig.*, 152 F. Supp. 3d 968, 983 (N.D. Ohio 2015).

361. Herbert Hovenkamp & Christopher R. Leslie, *The Firm as Cartel Manager*, 64 Vand. L. Rev. 813, 833 (2011).

362. *In re Coordinated Pretrial Proceedings in Petroleum Products Antitrust Litig.*, 906 F.2d 432, 452 (9th Cir. 1990); *U.S. v. Apple Inc.*, 952 F. Supp. 2d 638, 690 (S.D.N.Y. 2013).

363. *See, e.g.*, *In re Flat Glass Antitrust Litig.*, 385 F.3d 350, 368 (3d Cir. 2004); *Kleen Prod. LLC v. Georgia-Pac. LLC*, 910 F.3d 927, 936 (7th Cir. 2018); *Gelboim v. Bank of Am. Corp.*, 823 F.3d 759, 782 (2d Cir. 2016); *In re Bulk Popcorn Antitrust Litig.*, 783 F. Supp. 1194, 1196 (D. Minn. 1991).

Similarly, courts recognize price signaling as a plus factor.[364] Other plus factors include cartel enforcement mechanisms to detect and penalize cheating on the price-fixing agreement,[365] such as employing third-party auditors, using price-verification schemes,[366] and making intercompetitor sales that stabilize the defendants' relative market shares.[367]

Another major plus factor is that the defendants took actions that would be against their independent economic interests absent a conspiracy.[368] The Sixth Circuit has held that "[a] showing that the defendants' actions, taken independently, would be contrary to their economic self-interest will ordinarily 'tend to exclude the likelihood of independent conduct.'"[369]

Other plus factors include a high number of parallel price increases,[370] parallel price increases when defendants' costs are declining,[371] "a radical departure from the previous business practices of the industry,"[372] stable market shares,[373] and the defendants' price-fixing activities in foreign markets.[374] This list is not comprehensive; no exhaustive list exists because courts continue to recognize new plus factors through the common law process.

[3] Procedural Matters

In order to reach a jury, plaintiffs bringing price-fixing claims must survive the defendants' motions for dismissal and motions for summary judgment.

[a] Motion to Dismiss

In *Bell Atlantic Corp. v. Twombly*,[375] the Supreme Court discussed what antitrust plaintiffs bringing a § 1 claim must plead to survive a motion to dismiss. The Court noted that "conscious parallelism ... is not in itself unlawful."[376] Though parallel

---

364. *In re Coordinated Pretrial Proceedings in Petroleum Products Antitrust Litig.*, 906 F.2d 432, 446–47 (9th Cir. 1990); *In re Titanium Dioxide Antitrust Litig.*, 959 F. Supp. 2d 799, 828 (D. Md. 2013).

365. *In re Urethane Antitrust Litig.*, 768 F.3d 1245, 1265 (10th Cir. 2014).

366. *Penne v. Greater Minneapolis Area Board of Realtors*, 604 F.2d 1143, 1148–49 (8th Cir.1979).

367. *See, e.g.*, *In re* Ethylene Propylene Diene Monomer (EPDM) Antitrust Litig., 681 F. Supp. 2d 141, 168 (D. Conn. 2009); *In re Linerboard Antitrust Litig.*, 296 F. Supp. 2d 568, 579 (E.D. Pa. 2003); *In re High Fructose Corn Syrup Antitrust Litig.*, 261 F. Supp. 2d 1017 (C.D. Ill. 2003). Christopher R. Leslie, *Balancing the Conspiracy's Books: Inter-Competitor Sales and Price-Fixing Cartels*, 96 Wash. U.L. Rev. 1 (2018).

368. *Blomkest Fertilizer, Inc. v. Potash Corp. of Saskatchewan*, 203 F.3d 1028, 1037 (8th Cir. 2000).

369. *National Hockey League Players Ass'n v. Plymouth Whalers Hockey Club*, 419 F.3d 462, 475 (6th Cir. 2005).

370. *In re Titanium Dioxide Antitrust Litig.*, 959 F. Supp. 2d 799, 825 (D. Md. 2013).

371. *In re Text Messaging Antitrust Litig.*, 630 F.3d 622, 628 (7th Cir. 2010); *Starr v. Sony BMG Music Entm't*, 592 F.3d 314, 323 (2d Cir. 2010).

372. *Interstate Circuit v. United States*, 306 U.S. 208, 222 (1939).

373. *In re Text Messaging Antitrust Litig.*, 782 F.3d 867, 876 (7th Cir. 2015).

374. Christopher R. Leslie, *Foreign Price-Fixing Conspiracies*, 67 Duke L.J. 557, 591–96 (2017).

375. 550 U.S. 544 1964 (2007).

376. *Id.* at 553–54 (internal quotation marks omitted) (quoting *Brooke Group Ltd. v. Brown & Williamson Tobacco Corp.*, 509 U.S. 209, 227 (1993)).

behavior "is admissible circumstantial evidence," it does not establish conclusively an agreement nor does it alone constitute a violation of the Sherman Act.[377] The Court also noted that in pleading parallel conduct, the plaintiff must place the conduct "in a context that raises a suggestion of a preceding agreement" rather that just alleging "conduct that could just as well be independent action." The Court wrote:

> An allegation of parallel conduct is much like a naked assertion of conspiracy in a § 1 complaint: it gets the complaint close to stating a claim, but without some further factual enhancement it stops short of the line between possibility and plausibility of "entitle[ment] to relief."[378]

The Supreme Court made it clear in *Ashcroft v. Iqbal*,[379] that the pleading standard outlined in *Twombly* applies to all civil litigation, not just antitrust cases. In order to survive a 12(b)(6) motion for dismissal, a plaintiff must plead sufficient facts to show a plausible violation rather than simply a possible one.[380] The earlier standard, overturned by *Twombly* and *Iqbal*, called for the pleading to show only the "sheer possibility that a defendant has acted unlawfully."[381] The new standard requires a plaintiff's pleading reach the level of plausibility, a higher bar than a mere possibility. Nonetheless, the Court in *Iqbal* noted that this does not require the pleading to reach the level of probability.[382]

Debate continues in the lower courts as to where precisely the lines on the continuum fall between possible, plausible, and probable. A divided Sixth Circuit, in *Tam Travel, Inc. v. Delta Airlines, Inc.*,[383] applied the *Twombly* standard to dismiss antitrust conspiracy claims by a group of travel agents against several major airlines. In affirming the district court, the majority held that "allegations of parallel conduct and bare assertions of conspiracy no longer supply an adequate foundation to support a plausible § 1 claim."[384] The dissent argued that the majority had misapplied *Twombly* and required the plaintiff to show probability of success in their claims rather than simply plausibility as required by *Twombly*.

In later attempting to clarify the *Twombly/Iqbal* intersection, the Second Circuit reversed a dismissal by noting that the proper inquiry by the district court is "whether there are sufficient factual allegations to make the complaint's claim plausible," rather than "whether there is a plausible alternative to the plaintiff's theory."[385]

---

377. *Id.* at 553 (internal quotation marks omitted) (quoting *Theatre Enterprises, Inc. v. Paramount Film Distributing Corp.*, 346 U.S. 537, 540 (1954)).

378. *Id.* at 545–46.

379. 556 U.S. 662 (2009).

380. *See generally* Gregory G. Wroland, Michael J. Waters & Joshua Dunn, *Judicial Application of the* Twombly/Iqbal *Plausibility Standard in Antitrust Cases*, Antitrust 8 (Fall 2011).

381. *Iqbal*, 556 U.S. at 678.

382. *Id.*

383. 583 F.3d 896 (6th Cir. 2009).

384. *Id.* at 902.

385. *Anderson News, LLC v. American Media Inc.*, 680 F.3d 162, 189 (2d Cir. 2012).

In *In re Text Messaging Antitrust Litigation*,[386] the Seventh Circuit held that plaintiffs had satisfied the *Twombly* standard for surviving a motion to dismiss their price-fixing complaint because they had alleged "a mixture of parallel behaviors, details of industry structure, and industry practices, that facilitate collusion."[387] The court noted that the four defendants controlled 90 percent of the relevant market; the defendants detect cheating without any elaborate mechanisms; the defendants attended trade association meetings where they directly exchanged price information; prices were increasing despite steeply falling costs; defendants simplified their previously heterogeneous and complex pricing systems into "a uniform pricing structure, and then simultaneously jacked up their prices by a third."[388] These were all essentially individual plus factors that, when viewed holistically, made the plaintiffs' allegations of a price-fixing conspiracy sufficiently plausible to satisfy the pleading standard of *Twombly*.[389]

[b] Motion for Summary Judgment

The existence of the requisite agreement is an issue to be resolved by the trier of fact. The antitrust plaintiff must adduce sufficient evidence of an "agreement" to defeat both a directed verdict motion and post-trial motions directed to the sufficiency of the evidence. The Federal Rules of Civil Procedure provide that judgment as a matter of law will be granted only after a party has been fully heard on a particular issue and "the court finds that a reasonable jury would not have a legally sufficient evidentiary basis to find for the party on the issue."[390] On a motion for judgment as a matter of law, the court views the evidence in the light most favorable to the party opposing the motion.

Traditionally, a motion for summary judgment was disfavored as a means of terminating an antitrust action.[391] Courts recognized that antitrust litigation is often a fact-bound controversy with issues of intent and effect in dispute. Since the mid-1980s, however, the use of summary judgment as a means of preliminary disposition of the action has become more accepted, if not favored.[392] *Matsushita Electric Industrial Co., Ltd. v. Zenith Radio Corp.*,[393] held that defendants accused of conspiring

---

386. 630 F.3d 622 (7th Cir. 2010).

387. *Id.* at 627.

388. *Id.* at 628.

389. *Id.* at 627. Although the plaintiffs survived dismissal and received discovery, they eventually lost at summary judgment. *In re Text Messaging Antitrust Litig.*, 782 F.3d 867, 876 (7th Cir. 2015).

390. Fed. R. Civ. P. 50(a).

391. *Poller v. CBS*, 368 U.S. 464 (1962).

392. For a good discussion on the required showings for a summary judgment motion to succeed, including the good faith requirement, see *Reserve Supply Corp. v. Owens-Corning Fiberglass Corp.*, 971 F.2d 37, 49 (7th Cir. 1992).

The court in *Ideal Dairy Farms, Inc. v. John Labatt, Ltd.*, 90 F.3d 737, 747 (3d Cir. 1996), attributes this gradual acceptance of summary judgment as a means of efficiently adjudicating some antitrust claims to the abandonment of the "special standard" that the Supreme Court used to apply to summary judgment motions when trade restraints were involved.

393. 475 U.S. 574 (1986).

to charge below-cost prices to drive rivals from the market were entitled to summary judgment. In *Matsushita*, the plaintiffs were two American manufacturers of consumer electronics products (CEPs) that accused a group of twenty-one Japanese manufacturers of pricing their consumer electronics below cost in order to drive the plaintiffs out of business, so that the defendants could control the American market for CEPs. The plaintiffs argued that the defendants used their cartel profits from the Japanese market to subsidize their predatory pricing in the American market. The district court granted the defendants' motion for summary judgment, but the Third Circuit reversed. In a 5-to-4 decision, the Supreme Court reversed the Third Circuit.

The *Matsushita* majority noted that predatory pricing entails price cutting, which generally benefits consumers. With this concern in mind, the Court "emphasized that courts should not permit factfinders to infer conspiracies when such inferences are implausible, because the effect of such practices is often to deter procompetitive conduct."[394] The *Matsushita* Court announced a new summary judgment standard focused on plausibility and motive: if an antitrust conspiracy claim is implausible and "simply makes no economic sense," then the plaintiffs "must come forward with more persuasive evidence to support their claim than would otherwise be necessary."[395]

The Court then noted that although inferences must be drawn "in the light most favorable to the party opposing the motion,"[396] "antitrust law limits the range of permissible inferences from ambiguous evidence in a § 1 case."[397] The Court also linked implausibility to motive, holding that "the absence of any plausible motive to engage in the conduct charged is highly relevant to whether a 'genuine issue for trial' exists. . . ."[398] Ultimately, the announced standard for granting summary judgment is evidence produced by the plaintiff "that tends to exclude the possibility" that defendants acted independently of each other.[399]

Applying this standard to the predatory pricing conspiracy alleged by the plaintiffs, the *Matsushita* majority asserted that claims of predatory pricing conspiracies were inherently implausible because below-cost pricing entailed upfront losses with unlikely recoupment of those losses.[400] The Court then reiterated its concern that the fear of antitrust liability could deter firms from cutting prices, lest they be improperly condemned for participating in a predatory pricing conspiracy.[401]

---

394. *Id.* at 593 (quoting *Monsanto*, 465 U.S. at 762-764).

395. *Id.* at 587.

396. *Id.* at 587–88 (citing *United States v. Diebold, Inc.*, 369 U.S. 654, 655 (1962)).

397. *Id.* at 588.

398. *Id.* at 596.

399. *Id.* at 597–98 (citing *Monsanto Co. v. Spray-Rite Serv. Corp.*, 465 U.S. 752, 764 (1984)); *see also Blomkest Fertilizer, Inc. v. Potash Corp. of Sask., Inc.*, 203 F.3d 1028 (8th Cir. 2000) (holding that parallel pricing followed by price verification does not meet the burdens on plaintiff imposed by *Matsushita* and *Monsanto*).

400. *Id.* at 589 (quoting Frank Easterbrook, *Predatory Strategies and Counterstrategies*, 48 U. Chi. L. Rev. 263, 268 (1981)).

401. *Id.* at 594.

Courts have split on whether and how the *Matsushita* standard for summary judgment applies to traditional price-fixing claims. On the one hand, some courts hold that *Matsushita* has heightened the plaintiffs' burdens for surviving summary judgment only when the plaintiffs' antitrust claims are implausible, as the Court found predatory pricing conspiracy claims to be.[402] For example, the Seventh Circuit explained in *In re High Fructose Corn Syrup Antitrust Litigation* that *Matsushita*'s implausibility premise does not apply to "a garden-variety price-fixing conspiracy."[403] After all, unlike predatory pricing conspiracies, traditional price-fixing conspiracies do not entail upfront losses and are relatively common in the American marketplace.[404] Furthermore, there is little risk of deterring procompetitive or pro-consumer conduct because traditional price-fixing conspiracies raise prices in both the short run and the long run.

On the other hand, many courts apply *Matsushita*'s heightened standard to all antitrust claims, including traditional price-fixing conspiracies.[405] According to some courts, this is the majority rule.[406] Courts have justified this approach as appropriate to reduce deterrence of "pro-competitive conduct."[407] But courts have not explained what this "pro-competitive conduct" might be when the defendants are raising their prices in parallel under suspicious circumstances.[408] Applying these heightened standards, some courts are prone to granting summary judgment to price-fixing defendants even when plaintiffs have proven conscious parallelism and multiple plus factors.[409]

[4] Withdrawing from a Conspiracy

Another issue surrounding the conspiracy doctrine is determining the type of behavior sufficient to suggest a subsequent withdrawal from the conspiracy.[410] Withdrawal from a price-fixing conspiracy can operate as a defense against antitrust liability. However, "withdrawal through resumption of competitive activity constitutes

---

402. *In re Flat Glass Antitrust Litig.*, 385 F.3d 350, 358 (3d Cir. 2004) ("[A]n agreement among oligopolists to fix prices at a supracompetitive level makes perfect economic sense.").

403. 295 F.3d 651, 661 (7th Cir. 2002).

404. Leslie, *supra* note 268.

405. *See, e.g.*, *Kleen Prod. LLC v. Georgia-Pac. LLC*, 910 F.3d 927, 941–42 (7th Cir. 2018); *In re Chocolate Confectionary Antitrust Litig.*, 901 F.3d 383, 396 (3d Cir. 2015); *PepsiCo, Inc. v. Coca-Cola Co.*, 315 F.3d 101, 104 (2d Cir. 2002).

406. *Blomkest Fertilizer, Inc. v. Potash Corp. of Saskatchewan*, 203 F.3d 1028, 1032 (8th Cir. 2000) ("We are among the majority of circuits to apply *Monsanto* and *Matsushita*, broadly, and in both horizontal and vertical price fixing cases.").

407. *In re Citric Acid Litig.*, 191 F.3d 1090, 1094 (9th Cir. 1999); *Williamson Oil Co. v. Philip Morris USA*, 346 F.3d 1287, 1300 (11th Cir. 2003) (invoking *Matsushita*'s "chill the very conduct the antitrust laws are designed to protect" while affirming summary judgment for defendants).

408. Leslie, *supra* note 268 at 363 ("There is nothing procompetitive about exchanging price lists or raising prices in unison.").

409. Christopher R. Leslie, *The Decline and Fall of Circumstantial Evidence in Antitrust Law*, 69 Am. U. L. Rev. 1713 (2020); Christopher R. Leslie, *The Probative Synergy of Plus Factors in Price-Fixing Litigation*, 115 Nw. U. L. Rev. 1581 (2021).

410. For an example of an effective withdrawal, see *In re Potash Antitrust Litigation*, 954 F. Supp. 1334 (D. Minn. 1997).

something more than 'mere cessation' of activity in furtherance of the conspiracy."[411] The Supreme Court in *United States v. United States Gypsum Co.*[412] noted: "Affirmative acts inconsistent with the object of the conspiracy and communicated in a manner reasonably calculated to reach co-conspirators have generally been regarded as sufficient to establish withdrawal or abandonment."[413]

[B] Oligopoly Pricing and Facilitating Devices

As discussed in Chapters 2 and 6, an oligopoly is a market characterized by only a few sellers. Interdependence theory suggests that each seller takes into account the market reactions of the other competitors before price or output decisions are made. Anticipation, reaction, and coordination of a competitor's market moves are central to the theory of oligopoly pricing. If one seller were to increase output and lower price in order to capture more sales, other sellers would follow suit and, if the first price change were not concealed, the reaction to lower prices would be swift. A substantial increase in market share would not follow. The price cutter thus would gain little; incentives to price compete are reduced accordingly.

Given the structure of the market, producers are aware of the reaction of competitors to price changes and will take this into account when making price decisions. Common interest and mutual understanding dictate that competitors in concentrated markets forego price competition. Interdependent pricing, also known as oligopoly pricing, does not constitute an agreement or combination in violation of § 1 as long as firms make their decisions independently.[414] This creates a gap in antitrust coverage that some scholars and enforcers have suggested can be addressed by examining so-called facilitating devices.

[1] Facilitating Devices

One approach suggested by Judge Posner argued that while noncompetitive pricing by oligopolists may be facilitated by the structure of the market, it was not inevitably compelled.[415] The voluntary and coordinated action among the sellers was similar to conduct in a traditional cartel. The only missing link was an explicit agreement, but evidence of the structure of the market could bridge this gap by inferring an agreement through price signaling, tacit acceptances, and coordinated pricing decisions.

---

411. *United States v. Continental Group Inc.*, 603 F.2d 444 (3d Cir. 1979).

412. 438 U.S. 422 (1978).

413. *Id.* at 464-65.

414. *In re Chocolate Confectionary Antitrust Litigation*, 801 F.3d 383, 397 (3d Cir. 2015) ("The upshot is oligopolists may maintain supracompetitive prices through rational, interdependent decision-making, as opposed to unlawful concerted action, if the oligopolists independently conclude that the industry as a whole would be better off by raising prices."); *In re Flat Glass Antitrust Litig.*, 385 F.3d 350, 360 (3d Cir. 2004).

415. Richard A. Posner, *Oligopoly and the Antitrust Laws: A Suggested Approach*, 21 Stan. L. Rev. 1562 (1969).

These economic theories were the bases of federal enforcement actions in the early 1970s. Concentrated industries, characterized by inflated prices and reduced output, were targets of enforcement. Actions brought by the FTC were oriented toward the structure of the industry. They were litigated under a "shared monopoly" theory—a few sellers acting as though they were a single-firm monopoly with output restrictions, higher prices, and entry barriers.

The Department of Justice equated shared monopoly actions with oligopoly pricing and advanced enforcement actions when "facilitating devices" were used as a means to further price coordination among firms in an oligopoly. Two preconditions existed: (1) a noncompetitive price structure, and (2) little likelihood that independent action would result in increased profits and market share. The government urged that § 1 of the Sherman Act is violated when there was (1) parallel conduct by firms in a concentrated industry, (2) awareness by each firm that rivals are following lock-step in a parallel fashion, (3) anticompetitive benefits, and (4) actions contradictory to the independent self-interest of each firm.[416] Although its theories of shared monopoly and oligopoly pricing attempted to blend economic theories and traditional cartel agreements into an enforcement theme, the government's litigation successes were minimal.

In *In re Ethyl Corp.*,[417] the FTC brought an industry-wide suit directed at oligopoly pricing. The complaint alleged that four companies, with a total market share of 80%, maintained uniform prices for anti-knock gasoline compounds by "signing" future price changes to competitors. In addition, the Commission charged that the scheme was facilitated by defendants (1) using a 30-day price change advance notice clause in all contracts, (2) disclosing advance price changes, (3) selling only on a uniform delivered price basis, and (4) dealing on a most-favored customer arrangement with a customer entitled to the lowest price at which the manufacturer sells to other buyers. The pivotal theory was the price signaling, facilitated by advance price charge announcements in the press, which enabled coordination of prices throughout the industry.

On appeal to the Second Circuit,[418] the FTC's enforcement theory was rejected on the factual record presented. The court held that § 5 of the FTC Act is not violated by "non-collusive, non-predatory, independent conduct."[419] The court held, "The mere existence of an oligopolistic market structure in which a small group of manufacturers engage in consciously parallel pricing of an identical product does not violate the antitrust laws."[420] The court concluded that in order to find an unfair method of competition under § 5 of the Act, in absence of an agreement, there must be "1) evidence

---

416. *See, e.g.*, Complaint, *In re Ethyl Corp.*, 1976–77 Transfer Binder Trade Reg. Rep. (CCH) 21,579 (F.T.C., filed May 30, 1979); *United States v. G.E. Co.*, 1977 U.S. Dist. LEXIS 18147 (E.D. Wash. Sept. 20, 1977); *United States v. G.M. Corp.*, 1974 U.S. Dist. LEXIS 6569 (E.D. Mich. 1974).

417. 101 F.T.C. 425 (1983), *rev. sub nom., E.I. DuPont de Nemours & Co. v. F.T.C.*, 729 F.2d 128 (2d Cir. 1984); *see also infra* § 6.08[B].

418. 729 F.2d 128 (2d Cir. 1984).

419. *Id.* at 137.

420. *Id.* at 139.

of anticompetitive intent or purpose . . . , or 2) the absence of an independent legitimate business reason for the conduct."[421] Moreover, no § 1 Sherman Act violation occurred because the court refused to find a tacit agreement. To be sure, the court found that the challenged practices were adopted independently and for legitimate business reasons.

It is not clear whether the court in *Ethyl* sounded the death knell for the oligopoly pricing theory *per se*, especially where facilitating devices are present, but the court did order the Commission to first define the conditions under which such practices could be considered "unfair" under § 5 before other suits are brought.

A similar result was reached by the Ninth Circuit in *Boise Cascade Corp. v. FTC*,[422] where the court refused to enforce an FTC order prohibiting a delivered pricing system challenged under conscious parallel conduct theory. *Boise* required a finding of either (1) an overt agreement to avoid price competition or (2) an actual anticompetitive price effect caused by the challenged practice. A mere showing of parallel conduct in a concentrated or oligopoly industry is not enough. "Interdependence is consistent with the existence of a conspiracy but does not itself prove the traditional agreement."[423]

[2] Base Point Delivered Pricing

In *FTC v. Cement Institute*,[424] the Supreme Court provided a cogent explanation of base point delivered pricing, a mechanism sometimes used to determine the price of delivered industrial goods:

> Goods may be sold and delivered to customers at the seller's mill or warehouse door or may be sold free on board (f.o.b.) trucks or railroad cars immediately adjacent to the seller's mill or warehouse. In either event, the actual cost of the goods to the purchaser is, broadly speaking, the seller's "mill price" plus the purchaser's cost of transportation. However, if the seller fixes a price at which [it] undertakes to deliver goods to the purchaser where they are to be used, the cost to the purchaser is the "delivered price." A seller who makes the mill price identical for all purchasers of like amount and quality simply delivers [its] goods at the same place ([its] mill) and for the same price (price at the mill). [It] thus receives for all f.o.b. mill sales an identical net amount of money for like goods from all customers. But a "delivered price" system creates complications which may result in a seller's receiving different net returns from the sale of like goods. The cost of transporting 500 miles is almost always more than the cost of transporting 100 miles.[425]

---

421. *Id.*
422. 637 F.2d 573 (9th Cir. 1980).
423. VI Phillip E. Areeda, *Antitrust Law*, ¶ 1411 (1986).
424. 333 U.S. 683 (1948).
425. *Id.* at 696–97.

Base point pricing establishes the purchaser's cost predicated upon delivery costs from a standard shipping location which may not be the actual place from which the goods for a particular order are shipped.[426]

In *Cement Inst.*,[427] the Supreme Court reviewed a cease and desist order issued by the FTC against the 74 corporate members of a trade association, the Cement Institute, and 21 individuals associated with the Institute. The corporations manufactured, sold, and distributed cement employing a multiple base point pricing system that resulted in identical pricing by all competing corporations at any point in the United States, allegedly interfering with competition by means of an unlawful combination. The cement industry was highly concentrated, with 10 of its 80 domestic manufacturers controlling over half of the mills. The FTC charged that this conduct constituted an unfair method of competition in violation of § 5 of the FTC Act.[428]

The Court ruled first that the "[FTC] has jurisdiction to declare that conduct tending to restrain trade is an unfair method of competition even though the selfsame conduct may also violate the Sherman Act."[429] The Court then questioned whether there was sufficient evidence to warrant the Commission's finding of concerted conduct based upon defendants' parallel base point delivered pricing.

The defendants attempted to rebut an inference of unlawful concerted conduct through the testimony of economists who stated that precisely identical bidding will always result in the cement industry without either express or implied agreements among the bidders. The Commission disagreed and ruled that uniformity of bidding and lack of competition in the industry resulted from understandings or agreements among the defendants. The Supreme Court, upholding the Commission, held that an understanding, express or implied, could be inferred "from evidence that the industry's Institute actively worked, in cooperation with various of its members, to maintain the multiple basing point delivered price system; [and] that this pricing system is calculated to produce, and has produced, uniform prices and terms of sale throughout the country."[430]

The Court observed the highly concentrated structure of the cement industry and that cement is a fungible product. The Court eventually found that multiple basing point delivered pricing was an instrument to effectuate elimination of price competition. There was evidence of "[t]housands of secret sealed bids . . . received by public agencies which corresponded in prices of cement down to a fractional part of a penny."[431] One

426. *See generally* George J. Stigler, *The Organization of Industry* 147–70 (1968); David D. Haddock, *Basing-Point Pricing: Competitive vs. Collusive Theories*, 72 Am. Econ. Rev. 289 (1982); Carl Kaysen, *Basing-Point Pricing and Public Policy*, 63 Q.J. Econ. 289 (1948).

427. 333 U.S. 683 (1948).

428. 15 U.S.C. § 45 (2012).

429. 333 U.S. at 693.

430. *Id.* at 716.

431. *Id.* at 713.

example showed that eleven separate bidders quoted precisely $3.286854 per barrel of cement in a 1936 sealed bid to the government.[432]

In *Triangle Conduit & Cable Co. v. FTC*,[433] the Seventh Circuit applied the holding of *Cement Inst.* to review a FTC cease and desist order issued against fourteen corporate manufacturers of rigid steel conduit that controlled 93% of the conduit industry.[434] The alleged conduct by defendant corporation was the uniform quoting of delivered prices and parallel use of a formula for computing those delivered prices. The formula used a base price at one of only two cites in the United States, regardless of the actual originating point, plus transportation to the actual point of delivery. This scheme resulted in conduit manufacturers "match[ing] their delivered price quotations, and purchasers at or near a place of production could not buy more cheaply from their nearby producer than from producers located at greater distances."[435]

The court sustained the FTC's cease and desist order, holding that individual use of base point delivery pricing, with knowledge that parallel competitive conduct would yield identical delivered price quotations, constituted an unfair method of competition. The court stated that "price uniformity especially if accompanied by an artificial price level not related to the supply and demand of a given commodity may be evidence from which an agreement or understanding, or some concerted action of sellers operating to restrain commerce, may be inferred."[436] The court relied on an earlier Supreme Court case, *Cement Mfrs. Protective Ass'n v. United States.*[437]

In *Cement Mfrs.*, however, the Supreme Court held that information dissemination was not in itself a § 1 violation. The Court reasoned that the evidence in that case "fail[ed] to show any effect on price and production except such as would naturally flow from the dissemination of . . . that information [pertaining to sale and distribution of cement] . . . in the trade and its natural influence on individual action."[438] This, then, suggests that a Sherman Act plaintiff must show something more than "natural" influences on individual action in order to establish an inference of agreement.[439]

Likewise, the Ninth Circuit, in *Boise Cascade Corp. v. FTC*,[440] undercut *Triangle Conduit* by holding that evidence of a conspiracy must be present before industry-wide base point pricing is held illegal. "[I]n the absence of evidence of overt agreement to utilize a pricing system to avoid price competition, the Commission must

432. *Id.* at 713 n.15.
433. 168 F.2d 175 (7th Cir. 1948), *aff'd by an equally divided court*, 336 U.S. 956 (1949).
434. 15 U.S.C. § 45 (2012).
435. 168 F.2d at 180.
436. *Id.* at 179 (citing *Cement Mfrs. Protective Ass'n v. United States*, 268 U.S. 588, 606 (1925)).
437. 268 U.S. 588 (1925).
438. *Id.* at 606.
439. *Id.*
440. 637 F.2d 573 (9th Cir. 1980); *see also In re Plywood Antitrust Litig.*, 655 F.2d 627, 634 (5th Cir. 1981); *Crouse-Hinds Co.*, 46 F.T.C. 1114 (1950).

demonstrate that the challenged pricing system has actually had the effect of fixing or stabilizing prices. Without such effect, a mere showing of parallel action will not establish a section 5 violation."[441]

In 1996, the District of Columbia Circuit rejected a claim of base point pricing brought by local distribution companies of natural gas against the Federal Energy Regulatory Commission in *United Distribution Companies v. FERC*.[442] The plaintiffs alleged, among other things, that the FERC's act of removing "transportation costs from per unit charges at the supplier level amount[ed] to 'base point pricing,' which . . . 'would be a *per se* violation of the antitrust laws,' if done by agreement among private parties to fix the price of transportation added to the price of products."[443] In rejecting the challenge on this theory, the court noted that past base point pricing cases had dealt with "private agreements in otherwise unregulated markets, and commodities such as cement, expensive to transport as contrasted with natural gas."[444]

[C] The Plurality Requirement and Intra-Enterprise Conspiracy

The "contract, combination, . . . or conspiracy" language of § 1 requires proof of a relationship between at least two legally separate persons. Some courts have labeled this as the "plurality requirement." A literal interpretation of § 1 means that any two persons, even officers of the same corporation, could engage in unlawful conduct merely by agreeing to any course of conduct. But logic dictates that no corporation could survive if its officers and employees were not permitted to agree among themselves to engage in otherwise lawful conduct. As the Ninth Circuit has said, "[I]f the Sherman Act forbids such activities it: 'would be socially inconvenient and historically surprising. So long as the business enterprise is regarded as an individual economic unit, it must be permitted to act.'"[445]

A general rule has developed that a single corporation is incapable of conspiring with itself or through its officers, directors, employees, or agents within the meaning of § 1 of the Sherman Act. This general rule, however, does not answer whether the plurality requirement is met in numerous variations in the intra-enterprise structure.

441. *Boise Cascade*, 637 F.2d at 577.
442. 88 F.3d 1105 (D.C. Cir. 1996).
443. *Id.* at 1169 (quoting plaintiff's brief).
444. 637 F.2d at 577.
445. *Knutson v. Daily Review, Inc.*, 548 F.2d 795, 801 (9th Cir. 1976), (quoting Phillip E. Areeda, *Antitrust Analysis* 319 (2d ed. 1974)); *see also Nelson Radio & Supply Co. v. Motorola, Inc.*, 200 F.2d 911 (5th Cir. 1952).

[1] Corporate Parent and Wholly-Owned Incorporated Subsidiary

In *Copperweld Corp. v. Independence Tube Corp.*,[446] the Supreme Court, disapproving the Court's intra-enterprise conspiracy rationale in *Kiefer-Stewart Co. v. Joseph E. Seagram & Sons*,[447] held that as long as the initial parent-subsidiary combination was lawful, a parent and a wholly-owned subsidiary are a single entity incapable of combining or conspiring under § 1 of the Sherman Act.

> A parent and its wholly owned subsidiary have a complete unity of interest. Their objectives are common, not disparate; their general corporate actions are guided or determined not by two separate corporate consciousnesses, but one. They are not unlike a multiple team of horses drawing a vehicle under the control of a single driver. With or without a formal "agreement," the subsidiary acts for the benefit of the parent, its sole shareholder. If a parent and a wholly owned subsidiary do "agree" to a course of action, there is no sudden joining of economic resources that had previously served different interests, and there is no justification for § 1 scrutiny.[448]

Note that "wholly-owned" does not necessarily mean 100% ownership. In *Siegel Transfer, Inc. v. Carrier Express, Inc.*,[449] the court held that 99.92% ownership is the same as 100% ownership, and holding 8,993 shares out of 9,000 outstanding shares of stock constitutes complete control of the subsidiary company. If the differences are *de minimus*, courts will apply the "wholly owned" rule and bar a finding of conspiracy.

[2] Corporate Parent and Partially-Owned Incorporated Subsidiary

In post-*Copperweld* decisions, several circuit courts have addressed the conspiracy requirement in the context of corporate relationships other than a corporation and its wholly-owned subsidiary. Several cases have held that two corporations which are wholly-owned by the same parent corporation are not capable of conspiring within

446. 467 U.S. 752 (1984).

447. 340 U.S. 211 (1951). It should be noted that although the Court in *Copperweld* disapproves the reasoning of the *Seagram* Court it nonetheless approves of the ultimate finding of liability "on the ground that the subsidiaries conspired with wholesalers other than the plaintiff." 467 U.S. at 764.

448. 467 U.S. at 771. In *Copperweld*, the Court left little doubt, when it observed in *dictum*, that "[t]here is . . . general agreement that § 1 is not violated by the internally coordinated conduct of a corporation and one of its unincorporated divisions. Although this Court has not previously addressed the question, there can be little doubt that the operations of a corporate enterprise organized into divisions must be judged as the conduct of a single actor." 467 U.S. at 770. "A corporate division has no separate legal personality. It is simply a group of employees within the firm. And to say, as everyone does, that a single corporation acting unilaterally cannot conspire with itself is necessarily to say that it cannot conspire with its officers or employees who are its only means of acting." VII Phillip E. Areeda, *Antitrust Law*, ¶ 1470 (1986).

449. 54 F.3d 1125, 1133 (3d Cir. 1995).

the meaning of § 1. The Fifth Circuit, in *Hood v. Tenneco Texas Life Ins. Co.*,[450] held that because two corporations which are both wholly-owned by the same parent corporation share a common purpose with their parent corporation, "they cannot conspire with their parent in violation of the Sherman Act. By the same token, neither can they conspire with one another."[451] In *Greenwood Utils. v. Mississippi Power Co.*, another Fifth Circuit case, the court held that two sister corporations wholly-owned by the same corporate parent are incapable of forming a § 1 conspiracy.[452] Moreover, the Third Circuit, in *Weiss v. York Hospital*,[453] held that "[i]f the [two] businesses are controlled at both levels by the same firm, and the divisions at one level of production urge the parent corporation not to deal with their rivals, there is no 'concerted refusal to deal' under § 1."[454]

At least two circuit courts have considered alleged conspiracies between a parent corporation and its less than wholly-owned subsidiary. In *Tunis Bros. Co. v. Ford Motor Co.*,[455] Ford was accused of conspiring with Wenner Ford Tractor, Inc. Ford had established Wenner Ford Tractor and owned 100% of the voting stock, and 79% of the equity stock of Wenner Ford Tractor. Wenner Ford Tractor was an authorized Ford dealer for farm and industrial tractors, machinery, equipment, and parts. The Third Circuit held that *Copperweld* "does not ... preclude a conspiratorial relationship between Ford and Wenner Ford since Wenner Ford is not wholly-owned [by Ford]."[456] Thus, even though Ford owned all the voting stock of Wenner Ford Tractor, the fact that a mere 21% of Wenner Ford Tractor's equity stock was owned by other than Ford meant the two corporations were not protected by the reasoning in *Copperweld*.

The First Circuit avoided a direct ruling on whether a corporation and its less than wholly-owned corporation are capable of forming a Sherman § 1 conspiracy when it applied a functional rather than numerical test. In *Computer Identics Corp. v. Southern Pacific Co.*,[457] Southern Pacific and its 80% owned subsidiary, a computer consulting service, were accused of a § 1 conspiracy. The court, citing *Copperweld*, approved a lower court's jury instruction that there can be no conspiracy if "defendants were so closely related that *they were in fact one entity*.... [I]t is up to you jurors to decide whether the defendant corporations *acted as a single entity* sharing common management which made decisions controlling all [the defendants] or whether they operated as independent persons."[458] The *Computer Identics* jury found there was no conspiracy, but this does not suggest that the First Circuit would interpret *Copperweld*

450. 739 F.2d 1012 (5th Cir. 1984).

451. *Id.* at 1015.

452. 751 F.2d 1484, 1497, n.8 (5th Cir. 1985) (citing *Copperweld Corp. v. Independence Tube Corp.*, 467 U.S. 752 (1984) and *Century Oil Tool, Inc. v. Prod. Specialties, Inc.*, 737 F.2d 1316 (5th Cir. 1984)).

453. 745 F.2d 786 (3d Cir. 1984).

454. *Id.* at 819 n.57 (citing *Copperweld*, 467 U.S. 752).

455. 763 F.2d 1482 (3d Cir. 1985).

456. *Id.* at 1495 n.20.

457. 756 F.2d 200 (1st Cir. 1985).

458. *Id.* at 204–05.

to mean a parent and less than wholly-owned subsidiary are incapable of conspiring. To the contrary, the fact that the court approved the jury instruction means the jury could have found that Southern Pacific and its 80% owned subsidiary were capable of conspiring. Thus, at least in the First Circuit, *Copperweld* will not necessarily preclude the finding of a conspiracy between a parent and partially owned subsidiary so long as a jury is properly instructed to determine if the two entities were in fact one single entity.

In actual practice, however, it may not be necessary to satisfy the plurality requirement by focusing on the relationship of the parent and the partially-owned subsidiary. Partial ownership of the subsidiary means that the subsidiary has at least two owners. It might be argued that plurality is satisfied by the relationship of the two or more owners of the subsidiary, rendering unnecessary a ruling that the parent and subsidiary are not a single entity.

[3] Healthcare Operations as Single Entities

Several courts have addressed when the *Copperweld* doctrine applies to healthcare organizations. In *Oksanen v. Page Memorial Hospital*,[459] the court determined that the Board of Trustees and the medical staff of a hospital were not capable of conspiring to exclude the plaintiff through their peer review process. The court held, "Far from being a competitor with the hospital, the medical staff was in fact a natural component of the hospital's management structure."[460] The court cited *Copperweld*, stating that the Supreme Court cautioned against adopting a rule penalizing coordinated conduct "simply because [such a penalty] might well discourage corporations from creating divisions with their presumed benefits."[461] The plaintiff then argued that an exception to intra-enterprise immunity existed, since the physicians on the medical staff had personal stakes in the outcome of the peer process. The plaintiff suggested that the doctors' own practices would flourish through the elimination of the plaintiff's practice through an unfavorable peer review. The court declined to accept this argument, cautioning that the "independent personal stake" exception was one which "threaten[ed] to swallow the rule."[462] The court found only one of the physicians was a verifiable competitor to the plaintiff, and he had not taken part in the actions leading to the plaintiff's dismissal from defendant hospital. Any possible economic justifications for the medical staff to discharge the plaintiff were too indirect to be given any

---

459. 945 F.2d 696 (4th Cir. 1991)); *see also Mathews v. Lancaster Gen. Hosp.*, 87 F.3d 624, 639–41 (3d Cir. 1996) (evidencing a general intent to not hold peer review committees liable under § 1 unless the evidence is clear and excludes any inference of independent action); *Willman v. Heartland Hosp. E.*, 34 F.3d 605, 611 (8th Cir. 1994) ("Corrective action against a physician does not violate the antitrust laws if the physician's peer reviewers had legitimate medical reasons to believe that the physician provided substandard care.").

460. 945 F.2d at 703.

461. *Id.* (quoting *Copperweld*, 467 U.S. at 771).

462. *Id.* at 705.

serious consideration.[463] Furthermore, "because decision[-]making authority in [the plaintiff's] case was dispersed among a number of individuals, the personal stake exception [was] inapplicable."[464]

The court also denied any inference of a conspiracy within the medical staff itself. "Simply making a peer review recommendation does not prove the existence of a conspiracy; there must be something more such as a conscious commitment by the medical staff to coerce the hospital into accepting its recommendation."[465] Finally, the court found that even if a conspiracy had existed, the plaintiff's claim would still fail because the alleged restraint of trade could not be considered "unreasonable" as required under a rule of reason analysis. Even though the plaintiff was denied staff privileges, "[t]here [was] no evidence that competition as a whole in the relevant market has been harmed."[466] Hence, even setting aside the intraenterprise exception, the plaintiff still failed to prove a punishable violation of § 1.

In contrast, the Tenth Circuit in *Brown v. Presbyterian Healthcare Services*[467] found two defendant doctors who had participated in a peer review committee culminating in the revocation of the plaintiff's obstetrics privileges had conspired in violation of § 1. One of the doctors was a direct competitor of the plaintiff, and, although neither defendant voted in the final decision to exclude Dr. Brown from practicing obstetrics, the evidence showed that each "played an influential role in bringing about the revocation" and that there was not a "reasonable effort to obtain the facts of the matter."[468] The court affirmed the district court's denial of the defendant's motion for judgment as a matter of law on the antitrust claims, and the seeming blanket protection previously afforded peer review activities was qualified.

Of course, the *Copperweld* doctrine applies easily to healthcare defendants when one is a wholly owned subsidiary of the other. In *Boulware v. State of Nevada, Dep't of HR*,[469] the Ninth Circuit rejected the plaintiff physician's § 1 claim against a hospital and National Care Service Corporation, which was a wholly-owned subsidiary of the hospital. The plaintiff argued that the two entities had violated the Sherman Act by securing a permanent injunction forbidding him from constructing and running a Magnetic Resonance Imaging Unit. The court rejected the claim "at the outset," stating that Humana Hospital and NCSC were incapable of forming the requisite conspiracy to make their activities a violation of § 1.[470]

463. *Id.*

464. *Id.* at 706.

465. *Id.*

466. *Id.* at 709; *see also Nat'l Ass'n of Review Appraisers & Mortgage Underwriters, Inc. v. Appraisal Found.*, 64 F.3d 1130, 1135 (8th Cir. 1995) (holding that a decline in plaintiff's membership because of defendant's refusal to extend association benefits to plaintiff does not "establish harm to overall market").

467. 101 F.3d 1324 (10th Cir. 1996).

468. *Id.* at 1333, 1335.

469. 960 F.2d 793 (9th Cir. 1992).

470. *Id.* at 797.

[4] Corporation and Its Agents or Independent Consultants

A plurality of actors may not exist if a firm had agreed with its own agents. The Eighth Circuit interpreted the conspiracy requirement in the context of a corporation and its agents in *Pink Supply Corp. v. Heibert, Inc.*[471] The court held that a Sherman Act conspiracy cannot exist between a corporation and its agents, even if the agents are separately incorporated, when the agents function as an integral part of the corporate entity, do not represent separate steps in the corporation's chain of distribution, do act for the benefit of the corporate principle, and are functionally indistinguishable from the corporation's employees.[472] However, the Eighth Circuit recognized an exception when a corporation's and its agents' interests diverge and the agents act beyond the scope of their authority or for their own benefit. Under these circumstances, the corporation and its agents are capable of forming a § 1 conspiracy.[473]

In *Nurse Midwifery Assoc. (NMA) v. Hibbett*,[474] two nurse midwives, their supervising obstetrician, and three clients alleged that three hospitals, several members of their medical staffs, and a mutual insurance company all conspired to deny medical staff privileges for midwifery services at the defendant hospitals. The Sixth Circuit held that the members of the medical staff were acting as agents of the hospitals and that, therefore, the intracorporate conspiracy doctrine immunized their actions. In reaching this decision, however, the court specified,

> When the staff as a group, make decisions or recommendations for the hospital in areas that do not affect the market in which they compete as individuals, there is no reason not to treat them as agents of the hospital. However, when competing physicians are making privilege recommendations concerning another competitor, sufficient anticompetitive concerns are raised to warrant a conclusion that the members of the medical staff are not acting as agents of the hospital for purposes of applying the intracorporate conspiracy doctrine to preclude a conspiracy among staff members.[475]

In general, the agreement requirement may be satisfied if the agent has self-interest involved, is key to the effect on competition, and is an outsider to the corporation.[476]

---

471. 788 F.2d 1313 (8th Cir. 1986).

472. *Id.* at 1317.

473. *Id.* at 1318. Seven years later, the Eighth Circuit reaffirmed the holding in *Pink Supply* in *International Travel Arrangers v. NWA, Inc.*, 991 F.2d 1389, 1397–98 (8th Cir. 1993).

474. 918 F.2d 605 (6th Cir. 1990).

475. *Id.* at 614; *see also Muzquiz v. W.A. Foote Mem'l Hosp., Inc.*, 70 F.3d 422, 429–30 (6th Cir. 1995) (affirming *NMA v. Hibbet* in reasoning that, because the hospital was the only defendant and because *NMA* prevents the application of § 1 conspiracy claims to agreements between hospitals and agents or employees, the defendant hospital could not be held liable under a Sherman Act claim).

476. *See generally* VII Phillip E. Areeda, *Antitrust Law* § 1470, at 282–301 (1986). In *Crosby v. Hospital Authority of Valdosa & Lowndes County*, 93 F.3d 1515 (11th Cir. 1996), the Eleventh Circuit addressed an issue similar to that in *Hibbet*. Specifically, the court considered whether a hospital and its staff can be protected from § 1 as one legal entity incapable of conspiring. The court found that they

[5] Sports League Teams

Generally, competing sports league teams are capable of forming a conspiracy, but this rule is subject to statutory and court-directed exceptions. In *NCAA v. Bd. of Regents*,[477] the Supreme Court considered an allegation that the NCAA had unreasonably restrained trade in the televising of college football games. The Court's holding, that the NCAA's price and output restrictions were unlawful restraints of trade, implicitly recognizes that an association of sports league teams is capable of satisfying § 1.[478]

This implicit holding in *NCAA* was challenged in *Chicago Prof'l Sports Ltd. P'ship v. NBA*.[479] Plaintiffs challenged the NBA's ability to cap at thirty the number of games televised on Chicago television station WGN, and the NBA challenged the district court's ruling that the tax it imposed on those games televised nationwide was excessive. In considering the claim, the Court of Appeals held that the NBA bore a greater resemblance to a single firm than an independent group of firms.[480] This is true even though the teams are not subsidiaries of the national organization; they all have separate ownership.[481] The NBA submitted, and the court accepted, that it "functions as a single entity, creating a single product ("NBA Basketball") that competes with other basketball leagues . . . , other sports . . . , and other entertainments. . . ."[482] However, the court conceded that "[t]o say the league is 'more like a single bargaining employer' than a multi-employer unit is not to say that it necessarily is one, for every purpose.[483] Characterization of the league as a "single entity" serves to protect it from any § 1 liability.

The Supreme Court again addressed the issue of sport league conspiracy in *American Needle, Inc. v. Nat'l Football League*.[484] Finding that the NFL's licensing activities constitute concerted action that is not categorically beyond the coverage of antitrust law, the Court decided the league's joint licensing agreements should be subjected to rule of reason analysis. Justice Stevens, author of the Court's unanimous decision, stated that each NFL team is a substantial, independently owned, and independently managed business and that NFL teams "compete with one another, not only on the

could not be afforded intra-enterprise immunity, "but the staff physicians may in certain contexts be agents of the hospital for purposes of state action immunity." *Id.* at 1529. *See supra* § 3.07[A] for a further discussion of the state action doctrine.

477. 468 U.S. 85 (1984). *Compare* Myron C. Grauer, *Recognition of the National Football League as a Single Entity Under Sec. 1 of the Sherman Act: Implications of the Consumer Welfare Model*, 82 Mich. L. Rev. 1 (1983), *with* Gary R. Roberts, *Sports Leagues and the Sherman Act: The Use and Abuse of Section 1 to Regulate Restraints on Intraleague Rivalry*, 32 UCLA L. Rev. 219 (1984).

478. See also *O'Bannon v. National Collegiate Athletic Association*, 802 F.3d 1049 (9th Cir. 2015).

479. 95 F.3d 593 (7th Cir. 1996).

480. *Id.* at 600.

481. *Id.* at 597.

482. *Id.* at 599.

483. *Id.* ("[W]e do not rule out the possibility that an organization such as the NBA is best understood as one firm when selling broadcast rights to a network in competition with a thousand other producers of entertainment, but is best understood as a joint venture when curtailing competition for players who have few other market opportunities.").

484. 560 U.S. 183 (2010).

playing field, but to attract fans, for gate receipts and for contracts with managerial and playing personnel."[485] Although the Court acknowledged that NFL teams often share common interests regarding the promotion of NFL football, it concluded the teams' decision to license their separately owned trademarks collectively and to only one vendor deprived the marketplace of actual or potential competition.[486] In the wake of *American Needle*, leagues and their teams can be held capable of colluding when they behave as a collection of individual, self-interested actors.

Professional baseball, however, is viewed uniquely in antitrust law. Two Supreme Court cases have exempted professional baseball from the antitrust laws. First, *Fed. Baseball Club of Baltimore, Inc. v. Nat'l League of Prof'l Baseball Clubs*[487] found that interstate commerce was not involved in baseball; thus, baseball is exempted from the reach of the Sherman Act.[488] Second, *Flood v. Kuhn*[489] refused to repeal the professional baseball exemption of *Fed. Baseball*. In addition, Congress arguably approved implicitly the baseball exemption when it provided that nothing contained in an act relating to telecasting of sporting events "shall be deemed to change, determine, or otherwise affect the applicability or nonapplicability of the antitrust laws to . . . football, baseball, basketball, or hockey."[490] Professional sports other than baseball are not exempt from the antitrust laws.[491]

[6] Trade Associations

Several Supreme Court decisions leave little doubt that trade associations are capable of forming a conspiracy. In *Goldfarb v. Va. State Bar*,[492] the Court considered whether a minimum fee schedule for lawyers, which was enforced by the state bar association, violated the Sherman Act. The Court held that the bar association's rule prescribing minimum fees for legal services did violate § 1. Implicitly the association was capable of forming the requisite conspiracy.[493]

---

485. *Id.* at 2212.

486. *Id.* at 2205. *But see Washington v. Nat'l Football League*, 880 F. Supp. 2d 1004 (D. Minn. 2012) (finding that NFL and its teams are not capable of conspiring when marketing property the teams and the NFL can only collectively own).

487. 259 U.S. 200 (1922).

488. *Radovich v. Nat'l Football League*, 352 U.S. 445, 451 (1957) (restricting the holding in *Federal Baseball* to cases involving only the sport of baseball).

489. 407 U.S. 258 (1972).

490. 15 U.S.C. § 1294 (2012).

491. *See, e.g., Brown v. Pro Football, Inc.*, 518 U.S. 231 (1996); *Haywood v. Nat'l Basketball Ass'n.*, 401 U.S. 1204 (1971); *Clarett v. Nat'l Football League*, 369 F. 3d 124 (2d Cir. 2004); *Smith v. Pro Football, Inc.*, 593 F.2d 1173 (D.C. Cir. 1978); *Mackey v. Nat'l Football League*, 543 F.2d 606 (8th Cir. 1976); *N. Am. Soccer League v. Nat'l Football League*, 465 F. Supp. 665 (S.D.N.Y. 1979); *Denver Rockets v. All-Pro Mgmt., Inc.*, 325 F. Supp. 1049 (C.D. Cal. 1971).

492. 421 U.S. 773 (1975).

493. The Court in *Goldfarb* did not discuss directly the question whether the bar association was capable of forming a conspiracy or was merely a single entity incapable of conspiring, combining, or agreeing. The principal questions in the case were whether to apply the "state action" doctrine of *Parker v. Brown*, 317 U.S. 341 (1943), or whether the fact that defendants were members of a "learned

In *Nat'l Soc'y of Prof'l Eng'rs*,[494] the Court held that the Society's Code of Ethics, which banned competitive bidding by the Society's professional engineer members, was illegal under § 1 of the Sherman Act. As in *Goldfarb*, the Court's holding implies that the Society was capable of conspiring, combining, or agreeing for § 1 purposes. Thus, it is not a viable defense for a trade association faced with a § 1 charge to argue that the association is a single entity immune from the Act's coverage.[495] The combination inherent in the association satisfies the plurality requirement.

This idea was affirmed in *Alvord-Polk, Inc. v. F. Schumacher & Co.*[496] The Third Circuit held that trade associations are capable of conspiring as long as they are acting like an "entity" and that a full examination of the facts and circumstances would be necessary in such a case.[497]

In addition, an association cannot defeat a § 1 civil antitrust treble damage claim by arguing that it was unaware that one of its agents or employees engaged in the allegedly unlawful conduct. In *Am. Soc'y of Mech. Eng'rs, Inc. v. Hydrolevel Corp.*,[498] the Court held that an association, whether or not it is a nonprofit association, is civilly liable under the Sherman Act for the act of its agent who has apparent authority to act for the association, even when the association is unaware of, and has not ratified, the agent's act.

[7] Members of Non-Profit Foundations

In *Arizona v. Maricopa Cty. Med. Soc'y*,[499] the Court considered "whether § 1 of the Sherman Act . . . [was] violated by agreements among competing physicians setting, by majority vote, the maximum fees that they may claim in full payment for health services provided to policyholders of specified insurance plans."[500] The physicians were members of foundations which approved certain insurance plans. In considering whether the plurality requirement of § 1 was met, the Court reasoned as follows:

> The foundations are not analogous to partnerships or other joint arrangements in which persons who would otherwise be competitors pool their capital and share the risks of loss as well as the opportunities for profit. In such joint ventures, the partnership is regarded as a single firm competing with other sellers in the market. The agreement under attack is an agreement among hundreds of competing doctors concerning the price at which

---

profession," exempted them from the Sherman Act. *Goldfarb v. Va. State Bar*, 421 U.S. 773, 780 (1975). The implicit premise of the Court's holding, however, is that the association was not immune from § 1 of Sherman Act exposure on the basis that it was a single entity incapable of conspiring, agreeing, or combining.

494. 435 U.S. 679 (1978).

495. *See also FTC v. Ind. Fed'n of Dentists*, 476 U.S. 447 (1986).

496. 37 F.3d 996 (3d Cir. 1994).

497. *Id.* at 1007–08.

498. 456 U.S. 556 (1982).

499. 457 U.S. 332 (1982).

500. *Id.* at 335–36.

> each will offer his own services to a substantial number of consumers. . . . If a clinic offered complete medical coverage for a flat fee, the cooperating doctors would have the type of partnership arrangement in which a price-fixing agreement among the doctors would be perfectly proper. But the fee agreements disclosed by the record in this case are among independent competing entrepreneurs. They fit squarely into the horizontal price-fixing mode.[501]

Thus, even professional members of a nonprofit foundation are not immunized from § 1 through the argument that the foundation is a single entity incapable of combining or conspiring.

[8] Local Governmental Units

In *Fisher v. City of Berkeley California*,[502] the Supreme Court held that rent controls established by a city ordinance "lack[ed] the element of concerted action needed [to] be characterized as a *per se* violation of § 1 of the Sherman Act."[503] Plaintiff landlords challenged the constitutionality of an ordinance imposing rent ceilings on residential property. They argued that the ordinance "form[ed] a combination between [the City of Berkeley and its officials], on the one hand, and the property owners on the other" and that it also "create[d] a horizontal combination among the landlords."[504] The Court disagreed:

> A restraint imposed unilaterally by government does not become concerted action . . . simply because it has coercive effect upon parties who must obey the law. The ordinary relationship between the government and those who must obey its regulatory commands whether they wish to or not is not enough to establish a conspiracy. . . . There is no meeting of the minds here.
>
> . . . .
>
> Not all restraints imposed upon private actors by government units necessarily constitute unilateral action outside the purview of § 1. Certain restraints may be characterized as "hybrid," in that nonmarket mechanisms merely enforce private marketing decisions.[505]

Such "hybrid" restraints, in the form of a state statute or other government command that achieves the same result as a private agreement would, are subject to § 1.

The Court then reviewed two earlier "hybrid" decisions. First, in *Schwegmann Bros. v. Calvert Distillers Corp.*,[506] the Court reasoned that "when a state compels retailers to follow a parallel price policy, it demands private conduct which the Sherman Act

501. *Id.* at 356–57.
502. 475 U.S. 260 (1986).
503. *Id.* at 270.
504. *Id.* at 267 (quoting appellants' brief).
505. *Id.* at 267–68.
506. 341 U.S. 384 (1951).

forbids."[507] In *Schwegmann*, however, the price selections and power to enforce them were left by the state to the retailers. Thus, the retailers were capable of conspiring within the meaning of the Sherman Act. Second, in *Cal. Liquor Dealers Ass'n v. Midcal Aluminum, Inc.*,[508] the state required that all wine producers, wholesalers, and rectifiers file price schedules with the state, and state licensed wine merchants were required to sell wine to retailers at the scheduled prices. The Court found that the wine producers had the power to prevent price competition by dictating prices and that "the mere existence of legal compulsion did not turn California's scheme into unilateral action by the State."[509] "The national policy in favor of competition cannot be thwarted by casting such a cloak of state involvement over what is essentially a private price-fixing arrangement."[510]

The Court in *Fisher* found that the ordinance could not be viewed as a "cloak for any conspiracy among landlords or between the landlords and the municipality."[511] The Court characterized the *Schwegmann* and *Midcal* arrangements as "hybrid" and distinguished them from *Fisher*, where control over rent levels was in the hands of the city's Rent Stabilization Board and not within the landlord's power.

The *Schwegmann, Midcal*, and *Fisher* trilogy suggests that a local governmental entity and those who must obey its laws are not capable of forming a conspiracy unless the ostensibly municipally administered "scheme is really a private . . . conspiracy, concealed under a 'gauzy cloak of state involvement.'"[512]

[9] National Clubs and Affiliates

The *Copperweld* issue was considered again by the Ninth Circuit in the context of a national dog breed club in *Jack Russell Terrier Network of Northern Cal. v. Am. Kennel Club*.[513] The Jack Russel Terrier Club of America (JRTCA) required its affiliates and members not to register their dogs with "conflicting organizations such as the American Kennel Club."[514] An affiliate that allowed its members to register their dogs with the American Kennel Club (AKC), the Jack Russell Terrier Network of Northern California (JRTNNC), was terminated from the JRTCA.[515] The JRTNCC was threatened with legal action by two of its members who, because of the registration with a

507. *Id.* at 389.

508. 445 U.S. 97 (1980).

509. *Fisher v. City of Berkeley Cal.*, 475 U.S. 260, 269 (1986).

510. *Cal. Liquor Dealers v. Midcal Aluminum*, 445 U.S. 97, 106 (1980).

511. *Fisher*, 475 U.S. at 269.

512. *Cal. Liquor Dealers Ass'n.*, 445 U.S. 97, 106 (1980). See also *324 Liquor Corp. v. Duffy*, 479 U.S. 335 (1987), a vertical retail price maintenance case in which the defendant claimed state action exemption to antitrust liability. The Court held New York's statute providing that liquor retailers must charge at least 112% of wholesalers' posted bottle prices violates § 1 of the Sherman Act. The Court's opinion did not specifically address the conspiracy requirement, but did state that "[t]he antitrust violation in this case is essentially similar to the violation in *Midcal*." *Id.* at 724.

513. 407 F.3d 1027 (9th Cir. 2005).

514. *Id.* at 1029.

515. *Id.* at 1032.

conflicting club, were foreclosed from participating in the activities, shows, and other events organized by the JRTNNC.[516] The plaintiffs, the terminated affiliate and the individual members of the affiliate, claimed that "by boycotting all AKC-registered or dual AKC/JRTCA-registered dog owners and breeders from JRTCA membership and participation in JRTCA-sanctioned events, the JRTCA and participating JRTCA-regional affiliates unreasonably restrained Jack Russel Terrier commerce that would otherwise stem from those JRTCA-sanctioned events, the 'marketplace' of Jack Russel Terrier commerce."[517] The court concluded that the plaintiffs had not alleged sufficient facts to show that the national club and its affiliates were separate entities for the purposes of the antitrust analysis. The objectives of JRTCA and its affiliates were common, not different—to protect "the current and future value of the Jack Russell Terrier breed, as determined by JRTCA-breed standards."[518]

The court wrote:

> [T]he JRTCA's affiliates are best understood as extensions of the national club rather than independent economic actors. [. . .] By the terms of the affiliation agreement [. . .] the affiliates and the JRTCA share a unity of all relevant interests and policies, which are controlled entirely by the JRTCA.[519]

§ 4.16 Criminal Liability

Violations of § 1 of the Sherman Act can result in civil liability, criminal liability, or both. In *United States v. United States Gypsum Co.*,[520] the Supreme Court held that intent is an essential element of a criminal violation under § 1 of the Sherman Act. At issue was the exchange of current price data between competitors. Defendants argued that such an exchange was required in order to establish the "meeting competition" defense to a price discrimination charge under the Robinson-Patman Act.

The district court had instructed the jury that "if the effect of the exchanges of pricing information was to raise, fix, maintain, and stabilize prices, then the parties to them are presumed, *as a matter of law*, to have intended that result."[521] The Supreme Court rejected this instruction, holding that "an effect on prices, without more, will not support a criminal conviction."[522] The requisite intent could be established, the Court concluded, by a showing of "action undertaken with knowledge of its probable consequences [i.e., adverse effects on the market] and having the requisite

516. *Id.* at 1031.
517. *Id.* at 1033.
518. *Id.* at 1035.
519. *Id.*
520. 438 U.S. 422 (1978).
521. *Id.* at 430 (citation omitted) (emphasis added).
522. *Id.* at 435.

anticompetitive effects."[523] Thus, a general intent standard is acceptable when anticompetitive effects in fact are demonstrated. This is a lower burden of proof than that of showing "conduct undertaken with the 'conscious object' of producing such [anticompetitive] effects."[524] This specific intent standard, which the Court rejected, is applicable when no anticompetitive effects are established.[525] It requires a specific intent or conscious purpose to bring about the proscribed consequences.[526]

However, the intent requirement introduced in *Gypsum* usually does not extend to *per se* violations. As the Ninth Circuit held in *United States v. Brown*, "[w]here *per se* conduct is found, a finding of intent to conspire to commit the offence is sufficient; a requirement that intent go further and envision actual anticompetitive results would reopen the very questions of reasonableness which the *per se* rule is designed to avoid."[527]

The Court also stated that, in interpreting the language of criminal statutes, "far more than the simple omission of the appropriate phrase from the statutory definition is necessary to justify dispensing with an intent requirement."[528]

The First Circuit restated *Gypsum*'s requirement for the plaintiff's burden of proof regarding intent,[529] noting the plaintiff must prove the defendant had "an intent to agree and an intent to effectuate the commission of the substantive offense."[530]

In *United States v. Alston*,[531] the Ninth Circuit clarified the burden of proof requirements for criminal action in antitrust cases. In *Alston*, the Department of Justice initiated a criminal action against three dentists alleging they entered into a price-fixing conspiracy to increase the fee schedules for dental services provided to members of prepaid dental plans. Believing the jury instructions were "technically and legally correct," the Ninth Circuit reversed two motions for acquittal notwithstanding the verdict and a request for a new trial. With respect to the government's burden of proof, the Ninth Circuit commented:

> In order to convict any defendant, the government must prove beyond a reasonable doubt as to that each of the following: First, that the conspiracy charged existed at or about the time stated in the indictment; second, that the defendant knowingly—that is, voluntarily and intentionally—became a member of the conspiracy charged in the indictment, knowing of its goal and intending to help accomplish it; and third, that interstate commerce was involved.[532]

---

523. *Id.* at 444.
524. *Id.*
525. *Id.*
526. *Id.* at 444 n.21.
527. 925 F.2d 1182, 1188 (9th Cir. 1991).
528. *Id.* at 438; *see also United States v. Gendron*, 18 F.3d 955, 959 (1st Cir. 1994).
529. *United States v. Piper*, 35 F.3d 611 (1st Cir. 1994).
530. *Id.* at 615.
531. 974 F.2d 1206 (9th Cir. 1992).
532. *Id.* at 1210 (quoting the trial judge's instructions to the jury).

Based upon their review of the record, the Ninth Circuit held that the government presented sufficient evidence to enable the trier of fact to find the dentists guilty beyond a reasonable doubt.

The second element of the *Alston* three-part burden of proof requirement was clarified by the Fourth Circuit in *United States v. Whittington*.[533] The plaintiff need not prove the defendant had knowledge of every detail of the conspiracy in order to prove willful engagement in the conspiracy.[534] Rather, the plaintiff only need show "the defendant knew of the conspiracy's purpose and some action indicating his participation."[535] Circumstantial evidence like the defendant's relationship with other conspirators, the time span of his association, his attitude and behavior, and the nature of the conspiracy all can prove this second prong.[536]

Thus, the burden of proof in a criminal case is distinguishable from that in a civil antitrust case.[537] In the criminal case, a showing of anticompetitive effect is essential, absent specific intent. The general rule in a civil case is that the plaintiff needs to show either an unlawful purpose or an anticompetitive effect. Admittedly, there are few cases where there may be a finding of unlawful intent and no anticompetitive effects, perhaps because of lack of market power,[538] but it is frequently said that in litigating these cases one can infer effects from intent evidence and vice versa.[539]

---

533. 26 F.3d 456 (4th Cir. 1994).

534. *Id.* at 465 (citing *United States v. Goldman*, 750 F.2d 1221, 1227 (4th Cir. 1994)).

535. *Id.* (quoting *United States v. Collazo*, 732 F.2d 1200, 1205 (4th Cir. 1984)).

536. *Id.*

537. *Id.* For a general discussion on contemporary criminal enforcement under the antitrust laws, see Harry First, *Criminal Antitrust Enforcement, in* IX Occasional Papers from the Center for Research in Crime and Justice, New York University School of Law (1991).

538. *Id.* at 445–46. *See also United States v. Container Corp.*, 393 U.S. 333, 337 (1969), discussed at § 4.02[B].

539. *See Nw. Power Prods., Inc. v. Omark Indus. Inc.*, 576 F.2d 83, 90 (5th Cir. 1978) ("An evil intent alone is insufficient to establish a violation under the rule of reason, although proof of intent may help a court assess the market impact of defendants' conduct"); Milton Handler, *Antitrust 1978*, 78 Colum. L. Rev. 1363, 1402 (1978).

Chapter 5
Vertical Restraints

As discussed in Chapter 4, horizontal restraints—agreements between competitors—may be found unlawful under § 1 of the Sherman Act. Vertical restraints—agreements between firms at different levels in the production or distribution chain—may also violate the antitrust laws. Vertical agreements, however, are less likely to be inherently anticompetitive and thus the rule of reason is applied to purely vertical restraints. As a practical matter, this means that plaintiffs are very unlikely to prevail in cases involving vertical restraints.[1] It is in this area that antitrust has undergone the greatest change in the last 50 years.

Generally, vertical restraints are limitations placed on retailer activities by the manufacturer or distributor.[2] For purposes of analysis, it is useful to divide vertical restraints into two very broad categories. First are agreements in which a seller attempts to control a factor relating to the eventual resale of the product. The classic example is a manufacturer that only sells to retailers who agree to charge a specified resale price. These are called vertical price restraints. A manufacturer also may control the types of customers to whom the product is sold or the location of the reseller's store. These are called vertical nonprice restraints. Generally, the direct impact of this category of restraints is on competition among sellers of the same product, or intrabrand competition.

The second broad category includes efforts by sellers to limit interbrand competition. For example, in the typical tying arrangement, a seller sells one product to a buyer only on the condition that the buyer buys another separate product from the same seller. Another possibility is that the seller sells the product only on the condition that the buyer purchases all of its needs for that item from that seller. In addition, there are other methods of insuring the loyalty of the reseller. This Chapter is organized around these two types of restraints.

1. *See* Nicole McGuire, *An Antitrust Narcotic: How the Rule of Reason is Lulling Vertical Enforcement to Sleep*, 45 Loy. L.A. L. Rev. 1225 (2012).

2. In this chapter the terms "manufacturer" and "supplier" will be used to signify the "upstream" firm that is selling a product for resale. The terms "dealer," "retailer," and "reseller," will signify the "downstream" firm that purchases and resells the product.

§ 5.01 Intrabrand Distributional Restraints

Vertical restraints on distribution can be of the price or nonprice variety. Those in the first category include fixing minimum or maximum resale prices. Nonprice restraints appear in a number of forms, but typically involve the allocation of particular geographic areas or classes of customers to specified resellers. For nearly 100 years ending in 2007, the price/nonprice distinction was important. Nonprice restraints were assessed under the rule of reason, while minimum resale price setting (RPM)—in which a manufacturer fixes the price that retailers charge customers—was per se unlawful. Now, however, both price and nonprice vertical restraints are subject to the rule of reason.[3]

As with horizontal restraints, the first element of a § 1 claim challenging vertical restraints is whether an agreement exists. The agreement element is often not contested in vertical restraint cases because vertical agreements are commonly written down and publicly acknowledged. When the first element is contested, the agreement issue can be complex because the question often becomes one of how much circumstantial evidence is necessary to permit the inference of an agreement. The issue is somewhat less critical for defendants in the case of vertical restraints because even if there is an agreement, the rule of reason is applied. The rationale offered for both price and nonprice vertical intrabrand restraints is that they actually enhance interbrand competition. Before examining the law of restraints on distribution, a closer look at this justification is in order.

[A] Intrabrand Restraints and the Free Rider Problem

Vertical restraints can produce both competitive and anticompetitive effects. As in Chapter 4's discussion of horizontal territorial divisions, a key consideration is the theory of the "free rider." Generally in economics, the free rider problem occurs whenever an individual or firm is unable to enjoy the full advantage of the fruits of their work because someone else can use it without paying for the work. For example, without copyright laws, a composer would go uncompensated for the use of his or her works by someone else. The person using the composer's work would be "free riding" on the efforts of the composer. More technically, the composer would be unable to "internalize" the benefits of his or her efforts.

In theory, vertical restraints can increase intrabrand competition if suppliers are permitted to minimize intra-brand free riding. For example, suppose a distributor of

3. The *per se* status of vertical maximum price fixing ended in 1997. *State Oil Co. v. Khan*, 522 U.S. 3 (1997).

Xenox televisions and stereos locates in a high-rent area in the middle of a population center. It also elects to fully train its sales personnel, to carry a full line of Xenox brand equipment in stock, to maintain a service department, and to advertise every week in the local newspaper and on television. In contrast, another retailer locates in the low-rent industrial part of town, rarely advertises, carries very little stock and teaches its sales personnel little more than how to operate the cash register.

One would not be surprised to find that the second retailer is able to sell Xenox products for a lower price than the first. Furthermore, it seems likely that many consumers will go to the fully stocked store to see the equipment and to learn about it from the trained personnel. After gathering the information they need, they go to the retailer who has lower prices and make their purchases or order the equipment for future delivery. In this case, the free rider is the retailer in the industrial section of town; it benefits from the sales efforts of the downtown retailer.

When the downtown retailer is unable to internalize the benefits of the investment in rent, salesperson training, and maintaining a complete inventory and service department, its motivation to continue making such investments obviously will decline. The manufacturer of Xenox products may find that it is better able to compete with other manufacturers when its products are promoted, not by the lowest possible price, but through advertising, immediate availability and in-store sales efforts. The problem, then, is to shelter retailers who promote Xenox products in a manner that is consistent with the interests of the manufacturer from retailers who free ride on those efforts.

The sheltering can take two basic forms: price and nonprice. The manufacturer could require all retailers to observe a minimum resale price. If the high-service retailer and the low-service retailer are charging the same price, buyers would have little incentive to purchase from the low-service retailer. In order to compete effectively, other retailers are likely to find they must offer the same services. Another sheltering device is to assign sales territories to retailers or, in some other way, allow them to claim certain groups of potential customers as essentially their own. Again, the full-service retailer is able to internalize the benefits of its promotional efforts and will continue to sell in a manner that furthers the interests of the manufacturer.

Does this mean that price and nonprice vertical restraints are only procompetitive? Obviously not. First, such restraints definitely curtail *intrabrand* competition, which is competition among retailers who sell the same branded products. Second, vertical restraints may facilitate anticompetitive arrangements among manufacturers or be instigated by retailers who wish to indirectly engage in horizontal price fixing or territorial division through a dealer cartel. Third, vertical restraints on distribution may be used by a manufacturer to segregate a market in order to effectively practice price discrimination.[4]

A study of vertical intrabrand restraints requires close attention to the evolution of antitrust law. At various times over the last 100 years, intrabrand vertical restraints,

---

4. *See* H. Hovenkamp, *Federal Antitrust Policy* 454–55 (3d ed. 2005).

both price and nonprice, were treated as *per se* unlawful. In 1977, the Supreme Court made nonprice restraints subject to the rule of reason.[5] Maximum RPM remained in the *per se* category until 1997, and minimum RPM was *per se* unlawful until 2007, when the Supreme Court reversed a century-old precedent and held that RPM should be evaluated under the rule of reason. Quite clearly, though, the difference in the status of price and nonprice restraints was not as clear as this labeling suggests. During this period, the rationale for rule of reason treatment of nonprice restraints was thought by many to apply to vertical price restraints as well. Whether this view was completely shared by the Supreme Court is not clear but during the period, while maintaining the nominal *per se* status of vertical restraints on price, the Supreme Court made it increasingly difficult for plaintiffs to prevail in vertical price fixing claims. Part of the challenge of understanding modern antitrust law involves assessing the status of the steps the Court took in the 25-year period prior to shifting RPM to a rule of reason analysis.

[B] Vertical Restraints on Price: Shifting Positions

[1] Minimum Resale Price Maintenance (RPM)

The *per se* prohibition of RPM originated in the 1911 case of *Dr. Miles Medical Co. v John D. Park & Sons*.[6] The case involved efforts by the manufacturer of proprietary medicines to control the price at which the medicines were resold at the wholesale and retail levels. Dr. Miles argued that if it had the right to determine to whom it would sell, it should have a right to control the terms of resale. The Court rejected Dr. Miles' argument, concluding that a resale price restriction constituted an impermissible restraint upon alienation.[7] The majority offered no economic arguments for or against the arrangement, except to claim that the plan enhanced the profits of "favored dealers."[8] Essentially, the Court viewed vertical price fixing as indistinguishable from a horizontal agreement among the dealers reselling Dr. Miles' products.[9] After years of scholarly criticism,[10] in *Leegin Creative Leather Products v. PKS, Inc.*,[11]

---

5. *Continental T.V., Inc. v. GTE Sylvania*, 433 U.S. 36 (1977).

6. 220 U.S. 373 (1911), *overruled by Leegin Creative Leather Prod., Inc. v. PSKS, Inc.*, 551 U.S. 877 (2007). The impact of *Dr. Miles* was substantially abated in 1937 by the Miller-Tydings Fair Trade Amendment, ch. 690, 50 Stat. 693 (1937) (codified as amended at 15 U.S.C. § 1 (1976)), which permitted state legislation to authorize resale price maintenance for branded commodities. "Fair trade" was repealed in 1975 thus returning to *Dr. Miles*. Consumer Goods Pricing Act, Pub. L. No. 94-145. 89 Stat. 801 (codified at 15 U.S.C. § 45 (1976) (amending 15 U.S.C. §§ 1, 45)).

7. 220 U.S. at 404.

8. *Id.*

9. *Id.* at 408.

10. *See, e.g.*, R. Bork, *The Antitrust Paradox* 280–98 (1978); H. Hovenkamp, *supra* note 4, at 449–51; Orstein, *Resale Price Maintenance and Cartels*, 30 Antitrust Bull. 401 (1985); Posner, *The Next Step in the Antitrust Treatment of Restricted Distribution: Per Se Legality*, 48 U. Chi. L. Rev. 6 (1981).

11. 551 U.S. 877 (2007).

the Supreme Court rejected the restraint on alienation rationale as "formalistic" and lacking "demonstrable economic effect." In effect, it noted that the logic—the avoidance of free rider effects—applied to nonprice restraints in order to justify their analysis under the rule of reason was equally applicable to RPM.

In *Leegin*, the Supreme Court reversed the per se rule against RPM established in *Dr. Miles*. In a 5-to-4 opinion, the *Leegin* Court reasoned that the rule of reason was the default standard and that the *per se* rule should apply only to restraints that "always or almost always tend to restrict competition and decrease output"[12] and that "lack . . . any redeeming virtue."[13] The majority asserted that the economics literature theorized some procompetitive justifications for RPM, such as retailers investing more in promotional efforts that stimulate interbrand competition. Proponents of RPM argue that absent RPM, discount retailers will freeride on the advertising and promotional work of non-discount retailers. In other words, consumers will take advantage of promotional services offered by non-discount retailers but then purchase the product from lower-cost discount retailers, who can charge a lower price precisely because they are not paying for promotional services. This dynamic reduces the incentive for non-discount retailers to advertise the manufacturer's products. According to the *Leegin* majority, the manufacturer may use RPM to prevent free riding and encourage retailers to promote the manufacturer's products. The Court considered this to a procompetitive effect that counseled against *per se* condemnation of RPM.

The *Leegin* majority, however, conceded that vertical price fixing can have anticompetitive effects. First, it can stabilize a cartel among manufacturers because they can use RPM to identify manufacturers who are charging less than the cartel price. Second, vertical price fixing can stabilize a cartel among retailers who could use the manufacturer's RPM policy to penalize another retailer who cheats on their cartel agreement.

The *Leegin* opinion advised lower courts to consider three factors when applying the rule of reason to RPM. First, the number of manufacturers in a market using RPM is relevant; if many competing manufacturers are using RPM, this "should be subject to more careful scrutiny. . . ."[14] Second, the source of the restraint is important because if retailers convinced the manufacturer to impose RPM, that could be evidence of an underlying retailer cartel. Third, whether the manufacturer or the retailers have market power is important. If neither has market power, the RPM is less likely to have an anticompetitive effect.

Writing for the four Justices in dissent, Justice Breyer highlighted the anticompetitive effects of RPM, emphasizing the empirical evidence that RPM significantly raises the prices charged to consumers. Justice Breyer also noted that the stopping-free riding defense of RPM was largely theoretical, without real-world support. Finally, Justice Breyer wrote about the importance of stare decisis in antitrust and argued that reversing *Dr. Miles* was not warranted.

---

12. *Id.* at 886 (citation omitted).
13. *Id.* (citation omitted).
14. *Id.* at 897.

At this point, there is only preliminary information about the ultimate impact of changing the status of RPM.[15] The issue of the overall effects is complex. For example, some may argue that prices increasing under *Leegin* does not mean the decision was ill-advised—higher prices may be accompanied by better service. While others would respond that these higher prices represent antitrust injury and consumers—not manufacturers—should decide the proper balance between price and service. Moreover, those who favor RPM as a way of controlling free riding may be underestimating the ability of firms to internalize the benefits of services offered simply by charging for them separately. All that can be safely said is that, in some instances, RPM can increase overall efficiency while benefiting both producers and consumers. In others, it may increase overall efficiency but leave consumers worse off. Finally, it can decrease overall efficiency even though producers benefit by its use. Ultimately, there are many products for which free riding is unlikely if not impossible. In these instances, a more refined analysis of RPM would be one that shifts the burden of showing the procompetitve effects of RPM to those fixing prices.[16]

[2] Maximum Resale Price Maintenance

In 1967, in *Albrecht v. The Herald*,[17] the Court announced that the *per se* prohibition on price fixing extended to vertical maximum price fixing. The case arose when Albrecht, a newspaper carrier, charged subscribers a higher price than the maximum suggested by the publisher. In response, the publisher employed an independent circulation firm to solicit customers away from Albrecht and a new carrier to deliver to those customers.

It is useful to note that, at the time the *Albrecht* Court decided that vertical maximum price fixing was *per se* unlawful, vertical nonprice restraints were also *per se* unlawful. More specifically, manufacturers could not sell and then restrict the customers to whom or the areas in which the products were resold. When nonprice vertical restraints were shifted to the rule of reason standard, criticism of the so-called *Albrecht* rule became widespread. Manufacturers could now restrict the customers to whom or the areas in which their resellers sold but could not limit resale prices. This meant that a manufacturer could assign a retailer to a specific geography area but not prevent that same retailer from exploiting any market power it may enjoy in that market. This exploitation, because it would result in lower sales could defeat the purpose of the territorial restraint.

The *Albrect* rule was severely limited in 1990 when the Supreme Court decided *Atlantic Richfield Co. v. USA Petroleum Co (ARCO)*.[18] In *ARCO*, USA Petroleum, a retail

---

15. *See, e.g.*, Nathaniel J. Harris, *Leegin's Effect on Prices: An Empirical Analysis*, 9 J.L. Econ. & Pol'y 251 (2013). For a case illustrating the challenges facing plaintiffs under the rule of reason, see *Jacobs v. Tempur-Pedic Intern, Inc.*, 626 F.3d 1327 (11th Cir. 2010).

16. *See* McGuire, *supra* note 1, at 1269–1270.

17. 390 U.S. 145 (1968), *overturned*, 552 U.S. 3 (1997).

18. 495 U.S. 328 (1990).

seller of gasoline, complained that ARCO, an integrated oil company, had conspired with retailers to whom it supplied gasoline, to set retail prices that were "artificially low."[19] The effect of the scheme, according to USA, was to drive independent retailers from the market. USA did not claim that the prices charged were predatory or below cost. The Court noted that the essence of the problem faced by USA Petroleum was that it was unable to *raise* prices.[20] Any loss due to an inability to raise prices, the Court reasoned, could not be viewed properly as a form of antitrust injury. Although the Court seemed to defend the *Albrecht* rule in *ARCO*, it became less clear who could be a proper antitrust plaintiff.

Finally, in 1997, in *State Oil v. Khan*,[21] the Court overruled *Albrecht*. To some extent the Court's reasoning was a 20-year delayed response to its 1977 decision in *Continental T.V. v. GTE Sylvania*,[22] which marked the Court's acceptance of the free rider rationale for permitting vertical nonprice restraints on distribution. Much of the *Khan* Court's reasoning also reflected doubt about whether any of the original justifications offered in *Albrecht* were well-founded.[23] For example, in *Albrecht* the Court had expressed concern for the freedom of dealers. In *Khan*, however, the Court noted that one possible industry reaction to *Albrecht* was vertical integration and the elimination of dealers altogether. In addition, *Albrecht* was based on a supposition that maximum prices would be set so low as to make it impossible for the dealer to offer desirable services. The *Khan* Court questioned this rationale by suggesting that it would be irrational for manufacturers to set prices so low that sales-enhancing services would be sacrificed. Finally, the *Khan* Court questioned the *Albrecht* reasoning that maximum prices might become minimum prices. The Court conceded that this was a possible result but felt that assessment under the rule of reason would sufficiently recognize and punish those outcomes.

[C] The Treatment of Agreements in the Pre-*Leegin* Period

The period between *Dr. Miles* and *Leegin* can be broken into two periods: pre- and post-*Sylvania*, in which the Supreme Court held that nonprice vertical restraints were not *per se* illegal, but should be evaluated under the rule of reason. Prior to the Supreme Court's recognition of the possible procompetitive impact of vertical restraints, the Court seemed to guard against indirect ways of achieving RPM. After *Sylvania*, the Court changed direction and, in an effort to ensure that procompetitive nonprice vertical restraints were not condemned, it also made it easier for manufacturers to

19. *Id.* at 333.
20. *Id.* at 337–38.
21. 522 U.S. 3 (1997).
22. 433 U.S. 36 (1977).
23. 522 U.S. at 11–15.

influence resale prices. In this period, it also "protected" firms engaged in vertical price restraints by its interpretations of antitrust injury.

[1] Agreements: The Restrictive Period

[a] Consignment and the Use of Sales Agents

Because *Dr. Miles* was so firmly based on the concept of restraints on alienation, the decision seemed to open an important avenue for the control of resale prices through the mechanism of consignment or the use of independent sales agents. Traditionally, a manufacturer sells its products to a retailer, who now owns the products and has the power to set the price it will charge its customers. Under a consignment arrangement, the manufacturer does not actually sell its products to retailers; rather, the manufacturer retains ownership and pays the retailer a fee when customers buy the manufacturer's products from the shop owner. As long as the consignee or agent did not have title to the product, there was no resale and, therefore, no resale price maintenance. For many years, this avenue appeared to be broad enough to circumvent the *per se* rule. The leading case is *United States v. General Electric Co.*[24] in which G.E. employed "agents" for the wholesale and retail sale of light bulbs at prices determined by the manufacturer. The agents were often wholesalers or retailers in their own business and prior to the consignment they had resold G.E. light bulbs. Under the new arrangement, title passed directly from G.E. to the consumer. The Court found that the agents were not purchasers and not, therefore, within the scope of the prohibitions of *Dr. Miles*.[25]

In *Simpson v. Union Oil*[26] the Court returned to the use of consignment as a means of bypassing *Dr. Miles*. Union Oil leased retail outlets for the sale of its gasoline and entered into a consignment agreement with the lessees through which it controlled retail price. The arrangement was challenged by a retailer who was terminated when it "resold" for less than the price fixed by Union Oil. The Court distinguished *General Electric* as dealing with a patented product[27] and found Union Oil's arrangement to be a violation of § 1.

The Court declined to establish a "wooden formula" for determining when a consignment would be a permissible method of controlling prices. Instead, the Court, through an opinion by Justice Douglas, looked to the substance of the plan and concluded "[w]hen . . . a 'consignment' device is used to cover a vast gasoline distribution system, fixing prices through many retail outlets, the antitrust laws prevent calling the 'consignment' agency for then [the prohibition of price fixing] would be avoided merely by clever manipulation of words, not by differences in substance."[28]

---

24. 272 U.S. 476 (1926).

25. *Id.* at 485–87. The *G.E.* rule was controversial. *See* Herbert Hovenkamp, Mark Janis, Mark Lemley, Christopher Leslie & Michael Carrier, *Antitrust and IP: An Analysis of Antitrust Principles Applied to Intellectual Property Law* Chapter 31 (3d ed. 2016).

26. 377 U.S. 13 (1964).

27. *Id.* at 22–24.

28. *Id.* at 21–22.

In addition to the "vastness" of the distribution scheme involved, the Court seemed influenced by what it perceived to be an imbalance of bargaining power between Union Oil and the retail dealers[29] and the fact that business risks were ultimately borne by the dealers.[30] The critical issue after *Simpson* was not whether a consignment existed but whether the effect of the consignment was to circumvent antitrust policy. The *Simpson* Court expressly left open the possibility that smaller scale consignments could be legal.[31]

This suggestion, along with the particular facts of *Simpson* and the Court's refusal to officially overrule *General Electric*, left lower courts with sufficient flexibility to hold that consignments often serve legitimate business purposes.[32] A key factor that has been identified as distinguishing legitimate consignments from those designed to bypass the prohibitions of *Dr. Miles* is the allocation of business risks.[33] When most of the risk, unlike *Simpson*, remains with the manufacturer, the consignee is more likely to be a legitimate sales agent as opposed to an independent retailer through whom the manufacturer wishes to control resale prices. This approach makes a great deal of sense from the standpoint of both equity and efficiency; firms bearing the greatest risk in the marketplace probably should be permitted the leeway to make pricing decisions even if a consignment is involved.

Another factor the courts looked to is whether there are nonprice purposes for the consignment. For example, a consignment or the use of a sales agent may be part of a plan to maintain quality standards or simply an efficient method of marketing.[34] In a Seventh Circuit opinion, Judge Posner pinpointed the characterization problem in sales agent cases by noting that there is no clear line between independent distributors and agents. Accordingly, "distributors are permitted to operate as agents under consignments not intended to circumvent the antitrust laws."[35] Certainly, the problem of distinguishing the legitimate use of sales agents from efforts to circumvent the antitrust laws is complicated.[36]

In the pre-*Leegin* era, a court's approach was colored by its view of the *per se* status of resale price maintenance. Now, while consignment continues to be a useful method of distribution, it is seems less likely to be used as way to conceal RPM simply because engaging in overt RPM is now assessed under the rule of reason. An effort to conceal RPM as a consignment would be attractive only to a firm possessing a high market share. An illustration of how the issue remains relevant can be understood

---

29. *Id.* at 20–21.

30. *Id.* at 20.

31. *Id.* at 21.

32. *See generally* VII P. Areeda & H. Hovenkamp, *Antitrust Law* 269–70 (2003).

33. *Id.; see, e.g., Mesirow v. Pepperidge Farms, Inc.*, 703 F.2d 339 (9th Cir. 1983); *Greene v. General Foods*, 517 F.2d 635 (5th Cir. 1975).

34. *See, e.g., Illinois Corporate Travel, Inc. v. American Airlines*, 889 F.2d 751 (7th Cir. 1989); *Pogue v. International Industries, Inc.*, 524 F.2d 342 (6th Cir. 1975).

35. *Morrison v. Murray Biscuit Co.*, 797 F.2d 1430, 1438 (7th Cir. 1986).

36. For a relatively recent example, see *Day v. U-Haul Int'l Inc.*, 400 F.3d 1272 (11th Cir. 2005).

by considering *Day v. U-Haul Int'l Inc.*,[37] a 2005 case in which independent U-Haul dealers objected to the practice of U-Haul of fixing rental rates for local truck rentals. The court eventually held that dealers were legitimate sale agents because U-Haul retained significant risks.[38] On the other hand, had the court found differently, the practice could have been interpreted as RPM and the possibility that U-Haul would be found to be dominant in the market could have resulted in liability even under the rule of reason.

One possible interpretation of *Leegin* is that the agency defense is no longer viable. In *Valuepest.com of Charlotte v. Bayer Corp.*,[39] pest control companies complained that firms from whom they obtained chemicals were selling at minimum prices dictated by the manufacturer. Defendant relied on *General Electric* and responded that the sellers were "agents." Plaintiffs then claimed the *Leegin* had eliminated the agency defense and that even a true agency was subject to the rule of reason.[40] But if the agency relationship is genuine, no sale has taken place and technically no RPM. The court held that *Leegin* had no bearing on *General Electric*.[41]

[b] Vertical Agreements: The *Colgate* Doctrine and Dealer Termination

Use of consignment agreements and sales agents were ways for manufacturers to retain control over price as the product works its way through the distribution chain to the ultimate consumer. Another common method of controlling resale prices during the restrictive period was for the manufacturer to announce "suggested" resale prices and to refuse to deal with retailers who did not adhere to those prices. Because RPM falls within § 1 of the Sherman Act, there must be evidence that a pricing arrangement was the product of an agreement between the manufacturer and the retailer.

In the context of vertical restraints, there are at least two intertwined issues. First, what is sufficient evidence in the absence of an express agreement to permit the inference of an agreement? The "conscious parallelism" test used to infer horizontal agreements does not apply to vertical agreements because the manufacturer and retailers are not doing the same thing at the same time. Second, how closely associated with the actual restraint must the parties to the combination be?

The question of whether an agreement exists arises in the context of both price and nonprice vertical restraints. Prior to *Leegin*, it was a crucial determination in the context of RPM because fixing minimum resale prices was a *per se* violation of § 1 and the proof of an agreement essentially created antitrust liability. Because nonprice vertical restraints were assessed under the "rule of reason," the proof of an agreement

---

37. *Id.*

38. *Id.* at 1277.

39. 561 F.3d 282 (4th Cir. 2009).

40. *Id.* at 287–88.

41. *See generally* Jeffrey L. Harrison, *Dr. Miles's Orphans: Vertical Conspiracy and Consignment in the Wake of Leegin*, 45 Wake Forest L. Rev. 1125 (2010).

was only one, and possibly a minor, element of the plaintiff's case. Now that would be appear to be the same in the case of RPM.

[i] The "Colgate Doctrine"

When RPM was per se illegal, *United States v. Colgate*[42] provided a loophole to antitrust liability. Colgate had engaged in a number of practices designed to influence the resale price of its products including prior announcement of desired resale prices, persistent urging of dealers to adhere to those prices, and the termination of sales to dealers who did not observe the requested resale price. Although some of the practices seemed to involve actual agreements, the Supreme Court confined its analysis to the indictment as interpreted by the trial court.[43] The Court first determined that the trial court had not viewed the indictment as charging that any actual agreements had been made.[44] Instead a retailer could "after buying, if he chose, give away his purchase or sell it at any price that he saw fit . . . affected only by the fact that he might by his action incur the displeasure of the manufacturer who could refuse to make future sales to him. . . ."[45]

Thus, the issue became whether the dictates of *Dr. Miles* extended to a seller who announced desired resale prices and refused to deal with those who did not adhere to those prices. According to the Court, the *per se* rule did not apply because, under the Sherman Act, sellers were free to deal with whomever they wished and were similarly free to announce in advance under what circumstances they would refuse to deal.[46] As a general matter, *Colgate* permitted manufacturers to influence retail prices through unilateral conduct. The problem remained: how do we determine when conduct was no longer unilateral? Now that RPM is no longer *per se* illegal, *Colgate* would only seem to be important to a firm wishing to engage in RPM but concerned that it would be unlawful under the rule of reason.

Prior to *Sylvania*, most of the cases interpreting *Colgate* tended to narrow the protection it offered. For example, in *Frey & Sons, Inc. v. Cudahy Packing Co.*[47] the Court held that proof of a formal written or oral contract was not required. The agreement, according to the Court, "might be implied from a course of dealing or other circumstances."[48] Similar narrowing in subsequent cases suggested that *Colgate* was only available as a defense when a firm had literally done no more than indicate its wishes and refused to deal with those who did not go along.[49] In *United States v. Parke Davis & Co.*,[50] the Court considered an effort by a manufacturer of pharmaceutical products to control the prices charged by retailers by enlisting the aid of wholesalers.

42. 250 U.S. 300 (1919).
43. *Id.* at 304–06.
44. *Id.* at 307.
45. *Id.* at 306.
46. *Id.* at 307.
47. 256 U.S. 208 (1921).
48. *Id.* at 210.
49. *See United States v. Bausch & Lomb Optical Co.*, 321 U.S. 707, 722–23 (1944).
50. 362 U.S. 29 (1960).

Specifically, wholesalers were told that they would be cut off from supplies if they sold for less than suggested wholesale prices or if they sold to retailers who resold for less than the suggested retail prices. The Court found that Parke Davis had gone well beyond *Colgate* in that it used the threat of a refusal to deal as "the vehicle to gain the wholesalers' participation in the program" to maintain retail prices.[51]

As for the requirement under § 1 of the Sherman Act that an agreement exist, the Court concluded "an unlawful combination is not just as arises from a price maintenance *agreement*, express or implied; such a combination is also organized if the producer secures adherence to his suggested prices by means which go beyond his mere declination to sell to a customer who will not observe his announced policy."[52] In the period immediately after *Parke Davis*, it made sense to echo the concerns of the dissenting Justices in that case and question what was left of *Colgate*.[53]

[ii] The Parties Who Can Combine Under § 1

In the *Dr. Miles* era, not only did courts seem willing to find the required "combination" when threatened firms acquiesced in the wishes of the firm demanding adherence to prices, but parties that could come together to form the necessary plurality of actors were not necessarily those with a direct interest in the outcome of the price-fixing effort. The most telling Supreme Court decision with respect to the latter point is *Albrecht*, discussed above in the context of maximum resale price maintenance.[54] In *Albrecht*, the newspaper formed agreements with both a new carrier and a firm to solicit the customers of the carrier charging in excess of the maximum price. Although the *per se* prohibition of vertical maximum price fixing found in *Albrecht* has been overturned, its discussion of what constitutes an actionable agreement is still worth noting. The Court found that the necessary combination was formed between the newspaper, the circulation company, and the new carrier.[55] The Court relied on *Parke Davis*, reasoning that if the combination requirement was met in that case by threats to wholesalers, then it was surely met here as the solicitation company and the new carrier knew the purpose was to force Albrecht to observe the maximum price.[56] In addition, the Court suggested in a footnote the possibility of finding a combination between the plaintiff and the defendant "at least as of the day he [the plaintiff] unwillingly complied with the respondents's advertised price" or between the defendant and other carriers who "acquiesced" in the pricing policy.[57]

---

51. *Id.* at 46.

52. *Id.* at 43.

53. *Id.* at 49–57 (Stewart J., dissenting). *See* Pitofsky & Dam, *Is the Colgate Doctrine Dead?*, 37 Antitrust L.J. 772 (1968).

54. 390 U.S. 145 (1968), *overturned*, 552 U.S. 3 (1997).

55. *Id.* at 148–50.

56. *Id.* at 149–50.

57. *Id.* at 150 n. 6. Justice Harlan dissented noting that there would not have been a combination with the newspaper had it assigned one of its own employees the task of solicitation or delivery. Moreover, neither the solicitation company nor the new carrier had any special interest in the success of the maximum price setting plan. He charged that the majority had removed any significant meaning from

The language in *Albrecht* pertaining to agreements represents the highpoint of the Court's willingness to limit *Colgate* and find the necessary combination in vertical restraint cases. It is not surprising to find that it was decided in a period when both price and nonprice vertical restraints were categorized as *per se* violations. Its liberal view of a § 1 combination, along with a narrow interpretation of *Colgate* and an almost uniform *per se* approach to vertical restraints, made it very easy for any terminated dealer to make a colorable case that the termination was the result of a vertical conspiracy in violation of § 1.

[2] Agreements in the Less Restrictive Period

[a] Monsanto v. Spray-Rite Service Corp.

The Supreme Court announced a change in antitrust philosophy in 1977 in *Continental T.V. Inc. v. GTE Sylvania*,[58] which removed nonprice vertical restraints from the *per se* category. The Court accepted the possibility that some nonprice vertical restraints on distribution could be procompetitive. This meant that it was critical to distinguish RPM (which is a price restraint) from other nonprice restraints on intrabrand competition. In other words, the issue was not simply whether an agreement existed but what was the objective of the agreement. More specifically, was a *per se* unlawful combination found when competitors of a price-cutting dealer complained to their joint supplier and termination of the dealer resulted. After some conflicting decisions in the circuit courts,[59] the Supreme Court addressed the issue in 1984 in *Monsanto v. Spray-Rite Service Corp.*[60]

In *Monsanto*, the Court considered the Seventh Circuit's holding that "proof of termination following competitor complaints is sufficient to support an inference of concerted action."[61] The Supreme Court rejected the Seventh Circuit's standard because it would improperly allow inferences of agreement from retailer complaints and interfere with the manufacturer's freedom to engage in independent action. Proof of complaints from dealers, a common occurrence, was not enough to prove that termination was not the product of independent action allowable under *Colgate*. Instead, the plaintiff's evidence must tend "to exclude the possibility that the manufacturer

---

the concept of "combination." *Id.* at 160–63 (Harlan, J. dissenting). See *Russell Stover Candies, Inc. v. FTC*, 718 F.2d 256, 260 (8th Cir. 1983), where the Eighth Circuit stated: "If *Colgate* no longer stands for the proposition that a 'simple refusal to sell to customers who will not sell at prices suggested by the seller is permissible under the Sherman Act' . . . it is for the Supreme Court, not this court, to so declare." The court held that acquiescence through coercion did not constitute the requisite agreement.

58. 433 U.S. 36 (1977). *See* § 5.01[D][3], *infra*. *See generally* Harrison, *supra* note 41.

59. *Compare Edward J. Sweeney & Sons, Inc. v. Texaco, Inc.*, 637 F.2d 105 (3d Cir. 1980), *with Spray-Rite Serv. Co. v. Monsanto Co.*, 684 F.2d 1226 (7th Cir. 1982), 465 U.S. 752 (1984), *rehearing. denied*, 466 U.S. 994 (1984).

60. 465 U.S. 752 (1984). *See generally* Hay, *Vertical Restraints After* Monsanto, 66 Cornell. L. Rev. 418 (1985); Floyd, *Vertical Antitrust Conspiracies After* Monsanto *and* Russell Stover, 33 Kan. L. Rev. 274 (1985).

61. 465 U.S. at 758, *quoting* 684 F.2d at 1238.

and nonterminated distributors were acting independently."[62] *Monsanto* required direct or circumstantial evidence of "a conscious commitment to a common scheme to achieve an unlawful objective."[63] This could be shown by evidence "that the distributor communicated its acquiescence or agreement, and that this was sought by the manufacturer."[64]

The Court's decision was influenced by the difficulty of distinguishing vertical price restraints, which were *per se* illegal, from nonprice restraints, which were subject to the rule of reason. The Court reasoned that an overly permissive approach to proof of a combination could not only encroach on a manufacturer's rights under *Colgate* but endanger its ability to utilize procompetitive nonprice restraints. The Court recognized that manufacturers may have an interest, independent from complaining dealers, in protecting dealers from free riding discounters.[65] The facts of *Monsanto* serve to illustrate the commingling of price and nonprice restraints about which the *Monsanto* Court was concerned. The plaintiff, Spray-Rite, contended that its price discounts led to its termination. Monsanto, on the other hand, cited Spray-Rite's refusal to hire trained sales staff and promote sales adequately as the factors precipitating termination.[66] Depending on the perspective taken the case could be seen as either concerning a price or a nonprice restraint and, therefore, requiring either a *per se* or rule of reason analysis. The Court, however, chose to treat the case as one involving price restraints.[67]

Monsanto clearly revived *Colgate*. For example, the *Monsanto* Court noted that no agreement would arise from a manufacturer's announcement and a dealer's acquiescence[68]—a possibility that the *Albrecht* Court expressly suggested. Moreover, *Monsanto* opened the door to allowing discussions between manufacturers and dealers, even about price, as long as there was no agreement on a price. Indeed, the Court recognized the need for such contacts in order to further lawful nonprice restraints.[69] In essence, by reviving or broadening *Colgate* in the interest of protecting legal nonprice restraints, the Court implicitly discounted the dangers of vertical price restraints. Consequently, concerns about vertical price restraints became subordinate to an interest in promoting nonprice restraints. It seems clear the Court was beginning to recognize the difficulty of treating price and nonprice restraints differently when the rationale for rule of reason treatment of nonprice restraints (preventing free riders) was potentially applicable to vertical price restraints.

---

62. 465 U.S. at 764.

63. *Id.* (quoting *Edward J. Sweeney & Sons*, 637 F.2d at 111).

64. 465 U.S. at 764 n.9.

65. *Id.* at 762–63. *But see* Note, *A Functional Rule of Reason Analysis for the Law of RPM and its Application to* Spray-Rite, 1984 Wisc. Law. Rev. 1205.

66. *Id.* at 755–57.

67. For a criticism of the Court's characterization of the case as involving vertical price restraints *see* Hovenkamp, *Vertical Restrictions and Market Power*, 64 B.U. L. Rev. 521 (1984).

68. 465 U.S. at 761. *See also Russell Stover v. FTC*, 718 F.2d 256 (8th Cir. 1983).

69. *Id.* at 762–63. *See generally* Faruk, *The Defense of Terminated Dealer Litigation: A Survey of Legal and Strategic Considerations*, 46 Ohio State L.J. 925 (1985).

[b] Business Electronics v. Sharp Electronics Corp.[70]

The divergent approach to price and nonprice vertical restraints affected antitrust opinions. For example, in *Business Electronics v. Sharp Electronics Corp.*, defendant Sharp terminated the plaintiff, Business Electronics, for selling at prices below list and after a competing dealer threatened to drop Sharp products. The complaining dealer testified that it was less concerned about Business Electronics' discounts than it was about the free riding of Business Electronics on the complaining dealer's product promotion efforts. In its jury instructions, the trial court indicated that if an agreement existed between Sharp and the complaining dealer to terminate Business Electronics because of price cutting, there was a *per se* violation of the Sherman Act.[71] The issue on appeal concerned this instruction. Specifically, was it a *per se* violation to agree to terminate a dealer because of price cutting or was it necessary to find that the agreement was part of a scheme to fix an actual resale price? Noting that every vertical restraint could have an impact on price, the Supreme Court reasoned that the *per se* label must be reserved for a very narrow class of cases. To do otherwise, according to Justice Scalia, would "dismantle the doctrine of *GTE Sylvania*."[72] The Court concluded that "economic analysis supports the view, and no precedent opposes it, that a vertical restraint is not illegal *per se* unless it includes some agreement on price or price levels."[73] The Court emphasized that, without an agreement on the actual resale price, vertical agreements were unlikely to lead to a cartel at either the manufacturer's or retailer's level. It distinguished *Dr. Miles* as based on an impermissible restraint on alienation and *Albrecht v. Herald Co.* as involving an express agreement on price.[74] Finally, it rejected the arguments in dissent by Justices Stevens and White that the agreement should be treated as though it were horizontal in nature because it was a naked restraint involving coercion of the manufacturer in order to eliminate price competition among retailers.

Business Electronics and its interpretations greatly narrowed the *per se* rule prohibiting minimum vertical price fixing thereby decreasing even further the possibility that a terminated dealer could mount a successful action against a manufacturer. In fact, although *Leegin* officially overruled *Dr. Miles, Business Electronics* laid the groundwork establishing RPM as a de facto rule of reason offense.

After *Leegin, Monsanto* and *Business Electronics* became less important.[75] In a sense the cases served as a bridge between *Sylvania* and *Leegin*. In effect, they could be seen as efforts to rationalize an antitrust policy under which the free rider rationale was accepted for some vertical restraints but not for others. Although the cases could be relevant in the context of a concealed intrabrand vertical restraint, it is not clear why a modern nondominant business firm would attempt to conceal its agreements with its distributors.

70. 485 U.S. 717 (1988).
71. *Id.* at 725.
72. *Id.* at 727.
73. *Id.* at 735–36.
74. *Id.* at 731–35.
75. *See* Harrison, *supra* note 41.

[D] Territorial and Customer Restraints

The history of nonprice vertical restraints is quite different than that of RPM. Rather than RPM's nearly 100-year period of *per se* illegality, in considering the legal standard for evaluating nonprice vertical restraints, the Court changed course twice over a period of 15 years.

[1] White Motor Co. v. United States

The Supreme Court's jurisprudence on nonprice vertical restraints began in 1963 with *White Motor Co.*[76] White Motor Company, a manufacturer and seller of trucks and parts, required its dealers to sell only to customers who had places of business within the territory assigned to the dealer. In addition, no sales were to be made to government agencies. The former restriction is a classic example of a territorial clause; the latter is an example of a customer clause. White Motor Company argued that the territorial clause was necessary to develop a system of retail outlets in order to compete effectively with larger manufacturers. The customer clause, in effect, reserved to White Motor the opportunity to make fleet sales. The justification was that large scale buyers, if forced to purchase repair parts from dealers, would lose discounts and become "discontented" with White.[77]

The issue was whether the territorial and customer clauses should be regarded as *per se* violations of § 1 of the Sherman Act. In essence, the Court considered whether vertical restraints were sufficiently similar to horizontal restraints to be subject to the same standard.[78] By a 5-3 majority, the Court ruled that they were not and declined to apply the *per se* rule. The Court noted that *per se* treatment was reserved for practices with a "pernicious effect" on competition and a "lack of any redeeming virtue." It reasoned that horizontal territorial limitations were *per se* violations because they fit this description in that they were "naked restraints . . . with no purpose except to stifle competition." On the other hand, it concluded that it did not know "enough of the economic and business stuff out of which [vertical] arrangements emerge"[79] to rule that they too were virtually always anticompetitive in effect.

[2] United States v. Arnold, Schwinn & Co.[80]

Just four years later, in 1967, the Court in *Schwinn* reversed *White Motor*. *Schwinn* involved the contractual arrangements of a bicycle manufacturer for the distribution and final sale of its products. The system was three-pronged. Some bicycles were sold by distributors but shipped directly to the retailer by Schwinn with the distributor earning a commission. Others were sold to distributors for resale. Others were

---

76. 372 U.S. 253 (1963).
77. *Id.* at 257–58.
78. *Id.* at 263.
79. *Id.*
80. 388 U.S. 365 (1967).

consigned to the distributors for sale to retailers. In the latter two cases, the distributors were permitted to sell only to franchised dealers within designated territories. Retailers were permitted only to buy from the distributor in their area and permitted to sell only to consumers.

In a major stroke of judicial activism, since the question of *per se* illegality was not part of the appeal, the Court announced that vertical territorial and customer restraints were *per se* unlawful.[81] It struck down Schwinn's restrictions on resale as they applied to distributors and retailers who had purchased bicycles. It distinguished, however, sales made on behalf of Schwinn under consignment. The latter restraints remained under the "rule of reason." Although the Court had indicated in *White Motor Co.* that it would not declare vertical restraints *per se* unlawful without further knowledge of economic factors, the reasoning of the *Schwinn* Court left a great deal—perhaps everything—to be desired in this regard. The Court professed to examine the relevant "economic and business stuff," but its analysis went no further than to focus on the impact on intrabrand competition and to distinguish the case from *White Motor Co.*[82] In large measure, rather than rely on economic analysis at all, the Court reasoned that to permit continued vertical restraints when sales were involved "would violate the ancient rule against restraints on alienation."[83]

It is perhaps too easy to dismiss *Schwinn* as totally inconsistent with the promotion of economic benefits flowing from vertical restraints. Part of the rationale for leaving restraints associated with consignments in the "rule of reason" of category was to avoid "hampering smaller enterprises resorting to reasonable means of meeting the competition of giants."[84] In essence, the Court seemed to sense the procompetitive potential of vertical restraints and feel that they could be realized through the preservation of the right of manufacturers to invoke such restraints through consignment sales.

[3] Continental T.V., Inc. v. GTE Sylvania

After ten years of nearly uniform scholarly condemnation and judicial efforts at narrowing the reach of *Schwinn*, the Court overturned *Schwinn* in *Continental T.V. v. GTE Sylvania.*[85] The case is a landmark in antitrust because the Court embraced Chicago School-style economic analysis.[86] The Court declined to distinguish *Sylvania* from *Schwinn*, even though the cases concerned different types of vertical restraints, and manufacturers with significantly different market shares.[87]

---

81. *Id.* at 382.

82. *Id.* at 373–75.

83. *Id.* at 380.

84. *Id.*

85. 433 U.S. 36 (1977).

86. Another clear example came earlier in *United States Steel Corp. v. Fortner Enterprises, Inc.*, 429 U.S. 610 (1977). *See* § 5.02[B][2][b], *infra*.

87. Schwinn's market share was over 10% and it used both customer and territorial restraints. Sylvania's market share eventually reached 5% and its vertical restraint was a "location clause."

Sylvania was a struggling manufacturer of television sets with a market share of 1 to 2% in 1962. It then changed its marketing strategy to using a small group of franchisees. Franchisees could sell any brand of television from their stores and could sell to any class of customer. Under Sylvania's plan, however, they could not sell Sylvania televisions from other than approved locations.

The plan was designed to shield Sylvania dealers from competition by other Sylvania dealers in hopes that they would compete aggressively and promote Sylvania televisions. The "location clause" arrangement was eventually challenged by Continental T.V. when it was terminated as a dealer after selling from an unauthorized location.

The Court's analysis consisted of two steps. First, it discarded the sale/consignment distinction of Schwinn as difference with formal but not economic consequence.[88] Thus, whatever the merits or demerits of vertical restraints, the form—sale or consignment—was irrelevant. Having resolved to eliminate this inconsistency, the Court was not then required to upset *Schwinn's* *per se* standards. It could have classified both sales and consignments as *per se* unlawful. Instead it ruled that nonprice restraints associated with consignments and sales would be evaluated under the "rule of reason." The Court specifically cited the possible use of vertical restraints as a means of promoting interbrand competition by limiting the free rider effect.[89] Indeed, in this regard, it stated that interbrand competition was the "primary concern of antitrust law,"[90] thereby apparently reducing intrabrand competition to an ancillary concern.[91] Then, reverting to the analysis of *White Motor Co.*, it concluded that there was an absence of evidence generally, and with respect to the case at hand, to decide that vertical restraints had "a 'pernicious effect on competition' or that they 'lack . . . any redeeming virtue.'"[92]

There are several other facets of the opinion that deserve particular note. First, the Court did not rule out "the possibility that particular applications of vertical restraints might justify *per se* prohibition" in the future.[93] Second, in the process of explaining the result in *Sylvania*, it effectively undercut the rationale for *Dr. Miles' per se* treatment of vertical price restraints by reasoning that the notion of "restraints on alienation" had little antitrust significance. Still, it maintained that RPM could be distinguished from nonprice vertical restraints and left intact the *per se* status of RPM.[94] Obviously, in light of *Leegin*, the Court no longer holds this position.

---

88. *Id.* at 52–54.

89. *Id.* at 54–56.

90. *Id.* at 52 n.19.

91. This is inconsistent with the Court's opinion in *Topco*, which precluded plaintiffs from making this argument. *United States v. Topco Associates, Inc.*, 405 U.S. 596 (1972). *See* §4.13[A][2], *infra* (discussing *Topco*).

92. *Id.* at 58, *citing Northern Pacific R.R. v. United States*, 356 U.S. 1, 5 (1958).

93. 433 U.S. at 58.

94. *Id.* at 51 n.18.

Finally, and perhaps most importantly, the Court gave little direction to courts attempting to apply the rule of reason standard to nonprice vertical restraints. The limited advice offered by the Court came in three general forms. First, as noted, the Court asserted that interbrand competition was the primary concern of the antitrust laws, a position it has subsequently reiterated.[95] Thus, although the opinion certainly gives the impression that a balancing of intrabrand and interbrand effects is to take place, the Court's primary objective seemed to be the promotion of interbrand competition. This follows, the Court explained, from the fact that as long as there is aggressive interbrand competition, "it provides a significant check on the exploitation of intrabrand market power."[96]

Second, the Court quoted the general language of the leading rule of reason case, *Chicago Board of Trade v. United States*,[97] including its list of the factors that can influence a rule of reason analysis. Courts, however, do not apply this as a traditional factor test in which each factor is discussed and weighed. Instead, the list provides examples of considerations that can inform the antitrust analysis.

Third, the Court offered a list of procompetitive reasons for the adoption of vertical restraints. The list includes the use of restrictions during entry into a market in order to induce aggressive marketing by retailers. It also includes the use of vertical restraints as protection from free riders for retailers offering service and repair facilities that might generate good will for the manufacturer. In addition, the Court suggested that vertical restraints could play a role in assuring the safety and quality of the manufacturer's product.[98] This last suggestion, found in a footnote, can be interpreted as an indication that product safety was to have some weight in an antitrust review, a possibility supposedly discarded the following year in *National Society of Professional Engineers v. United States.*[99]

Sylvania left open the issue of how one balances the decrease in intrabrand competition against a possible increase in interbrand competition.[100] Presumably, a system without vertical restraints would mean lower prices. If the imposition of restraints does encourage nonprice competition, prices will be higher, but the product will be "different" in the sense that it will be accompanied by service and repair opportunities or have enhanced appeal due to promotional activities.[101] Although the problem may not be exactly like the proverbial one of comparing apples and oranges, it is uncomfortably close. What is clear, is that any anticompetitive impact on intrabrand competition is unlikely to outweigh procompetitive interbrand affects.

95. For a recent example, see *Volvo Trucks North America, Inc. v. Reeder-Simco GMC, Inc.*, 546 U.S. 164 (2006).

96. 433 U.S. at 52 n.19.

97. 246 U.S. 231, 238 (1918), quoted at 433 U.S. at 49 n.15.

98. 433 U.S. at 55 n.23.

99. 435 U.S. 679 (1978).

100. Frank Easterbrook, *Vertical Arrangement and the Rule of Reason*, 53 Antitrust L.J. 135 (1984).

101. *See* Posner, *The Next Step in the Antitrust Treatment of Restricted Distribution: Per Se Legality*, 48 U. Chi. L. Rev. 6, 19 (1981).

[4] *The Aftermath of* Sylvania

To find the result of the "full" rule of reason approach flowing from *Sylvania*, one need look no further than Professor Robert Pitofsky's prediction issued in 1978, on the heels of the Court's decision:

> A standard under which all circumstances are weighed, and violations found only upon demonstration of specific anticompetitive effects, may sound sober and moderate, but in the real world it has little deterrent effect, produces trials of inordinate length and expense, and often undermines antitrust enforcement. Business practices tested under a full rule of reason, with no presumptions based on any set of facts and with the burden of showing anticompetitive effect on the plaintiff, will usually turn out to be legal.[102]

Professor Pitofsky's prediction of "usual" legality has turned out to be accurate. Antitrust liability based on nonprice vertical restraints on distribution is, in fact, rare.[103] Furthermore, it would be misleading to suggest that the courts have arrived at a uniform method of applying the rule of reason to nonprice vertical restraints. In addition, after *Leegin*, liability based on RPM is also likely to be very rare.

The notion that the anticompetitive effects of vertical restraints on intrabrand competition would be placed on a scale opposite the procompetitive interbrand effects has given way to an approach that focuses directly on interbrand impact.[104] The logic, which can be gleaned from *Sylvania* itself,[105] and which now finds support in most circuits, is that there can be no detrimental interbrand effects unless the manufacturer has market power.[106] For example, a manufacturer's actions vis-à-vis vertical restraints cannot result in increased prices and restricted output as long as there are aggressive sellers of other brands. The market power of the firm imposing the restraint has become the "threshold issue" because, in the absence of power, a firm "is unlikely to adopt policies that disserve its customers."[107]

---

102. Pitofsky, *The* Sylvania *Case: Antitrust Analysis of Non-Price Vertical Restraints*, 78 Colum. L. Rev. 1, 2 (1978). *See also* William F. Baxter, *The Viability of Vertical Restraints Doctrine*, 75 Cal. L. Rev. 933, 949 (1987).

103. Two early exceptions are *Graphic Products Distributors, Inc. v. Itek Corp.*, 717 F.2d 1560 (11th Cir. 1983), and *Eiberger v. Sony Corp.*, 622 F.2d 1068 (2d Cir. 1980). Modern cases have been deferential to defendants.

104. *See, e.g., Eastern Food Services, Inc. v. Pontifical Catholic Univ. Serv Ass'n Inc.*, 357 F.3d 1 (1st Cir. 2004); *Menasha Corp. v. News America Marketing In-Store, Inc.*, 354 F.3d 661 (7th Cir. 2004); *JBL Enterprises, Inc. v. Jhirmack Enterprises, Inc.*, 698 F.2d 1011 (9th Cir. 1983); *Valley Liquors, Inc. v. Renfield Importers, Ltd.*, 678 F.2d 742 (7th Cir. 1982); *Daniels v. All Steel Equipment Co.*, 590 F.2d 111 (5th Cir. 1979).

105. 433 U.S. at 52 n.19.

106. *See* H. Hovenkamp, *supra* note 4, at 483–85.

107. *Valley Liquors*, 678 F.2d at 745. *See also Muenster Butane, Inc. v. Stewart Co.*, 651 F.2d 292 (5th Cir. 1980); *Graphic Products Distributors v. Itek Corp.*, 717 F.2d 1560 (11th Cir. 1983).

In theory, the analysis of market power serves to screen or filter out cases in which competitive harm is unlikely.[108] Specifically, vertical restraints are likely lawful when the firm imposing them has little market power in the interbrand market because competitors in the market can respond. If, for example, the restraint shields dealers from free riding and, therefore, encourages their promotional efforts, this would raise little concern if the restraint is employed by a firm with 5% of the market. Conversely, if the firm has a 60% market share, there would be reason for much greater concern. In some cases, courts have approved implicitly of justifications that generally mirror the suggestions in *Sylvania* itself without a detailed market analysis.[109] In any event, in the post-*Sylvania* era, plaintiffs objecting to vertical restraints on distribution (and presumably, after *Leegin*, on price) will rarely prevail.

[E] Dual Distribution

Because of *Sylvania* and *Leegin*, courts view horizontal and intrabrand vertical restraints very differently. Vertical restraints are assessed under the rule of reason, while many horizontal restraints are viewed as *per se* unlawful. Some horizontal restraints, however, are only nominally *per se* unlawful and receive a broader examination.

Nevertheless, the different treatment means that the classification of a restraint as vertical or horizontal can be critical. Unfortunately, it also can be very difficult.[110] For example, suppose a manufacturer of shoes owns a chain of retail outlets. Plus, it sells shoes to independent retailers who are assigned specific territories in order to decrease intrabrand competition both with each other and with the manufacturer's own outlets. The restraint could be designed to reserve to the manufacturer, and each distributor, an area in which it has monopoly power at the retail level. Or, it could be designed to protect retailers from free riders as means of encouraging promotion of the manufacturer's product. The situation, in either case, is called "dual distribution" because the manufacturer operates on the same level as the firms it supplies. The question is whether the territorial restraint is horizontal or vertical.[111]

Because the Supreme Court has yet to rule on the proper treatment to be afforded a system of dual distribution, lower courts have employed a variety of approaches to the classification problem resulting in a trend toward rule of reason treatment.[112] One

108. Steuer, *The Turning Points in Distribution Law*, 35 Antitrust Bull. 467, 478 (1990).

109. *See, e.g., Mendelovitz v. Aldolph Coors Co.*, 693 F.2d 570, 576 (5th Cir 1982); *Red Diamond Supply, Inc. v. Liquid Carbonic Corp.*, 637 F.2d 1001, 1005 (5th Cir. 1981).

110. Mark A. Lemley & Christopher R. Leslie, *Categorical Analysis in Antitrust Jurisprudence*, 93 Iowa L. Rev. 1207 (2008).

111. *See generally* Barbara O. Bruckman, *Fresh Perspectives on Dual Distribution: Managing Antitrust Risks of Price-Related Restraints*, 17 Antitrust 19 (2003); Alan J, Meese, *Property Rights and Intrabrand Restraints*, 89 Corn. L. Rev. 553 (2004).

112. *See, e.g., PSKS, Inc. v. Leegin Creative Leather Prod., Inc.*, 615 F.3d 412 (5th Cir. 2010); *AT & T Corp. v. JMC Telecom, LLC*, 470 F.3d 525 (3d Cir. 2006); *Donald B. Rice Tire Co. v. Michelin Tire Corp.*, 638 F.2d 15 (4th Cir. 1981); *Krehl v. Baskin-Robbins Ice Cream Co.*, 664 F.2d 1348 (9th Cir. 1982); *Red Diamond Supply, Inc. v. Liquid Carbonic Corp.*, 637 F.2d 1001 (5th Cir. 1981).

approach, evidently inspired by *Schwinn*, involves ascertaining whether the arrangement is primarily the result of an agreement among competitors or whether it was instituted primarily by the manufacturer.[113] The logic is that a restraint imposed by a manufacturer is likely to be driven by the desire to encourage interbrand competition.[114] On the other hand, competitors may enter into the same arrangement for anticompetitive purposes. In a sense, the determination of the source of the restraint is used as a surrogate for an examination of the function of the restraint.[115]

Other courts have been less trusting of a correlation between the source of restraint and its purpose. Thus, rather than a bright line test, a trend toward evaluating dual distribution under the rule of reason has developed.[116] The Fourth Circuit Court of Appeals, for example, has observed, "it is important to distinguish between a conspiracy among dealers and their supplying manufacturer . . . that would benefit the dealers and one involving the same parties but redounding primarily to the benefit of the manufacturer as a result of increased interbrand competition."[117] Implicit in such an approach is the belief that a "vertical" restraint could result from the power wielded by a cartel of dealers. The court admitted that this substantive analysis is essentially an application of the rule of reason.[118]

Similarly, in one of the more influential dual distribution cases, *Krehl v. Baskin-Robbins Ice Cream Co.*,[119] the court observed, "our inquiry focuses not on whether the vertical or horizontal aspects of the system predominate, but rather, on the actual competitive impact."[120] The court essentially skipped the classification step or replaced it with the rule that "in the absence of proof of anti-competitive purpose or effect, dual distribution must be evaluated under the traditional rule of reason standard."[121]

Finally, in a Seventh Circuit opinion, Judge Easterbrook reasoned that "[d]ual distribution . . . does not subject to the *per se* ban a practice that would be lawful if the manufacturer were not selling directly to customers; antitrust laws encourage rather than forbid this extra competition."[122] The rule-of-reason treatment of dual distribution finds considerable support in economic theory. The question is whether a

---

113. *See, e.g., H & B Equipment Co. v. International Harvester Co.*, 577 F.2d 239 (5th Cir. 1978).

114. *Red Diamond Supply Co. v. Liquid Carbonic Corp.*, 637 F.2d 1001, 1004 n.4 (5th Cir. 1981).

115. The Fifth Circuit Court of Appeals, the leading proponent of the "source" approach to classification has altered its course somewhat to one that focuses more on actual impact. *See Abadir & Co. v. First Mississippi Corp.*, 651 F.2d 422 (5th Cir. 1981).

116. *See, e.g., Elecs. Commc'ns Corp. v. Toshiba Am. Consumer Prods., Inc.*, 129 F.3d 240, 243 (2d Cir. 1997); *Vital Pharms., Inc. v. Berlin Packaging LLC*, 632 F. Supp. 3d 780, 785 (N.D. Ill. 2022). *See also United States v. Brewbaker*, 87 F.4th 563, 583 (4th Cir. 2023) ("While sometimes applying different analyses, this Court and nearly all other lower courts have adjudged hybrid restraints with vertical and horizontal aspects under the rule of reason.").

117. *Donald B. Rice Tire Co. v. Michelin Tire Corp.*, 638 F.2d 15, 16 (4th Cir. 1981).

118. *Id.* at 16–17.

119. 664 F.2d 1348 (9th Cir. 1982).

120. *Id.* at 1356.

121. *Id.* at 1357. *Accord Copy-Data Systems, Inc. v. Toshiba America, Inc.*, 663 F.2d 405 (2d Cir. 1981); *Davis-Watkins Co. v. Service Merchandise Co.*, 686 F.2d 1190 (6th Cir. 1982).

122. *Illinois Corporate Travel, Inc. v. American Airlines*, 889 F.2d 751, 753 (7th Cir. 1989).

manufacturer who institutes dual distribution is after the same types of gains normally associated with typical horizontal agreements. Some commentators argue that this is extremely unlikely.[123] First, if a manufacturer does not have market power, there is nothing magical about dual distribution that will suddenly enable it to raise prices and restrict output. Second, even if it does have market power, economic theory suggests that the firm can reap the full benefits of that power by its pricing as a manufacturer.[124]

[F] Exclusive Dealerships

A territorial or customer restraint limits the area in which a dealer may compete. This does not necessarily mean that there will not be other dealers sharing that territory. In fact, the manufacturer can "regulate" the amount of intrabrand competition by adjusting the number of sellers sharing a market. Under another type of vertical restraint, the exclusive dealership, the dealer is the exclusive representative of the manufacturer.

Both territorial restraints and exclusive dealership agreements can shield a dealer from intrabrand competition and free rider problems. Thus, either one can be used to promote interbrand competition. A combination of the two means even greater protection. Here the retailer is assigned not only a territory but is the only retailer permitted to sell within that territory. In theory, this completely eliminates intrabrand competition.[125]

Three questions are raised by exclusive dealerships. First, how are they to be treated when unaccompanied by a vertical restraint that makes them "absolute" or "airtight?"[126] Second, does it make a difference how the exclusive dealership is achieved. For example, does it matter whether it comes about by terminating all but one dealer or by the initial appointment of a single dealer and refusals to deal with subsequent applicants. Finally, how is the exclusive dealership to be treated when it is superimposed over a vertical territorial restraint?

With respect to the first question, there is language in *Schwinn*, the case taking the *least* charitable approach to vertical restraints, suggesting that exclusive dealerships are *per se* legal. According to that Court, "a manufacturer of a product other and equivalent brands of which are readily available in the market may select his customers, and for this purpose he may 'franchise' certain dealers to whom, alone he will sell his goods."[127] Challenging exclusive dealerships under § 1 is theoretically possible, but unlikely. For example, in *Paddock Publications v. Chicago Tribune*,[128] a Chicago

---

123. *See* H. Hovenkamp, *supra* note 4, at 490.

124. The argument here is the same one made with respect to the economics of tying, *see infra*, § 5.02[B][1], and vertical integration by a monopolist, *infra* § 6.05[G].

125. The exclusive dealership should be distinguished from "exclusive dealing." Exclusive dealing requires a buying (or selling) firm to buy from (or sell to) one other firm.

126. *See generally* Pitofsky, *supra* note 102, at 17.

127. 388 U.S. at 376.

128. 103 F.3d 42 (7th Cir. 1996).

newspaper sought relief because a rival newspaper had exclusive rights in the Chicago area to the New York Times News Service as a source of stories. The argument by the plaintiff was that this exclusive access rendered the newspaper market less competitive. In finding the exclusivity arrangement lawful, the court did not engage in a detailed market analysis. Instead, it questioned the general anticompetitive potential of the agreement and concluded that the plaintiff had simply lost the "competition-for-the-contract."[129] The same would appear to be true in most instances in which there are exclusive dealers. Although not expressly finding the agreement *per se* lawful, the court's analysis left seemed to leave little room for a successful attack on this type of exclusivity.[130]

With respect to the second question, a manufacturer that simply appoints an exclusive dealer would fall within the protections of *Colgate* as expanded by *Monsanto*. On the other hand, when an exclusive dealership arises as the result of the insistence of a powerful dealer that a competitor be terminated, the scheme has a horizontal flavor.[131] Indeed, this was addressed in *Klor's Inc. v. Broadway Hale Stores.*[132] If buyers combine to pressure a manufacturer to terminate a cost-cutting competitor, the makings of a horizontal price-fixing case would be especially evident. In the absence of a horizontal agreement, though, the arrangement must be analyzed from the standpoint of a vertical restraint. Two problems for the terminated dealer emerge. First, there must be an agreement, and after *Monsanto*, proof that one or more competitors urged that another be terminated would not be sufficient.[133] Second, even if a vertical agreement to terminate other dealers is shown, procompetitive justifications may allow the agreement to stand. Clearly, at most what would be called for would be a rule of reason analysis, a practical dead end for plaintiff in most of these cases.

Finally, an argument can be made that a scheme of vertical distribution in which a territorial restraint is combined with an exclusive dealership should be scrutinized more closely than either restraint separately.[134] Whatever anticompetitive effects result from either restraint are compounded when they are combined. On the other hand, there is hardly a more effective way to free a dealer from the threat of free rider problems than a territorial restraint combined with an exclusive dealership. Thus, the arrangement may be attractive especially when a manufacturer is attempting to enter a new market or is depending on a dealer to enhance the product's attractiveness

129. *Id.* at 45.

130. The court distinguished exclusive dealing arrangements which are discussed in § 5.02[A], *infra*. A comparable analysis is found in *NYNEX Corp., v. Discon, Inc.* 525 U.S. 128 (1998), in which the Supreme Court also ruled out the possibility that a single firm's refusal to deal with more than one buyer or seller is not a *per se* unlawful boycott.

131. It is possible that the case could be analyzed under § 2 as monopolization or attempt to monopolize.

132. 359 U.S. 207 (1959). See discussion in § 4.12.

133. Even pre-*Monsanto* cases illustrate the problem the plaintiff faces in this regard. *See, e.g., Valley Liquors, Inc. v. Renfield Importers, Ltd.*, 678 F.2d 742 (7th Cir. 1982); *Packard Motor Car Co. v. Webster Motor Car Co.*, 243 F.2d 418 (D.C. Cir. 1957).

134. *See* Pitofsky, *supra*, note 102, at 18–25.

through efforts that require a substantial investment. In these instances, the dealer may only be willing to take on the risk and expense involved if it is fully protected from intrabrand competition. This means that the rule of reason analysis is more complicated, a happenstance that favors defendants.[135]

§ 5.02 Interbrand Vertical Foreclosure

The previous section addressed intrabrand vertical restraints—that is, agreements between a manufacturer and its retailers that restrict competition among retailers selling the same brand of products. This section discusses interbrand vertical restraints, which restrict competition across brands. Antitrust law focuses primarily on two types of interbrand vertical restraints: exclusive dealing arrangements and tying arrangements. One example of exclusive dealing is when a manufacturer conditions the sale of a product to a retailer on the promise by the retailer that it will purchase all of its requirements for that product from the manufacturer. A variation on this practice includes offering discounts based on quantities purchased. As you will see in Chapter 6, exclusive dealing in one form or another may form the basis for a monopolization or attempt to monopolize claim. Exclusive dealing is different from the exclusive dealership discussed earlier; the latter does not involve a conditional sale. Under a tying arrangement, a manufacturer sells a product—the tying product—to a buyer only on condition that the buyer also purchase another specified product—the tied product. The chief antitrust concern in the case of exclusive dealing and tying is that the arrangement makes it more difficult for competing manufacturers to find outlets for their products; in effect, they are "foreclosed."

Much of exclusive dealing and tying are prohibited by § 3 of the Clayton Act. Under the Act:

> It shall be unlawful for any person engaged in commerce, in the course of such commerce, to lease or make a sale or contract for sale of good, wares, merchandise, machinery supplies, or other commodities ... or fix a price charged therefore, or discount from, or rebate upon, such price on the condition, agreement, or understanding that the lessee or purchaser thereof shall not use or deal in the goods, wares, merchandise, machinery, supplies, or other commodities of a competitor or competitors of the lessor or seller,

135. For a case that deals with an exclusive dealership and a trademarked brand, see *Generac Corp. v. Caterpillar, Inc.* 172 F.3d 971 (7th Cir. 1999) (applying the rule of reason to an agreement between a small generator manufacturer and a trademark holder, in which the manufacturer developed generators that would be marketed under the trademarked name and agreed to restrict sale of the trademarked brand generator to designated dealers and also agreed to restrict sales of its own brand generators to the trademark holder's dealers).

> where the effect . . . may be to substantially lessen competition or tend to create a monopoly.[136]

It is important to note some limitations on the application of the Clayton Act. First, the Act only applies to conditions imposed by sellers. Thus, a contract under which a buyer agrees to buy the output of a seller only if that seller sells all of its output to him would not fall within the Act. However, it may fall under § 1 of the Sherman Act or § 5 of the Federal Trade Commission Act.[137] Second, the Clayton Act applies to goods or commodities, but not services. The Sherman Act or the Federal Trade Commission Act would be the statute applicable for conduct involving services. Finally, the Clayton Act indicates that the arrangements described therein are prohibited when they "may be to lessen competition or tend to create a monopoly." The Sherman Act, on the other hand, does not include comparable language. Thus, the possibility of different treatment for similar activities exists depending upon whether the Sherman Act or Clayton Act is applied.

[A] Exclusive Dealing

[1] Economic Issues

The primary economic concern raised by exclusive dealing is foreclosure of manufacturers because they are unable to find outlets for their products. A related concern is that entry into the industry will become more difficult because, in order to enter, the firm will have to be vertically integrated. That is, it will have to operate at both the manufacturing and retailing level—a prospect that increases the costs of entry. These are, as one would expect, precisely the concerns expressed about vertical mergers.[138] After all, exclusive dealing is essentially a method of vertical integration by contract.

There are two responses to the concerns about anticompetitive effects. The first merely notes that exclusive dealing is not uniformly anticompetitive and that the anticompetitive and procompetitive effects should be weighed. For example, both buyers and sellers may find exclusive dealing attractive. For sellers it will mean an assured outlet and for buyers it means a dependable source of supply. The effect may be to lower transaction costs which could translate into lower prices for consumers.[139] In addition, if the retailer is obligated to purchase only one brand of merchandise, it will be inclined to promote that brand, thus enhancing interbrand competition.[140]

Finally, the use of exclusive dealing may help prevent a type of "free riding" that is different from that already discussed. In the case of RPM, the concern was the free

---

136. 15 U.S.C. § 14 (1976).

137. 15 U.S.C. § 45 (1976).

138. *See* § 7.04[B].

139. In a sports context, exclusivity may be linked to standards for equipment used competitors. *See generally, Race Tires America, Inc. v. Hoosier Racing Tire Corp.*, 614 F.3d 57 (3d Cir. 2010).

140. *See* R. Blair & D. Kaserman, *Antitrust Economics*, 409–10 (1985).

riding of retailers on the efforts of other retailers. Conversely, a manufacturer may use exclusive dealing to prevent free riding by a retailer on the promotional efforts of a manufacturer from whom it purchases. For example, suppose Xenox is a manufacturer of televisions and advertises its product nationally. If it sells to retailers who sell other brands, it may find that consumers go to those retailers because of the advertising by Xenox but, once there, they are sold a different brand of television. In essence, the retailer is the free rider and the manufacturer is unable to "internalize" the benefits of its promotional efforts.

The second response to the anticompetitive concerns about exclusive dealing goes much further and suggests that there are no substantial anticompetitive effects in the first place.[141] For example, if the manufacturer has no market power, the manufacturer will have to offer the retailer something in return for its agreement not to make purchases from others. Theoretically, the manufacturer will supply the product at a lower price or perhaps lower the retailer's cost by absorbing promotional expenses. Accordingly, even if the manufacturer has market power, there is still no real cause for concern. The key is that the market power possessed by the manufacturer which enables it to charge a supracompetitive price is limited. Price can be "charged" as traditionally understood, by simply asking for more money for each unit. Or, the manufacturer can demand something else, such as an exclusive dealing agreement. Therefore, market power can be exploited only to a certain degree. If the manufacturer demands an exclusive dealing agreement, the argument is that it cannot be motivated simply by a desire to charge higher prices since the profit maximizing price can be exacted through the direct use of the firm's market power.

The first group of procompetitive justifications for exclusive dealing do not suggest *per se* legality, only that exclusive dealing may have procompetitive and anticompetitive effects that must be balanced. The latter reasoning so undercuts the economic concerns about exclusive dealing that it suggests that exclusive dealing should be *per se* lawful.

[2] Exclusive Dealing and the Supreme Court

The two most influential Supreme Court decisions in the area of exclusive dealing are *Standard Oil Co. v. United States (Standard Stations)*[142] and *Tampa Electric Co. v. Nashville Coal Co.*[143] In *Standard Stations*, the Court reviewed the contracts between Standard Oil and independent retailers that required all purchases of gasoline to be from Standard Oil. Standard Oil was the largest seller of gasoline in the "Western Area" which included Arizona, California, Idaho, Nevada, Oregon, Utah, and

141. *See* R. Bork, *supra*, note 10, at 299–309.

142. 337 U.S. 293 (1949). *Standard Stations* was preceded by *Standard Fashion Co. v. Magrane-Houston Co.*, 258 U.S. 346 (1922) in which the Court condemned an exclusive dealing arrangement resulting in a 40% foreclosure. It is difficult from the decision, however, to discern a standard for the analysis of exclusive dealing.

143. 365 U.S. 320 (1961).

Washington. Sixteen percent of the retail stations in the area were covered by exclusive dealing arrangements with Standard Oil. This accounted for 6.7% of the total taxable gallonage sold in the area.

The issue was whether a showing that a "substantial portion" of the market was affected was enough to satisfy the statutory requirement that the effect of the arrangement "may be to substantially lessen competition."[144] The Court, in short, was faced with the issue of whether the standards then applied to tying agreements should be extended to exclusive dealing.[145] Justice Frankfurter, writing for the majority, reasoned that tying agreements "serve hardly any purpose beyond the suppression of competition."[146] Requirement contracts, on the other hand, could be economically beneficial to both buyers and sellers and, ultimately, to consumers. He observed that this would seem to require an evaluation of competitive effects on a case-by-case basis.

The Court, however, in a five-to-four decision, opted not to require plaintiffs to show actual anticompetitive effects.[147] Justice Frankfurter noted the difficulty the courts were likely to have in analyzing economic effects. In addition, any error made by prohibiting beneficial agreements could be overcome by legal agreements with similar effects. Finally, he reasoned that a plaintiff would typically find it virtually impossible to show that "but for" the agreement, competition would be more vigorous. However, rather than announce a rigid *per se* standard, he opted for the rule that "§ 3 is satisfied by proof that competition has been foreclosed in a substantial *share* of the line of commerce affected."[148] He concluded that Standard Oil's actions had violated this standard.

Justice Jackson dissented, contending that the majority's announced standard and its application amounted to the establishment of a *per se* rule.[149] He agreed that the requirements contracts, which foreclosed 6.7% of the defined market, did affect a substantial share of commerce. On the other hand, he did not believe that this showing alone met the § 3 requirement of a substantial lessening of competition. Justice Douglas also dissented, arguing that the majority, by closing the door to exclusive dealing had, in effect, invited firms to achieve the same result through vertical integration—a more harmful alternative.[150]

In *Tampa Electric*, a public utility contracted with Nashville Coal Co. for all its coal requirements over a twenty-year period.[151] The supplier refused to perform, after which it sought and received a declaratory judgment that the contract violated § 3 of

144. 337 U.S. at 299.

145. As will be seen, at the time of *Standard Stations*, tying agreements were treated under a modified *per se* rule. *See* § 5.02[B][2][a], *infra*.

146. 337 U.S. 293 at 305.

147. *Id.* at 308–12.

148. *Id.* at 314 (emphasis added).

149. *Id.* at 323 (Jackson, J. dissenting).

150. *Id.* at 320–21 (Douglas, J. dissenting).

151. 365 U.S. at 322.

the Clayton Act.[152] The lower courts concentrated on the competitive impact within Florida where the coal was consumed. The Supreme Court rejected this analysis in favor of one focusing on the impact on suppliers who were in competition with Nashville Coal in serving the Tampa area.[153] Under this market definition, the share of commerce affected was 0.77%.

The Court concluded that the contract plainly did not tend to substantially foreclose competition in the relevant market.[154] Two aspects of the case are important. First, the Court viewed market definition as an indispensable step in its foreclosure analysis. Second, it was willing to review a range of factors regarding the competitive impact of the arrangement. For example, it noted that unlike *Standard Stations* the exclusive dealing here was not industry wide, nor was Nashville Coal a dominate seller. In addition, it suggested that the length of the exclusive dealing contract could be a relevant consideration. In general, the approach taken involved the consideration of a broader range of factors than was the case in *Standard Stations*. The Court, perhaps due to the very limited foreclosure involved, found it unnecessary to give specific indication of the weight to be attributed to these factors.

[3] Exclusive Dealing as an Unfair Method of Competition

Exclusive dealing also has been examined by the Federal Trade Commission under § 5 of the Federal Trade Commission Act. One case, *FTC v. Motion Picture Advertising Service*,[155] is particularly interesting because it dealt with exclusive dealing in the form of an outputs contract. The case involved a producer/distributor of advertisements that were shown in movie theaters. The terms of the contracts required theaters to show only the advertisements made by the producer. In essence, the producer was the exclusive buyer of a theater's advertising display time. The relevant foreclosure took place at the level of buyers. Motion Picture Advertising had exclusive contracts with 40% of the theaters in its area of operation.

The FTC issued a cease and desist order that limited the duration of the agreements to no more than one year. The Supreme Court generally deferred to the Commission and upheld its order.[156] It seemed influenced, however, by the fact that 75% of the available outlets for exhibiting film advertisements in the United States were foreclosed by similar agreements. The Court seemed unimpressed by the fact that the exclusive arrangements were preferred by both theater owners and advertising film producers.[157]

---

152. *Id.* at 321.

153. *Id.* at 330–33.

154. *Id.* at 334.

155. 344 U.S. 392 (1953).

156. *Id.* at 395–97. In so doing it reversed *Motion Pictures Advertising Service v. FTC*, 194 F.2d 633 (D.C. Cir. 1952).

157. 344 U.S. at 395–96.

In *Motion Picture Advertising* the Court noted that the Commission, under § 5 of the Federal Trade Commission Act, could prohibit activities beyond those subject to § 1 of the Sherman Act or § 3 of the Clayton Act.[158] Under the facts of the case and its timing—between *Standard Stations* and *Tampa Electric*—it probably was unnecessary to stretch § 5 that far. The Commission did seem to rely on this extra authority, however, in a post-*Tampa Electric* case, *FTC v. Brown Shoe Co.*[159] The Commission ordered Brown Shoe to cease and desist from entering into exclusive dealing arrangements with 650 retail outlets. The order was challenged as unsupported by sufficient evidence that the effect of the practice may have been to substantially lessen competition.[160] The Court, relying on *Motion Picture Advertising Services*, unanimously recognized the distinction between the requirements of § 3 of the Clayton Act and § 5 of the Federal Trade Commission Act. It upheld the Commission's action, observing that "the Commission has power under § 5 to arrest trade restraints in their incipiency."[161]

Although the Court suggested that the Commission was to be afforded broad leeway in applying § 5 to exclusive dealing, the Commission has not made full use of that power.[162] Indeed, the trend has been for the Commission to apply an analysis similar to that used under the Clayton Act or Sherman Act. An example of this is *Beltone Electronics Corp.*[163] in which the Commission considered the exclusive dealing arrangement between a manufacturer of hearing aids and its dealer. The Commission went well beyond the analysis suggested in *Tampa Electric* and drew on *Sylvania*. Accordingly, the Commission emphasized the importance of viewing foreclosure in the context of "reasonable justifications" including possible procompetitive effects on interbrand rivalry.[164]

*[4] Exclusive Dealing in the Post-*Tampa Electric *and* Sylvania *Era*

Tampa Electric suggested that exclusive dealing should be analyzed under an approach very similar to the rule of reason. *Sylvania* stressed the importance of economic factors in applying the rule of reason and expanded the scope of the analysis. Both cases have influenced lower court evaluations of exclusive dealing resulting in a general acceptance of a rule of reason approach.

An ambitious attempt to articulate the relevant factors under a modern exclusive dealing analysis is found in a Seventh Circuit decision, *Roland Machinery v. Dresser Industries.*[165] Judge Posner contrasted what he regarded as the current approach to

---

158. *Id.* at 394.
159. 384 U.S. 316 (1966).
160. *Id.* at 322–23.
161. *Id.* at 322; *See generally* Steuer, *Exclusive Dealing in Distribution*, 69 Cornell L. Rev. 101, 106–07 (1983).
162. *See* Steuer, *supra* note 161, at 106–16.
163. 100 F.T.C. 68 (1982). For a complete analysis, see Steuer, *supra* note 161, at 108–11.
164. 100 F.T.C. at 204–18.
165. 749 F.2d 380 (7th Cir. 1984).

exclusive dealing with that previously applied. Originally the issue was whether the agreement covered "a large fraction of the market."[166] Under Judge Posner's formulation, the plaintiff must show that (1) the agreement excludes at least one "significant competitor of the defendant from doing business in a relevant market," and (2) the anticompetitive effects outweigh the procompetitive effects.[167] In effect, exclusive dealing was to be assessed under the rule of reason.

There are variations on traditional exclusive dealing as in requirements contract. For example, if competitors agree to impose a requirements contract on a buyer so that they both act as suppliers while excluding other suppliers, the case fits the model of a horizontal boycott. In another variation, the supplier may not be the sole supplier but may condition sales on the requirement that specific suppliers be excluded. This was the case in *United States v. Visa, U.S.A.*,[168] in which the Justice Department challenged the practice of Visa and MasterCard of requiring member banks not to issue American Express or Discover cards. The court applied the rule of reason and found the practice unlawful.

As suggested earlier, exclusivity can refer to buying (requirements contract) or selling (outputs contract). *Geneva Pharmaceuticals Technology Corp. v. Barr Laboratories, Inc.*[169] applied an approach that may be less demanding than a full rule of reason. The case involved an agreement under which the supplier of a compound that was critical in the production of a prescription drug sold all of its output to one producer of that drug. The drug was a generic drug and potential competitors in the generic market complained that their entry into the market was retarded as a result of the agreement. Here the court noted that "Exclusive dealing is an unreasonable restraint of trade and a § 1 violation only when the agreement freezes out a significant fraction of buyers or sellers from the market."[170] It held that plaintiff had presented an issue of material fact of supplier's market power and had demonstrated that the supplier was prepared to produce more of the critical compound than required by the generic manufacturer but this output was kept out of the market due to the agreement.[171]

An issue that may be important in an exclusive dealing case is whether it arises under the Clayton Act or the Sherman Act. Recall that the Clayton Act only applies if the transaction is for the sale of goods. For example, in a recent case, *CDC Technologies v. Idexx Laboratories*, Inc.,[172] the plaintiff complained that the defendant, a competing manufacturer of blood analysis machines, had entered into exclusive dealing arrangements with a network of distributors in violation of § 3 of the Clayton Act. The Clayton Act claim was dismissed since the distributors did not actually buy the

166. *Id.* at 393.

167. *Id.* at 394.

168. 344 F.3d 229 (2d Cir. 2003).

169. 386 F.3d 485 (2d Cir. 2004). Defendants had been granted summary judgment by the lower court.

170. *Id.* at 508.

171. *Id.*

172. 186 F.3d 74 (2d Cir. 1999).

equipment. This leaves open a Sherman Act possibility and leads to the question of whether the Sherman Act standard is different. Language in *Tampa Electric* indicates that there is a difference. There the Supreme Court made reference to the Clayton Act's "broader proscription"[173] meaning that, whatever the standard under the Clayton Act, it was less burdensome to plaintiffs than the rule of reason which would be applied under the Sherman Act. Since that time, it is clear that exclusive dealing, even under the Clayton Act, has gravitated to a rule of reason-like analysis but the possibility remains that there could be a difference depending on whether the exclusivity involves good or services.[174]

As noted, the incentive for a buyer to enter into an exclusive dealing arrangement can be in the form of a discounted price. For example, a seller may offer a 5% discount if a buyer purchases 80% of its needs for a specific item from that seller. Two cases, *Masimo Corp. v. Tyco Healthcare Group*[175] and *Allied Orthopedic Appliances Inc. v. Tyco Healthcare Group*,[176] illustrate the complexity of the analysis and, perhaps, the shifting view of courts. In *Masimo*, Tyco sold patented pulse monitoring systems that required replaceable sensors. Buyers of the monitoring systems could use only Tyco sensors. Tyco offered discounts to those who purchased no more than a certain percentage of their requirements from competitors and those who treated Tyco as a sole source. The Ninth Circuit Court of Appeals upheld a jury verdict for plaintiff based on an exclusive dealing theory and a finding that a substantial share of the market was foreclosed. The court did not announce a bright test for percentage foreclosure and noted the length of the contracts was relevant.[177]

The same industry was involved in *Allied* shortly thereafter. The patents now had expired on Tyco's original monitoring system and manufacturers of generic sensors were able to sell sensors to hospitals and other users of the Tyco monitor.[178] In order to maintain its position in the industry, Tyco stopped producing the formerly patented monitor and offered a new one. Some of the functions of the monitor were shifted to a new patented sensor that was compatible with both the old and new monitors. Tyco still offered discounts based on the percentage of requirements purchased or for using Tyco as the sole source for sensors. Plaintiffs, who were buyers, claimed prices were higher as a result of the exclusion of competing sellers. Here the court affirmed summary judgment for Tyco noting that no customers were required to enter into the agreements, the agreements could be terminated on short notice, and that lower priced generic sensors were available on the market.[179] The court rejected the argument that buyers would not shift to competing suppliers for fear of losing their Tyco

173. 365 U.S. at 335.

174. *See CDC Technologies*, 186 F.3d 74; *Twin City Sportservice, Inc., v. Charles O. Finley & Co.*, 676 F.2d 1291 (9th Cir. 1982).

175. 350 F. App'x 95 (9th Cir. 2009).

176. 592 F.3d 991 (9th Cir. 2010).

177. Conversely, the court rejected a claim based on "bundling." For a discussion see Chapter 6.

178. *Id.* at 995.

179. *Id.* at 996–98.

discounts.[180] Instead, it reasoned that buyers could always buy lower priced generic sensors for use with the older monitors. It distinguished *Masimo* by noting that in that case users of the patented monitor were required to purchase Tyco sensors. In addition, in the earlier case, buyers were obligated to purchase a set percentage of their requirements from Tyco.[181]

It is impossible to formulate a bright line test when a substantial share of a market is foreclosed. For example, a 30% foreclosure for 10 years may have more anticompetitive consequences than a 40% foreclosure for five years. In addition, cost reducing effects must also be considered. Nevertheless, there is a core issue: are firms that are likely to be more efficient excluded from the market? One response may be that more efficient firms, in the long run, will always find a way, through lower prices to unseat incumbents. This misses a critical point. Suppose an incumbent supplies 60% of the market and is able to charge lower prices than a competitor because it is able to produce at a higher scale. If the challenger were able to supply 60% of the market, perhaps economics of scale would permit it to charge even lower prices. At the very least, the incumbent's exclusive dealing will raise the entry of competitors and possibly preclude them completely. This suggests that exclusive dealing should focus not simply on the market share foreclosed and the length of the foreclosure but on the economics of production in the market.[182]

[B] Tying Arrangements

A "tie-in," or tying arrangement, occurs when a seller sells a good to a buyer only on the condition that the buyer also buy a second good from the seller. The threshold issue is whether the transaction involves two separate products. The product that the purchaser finds more desirable is the tying product. The product that the buyer must purchase in order to buy the tying product is called the tied product. Like exclusive dealing, tying one good to another is expressly prohibited by § 3 of the Clayton Act.[183] Section 1 of the Sherman Act also condemns anticompetitive tying arrangements, and—unlike the Clayton Act—it applies to both goods and services. Tying can also be analyzed under § 5 of the Federal Trade Commission Act. Although historical factors suggest that the analysis of tying may vary depending upon the statute invoked, today it seems likely that any variation in analysis is likely to be negligible. As in the case of other vertical restraints, the law of tying has undergone considerable change. Although tying was once regarded as *per se* illegal, and even today is nominally in that

180. *Id.* at 997.

181. *Id.* at 997 n.4. In *Masimo*, the lower court found that "A number of hospitals were financially locked into purchasing a fixed amount of Tyco sensors to support their installed Tyco monitors." 2006 U.S. Dist. LEXIS 29977, at *17 (C.D. Cal. Mar. 22, 2006).

182. *See generally* Daniel A. Crane & Graciela Miralles, *Toward a Unified Theory of Exclusionary Vertical Restraints*, 84 S. Cal. L. Rev. 605 (2011).

183. 15 U.S.C. § 14 (1976).

category, the *per se* rule applied to tying is considerably different than that applied to horizontal restraints.

The classic tie involves the two product example just described. Tying arrangements, however, can take a number of more complicated forms. For example, in the case of a "full line force" the seller permits a dealer to carry some of its products only if the dealer is willing to carry a complete line of the seller's products. In other cases, the tie occurs when related products are only offered as a bundle for a single price. Some transactions are not technically ties but have tying-type qualities. For example, the seller may sell its product only on the condition that the buyer purchase a product from a designated third party. Finally, in an arrangement labeled "reciprocal dealing," one firm agrees to buy from another only if the second firm makes purchases from the first. The following pages consider these special cases along with the general development of tying law and the defenses that have evolved. First, however, it is important to discuss the economic consequences of tying.

[1] The Economics of Tying

The changing level of judicial tolerance toward tying can be traced to the fact that there are a great number of reasons why a firm might wish to engage in tying and a variety of economic consequences may follow. Some of the consequences may harm consumers; others are unlikely to produce anticompetitive effects. The difficult task is to segregate those ties that are anticompetitive from those that are not. The Court initially condemned tying based on the belief that a firm with monopoly power in one market would be able to use that power to gain monopoly power in another market.[184] For example, suppose a firm manufactures lamps and possesses monopoly power in that market. Suppose further that the market for lampshades is competitive. The question then becomes: can the firm use its power in the market for lamps as leverage to gain monopoly power in the lampshade market?

Some economists and antitrust scholars would answer "no," arguing that the power associated with the desirability of the tying product enables the monopolist to collect only a single monopoly profit. For example, suppose the lamp manufacturer has discovered that the profit maximizing price for its lamps is $50. Lampshades are $10 each in the competitive market. If it packages them together, the total price will be $60. To charge a price that is any higher than $60 when lampshades are available for $10 would be tantamount to charging more than $50 for the lamps.[185] Some consumers would go elsewhere and the firm would no longer maximize profits. To be sure, it sells more lampshades and increases its share of the lampshade market. It does not,

---

184. *See Northern Pac. Ry.*, 356 U.S. at 11 ("the vice of tying arrangements lies in the use of economic power in one market to restrict competition on the merits in another"); Kurt A. Strasser, *Antitrust Policy for Tying Arrangements*, 34 Emory L.J. 253, 267 (1985); Donald Turner, *The Validity of Tying Arrangements Under the Antitrust Laws*, 72 Harv. L. Rev. 50, 62 (1958).

185. *See* Ward Bowman, *Tying Arrangements and the Leverage Problem*, 67 Yale L.J. 19, 21–23 (1957).

however, acquire monopoly power in the lampshade market in the sense that it can now increase its price and restrict output in that market. Other scholars, however, have rebutted the single monopoly profit theory.[186]

Even if the monopolist is unable to use its power to become a monopolist in another market it may increase its share of sales in the tied product market. In the lamp/lampshade example, this can mean the elimination of sales opportunities for competing manufacturers of lampshades. In other words, if lampshades are sold by the lamp monopolist whenever it sells a lamp, there is less room in the market for a firm that only produces lampshades. The foreclosure of sales or sales opportunities makes it more difficult for firms already in the lampshade market to survive and also raises barriers to the entry of new producers.

Opponents of leverage theory proffer alternative explanations for why firms use tying arrangements. For example, one possibility would be when the monopolist is confronted by price regulation and a price ceiling that is below the profit maximizing price for the tying product.[187] For example, suppose that state regulation prohibits hotels from charging more than $100 per night for a room. A hotel in a scenic area may find that it has market power and that its profit maximizing rate is higher than the maximum allowed. It might attempt to bypass the regulation and take greater advantage of its market power by only offering a rate that includes breakfast at a total charge in excess of $100.

Tying may also be used as a metering device to effect price discrimination, effectively charging different prices to different consumers. Suppose a monopoly manufacturer of commercial ice cream making machines has a policy of only leasing machines at a flat rate per month and only leases on the condition that lessees also buy all their ice cream ingredients from it. One reason for doing this is that the manufacturer's actual costs of serving each customer vary with the intensity with which the machine is used. The life of each machine is, in effect, inversely related to how much it is used. Here the sale of ingredients is a method of "metering" the use of each machine so that each user is charged in proportion to the speed with which the machine they have leased becomes obsolete.[188] The tie can be seen as permitting the manufacturer to collect information that will be useful in legitimate pricing decisions.

On the other hand, suppose the useful life of a machine is unrelated to its intensity of use. Again, tying ingredients to the lease means that high intensity users will pay more than low intensity users. Unless the difference in cost for each lessee precisely reflects the difference in the amount of ingredients purchased, the manufacturer is engaged in price discrimination. In effect, rather than trying to match each lessee with the costs of serving that lessee, the manufacturer charges different prices depending on the lessee's willingness to pay. The key factors in successful price discrimination are

186. Einer Elhauge, *Tying, Bundled Discounts, and the Death of the Single Monopoly Profit Theory*, 123 Harv. L. Rev. 397 (2009).

187. *See generally* Bowman, *supra* note 185, at 22.

188. For discussion see R. Bork, *supra* note 10, at 376–78; R. Blair & D. Kaserman, *supra* note 140, at 384–86; H. Hovenkamp, *supra* note 4, at 428–30.

identifying groups that will pay different amounts and segregating the groups so that those paying the lower price will not sell to those paying more. Tying can be a method of overcoming both of these obstacles. As discussed at length in Chapter 8, it is not clear that price discrimination always leads to an inefficient result.[189] In fact, price discrimination may lead to higher output and, for some consumers, lower prices. Some forms of price discrimination do, however, violate § 2 of the Clayton Act as amended by the Robinson-Patman Act.

Tying also may be used to aid interbrand competition. For example, a restaurant franchiser may only license franchisees who agree to serve food purchased from the franchiser. The franchiser's argument will be that the tie is necessary to ensure the uniform quality of the product, thereby enhancing the goodwill of the franchise and encouraging interbrand competition.[190]

Alternatively, a transaction that resembles tying may be used to facilitate predatory pricing.[191] As discussed in Chapter 6, predatory pricing involves an effort to eliminate competitors by charging prices below cost. Tying can be useful if the seller wishes to achieve the same result but disguise the effect on prices. Thus, instead of lowering the price of a single product it might offer that item in a package with another item for a total price much less than the price of the two sold separately. While this example suggests a tie-in, it is questionable whether the transaction is a tie in the usual sense of forcing a consumer to buy an unwanted product.

Finally, a firm may impose a tying requirement to sell more of the tied product. Assume that a firm possesses monopoly power in the tying product market but faces competition in the tied product market. A tying arrangement allows the firm to link two different market structures. The seller can use its market power over the tying product to increase sales of the tied product at the competitive price.[192] That can increase the firm's overall profits.

[2] Tying and the Supreme Court

[a] Early Interpretations

With this array of reasons for tying, it is not surprising that the Supreme Court was initially not entirely consistent in its approach. The wavering of the Court, although far less dramatic than that exhibited with respect to nonprice restraints on distribution, has followed the same basic pattern. One of the first indications of the Court's direction in tying cases came in *Motion Picture Patents v. Universal Film Co.*[193] A holder of

---

189. See discussion at § 8.02, *infra*.

190. *See* § 5.02[B][4], *infra*.

191. *See* H. Hovenkamp, *supra* note 4, at 423.

192. Christopher R. Leslie, *Cutting Through Tying Theory with Occam's Razor: A Simple Explanation of Tying Arrangements*, 78 Tul. L. Rev. 727 (2004).

193. 243 U.S. 502 (1917). *Motion Picture Patents* was preceded by two pre-Clayton Act cases in which tying was a relevant consideration. In *Henry v. A.B. Dick*, 224 U.S. 1 (1912), the Court felt that

a patent for movie projection equipment attempted to preclude licensees from using film other than that produced by the patent holder. It claimed that those licensees who had not acted in accord with this condition were guilty of infringing the patent held on the projection equipment. The Court held there was no infringement.[194] In so doing, it noted the recent passage of the Clayton Act reflecting legislative intent to prohibit tying arrangements.[195] More importantly, the Court, in *dicta*, reasoned that permitting the restraint would allow the plaintiff to become a monopolist in the motion picture film market.[196] Thus, the Court accepted the "leverage" theory of monopoly power, the primary economic premise for all of its future responses to tying.

The same concerns were reflected in *International Business Machines Corp. v. United States* in 1936.[197] IBM conditioned the lease of its machines on use by lessees of tabulating cards also manufactured by IBM. The Court directly addressed the issue of whether the arrangement "may . . . substantially lessen competition" thereby violating § 3 of the Clayton Act.[198] Although it announced no particular formula for the application of § 3, it focused on the dangers of "monopolistic tying clauses."[199] The clear suggestion was that without monopoly power in the tying product market, this danger would not be present. The Court mentioned the volume of commerce involved but did not, with any degree of clarity, indicate the weight to be afforded this factor.

Eleven years later, the Court took an even harsher view of tying. In *International Salt Co. v. United States*[200] the defendant, International Salt, leased its patented machines[201] only on the condition that lessees purchase from International Salt all the salt to be used in the machines. In 1944, the defendant had sold $500,000 worth of salt for use in its machines. The Court affirmed the lower court's award of a summary judgment in favor of the plaintiff based on a violation of both § 1 of the Sherman Act and § 3 of the Clayton Act. In so doing, it announced that it was "unreasonable, *per se*, to foreclose competitors from any substantial market."[202] The Court made note of the "limited monopoly"[203] held by International Salt but did not expressly indicate that

---

a patent gave the holder tying-type powers. In *United States v. Winslow* 227 U.S. 202 (1913), the Court similarly was unresponsive to the dangers of tying again indicating the broad power inherent in the holding of a patent.

194. 243 U.S. at 515–19.

195. *Id.* at 516–17.

196. *Id.* at 518.

197. 298 U.S. 131 (1936).

198. *Id.* at 134.

199. *Id.* at 140.

200. 332 U.S. 392 (1947).

201. *Id.* at 394–95. The "Saltomat" injected salt into canned products. The "Lixator" dissolved rock salt into brine.

202. 332 U.S. at 396. The Court cited *Fashion Originators' Guild v. FTC*, 312 U.S. 457 (1941). See discussion in § 4.12, *supra*.

203. 332 U.S. at 395.

such a finding was necessary for applying the *per se* standard under either the Clayton or Sherman Acts.

In 1953, in *Times-Picayune Publishing Co. v. United States*,[204] the Court considered the requirement of a New Orleans publisher that advertisers buy space in both its morning and evening newspapers. It reviewed the case under § 1 of the Sherman Act. First, however, it interpreted *International Salt* as indicating that the test for tying was different under the Sherman Act than under the Clayton Act. Under the Clayton Act, a tying arrangement was illegal if the tying firm held a "monopolistic" position in the tying good market or "restrained" a substantial volume of commerce in the tied product market.[205] Under the Sherman Act, however, the "rule of *International Salt* [would] only apply only if both conditions are met."[206]

The Court assumed that the "substantiality" test was met and turned its attention to the issue of market dominance, concentrating on the question of whether the publisher had "wielded monopoly leverage."[207] The Court found two flaws in the Government's case. First, it noted that there were three newspapers in New Orleans and that an equal division of the relevant market—advertising in New Orleans dailies—would result in a 33% share for each newspaper. The alleged dominant newspaper, the Times-Picayune, had a market share of only 40% which was insufficient to establish dominance. Second, the Court reasoned that advertisers were purchasing access to readers and that the readers, whether morning or evening, were viewed by advertisers as "fungible customer potential."[208] In essence, there was no tying or use of leverage to gain power in another market because both newspapers were selling the same service and, therefore, occupied the same market.

In 1958, the Supreme Court again considered tying in *Northern Pacific Railway Co. v. United States*.[209] Northern Pacific leased land for various uses on the condition that lessees use Northern Pacific to ship all commodities produced or manufactured on the land as long as Northern Pacific's rates were equal to those of competitors. Like *Times-Picayune*, review was under the Sherman Act and the Court looked to *International Salt* for guidance. The rule the Court devised seemed to be the result of merging the dual approaches announced in *Times-Picayune*: "[tying arrangements] are unreasonable in and of themselves whenever a party has sufficient economic power with respect to the tying product to appreciably restrain free competition in the market for the tied product and a 'not insubstantial' amount of interstate commerce is affected."[210]

---

204. 345 U.S. 594 (1953).
205. *Id.* at 606.
206. *Id.* at 608–09.
207. *Id.* at 611.
208. *Id.* at 613–14.
209. 356 U.S. 1 (1958).
210. *Id.* at 6.

[b] Fortner I and II

In *Fortner Enterprises v. United States Steel*, (*Fortner I*)[211] the Supreme Court considered a summary judgment that U.S. Steel had not violated § 1 of the Sherman Act when the extension of credit by its wholly-owned credit subsidiary was conditioned on the purchase of prefabricated homes from its Home Division. The tying "product" was credit and the "tied" product was prefabricated homes. The 100% financing offered by U.S. Steel made its credit especially desirable. The trial court ruled that the plaintiff had not shown that the defendant had sufficient power in the credit market or that a "not insubstantial amount of commerce" was involved.

In a 5-to-4 decision, the Supreme Court reversed and remanded for trial. It found that the $190,000 involved in sales of the tied product to the defendant was not insubstantial. In addition, the total annual dollar figure for the arrangement when other buyers were included was in the range of $2,000,000 to $4,000,000. The remand, therefore, was on the issue of whether U.S. Steel possessed power in the tying product market. On this issue, the Court observed that the lower court had applied too strict a standard. The Supreme Court emphasized that the search was not for dominant market power or monopoly power as traditionally understood. Instead, sufficient power could be found even if that power extended to some buyers, "whether few or many, whether scattered throughout the market or part of some group within the market."[212] Power could be "inferred from the tying product's desirability to consumers or uniqueness in its attributes."[213]

Uniqueness alone, according to the Court, was not determinative. Instead, the uniqueness had to be the product of an economic advantage that U.S. Steel had over competitors. More precisely, it had to flow from barriers that precluded competitors from offering the same product.[214] The Court offered the examples of land and patents[215] and also suggested that the inability of competitors to offer the same product profitably could provide the requisite power. In the case at hand, it suggested that the plaintiff could prevail by showing that local lending institutions would regard such financing as too risky to be profitable or were unable to offer competitive terms because of state or federal regulation. The majority opinion, written by Justice Black, was in many respects as hostile toward tying as any that it followed. On the other hand, it clearly reestablished assessment of economic power in the tying good market as an independent step in tying analysis. On remand, the trial court held for the plaintiff.[216]

---

211. 394 U.S. 495 (1969). Prior to *Fortner I*, the Court encountered "block booking" in *United States v. Loew's, Inc.* 371 U.S. 38 (1962). It applied a standard that was consistent with that applied in *Northern Pacific*. *See* § 5.02[B][2][a], *supra*.

212. *394 U.S.* at 503.

213. *Id.* (quoting *United States v. Loew's, Inc.*, 371 U.S. 38, 45).

214. 394 U.S. at 505 n.2.

215. For the more recent view of patents as a source of market power, see *Illinois Tool Works Inc. v. Independent Ink, Inc.*, 547 U.S. 28 (2006).

216. The case was twice considered by the trial court with its decision eventually being affirmed by the Sixth Circuit Court of Appeals in 1975. *United States Steel Corp. v. Fortner Enterprises, Inc.*, 523 F.2d 961 (6th Cir. 1975).

Eight years later the case returned to a Supreme Court which now included only four Justices who had participated in *Fortner I*.[217] The issue in *Fortner II*[218] was whether the evidence supported the finding that U.S. Steel did have power in the credit market. This time the Supreme Court engaged in a step-by-step analysis of the factors that had led the trial court to conclude that U.S. Steel did have the requisite power. The first factor cited was that it was one of the nation's largest corporations. Here the Court observed that there was nothing about the affiliation of the credit subsidiary with U.S. Steel that enabled it to borrow funds on more favorable terms than its competitors or to otherwise operate more efficiently.[219]

The Court also was not persuaded that economic power was shown by the fact that a significant number of customers, in addition to the plaintiff, had entered into the agreement.[220] According to the Court, disproportionately large sales of the tied product in relation to the tying product would be indicative of the type of leverage associated with economic power. Here, though, the plaintiff was only obligated to purchase houses to the extent that it applied for and received financing.

The third factor considered by the Court was whether the above-market prices for the tied product meant that U.S. Steel had the requisite power in the credit market. The Court reasoned that higher than market prices were to be expected since the credit terms were unusually attractive. Thus, the above-market prices were not inconsistent with a competitive price for the package.

Finally, the Court responded to the argument that power was inherent in the offering of financing that was unlike that available from other lenders. The Court, recalling its reasoning in *Fortner I*, explained that the power issue was not whether the credit terms were unique but whether the power exercised by U.S. Steel was market power as traditionally defined.[221] The Court, however, went a step further than it had in *Fortner I*. There the Court spoke of power *vis-à-vis* few or scattered buyers. In *Fortner II*, however, the power issue was framed in terms of whether U.S. Steel possessed the type of power in the credit market that would enable it to raise prices and restrict output. In particular, was the price it was exacting from buyers the purchase of homes that otherwise would not be purchased?

The Court held that the evidence did not support a finding that U.S. Steel possessed this type of power. Instead, all that was suggested by the evidence was that U.S. Steel was willing to take a lower profit and accept a greater risk than were competitors when offering credit. Thus, the Court emphatically injected traditional market power

---

217. *See generally* Kramer, *The Supreme Court and Tying Arrangements: Antitrust as History*, 69 Minn. L. Rev. 1013, 1045–50 (1985).

218. *United States Steel Corp. v. Fortner Enterprises, Inc.*, 429 U.S. 610 (1977).

219. *Id.* at 617.

220. *Id.* at 617–18. This had been a persuasive argument in earlier cases. *See, e.g.*, *United States v. Loew's, Inc.*, 371 U.S. 38 (1962); *Northern Pacific Railway v. United States*, 356 U.S. 1 (1958).

221. *Id.* at 620.

analysis into the consideration of tying. Although the *per se* rule survived, it was far from that envisioned in *International Salt* thirty years earlier.[222]

[c] Jefferson Parish Hospital v. Hyde

In 1984, the Supreme Court once again considered the standards applicable to tying arrangements. In *Jefferson Parish Hospital v. Hyde*,[223] the defendant, East Jefferson Hospital, contracted with a firm of anesthesiologists to provide all the hospital's anesthesiological services. An excluded anesthesiologist charged the hospital with tying anesthesiological services to hospital services. The plaintiff lost at the trial court level. That decision was reversed by the Court of Appeals for the Fifth Circuit which labeled the arrangement *per se* unlawful.[224]

In arriving at its decision, the appellate court declined to apply the type of analysis that might be involved in more typical markets. It reasoned that the requisite power was present as a result of both the preference of consumers for the closest hospital and the presence of imperfections in the medical care market. In particular, the Court of Appeals believed that the prevalence of third-party payers and the relative ignorance of consumers about the quality of medical care increased the power of the hospital to influence consumers' decisions.

The Supreme Court unanimously reversed. There was, however, a 5-to-4 split on the Court, with four Justices arguing that tying should be lifted from the *per se* category.[225] The majority of the Court reaffirmed, at least nominally, the *per se* status of tying. The majority opinion, written by Justice Stevens, focused on whether hospital services and anesthesiological services should be regarded as two products for tying analysis purposes and whether East Jefferson Hospital possessed sufficient power in the tying product market.

With respect to the first issue, the question was whether the hospital's services could be meaningfully separated from anesthesiological services. In effect, if the services were functionally inseparable, the harm to be avoided by prohibiting tying could not occur in the first place; consumers could not be forced to buy something they would not otherwise buy. The hospital argued that it offered "a functionally integrated package of services"[226]—in essence, a single product. The Court viewed the issue as whether hospital services and anesthesiological services were sufficiently distinguished in the eyes of consumers to be subject to separate demands. It concluded

---

222. *See generally* Bauer, *A Simplified Approach to Tying Arrangements: A Legal and Economic Analysis*, 33 Vand. L. Rev. 283, 288–91 (1980); Hovenkamp, *Tying Arrangements and Class Actions*, 36 Vand. L. Rev. 213 (1983); Kramer, *supra* note 217, at 1048–49; Melican, *Tying Arrangements and Related Restrictions After* Fortner II, 51 Antitrust L.J. 157 (1982).

223. 466 U.S. 2 (1984).

224. *Jefferson Parish v. Jefferson Parish Hospital Dist No. 2*, 686 F.2d 286 (5th Cir. 1982).

225. The four group included Justices O'Conner, Powell and Rehnquist along with Chief Justice Burger. 466 U.S. at 32–47.

226. *Id.* at 18–19.

the ability of patients to request specific anesthesiologists as well as other factors, such as separate billing for surgical services and anesthesiological services, established that there were two products.

On the issue of market power, the Court began its analysis by invoking the *Fortner II* view that the relevant power was whether a firm could raise prices above competitive levels.[227] The Court believed the question was whether the defendant possessed this type of power and used it to coerce the purchase of a tied product that would otherwise not have been purchased.[228] This theme of coercion distinguishes *Jefferson Parish* from *Fortner II*. In the latter case, the Court was most clearly concerned with the simple possession of market power. In *Jefferson Parish* the use of this power for coercive purposes is emphasized. Accordingly, the question was whether the hospital's power was used to "force" consumers to purchase an "unwanted product."[229] The Court conceded that the market imperfections the Fifth Circuit had found persuasive would mean that consumers' decisions were less likely to be made on the basis of competitive merit. In effect, third-party payers and ignorance insulated consumers from questions of price, value, and quality of service. In this context, the hospital could influence decision making. But, "power" resulting from consumer indifference could hardly be used to force consumers to forego choices that they would have otherwise preferred.[230]

Where the Court stands on the separate issue of what constitutes sufficient power in the tying product market is less clear. On the one hand, the Court indicated that the 30% market share possessed by East Jefferson Hospital did not constitute sufficient power in the tying product market.[231] If this is the case, the Court was announcing a standard that would be inconsistent with that applied in virtually every prior case in which it has found that the defendant possessed the requisite level of power. On the other hand, the Court cited those earlier cases with approval,[232] suggesting that they could be reconciled with its analysis.

Four of the concurring Justices in *Jefferson Parish* argued for abandoning the *per se* approach to tying. Justice O'Connor's concurrence is noteworthy because she questioned the "leverage" theory as a justification for barring tying.[233] Moreover, she noted the possible beneficial effects of tying. For example, in *Jefferson Parish* the packaging of hospital services and anesthesiological services could increase the efficiency of hospital operations. A rule of reason approach, she concluded, would permit the proper weighing of harmful and beneficial effects.

---

227. *Id.* at 27 n.46.

228. *Id.* at 26.

229. *Id.* at 18.

230. *Id.* at 27–28.

231. Thirty per cent of the patients living in Jefferson Parish entered East Jefferson Parish Hospital. *Id.* at 26.

232. *Id.* at 13–18. *Cf.* Bern, *Jefferson Parish Hospital District No. 2 v. Jefferson Parish: Return to Reality in Economic Power Analysis in Tying Cases*, 53 UMKC L. Rev. 145, 164–69 (1985).

233. 466 U.S. at 35–36 (O'Connor, J. concurring). Justices Brennan and Marshall concurred in an opinion that supported continued *per se* treatment of tying.

[d] Eastman Kodak Co. v. Image Technical Services

The issue of market power in a tying context also arose in *Eastman Kodak Co. v. Image Technical Services Co.*,[234] a 1992 case. Kodak manufactured office machinery including photocopiers. It also sold parts for and serviced the machines. In the mid 1980s, Kodak instituted a policy of selling parts for its equipment only to buyers who repaired their own machines or used Kodak service. The independent service organizations (ISOs) that repaired Kodak equipment sued, charging Kodak with tying replacement parts to service, thereby foreclosing ISOs from the repair market. Since only Kodak parts could be used in Kodak equipment, the argument was that once purchasers bought Kodak's equipment, they constituted a "captive market" with respect to the aftermarkets in Kodak replacement parts and service.

The Court considered whether it was proper to grant Kodak summary judgment under the theory that, since Kodak did not have market power in the original equipment market, it could not have market power in the market for replacement parts. Kodak argued that forcing purchasers to use Kodak service in order to obtain Kodak replacement parts was comparable to raising the price of the original purchase. Since Kodak did not have market power in the original equipment market, any purchasers who would prefer not to use Kodak service would just shift to competing suppliers of office equipment. Thus, as a matter of law, according to Kodak, the absence of market power in the original equipment market would mean that a seller could not have market power in the aftermarket.

The Supreme Court rejected Kodak's reasoning. First, it noted that even if the tie was viewed as comparable to an increase in the price of the original equipment and led to a decrease in original equipment sales, it did not follow that Kodak did not have market power in the aftermarket. The Court explained that all firms, including monopolists, face downward sloping demand curves meaning that higher prices result in fewer sales. This alone did not rule out the presence of market power.[235] Second, the Court noted that Kodak had increased the price of service without incurring decreased equipment sales, a combination that was inconsistent with its theory.[236]

Most important, however, was the Court's response to Kodak's effort to reconcile the phenomenon of higher service prices without a loss in equipment sales with its theory that it did not have market power in the replacement parts market. Kodak attempted the reconciliation by arguing that the cost of its equipment was evaluated by purchasers over the life of the equipment, and was composed of the price of the original equipment, and anticipated aftermarket purchases of replacement parts and service. Thus, higher service costs would be off-set by lower original equipment prices and the entire cost of the package would be competitively determined.

---

234. 504 U.S. 451 (1992). *See also* Hovenkamp, *Market Power in Aftermarkets: Antitrust Policy and the Kodak Case*, 40 UCLA 1447 (1993).

235. *Id.* at 470–71.

236. *Id.* at 472.

The Court responded by noting the importance of information and switching costs as sources of market power. With respect to information costs, the Court explained that the type of "lifecycle pricing" suggested by Kodak required a significant investment by buyers in the acquisition of information about repair costs, breakdown frequency, and losses incurred during downtime. If these costs were sufficiently high, or at least high enough that their acquisition was not cost justified, the price of the package could exceed competitive levels.[237] In addition, the Court noted that the cost of switching to a different brand of equipment in response to the tie or higher repair service costs could be high enough that "locked-in" buyers would elect to pay supracompetitive prices.[238] These factors, the Court ruled, meant that the extent of Kodak's market power in the aftermarket was a question of fact.

In adopting the information cost rationale, the Court may have taken a position that is at odds with that stated in *Jefferson Parish*.[239] In *Jefferson Parish*, the indifference of consumers to price due to the presence of third-party payers was not viewed as a source of market power. Yet, in *Kodak* the Court recognized that information costs "could create a less responsive connection between service and parts prices and equipment sales,"[240] and viewed that lack of responsiveness as source of market power giving rise to antitrust concerns. The market imperfections in *Jefferson Parish* can be distinguished from those in *Kodak*, but not so completely as to eliminate the possibility that the Court has broadened the scope of factors to be considered in assessing market power.

Another question that remained after *Kodak* was whether it would make a difference if the defendant's policy with respect to the alleged tie was known at the time the sale was made. In a footnote and in response to Justice Scalia, the Court noted that it was "crucial" that the change came after initial sale.[241] For example, in *Kodak*, the policy objected to was instituted after many buyers had committed to the original equipment. On the other hand, had the policy been in place at the time of the purchase, so the argument goes, the tying product would more obviously be the original equipment and market power in the original equipment market would be critical. Some courts have interpreted the holding in *Kodak* as limited only to instances in which the seller's policy was not known or was instituted after the sale.[242] In effect, while it is possible that buyers may become "locked-in," they generally may not create market power for tying purposes by volunteering at the outset to forgo buying aftermarket goods from supplier other than the seller of the original equipment.

---

237. *Id.* at 473–74.

238. *Id.* at 476.

239. This point was made by Justice Scalia in dissent. *Id.* at 496.

240. *Id.* at 473.

241. *Id.* at 477 n.24.

242. *See Queen City Pizza Inc., v. Domino's Pizza, Inc.*, 124 F.3d 430 (3d Cir. 1997); *PSI Repair Servs v. Honeywell, Inc.*, 104 F.3d 811 (6th Cir. 1997); *Digital Equipment Co. v. Uniq Digital Tech.*, 73 F.3d 756 (7th Cir. 1996). *See generally* Jeffrey L. Harrison *An Instrumental Theory or Market Power and Antitrust Policy*, 59 S.M.U. L. Rev. 1673 (2006).

[e] Illinois Tool Works, Inc. v. Independent Ink[243]

In 2006, the Supreme Court revisited the issue of whether a firm necessarily has market power in the tying product market if the tying product is patented. The case involved a claim that the defendant had tied its unpatented ink to its patented print heads and ink containers. The lower court, following well-established precedent, held that the use of a patented tying product to require usage of a tie product was per se unlawful. The implication in the earlier cases was that a patent conferred market power on the owner of the patent.[244]

In *Illinois Tool Works*, the Court noted the inference that a patent created market power was incorrect as an economic matter. Instead, patented tying products should be subjected to the same type of market analysis applied in *Fortner II* and in *Jefferson Parrish*. The strength of the Court's conviction that tying is not as pernicious at suggested in earlier cases is evident from its refusal to place patented products in a middle category by allowing the presumption of market power to be rebutted or by only condemning the "tying" when the two products are not purchased simultaneously.[245] In making its decision the Court relied on a change in patent law that also recognized that a patent did not necessarily result in market power.[246]

[f] Modern Tying Doctrine

The *Jefferson Parish* Court's emphasis on coercion seemed to resolve an issue surrounding the application of the *per se* rule to tying. Some courts, with support from *International Salt* and *Northern Pacific*, have confined their analyses to the defendant's power in the tying product market and the level of commerce affected in the tied product market.[247] Others have regarded the additional question of whether the tie precluded the buyer from considering the tied product on its competitive merits as a required inquiry.[248] After *Jefferson Parish*, coercion is an independent prerequisite for application of the *per se* rule. This is not to say, however, that coercion can be demonstrated only by direct evidence.[249]

Lower courts have converted the Supreme Court's opinion into structured legal tests. The First Circuit in *Borschow Hosp. and Medical Supplies, Inc. v. Cesar Castillo Inc.*, for example, explained:

---

243. 547 U.S. 28 (2006).

244. *Id.*

245. The idea here was the simultaneously purchased products could be viewed as a single product and, thus, not subject to further tying analysis.

246. *Id.* at 42.

247. *See, e.g., Siegel v. Chicken Delight. Inc.*, 448 F.2d 43, 47 (9th Cir. 1971); *see also In re Visa Check/ Mastermoney Antitrust Litigation*, 280 F.3d 124 (2d Cir. 2001) (upholding certification of class action by four million retailers who allege illegal tying of credit card and debit card products due to Visa and Mastercard "honor all cards" requirement).

248. *See, e.g., Yentsch v. Texaco, Inc.*, 630 F.2d 46, 56–57 (2d Cir. 1980).

249. *See, e.g., Tic-X-Press, Inc. v. Omni Promotions Co.*, 815 F.2d 1407, 1418 (11th Cir. 1987).

> There are essentially four elements to a per se tying claim: (1) the tying and the tied products are actually two distinct products; (2) there is an agreement or condition, express or implied, that establishes a tie; (3) the entity accused of tying has sufficient economic power in the market for the tying product to distort consumers' choices with respect to the tied product; and (4) the tie forecloses a substantial amount of commerce in the market for the tied product.[250]

Technically, if the plaintiff is unable to establish all of the elements for a *per se* ruling, it may still proceed under the rule of reason. Needless to say, this is not a promising alternative for plaintiffs wishing to pursue a tying claim.[251]

One issue theoretically left open after *Fortner II* was whether the standards to be applied to tying under the Sherman Act and Clayton Act are different. That suggestion, of course, originally appeared in Justice Clark's opinion in *Times-Picayune.* The Supreme Court seemed to foreclose this possibility in *Jefferson Parish* by observing that even though *Jefferson Parish* did not arise under the Clayton Act, "the congressional finding made therein concerning the competitive consequences of tying is illuminating, and must be respected."[252]

[g] Tying in Technology Markets: United States v. Microsoft

In *United States v. Microsoft Corp.*,[253] the lower court found Microsoft's tying practices to be *per se* unlawful. Microsoft required licensees of Windows 95 and 98 also to license Internet Explorer (IE), refusing to allow equipment manufacturers to uninstall from the desktop, designing Windows 98 so that IE could not be removed by use of the add/remove program, and designing Windows 98 to override a user's efforts to choose a default web browser.[254] The D.C. Circuit reversed, indicating that these tying agreements should be assessed under the rule of reason. The court's concern was not with the issue of market power, or impact on the tied product market but with the wisdom of treating the operating system and the browser as separate products. As noted earlier, for tying to be illegal there must be two products. The court reasoned that the separate demands test of *Jefferson Parish* was essentially a screening mechanism.[255] Ideally, what were screened out of the *per se* category were instances in which

---

250. Borschow Hosp. and Medical Supplies, Inc. v. Cesar Castillo Inc., 96 F.3d 10, 17 (1st Cir.1996) (quoting *Data General Corp. v. Grumman Systems Support Corp.*, 36 F.3d 1147, 1178–79 (1st Cir.1994)). *See also United States v. Microsoft Corp.*, 253 F.3d 34, 85 (D.C. Cir. 2001) (articulating similar test) (citing *Eastman Kodak Co. v. Image Tech. Servs., Inc.*, 504 U.S. 451, 461–62 (1992); *Jefferson Parish Hosp. Dist. No. 2 v. Hyde*, 466 U.S. 2, 12–18 (1984)); *Siva v. Am. Bd. of Radiology*, 38 F.4th 569, 574 (7th Cir. 2022); *United States v. Google LLC*, No. 1:23-CV-108 (LMB/JFA), 2025 WL 1132012, at *38 (E.D. Va. Apr. 17, 2025); *Fotobom Media, Inc. v. Google LLC*, 719 F. Supp. 3d 33, 50 (D.D.C. 2024).

251. *See, e.g., Jefferson Parish*, 466 U.S. at 29–32; *Times-Picayune*, 345 U.S. at 614–26; *Digital Equipment Corp. v. Uniq Digital Technologies*, 73 F.3d 756 (7th Cir. 1996).

252. 466 U.S. at 10–11.

253. 253 F.3d 34 (D.C. Cir. 2001).

254. 253 F.3d at 84–85.

255. *Id.* at 87.

significant efficiencies were made available by integrating products. According to the court, an unrefined separate products analysis would mean that even the integration of spell checkers in work processing programs could potentially violate the tying prohibitions. The problem, according to court, is to balance a loss in consumer choice against the gains made possible by integration. The court also recognized the possibility that the *per se* rule could stifle innovation in the sense that producers would be reluctant to experiment with new and possibly beneficial integrations. Given these considerations and others, the court indicated that it was not confident that bundling in computer software markets has sufficiently negligible "redeeming virtue" as to warrant *per se* treatment.[256]

[3] Package Transactions: Block Booking and Bundling

Tying analysis is relatively simple when the case involves the basic model of a single tying product and a single tied product. Tying, however, sometimes involves a bundle of products. A leading case in this regard is *United States v. Loew's, Inc.*[257] in which the Supreme Court discussed block booking by distributors of motion picture feature films. Block booking occurs when a distributor conditions the licensing or sales of commercially popular films to television stations on the acceptance of a block of films including movies with limited appeal. For example, in order to get "Casablanca" the buyer had to accept a block which also included "Tugboat Annie Sails Again."

The Supreme Court primarily focused on whether the defendants possessed sufficient economic power to satisfy the *Northern Pacific* test.[258] The defendants argued that, since films made up only 8% of television programming and were interchangeable with other types of programming, they had no market power. The Court responded that "a copyrighted feature film does not lose its legal or economic uniqueness because it is shown on a television rather than a movie screen."[259] The Court did not prohibit block booking but only as long as films were also available individually and the price differences between single films and groups of films were cost justified.[260]

Loew's is interesting from a number of perspectives. First, the case was decided in 1962 and the Court's standard for determining the presence of sufficient power in the tying product market is reflective of the then-prevailing hostility toward tying. The Supreme Court in *Illinois Tool Works*, however, eliminated the presumption that copyrights necessarily indicate market power. Second, the Court's reasoning is based largely on the potential coercive effect of the arrangement. That is, purchasers would not have the option to accept or reject the less popular films on their individual merit.

---

256. *Id.* at 94.

257. 371 U.S. 38 (1962).

258. *Id.* at 45.

259. *Id.* at 47–48.

260. *Id.* at 53–55. For subsequent interpretations of *Loew's*, see *Coniglio v. Hollywood Services, Inc.*, 495 F.2d 1286 (2d Cir. 1974), and *American Manufacturers Mutual Insurance Co. v. American Broadcasting-Paramount Theatres, Inc.*, 388 F.2d 272 (2d Cir. 1967).

Even though the Court permitted cost-justified block sales, it noted that price could not be manipulated to have a coercive effect. Under *Jefferson Parish*, the notion of coercion becomes central to tying analysis.

Finally, the facts of the case are ideal for raising the issue of how the tie could benefit the seller. In particular, using the "one monopoly profit" theory, any distributor would seem to be able to maximize profit by pricing individual films at their profit maximizing level. If this were the case, why would the seller insist on block sales? The suggestion has been made that the block sales actually facilitated a form of price discrimination.[261] More specifically, suppose a seller has two films, "Hangover" and "Aunt Julie's Vacation." One buyer will pay $1,000 for "Hangover" and $500 for "Aunt Julie's Vacation." Another will pay $1,500 for "Hangover" and $200 for "Aunt Julie's Vacation." If the seller must sell them separately, the maximum revenue it could hope for would be $2,500—$2,000 for "Hangover" and $500 for "Aunt Julie's Vacation."[262] On the other hand, a package price of $1,500 would result in both buyers buying both films and a total revenue of $3,000.[263]

A more modern version of block booking occurs in the context of cable and satellite television, in which programmers sell to distributors who sell to users. At each stage, access to stations is sold in groups. In *Brantley v. NBC Universal*,[264] cable subscribers claimed that providers were grouping high demand and low demand stations together and, therefore, were engaged in a form of tying.[265] For reasons that are not completely clear, the plaintiffs conceded that the arrangement did not amount to "*per se* tying,"[266] and the rule of reason was applied. Plaintiffs claimed the arrangement was anticompetitive because prices were higher, distributors did not compete by offering a la carte choices, and the methods of competition among distributors were limited. The court distinguished *Loew's* as follows:

> The Court [in *Loew's*] observed that the restraint injured competition because the movie studios' block booking forced the television stations to forego purchases of movies from other distributors. The relevant injury in *Loew's* was to competition, not to the ultimate consumers, because the challenged practice forced television stations to forego the purchase of

261. *See* Stigler, *United States v. Loew's, Inc.: A Note on Block-Booking*, 1963 Sup. Ct. Rev. 152 (1963).

262. A price of $1,000 maximizes the possible revenue for "Hangover" and a price of $500 maximizes the possible revenue for "Aunt Julie's Vacation." Assuming that seller must charge the same price to all buyers, charging $1,000 for "Hangover" for means both buyers purchase the film, yielding $2,000, which is greater than charging $1,500 to the high-value buyer. Conversing, charging $500 for "Aunt Julie's Vacation" and making one sale is more profitable than reducing the price to $200 and making two sales.

263. Both buyers value the bundle of two films at $1,500 (or more) and would be willing to pay this price.

264. 675 F.3d 1192 (9th Cir. 2012).

265. Programmers sold to distributors who sold to subscribers. Programmers insisted in block selling groups of stations and this was passed through by distributors to subscribers.

266. *Id.* at 1196 n.7.

> other movies, and therefore created barriers to entry for competing movie owners.[267]

The Ninth Circuit ruled against plaintiffs. It reasoned that consumers were not literally barred from purchasing channels other than those offered in groups. Instead, they were required to purchase channels they did not want. Relying on the single monopoly profit theory, it concluded that being forced to buy unwanted channels was not different from charging a higher price for desired channels. Charging high prices for desired channels was not a violation of the antitrust laws.[268]

On final note of clarification is in order. Tying is sometimes referred to as "bundling" but it is best to keep two different practices that raise similar concerns separate. For bundling to be subject to a tying analysis as discussed here it should involve selling one product only on the condition that another is purchased. On the other hand, suppose two products are sold together at a discount and they are also offered separately. This is more appropriately referred to as a "bundled discount" and is more effectively analyzed as form of monopolization. That subject is reserved for the discussion of attempted monopolization in the next chapter.[269]

[4] "Defenses" and Justifications

Courts have accepted at least two arguments to justify an arrangement that might otherwise be condemned as a tying agreement. The first focuses on whether the transaction involves one or two products. This issue has been raised repeatedly in the context of franchise agreements. In a technical sense, an argument by a defendant that the exchange involves a single product is not a defense to tying because without two products the plaintiff has not established the *prima facie* elements for a tying claim. In some cases, however, the issue has come to resemble a defense because the question addressed by the court is not so much whether two products are involved but whether the sale should be regarded as involving two products for tying purposes. The second more traditional defense seeks to justify an arrangement that clearly involves two products and would otherwise fall within the Sherman or Clayton Act prohibitions against tying.

[a] The Single Product "Defense"

When courts have allowed the single product issue to become an indirect defense, there appear to be two underlying justifications. One is based on the fact that a single product classification may protect the goodwill of the seller and enhance interbrand competition. The other suggests that joint sale of two items results in efficiencies in supplying the good that could mean lower prices for consumers. A leading example

---

267. *Id.* at 1202–03.
268. *Id.* at 1203.
269. *See* §6.05[M], *infra*.

of the first type of reasoning is found in *United States v. Jerrold Electronics Corp.*[270] in which the seller of community antenna systems required purchasers to buy the complete system although several components could be sold, and were available, separately. The defendant's unique "head end equipment" provided the necessary economic power for demanding full system sales. The issue for the court was "whether this should be treated as a case of tying the sale of one product to another product or merely as the sale of a single product."[271] One of the factors the court considered was whether there was a "business justification" for complete system sales. Jerrold argued that it was necessary to sell its product as a complete system in order to assure its proper functioning and to protect the goodwill of the firm.[272] The court concluded that during the start-up stage of the firm, it was appropriate to classify the system as a single product.[273]

Similar reasoning is found in *Krehl v. Baskin-Robbins Ice Cream Co.*[274] in which the defendant conditioned the grant of a franchise on the purchase of ice cream. The issue considered by the Ninth Circuit Court of Appeals was whether the Baskin-Robbins trademark could be treated as a product separate from the ice cream itself. The court distinguished franchises that were "business format systems" from those that were "distribution systems."[275] In the latter case, the franchiser uses the franchised outlet as a "conduit" for final distribution of its products. Baskin-Robbins was in this category because the trademark was merely a means of identifying its product.[276] Control over the ice cream sold was the *sine qua non* of protecting the goodwill afforded the trademark itself. In effect, the trademark could not be regarded as having an independent value or an identity separate from the ice cream sold under it. The court distinguished *Siegel v. Chicken Delight*[277] in which it held that the two product requirement was met. The franchise in that case, according to the court, was a "business format system" which served only to conduct business under a common name. The tied items were, in many instances, not likely to have a direct influence on the goodwill of the Chicken Delight name.[278]

The second category of single-product issue cases addresses situations in which tying creates efficiencies in production or distribution and lower prices for consumers. For example, Justice O'Connor's concurring opinion in *Jefferson Parish* discussed the efficiency of tying anesthesiology services to hospital services. The majority

---

270. 187 F. Supp. 545 (E.D. Pa.), *aff'd per curiam*, 365 U.S. 567 (1961).

271. 187 F. Supp. at 559.

272. Jerrold's sales effort included both full system sales and the requirement that all maintenance and installation services be purchased from Jerrold as well.

273. In an earlier part of the opinion, the court had already accepted Jerrold's justification for tying installation and maintenance service to the equipment. The court regarded the full system requirement as necessary to achieve the beneficial effects of that tie. *Id.* at 560.

274. 664 F.2d 1348 (9th Cir. 1982).

275. *Id.* at 1353.

276. *Id.* at 1353–54.

277. *Id.* at 1352–54, distinguishing *Siegel v. Chicken Delight*, 448 F.2d 43 (9th Cir. 1971).

278. 664 F.2d at 1352.

determined that two products were involved since there could be separate demands for each product. Justice O'Connor framed the issue as whether there is a "coherent economic basis for treating the products as distinct."[279] Economies associated with offering the products together would be the type of factor that would favor treating them as a single product. For example, automobiles could easily be sold without wheels leaving purchasers to buy wheels from the automobile dealer or from independent wheel producers. Indeed, the near universal tying of wheels to automobiles arguably forecloses an industry of wheel manufacturers. On the other hand, it is probably less costly for a manufacturer of automobiles to produce all its automobiles with wheels intact as opposed to delivering to the dealer automobiles and wheels as separate products. Ultimately, the result could be lower prices for consumers. When faced with these types of cases the courts have often found some basis for avoiding a tying analysis.[280] Most recently in *Microsoft*, the court framed the issue in terms of a trade-off between the economic efficiency of integration and the losses in consumer choice.

Efficiency concerns clearly played a pivotal role in *Principe v. McDonald's Corp.*,[281] one of the most influential franchise cases. McDonald's required licensees to operate their restaurants in premises leased from McDonald's. Both royalties under the license and rent for the premises were calculated as a percentage of gross receipts.[282] The Fourth Circuit Court of Appeals upheld the decision of the lower court that the license contract and the rental agreement constituted a single product. The court applied the standard that "[w]here the challenged aggregation is an essential ingredient of the franchised system's formula for success, there is but a single product. . . ."[283]

The Court was impressed by the extensive research conducted by McDonald's before deciding on a location and the fact that eventual franchisees were not involved in the process. According to the court, McDonald's system enabled it to (1) obtain superior sites, (2) assure that all the restaurants remained in the system therefore ensuring uniformity and consequent goodwill of the system, and (3) select franchisees on the basis of managerial skills rather than financial resources.[284] Moreover, not only did McDonald's train franchisees but it engaged in frequent inspections of

279. 631 F.2d 303 (4th Cir. 1980). *See also Kypta v. McDonald's Corp.*, 671 F.2d 1282 (11th Cir. 1982).

280. This seems to be the case in "physical ties," in which two components are actually combined, *see, e.g., ILC Peripherals Leasing Corp. v. IBM Corp.*, 444 F. Supp. 110 (N.D. Cal. 1978), *aff'd*, 636 F.2d 1188 (9th Cir. 1980); and in cases with products that must be used together because of technological comparability, *see, e.g., Foremost Pro Color v. Eastman Kodak Co.*, 703 F.2d 534 (9th Cir. 1983).

281. 631 F.2d 303 (4th Cir. 1980). *See also Kypta v. McDonald's Corp.*, 671 F.2d 1282 (11th Cir. 1982).

282. 631 F.2d at 304. The agreement was probably a means of practicing price discrimination since a franchisee's rent increased with its volume of business. As indicated in Chapter 8, the practice of price discrimination may result in higher output—in this case more franchisees—than would be the case if a single price were charged.

283. 631 F.2d at 309.

284. *Id.* at 310. The court noted that the arrangement resulted in a "sort of partnership" between McDonald's and the franchisee.

each store during operation. What McDonald's offered franchisees was "a complete method of doing business" and virtual guaranteed success.[285] In short, the license/lease aggregation was an essential ingredient of the "formula for success."[286]

A different type of efficiency seemed to play a role in the Seventh Circuit Court of Appeal's decision in *Johnson v. Nationwide Industries, Inc.*[287] Buyers of condominium units were required to assume a proportionate obligation under a pre-existing building management agreement. The court held that a single product was involved as long as the management agreements were of reasonable duration. It noted the difficulty of selling individual units over a period of time without being able to assure purchasers of stability in building management.[288] Without the aggregation, prospective purchasers would have to weigh the risk of not knowing about future building management arrangements and would face the transaction costs resulting from the necessity of combining with other owners and then searching and contracting for management services. By declining to classify the case as one involving two products, the court seemed cognizant of the savings to consumers of combining individual units with building management.

Finally, in *Digital Equipment Corporation v. Uniq Digital Technologies*[289] the Seventh Circuit Court of Appeals responded to a claim that a computer manufacturer was tying its operating system to the computer. Judge Easterbrook focused on the purposes of the antitrust laws and questioned whether it was "useful" to call the practice a tie reasoning that "[a]n operating system is essential to making a bunch of silicon chips a computer."[290] Accordingly, he went on to compare the operating system of the computer to the electrical system of a car. The result of viewing such a combination as a tie, he concluded, would not "help to uncover practices that restrict output, drive up prices, and transfer wealth from consumers to producers." As suggested earlier in the context of the Microsoft litigation, an economic approach to the question of whether the transaction should be regarded as one or two products may become increasingly significant in tying analysis.

---

285. *Id.* at 309.

286. *Id.* An extensive discussion by Judge Posner of the efficiency justification for finding that an arrangement involves two products is found in *Jack Walters & Sons Corp. v. Morton Building, Inc.*, 737 F.2d 698 (7th Cir. 1984). Morton had tied prefabricated building components to the Morton trademark. The actual rationale for finding that there was not a tie seemed to rest on the inherent inseparability of a product and its name, not on Judge Posner's discussion of efficiencies.

287. 715 F.2d 1233 (7th Cir. 1983).

288. *Id.* at 1237. The court affirmed denial of the defendant's motion for summary judgment indicating the necessity of determining whether the duration of the management contract was reasonable. One year later, in *Jack Walters v. Morton*, Judge Posner characterized the holding as "a condominium and a contract for the provision of management services to the condominium owner was a single product." 737 F.2d at 703. Judge Posner's interpretation of the *Nationwide Industries* holding attributes to that panel less flexibility on the "one product issue" than is actually reflected in the opinion.

289. 73 F.3d 756 (7th Cir. 1996).

290. *Id.* at 761.

[b] Goodwill

In case of obviously separate products, some courts have considered directly whether "goodwill" is a defense for what would otherwise be an illegal tie. In *IBM v. United States*,[291] the Supreme Court evaluated the requirement that lessees of IBM's tabulating and other machines use only tabulating cards produced by IBM. The cards had to be manufactured to precise specifications in order to perform properly in the machines. IBM argued that § 3 was not applicable because its goal was to protect goodwill by insuring the successful performance of the machines. The Court seemed to leave open the possibility that a goodwill defense could be successfully asserted when protection of good will could not be achieved by a less restrictive means.[292] IBM's case was weak on this point since it permitted the Government to make its own cards in exchange for higher rent. In all likelihood, tying cards to the machines was designed to facilitate price discrimination.[293]

In *Jerrold Electronics*, discussed above in the context of the single product issue, the defendant also tied its antenna system to a service contract that covered installation and maintenance.[294] The supplier wanted to avoid do-it-yourself installation and service in order to minimize system failure. Two factors, in particular, seemed to make Jerrold's justification compelling. First, the industry itself was in a developmental period.[295] Second, the investment was substantial and payment to Jerrold was essentially contingent on successful functioning of the equipment.[296] These factors persuaded the court that, at least at their inception, the restrictions were reasonable. In many respects, the court's statement in 1961 provided an introduction to future developments in the law of tying: "while the *per se* rule should be followed in almost all cases, the court always must be conscious of the fact that a case might arise in which the facts indicate that an injustice would be done by blindly accepting the *per se* rule."[297]

[5] When the Tying Product Is Sold by a Third Party

It is fairly common for sellers to sell goods or services on the condition that the buyer purchase the "tied" good from a third party. As one might expect, however, the firm selling the tying product may receive payment from the seller of the "tied" product. The danger, as in the tying cases, is that the producer of the tying product is using its power in that market to reduce competition in the tied product market. The economic concerns of tying—foreclosure, entry barriers, etc.—also are raised by this

291. 298 U.S. 131 (1936).
292. *Id.* at 140.
293. *See* R. Bork, *supra* note 10, at 376–78.
294. 187 F. Supp. at 554–58.
295. *Id.* at 556.
296. *Id.*
297. *Id.* at 556.

form of conditional sale. On the other hand, the arguments that tying really is not anticompetitive also are equally applicable.

The leading cases dealing with this type of arrangement concern requirements by major oil companies that their wholesale and retail outlets purchase tires, batteries and accessories from specified major tire manufacturers. The FTC labeled the practice an unfair method of competition under § 5 of the Federal Trade Commission Act. In two cases, *Atlantic Refining Co. v. FTC*[298] and *FTC v. Texaco*[299] the Supreme Court affirmed the position taken by the Commission. The facts of the cases were substantially the same, with the former involving more coercion than the latter.

The Court's approach mirrored that applied to tying during the mid-1960s with particular attention paid to the pervasive control the oil companies had over their outlets.[300] It reasoned that "just as the effect of this plan is similar to that of a tie-in, so is it unnecessary to embark upon a full-scale economic analysis."[301] The Court also indicated that it had been proper for the Commission to refuse to consider economic justifications for the program.[302] The approach taken today to such cases would be influenced by the decisions in *Fortner II* and *Jefferson Parish*. In particular, after those cases, proof of market dominance and coercion play a greater role in the analysis of such sales. In addition, possible procompetitive aspects of protecting goodwill by such an agreement also would seem to have increased relevance.

One issue lower courts face with increasing frequency is the relevance of the relationship between the sellers of the tying and tied products. For example, in *County of Toulumne v. Sonora Community Hospital*,[303] a hospital required that all caesarian sections be performed by certified obstetricians or specially qualified physicians. The lower court held that the per se standard should not apply since the hospital had no economic interest in the business success of the obstetricians. The appellate court agreed, indicating that without a financial interest there was little likelihood that the tying firm would attempt to acquire market power in the tied product market.[304]

Similarly, in *Abraham v. Intermountain Health Care, Inc.*,[305] optometrists challenged the requirement of a managed care organization that enrollees purchase nonsurgical eye care from a designated panel of ophthalmologists. The optometrists could provide the care and claimed that defendant had tied nonsurgical eye care to the sale of membership in the organization. After the court rejected the claim that membership and care should be treated as one product,[306] it addressed the "economic interest" question. It noted the requirement in most circuits that the firm engaged in tying receive

298. 381 U.S. 357 (1965).
299. 393 U.S. 223 (1968).
300. *Id.* at 228–30.
301. *Atlantic Refining Co.*, 381 U.S. 357, 371.
302. *Id.*
303. 236 F.3d 1148 (9th Cir. 2000).
304. *Id.* at 1158.
305. 461 F.3d 1249 (10th Cir. 2006).
306. *Id.* at 1265.

some economic benefit from the sale of the tied product.[307] Then, reasoning that the organization actually paid the physicians who administered nonsurgical eye care to members, it found the economic interest lacking.[308] In some respects the analysis raises the issue of what is meant by "economic interest." The inclusion of nonsurgical eye care in its coverage was clearly in the economic interest of the managed care organization. On the other hand, unlike a conventional tying arrangement, here the seller of the tying product was actually better off if less of the tied product were sold.

As an economic matter, it is not clear what function the economic interest test serves. If one seller ties the purchases of its tying product to the purchase of a tied product from a different seller, the relevant economic question is the impact on the tied product market. Certainly, the fact that the tying firm is not made more profitable is of little comfort to foreclosed sellers of the tied product or customers who would like to deal with those foreclosed suppliers.

[6] Reciprocal Dealing

Another arrangement, somewhat rare, that has a tying-type quality is reciprocal dealing. Here firm A agrees to make purchases from firm B only on the condition that firm B make purchases from firm A. In these instances, the "leverage" involved lies in firm A's ability to purchase or withhold its purchases from firm B. In other words, firm A uses its monopsony power—power as a buyer—to coerce firm B to buy its product. The alleged damage occurs to competitors of firm A who will find it more difficult to find outlets for their products. In effect, monopsony leverage is used to promote the sales of A's product on the basis of a factor other than competitive merit. Courts have used tying analysis in such cases.

The principal Supreme Court case regarding reciprocal dealing is *FTC v. Consolidated Foods Corp.*,[309] in which the FTC challenged the acquisition of a producer of dehydrated vegetables by a major food processor because the acquisition created the threat of reciprocal dealing. More specifically, Consolidated Foods could condition its purchases from other food processors on their purchase of dehydrated onion and garlic from Consolidated's subsidiary. The Court reasoned that, "reciprocity made possible by such an acquisition is one of the congeries of anticompetitive practices at which the antitrust laws are aimed."[310] Accordingly, it upheld the Commission's divestiture order citing *International Salt* and *Northern Pacific*.

---

307. *Id.* at 1265. *See also Sports Racing Services, Inc. v. Sports Car Club of America, Inc.*, 131 F.3d 874 (10th Cir. 1997). *But see Gonzalez v. St. Margaret's Housing Development Fund Corp.*, 880 F.2d 1514 (2d Cir. 1989).

308. *Id.* at 1266.

309. 380 U.S. 592 (1965).

310. *Id.* at 594–95. One year later *Consolidated Foods* was relied upon to condemn a purely reciprocal dealing arrangement. *United States v. General Dynamics*, 258 F. Supp. 36 (S.D.N.Y. 1966). *See generally* Note, *A Reevaluation of Reciprocal Dealings, Under the Federal Antitrust Laws*: Spartan Grain v. Ayers, 11 Loy. U. Chi. L.J. 577 (1980). For more recent discussions of reciprocal dealing, see *Intergraph*

The economic issues raised by reciprocal dealing are similar to those that arise in the tying context. The single monopoly profit rule can be applied to the firm with monopsony power. Whatever profit producing capabilities the firm has due to monopsony power can be fully realized by making purchases at low prices.[311] In effect, firm A, in the example, may receive its profit by acquiring the goods of firm B at a low price or by selling its own product. In either case, so the argument goes, the total profit is the same. The possibility also exists that reciprocal dealing may promote efficiency.[312] This is likely to be the case when the arrangement, rather than being the result of coercion, is voluntary. Although *Consolidated Foods* did not distinguish between voluntary and involuntary reciprocal dealing and was decided before *Jefferson Parish*, now issues of market power and "forcing" are important in a reciprocal dealing case.

In *Brokerage Concepts Inc. v. United States Healthcare, Inc.*,[313] the Third Circuit applied all the elements of a modern tying analysis to a reciprocal dealing case. An HMO had agreed to buy drugs for its members from a group of pharmacists if the pharmacists made use of a third-party administrator that was a subsidiary of the HMO.[314] The plaintiff was a competing third-party administrator. The court evaluated whether this arrangement should be assessed under the *per se* or rule of reason standard and focused specifically on the market power of the defendant. In this instance, leverage used by the defendant resulted from its ability to steer its membership to a specific group of pharmacists. In a sense, the defendant was seen as "selling" access to its members. Thus, the court examined whether there were other reasonable substitutes in the market and reasoned that members of any managed care organization were reasonably interchangeable from the perspective of pharmacists with those of the defendant. In a properly defined market, the defendant's market share was, at most, 25% which was too small to warrant a *per se* ruling. The court then applied the rule of reason and found that the plaintiff had not demonstrated harm to competition.

[C] Antisteering Requirements

In *Ohio v. American Express Co.*,[315] the Supreme Court considered whether antisteering requirements violate § 1 of the Sherman Act. American Express forbade merchants that accepted the American Express card from informing customers that other credit card companies charge the merchant less and that this might be reflected in the

---

Corp. v. Intel Corp., 195 F.3d 1346 (Fed. Cir. 1999), *Betaseed, Inc. v. U and I, Inc.*, 681 F.2d 1203 (9th Cir. 1982), and *Spartan Grain & Mill Co. v. Ayers*, 581 F.2d 419 (5th Cir. 1978).

311. *See generally* R. Posner & F. Easterbrook, *Antitrust* 855 (2d ed. 1981).

312. *See* H. Hovenkamp, *supra* note 4, at 427–30.

313. 140 F.3d 494 (3d Cir. 1998).

314. The Court viewed the practice as falling somewhere between tying and reciprocal dealing. *Id.* at 511.

315. 585 U.S. 529 (2018).

final sales price. In effect, merchants were not permitted to steer customers to cards that charged the merchant lower fees. Withholding this information obviously limited the ability of customers to enjoy lower prices.

The majority characterized Amex as a two-sided transaction platform, which is an intermediary that offers different products or services to two different groups who both depend on the platform to make sales. This type of market may have "indirect network effects" whereby the value of the two-sided platform to one group of participants depends on how many members of another group participate.[316] In this case, the value of a credit card for consumers depends on how many businesses accept that card, and the value for merchants depends on how many consumers will use that particular credit card. Amex induced consumers to use its card by offering rewards. Amex paid for these rewards by charging merchants relatively high merchant fees. Some merchants resented Amex's high fees and encouraged their customers to use other credit cards. Amex responded by adopting a no-steering policy that forbade merchants from doing this. And the merchants sued.

After a 7-week trial, the district court held that Amex's antisteering provisions violated § 1. The district court treated the market for credit-card transactions as two separate markets—one for merchants and one for cardholders. The court found that Amex's antisteering policy injured competition on the merchant side of the market, because the policy resulted in higher merchant fees. The Second Circuit reversed, holding that credit-card market was one market, not two.

The Supreme Court granted certiorari and first held that, because the antisteering policy is a vertical restraint, the challenged restraint should be evaluated under the rule of reason. The Court used this case to articulate that the rule of reason is operationalized through "a three-step, burden-shifting framework" comprising these three inquiries:

> [1] the plaintiff has the initial burden to prove that the challenged restraint has a substantial anticompetitive effect that harms consumers in the relevant market. [2] If the plaintiff carries its burden, then the burden shifts to the defendant to show a procompetitive rationale for the restraint. [3] If the defendant makes this showing, then the burden shifts back to the plaintiff to demonstrate that the procompetitive efficiencies could be reasonably achieved through less anticompetitive means.[317]

Writing for a 5-to-4 majority, Justice Thomas held that the two-sided market for credit-card transactions is a single market that must be examined "as a whole to determine whether the plaintiffs have shown that Amex's antisteering provisions have anticompetitive effects."[318] Justice Thomas held that to make this showing, "the plain-

---

316. *Id.* at 535.
317. *Id.* at 541–42 (citations omitted).
318. *Id.* at 547.

tiffs must prove that Amex's antisteering provisions increased the cost of credit-card transactions above a competitive level, reduced the number of credit-card transactions, or otherwise stifled competition in the credit-card market."[319] Showing that merchants were paying more, by itself, was not enough. The majority reasoned that if these merchant fees subsidized cardholder rewards, then one of the market participants was benefitting from the Amex system and therefore there was not an overall anticompetitive effect.

Writing for the four Justices in dissent, Justice Breyer emphasized several of the factual findings of the district court. These included that American Express did not increase benefits (or cut credit-card prices) to American Express cardholders in tandem with its merchant fee increases; that antisteering policy blocked price competition by rival credit cards; that the policy eliminated the incentive for other credit card to lower their merchant fees; that there was "no offsetting pro-competitive benefit to shoppers"; and that "[c]onsumers throughout the economy paid higher retail prices as a result, and they were denied the opportunity to accept incentives that merchants might otherwise have offered to use less-expensive cards."[320] Regarding market definition, Justice Breyer reasoned that plaintiffs did not need to define markets when they presented direct evidence of anticompetitive effects. In this case, the district court had found strong direct evidence of anticompetitive effects—namely the higher merchant fees—and this operated as proof of market power. Justice Breyer also noted that even if market definition was relevant, the plaintiffs made the necessary factual showing by proving that Amex "increased the percentage of the purchase price that it charges merchants . . . and that this increase was not entirely spent on cardholder rewards."[321]

The *Amex* opinion has proven controversial.[322] The majority improperly elevated the issue of market definition over anticompetitive effects—given that the district court found actual anticompetitive effects, which the majority did not refute. This is odd because the reason that courts define the market is to help find or predict anticompetitive effects. When antitrust plaintiffs prove anticompetitive effects through direct evidence, market definition is arguably unnecessary and may prove to be a distraction. The opinion creates a strong incentive for antitrust defendants to characterize their markets as two-sided transaction platforms in order to minimize the significance of anticompetitive effects on one side of the market.

The *Amex* opinion also mishandles the issue of "negative externalities." According to Justice Thomas, "[w]hen merchants steer cardholders away from Amex at the point of sale, it undermines the cardholder's expectation of 'welcome acceptance'—the

319. *Id.*

320. *Id.* at 560 (Breyer, J., dissenting).

321. *Id.* at 572.

322. *See, e.g.*, John B. Kirkwood, *Antitrust and Two-Sided Platforms: The Failure of American Express*, 41 Cardozo L. Rev. 1805, 1815 (2020) (describing *Amex* as "deeply flawed"); Chris Sagers, *Platforms, American Express, and the Problem of Complexity in Antitrust*, 98 Neb. L. Rev. 389, 389 (2019) ("Everything about *Ohio v. American Express* was wrong and the adoption of 'two-sided platform' reasoning into American antitrust law might be one of its worst, most regrettable wrong turns in decades.").

promise of a frictionless transaction." This may, so the argument goes, make the American Express card less attractive generally and endanger the viability of the American Express network. In effect, the Court seems to reason that lower price alternatives to American Express may mean American Express loses out in the competitive process. This rationale is inconsistent with the view that the antitrust laws protect competition but not individual competitors.[323]

323. 585 U.S. at 551.

Chapter 6
Monopolization and Related Offenses

§ 6.01 Introduction

Section 2 of the Sherman Act makes it illegal to monopolize, to attempt to monopolize, or to conspire to monopolize.[1] The statute, however, never defines any of these terms. The legislative history provides no insights, as the senators and representatives did not define the terms in their floor debates. Initially, two strands of thought emerged as to the meaning of "monopolize." First, "monopolize" could mean to have a monopoly, in which case the Sherman Act would make all monopolies illegal. Second, "monopolize" could mean to acquire or maintain a monopoly through anticompetitive conduct. Under this approach, possessing a monopoly is not illegal. Instead, the focus is on the monopolist's conduct.

Treating all monopolies as illegal would be problematic because the competitive process sometimes results in a single winner, who then charges a monopoly price. Should this be illegal? As Judge Learned Hand explained, "The successful competitor, having been urged to compete, must not be turned upon when he wins."[2] As explained in this chapter, the Supreme Court has held that illegal monopolization requires proof of anticompetitive conduct, not simply proof of monopoly power.

This chapter considers all three prohibitions of § 2—monopolization, attempt to monopolize, and conspiracy to monopolize. The first section is a brief review of the economic concerns raised by the existence of monopoly.[3]

1. 15 U.S.C. § 2 (1983).
2. *United States v. Aluminum Co. of Am.*, 148 F.2d 416, 430 (2d Cir. 1945).
3. For greater depth, see Chapter 2.

§ 6.02 The Economics of Monopoly

Antitrust is concerned about monopolization because, as explained in Chapter 2, monopolies raise price and reduce output below the efficient level. This can be explained through logic as well as through supply and demand curves. These two ways of explaining the effects of monopolization reinforce each other. They tell the same story, one through words and the other through diagrams. While economists rely heavily on supply and demand graphs to explore the consequences of monopolization, lawyers do not generally use supply and demand graphs in their briefs, and judges do not include them in their antitrust opinions. Still, understanding supply and demand graphs can help one comprehend and explain the effects of monopolization.

Before examining the economic graphs, consider logically how firms will behave differently based on whether or not they face competition in the market. If a firm has several competitors, it cannot profitably raise its prices above the competitive level. If a firm unilaterally raises its price, consumers will simply purchase their products from the competitors who are charging a lower price. With each firm similarly constrained in its ability to raise prices unilaterally, all firms will end up charging the competitive price.

When firms charge a competitive price instead of a supracompetitive price (which is, by definition, higher than the competitive price), consumers generally purchase greater quantities because products are more affordable. For each product, every consumer has a reservation price, which is the highest price that a consumer is willing to pay for a particular product. Different consumers have different reservation prices. For example, some consumers are willing to pay $20 for an insulated water bottle, while others are willing to pay $40, and some are willing to pay $50. If the price of insulated water bottles is $40, then those with the reservation price below $40 will not purchase the product. Reducing the price from $40 to $20 increases the pool of consumers who are willing and able to purchase an insulated water bottle at that price. In this way, lowering price increases consumption.

Suppose that in a competitive market, the prevailing price is $20. Then, every consumer with a reservation price $20 or higher will purchase the product. Those consumers that have a relatively high reservation price are getting a particularly good deal. For example, those consumers with the highest reservation price, $50, are willing to pay $30 more than the price they actually pay. (In economic parlance, this $30 is called consumer surplus.)

Now, suppose that this market is not competitive, but is instead controlled by a monopolist. If the monopolist's goal is to maximize its profits, it will not continue to charge the competitive price. A monopolist maximizes its profits by raising its price. (Essentially, it is trying to take some of the consumer surplus the consumers receive at the competitive price and convert it into monopoly profit.) The monopolist, for example, may raise its price to $40. At this higher price, consumers with a reservation price below $40 will be priced out of the market. The monopolist will consequently make fewer sales. But the monopolist will make significantly greater profits on the sales that it does make. These greater profits per sale can outweigh any losses associated with reduced sales volume. Of course, the monopolist cannot raise price too high, because if it prices too many consumers out of the market, its profits will decline.

Each monopolist has a profit-maximizing monopoly price, a price that captures enough profits per sale to outweigh the losses associated with reduced sales, but not so high that it loses too many sales. When a monopolist charges this profit-maximizing price, overall output is reduced and consumers pay a higher price. Monopoly pricing makes all consumers worse off. Consumers fall into one of two camps. First, some consumers are priced out of the market and cannot afford the product. These consumers are denied access to products, even though they are willing and able to pay a price that covers the cost of the product. Second, those consumers that continue to purchase the product are worse off because they are forced to pay a higher price than they would pay in a competitive market.

In short, monopolization has two effects: reduced output and higher prices. Each of these effects harms consumers in a different way. If you understand this explanation, then you understand why antitrust law condemns monopolization. Economists tell this story using supply and demand curves. It is the same story; it is simply told using the language of economics.

In Figure 6-1, D is the demand and S is the supply for bagels. From Chapter 2, you know that the supply curve under competitive conditions is actually the horizontal summation of the supply curves of all the manufacturers of bagels. These individual supply curves are the marginal cost curves of the firms. Under competitive conditions, the equilibrium market price will be Pc and output will be Qc. Each firm would sell all it wants at price Pc. By definition, no firm is large enough to affect price by increasing or decreasing the number of bagels it offers for sale. Under competitive conditions, all producers are "price takers" and price will tend to equal marginal cost.

The area of triangle PcAB in Figure 6-1 indicates the total value to consumers of bagels above the amount they are required to pay. This is called "consumer surplus." For example, in Figure 6-1, the first bagel is sold for Pc as are all the others. The demand curve, however, shows that a purchaser would have been willing and able to pay up to price P1 for the bagels. The consumer surplus would be the difference between Pc and P1; it measures the gain to the consumer from the exchange of Pc for a bagel. There must be consumer surplus associated with every bagel sold or the exchange would not take place.

Suppose, through some huge and highly unlikely merger, all the firms producing bagels became a single firm and each plant maintained its own production system. Now the monopolist—the single firm supplier of the product—would face the entire demand curve for the industry, D. Since the monopolist faces a downward sloping demand curve and must lower price in order to sell additional output, its marginal revenue curve becomes an important decision-making tool. Its marginal cost curve (MC) would be what was formerly the industry supply curve.[4] Its profit maximizing

4. This assumes that the monopolist does not experience any economies in production over those available when the industry is competitive.

Figure 6-1.

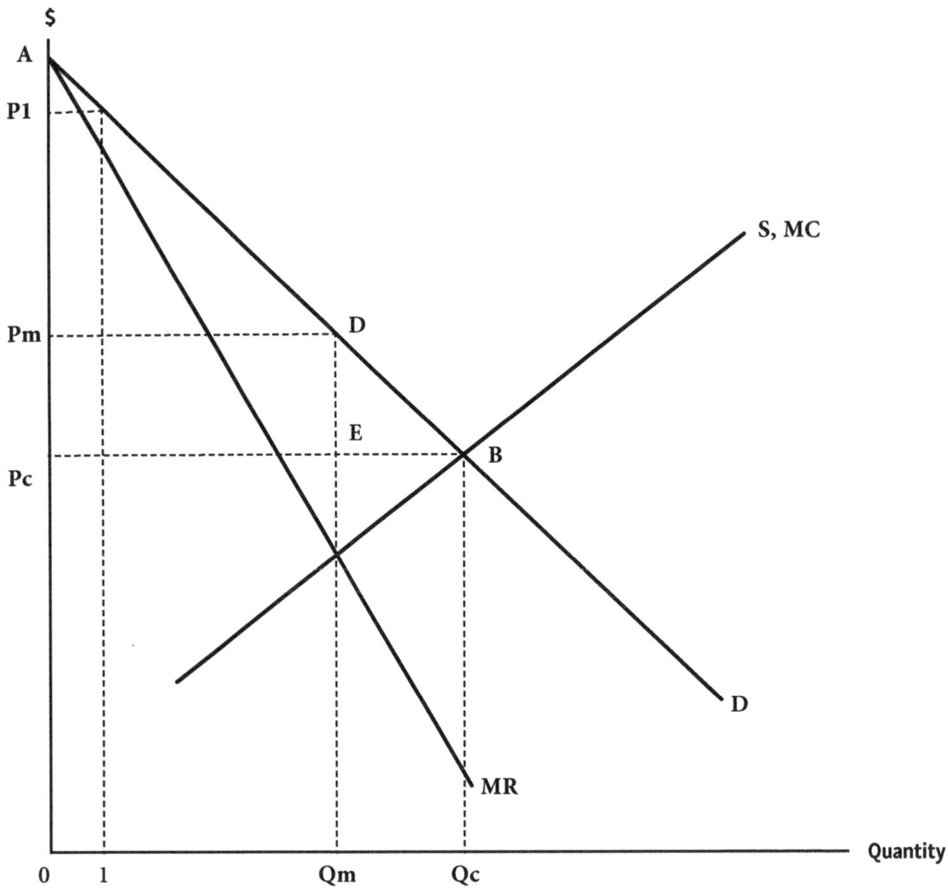

level of output is Qm, where the marginal cost and marginal revenue curves intersect. The monopolist then sells the profit maximizing output for Pm, the highest price consistent with selling that quantity. In fact, the primary way the monopolist differs from the competitive firm is in this ability to be a price setter, not a price taker. Consequently, the concept of monopoly power is reduced to "market power," which is a measure of the firm's ability to raise price above what it would be under competitive conditions.

The most important aspect of the change from competition to monopoly is the impact on consumer surplus. The former consumer surplus was PcAB. Under monopoly it has declined to PmAD. What has happened to the remainder? A portion of it, PcPmDE has been transferred to the monopolist. One's reaction to this will depend on whether one feels that antitrust should be guided by distributive goals or should be indifferent to them. Another portion of what was consumer surplus, EDB, is not transferred to the monopolist but simply eliminated. In short, it was a gain to consumers that now does not exist, even in the form of a benefit to the monopolist. This "deadweight" loss, the quantity of which is of some dispute, is most frequently held out as the true social cost of monopoly.

There are two other factors that complicate the evaluation of monopoly. First, although the "deadweight" loss is important, it may not be the only social cost of monopoly. In particular, the lure of capturing some of the consumer surplus resulting from the exchange could be quite tempting to an incumbent and a potential monopolist. Consequently, a monopolist may find it worthwhile to invest a great deal of effort in maintaining or gaining a share of what otherwise would be consumer surplus. In theory, it may use some or nearly all the surplus it has captured—PcPmDE in Figure 6-1—in this effort. To the extent that the process involves the use of resources and has no other impact than the transfer of income, the cost may be regarded as an additional form of "deadweight" loss.[5]

Finally, in the simple model examined here, the economies of production for the merged firm are the same as they were for the industry under competitive conditions. However, the larger firm producing bagels may be able to operate at a scale that enables it to produce each unit at a lower per unit cost than several firms operating under competition. The most extreme version of this is called "natural monopoly," a condition under which the lowest per unit cost of production is achieved when one firm serves the entire market. Thus, production by a monopolist may mean higher prices and lower output and a deadweight loss that would not exist under competition. On the other hand, due to efficiencies in production, the actual cost per unit may be lower; resources may be used more effectively.[6] If a market is a natural monopoly, a single supplier is the most efficient way to supply the market. This raises important questions. What economies are derived from having a single producer of the good? How does the deadweight loss compare with the possible gains from more efficient production? To what extent do consumers value the presence of a large number of possibly "inefficient" competitors over a relatively efficient monopolist?[7] Only by answering these questions—a practical impossibility—can one be sure about the actual gains or losses due to monopoly.

---

5. *See* R. Posner, *Antitrust Law: An Economic Perspective* 11–14 (1976).

6. *See* R. Bork, *The Antitrust Paradox* 107–10 (1978); see *supra* Chapter 2.

7. This point and others that question the soundness of current economic approach to antitrust are made in Jeffrey L. Harrison, *Other Markets, Other Costs: Modernizing Antitrust*, 27 J. L. & Pub. Policy 373 (2016).

§ 6.03 The Modern Offense of Monopolization: The Search for Standards

[A] Early Interpretations

[1] Preliminary Issues

Because the text of § 2 of the Sherman Act is so vague, early courts had to address two questions with no meaningful guidance from Congress. First, does § 2 condemn the mere possession of monopoly power? In short, is bigness *per se* to be condemned? Second, if there is a separate conduct component of the monopolization offense, what types of behavior are prohibited? Specifically, do the prohibitions of § 2 extend only to behavior that would violate § 1 if engaged in by more than one actor or does it prohibit a broader range of conduct? As a corollary: are otherwise lawful acts prohibited if engaged in by a firm with monopoly power?

Different answers to these questions create a continuum of possible interpretations. At one end lies the possibility that merely having a monopoly violates § 2. This is not an unreasonable position.[8] As a matter of economic theory, in most situations, when an industry moves from being competitive to monopoly, consumers are worse off by more than the monopolist is better off. Thus, unless there are specific advantages of allowing monopolies to exist, it is inefficient to do so.[9]

At the other extreme is the requirement that the firm possess monopoly power and engage in practices that would otherwise violate § 1. Today, we know that courts have opted for a point somewhere between these extremes. Monopolies are only illegal if the monopolist has engaged in anticompetitive conduct to acquire or maintain its monopoly power; that conduct is not viewed through the lens of § 1 jurisprudence. Before discussing how courts apply this standard today, this chapter briefly reviews the evolution of the case law that brought us to the current legal test.

[2] Standard Oil v. United States[10]

In 1911, in *Standard Oil v. United States*, the Supreme Court began the process of defining the purpose and reach of § 2. The case addressed the federal government's effort to break up Standard Oil as an illegal monopoly. At points, the Court seemed to view § 2 as a complement to § 1. Thus, "the 2nd section seeks, if possible, to make the

---

8. *See* Robert H. Lande & Richard O. Zerbe, *The Sherman Act Is a No-Fault Monopolization Statute: A Textualist Demonstration*, 70 Am. U. L. Rev. 497, 497 (2020).

9. *See* Jeffrey L. Harrison, *An Instrumental Approach to Market Power and Antitrust Policy*, 59 SMU L. Rev. 1673, 1673–74 (2006).

10. 221 U.S. 1 (1911).

prohibition of the act all the more complete and perfect by embracing all attempts to reach the end prohibited by the 1st section."[11]

Although the Court stressed the importance of interpreting §§ 1 and 2 in parallel fashion, it opened the door for an expanded application of § 2 by noting that the evil to be avoided was achievement of monopoly power through other than "normal methods of industrial development."[12] This implicitly set § 2 on separate footing from § 1. Ultimately, the decisions in *Standard Oil*, as well as *American Tobacco*,[13] which was decided the same term, seemed to tie § 2 to § 1 without precluding a broader application.

[3] United States v. United States Steel Corp.

The parameters of § 2 became slightly more focused in *United States v. U.S. Steel Corp.*[14] There, all of the Justices agreed that ". . . the law does not make mere size an offense, or the existence of unexercised power an offense. It . . . requires overt acts."[15] Interestingly, as the following discussion of *Alcoa* demonstrates (§ 6.03[B], *infra*), this did not entirely lay to rest the question of whether § 2 could be a response to bigness *per se*.

Although the Court in *United States Steel* was unanimous in its view that § 2 required both power and conduct, it was deeply divided on the application of this standard to the emergence and practices of U.S. Steel. The majority took the view that U.S. Steel had not achieved power over price, the measure of monopoly power,[16] because various collusive activities engaged in by U.S. Steel would not have been necessary if it had possessed monopoly power. Furthermore, according to the majority, the practices of U.S. Steel could be distinguished from those in *Standard Oil* and *American Tobacco* because the latter cases involved "a persistent and systematic lawbreaker masquerading under legal forms."[17] Finally, the majority was not concerned with practices leading to the accumulation of power because, in their view, the effort to gain control of the market had failed. As a general matter, the majority stressed the need to find wrongdoing by the defendant and suggested a close parallel between the type of conduct condemned by § 1 and the proper scope of § 2.

---

11. *Id.* at 61.
12. *Id.* at 72.
13. *United States v. American Tobacco*, 221 U.S. 106 (1911).
14. 251 U.S. 417 (1920).
15. *Id.* at 451.
16. *Id.* at 444–46.
17. *Id.* at 457.

[B] *United States v. Aluminum Co. of America (Alcoa)*

The 1945 case of *United States v. Aluminum Co. of America*[18] *(Alcoa)* is typically regarded as the landmark monopolization case and the starting point for modern monopolization law. This is ironic because, read as a whole, Judge Hand's opinion would still leave any corporate counsel or antitrust scholar confused about the type of behavior that would lead to antitrust liability. Nevertheless, *Alcoa* is critical as a foundation for further development of the monopolization offense. *Alcoa* emphasized market power analysis as a component of the monopolization offense. More significantly, it made clear that § 2 would be applied to conduct beyond that condemned for multiple firms under § 1.

[1] Background

Alcoa was founded in 1888. It sold virgin "ingot" aluminum and, after 1895, produced aluminum products. Through patents, Alcoa effectively possessed a legal monopoly on the production of aluminum until 1909. Alcoa's dominance was bolstered and extended by agreements with foreign competitors limiting competition and with power companies restricting the sale of electricity to potential domestic producers.[19] These activities were enjoined by a consent decree in 1912. After 1912, Alcoa continued to be the only domestic producer of virgin ingot.[20] The Justice Department charged that Alcoa's continued existence as sole domestic producer violated § 2 of the Sherman Act.[21]

[2] Market Definition

The market share issue in *Alcoa* centered on the product and geographic markets for aluminum ingot. In addressing the market, Judge Hand saw three choices. The first was a market composed of all the virgin ingot sold in the United States. This possibility would include all ingot produced by Alcoa including that which it used to produce aluminum products. That market definition would mean a 90% market share for Alcoa because only 10% of the ingot sold domestically was produced outside the U.S. The second choice was a market consisting of all virgin ingot plus "secondary" ingot (made from scrap). In this case, Aloca's share was 64%. The final possibility was all virgin and secondary ingot sold in the United States excluding Alcoa's own consumption. Here Alcoa's share was 33%.

---

18. 148 F.2d 416 (2d Cir. 1945). *Alcoa* was heard by the Second Circuit Court of Appeals after four members of the Supreme Court disqualified themselves.

19. Aluminum production requires bauxite (a mineral) and massive amounts of electricity to convert that bauxite into aluminum.

20. 148 F.2d at 422–23.

21. The complaint was filed in 1937, before the beginning of World War Two.

Judge Hand defined the relevant market as all the virgin ingot sold in the United States resulting in a market share of 90% for Alcoa. In settling on that choice, he recognized that secondary ingot was an acceptable substitute for virgin ingot for many buyers and this could influence Alcoa's power *vis-à-vis* the sales of virgin ingot. He reasoned, however, that it was inappropriate to include secondary ingot in the market because Alcoa, as the sole producer of virgin ingot, ultimately controlled the amount of secondary ingot that was available.[22] The second step in his analysis was to include Alcoa's internal consumption of virgin ingot as part of the total market although it was not actually sold as ingot. Judge Hand noted that the market analysis was undertaken to determine Alcoa's control over price. Alcoa's use of its own ingot, according to Judge Hand, reduced demand for ingot and affected Alcoa's power.[23] Finally, although he recognized the possible limiting effect of foreign production on Alcoa's pricing, he concluded that—because of transportation costs and tariffs—this competition was not sufficiently threatening to keep Alcoa from wielding significant power over price.[24]

Judge Hand's market definition was pivotal because he deemed it "doubtful" that 64% would constitute a monopoly. Accordingly, 33% was definitely not a monopoly.[25] Some assumptions used in his market analysis are questionable. For example, the availability of secondary ingot was likely to influence Alcoa's pricing behavior and probably should not have been excluded entirely from the market.

While people may disagree with some of Judge Hand's reasoning on what to include and exclude from the relevant market, the *Alcoa* opinion is foundational to modern antitrust law because the court performed this extensive market definition analysis. Prior opinions largely took market definition and the defendant's monopoly status as a given without performing an individualized analysis. The *Alcoa* decision started courts down the path of meticulously defining the relevant market and calculating defendants' market shares.

[3] Alcoa's Conduct

After finding that Alcoa's 90% market share constituted a monopoly, Judge Hand turned to whether that alone violated § 2. Much of Hand's opinion is an indictment of bigness *per se*. This follows from his view that "great industrial consolidations are inherently undesirable, regardless of their economic results" and that the antitrust law was designed to preserve an "organization of industry in small units."[26] He reasoned that § 2, at a minimum, prohibits single firms from engaging in acts prohibited under § 1. Since § 1 prohibits a combination of firms from fixing prices, § 2 can be read as

---

22. 148 F.2d at 425.
23. *Id.* at 424.
24. *Id.* at 426.
25. *Id.* at 424.
26. *Id.* at 429.

applying to the same actions by a monopolist.[27] Merely by operating, a monopolist would seem, therefore, to violate § 2.

But Judge Hand noted that some monopolies were legal. Notably, liability would not attach to a monopolist which had market power "thrust upon it,"[28] or which gained its market power by "force of accident,"[29] or was a "passive beneficiary."[30] More significantly, Judge Hand observed that market dominance resulting from "skill, foresight and industry"[31] was not to be condemned. He reasoned that "[t]he successful competitor, having been urged to compete, must not be turned on when he wins."[32]

Judge Hand held that illegal monopolization requires affirmative conduct—or misconduct—by the monopolist. In Alcoa's case, he saw evidence of "persistent determination to maintain control."[33] Two of Alcoa's practices in particular seemed compelling to Judge Hand. The first was Alcoa's practice of maintaining excess capacity in order to meet increases in demand for ingot, thereby forestalling entry by potential competitors.[34] The second was Aloca's "price squeeze" or the practice of selling ingot to competing fabricators of "sheet" at prices that made it difficult for them to compete with Alcoa in the sale of sheet.[35] Judge Hand also addressed the intent requirement in monopolization cases. He rejected the notion that the intent requirement could be equated with the traditional concept of "specific intent" in criminal law. In Judge Hand's words, "no monopolist monopolizes unconscious of what he is doing."[36]

Judge Hand's opinion ranges from a condemnation of bigness *per se* to a call for an analysis of market structure and the defendant's conduct. Whether Judge Hand applied his elusive standards in a way that would satisfy today's judges and antitrust scholars is debatable. Neither the maintenance of excess capacity nor the "price squeeze" would probably violate § 2 today. Nevertheless, the case stands as a milestone in the development of monopolization law. Its importance lies in its structural analysis and its signal that § 2 and § 1 are separate offenses with differing standards.

Judge Hand's views of monopolization received sweeping Supreme Court approval in 1946 in *American Tobacco Co. v. United States*.[37] The Court addressed the issue of whether actual exclusion was a necessary element of monopolization.[38] It determined

27. *Id.* at 428.
28. *Id.* at 429.
29. *Id.* at 430.
30. *Id.*
31. *Id.*
32. *Id.*
33. *Id.* at 430.
34. *Id.* at 431.
35. *Id.* at 436–37.
36. *Id.* at 432.
37. 328 U.S. 781 (1946).
38. *Id.* at 808–09.

that it was not, and it drew guidance from *Alcoa*.[39] In fact, the Court quoted so extensively from Judge Hand's opinion that it can be seen as endorsing either the view that only passive monopoly is permissible or that a more searching examination of actual conduct is required.

[C] The Search for Standards in the Aftermath of *Alcoa*

[1] United States v. Griffith

The Supreme Court once again addressed the issue of monopolization in *United States v. Griffith*.[40] A monopolization charge was leveled at theater owners who were monopolists in some towns but who faced competition in others. Through the mechanism of booking films for the entire chain, defendants were able to force film distributors to make concessions as a condition of having their films shown in the towns where the defendants were the only exhibitors. In essence, the monopoly possessed by the defendants in some towns arguably enabled them to gain an advantage in the towns in which they faced competition.[41]

Unfortunately, Justice Douglas's articulation of the guiding standard was no more enlightening than Judge Hand's in *Alcoa*. At one level, he seemed to add credence to the view that § 2 is aimed at bigness alone: "[M]onopoly power, whether lawfully or unlawfully acquired, may itself constitute an evil and stand condemned under § 2. . . ."[42] On the other hand, he offered the seemingly inconsistent view that "the existence of power 'to exclude competition when it is desired to do so' is itself a violation of § 2, provided it is coupled with the purpose or intent to exercise that power."[43]

Griffith also raised an issue that was not addressed by the Court for several more years. In *Griffith*, the defendants were using power in some markets in order to gain competitive advantage in other markets. The issue left open was whether this use of "leverage" is itself a violation of § 2 of the Sherman Act or is it a violation only if the defendant is likely to become a monopolist in the second market.[44] In the 1993 decision, *Spectrum Sports v. McQuillan*, the Court appeared to answer this question by ruling that the leverage must create a dangerous probability that the firm will become a monopolist in the second market,[45] which provides a basis for an attempted monopolization claim.

39. *Id.* at 811–14.
40. 334 U.S. 100 (1948).
41. See the discussion of monopsony power *supra* at § 2.06[B][10].
42. 334 U.S. at 107.
43. *Id.*
44. *See* Hovenkamp, *Federal Antitrust Policy* 321–22 (3d ed. 2005).
45. 506 U.S. 447 (1993).

[2] United States v. United Shoe Machinery Corp.

In 1954, in *United States v. United Shoe Machinery Corp.*,[46] Judge Wyzanski reviewed the possible interpretations of § 2 that seemed to be available after *Alcoa* and *Griffith*. First was the "classic" test under which § 2 prohibited single firm conduct that would be deemed illegal under § 1 if undertaken by two or more firms. Judge Wyzanski felt precluded from applying this test due to prior cases involving *United Shoe*. A second approach, which Judge Wyzanski derived from Justice Douglas's *Griffith* opinion, was that monopolization entailed (1) the power to exclude competition and (2) the exercise or purpose to exercise that power.[47] A third option was that monopolization occurs whenever the monopolist does business or acts deliberately even if the conduct is not exclusionary. Judge Wyzanski regarded this approach as having been "softened by Judge Hand's suggestion that the defendant may escape statutory liability if it bears the burden of proving that it owes its monopoly solely to superior skill, superior products, natural advantages, . . . economic or technological efficiency. . . ."[48] Under the facts of *United Shoe* in which exclusionary conduct was found, Judge Wyzanksi reasoned it was unnecessary to choose between the second and third approaches because the government satisfied both.[49]

[3] United States v. Grinnell

The Supreme Court announced the modern test for illegal monopolization in *United States v. Grinnell*.[50] The Court held:

> The offense of monopoly under § 2 of the Sherman Act has two elements: (1) the possession of monopoly power in the relevant market and (2) the willful acquisition or maintenance of that power as distinguished from growth or development as a consequence of a superior product, business acumen, or historic accident.[51]

The threshold issue is whether the firm has monopoly power. The second requirement—monopoly conduct—requires conduct that excludes competitors by means that are predatory in nature, not competition on the merits. Courts have defined what constitutes monopoly conduct through the common law process, in which courts determine whether the defendant's conduct satisfies the second element of *Grinnell* on a case-by-case basis. An extensive body of common law has developed.

---

46. 110 F. Supp. 295 (D. Mass. 1953), *aff'd per curiam*, 347 U.S. 521 (1954).
47. 110 F. Supp. at 342.
48. *Id.*
49. *Id.* at 343.
50. 384 U.S. 563 (1966) (affirming except as to decree 236 F. Supp. 244 (D.R.I. 1964)). For additional discussion of the facts of *Grinnell*, see *supra* § 6.03[C][3].
51. *Id.* at 570–71.

§ 6.04 Monopoly Power and Market Definition

The first element of a monopolization claim is that the defendant possesses monopoly power in a relevant market. "Monopoly power is the power to control prices or exclude competition."[52] To determine whether the defendant has such power, courts generally require the antitrust plaintiff to define the relevant market that the defendant has allegedly monopolized. The relevant market has two components: the product market and the geographic market.

The technical economic matters of market definition and assessing market power are the same regardless of the applicable provision of the antitrust laws. Most of the judicial discussion of market definition and market power, up until the mid-1970s, took place in the context of § 2 cases. After the mid-1970s and the emergence of the rule of reason as the predominant analytical method, market analysis also became a focus of cases arising under § 1. The history of judicial interpretations of market power is discussed in some depth in Chapter 2. Thus, the principal focus throughout the remainder of this Chapter is the conduct component of § 2.

§ 6.05 Monopoly Conduct

Merely possessing monopoly power does not violate § 2 of the Sherman Act. The second element of the *Grinnell* test requires the plaintiff to prove that the monopolist willfully acquired or maintained its monopoly power through anticompetitive conduct. Courts have referred to this conduct by several different names: monopoly conduct, anticompetitive conduct, exclusionary conduct, and predatory conduct. All these phrases mean the same thing. No significance should be inferred based on which phrasing the court uses. The Supreme Court has never clearly defined what exactly constitutes monopoly conduct. In *Grinnell*, the Court noted that monopoly conduct does not include acquiring monopoly power through making "a superior product, business acumen, or historic accident."[53] The closest the Supreme Court has come to defining monopoly conduct in the abstract is its statement in *Aspen Skiing* that "'exclusionary' comprehends at the most behavior that not only (1) tends to impair the opportunities of rivals, but also (2) either does not further competition on the merits or does so in an unnecessarily restrictive way.'"[54] While helpful, this language does not clearly define the boundary between legal and illegal conduct.

---

52. *United States v. E.I. DuPont de Nemours & Co.*, 351 U.S. 377, 391 (1956).

53. 384 U.S. 563, 570–71 (1966).

54. *Aspen Skiing Co. v. Aspen Highlands Skiing Corp.*, 472 U.S. 585, 605 n. 32 (1985) (quoting 3 P. Areeda & D. Turner, *Antitrust Law* 78 (1978)).

Like so many areas of the law in which only general guidelines are available, monopoly conduct is most likely to be something that a court "knows when it sees it." A systematic analysis is made difficult because of the diversity of conduct arguably characterized as exclusionary.

Antitrust law is common law. The 1890 Congress intended courts to flesh out the meaning of the word "monopolize," as used in § 2 of the Sherman Act. With the authority delegated to it by Congress, the Supreme Court created the two-element *Grinnell* test, which requires plaintiffs to prove that the defendant possesses monopoly power and engaged in monopoly conduct. To determine what constitutes monopoly conduct, one must be familiar with antitrust case law, in which courts condemn or exonerate conduct engaged in by monopolists one case at a time.

Another guiding principle is whether the monopolist's conduct serves to benefit the firm *only* by virtue of the harm it does to its competitors. In a 1997 case, *American Professional Testing Service v. Harcourt, Brace and Jovanovich Legal and Professional Publications*,[55] a bar review service alleged a rival had engaged in monopolizing conduct by hiring away one of its professors. The court distinguished an instance in which a firm hires a key employee of another but does not use that employee itself from one in which the employee does actually perform services for the new employer. In both cases, the expense of the hiring only makes economic sense if the increased revenues are higher than the cost. The problem is that in the first instance, the increased profit will not be the result of anything that can be said to make the market more competitive or be of benefit to consumers. In the second case—the firm making use of the professor—the hiring firm can be said to be motivated by the belief that it can make better use of the professor than the first employer.

In *United States v. Microsoft Corp.*,[56] the D.C. Circuit laid out five "principles" to determine whether a monopolist's conduct "is exclusionary, rather than merely a form of vigorous competition": (1) "a monopolist's act must have an 'anticompetitive effect.' That is, it must harm the competitive process and thereby harm consumers"; (2) the plaintiff has the burden of proof for demonstrating that the monopolist's conduct has the requisite anticompetitive effect; (3) if a plaintiff successfully demonstrates this anticompetitive effect, then the monopolist may proffer a nonpretextual "procompetitive justification" for its conduct, such as greater efficiency or enhanced consumer appeal, which shifts the burden back to the plaintiff to rebut that claim; (4) if the monopolist's procompetitive justification stands unrebutted, then the plaintiff must demonstrate that the anticompetitive harm of the conduct outweighs the procompetitive benefit; and (5) in doing this balancing, the "focus is upon the effect of that conduct, not upon the intent behind it."[57]

---

55. 108 F.3d 1147 (9th Cir. 1997).

56. 253 F.3d 34 (D.C. Cir. 2001).

57. *Id.* at 58–59. On procompetitive justifications, see John M. Newman, *Procompetitive Justifications in Antitrust Law*, 94 Ind. L.J. 501 (2019).

The remainder of this section reviews challenged conduct that courts have condemned or exonerated in specific cases. Because antitrust law is common law, one cannot appreciate the reach of § 2 without knowing the antitrust caselaw. The following case discussions are not exhaustive, but they present some of the most important cases in § 2 jurisprudence.

[A] Maintenance of Excess Capacity: *Alcoa*

The *Alcoa* opinion illustrates the difficulty of separating illegal anticompetitive conduct from desirable competitive conduct. Judge Hand found fault in Alcoa's strategy of expanding its production capacity and supplying new demand for aluminum. He reasoned: "we can think of no more effective exclusion than progressively to embrace each new opportunity as it opened, and to face every newcomer with new capacity already geared into a great organization. . . ."[58] Maintenance of excess capacity enabled Alcoa to meet new demands faster and less expensively than competitors and allegedly impeded the entry of new producers. Depending on one's viewpoint, Alcoa's conduct can be seen as anticompetitive or procompetitive. Judge Hand viewed Alcoa's strategy as predatory in nature, believing that its ultimate profitability was dependent on blocking new entry. On the other hand, one could view Alcoa's conduct as "skill, foresight, and industry," which Judge Hand had elsewhere described as appropriate. After all, Alcoa's maintenance of excess capacity arguably benefited consumers by giving them quicker access to aluminum. Tension exists between these two viewpoints because Alcoa may have discouraged entry but did so by being a more attractive supplier in the eyes of buyers than any other firm. Indeed, Alcoa's activity even can be seen as a response to competition, albeit potential competition. Whether *Alcoa*, at least as far as the excess capacity issue is concerned, would be decided the same way today is open to serious question.

[B] Exclusivity: *United Shoe*

In *United Shoe*, Judge Wyzanski articulated the competing conduct standards in monopolization cases and offered additional insight into when the erection of entry barriers constitutes monopoly conduct. The defendant, a monopolist in the production of shoe-manufacturing equipment, leased its equipment to shoe manufacturers for a term of ten years, but would not make the equipment available for purchase. Machines could be returned before the expiration of the lease with the payment of a return charge. This charge was reduced if the lessee replaced the machine with another United Shoe machine. Repair services were included as part of the rental arrangement. In addition, United Shoe evidently charged different prices for different

58. 148 F.2d at 431.

machines depending upon competitive conditions.[59] The leases also required that shoe manufacturers use United Shoe's machines at their full capacity.

The cumulative effect of these practices impeded the entry of other producers of shoe-manufacturing equipment. The lease-only policy precluded shoe manufacturers from owning their machines and later selling them; this prevented the creation of a secondary market for used machines that would compete against United Shoe's machines. The long-term lease with reduced return charge possibilities had the effect of tying individual shoe manufacturers to United Shoe. The automatic inclusion of repair service foreclosed the development of an independent repair industry and meant that a new entrant into the shoe machinery industry would have to also provide repair service, a significant undertaking that it may be unable to do. The full-capacity clause precluded shoe manufacturers from trying out competing machines. Judge Wyzanski concluded that the practices, "instead of encouraging competition based on pure merit, further[ed] the dominance of a particular firm."[60] Thus, the lease arrangement created "unnatural barriers" to entry.[61]

Judge Wyzanski noted other barriers to entry but did not condemn them. For example, he observed that entering the market for shoe-manufacturing equipment required significant capital and a labor force with engineering skills. These barriers to entry, however, were not erected by United Shoe. Conversely, some additional barriers to entry were created by United Shoe, such as satisfied customers who were content to continue purchasing their equipment from United Shoe. The fact that its customers were happy to eschew other suppliers is United Shoe's "fault," but it is not blameworthy; it is competition on the merits and does not constitute anticompetitive conduct even though it makes it harder for rivals to enter the market and secure sales.

[C] Product Innovation and Predisclosure

In *Berkey Photo Inc. v. Eastman Kodak Co.*,[62] a camera maker (Berkey) accused Kodak of using its monopoly power in the film market to gain an advantage in the market for cameras by introducing a new film (Kodacolor II) that was cut to a new size (the 110 format). For several months, only Kodak made 110 cameras that fit the Kodacolor II film. So, consumers who wanted to take photographs with the new Kodacolor II film needed to purchase a 110 camera from Kodak. Kodak's strategy is sometimes referred to as "leveraging"—the use of power in one market to gain an advantage in another market. The specific question was whether Kodak had monopolized the market for amateur still cameras by not disclosing to competing camera manufacturers the upcoming introduction of the new film and the fact that it was

59. 110 F. Supp. at 314–29.

60. *Id.* at 345.

61. *Id.*

62. 603 F.2d 263 (2d Cir. 1979).

being cut to a new size.[63] In a sense, Kodak possessed unique information without which competitors would be unable to compete effectively. As such, *Berkey* represents one of many cases in which a court must determine whether a firm must cooperate, share its resources, or otherwise deal with competitors.[64]

The Second Circuit Court of Appeals held that Kodak did not have a predisclosure duty. First, it disassociated Kodak's introduction of the new film from its market power. It found that even if Kodak had possessed a much smaller share of the market, it would have been able to develop and market the new film and camera. Thus, even though Kodak had the requisite power in the film market, nondisclosure was not the use of that power.[65]

The court then considered the argument that predisclosure was required because Kodak had, in the past, excluded competitors by refusing to sell film in certain formats suitable for competing cameras or materials necessary for production of suitable film. In short, the question posited was whether past refusals to deal give rise to a predisclosure obligation. The court noted that refusal to sell Berkey rolls of uncut Kodacolor II film—which Berkey could cut to fit its cameras—could support a § 2 charge. It found, however, that "the benefits that would flow to Kodak's rivals in the camera market from [predisclosure] bear no relationship to the injury caused them by the monopolist's refusal to sell film."[66] The possible evil inherent in Kodak's past conduct was not sufficiently connected with the current issue of disclosure to warrant a finding that nondisclosure was violative of § 2.

Three facets of *Berkey* are worth noting. First, although it is hard to imagine a case in which predisclosure would be required, as a technical matter, neither of the lines of reasoning offered by the court rule out that possibility. Second, and far more important, is the *Berkey* court's vision of allowable monopoly conduct:

> So long as we allow a firm to compete in several fields, we must expect it to seek the competitive advantages of its broad based activity—more efficient production, greater ability to develop complementary products, reduced transaction costs and so forth. These are gains that accrue to any integrated firm, regardless of its market share, and they cannot by themselves be considered uses of monopoly power.[67]

This is obviously a very different view than that expressed by Judge Hand for the same court in *Alcoa* 35 years earlier. In his view, the only permissible monopolies were essentially passive. The *Berkey* court laid this approach to rest in favor of one

---

63. *Id.* at 279–85. On the issue of leverage, see generally Kaplow, *Extension of Monopoly Power Through Leverage*, 85 Colum. L Rev. 515 (1985).

64. *See infra* § 6.05[G].

65. 603 F.2d at 283.

66. *Id.* at 284.

67. *Id.* at 276.

that permits the monopolist competitive latitude approaching that of its smallest competitor.[68]

Finally, as already noted, the *Berkey* court recognized the viability of a monopoly claim based on leverage. Under this theory, the use of monopoly power in one market to gain an advantage over competitors in another market could constitute monopolization without regard for the market power possessed in the second market. The Supreme Court in *Spectrum Sports v. McQuillan*[69] ruled that an attempt to monopolize claim cannot succeed without a showing that the defendant had a dangerous probability of monopolizing the market, not merely gaining a competitive advantage in that market. For practical purposes, this means that a leverage theory is only to be available in "attempt to monopolize" cases.[70] Even in that context, a court is likely to require some showing that the defendant's practice had a predatory element.

The principal criticism of the leverage theory under § 2 is the same as that offered in the context of tying, as discussed in Chapter 5. If a firm has monopoly power in one market, so the argument goes, it is can exact its full monopoly profit in that market.[71] It supposedly sets a price to achieve that end. The leverage applied to a secondary market, to the extent it affects customers in the monopoly market is comparable to raising prices in the market in which there is market power. In *Schor v. Abbott Laboratories*,[72] the Seventh Circuit Court of Appeals applied this reasoning to reject a claim that a firm selling two AIDS medications had raised price in a market in which it possessed power in order to lower the price and monopolize the market for the drug in which it did not possess power.

[D] Physical and Technological Ties

The facts in *Berkey* also gave rise to another monopolization claim against Kodak founded on a different theory. In *Foremost Pro Color Inc. v. Eastman Kodak Co.*,[73] a competitor sued Kodak for monopolizing the "amateur photographic market" by creating technological incompatibilities. The plaintiff argued that by producing a desirable film in a format that was only usable in cameras produced by Kodak and which required different paper, chemicals, and photofinishing equipment than generally in use, Kodak was able to extend its power by rendering obsolete the cameras and photofinishing services of competitors. Although there was no requirement that

---

68. *See also Olympia Equip. Leasing v. Western Union Tel.*, 797 F 2d 370, 375 (7th Cir. 1986); *Foremost Pro Color Inc. v. Eastman Kodak Co.*, 703 F.2d 534, 544 (9th Cir. 1983).

69. 506 U.S. 447 (1993).

70. *See also Pacific Bell Telephone Co. v. linkLine Communications, Inc.*, 555 U.S. 438 (2009); *Safeway v. Abbott Labs*, 761 F. Supp. 2d 874, 895–97 (N.D. Cal. 2011); *Doe v. Abbott Laboratories*, 571 F.3d 930 (9th Cir. 2009).

71. For a critique of this theory, see Einer Elhauge, *Tying, Bundled Discounts, and the Death of the Single Monopoly Profit Theory*, 123 Harv. L. Rev. 397 (2009).

72. 457 F.3d 608 (7th Cir. 2006).

73. 703 F.2d 534 (9th Cir. 1983).

a purchaser buy film, cameras, and processing from Kodak, the plaintiff claimed that the incompatibility produced the same result. The Court of Appeals for the Ninth Circuit, while recognizing that in some instances product innovation could violate § 2, ruled that the introduction of incompatible products, without additional abusive conduct, was not violative.[74]

A "tie" that was more physical than technical was addressed by the same court in *California Computer Products Inc. v. IBM Corp.*[75] In the early generations of computers, disk drives and memory storage were physically separate peripheral devices that plugged into the central processing unit. Many peripheral devices were manufactured by independent companies that made IBM-compatible peripheral devices. When IBM began to market computers with the disk drives and memory units integrated into the central processing unit, independent manufacturers of disk drives and memory units for computers charged IBM with monopolization. According to the plaintiffs, this "technological manipulation" allowed IBM to monopolize the market but did not improve performance. The evidence indicated, however, that the integrated computer was less expensive to produce and priced lower than nonintegrated models.[76] The court reasoned that IBM "had the right to redesign its products to make them more attractive to buyers—whether by reason of lower price or improved performance" and upheld a directed verdict for IBM.[77]

Courts are generally deferential to manufacturers' design decisions, and product redesigns that improve quality do not generally constitute monopoly conduct. But predatory design by a monopolist can violate § 2. In *C.R. Bard, Inc. v. M3 Systems, Inc.*,[78] Bard manufactured a patented biopsy gun (trademarked as the Biopty gun) for taking samples of body tissue. Biopsy guns require biopsy needles that are one-time use. The antitrust plaintiff accused Bard of attempting to monopolize the market for replacement biopsy needles, which are unpatented and were the relevant product market. M3 Systems, a competing maker of needles used in biopsy guns alleged that Bard violated § 2 by modifying its gun to accept only Bard needles. The jury found that Bard had monopoly power in the relevant market for replacement biopsy needles and that Bard's modifications to its Biopty gun constituted monopoly conduct. The Federal Circuit required M3 to prove that Bard made a change in its Biopty gun for predatory reasons, i.e., for the purpose of injuring competitors in the replacement needle market, rather than for improving the operation of the gun. Bard claimed that it had modified its Biopty gun to make it easier to load and unload. But there was substantial evidence that Bard's real reasons for modifying the gun were to raise the cost of entry to potential makers of replacement needles, to make doctors apprehensive about using non-Bard needles, and to preclude the use of "copycat" needles. The Federal Circuit affirmed the jury verdict, concluding that "[i]n view

74. *Id.* at 544–45.

75. 613 F.2d 727 (9th Cir. 1979).

76. *Id.* at 744.

77. *Id.*

78. 157 F.3d 1340 (Fed. Cir. 1998).

of that evidence, the jury could reasonably conclude that Bard's modifications to its guns constituted 'restrictive or exclusionary conduct' in a market over which it had monopoly power."

[E] Thwarting Nascent Threats: *United States v. Microsoft*[79]

The issue of monopolistic conduct came to the forefront in the *Microsoft* case.[80] The government accused Microsoft of illegally monopolizing the market for Intel-compatible personal computer (PC) operating systems. Microsoft's monopoly position was protected by the so-called applications barrier to entry. As long as there is one dominant operating system, developers are highly motivated to write software for that operating system. Conversely, as long as software is predominately written for a specific operating system, customers will purchase that operating system, and it is difficult for new operating systems to emerge. The court described this as a chicken-and-egg relationship.

Microsoft worried that technological advances could undermine the applications barrier to entry. Netscape had the dominant share of the browser market through its Navigator browser. Microsoft considered Navigator a long-term threat to Microsoft's operating system monopoly because browsers can include protocols—Application Programming Interfaces (APIs)—that are widely used in operating systems. If written expansively enough, a browser (or other versions of what is called middleware) could take over many of the functions of an operating system. Software written for a specific operating system would not then be dependent on the user actually using that specific operating system. The lower cost of writing software that could be used on a variety of operating systems would then mean other operating systems could emerge as reasonable substitutes.

Microsoft maintained its monopoly position by thwarting the development of middleware, namely browsers and the Java Virtual Machine. The label "middleware" describes "software products that expose their own APIs."[81] Microsoft sought to control the browser market in order to prevent browsers from evolving in a manner that exposed APIs and allowed software to be written for browsers instead of operating systems. Microsoft engaged in several types of anticompetitive conduct to have its own browser, Internet Explorer (IE), replace Netscape's Navigator as the dominant browser. The court broke these practices into a number of categories. For example, one category concerned Microsoft's relationship with original equipment manufacturers (OEMs). These generally involved packaging IE with Windows in order to make it unlikely that a user would substitute another browser. For instance, in its licensing agreements with OEMs, Microsoft required that the start up icons for IE not

79. 253 F.3d 34 (D.C. Cir. 2001).

80. For a comprehensive treatment see William Page & John Lopatka, The *Microsoft* Case (2009).

81. 253 F.3d at 53.

be removed and that the OEM not create a boot-up sequence that would allow users to choose from a variety of competing browsers.

A second category concerned the actual physical integration of the operating system and the browser. In effect, Microsoft integrated Windows and IE to make it difficult for consumers to delete IE. OEMs were disinclined to preinstall another browser if IE could not be removed because that would raise the OEMs' customer support costs. Microsoft also did not include IE in the add/remove menu; so, consumers could not easily remove IE from their PCs. Another category concerned the agreements Microsoft had with internet access providers (IAPs), like America On Line. Microsoft offered IE free to the IAPs, offered financial incentives for signing customers up for services using IE, and entered into reciprocal agreements that guaranteed the promotion of IE. Under these later agreements, Microsoft provided easy desktop access to IAPs that promoted the IE browser.[82]

The unanimous appeals court sitting *en banc* held that Microsoft violated § 2 by using anticompetitive conduct to maintain its monopoly in the operating system market. The court largely rejected Microsoft's arguments that it did not possess monopoly power or that there should be an exception for network effects.[83] With respect to conduct, the court found unlawful the licensing and contractual agreements with OEMs and IAPs. Microsoft's licenses had the effect of reducing usage share of Netscape's browser by preventing OEMs from distributing browsers other than Microsoft's IE. In addition, the court held that the contracts with the IAPs were also exclusionary, as were exclusive dealing arrangements with Apple and threats directed to Intel.

The analytical approach of the appellate court to monopoly conduct seemed consistent with the idea of determining whether Microsoft's efforts amounted to "competition on the merits," likely to benefit consumers, or were more designed to promote Microsoft's ends by harming competitors. In analyzing each of Microsoft's practices, the court first assessed whether there was an anticompetitive effect and then whether Microsoft had a procompetitive or valid business purpose.

To take a simple example, as already described, Microsoft required OEMs not to alter the desktop icons. In effect, if an OEM wanted to prepackage a browser other than IE, it would have to prepackage and be ready to support two browsers. The anticompetitive effect was that OEMs were unlikely to prepackage two browsers because of increased support costs and the risk of consumer confusion.[84] In effect, by requiring the maintenance of IE, Microsoft was blocking the entry of other browsers. In addition to some copyright justifications that the court rejected, Microsoft argued

82. Other categories included (1) Microsoft's dealings with Internet content providers, independent software vendors, and Apple Computer and (2) efforts to retard the development of Java.

83. *See* discussion in Chapter 2, *supra*. *See also* E.T. Sullivan, *The Jurisprudence of Antitrust Divestiture: The Path Less Traveled*, 86 Minn. L. Rev. 565, 568 (2002).

84. 253 F.3d at 61. *See* Ronald Cass, *Preserving Competition: Economic Analysis, Legal Standards and Microsoft*, 8 Geo. Mason L. Rev. 1 (1999); Steve C. Salop & Craig Romaine, *Preserving Monopoly: Economic Analysis. Legal Standards and Microsoft*, 8 Geo. Mason L. Rev. 617 (1999).

that the restrictions were designed to prevent OEMs from reducing the value of the operating system by undermining its stability and consistency.

Developed by Sun Microsystems, Java is a programming language as well as a set of programs written in that language that expose APIs. The Java Virtual Machine ("JVM") translates bytecode into instructions to the operating system. Programs written in Java can run on multiple operating systems. Microsoft worried that programmers would write their applications in Java, instead of specifically for the Microsoft operating system. This would eliminate the application barriers to entry that protected Microsoft's monopoly. Consequently, Microsoft took several actions "to exclude Java from developing as a viable cross-platform threat."[85] For example, after licensing Java from Sun Microsystems, Microsoft developed a JVM that was incompatible with Sun's, "but Microsoft deceived Java developers regarding the Windows-specific nature of the tools."[86] Microsoft lied to developers, telling them their programs were "cross-platform applications," but in reality they "ended up producing applications that would run only on the Windows operating system."[87] Microsoft's internal documents showed that "Microsoft's ultimate objective was to thwart Java's threat to Microsoft's monopoly in the market for operating systems. One Microsoft document, for example, states as a strategic goal: 'Kill cross-platform Java by grow[ing] the polluted Java market.'"[88] The D.C. Circuit noted: "Unsurprisingly, Microsoft offers no procompetitive explanation for its campaign to deceive developers. Accordingly, we conclude this conduct is exclusionary, in violation of § 2 of the Sherman Act."[89]

In an extensive opinion, the D.C. Circuit held that many other actions by Microsoft constituted monopoly conduct and were not supported by any procompetitive justifications. But this discussion provides a sense of some of the conduct that the court found objectionable.

[F] Abuse of Patents and Other Intellectual Property Rights

Intellectual property (IP) law is the foundation of innovation policy. Patents and copyrights—and to a lesser extent trademarks—grant exclusionary rights to their owners. These rights to exclude encourage inventors and other businesses to invest in research and development, knowing that rivals will not be able to copy their inventions and undersell them. Absent IP rights, many market sectors would likely underinvest in innovation. Armed with the right to exclude competitors, the owners of valuable IP can reduce output and raise price, maximizing their profits but causing inefficiency in the form of deadweight loss because less product is being sold than would be sold at

85. *Id.* at 74.
86. *Id.* at 76.
87. *Id.*
88. *Id.*
89. *Id.* at 77.

the efficient equilibrium in a competitive market. Congress has determined that these consequences are justified by the increase in innovation.

Because IP rights give firms the ability to exclude rivals, firms may misuse them to illegally monopolize a market. Several types of monopoly conduct involve IP rights. Most famously, in *Walker Process Equipment v. Food Machinery & Chemical*,[90] the Supreme Court held that "the enforcement of a patent procured by fraud on the Patent Office may be violative of § 2 of the Sherman Act provided the other elements necessary to a § 2 case are present."[91] Thus, enforcement of a fraudulently procured patent constitutes monopoly conduct that can satisfy the second element of the *Grinnell* test.[92] Subsequent courts have emphasized the enforcement language of *Walker Process*.[93] Courts have reasoned that "[w]ithout some effort at enforcement, the patent cannot serve as the foundation of a monopolization case."[94]

The enforcement requirement is arguably both unnecessary and counterproductive. Even if they are not actively enforced through litigation, fraudulently procured patents can deter competitive entry by creating unacceptable litigation risks for potential entrants, raising entry costs, and deterring customers and business partners from contracting with rivals. Indeed, even when a potential competitor knows or suspects that a monopolist's patent is invalid, the vagrancies of patent litigation—especially pro-patentholder legal rules—can create an intolerable risk that an infringement defendant that should prevail on the merits will lose. Appreciating that risk, rational competitors will stay out of the market instead of challenging a patent they know or strongly suspect to have been fraudulently procured.[95]

Antitrust law cannot sufficiently deter patent fraud if wrongdoers can evade antitrust liability by harnessing the anticompetitive powers of their invalid patents in ways that do not trigger the *Walker Process* enforcement requirement. Given the exclusionary effects of unenforced, fraudulently procured patents, a strong argument can be made that courts should eschew the enforcement element altogether. At a minimum, the concept of patent enforcement should be viewed broadly to encompass all of the various ways that patentholders use patents to exclude competitors, including those that fall short of actual infringement litigation or explicit threats thereof.[96]

To ensure that various products are compatible with each other and the networks they use, industries develop technological standards for technologically complex products, such as cell phones. To make sales, manufacturers must make products that comply with those standards. Most technical standards are adopted through

---

90. 382 U.S. 172 (1965).

91. *Id.* at 172.

92. In addition to patent fraud, patent theft can also constitute monopoly conduct. Christopher R. Leslie, *Monopolization Through Patent Theft*, 103 Geo. L.J. 47 (2014)

93. *Struthers Scientific & Intl Corp. v. General Foods Corp.*, 334 F. Supp. 1329, 1331 (D. Del. 1971).

94. *California E. Lab., Inc. v. Gould*, 896 F.2d 400, 403 (9th Cir. 1990).

95. Christopher R. Leslie, *The Anticompetitive Effects of Unenforced Invalid Patents*, 91 Minn. L. Rev. 101 (2006).

96. Christopher R. Leslie, *Patents of Damocles*, 83 Ind. L.J. 133 (2008).

deliberative processes run by standard-setting organizations (SSOs), which are largely composed of industry participants. These SSO-adopted standards will often include requirements that read on patents owned by SSO members. When that happens, once an SSO adopts a standard, some members may possess standard essential patents (SEPs), which are necessary to make standard-compliant products. This gives potential market power to SEP owners who may engage in "patent holdup" by demanding unreasonably high royalties from manufacturers seeking to make standard-compliant products. Patent holdup is bad because it raises prices for consumers, reduces output, and threatens the efficiency and viability of the entire standard-setting process.

To minimize the risk of patent holdup, many SSOs have taken a two-pronged approach. First, many SSOs require their members to disclose their IP rights during the standard-setting process. Second, they require that their members commit to charging a fair, reasonable, and non-discriminatory (FRAND) royalty for their patents on technology that is eventually incorporated into the standard. These steps allow an SSO to choose an alternative non-proprietary standard if the SSO member declines to commit to charging a FRAND royalty.

SSO members sometimes try to acquire monopoly power by manipulating the SSO process to adopt a standard that reads on that member's patents, thus making them SEPs. For example, an SSO member may conceal its relevant patents or make a FRAND commitment that it ignores after the standard is adopted. Courts have addressed whether such misconduct constitutes monopoly conduct. In *In re Rambus, Inc.*,[97] Rambus was a member of the Joint Electronic Device Engineering Council ("JEDEC"), a standard setting organization (SSO). Although Rambus actively participated in JEDEC standard setting discussions, it did not disclose its patents or patent applications. After JEDEC adopted and implemented its standard, Rambus disclosed its patents and sued JEDEC members who made standard-compliant products. The FTC held that Rambus's intentional deception of JEDEC was not competition on the merits. The D.C. Circuit reversed, suggesting that antitrust plaintiffs must show that the SSO would have adopted a standard that did not include the defendant's patented technology but for the defendant's deception.

In contrast, in *Broadcom Corp. v. Qualcomm Inc.*,[98] the Third Circuit considered whether violating FRAND commitments constitutes monopoly conduct. In order to have its technology accepted as the standard for one of two technology paths, Qualcomm, a competitor in the market for chip sets used in the cellular telephone market, agreed to license that technology on FRAND terms. One or more chip sets are necessary for a cellular phone to operate. Broadcom complained that Qualcomm had, in fact, charged higher prices for use of the technology to competitors and customers who did not use Qualcomm's chip sets in their cell phones. In effect, Qualcomm used this leverage as a means of maintaining market power in the chip set market. The Third Circuit held:

97. 2006 WL 2330117 (FTC 2006), *rev'd*, 522 F.3d 456 (D.C. Cir. 2008).
98. 501 F.3d 297 (3d Cir. 2007).

> that (1) in a consensus-oriented private standard-setting environment, (2) a patent holder's intentionally false promise to license essential proprietary technology on FRAND terms, (3) coupled with an [SSO's] reliance on that promise when including the technology in a standard, and (4) the patent holder's subsequent breach of that promise, is actionable anticompetitive conduct. This holding follows directly from established principles of antitrust law and represents the emerging view of enforcement authorities and commentators, alike. Deception in a consensus-driven private standard-setting environment harms the competitive process by obscuring the costs of including proprietary technology in a standard and increasing the likelihood that patent rights will confer monopoly power on the patent holder.[99]

Under this test, violating a FRAND commitment to an SSO can constitute monopoly conduct.

[G] The Refusal to Supply an Essential Facility or Input

A number of antitrust cases center around one firm's refusal to supply something to another that the second firm needs to be competitive. In some of these cases, the issue is whether the "essential facilities" doctrine is applicable. In others, the issue is whether the firm has engaged in illegal "refusal to deal." In some ways, the essential facilities doctrine is a specific type of refusal to deal. But courts generally treat the two doctrines separately, and so shall we.

[1] The "Essential Facilities" Doctrine

The general proposition that monopolists may in certain circumstances be required to cooperate with competitors dates to the 1912 case of *United States v. Terminal Railroad.*[100] A group of railroads acquired control of St. Louis' rail terminal facilities and a bridge crossing the Mississippi River. By controlling this "essential facility" the combination was able to discriminate against competitors and gain an advantage in rail service. The Court held that acquisition and control of the terminal facilities by a group of railroads smaller than the total number dependent on the facilities was a violation of §§ 1 and 2 of the Sherman Act. The Court ordered that any existing or future railroad be allowed to participate in ownership and control.[101]

---

99. *Id.* at 314.

100. 224 U.S. 383 (1912); *see generally* IIIA P. Areeda & H. Hovenkamp, *Antitrust Law* 164–227 (2d ed. 2002).

101. 224 U.S. at 411.

The Court's unitary analysis of §§ 1 and 2 of the Sherman Act reflects the Court's early conflation of the Sherman Act's two sections.[102] Today, most cases discussing the essential facilities doctrine involve § 2 claims because a single monopolist is denying its rivals access to an essential facility. If multiple entities are controlling an essential facility, however, an agreement among them to deny access to rivals could trigger § 1 liability. Finally, *Terminal Railroad* raised an antitrust issue with enormous political implications and one that the courts may prefer to avoid: When does a monopolist attain quasi-public utility status?

Otter Tail v. United States[103] is a case of a refusal to deal that can also be seen as involving an essential facility. The defendant was a monopolist operator of electric transmission lines and producer of electricity selling electricity directly to retail customers. When Otter Tail's franchise to sell electricity in four municipalities terminated, the municipalities attempted to set up their own retail distribution schemes selling electricity produced or transmitted by Otter Tail. Otter Tail refused to sell electricity to the municipalities or to transmit electricity the municipalities had purchased from other producers.[104] The Supreme Court held that Otter Tail's refusal to deal violated § 2 because it involved the use of monopoly power in one market as leverage to gain power in another market.[105] Otter Tail's status as a regulated firm possibly influenced the Court's decision.[106] The case indicates, however, that in some instances, a monopolist supplier may not refuse to sell when the effect is to destroy competitors.

In *Verizon Commc'ns Inc. v. Law Offices of Curtis V. Trinko, LLP*, Justice Scalia said that the Supreme Court has "never recognized" the essential facilities doctrine.[107] His statement is deceptive and misleading. Although the Court did not use this precise expression in either *Terminal Railroad* or *Otter Tail*, these cases created and recognized the doctrine. The phrase "essential facilities doctrine" is simply the label that lower courts attached to the holdings of these Supreme Court cases. Federal circuits recognize the essential facilities doctrine and identify either *Terminal Railroad or Otter Tail* or both as the origin of the doctrine.[108]

Lower courts have announced various formulations of the essential facilities doctrine. For example, in *MCI Communications Corp. v. American Telephone and*

102. In *Otter Tail Co. v. United States*, 410 U.S. 366 (1973), the Supreme Court considered the essential facilities issue in the context of a single firm.

103. 410 U.S. 366 (1973).

104. *Id.* at 368–77.

105. *Id.* at 377.

106. Professors Areeda and Hovenkamp suggest that vertical integration by Otter Tail may have been motivated by a desire to side-step federal regulation and collect monopoly profits at the retail level. IIA P. Areeda & H. Hovenkamp, *Antitrust Law* 355 (2d ed. 2002).

107. *Verizon Commc'ns Inc. v. Law Offices of Curtis V. Trinko, LLP*, 540 U.S. 398, 411 (2004).

108. *See, e.g., Novell, Inc. v. Microsoft Corp.*, 731 F.3d 1064, 1074 (10th Cir. 2013) (describing *Otter Tail* as the "forebearer of essential facilities doctrine"). In *Aspen Skiing Co. v. Aspen Highlands Skiing Corp.*, 472 U.S. 585 (1985), the Supreme Court acknowledged the existence of the essential facilities doctrine but found it unnecessary to apply it because it had already affirmed the jury verdict on other grounds. *Id.* at 611 n.44.

Telegraph,[109] the Seventh Circuit Court of Appeals indicated that the doctrine would apply when (1) the essential facility is controlled by a monopolist, (2) a competitor cannot reasonably duplicate the facility, (3) the monopolist denies access to the facility and (4) it would be feasible for access to be provided.[110] This later requirement would seem to preclude requiring a firm to provide access that would lower the quality of its own offering in the market.

The Ninth Circuit applied these factors in *Aerotec International v. Honeywell*,[111] in which Honeywell was a producer of auxiliary power units for aircraft. Aerotec provided maintenance for the units in competition with Honeywell. Aerotec claimed that Honeywell used its power in the parts market for the units in order to monopolize the market for maintenance services.[112] Here, the alleged essential facility was the parts which were manufactured by Honeywell. Aerotec failed the four-part test, because it had access to parts through sources other than Honeywell.[113]

An element of this test that was critical recently is the relationship between the firm desiring access and the firm denying access. In *Intergraph Corporation v. Intel Corporation*,[114] the plaintiff complained that the refusal by Intel to continue supplying Advance Chip Samples and design and technical information violated § 2.[115] The Federal Circuit Court of Appeals refused to apply the essential facilities doctrine, reasoning that Intergraph and Intel were not competitors in the market affected by the essential facility. This is an important distinction. The question is not whether the market in which Intergraph operated was likely to become less competitive. Instead it was whether Intel was making an effort to monopolize that market. This is because the concept of "monopolization" must be in reference to a specific market. In this instance, Intel could not be viewed as monopolizing or attempting to monopolize a market in which it did not compete.

[2] Refusal to Deal Doctrine

In *Aspen Skiing Co. v. Aspen Highlands Skiing Corp.*[116] The plaintiff, Aspen Highlands (Highlands), was the operator of a single mountain ski facility in Aspen, Colorado. The defendant, Aspen Skiing (Ski Co.), owned the three remaining ski areas. For a period of time they cooperated in offering an "all-Aspen" ticket which enabled the

---

109. 708 F.2d 1081 (7th Cir. 1983).

110. *Id.* at 1132–33. The plaintiff's failure to prove its inability to duplicate the essential facility dooms its antitrust claim. *Buccaneer Energy (USA) Inc. v. Gunnison Energy Corp.*, 846 F.3d 1297, 1310 (10th Cir. 2017) (context is § 1).

111. *Aerotec International, Inc. v. Honeywell International, Inc.*, 836 F.3d 1171, 1185 (9th Cir. 2016). *See also MCI Commc'ns Corp. v. Am. Tel. & Tel. Co.*, 708 F.2d 1081, 1132–33 (7th Cir. 1983).

112. *Id.* at 1176.

113. *Id.* at 1185. *See also VBR Tours, LLC v. National Railroad Passenger Corp.*, 2016 WL 4945015 (N.D. Ill. 2016). *But see Buccaneer Energy (USA) Inc. v. Gunnison Energy Corp.*, 846 F.3d 1290 (10th Cir. 2017).

114. 195 F.3d 1346 (Fed. Cir. 1999).

115. *Id.* at 1356.

116. 472 U.S. 585 (1985).

purchaser to ski on any of the four areas. The allocation of revenues between the parties was based on skiers' relative use of each mountain. Eventually Ski Co. offered to continue the all-Aspen pass only if Highlands accepted a fixed percentage of the revenues, which reimbursed Highlands at a lower rate than actual use. Highlands found the percentage offered unacceptable, and the all-Aspen ticket was discontinued. Ski Co. interfered with Highland's attempts to duplicate the all-Aspen pass by offering a package which included passes for its single mountain and negotiable instruments that could be used to purchase passes from Ski Co., and Highland's market share fell from 20% to 11% over a four year period.[117]

Highlands claimed that Ski Co. had monopolized the market for downhill skiing in Aspen by terminating the all-mountain pass (and interfering with Highland's attempts to replicate it). The Tenth Circuit upheld a jury verdict for Highlands based on two separate theories: (1) under *Terminal Railroad* and the essential facilities doctrine, Ski Co. was required to cooperate in offering the multi-area pass and (2) there was sufficient evidence to support the jury's finding that Ski Co.'s refused to continue the four-mountain pass with an intent to "create or maintain a monopoly."[118] On review, the Supreme Court declined to address the first theory because it affirmed the jury verdict based on the second theory. Ski Co. argued that the jury's finding was "erroneous as a matter of law because it rests on an assumption that a firm with monopoly power has a duty to cooperate with its smaller rivals. . . ."[119]

The Court began its analysis by observing that there was no general duty for a monopolist to cooperate with a rival and that the trial court unambiguously had instructed the jury to that effect. The right to refuse to deal, however, was not unqualified. The Court relied on its earlier opinion in *Lorain Journal v. United States*.[120] The Lorain Journal was a newspaper that was the primary source of advertising in the local market. When advertisers started spending some of their budgets on a local radio station, the Lorain Journal refused to sell advertising to firms that patronized the local radio station in an effort to destroy its competitor in the advertising market. The Court acknowledged the paper had a general right to refuse to accept ads from whomever it pleases, but this right is neither absolute nor exempt from regulation. On the facts of the case, the Court concluded that Lorain Journal's refusal to deal constituted anticompetitive conduct.

In *Aspen Skiing*, the trial court had instructed the jury that Ski Co. had not violated § 2 if there were valid business reasons for the refusal to cooperate. The jury found that there were no valid business reasons. The Supreme Court reviewed the business justifications offered by Ski Co. and considered whether the change in policy created a gain in efficiency. It held that the jury's finding, that there was an absence of a valid

---

117. *Id.* at 593–95.

118. 738 F.2d 1509, 1520–23 (10th Cir. 1984).

119. 472 U.S. at 587. The approach taken by the Court meant that it was unnecessary to address the relevance of the "essential facilities" doctrine. *Id.* at 611, n. 44.

120. 342 U.S. 143 (1951).

business reason, was not clearly erroneous and therefore must be upheld. The Court suggested that Ski Co.'s conduct was essentially predatory because the change in policy resulted in losses to Ski Co. which it evidently hoped to recoup once the damage to Highlands had been accomplished.[121]

Some courts have converted the holding of *Aspen Skiing* into a three-element test. The Ninth Circuit in *FTC v. Qualcomm Inc.*,[122] for example, asserted that "a company engages in prohibited, anticompetitive conduct when (1) it unilateral[ly] terminat[es] . . . a voluntary and profitable course of dealing; (2) the only conceivable rationale or purpose is to sacrifice short-term benefits in order to obtain higher profits in the long run from the exclusion of competition; and (3) the refusal to deal involves products that the defendant already sells in the existing market to other similarly situated customers."[123] Not everyone agrees that this statement accurately reflects the breadth of the *Aspen Skiing* opinion.

In *Verizon Communications, Inc. v. Law Offices of Curtis V. Trinko, LLP*,[124] the Supreme Court seemed to limit the reach of *Aspen Skiing*, describing the case as "at or near the outer boundary of § 2 liability."[125] The case arose in the context of the Telecommunications Act of 1996. Under that Act, local exchange carriers (LECs), which were regional monopolies, could not enter the market for long-distance telephony unless they allowed competitors in the local exchange market to have access to their networks. The plaintiff alleged that Verizon was filling the orders of customers of competing LECs last or not at all.[126] The district court dismissed the case, and the Second Circuit reversed. The Supreme Court held that Verizon did not violate § 2. The Court relied in part on "the existence of a regulatory structure designed to deter and remedy anticompetitive harm. Where such a structure exists, the additional benefit to competition provided by antitrust enforcement will tend to be small, and it will be less plausible that the antitrust laws contemplate such additional scrutiny."[127]

[H] Price Squeeze

"Price squeeze" is the term used when a manufacturer of an input that both fabricates that input into an output and sells it to others for fabrication, raises the price of the input to competing fabricators while lowering its own price of the finished product in order to make it impossible for independent fabricators to match the manufacturer's output price. Indeed, in *Alcoa*, Judge Hand found such a practice to be an abuse of Alcoa's power in the ingot market.

---

121. 472 U.S. at 610–11.
122. 969 F.3d 974 (9th Cir. 2020).
123. *Id.* at 993–94 (cleaned up).
124. 540 U.S. 398 (2004).
125. *Id.* at 409.
126. *Id.* at 404.
127. *Id.* at 412.

In *Pacific Bell Telephone Co. v. linkLine Communications, Inc.*, the Supreme Court made it more difficult for antitrust plaintiffs to pursue cases based on a price squeeze theory.[128] Digital subscriber line (DSL) service connects consumers to the Internet at high speeds over phone lines. AT&T owned much infrastructure in California, including the last link between the telephone network and users, such as homes and businesses. Competing DSL providers needed access to AT&Ts facilities. Pursuant to its agreement with the Federal Communications Commission (FCC) that AT&T negotiated to secure approval of an earlier merger, AT&T was "obligated to provide wholesale 'DSL transport' service to independent firms at a price no greater than the retail price of AT&T's DSL service."[129] AT&T participated in the DSL market at both the wholesale and retail levels.

The plaintiffs were four independent Internet service providers (ISPs) that competed with AT&T in the retail market, but leased DSL transport service from AT&T pursuant to the merger condition that AT&T had agreed to with the FCC. Plaintiffs sued AT&T for monopolizing the DSL market in California, alleging in part that AT&T engaged in price squeezing by setting high wholesale prices for DSL transport and low retail prices for DSL Internet service. The district court denied AT&T's motion to dismiss but allowed an interlocutory appeal, and the Ninth Circuit affirmed the district court's denial of the motion. The Supreme Court, however, reversed.

The Supreme Court disaggregated the price squeeze claim into its two parts: wholesale (input) and retail (output). Regarding the wholesale market, the Court held that a plaintiff cannot bring a § 2 price squeeze claim unless the defendant has an "antitrust obligation to sell the inputs to the plaintiff in the first place."[130] The Court reasoned that AT&T did not have a so-called antitrust duty to deal with the plaintiffs because any duty of AT&T arose "only from FCC regulations, not from the Sherman Act."[131] The Court found this alone was sufficient to defeat the plaintiffs' antitrust claim, but it went on to discuss the retail market. The Court suggested that to show an anticompetitive effect in the retail market, plaintiffs bringing price squeeze claim must satisfy the 2-element test from *Brooke Group*: (1) a price below cost, and (2) a dangerous probability of recoupment. The Court noted that the plaintiffs' complaint alleged neither of these elements. Ultimately, the Court held: "If there is no duty to deal at the wholesale level and no predatory pricing at the retail level, then a firm is certainly not required to price *both* of these services in a manner that preserves its rivals' profit margins."[132] Finding that the plaintiffs failed to satisfy either of these components, let alone both, the Court held that they had not stated an antitrust claim.

---

128. 555 U.S. 438 (2009).

129. *Id.* at 442.

130. *Id.*

131. *Id.* at 450.

132. *Id.* at 452 (citing *Brooke Group Ltd. v. Brook Group Corp.*, 509 U.S. 209 (1993), discussed *infra* § 6.05[L]).

[I] Raising Rivals' Costs

Monopolization and attempt to monopolize claims involve anticompetitive conduct that makes it more difficult or costly for a competitor to survive in the market. For example, the denial of access to "essential facilities" and refusals to deal generally also can be viewed as efforts to increase the costs of rivals. Sometimes this effort is costly to the defendant, in which case it can be analyzed as ordinary predation, i.e., is it an expenditure that only makes sense if the effect is to eliminate competitors and permit the exploitation of market power. Other times the goal is to raise the costs of competitors without raising the cost of the defendant. The label "raising rival's costs" has been attached to this effort. The theory has received more attention from commentators,[133] than from courts.

The theory posits that a firm may cause the costs, and ultimately the prices, of a competitor to increase. The effect is to create an umbrella under which the firm then has the freedom to raise its own prices above competitive levels. Raising the costs of a rival could either increase the market power of the firm or simply enable it to maintain existing power. Moreover, possession of market power is not required necessarily in order to cause the costs of a rival to increase. Thus, the activity could fulfill the conduct component of a charge of either monopolization or attempted monopolization. The general argument has been advanced that "[r]aising [a] rival's costs is a more credible way to market power than is predatory pricing because it is not necessary to cause the rival to exit, no 'deep pocket' is required, and additional profits are gained immediately."[134]

In order to be effective, the firm must be able to raise substantially its rival's costs. This means that the firm must have considerable direct or indirect control over an input that makes up a not insignificant portion of its rival's total cost of production. The difficulties of establishing this factor and a resulting anticompetitive impact likely have caused the theory to be difficult to apply in litigation.[135]

The purest example of raising a rival's costs is an instance in which a firm simply refuses to supply an input or causes other firms to refuse to supply an input, thus causing the competitor to rely on a more expensive source.[136] The theory can, however, have much broader applications. For example, *Aspen* could be interpreted as a case in which the defendant engaged in such conduct. Similarly, *Berkey Photo* can be viewed as a case in which product innovation led to increased costs for rivals who would have

---

133. *See, e.g., Nonprice Predation Under Section 2 of the Sherman Act* (E.T. Sullivan, ed. 1991); Hovenkamp, *Antitrust Policy, Restricted Distribution and the Market for Exclusionary Rights*, 71 Minn. L. Rev. 1293 (1987); Salop, *New Economic Theories of Economic Exclusion*, 56 Antitrust L.J. 57 (1967); Salop & Scheffman, *Raising Rival's Costs*, 73 Am. Econ. Rev. 267 (1983); *see also* Calkins, *A Comment on the Presentation of Steven C. Salop*, 56 Antitrust L.J. 65 (1987).

134. Krattenmaker & Salop, *Competition and Cooperation in the Market for Exclusionary Rights*, 76 Am. Econ. Rev. 109 (1986). *See also Aspen*, 472 U.S. at 610–11.

135. *See* Calkins, *supra* note 133, at 66–67; Salop, *supra* note 133, at 59–60.

136. *Klor's v. Broadway-Hale Stores, Inc.*, discussed *supra* § 4.12, has been offered as an example. *See* Salop, *supra* note 133, at 60–61.

to engage in extraordinary research efforts in order to compete effectively. Herein lies a major problem with the theory. Many activities that cause the costs of competitors to increase are simply side effects of "competition on the merits." Others may be specifically designed to harm competitors without benefiting consumers. The mere fact that an action raises the costs of rivals does not mean one can escape the issue that plagues monopolization law: when is the activity ultimately beneficial and when is its primary purpose the exclusion or hampering of others?

In *Ball Memorial Hospital Inc. v. Mutual Hospital Inc.*,[137] the Seventh Circuit Court of Appeals considered the argument that the low rates paid by a health care insurer to hospitals providing service to its subscribers would force the hospitals to shift costs to patients covered by other insurers, thereby making it more difficult for those insurers to compete. The court declined to apply the theory of raising a rival's costs to find liability, noting that shifting costs was only possible if the insurer possessed market power which, in the case at hand, it did not.[138] In contrast, the notion of raising a rival's cost played an important role in *McWane v. FTC* (discussed *infra* §6.05[J], where the Eleventh Circuit Court of Appeals noted that the impact of exclusive dealing was to raise the costs to new competitors of entering a market.

[J] Blocking Distribution Channels

A monopolist may illegally inhibit its rivals from being effective competitors by blocking the most efficient means of distribution. The *Microsoft* case, *supra*, implicates this form of monopoly conduct, as the court condemned Microsoft's efforts to restrict Netscape's most efficient ways for distributing its Navigator browser to consumers. While the *Microsoft* case involved multiple forms of anticompetitive conduct, some cases revolve exclusively around the monopolist's moves to block distribution channels.

In *United States v. Dentsply International. Inc.*,[139] Dentsply had a monopoly over the sale of prefabricated artificial teeth in the United States. Dentsply sold to dealers who then sold to dental laboratories who converted Dentsply's artificial teeth into dentures and other products for dentists. Dealers are the most effective distribution channel because: dealers provide laboratories the benefit of "one stop-shopping," which reduces transaction costs and time; dealers provide extensive credit services; dealers take tooth returns more efficiently than manufacturers; dealers reduce the manufacturer's distribution costs and credit risks; and dealers provide marketing and sales representatives for the manufacturers' products. In order to block its rivals from being able to use dealers for their distribution, Dentsply created "Criterion 6," which

---

137. 784 F.2d 1325 (7th Cir. 1986). *But see Reazin v. Blue Cross & Blue Shield of Kansas, Inc.*, 635 F. Supp. 1287 (D. Kan. 1986) (jury award on theory of raising rival's costs).

138. A recent example of raising rivals' costs is *Safeway Inc. v. Abbott Labs*, 761 F. Supp. 2d 874 (N.D. Cal. 2011).

139. 399 F.3d 181 (3d Cir. 2004).

forbade dealers from adding non-Dentsply tooth lines to their offerings. Dentsply terminated dealers who expanded their lines to include competing products. Because Dentsply had such market power over prefabricated artificial teeth, many dealers submitted to Criterion 6.

The Third Circuit held that foreclosing distribution channels can be anticompetitive conduct, and it found that Criterion 6 created an illegal barrier to entry, developed by Dentsply to undermine effective competition. The court noted that it was "not necessary that all competition be removed from the market. The test is not total foreclosure, but whether the challenged practices bar a substantial number of rivals or severely restrict the market's ambit."[140] The court found that direct sales from manufacturers to laboratories did not allow for effective competition.

Although Dentsply claimed that Criterion 6 increased efficiency, the court rejected Dentsply's proffered justification as pretextual. Dentsply had exempted some of its suppliers from the new exclusionary policy. The court found that these "grandfathered dealers were no less efficient than the exclusive ones, nor was there any difference in promotional support."[141] This fact disproved Dentsply's efficiency claims.

In *McWane v. FTC*,[142] a producer of pipe fittings sold through distributors. In response to a new entry at the manufacturing level, the defendant, McWane, indicated to distributors that if they sold the pipe fittings of the new entrant, they would lose rebates or the right to sell McWane's products at all. The effect of McWane's action was to deter entry by raising the costs of its new rival.[143] Although assessed as a monopolization case, the court applied a rule of reason approach that first required the FTC to demonstrate that the monopolist's action harmed competition. The defendant's justifications were then noted, and the procompetitive and anticompetitive effects weighed.[144] The court affirmed the FTC's finding that there was substantial foreclosure that harmed competition and that this impact was not offset by procompetitive justifications.

[K] Product Hopping

A relatively new theory with which courts have dealt is called "product hopping" and occurs in the pharmaceutical industry. When patents for brand name drugs expire, generic substitutes are available as long as they are bioequivalent. Pharmacists often switch patients to those substitutes (in some cases because state law requires it). Some drug manufacturers have sought to prevent this generic substitution by

---

140. *Id.* at 191.

141. *Id.* at 197.

142. 783 F.3d 814 (11th Cir. 2015). The case was brought under § 5 of the Federal Trade Commission Act.

143. *Id.* at 832.

144. *Id.* at 833.

discontinuing the formerly patented drug in its original form and, instead, offer a version that is slightly different and has no therapeutic advantage over the original. Since generic substitution is only possible when the generic is a bioequivalent, competition between the brand name drug and the generic is eliminated or at least delayed.[145] Courts refer to this conduct as "product hopping."

The issue of whether product hopping violates §2 of the Sherman Act has been addressed by a number of courts. In *New York v. Actavis*,[146] the manufacturer of Namenda IR, a drug for the treatment of Alzheimer's disease, withdrew it from the market and replaced it with Namenda XR, the same drug in a time release version. This forced users of the drug to switch. At that point, generic equivalents of Nemenda IR were ready to enter the market. The replacement of Namenda IR with Namenda XR meant that the generics could not be substituted by pharmacists, thereby effectively extending the monopoly of the manufacturer beyond the patent term.[147] It is important to note that patients could switch back to the generic version of the Nemenda IR, but this would require obtaining a different prescription from a doctor. The Second Circuit relied on the high transaction costs of switching first to Namenda XR and then back to generic Namenda IR as the source of market power[148] and upheld the lower court's grant of a preliminary injunction prohibiting the withdrawal of Nemenda IR from the market prior to the entry of generic versions. The court cited *Berkey Photo*,[149] noting that "when a monopolist combines product withdrawal with some other conduct, the overall effect of which is to coerce consumers rather than persuade them of the merits and to impede competition, its actions are anticompetitive."[150]

In *Mylan Pharmaceuticals, Inc. v. Warner Chilcott Co.*,[151] the same pattern emerged in the context of Doryx, a drug for the treatment of acne. The changes made to the drug included switching from capsules to tablets and scoring the tablets.[152] Each change required generic manufacturers to catch up and allegedly meant the defendant extended its monopoly power. In this case, however, the Third Circuit Court of Appeals found that the defendant did not possess monopoly power in the relevant market which included all oral tetracyclines. In addition, the court further noted that the defendant's version of "product hopping" was not anticompetitive.[153] Specifically, the defendant's reasons for the changes did not appear to be pretextual.[154] In addition, the plaintiff had been afforded a number of opportunities to compete in the market.

---

145. *See* Jessie Cheng. *An Antitrust Analysis of Product Hopping in the Pharmaceutical Industry*, 108 Colum. L. Rev. 1471,1487–89 (2006).

146. 787 F.3d 638 (2d Cir. 2015).

147. *Id.* at 649.

148. *Id.* at 656.

149. *See* §6.05[C], *supra.*

150. 787 F.3d at 653–54.

151. 838 F.3d 421 (3d Cir. 2016).

152. *Id.* at 430.

153. *Id.* at 439.

154. *Id.*

[L] Predatory Pricing

Predatory pricing is a two-step strategy. The first step is predation, in which a firm charges a price below its costs to drive its competitors from the market because they are unwilling or unable to sustain the losses that the predator is willing to endure. The second step is the recoupment phase. This begins after the predator has succeeded in monopolizing the market and can now charge a monopoly price. Actual recoupment occurs if the predator earns enough monopoly profits to cover its losses from the predation phase.[155]

Because the first stage of predatory pricing entails losses, this can be an expensive and risky endeavor. In Figure 6-2, the profit maximizing price is P1 and the profit maximizing quantity is Q1. Suppose the firm lowers price to P2 in hopes of eliminating a competitor or competitors. Note that this necessitates selling quantity Q2. Thus, it is not a matter of simply lowering price to existing customers; it also requires preparation to sell to all those wishing to buy at the new lower price. Two factors influence just how burdensome this undertaking may be. First, the more elastic the industry demand, the more responsive buyers will be to the lower price. Second, if the predator has a relatively small market share, it will find that the percentage increase in its own output may have to be quite large to even make a dent in the sales of its competitors.[156]

The problem facing the firm may not be simply one of increased sales at a lower price but one of increased costs as well. For example, as Figure 6-2 illustrates, as the firm begins to exceed its optimal level of output, the average cost of each unit sold (AVC) will increase. A further possibility is that increases in sales may require additions to capacity which, if things go as planned, will not be needed at the eventual profit maximizing price and output.[157]

Another issue is whether, once the firm has eliminated competitors, it can raise price sufficiently and deter entry by old or new competitors long enough to justify the losses incurred during the period of predatory behavior. Again, it is basically an investment decision: current losses or foregone profits must be exceeded by the discounted present value of future increases in profits. Given how heavily the odds are against the predator, most scholars share the view that predatory pricing is a rarity. Some even believe that it is so unlikely that no serious judicial concern is warranted.[158] Those who claim that it may occur, even if only occasionally, believe that the investment can be worthwhile to the predator either because entry can be sufficiently

---

155. *Transamerica Computer Co., Inc. v. IBM Corp.*, 698 F.2d 1377, 1384 (9th Cir. 1983) ("Predatory pricing occurs when a company that controls a substantial market share lowers its prices to drive out competition so that it can charge monopoly prices, and reap monopoly profits, at a later time.").

156. *See generally* R. Bork, *supra* note 6, at 149–52.

157. It may, however, serve as a continuing deterrent to competitors considering entering the market. *See generally* Williamson, *Predatory Pricing: A Strategic and Welfare Analysis*, 87 Yale L.J. 284 (1977).

158. *See* Bork, *supra* note 6, at 186: Easterbrook, *Predatory Strategies and Counterstrategies*, 48 U. Chi. L. Rev. 263 (1981).

Figure 6-2.

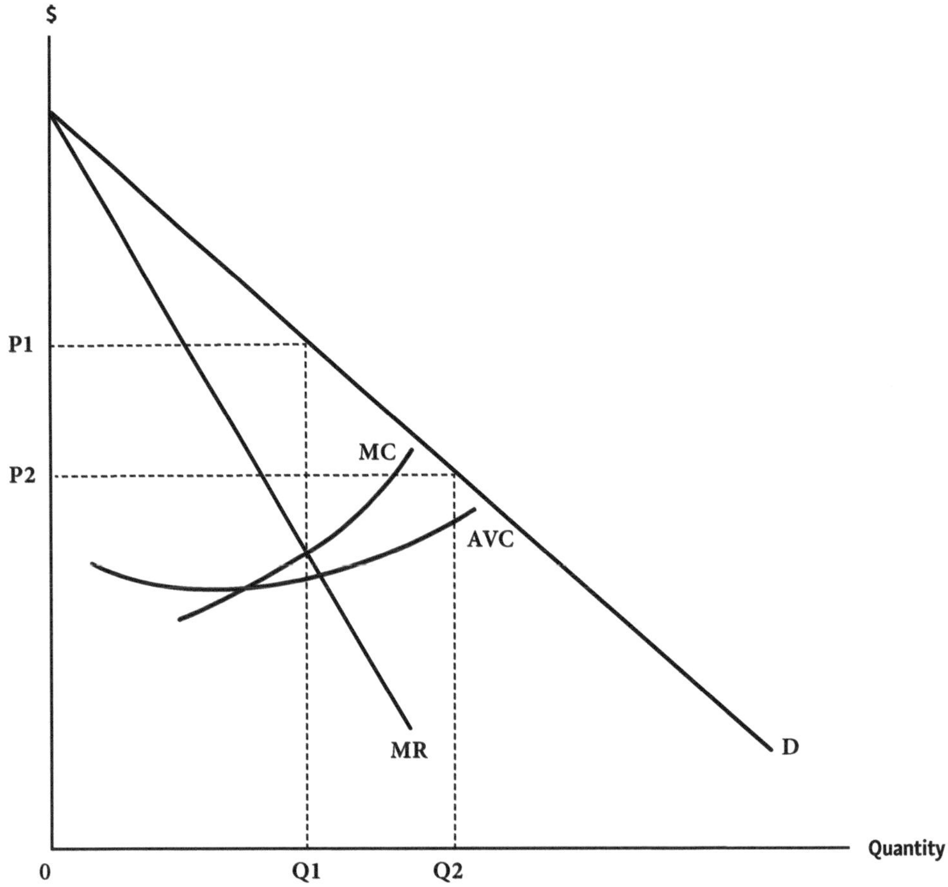

retarded through economic or legal barriers[159] or because predatory pricing can be used as a disciplinary device by a firm to discourage price cutting by competitors.[160]

Over the last 50 years, the Supreme Court has questioned predatory pricing as a theory for liability under § 2. In *Matsushita Electric Industry Co. v. Zenith Radio*,[161] Japanese manufacturers of televisions were accused of conspiring to charge predatory prices for televisions sold in the United States. In reversing the court of appeal's refusal to grant the defendant summary judgment, the Court asserted that "predatory pricing schemes are rarely tried, and even more rarely successful."[162] This claim

---

159. *See* Joskow & Klevorick, *A Framework for Analyzing Predatory Pricing Policy*, 89 Yale L.J. 213 (1979).

160. *See* Posner, *supra* note 5, at 186; *cf.* Williamson, *supra* note 157.

161. 475 U.S. 574 (1986).

162. *Id.* at 589. The Court seemed to embrace the views expressed by Robert Bork. *See* Bork, *supra* note 6.

is debatable.[163] The Court was skeptical about the likelihood that firms engaged in predatory pricing could achieve and maintain monopoly power for a period long enough to recoup the losses sustained during the period of predation.[164] Although the Court was concerned with a conspiracy, it added that its observations applied to single firms as well.[165]

In a similar vein but expressing less skepticism about the theory of predatory pricing is the Court's opinion in *Cargill v. Monfort of Colorado, Inc.*[166] There, a firm challenged the merger of two rivals, claiming that the newly merged firm could engage in predatory practices "by lowering its prices to some level at or slightly above its costs in order to compete . . . for market share. . . . In order to remain competitive [plaintiff] would have to lower its prices; as a result [plaintiff] would suffer a loss in profitability, but would not be driven out of business."[167] The Court held that a competitor does have standing to seek an injunction against threatened injury but found unpersuasive the argument that there was a threat of predatory pricing. The Court reasoned that the record did not support a finding of "antitrust injury"[168] because the threat of less profit was due to increased, not decreased competition. The Court noted, however:

> [P]redatory pricing is an anticompetitive practice forbidden by the antitrust laws. While firms may engage in the practice only infrequently, there is ample evidence suggesting that the practice does occur. It would be novel indeed for a court to deny standing to a party seeking an injunction against threatened injury merely because such injuries rarely occur.[169]

In *Brooke Group Ltd. v. Brown & Williamson Tobacco Co.*,[170] a 1993 case, the Court repeated many of the reservations it had expressed in *Matsushita*. It laid out a framework for analyzing predatory pricing claims that plaintiffs found especially burdensome. Plaintiffs are required to show that the defendant (1) charged prices "below an appropriate measure" of the defendant's costs[171] and (2) "had . . . a dangerous probability of recouping its investment in below-cost prices."[172] Since *Brooke Group*, lower courts have stressed the issue of whether the firm allegedly engaged in predatory

163. *See* Christopher R. Leslie, *Revisiting the Revisionist History of Standard Oil*, 85 S. Cal. L. Rev. 573 (2012); Sandeep Vaheesan, *Reconsidering Brooke Group: Predatory Pricing in Light of the Empirical Learning*, 12 Berkeley Bus. L.J. 81 (2015).

164. The *Matsushita* Court asserted that "because the alleged losses have accrued over the course of two decades, the conspirators could well require a correspondingly long time to recoup." 475 U.S. at 592. The Court's assumption is flawed because recoupment can occur much more quickly than predation. Christopher R. Leslie, *Predatory Pricing and Recoupment*, 113 Colum. L. Rev. 1695, 1719 (2013).

165. 475 U.S. at 590.

166. 479 U.S. 104 (1986).

167. *Id.* at 114–15.

168. *See* discussion *supra* § 3.02[B].

169. 479 U.S. at 121, *citing* Koller, *The Myth of Predatory Pricing: An Empirical Study*, 4 Antitrust L. & Econ. J. 105 (1971); Miller, *Comments on* Baumol *and* Ordover, 28 J. Law & Econ. 267 (1985)).

170. 509 U.S. 209 (1993). The case actually dealt with a charge of predatory pricing. For additional discussion, see *infra* § 8.04[A][2].

171. 509 U.S. at 222.

172. *Id.* at 224.

pricing can reasonably expect to recoup its losses.[173] To a great extent, this emphasis involves an examination of possible entry barriers encountered by firms seeking to compete with the predator once it begins raising prices to supracompetitive levels.

[1] Price Below Cost

The Court in *Brooke Group* held that a plaintiff bringing a predatory pricing claims must prove that the defendant charged a price below an appropriate measure of cost.[174] This was the third predatory pricing case in a row in which the Supreme Court required this element but refused to define it.[175] Lower courts have taken various approaches to defining cost in predatory pricing cases.

Most discussions of the appropriate measure of cost for predatory pricing claims flow from the proposals of Professors Areeda and Turner in their seminal 1975 article.[176] The test is actually the application of the logic of elementary economic price theory as a means of identifying a range of prices that a rational nonpredatory competitor might charge and a range that suggests predatory intent. The primary Areeda-Turner guideline is that prices below "reasonably anticipated short run marginal costs" are predatory.[177] Figure 6-3 illustrates the test. The profit maximizing price would be Pl and the profit maximizing quantity would be Q1. Any price at or above marginal cost, even though not profit maximizing, would be regarded as nonpredatory. The general standard has the major exception that prices below short run marginal cost are not predatory if they are equal to or exceed average total cost (ATC).[178] Thus, in Figure 6-3, P2 would be regarded as nonpredatory even though it is below marginal cost. The marginal cost test applies strictly to prices below average total cost. A firm need not earn an economic profit in order to escape the presumption of predatory pricing. The demand and cost curves may be such that the profit maximizing firm is really minimizing losses. As long as price is at or above short run marginal cost, though, the behavior is not predatory.

Because of the difficulties of computing marginal cost, Areeda and Turner propose using average variable cost (AVC) as a surrogate. Thus, "[a] price at or above reasonably anticipated average variable cost should be presumed lawful" and "[a] price below reasonably anticipated average variable cost should be conclusively presumed

---

173. *See, e.g., Israel Travel Advisory Service v. Israel Identity Tours*, 61 F.3d 1250 (7th Cir. 1995); *Multistate Legal Studies, Inc. v. Harcourt Brace Jovanovich*, 63 F.3d. 1540 (10th Cir. 1995), *cert denied*, 516 U.S. 1044 (1996); *Bathke v. Casey's Central Store*, 64 F.3d 340 (8th Cir 1995); *Advo v. Philadelphia Newspapers*, 51 F.3d 1191 (3d Cir. 1995).

174. 509 U.S. at 222 n.1.

175. *See* Christopher R. Leslie, *False Analogies to Predatory Pricing*, 172 U. Pa. L. Rev. 329 (2024) (discussing cases).

176. Areeda & Turner, *Predatory Pricing and Related Practices Under Section 2 of the Sherman Act*, 88 Harv. L. Rev. 687 (1975).

177. III P. Areeda & D. Turner, *Antitrust Law* 153 (1978).

178. *Id.* at 154.

Figure 6-3.

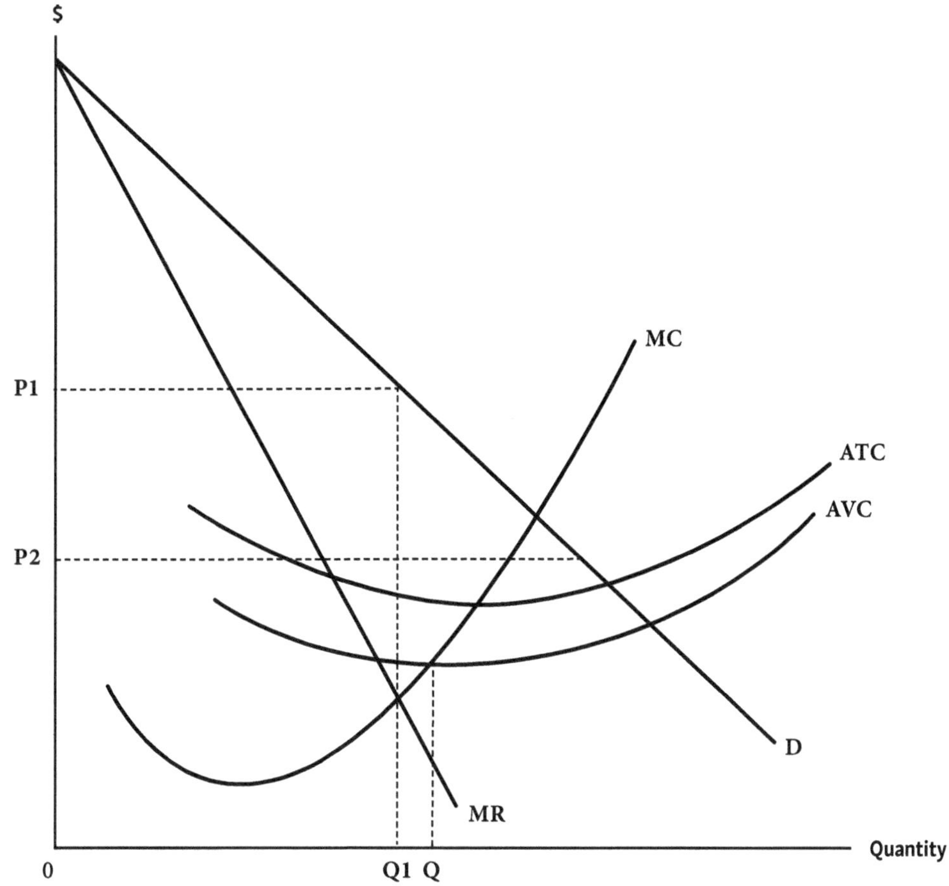

unlawful."[179] Average variable cost and short run marginal cost may be similar for extended ranges of production. The implications when marginal cost and average variable cost deviate are discussed below.

The Areeda-Turner test has been debated by courts[180] and commentators.[181] The test raises three questions. The first stems from the fact that the firm is permitted to charge a price below the short run profit maximizing level. Yet, any price—even one above marginal cost—other than the short run profit maximizing price signals an

179. Areeda & Turner, *supra* note 177, at 154.

180. *See, e.g., Barry Wright Corp. v. ITT Grinnell Corp.* 724 F.2d 227 (1st Cir. 1983); *William Inglis & Sons Baking Co. v. ITT Continental Baking Co.*, 668 F.2d 1014 (9th Cir. 1981); *Pacific Engineering & Prod. Co. v. Kerr McGee Corp.*, 551 F.2d 790 (10th Cir. 1977).

181. *See, e.g.*, Posner, *supra* note 5, at 191–93; Joskow & Klevorick, *supra* note 159; Scherer, *Predatory Pricing and the Sherman Act: A Comment*, 89 Harv. L. Rev. 869 (1976); Williamson, *supra* note 157. For an interesting application of these theories, see Brodly, *The Goals of Antitrust—Pretrial Hearing No. 1: A Verbatim Account of an Imagined Proceeding*, 28 Antitrust Bull. 823 (1983).

effort to exclude competitors. The firm could hold price constant at a level below the short run profit maximizing level in order to deter entry[182] or, capacity permitting, increase and decrease prices in this range to discourage potential entrants.[183] These are forms of what is called "limit pricing." Whether either of these activities should be condemned is problematic. If a firm has excess capacity and lowers prices when entry seems likely and raises them to monopoly levels when the threat has passed, the usual efficiency objections to monopoly pricing are applicable. On the other hand, one can argue that such behavior is, in essence, competitive and only injures those firms with higher production costs than the price cutter. Thus, prohibiting above-cost pricing would do little more than shield less efficient firms. For now, the latter view seems to be the one held by the Supreme Court.[184]

A more serious problem with the Areeda-Turner test is presented when the average variable cost surrogate is invoked. Figure 6-3 illustrates the leeway available. Any price at or above average variable cost is presumed nonpredatory. But, at every point to the right of quantity Q on the graph, marginal cost exceeds average variable cost. Thus, the test permits a great range of prices to be regarded as nonpredatory even though they are below marginal cost and are irrational unless made up in the future when prices can be increased.[185]

The Areeda-Turner test, and any other cost-based or objective test for predation, encounter problems when the issue is one of precision. For example, when reasonably anticipated average variable cost is substituted for short run marginal cost, the test loses some of its consistency with sound economic theory. The substitution is necessary, though, because average variable cost data are more generally available than marginal cost data. But problems remain of ascertaining what was "reasonably anticipated" and which costs are variable with respect to a particular product of a multiproduct firm. Economists and accountants can provide answers, but the estimates depend upon assumptions about the future and cost classifications which are often arbitrary. Thus, an admirable, though fallible, theoretical basis also is subject to practical imprecision.

Other than the predictable issues, there is a fundamental question of how to calculate the cost basis. For example, suppose a seller charges $500 for a stereo system and the $500 is above any measure of cost. It then adds to the system a sound filtering

---

182. This is commonly called "limit" pricing. *See generally* Gunther, *Limit Pricing and Predation in the Antitrust Laws: Economic and Legal Aspects*, 35 Ala. L Rev. 211 (1984).

183. This is a variation of "limit" pricing which involves strategic use of price and capacity to deter entry. *See* Williamson, *supra* note 157; *see also* IIA P. Areeda & H. Hovenkamp, *Antitrust Law* 178–79 (2d ed. 2002); Baumol, *Quasi-Permanence of Price Reductions: A Policy for Prevention of Predatory Pricing*, 89 Yale L.J. 5 (1979).

184. *See Brooke Group Ltd. v. Brook Group Corp.*, 509 U.S. 209 (1993); *Atlantic Richfield v. USA Petroleum*, 495 U.S. 328, 340 (1990).

185. Professors Areeda and Turner have attempted to off-set this difficulty by suggesting that "a monopolist relying on a defense that price was not less than average variable cost should be required to offer proof that his marginal cost . . . did not exceed average variable cost." *See generally* Areeda & Turner, *supra* note 177, at 176.

device that costs $20 but does not raise the price of the system, the average cost of which is still less than $500. In one sense, the firm has just engaged in competition by increasing the quality of the product and not raising the prices. On the other hand, the incremental improvement was provided at a price that was below average marginal cost. At least one court has been interpreted as viewing this activity as predatory pricing.[186]

A final limitation on predatory pricing standards is that they only consider the costs actually incurred by the firm. More specifically, in the process of production, firms may give rise to external costs. These are cost to society that are not internalized by the firm giving rise to them. So, suppose we have two firms. Both pollute the air in their production process. Their total costs—public and private—are the same. One firm, however, pays fines for its pollution, while one is in a jurisdiction in which fines are not levied in response to air pollution. The second firm will appear to be more efficient and charge a lower price. It will not be engaged in predatory pricing, because it is able to shift some of its costs to others. In fact, maybe the firm paying the fines is actually the more efficient producer when all costs are accounted for. That firm's claim that the firm not paying fines for polluting is engaged in predatory pricing will fail as long as the second firm can externalize its costs.[187]

This possibility may explain the outcome in *Philadelphia Taxi Assoc., Inc. v. Uber Technologies, Inc.*[188] There, incumbent taxi drivers complained that Uber had "flooded" the market with lower cost options. Lower costs were made possible because Uber did not pay for medallions and failed to comply with statutory requirements and regulations. The lower court dismissed the action and was affirmed by the Court of Appeals for the Third Circuit. Basically, the court noted that operating at a lower cost could not be the basis of a colorable claim unless the pricing was predatory. In this instance, though, it seems possible that the incumbents were disadvantaged by regulations designed to control external costs, while Uber was able to shift these costs to the public more generally.

[2] Dangerous Probability of Recoupment

The recoupment requirement for predatory pricing claims is unusual. It suggests that even if a firm monopolizes a market through below-cost pricing, antitrust law is indifferent unless the monopolist made a wise business decision. No other area of antitrust requires proof that a monopolist's anticompetitive conduct was profitable. In general, antitrust law cares about anticompetitive effects, not the monopolist's profits. The recoupment requirement is based on the assumption that "[p]redatory pricing is only harmful when the predator succeeds in recouping the losses it suffered by its earlier below-cost pricing." That, however, is not strictly true. Consumers who pay

---

186. *See Multistate Legal Services v. Harcourt Brace Jovanovich*, 63 F.3d 1540 (10th Cir. 1995).

187. *See* Jeffrey L. Harrison, *Some Inconvenient Truths About Antitrust Economics*, 2 Italian L.J. 471 (2016).

188. 886 F.3d 332 (3d Cir. 2018).

the monopoly price during the recoupment phase suffer antitrust injury regardless of the fact that consumers who paid a below-cost price during the predation phase got a bargain.[189] Nevertheless, the recoupment requirement exists.

Courts have often rejected predatory pricing claims by finding that there was no dangerous probability that the defendant could recoup losses incurred during predation. For example, in *Dial A Car v. Transportation, Inc.*,[190] the District of Columbia Circuit Court of Appeals denied a predatory pricing claim by the provider of limousine services noting that the plaintiff had failed to allege that the defendant would be able to recoup its losses. Specifically, the court focused on both the ease of entry of new competitors if prices were raised and the presence in the market of other service providers.[191] Similarly, in *Advo v. Philadelphia Newspapers*,[192] a firm engaged in the distribution of advertising circulars claimed that a newspaper was offering the same service on a predatory basis. The court directed its attention to the issue of dangerous probability of success by discussing the problem of recoupment. It noted that, even if the prices charged were predatory, entry barriers into the market were sufficiently low to prevent recoupment.[193] Finally, in *Taylor Publishing Co. v. Jostens, Inc.*,[194] a rival school yearbook publisher claimed that its competitor had sold at prices below average variable cost and, in so doing, had lured away 27 customers per year in the period 1995–1997. As this was out of a total of 6,500 customers, the court reasoned that recoupment could not occur because the likelihood that the plaintiff actually would be forced out of business was extremely remote.[195]

In *Multistate Legal Services v. Harcourt Brace Jonvaovich*,[196] the Tenth Circuit Court of Appeals addressed predatory pricing with respect to bar review courses. In a fairly detailed matter, the court discussed the economic determinants of the possibility for successful recoupment. It identified those determinants as the defendant's market share, the defendant's resources, and entry barriers. Plaintiff provided sufficient evidence as to all three to create an issue of fact.[197] Similar, is *Spirit Airlines, Inc. v. Northwest Airlines, Inc.*[198] which is an instructive case in a number of respects. First, the Sixth Circuit Court of Appeals adopted the Ninth Circuit's set of presumptions with respect to what constitutes a predatory price. Second, in defining the relevant market, the court held that Spirit had raised an issue of fact with regard to whether the market was composed of low-cost and leisure travelers over specific air routes rather than all travelers.

---

189. Christopher R. Leslie, *Predatory Pricing and Recoupment*, 113 Colum. L. Rev. 1695, 1741-44 (2013).

190. 82 F.3d 484 (D.C. Cir. 1996).

191. *See also Israel Travel Advisory Serv., Inc. v. Israel Identity Tours, Inc.*, 61 F.3d 1250 (7th Cir. 1995).

192. 51 F.3d 1191 (3d Cir. 1995).

193. *Id.* at 1191–1200.

194. 216 F.3d 465 (5th Cir. 2000).

195. *Id.* at 478.

196. 63 F.3d 1540 (10th Cir. 1996).

197. *Id.* at 1554–55.

198. 431 F.3d 917 (6th Cir. 2005).

This was a critical question because the cost/revenue comparison required under the first step of the predatory pricing analysis can vary depending on whether high fare passengers were included in the relevant market. Third, there was no dispute that Spirit had entered the market with fares that were substantially below those of Northwest. Northwest then lowered its fare and added capacity, and Spirit left the market. Finally, the court correctly noted the importance of entry barriers in assessing recoupment.

[M] Bundled Rebates and Other Conditional Discounts

Dominant firms sometimes attach conditions to their discounts. Examples of conditional discounts include requiring customers to purchase a bundle of different products (often called a bundled rebate), making a specified percentage of their purchases from the seller (sometimes called a market-share discount), or other forms of loyalty discounts.[199] Although some courts have asserted that "[b]undled discounts are generally pro-competitive because they result in lower prices to consumers,"[200] this overlooks the fact that conditional discounts may be anticompetitive not because of the discount but because of the condition that the dominant firm has attached to the discount.[201]

To understand why a bundled rebate can be anticompetitive, suppose firm A produces both computers, a market in which it has market power, and monitors. The average variable cost of producing a computer is $500, and the average variable cost of producing a monitor is $100. Firm B produces monitors only, and the average variable cost is $90. It sells them for $120. Firm A prices computers at $700 and monitors at $150 if they are purchased separately. They are also packaged together for a price of $650. A person wishing to buy a computer and monitor has the choice of buying the combination from A for $650 or the computer from A for $700 and the monitor from B for a total of $820. Obviously, the bundled opportunity is more attractive. More importantly, even if firm B charged a price equal to its costs, the total price of $790 would exceed the bundled price. In effect, even though B is the more efficient producer of monitors, the bundling by A makes it impossible for it to remain in the industry.

Bundled discounting has drawn considerable attention.[202] One influential case is *LePage's, Inc. v. 3M Corp.*[203] in which 3M, a monopolist in the sale of transparent tape, offered a discounted bundle (via rebates) which included that tape. 3M dominated the transparent tape market in the United States, maintaining a market share above 90%.

---

199. Steven C. Salop, *The Raising Rivals' Cost Foreclosure Paradigm, Conditional Pricing Practices, and the Flawed Incremental Price-Cost Test*, 81 Antitrust L.J. 371, 372 (2017).

200. *Inline Packaging, LLC v. Graphic Packaging Int'l, LLC*, 351 F. Supp. 3d 1187, 1206 (D. Minn. 2018).

201. Christopher R. Leslie, *False Analogies to Predatory Pricing*, 172 U. Pa. L. Rev. 329, 394 (2024).

202. *See, e.g.*, See Daniel Crane, *Multiproduct Discounting: A Myth of Nonprice Predation*, 72 U. Chi. L. Rev. 27 (2005); Thomas A, Lambert, *Evaluating Bundled Discounts*, 89 Minn. L Rev. 1688 (2005); Barry Nalebuff, *Exclusionary Bundling*, Antitrust Bull. 321 (2005).

203. 324 F.3d 141 (3d Cir. 2003) (*en banc*).

LePage's sold private label transparent tape, which is tape sold under the retailer's name rather than under the name of the manufacturer. Private label tape sold at a lower price to the retailer and the customer than branded tape. By 1992, LePage's sold 88% of private label tape sales in the United States, which represented but a small portion of the transparent tape market. 3M also entered the private label business during the early 1990s and sold its own second brand under the name "Highland."

3M offered many of LePage's major customers substantial rebates to induce them to eliminate or reduce their purchases of tape from LePage's. 3M, however, conditioned these discounts on customers making sufficient purchase across all six of 3M's diverse product lines: Health Care Products, Home Care Products, Home Improvement Products, Stationery Products (including transparent tape), Retail Auto Products, and Leisure Time. 3M's rebate programs set customer-specific target growth rates in each product line. If a customer failed to meet the target for any one product, it would lose the rebate across the line. This created a substantial incentive for each customer to meet the targets across all product lines to maximize its rebates. If stores purchased tape from LePage's, they would have lost hundreds of thousands of dollars in rebates from 3M. Because of 3M's rebate scheme, many of LePage's former customers refused even to meet with LePage's sales representatives. The Third Circuit considered 3M's bundled rebates to be monopoly conduct, and it affirmed a jury verdict for LePage's.

In *Cascade Health Solutions v. Peacehealth*,[204] the Ninth Circuit held that bundled rebates should be evaluated under the "discount attribution standard." Under this test, "the full amount of the discounts given by the defendant on the bundle are allocated to the competitive product or products. If the resulting price of the competitive product or products is below the defendant's incremental cost to produce them, the trier of fact may find that the bundled discount is exclusionary for the purpose of § 2."[205] The Ninth Circuit reasoned that the discount attribution "standard makes the defendant's bundled discounts legal unless the discounts have the potential to exclude a *hypothetical* equally efficient producer of the competitive product."[206]

In the computers and monitors example described above, this discount attribution approach would mean subtracting the $200 discount for the package from the unbundled price ($100) of the monitor. Obviously, in this example, the bundled price would be viewed as exclusionary because the monitor is priced below the cost of its production. This approach labels bundles exclusionary when the impact would be to eliminate an equally efficient or more efficient producer.

In the process of making its decision, the Ninth Circuit considered and rejected what it referred to as the "aggregate discount rule."[207] Under this approach, the entire cost of producing the components of the bundle is compared to the cost. In effect, it treats the bundle as a single product and asks whether the price can be regarded as

204. 502 F.3d 895 (9th Cir. 2007).

205. *Id.* at 906.

206. *Id.*

207. *Id.* at 914.

predatory. The court correctly noted that the approach hardly serves the function of protecting the more efficient producers.[208]

In a 2015 case, the Sixth Circuit applied an approach much like the Ninth Circuit's to what might more accurately be viewed as an instance of tying. In *Collins Inkjet Corp. v. Eastman Kodak Co.*,[209] Kodak sold printers, printheads and ink. Customers who bought ink from Kodak received a reduced price for printheads, while customers who purchased ink from Collins were charged a higher price for Kodak printheads. The net effect was to make it more expensive to buy ink from Collins and printheads from Kodak than to buy them from Kodak. In a sense, Kodak had bundled ink and printheads. The court affirmed a preliminary injunction against Kodak noting that "a bundled pricing scheme may be unlawful under the discount attribution standard even if the bundle's aggregate price is above cost, so long as the discount is significant enough to take the competitive (or tied) product's price below cost."[210]

Although some defendants have argued that discounts are per se legal so long as price remains above cost, some courts have explained why conditional discounts are a distinct form of monopoly conduct, separate from predatory pricing. A good example is *ZF Meritor v. Eaton Corporation*,[211] which involved the sales by a monopolist producer of truck transmissions to four truck manufacturers. These were the only purchasers. After a new seller, ZF Meritor, entered the market with some success, Eaton entered into long term supply contracts with the four buyers. These were not requirements contracts, but a buyer would only receive a discount if it bought a certain percentage of its requirements from Eaton. In effect, their loyalty was rewarded. Buyers of trucks were able to select various components from a list. As part of its agreement with truck manufacturers, Eaton required that its transmissions be offered at a preferred price or lower prices than that of its competitors and that it be permitted to match any lower prices offered by competitors.[212] In combination, these practices and others, it was alleged, led to the departure of the plaintiff from the market.

Eaton argued that liability should be determined in the same manner as it would be in a more standard predatory pricing case. In other words, were its prices below cost? There was no allegation that they and plaintiff adopted the position that the combination of agreements should be assessed under the rule of reason typically applied to vertical restraints cases involving exclusive dealing. The court distinguished other predatory pricing cases by noting that, in those cases, "price itself" was the sole exclusionary factor. It went on to reason:

> [W]e find nothing in the Supreme Court's recent predatory pricing decisions to indicate that the court intended to overturn decades of other

208. See also *Southeast Missouri Hospital v. Bard*, 616 F.3d 888 (8th Cir. 2010), for a misuse of the "discount attribution standard."

209. 781 F.3d 264 (6th Cir. 2015).

210. *Id.* at 274.

211. 696 F.3d 254 (3d Cir. 2012).

212. *Id.* at 265–66.

precedent holding that conduct that does not result in below-cost pricing may nevertheless be anticompetitive.[213]

The exclusionary impact of discounts is also explored in *Church & Dwight Co. v. Mayer Labs.*[214] In *Mayer*, the practice was discounting prices in exchange for guarantees of shelf space for the sale of condoms. Shelf space is essential for successful sales, and the question was whether a dominant firm offering discounts in exchange for shelf space was unlawfully excluding competitors. Here again, the defendant asked that the claim be dismissed because there was no allegation that its net prices were below costs. The court noted that the case was not to be assessed under predatory pricing standards because the plaintiff's claim was not "price based." Instead, it was an objection to the restrictions required to obtain the discount.[215] The court shifted the analysis from predatory pricing to the rule of reason and held that the plaintiff survived a motion to dismiss. Of course, a rule of reason standard is a very difficult one for plaintiffs to prevail on and summary judgment was eventually granted to the defendant.[216]

[N] Monopsony Power and Monopsony Conduct

To this point in the discussion of monopoly conduct, the emphasis has been only on monopoly conduct. Technically, the concept of monopoly refers to the power of sellers of a good or service. In some instances, however, the "predatory conduct" involves firms trying to acquire or maintain power on the buying side or demand side of the market.[217] A buyer having power over price and quantity is said to have monopsony power.[218] Monopsony power falls within the ambit of § 2 and has been examined by courts in much the same manner as monopoly conduct.

One of the more influential early § 2 cases involving monopsony power is *United States v. Griffith.*[219] Defendants operated movie theaters in a number of towns. In some towns (closed towns), they were the only exhibitor. In others, they faced competition. Of course, as an exhibitor-seller in the closed towns, they possessed some degree of monopoly power. Similarly, as purchasers of films from distributors wishing

213. *Id.* at 279.

214. *Church & Dwight Co., Inc. v. Mayer Laboratories, Inc.*, C-10-4029 EMC, 2011 WL 1225912 (N.D. Cal. Apr. 1, 2011).

215. *Id.*

216. 868 F. Supp. 2d 876 (N.D. Cal. 2012).

217. *See generally* Blair & Harrison, *Antitrust Policy and Monopsony*, 76 Cornell L. Rev. 297 (1991).

218. The issues that arise in determining market power in the case of monopsony mirror those encountered when the market power of sellers is examined. *See* Blair & Harrison, *Cooperative Buying, Monopsony Power, and Antitrust Policy*, 86 Nw. Univ. L. Rev. 331 (1992).

219. 334 U.S. 100 (1948). For an application of the concept of monopsony to college sports, see McKenzie & Sullivan, *Does the NCAA Exploit College Athletes: An Economic and Legal Analysis*, 32 Antitrust Bull. 373 (1987).

to have their films shown in those towns, they possessed monopsony power. By linking closed and competitive towns in their negotiations with distributors, the defendants were able to obtain the first run rights to films for exhibition in both closed and competitive towns. The alleged effect was to increase the market power of the exhibitors in competitive towns. The Supreme Court held that a violation of § 2 had been shown. Although it did not discuss expressly the concept of monopsony power, it did so implicitly by condemning the use of "the buying power of the entire circuit" and "[l]arge scale buying."[220]

In *Griffith*, the exhibitors used their monopsony power to increase their market power in towns where they competed with other sellers. Monopsony power also may be used to achieve vertical integration. In the vertical integration cases discussed above, monopolists tended to integrate forward—manufacturing to retailing. In the case of the monopsonist, however, the temptation is to integrate backward. Thus, in the case of the monopsonist exhibitors, the expectation would be that the firm would set up its own distribution scheme and begin to either refuse to deal with or drastically lower the price they offer existing distributors in hopes of excluding them. For the most part, the arguments for and against prohibiting vertical integration by monopolists apply with equal force to vertical integration by monopsonists.

The First Circuit addressed monopsony power in *Kartell v. Blue Shield of Massachusetts*.[221] Blue Shield provided health insurance for about 74% of the Massachusetts residents who were privately insured. Under the agreement Blue Shield made with physicians, Blue Shield paid for the physicians' services as long as the physicians did not charge subscribers more than the amount paid by Blue Shield. The Blue Shield plan accounted for 14% of all physician practice revenue. The issue was whether Blue Shield's "ban on balance billing" violated §§ 1 or 2 of the Sherman Act.[222] Under the court's analysis, Blue Shield was viewed as a buyer of physicians' services. The plaintiffs argued that, as a buyer, Blue Shield possessed market power that forced prices below those that would exist in a "freely competitive market," with the consequence of discouraging the entry of new doctors and the utilization of new medical techniques. Essentially, the plaintiffs complained that Blue Shield had used its monopsony power to obtain a low price. The court held that, even if Blue Shield had the power attributed to it, it had not violated the Sherman Act. To hold otherwise, the court noted, would be comparable to extending § 2 to monopoly[223] pricing *per se*, an option long since foreclosed. The court observed:

> Antitrust law rarely stops the buyer of a service from trying to determine the price or characteristics of the product that will be sold. Thus, the more closely Blue Shield's activities resemble, in essence, those of a purchaser, the less likely that they are unlawful.... [C]ourts at least should be

---

220. 334 U.S. 100 at 108.
221. 749 F.2d 922 (1st Cir. 1984).
222. *Id.* at 926.
223. *Id.* at 927.

> cautious—reluctant to condemn too speedily—an arrangement that, on its face, appears to bring low price benefits to the consumer.[224]

Although mere price setting by either single buyers or sellers with market power does not violate § 2 of the Sherman Act, it is incorrect as a matter of economic theory to believe that monopsonistically determined prices always will benefit consumers. This is particularly true when the buyer is in the market for inputs and employs monopsony power to obtain lower prices than would exist under competitive conditions. If the buyer offers a lower price, chances are that the seller will sell a lower quantity. Of course, fewer inputs typically mean a lower level of output. And restrictions in output are generally associated with higher prices for the final good. Thus, the same kinds of welfare losses experienced under monopoly conditions also can be found under conditions of monopsony.[225]

In a 2007 case, the Supreme Court dealt directly with the issue of illegal monopsonization. In *Weyerhaeuser Co. v. Ross-Simmons Hardwood Lumber Co.*,[226] the Supreme Court addressed predatory bidding as an illegal method of acquiring monopsony power. The defendant (Weyerhaeuser), an operator of saw mills, bid up the prices of sawlogs to the point that a competing buyer claimed to be unable to purchase the sawlogs as an input that could be converted into a profitable output. The plaintiff claimed that Weyerhaeuser had used predatory bidding—overpaying for an input—to monopsonize the market and that, after it was the only buyer of sawlogs, Weyerhaeuser would have sufficient market power to drive down the price of the sawlogs it purchased in the future. The lower court had instructed the jury that Weyerhaeuser had violated § 2 if it had purchased more sawlogs than needed or paid a higher price in an effort to prevent the plaintiff from obtaining sawlogs. The Ninth Circuit affirmed a jury verdict for the plaintiff.

The Supreme Court reversed, analogizing predatory bidding to predatory pricing and applying the two-step *Brooke Group* approach to predatory bidding claims. Thus, the *Brooke Group* test in the context of monopsony consists of two steps: (1) a period of excess buying prices that result in costs of production that exceed the selling price of output, and (2) a period of recoupment by virtue of paying less for the input in the future.

Writing the majority opinion, Justice Thomas also analogized predatory pricing and predatory bidding because "both claims logically require firms to incur short-term losses on the chance that they might reap supracompetitive profits in the future."[227]

---

224. *Id.* at 925, 931. This logic may be inconsistent with the Supreme Court's decisions in *Maricopa* and *Catalano*. *See supra* § 4.04[B]. More recently, in a pattern common to professional sports, professional soccer players challenged the use of power on the buying side of the market when soccer teams acted as a single entity in hiring players. Plaintiffs sought to define the market as Division I professional soccer players in the United States. The market definition was rejected by the jury. *Fraser v. Major League Soccer*, 284 F.3d 47 (1st Cir. 2002).

225. *See generally* R. Blair & J. Harrison, *Monopsony: Antitrust Law and Economics* 39–42 (1993).

226. 549 U.S. 312 (2007).

227. *Id.* at 322.

This similarity is true but irrelevant; most business strategies—such as product development and marketing—involve short-term losses incurred with the hope of long-term profits. Justice Thomas also asserted that, like the initial low prices charged during the predation phase of a predatory pricing scheme, predatory bidding benefits consumers and, thus, prohibiting this conduct would deter procompetitive behavior.[228] This odd argument is demonstrably false: unlike predatory pricing, predatory bidding never results in lower prices for consumers.[229] Predatory bidding immediately drives up input costs and likely leads to higher prices for consumers buying the relevant outputs. Moreover, Justice Thomas never identifies any procompetitive behavior that could be deterred by condemning monopsonization through predatory bidding.[230]

§ 6.06 Attempt to Monopolize

Attempted monopolization is a separate cause of action under Section Two of the Sherman Act. For over a century, federal courts struggled to articulate a clear legal test for what constitutes an illegal attempt to monopolize a market. The Supreme Court's most important early endeavor to describe attempted monopolization is found in an oft-quoted passage from Justice Holmes in *Swift & Co. v. United States*:

> Where acts are not sufficient in themselves to produce a result which the law seeks to prevent—for instance, the monopoly—but require further acts in addition to the mere forces of nature to bring that result to pass, an intent to bring it to pass is necessary in order to produce a dangerous probability that it will happen. But when that intent and the consequent dangerous probability exist, this statute, like many others and like the common law in some cases, directs itself against that dangerous probability as well as against the completed result.[231]

Courts and commentators interpreted this passage in various—and sometimes conflicting—ways. In 1993, the Supreme Court in *Spectrum Sports v. McQuillan*[232] laid out the current legal test for attempted monopolization. The Court interpreted its prior precedent as holding that "it is generally required that to demonstrate attempted monopolization a plaintiff must prove (1) that the defendant has engaged in predatory or anticompetitive conduct with (2) a specific intent to monopolize and (3) a dangerous probability of achieving monopoly power."[233] Lower courts apply this three-element test when evaluating attempted monopolization claims.

---

228. *Id.* at 324, 320.
229. Christopher R. Leslie, *False Analogies to Predatory Pricing*, 172 U. Pa. L. Rev. 329, 383 (2024).
230. *Id.* at 383–84.
231. 196 U.S. 375, 396 (1905) (citation omitted).
232. 506 U.S. 447 (1993).
233. *Id.* at 456.

Although worded differently, these elements for attempted monopolization are very similar to the elements for actual monopolization articulated in the Supreme Court's *Grinnell* decision. *Grinnell* starts by asking whether the defendant possesses monopoly power. This is similar to *Spectrum Sports*' inquiry into whether the defendant possesses a dangerous probability of achieving monopoly power. As discussed below, the legal analysis is the same, though the market share thresholds differ. *Grinnell*'s second element focuses on the defendant's conduct, as does the first element of *Spectrum Sports*. Indeed, these elements are identical. Any conduct that satisfies the second element of *Grinnell* necessarily satisfies the first element of *Spectrum Sports*. Unlike *Grinnell*, *Spectrum Sports* explicitly articulates an intent element—specific intent to monopolize. That is a major difference between the *Grinnell* test and the *Spectrum Sports* test.

It is often best to consider the elements of *Spectrum Sports* in this order: dangerous probability of monopoly; anticompetitive conduct; and specific intent to monopolize. This mimics the order of the *Grinnell* test, which correctly acknowledges that the analysis must start with market definition (which is the first element of *Grinnell* but listed third in *Spectrum Sports*). In an older opinion, the FTC Commissioners noted that "the Commission has taken the position that in attempted monopolization cases, the dangerous probability of success element should be evaluated 'before proceeding to the other two elements.'"[234] The following discussion proceeds accordingly.

[A] Dangerous Probability of Success

The *Spectrum Sports* test requires that the plaintiff prove the defendant possesses "a dangerous probability of achieving monopoly power."[235] This element generally entails that the plaintiff define the relevant market. Quoting its opinion in *Walker Process*, the *Spectrum Sports* Court noted that "'[w]ithout a definition of that market there is no way to measure [the defendant's] ability to lessen or destroy competition.'"[236] The process of defining the market for an attempted monopolization claim is the same process used in monopolization cases. This requires the plaintiff to define the relevant product market and the relevant geographic market. These two components comprise the relevant market. Next, the defendant's market share in that relevant market is calculated.

This is where the legal tests for monopolization and attempted monopolization part ways. As the Second Circuit explained in *Tops Markets, Inc. v. Quality Markets, Inc.*, "[d]espite the similar approaches, a lesser degree of market power may establish an attempted monopolization claim than that necessary to establish a completed

---

234. *Matter of Int'l Tel. & Tel. Corp.*, 104 F.T.C. 280, 380 (1984) (quoting *General Foods Corp.*, 3 Trade Reg. Rep. (CCH) ¶ 22,142 (April 6, 1984), at 22,977).

235. *Spectrum Sports, Inc. v. McQuillan*, 506 U.S. 447, 456 (1993).

236. *Id.* (quoting *Walker Process Equipment, Inc. v. Food Machinery & Chemical Corp.*, 382 U.S. 172, 177 (1965)).

monopolization claim."[237] In other words, the plaintiff must show that the defendant possesses a higher market share to satisfy the "monopoly power" element of the *Grinnell* test than the "dangerous probability" element of the *Spectrum Sports* test. Under either cause of action, however, the federal circuits have not agreed on what these market share thresholds are.

Different courts have approached the market share requirement differently. The Fourth Circuit "has offered a 'general scale that a court may cautiously apply': '(1) claims of less than 30% market shares should presumptively be rejected; (2) claims involving between 30% and 50% shares should usually be rejected, except when conduct is very likely to achieve monopoly or when conduct is invidious, but not so much so as to make the defendant *per se* liable; [and] (3) claims involving greater than 50% share should be treated as attempts at monopolization when the other elements for attempted monopolization are also satisfied.'"[238] This quotation, however, provides an illusion of precision. Courts have not generally agreed on what market share threshold is necessary to constitute "a dangerous probability of achieving monopoly power." For example, other courts are more receptive to the possibility that a firm with less than 50 percent market share can still possess a dangerous probability of monopolizing that market.[239]

Although courts differ on the numerical thresholds, if the defendant's market share is deemed "too low," the § 2 claim will fail. But even if the defendant's market share is deemed sufficiently high, that does not automatically mean that it has a dangerous probability of achieving monopoly power. As with monopolization claims, the plaintiff must also show that barriers to entry exist. If barriers to entry are sufficiently low, then courts often conclude that the defendant is unlikely to monopolize the market. For example, the Ninth Circuit has opined that despite the defendant's "high market share, neither monopoly power nor a dangerous probability of achieving monopoly power can exist absent evidence of barriers to new entry or expansion."[240]

Whether the defendant possesses a dangerous probability of achieving monopoly power should be evaluated with reference to the time that the defendant began engaging in the challenged anticompetitive conduct.[241] For example, the Eleventh Circuit has explained that "[w]hen determining whether an issue of fact exists as to whether defendant's actions presented a dangerous probability of defendant achieving a monopolist's market power, a court examines the relevant market and

237. 142 F.3d 90, 100 (2d Cir. 1998).

238. *Fotobom Media, Inc. v. Google LLC*, 719 F. Supp. 3d 33, 52 (D.D.C. 2024) (quoting *M & M Med. Supplies & Serv., Inc. v. Pleasant Valley Hosp., Inc.*, 981 F.2d 160, 168 (4th Cir. 1992)).

239. *In re Pool Prod. Distribution Mkt. Antitrust Litig.*, 940 F. Supp. 2d 367, 386 (E.D. La. 2013) ("The Fifth Circuit agrees that a market share of less than 50 percent can support an attempt claim if other circumstances are present. With the complaint supporting a market share of 33 percent, the Court must look holistically at the market characteristics and Pool's conduct to determine whether plaintiffs have alleged an attempted monopolization claim." (citation omitted)).

240. *Am. Pro. Testing Serv., Inc. v. Harcourt Brace Jovanovich Legal & Pro. Publications, Inc.*, 108 F.3d 1147, 1154 (9th Cir. 1997).

241. *See HDC Med., Inc. v. Minntech Corp.*, 474 F.3d 543, 550 (8th Cir. 2007).

defendant's market power before the attempt to monopolize began."[242] Despite this well-established rule in antitrust law,[243] courts sometimes improperly analyze the element in hindsight, reasoning that there must not have been a dangerous probability of the defendant achieving monopoly power because it eventually failed in its efforts.[244]

[B] Anticompetitive Conduct

In *Spectrum Sports*, the Court noted that the Sherman Act "directs itself not against conduct which is competitive, even severely so, but against conduct which unfairly tends to destroy competition itself."[245] Although "[a]n attempted monopolization claim necessarily involves conduct which has not yet succeeded,"[246] courts treat the conduct element similarly for both monopolization and attempted monopolization claims. In evaluating an attempted monopolization claim, the Fifth Circuit, for example, noted: "'"Exclusionary" conduct is conduct, other than competition on the merits or restraints reasonably "necessary" to competition on the merits, that reasonably appear[s] capable of making a significant contribution to creating or maintaining monopoly power.'"[247]

In essence, the element of the *Spectrum Sports* test is effectively the same as the second element of the *Grinnell* test. That said, some forms of anticompetitive conduct are more frequently seen in attempted monopolization cases. Most notably, predatory pricing cases appear more likely to be brought as attempted monopolization claims, but predatory pricing can satisfy the conduct element of either a monopolization or an attempted monopolization cause of action.

One recent case evaluating allegedly anticompetitive conduct in the context of an attempted monopolization claim is *Philadelphia Taxi Association, Inc. v. Uber Technologies, Inc.*,[248] in which Philadelphia taxicab drivers sued Uber for attempted monopolization. The plaintiffs claimed that Uber engaged in anticompetitive conduct because "it failed to comply with statutory and regulatory requirements, failed to purchase medallions, failed to pay drivers a minimum wage, and failed to obtain the proper insurance, among other actions."[249] They also accused Uber of "flood[ing]

---

242. *McGahee v. N. Propane Gas Co.*, 858 F.2d 1487, 1505 (11th Cir. 1988).

243. *See, e.g.*, *Taylor Publ'g Co. v. Jostens, Inc.*, 216 F.3d 465, 475 (5th Cir. 2000) ("[W]e look to the defendant's conduct and the market *at the time the conduct occurred*, rather than evaluating the conduct's effects after-the-fact." (emphasis added)); *Int'l Distribution Ctrs., Inc. v. Walsh Trucking Co.*, 812 F.2d 786, 791 (2d Cir. 1987) ("A dangerous probability of monopoly may exist where the defendant firm possesses a significant market share *when it undertakes* the challenged anticompetitive conduct." (emphasis added)).

244. Christopher R. Leslie, *Hindsight Bias in Antitrust Law*, 71 Vand. L. Rev. 1527 (2018).

245. *Spectrum Sports, Inc. v. McQuillan*, 506 U.S. 447, 458 (1993).

246. *Taylor Pub. Co. v. Jostens, Inc.*, 216 F.3d 465, 474 (5th Cir. 2000).

247. *Id.* at 475 (quoting 3 Phillip E. Areeda & Herbert Hovenkamp, *Antitrust Law* ¶ 651, at 82 (1996)).

248. 886 F.3d 332 (3d Cir. 2018).

249. *Id.* at 340.

the Philadelphia taxicab market by improperly luring drivers away from" traditional taxicab companies.[250] The Third Circuit held that none of these actions constituted anticompetitive conduct. The court characterized Uber's actions as competitive, not anticompetitive, because they increased supply and "bolstered competition by offering customers lower prices, more available taxicabs, and a high-tech alternative to the customary method of hailing taxicabs and paying for rides."[251] By lowering its costs, Uber was operating "with greater economic efficiency."[252]

The claim that Uber was luring taxicab drivers away from their former employers is called predatory hiring. The Third Circuit noted that "hiring rivals may be anticompetitive, but only in certain cases. For example, if rival employees were hired in an attempt to exclude competitors from the market for some basis other than efficiency or merit, such as to acquire monopoly power or to merely deny the employees to the rival, this could violate the antitrust laws if injurious to the rival and to competition at large."[253] Because Uber was actually using the former taxicab drivers as Uber drivers, its recruitment tactics did not constitute predatory hiring.

As with actual monopolization claims, defendants accused of attempted monopolization can proffer a defense that their conduct is justified by a legitimate business justification unrelated to the suppression of competition.

[C] Specific Intent to Monopolize

The role of intent in monopolization claims is unclear. But it is, at most, general intent, not specific intent. *Spectrum Sports* requires plaintiffs bringing attempted monopolization claims to prove that the defendant had "a specific intent to monopolize." This is consistent with the Court's earlier pronouncement in *Times-Picayune Co. v. United States*:[254] "While the completed offense of monopolization under s 2 demands only a general intent to do the act, 'for no monopolist monopolizes unconscious of what he is doing', a specific intent to destroy competition or build monopoly is essential to guilt for the mere attempt now charged."[255] The Court considered the actions actually taken, however, and found that they were motivated by "legitimate business aims,"[256] thus suggesting that attempt extended only to efforts to achieve market power by illegitimate means.

Another solid early effort to provide substance to the intent component of attempted monopolization is found in *Union Leader Corp. v. Newspapers of New England Inc.*[257]

---

250. *Id.*

251. *Id.*

252. *Id.*

253. *Id.* at 340–41.

254. 345 U.S. 594 (1953).

255. *Id.* at 626 (1953) (quoting *United States v. Aluminum Co. of America*, 148 F.2d 416, 431–32 (2d Cir. 1945))

256. *Id.* at 627.

257. 180 F. Supp 125 (D. Mass. 1959), *modified*, 284 F.2d 582 (1st Cir. 1960).

According to Judge Wyzanski, "a person does not necessarily have an exclusionary intent merely because he foresees that a market is only large enough to permit one successful enterprise."[258] Instead, § 2 comes into play only when "the person who foresees a fight to the death intends to use or actually does use unfair weapons."[259] In short, the intent must go further than just a desire to displace competitors. It requires, in the words of the *Spectrum Sports* Court, "something more than an intent to compete vigorously."[260]

In *Philadelphia Taxi Association, Inc. v. Uber Technologies, Inc.*,[261] discussed above, the plaintiffs alleged that Uber's specific intent to monopolize was proven by its decision to evade local regulations for taxi services. The Third Circuit held that "[w]hile Uber's alleged conduct might have formed the basis of a regulatory violation, its knowledge of existing regulations alone cannot reasonably be said to demonstrate specific intent to monopolize."[262] The court characterized Uber's decisions as helping it "operate more efficiently," which was a legitimate business aim.[263] The court, thus, concluded that "Uber's alleged competitive strategy of creating a vehicle-for-hire business model, presumably to acquire customers, does not reflect specific intent to monopolize."[264]

§ 6.07 Procompetitive Justification Defense

After a plaintiff has established the prima facie elements of a § 2 claim for monopolization or attempted monopolization, the defendant is afforded an opportunity to present a procompetitive justification for its anticompetitive conduct.[265] Using this defense, the defendant asserts that its conduct was "a form of competition on the merits because it involves, for example, greater efficiency or enhanced consumer appeal."[266] One common justification is that the defendant's conduct is necessary to solve a market failure, such as free riding.[267]

This justification must be nonpretextual; in other words, it must accurately reflect the defendant's rationale for engaging in the challenged conduct. Courts will reject the defendant's proffered rationale for its anticompetitive conduct if that rationale is

258. 180 F. Supp. at 140.
259. *Id.*
260. 506 U.S. at 459.
261. 886 F.3d 332 (3d Cir. 2018).
262. *Id.* at 341.
263. *Id.*
264. *Id.*
265. *U.S. v. Microsoft Corp.*, 253 F.3d 34 (D.C. Cir. 2001).
266. *Id.* at 59.
267. *See* John M. Newman, *Procompetitive Justifications in Antitrust Law*, 94 Ind. L.J. 501 (2019).

pretextual. Recall *C.R. Bard, Inc. v. M3 Systems, Inc.*,[268] in which Bard manipulated the interface for replacement needles used in its patented biopsy guns in an attempt to monopolize the market for replacement biopsy needles. Bard argued that it redesigned its interface to reduce injuries and "to make [the biopsy gun] easier to load and unload," which, if true, would have been a legitimate business justification for Bard's conduct.[269] The Federal Circuit, though, rejected Bard's defense as pretextual because "there was substantial evidence that Bard's real reasons for modifying the gun were to raise the cost of entry to potential makers of replacement needles, to make doctors apprehensive about using non-Bard needles, and to preclude the use of 'copycat' needles."[270] Moreover, Bard's own internal documents "showed that the gun modifications had no effect on gun or needle performance" and that using non-Bard needles could not cause injuries to either patients or physicians.[271]

Courts reject proffered procompetitive justifications as pretextual not only when they are contradicted by the record, but also when they are not supported by evidence. For example, in *LePage's Inc. v. 3M*,[272] in which a jury held that 3M illegally monopolized the market for transparent tape by using bundled rebates, the defendant argued that the anticompetitive bundling was justified because its customers wanted single invoices and single shipments. The Third Circuit discounted 3M's proffered business justification because the defendant cited no testimony or other evidence that either single invoices or single shipments would create any actual economic efficiencies. Moreover, the court noted that it was "highly unlikely that 3M shipped transparent tape along with retail auto products or home improvement products ... or that, if it did, the savings stemming from the joint shipment approaches the millions of dollars 3M returned to customers in bundled rebates."[273]

Even if the proffered procompetitive justification is not pretextual, plaintiffs can defeat this defense by showing that "the anticompetitive harm of the conduct outweighs the procompetitive benefit."[274] Federal courts have not explained how exactly to perform this weighing. Plaintiffs can also rebut a legitimate business justification defense by showing that "a less restrictive alternative exists that achieves the same legitimate competitive benefits."[275] However, the Supreme Court in *Alston* stated that "antitrust law does not require businesses to use anything like the least restrictive means of achieving legitimate business purposes."[276] It is difficult to reconcile these two principles, and courts have not done so yet.

---

268. 157 F.3d 1340 (Fed. Cir. 1998), *supra* § 6.05[D].
269. *Id.* at 1382.
270. *Id.*
271. *Id.*
272. 324 F.3d 141 (3d Cir. 2003) (*en banc*).
273. *Id.* at 164.
274. *Microsoft Corp.*, 253 F.3d at 59.
275. *1-800 Contacts, Inc. v. Fed. Trade Comm'n*, 1 F.4th 102, 120–21 (2d Cir. 2021).
276. *NCAA v. Alston*, 594 U.S. 69, 98 (2021).

§ 6.08 Oligopoly and "Shared Monopoly"

Section 2 of the Sherman Act is designed to prevent anticompetitive behavior by a single firm. Section 1 concerns the behavior of more than one firm operating under an agreement. The net result is a gap in antitrust coverage for markets characterized by a few large competitors. These markets are called oligopolies. This oligopolistic market structure is not without consequence. Because of their high visibility to each other and their interdependence, the firms may charge supracompetitive prices and restrict output without an express agreement. Without an agreement, though, § 1 is not applicable. And, unless one of the firms approaches a monopoly market share and begins to act in a manner that is not "honestly industrial," § 2 likewise offers no protection for a plaintiff.

[A] Oligopolistic Behavior

The key to oligopolistic behavior[277] is the limited number of competitors and the interdependence it breeds. For instance, consider three airlines all serving the route from Chicago to St. Louis. Any one might consider lowering fares in order to gain a larger share of the market. It must contend, however, with the very real possibility that if it does decrease fares, its competitors will shortly follow suit. As a result, the firm will not increase its market share but, quite possibly, it may find that it has lower total revenue.[278] If it raises fares, competitors may or may not follow suit. If they do not, the firm will find itself losing ground and will have to return to the original fare in order to regain its position. On the other hand, the firms may follow the leadership of the airline initially increasing prices with the outcome being higher fares and lower output for the whole industry. As a result of this interdependence, fares are likely to be rigid. When they are not, the outcome will tend to be similar to what one would expect to find under conditions of monopoly. Yet this parallel behavior, which would seem to require some kind of agreement in a less concentrated industrial context, can be the product of independent reaction to market conditions.

[B] "Shared Monopoly"

As a result of this interdependence, oligopolistic industries are characterized by a lack of price competition and may be regarded as "shared" monopolies.[279] A range of approaches designed both to fill the gap between §§ 1 and 2 of the Sherman Act and

277. For a more detailed discussion, see *supra* Chapter 4.

278. The impact on sales and total revenue will be determined by the elasticity of demand for the entire "industry."

279. *See generally* George Hay, *Oligopoly, Shared Monopoly, and Antitrust Law*, 67 Cornell L. Rev. 439 (1982).

to respond to the problem of shared monopoly have evolved; however, almost all ultimately have proven unsuccessful. For the most part, these attempts to supplement the Sherman Act have been made by the Federal Trade Commission through application of § 5 of the Federal Trade Commission Act.[280]

Although all of the theories experimented with by the FTC examine both structure and conduct, there is a difference in emphasis. Those that are conduct oriented seem to respond to the problem presented by the § 1 requirement that an agreement exist. Efforts which emphasize structure on the other hand, can be viewed as attempts to supplement § 2 with the focus on market power possessed collectively by a small group of firms.

Cases in the former category are related to the general issue of when an agreement can be found and how closely § 1 comes to condemning consciously parallel behavior.[281] In *E.I. Du Pont de Nemours & Co. v. FTC*,[282] the Second Circuit considered an FTC order that Du Pont and Ethyl Corporation, dominant firms in the lead antiknock gasoline additive industry, had engaged in unfair business practices by pursuing practices that facilitated price parallelism at noncompetitive levels. The practices included (1) sales at delivered prices, (2) the giving of advance notice of price increases beyond that contractually provided for, and (3) the use of "most favored nation" clauses under which buyers were promised that they would not be charged a higher price than any other customer.[283] The Commission did not allege that the practices were adopted as the result of an agreement nor did it categorize the practices as predatory or deceitful. The theory was, in effect, that certain practices in a concentrated industry were "unfair" under § 5 because of the probable anticompetitive result. The practices amounted to consciously parallel adoption of practices that facilitated price uniformity or, as it has been labeled, "indirect collusion."[284]

The Second Circuit vacated the Commission's order, noting a lack of standards upon which competitors could depend as to what was acceptable and unacceptable conduct in oligopolistic markets.[285] It announced a general rule that "in the absence of proof of a violation of the antitrust laws or evidence of collusive, predatory, or exclusionary conduct, business practices are not 'unfair' in violation of § 5 unless those practices either have an anticompetitive purpose or cannot be supported by an independent legitimate reason."[286] The court found that the FTC's conclusion that the practices led to a lessening of competition was not supported by substantial evidence. Moreover, there was overwhelming evidence that the practices were adopted for legitimate independent business reasons. The decision comes very close to rendering the existence of an oligopolistic market structure inconsequential under § 5. Indeed,

280. 15 U.S.C. § 45 (1983).
281. *See supra* § 4.15[A][2][b].
282. 729 F.2d 128 (1984).
283. *Id.* at 133.
284. *See* Hay, *supra* note 279, at 468.
285. 729 F.2d at 138–39.
286. *Id.* at 140.

according to the court, "an oligopolistic market structure in which manufacturers engage in consciously parallel pricing" is indicative of a "condition, not a 'method.'"[287]

Undoubtedly, the Commission's most publicized effort at filling the gap between §§ 1 and 2 by way of an extension of § 2 was its prolonged attack on cereal manufacturers during the 1970s.[288] The four cereal manufacturers involved possessed a combined 90% market share and were charged with excluding entry by engaging in the following activities: brand proliferation, misleading advertising, controlling retail shelf space, and acquisition of competitors.[289] At least, initially, there was no claim that there was a horizontal agreement.[290] Instead, the focus was on a "shared monopoly," as opposed to a single-firm monopoly, that engaged in activity that was not competition on the merits. The requested remedy was divestiture and compulsory trademark licensing. The case was eventually dismissed by an administrative law judge.[291] Although it was noted that the Commission, in enforcing § 5 of the Federal Trade Commission Act, was not bound by the limits of § 2 of the Sherman Act, the Judge ruled that there was no showing of monopoly profits in the industry—a condition that would invite entry but for exclusionary conduct. Thus, the cereal manufacturers could not be regarded as responsible for the lack of entry.[292] Nor was there proof that the performance of the industry was consistent with what might be expected under monopoly conditions.[293]

Although the theory of shared monopoly was left alive in the cereal case, the outcome of that litigation read in light of the Second Circuit opinion in *Du Pont* suggests that the FTC's ability to plug the gap between §§ 1 and 2 of the Sherman Act is very limited. The difficulty of determining a workable remedy in such cases may underlie the reluctance to permit Commission expansion of § 5. If an agreement exists, it can be enjoined, as can predatory practices. When, however, the practice is not predatory and is essentially the result of interdependent behavior, the remedy would have to be one that precludes rational independent profit maximizing behavior. The suggestion has been made that an effective remedy may be to restructure the industry so that sufficient competitors exist to make oligopoly behavior difficult or impossible.[294] Of course, this too has efficiency implications if the industry is one in which substantial economics of scale cannot be enjoyed unless each firm serves a substantial share of the market.[295]

---

287. *Id.* at 139.

288. *In re Kellogg Co.*, 99 F.T.C. 8 (1982). *See generally* Paul Connuck, *"Shared Monopoly," "Conscious Parallelism" and an Approach to Oligopoly Under Section 5 of the FTC Act*, 9 Rut. Computer & Tech. L.J. 165 (1982).

289. 99 F.T.C. at 12–15.

290. *See* Connuck, *supra* note 288, at 205–06.

291. 99 F.T.C. at 269.

292. *Id.* at 267.

293. *Id.* at 258–61.

294. *See* II P. Areeda & D. Turner, *Antitrust Law* at 377–78.

295. There also have been attempts to employ the "shared monopoly" theory by private parties. *See Harkins Amusement Enterprises v. General Cinema*, 850 F.2d 477 (9th Cir. 1988). In addition, the term is used to denote an agreement. *See In re Tamoxifen Citrate Antitrust Litigation*, 429 F.3d 370 (2d Cir. 2005).

For decades there has been "a split in authority" on the issue of whether "an actual monopolization claim must be predicated on the market domination of a single defendant or single economic entity and cannot be established by combining the market power of multiple defendants."[296] Some courts have reasoned that "When two or more persons agree to monopolize, they have committed the offense of joint monopolization provided that they have jointly acquired monopoly power. Joint monopolization claims do not require that the Plaintiffs allege that each Defendant has at least fifty-percent market share."[297] On the other hand, "[t]he Second Circuit has stated that a shared monopoly theory may not support a monopolization or attempted monopolization claim under Section 2, and numerous district courts ... have repeatedly rejected the viability of a Section 2 conspiracy claim based on a shared monopoly theory."[298] It is fair to say that shared monopoly is not a widely accepted theory of antitrust liability.

§ 6.09 Conspiracy to Monopolize

Section 2 of the Sherman Act expressly prohibits combinations or conspiracies to monopolize. This infrequently invoked portion of § 2 duplicates a great deal of the behavior prohibited by § 1. In fact, in practice, it is commonly attached to a § 1 claim, making difficult an independent analysis of the elements of conspiracy to monopolize.[299] The Third Circuit has observed that "to the extent it bans *conspiracies* to monopolize, section 2 is largely superfluous, as conspiracies to monopolize will usually—if not always—run afoul of section 1's prohibition of conspiracies that unreasonably restrain trade."[300] When it is separately considered, it is clear that the essential elements of a conspiracy to monopolize are: "(1) the existence of a combination or conspiracy to monopolize; (2) an overt act in furtherance of the conspiracy; (3) the specific intent to monopolize; and (4) causal antitrust injury."[301] As with attempted monopolization, specific intent can either be shown through actual agreement or inferred from conduct.[302] It is the specific intent requirement that makes the offense harder to prove than a § 1 charge which does not require intent evidence.

---

296. *Morgenstern v. Wilson*, 29 F.3d 1291, 1295 n.2 (8th Cir. 1994).

297. *Stewart Glass & Mirror, Inc. v. U.S.A. Glas, Inc.*, 940 F. Supp. 1026, 1037 (E.D. Tex. 1996) (citation omitted).

298. *In re Zinc Antitrust Litig.*, 155 F. Supp. 3d 337, 382 (S.D.N.Y. 2016) (citations omitted).

299. *See* Daniel A. Crane, *Criminal Enforcement of Section 2 of The Sherman Act: An Empirical Assessment*, 84 Antitrust L.J. 753, 757 (2022) ("[T]here is no obvious reason to bring a separate Section 2 conspiracy to monopolize case if the same behavior is *per se* illegal under Section 1.").

300. *W. Penn Allegheny Health Sys., Inc. v. UPMC*, 627 F.3d 85, 110 n.7 (3d Cir. 2010).

301. *In re Nat'l Football League's Sunday Ticket Antitrust Litig.*, 933 F.3d 1136, 1159 (9th Cir. 2019) (quoting *Paladin Assocs., Inc. v. Mont. Power Co.*, 328 F.3d 1145, 1158 (9th Cir. 2003)).

302. *See, e.g.*, *American Tobacco Co. v. United States*, 328 U.S. 781 (1946); *International Distribution Centers v. Walsh Trucking Co.*, 812 F.2d 786 (2d Cir. 1987); *cf. Instructional Systems Development Corp. v. Aetna Casualty Surety Co.*, 817 F.2d 639 (10th Cir. 1987).

As a general matter, courts have not always agreed on the level of sophistication with respect to market definition when the claim is conspiracy to monopolize.[303] Because market analysis is now a pivotal part of most § 1 claims as well as § 2 claims, the standard should not vary. It may be that the Supreme Court's emphasis on market definition in *Spectrum Sports* in attempt cases will be extended to conspiracy cases as well. This was clearly the view taken by the Tenth Circuit in a recent decision.[304] The court noted that after *Spectrum Sports*, it could no longer apply a lenient standard with respect to market definition in § 2 conspiracy cases.[305] Moreover, this appears to be the majority position.[306] In any case, it is clear that plaintiffs claiming a conspiracy to monopolize, whether or not joined with a § 1 claim, should not be able to escape by careful pleading the burdens of § 1.

---

303. *See, e.g., Fraser v. Major League Soccer*, 284 F.3d 47 (1st Cir. 2002); *Levine v. Central Florida Medical Affiliates, Inc.*, 72 F.3d 1538 (11th Cir. 1996); *Intergraph Corp. v. Intel Corp.*, 195 F.3d 1346 (Fed. Cir. 1999). *See generally* P. Areeda & H. Hovenkamp, IIIA *Antitrust Law* 390 (2d ed. 2002); David Woods, *Hybrid Single Entities and the Market Power Requirement for Conspiracies to Monopolize Following Fraser: Are Courts Putting Form over Substance?* 2004 U. Ill. L. Rev. 1261 (2004).

304. *Auraria Student Housing at the Regency v. Campus Village Apartments*, 843 F.3d 1225 (10th Cir. 2016). *See also Buccaneer Energy (USA) Inc. v. Gunnison Energy Corp.*, 846 F.3d 1297, 1320 (10th Cir. 2017) ("[A] claim of conspiracy to monopolize under § 2, like a claim under § 1, requires proof of a relevant antitrust market.").

305. *Auraria Student Housing*, 843 F.3d at 1239.

306. Earl W. Kintner et al., *Federal Antitrust Law*, § 16.39 (2d ed. 2015).

Chapter 7
Mergers and Acquisitions

§ 7.01 Introduction

In order to expand business, reduce costs or increase market power, firms often seek to merge with or acquire other firms. Generally, mergers occur through either a stock or asset purchase of one firm by another. Mergers may threaten to substantially reduce competition, depending on the type of merger and the size and strength of the companies involved. The entire structure of an industry can be altered by a merger. Mergers are generally characterized as horizontal (between competitors), vertical (between a firm and its supplier or distributor), or conglomerate (between firms in unrelated markets). Each type of merger raises varying levels of antitrust concerns.

§ 7.02 Horizontal Mergers

Horizontal mergers involve firms selling the same or similar products in the same geographical market; these firms compete against each other directly. By merging, firms eliminate competition between themselves. Because of the direct impact on competition within a given market, horizontal mergers receive the most intense scrutiny.

On the other hand, horizontal mergers may serve useful economic purposes. They can result in joint operating efficiencies, economies of scale, and financial economies. Price reductions to consumers may follow. Courts must balance the beneficial effects of horizontal mergers against threats to competition created by the merger. They must determine how much of an effect the merger will have on competition within the defined market. To do this, courts must examine the market size and power of the firms involved and attempt to predict the consequence of the merger. Horizontal mergers can raise one of two anticompetitive risks: (1) unilateral effects: the resulting firm will have sufficient market power to enable the combined enterprise to act like a monopolist, or (2) concerted effects: the merger will result in a concentrated market that facilitates collusion among the remaining competitors. The test under § 7 of the Clayton Act is whether there is a reasonable probability the merger will reduce competition.[1]

1. It should be noted that the government through the FTC or the Department of Justice, a competitor to the firms proposing a merger, or the very firm targeted for merger can sue for a preliminary

§ 7.03 Non-Horizontal Mergers

Non-horizontal mergers do not present the same overt threat to competition. Although horizontal mergers directly remove one competitor from a market and increase the market share of the merged firm, non-horizontal mergers involve firms that do not compete directly with each other. Because the number of competitors within a given market remains the same, the direct, overt threat of monopoly or oligopolistic collusion apparent in horizontal mergers does not exist. However, non-horizontal mergers may restrain competition in other ways.

Traditionally, courts distinguish between two types of non-horizontal mergers: vertical and conglomerate. In reviewing non-horizontal mergers, courts consider whether the merger results in a loss of a potential competitor and the effect that will have on the market. In terms of anticompetitive consequences, non-horizontal mergers may create barriers to entry, facilitate collusion or make it possible to evade rate regulation. They may also create transaction cost efficiencies that lead to procompetitive effects. In determining the legality of proposed mergers, courts attempt to balance the harms and benefits of the merger and determine whether there may be a procompetitive effect or a lessening of competition.

[A] Vertical Mergers

Vertical mergers occur when one firm purchases either a customer or a supplier, with the result that the acquiring firm expands into a new market. When a concrete producer purchases a sand plant it then operates in two markets—sand and concrete production. Mergers may be upstream or downstream. Upstream mergers occur when a consumer acquires a supplier—the concrete company purchases the sand operation. Downstream mergers occur when the supplier acquires the purchaser—the sand company acquires the concrete firm.

By merging with a customer or supplier, a firm integrates different stages of the production process. On its face, this type of merger leaves competitive levels unchanged in each market.[2] To use the above example, both the concrete and sand markets have the same number of competitors as before, only the ownership has changed.

Competition may be affected in other ways by the vertical integration. Two firms in the distribution chain have now become one. Each is assured of a source of supply and demand for its production. The integration may produce advantages over nonintegrated firms, such as economies of scale, distribution efficiencies and reduced

injunction to prevent the merger. *See Anago, Inc. v. Tecnol Med. Prods., Inc.*, 976 F.2d 248 (5th Cir. 1992); *see also infra* § 7.10 on private enforcement of § 7. The firms must prove both standing and antitrust injury like any other antitrust plaintiff. 976 F.2d at 249–50.

2. *See generally Brown Shoe Co. v. United States*, 370 U.S. 294 (1962); *United States v. E.I. du Pont de Nemours & Co.*, 353 U.S. 586 (1957); Thomas W. Brunner, Thomas G. Krattenmaker, Robert A. Skitol & Ann Adams Webster, *Mergers in the New Antitrust Era* (1985).

transaction costs.[3] To remain competitive, the nonintegrated firms also may have to integrate.

Other, less obvious, secondary effects also may occur through vertical integration. One type of threat exists when the downstream firm has monopoly power and is rate regulated on a cost-plus basis. The regulated firm may use the acquisition of a supplier to spread its profits over several transactions. Instead of making all the profits on sales of concrete, a monopolist could transfer some of the profits to the sand company by purchasing at inflated prices. In rate regulated industries, this spreading of profits would look like increased costs incurred by the downstream firm. These increased costs could be presented to the rate-making authority to justify a higher rate. Vertical integration with supply sources for rate-regulated monopolists makes proper rate base computation more complex and allows the monopolist more opportunities to inflate costs.[4]

Vertical integration can result in what courts speak of as "foreclosure." This occurs when the patronage or custom of the acquired firm is no longer available to competitors of the acquiring firm. If the acquiring firm supplies the acquired firm, other suppliers may be deprived of the ability to sell to that firm. Similarly, if the acquiring firm purchases from the acquired firm, competitors of the acquiring firm will be deprived, to a greater or lesser degree, of the ability to obtain needed supplies from the acquired firm. Whether or not this actually occurs, and to what extent this harms consumers by increasing the monopoly power of the firm will be discussed in § 7.04, *infra*, on economic theory in mergers.

[B] Conglomerate Mergers

Conglomerate mergers are those in which the merging firms had no prior relationship. The firms may have been potential competitors, but they were not customers or suppliers of each other. "Pure" or "true" conglomerate mergers have no overt effect upon competition or market shares; they merely change the ownership of firms in the markets. We are, nevertheless, concerned with the effects of such a merger in concentrated markets.

Examples of conglomerate mergers include product market extension mergers, involving products closely identified with each other, and geographic market extensions. An example of the first includes when a manufacturer of detergents merges with a bleach producer. The second occurs when a bank in one market decides to enter and compete in another geographical market.[5]

---

3. *Paschall v. Kan. City Star Co.*, 727 F.2d 692 (8th Cir. 1984); *see also infra* § 7.04[B] (discussing vertical integration).

4. *See, e.g., Application of Montana-Dakota Utils. Co. for Auth. to Establish Increased Rates for Elec. Serv.*, 278 N.W.2d 189 (S.D. 1979).

5. *See generally FTC v. Procter & Gamble Co.*, 386 U.S. 568 (1965); *United States v. Cont'l Can Co.*, 378 U.S. 441 (1964); *United States v. El Paso Natural Gas Co.*, 376 U.S. 651 (1964).

Several theories have been used to challenge conglomerate mergers. Reciprocity and entrenchment are two of the traditional theories.[6] Reciprocity may occur when one firm agrees to purchase items from another firm that purchases from it. For example, a silicon chip manufacturer may purchase computers for its office use from a computer firm that purchases silicon chips from it. Courts have feared that certain conglomerate mergers would facilitate these types of actions. A merger between two firms may increase the reciprocal purchasing that exists between those two firms; neither may buy from outside competitors. Those competitors (suppliers) may be foreclosed from supplying products to the two firms. From an antitrust perspective, we are concerned with a firm using its size to influence suppliers or customers to deal with the newly acquired firm in a manner which actually exploits the firm size and structure. The mere possibility of exploitation alone is not enough to warrant a finding of an illegal merger but "a finding of probability of reciprocal buying . . . should [warrant a finding of illegality] if there is substantial evidence to support it."[7]

Another traditional theory used to condemn conglomerate mergers is based on entrenchment. If a firm acquires another firm that already has substantial market share, the resulting acquisition may permit the acquired firm's market position to be further entrenched and reinforce the position of the dominant firm. Generally, however, we are concerned, under this theory, only if a dominant firm in one market is purchased by a large firm in another market. Size alone may discourage competitors from expanding or it may create barriers to entry for new competitors.[8] Certain economies may result, however, because of the vast resources resulting from the merger such as volume discounts, or advertising incentives that permit lower pricing. Cost saving may be passed on to the customer, but other competitors may be injured by this increased competition.

[C] Loss of Potential Competitors

Another theory used to challenge mergers centers on diminished competition resulting from a loss of a potential competitor. Mergers involving potential competitors are acquisitions between firms that are not in competition with each other but which are "actual potential entrants" in the market of the other or "perceived" as such.

The potential competitor, but for the merger, would have entered the market through some less anticompetitive means than through the challenged merger. This model of analysis is applied to mergers in concentrated industries. Examples include "de novo" entry where entry is without an acquisition of an existing competitor and a "toehold" entry through purchase of a smaller competitor. At the least, the firm is perceived as a potential competitor—one that had the ability to enter the market and would have done so within a reasonable period of time. The argument is that entry

---

6. *See supra* § 5.02[B][6].
7. *FTC v. Consol. Foods Corp.*, 380 U.S. 592, 600 (1965).
8. *FTC v. Procter & Gamble Co.*, 386 U.S. 568, 579 (1967).

through these means, rather than by merger, would have resulted in a more deconcentrated, and hence, competitive market.[9]

The merger of a potential entrant may be anticompetitive because the potential entrant sitting on the sidelines of a market helps keep prices lower in that market in two ways. The firms in that market may believe that the potential competitor will enter the market if they raise prices. Thus, the existence of potential competition creates a restraining effect on prices. Additionally, even if the firms in that market do not believe the outside firm will enter, that firm may enter if the other companies raise their prices. Consequently, the new entrant will increase supply in the market and will help drive prices down.

Many cases that previously would have been decided under the conglomerate mergers theories of reciprocity or entrenchment are today viewed under the potential competitor doctrine.

§ 7.04 Economic Analysis of Mergers

[A] Horizontal Mergers

Horizontal mergers realign competitive relationships within markets. Firms that once competed with each other unite and operate as a single entity. The realignment can have substantial economic impact in the market. For example, it would have been illegal for the two firms to agree on price before a merger. After a merger, coordinated pricing is expected from unified management. The market power of the resulting firm will increase. Increased market power may result in enhanced economic efficiency or it may create a threat of predatory or oligopolistic pricing within the market, either through sheer size, market control, or by collusion between the combined firm and other firms within the market.

Market power is the ability to set price without a resulting decrease in sales that causes a net reduction in profits. A measure of market power is the ability to price above marginal costs. The antitrust concern is that as a firm's market power grows, prices will increase above competitive levels.

Economic benefits may result from horizontal mergers that increase efficiency. Several theories have been advanced in support of mergers. First, mergers permit the movement of assets from lower to higher-valued uses through increased efficiencies and redeployment of assets. Second, mergers serve as a means to replace or discipline ineffective and entrenched corporate management. Third, mergers can produce efficiencies through joint operating agreements, economies of scale, financial economies, and economies of scope. Finally, mergers can provide resource and service access for

9. *United States v. Marine Bancorporation, Inc.*, 418 U.S. 602 (1974); *FTC v. Procter & Gamble Co.*, 386 U.S. 568 (1967); *United States v. El Paso Natural Gas Co.*, 376 U.S. 651 (1964).

both the acquiring and acquired firms.[10] However, the amount of enhancement may be difficult to determine, even for a trained economist.

Restraints on competition, if they exist, are similar to those created by contractual agreements between competitors that result in cartels. The underlying theories against a liberal merger policy argue that mergers (1) force management to operate only on short-term goals and protect against hostile takeovers, thereby diverting management attention away from long-term goals such as technological change; (2) damage management and personnel morale; (3) misallocate financial resources of lending institutions, "crowding out" more productive investments; (4) increase concentration and market power; and (5) permit leveraging to finance the acquisition which increases the debt to equity ratio to unacceptable levels.[11] A reviewing court will attempt to balance the costs of a merger against its benefits and determine whether there is a reasonable probability of the merger creating a substantial lessening of competition.[12] Some scholarship demonstrates that the actual negative effects of mergers outweigh the theoretical benefits.[13]

[B] Vertical Integration Through Merger

Vertical integration usually occurs because a firm believes it can reduce costs by supplying itself a service or product.[14] A television manufacturer builds its own electronic components because it is cheaper than buying them from electronics suppliers. By supplying retail outlets itself, the manufacturer saves mark-up costs added by a wholesale distributor. When a supplier acquires a customer or potential customer, a forward vertical integration has occurred. When a customer acquires a supplier or potential supplier, a backward vertical integration occurs.[15]

---

10. Alan A. Fisher & Robert H. Lande, *Efficiency Consideration in Merger Enforcement*, 71 Calif. L. Rev. 1580, (1983); Alan A. Fisher, Robert H. Lande & Walter Vandaele, *Afterword: Could a Merger Lead to Both a Monopoly and a Lower Price?*, 71 Calif. L. Rev. 1697 (1983); Robert Pitofsky, *Proposals for Revised United States Merger Enforcement in a Global Economy*, 81 Geo. L.J. 195 (1992); E. Thomas Sullivan, *The Antitrust Division as a Regulatory Agency: An Enforcement Policy in Transition*, 64 Wash. U. L.Q. 997 (1986) and authorities cited therein; *see also* Oliver E. Williamson, *Economies as an Antitrust Defense: The Welfare Tradeoffs*, 58 Am. Econ. Rev. 18 (1968).

11. Sullivan, *supra* note 10.

12. For the economic theories outlining these costs and benefits *see* Ernest Gellhorn, *Antitrust Law and Economics in a Nutshell* 402–76 (5th ed. 2004); Herbert Hovenkamp, *Federal Antitrust Policy* ch. 12 (3d ed. 2005); F.M. Sherer & David Ross, *Industrial Market Structure and Economic Performance* (3d ed. 1990); Williamson, *supra* note 10.

13. See Chris Sagers, *Why Do Corporations Merge and Why Should Law Care?*, 56 U. Mich. J.L. Reform 291 (2023).

14. Oliver E. Williamson, *Markets and Hierarchies: Analysis and Antirust Implications* (1975); Oliver E. Williamson, *The Economic Institutions of Capitalism*, 15–41 (1985); Robert Bork, *Vertical Integration and the Sherman Act: The Legal History of An Economic Misconception*, 22 U. Chi. L. Rev. 157 (1954); Pablo T. Spiller, *On Vertical Mergers*, 1 J. L., Econ. & Org. 285 (1985); *see also supra* § 6.05[I].

15. 1995-2 Trade Reg. Rep. (CCH) ¶ 4330, 8097.

Efficiency is one of the expected by-products of vertical integration. Whether done through internal expansion or through the acquisition of an existing firm, a firm is not likely to expand unless there is a cost reduction to be gained; otherwise, it will be cheaper and more efficient to continue to purchase the product or service from outside suppliers. Cost reductions may occur through technological, transactional, or distributional efficiencies.

Technological efficiencies in the above example would result if the television manufacturer could have the electronic components built into the chassis of its sets. This would reduce the cost of placing and anchoring the components onto the chassis later. These efficiencies usually occur when a plant expands internally; the electronics plant operations would have to be added physically at some point on the chassis assembly line or the electronics components would still have to be manufactured and placed on the chassis in two different steps. Acquiring an existing firm will usually not result in technological efficiencies.

Vertical mergers that do not result in technological efficiencies can still result in transactional efficiencies—costs saved by avoiding contracting in the marketplace.[16] These costs saved are often more substantial than any technological savings. In the above example, the electronics producers include a profit in their prices. These profits represent a cost to the television manufacturer. The profit the electronics company makes does not go into the revenues of the television company, nor does it contribute to the quality of electronics supplies available to the television company. By making its own electronic components, the television company can take the money saved by avoiding a contract with the electronics firms and either improve the quality of its product, or redeploy the savings elsewhere.

Firms can obtain other transactional cost savings through vertical mergers. State and federal governments may require recordkeeping and payment of taxes for products purchased from other firms. Internal records must be kept of sales or purchases. By incorporating these other levels into its operations, a firm reduces the tax payments, the tax accounting costs and many of the internal accounting costs that result from outside purchases.

Finally, mergers may result in transactional cost savings in one other very significant area—market use costs. When purchasing products on the open market, a firm must expend time and effort obtaining information about, and negotiating with, other firms. Negotiating a contract with another firm involves time and risks that must be included in a firm's costs. One firm wants to produce the least expensive product that another firm will accept at the highest possible price. The other wants the best product at the lowest possible price. Arriving at a compromise between these two conflicting interests involves the costs of transacting. There is also the risk that one or the other may be taken advantage of in the negotiations because of superior bargaining skills or position.

---

16. *See generally* Williamson, *supra* note 14, at 85–130.

Furthermore, firms want to deal with reliable entities; they want to be assured of adequate future supplies or markets for their products. Obtaining financial information about another firm always involves some risk; no one can be certain of the reliability of another firm's financial records. Checking the information increases costs and may not yield correct predictions. The risk created by dealing with other firms must figure into a firm's cost analysis.

Even after a firm begins to deal with another firm, negotiation and information costs can continue to increase. As technology and markets change, the firms involved in the original contract may wish for revisions of the product. Using the previous television manufacturer example, an improved screen display may become available. This display may require higher electrical charges to function efficiently. The television manufacturer may be locked into a contract for electronics that supply lower level electrical charges. Changing the contract specifications will involve additional negotiation costs. For a manufacturer that owned its own electronics plant, an immediate change of electronic specifications may be less costly.

In the past, courts often condemned vertical mergers because increased efficiencies can be used to increase market power. Increases in market power allow firms to charge monopoly prices, to foreclose other rivals by restricting their source of supply, or to erect barriers to entry in either or both levels of the market.

Economists have attacked these theories on several grounds. They point out that increased efficiency most often results in benefits to the consumer. Even a monopolist may decrease prices and increase supply when its costs are reduced.[17]

Economists also point out that in even modestly competitive markets, vertical acquisitions do not foreclose transactions. Unless both firms involved have substantial market power and the ability to expand production, or supply, a certain amount of readjustment takes place. If a manufacturer has 10% of the market and merges with a purchaser taking 50% of the manufactured market, the purchaser will still need to purchase 40% of its supply from others. Even if the manufacturer originally sold nothing to the purchaser, the 10% it now sells to the purchaser will no longer be available to other purchasers. Unless the manufacturer can significantly expand production, those other purchasers will go to other manufacturers for their supply. Thus, foreclosure in this type of transaction is nominal.

Vertical integration can be anticompetitive in some instances. It may facilitate price discrimination, an activity condemned by § 2 of the Clayton Act.[18] Usually, firms must charge approximately the same price to all purchasers. Otherwise, arbitrage takes place: purchasers that buy cheaply sell to other purchasers at a price between what the first purchasers paid and what the other purchasers have to pay. A manufacturer may circumvent arbitrage through a vertical merger in which it can then segregate different types of buyers. The television manufacturer may sell its products to retail firms for $50. However, a manufacturer of entertainment consoles may be able to include

---

17. *But see* Fisher, Lande & Vandaele, *supra* note 10.

18. See Chapter 8.

the television in the console and sell it for a price that would permit it to pay $100 for the television. If the television manufacturer begins to charge $100 to the manufacturer of the entertainment consoles, the latter will substitute suppliers and will be supplied by other purchasers of the TV at a price between $50 and $100. A merged television manufacturer and entertainment console manufacturer could segregate buyers and thereby pass on $100 for the cost of the television to purchasers of entertainment consoles and continue to charge $50 to retail firms. Thus, the merged firm would not lose sales to the entertainment console manufacturer by arbitrage sellers.

Not all price discrimination is necessarily bad. If the television manufacturer determined that its profit-maximizing price before the merger encouraged selling to the entertainment console manufacturer at $100, it would make as many, albeit few, sales as it could get in the retail market at the $100 price. As a merged firm, the television manufacturer may then be able to maximize profits by selling to retail stores at $50 and by getting $100 for televisions sold to the entertainment console manufacturer. This would increase supply and decrease price to the consumer.

Vertical integration also may foreclose competition in either the supply or the customer markets. It also may erect barriers to entry that chill incentives for potential competitors to enter the market, and it may serve as a device to evade a regulatory scheme. Finally, although an entity is not forbidden under § 7 from making a series of small vertical acquisitions, if the combination of the acquisitions becomes large enough to have an adverse effect on trade, a violation may occur.[19] A large collection, or pattern, of independent vertical integrations over time can have the same effect as a single trade-restraining merger in some cases.[20]

§ 7.05 Legal Analysis of § 7: An Overview

Section 7 of the Clayton Act proscribes mergers or acquisitions that have a reasonable probability of substantially lessening competition within a market.[21] This standard allows courts to invalidate mergers only if they threaten to reduce competition in a market by a substantial amount.

In interpreting this standard, courts must estimate what effect a merger will have on competition within the affected market. To accomplish this, courts first determine the relevant market and then estimate the effect the merger will have on that market. In making the first determination, courts must define both the geographical and the product markets.

---

19. *Chateau De Ville Prod., Inc. v. Tams-Witmark Music Library, Inc.*, 586 F.2d 962 (2d Cir. 1978).
20. *Id.*
21. 15 U.S.C. § 18 (2011).

[A] Product Market

Courts must first determine the relevant product market.[22] The relevant product market is the smallest market where the hypothetical monopolist having all the total production of that product could increase price but not lose enough customers to decrease profits. In other words, the product market must be large enough to include all the effective substitutes that buyers would turn to should price increase. "Where an increase in the price of one product leads to an increase in demand for another product, both products should be included in the relevant product market."[23] This is a thin distinction. Products need not be fungible in order to be part of the same product market, but a minute increase in demand in response to a product's increase in price does not necessarily place the goods in the same product market.[24] As the court found in *United States v. Bethlehem Steel*,[25] distinct products like iron and steel can be part of the same relevant market when sold in a market that is recognized and has its own competitive standards.

The relevant product market, for example, defined for television sets, would be larger than the market for a certain brand or even a certain type. If price increased for these brands or types, the consumer may switch to others. If the quantity demanded in a product is affected by price changes of other products, then the two are defined within the same product market. The relevant market may even be larger than plasma or LED televisions; if plasma television prices increased, consumers may substitute LED. The market would not probably include other electronic entertainment devices; radios, for instance, may not be viewed by customers as an adequate substitute for televisions. However, if consumers did substitute or if radio manufacturers could cheaply and easily switch their plants to television production in response to a price change in televisions, then a court might include the production capabilities of radio manufacturers in the relevant product market for televisions.

Finally, courts have held that, in some situations, when the product is truly unique and without adequate substitution, a single product brand can constitute the entire relevant product market.[26] Also, products and their parts do not need to be peculiar to a market in order to be part of it.[27] Thus, even generic products may have enough similarity with the product in question to be "reasonably interchangeable" with it.[28]

---

22. *See generally United States v. E.I. du Pont de Nemours & Co.*, 351 U.S. 377 (1956).
23. *Olin Corp. v. FTC*, 986 F.2d 1295, 1298 (9th Cir. 1993).
24. *Id.* at 1299.
25. 168 F. Supp. 579 (S.D.N.Y. 1958).
26. *See Tarrant Serv. Agency, Inc. v. Am. Standard, Inc.*, 12 F.3d 609, 614 (6th Cir. 1993).
27. *Id.*
28. *Id.*

[B] Geographic Market

The size of the relevant geographic market depends on the type of product sold and the capabilities of firms selling that product. The geographic market includes the area that consumers will look to when satisfying a consumption need: If St. Louis consumers shopping for televisions look as far as Chicago to satisfy their needs, then Chicago must be included within the geographic market for televisions sold in the St. Louis area.[29] Likewise, if Chicago suppliers would increase or decrease production because of prices in St. Louis then the geographic market is the same.[30] "The proper definition of a geographic market is determined by a 'factual inquiry into the "commercial realities" faced by consumers.'"[31] Presenting evidence concerning only the individual perspectives of certain competitors will not be sufficient in defining the relevant geographic market.[32] Similarly, evidence concerning the present-day habits of consumers of the product or service at hand alone will not suffice to detail the parameters of the market.[33] The main concern is the practicable alternatives of which the consumer is aware.

The relevant geographical area can include distant supply points. If a manufacturer in Los Angeles can supply easily and cheaply the needs of consumers in St. Louis, then Los Angeles becomes an extension of the St. Louis geographic market, even though consumers in St. Louis would not look to Los Angeles to shop for their needs. The price of the product relative to transportation and other market costs significantly affects the supply accessibility to markets. The cheaper the relative costs of selling the product in St. Louis, the more likely Los Angeles manufacturers are to ship that product to St. Louis. Conversely, as the cost of shipping the product to St. Louis rises above what St. Louis manufacturers sell the product for, the more likely it is that the Los Angeles manufacturers will not enter or continue in the St. Louis market.

A study of the marginal, relative movements of firms in two geographical locations often helps determine whether the two are in the same geographical market.

[C] Market Power

Once the relevant markets, both product and geographic, have been established, courts examine the percentage of the market, or market shares, controlled by the merging firms. Market share is used frequently as a proxy for market power. Price elasticity of demand and cross-elasticity of demand are also measures of market power. Depending on the relevant product market, other factors also may serve as evidence of market power.

---

29. *See generally United States v. Grinnell Corp.*, 384 U.S. 563 (1966).

30. *See generally United States v. Columbia Steel*, 334 U.S. 495 (1948); *Twin City Sportservice Inc. v. Charles O. Finley & Co.*, 512 F.2d 1264 (9th Cir. 1975).

31. *Bathke v. Casey's Gen. Stores, Inc.*, 64 F.3d 340, 345 (8th Cir. 1995) (citations omitted).

32. *Id.*

33. *Id.*

The purpose of antitrust merger law is to deter monopoly and oligopolistic pricing and conditions that facilitate collusion. High concentration of market share in the hands of a single dominant firm or a few competitors threaten competitive pricing. Courts, therefore, look to the market shares of the merging firms and to the market as a whole. Traditionally, courts used a four-firm concentration ratio to measure market concentration. Under this approach, courts added the shares of the four top competitors in the market. If those firms respectively held 25%, 20%, 15% and 10% of the market, then the concentration ratio was 70%. This would be considered a highly concentrated market, and any merger in that market would fall under close scrutiny.

The original Department of Justice *Merger Guidelines* issued in 1968 considered mergers of two firms with 4% market shares each presumptively illegal in concentrated markets. In less concentrated markets, the shares had to be at least 5% each. Either standard was more lenient than the previous case law suggested. The *Guidelines* were an attempt to identify mergers which would alter market structure towards noncompetitive conduct.[34]

The 1982, 1984, 1992, 2010, and 2023 *Guidelines* abandoned the use of this traditional four-firm concentration analysis. The *Guidelines* instead use the Herfindahl-Hirschman Index (HHI) to determine market concentration. Under the HHI, market concentration equals the sum of the squares of the market percentage of every firm in the market. The HHI analysis is explained *infra*, § 7.09[C].

§ 7.06 Mergers Under the Sherman Act: The Early Years

The history of law governing mergers begins with the railroad merger cases in the early 1900s. In applying the Sherman Act, the Supreme Court originally held that all mergers between competitors violated the law. The Court in *Northern Securities Co. v. United States*[35] reasoned that every time competing firms combined, they lessened competition by eliminating competition between the merging firms.[36] These results bespoke of a rigid test that would condemn any merger and indeed there seemed to be a significant decrease in merger activity after the 1904 decision.[37] In the 1911

34. *U.S. Department of Justice Merger Guidelines*, 2 Trade Reg. Rep. (CCH) 4510 (May 30, 1968); *see U.S. v. Pabst Brewing Co.*, 384 U.S. 546 (1966). The 1968 *Merger Guidelines* employed the four-firm concentration ratio, while the 1982, 1984, 1992, and 2010 *Guidelines* examine the entire market share distribution for all firms. *See generally* Neil B. Cohen & Charles A. Sullivan, *The Herfindahl-Hirschman Index and the New Antitrust Merger Guidelines: Concentrating on Concentration*, 62 Tex. L. Rev. 453 (1983); John E. Kwoka, Jr., *The Effect of Market Share Distribution on Industry Performance*, 61 Rev. Econ. & Stat. 101 (1979).

35. 193 U.S. 197 (1904). This approach was similar to that of *Trans Missouri*, discussed *supra*, ch. 1, 4.

36. *Id.* at 327.

37. *See* Sullivan, *supra* note 10. *See generally* 221 U.S. 1 (1911).

decision of *Standard Oil Co. v. United States*,[38] the Court struck down a merger under the Sherman Act because the merger resulted in a monopoly in violation of § 2. But in *Standard Oil* the Court announced a broad rule of reason approach, which suggested the approval of some mergers.

In *United States v. United States Steel Corp.*,[39] the Court upheld a merger that resulted in a post-merger firm controlling at least 80% of the market, even after finding that the merger occurred with the intent to gain monopoly control of the steel industry. Unless a merger actually resulted in monopoly control, the Court seemed willing to permit it. In *United States v. Columbia Steel Co.*,[40] the Court allowed a merger that brought control of approximately one-quarter of the steel fabrication market into one firm. The Court held that a large market share in and of itself does not constitute unreasonable restraint. Instead, the Court looked to characteristics of the market, including the strength of remaining competition, consumer demands, development in the industry, and most importantly, whether the merger resulted from an intent to monopolize or from business requirements. After these cases, it seemed that the Sherman Act would prevent mergers only where the firms actually intended to, and did, accomplish a monopoly. Congress responded to the Court's permissive treatment in *Standard Oil* with new legislation.

§ 7.07 The Clayton Act

In 1914, Congress passed § 7 of the Clayton Act in response to the rule of reason standard used by the Supreme Court in *Standard Oil*. The original § 7 was easily circumvented, though, as many believed that it applied only to stock purchases. If a company acquired the assets of another company rather than its stock, the merger was still tested under the more lenient rule of reason under the Sherman Act.[41]

Furthermore, the Clayton Act only applied to mergers that lessened competition between competing firms. It failed to reach vertical mergers or other non-horizontal mergers when the merging firms were not in competition with each other. Even if the merger lessened competition between the post-merger firm and other businesses in the market, the Clayton Act did not apply.[42]

Concerned with the rising tide of industrial concentration and pushed by a 1948 Federal Trade Commission report concluding that giant corporations were taking

38. 221 U.S. 1 (1911).

39. 251 U.S. 417, 451 (1920) ("[T]he law does not make mere size an offence or the existence of unexerted power an offence.").

40. 334 U.S. 495 (1948).

41. *See, e.g.*, *FTC v. W. Meat Co.*, 272 U.S. 554 (1926).

42. "Lessening of competition" has been defined broadly to mean having "an effect on competition [which is] injurious to the public." 1995-2 Trade Cas. (CCH) ¶ 4270, 7965. In proving such an effect on competition, it is not necessary to prove intent on the part of the acquiring company or individual. *Id.* at 7966.

over the country,[43] Congress amended § 7 in 1950 with the Celler-Kefauver Act. The legislative history illustrates that Congress was concerned that large corporations would drive smaller competitors out of the market through predatory conduct, as well as with the threat of monopolistic or oligopolistic pricing. Controlling increased business concentration was the focus of the Act. Congress favored local control over markets and protection for small businesses.[44] The Celler-Kefauver amendments to § 7 were designed to reach both horizontal and vertical acquisitions, to cover mergers in their incipiency when there was a tendency toward a monopoly, and to allow courts to enjoin mergers with only a showing of a reasonable probability of anticompetitive effects.[45]

The first case to embrace the expanded coverage of § 7 was *United States v. E.I. du Pont de Nemours & Co.*,[46] even though it was decided under the original § 7. DuPont sold fabrics and paint to automobile manufacturers. In *Du Pont*, the Court held that stock acquisitions by Du Pont of 23% of General Motors stock before 1920 had an anticompetitive effect because the merger had the reasonable probability of foreclosing other sellers of automobiles (competitors of General Motors) from dealing with Du Pont and foreclosing Du Pont from selling fabrics and paints to General Motors' competitors. Plaintiff was not required to show an actual restraint as long as there was a reasonable probability of a substantial lessening of competition.

Interestingly, the behavior challenged in *Du Pont* occurred in 1918–1920, but the suit was not brought until 1949. As explained in *United States v. ITT Continental Baking Company*,[47] the Court in *Du Pont* interpreted the words "acquire" and "acquisition" to encompass more than just the original shifting of control of the entity. Rather,

> the Court held that there is a violation "any time when the acquisition threatens to ripen into a prohibited effect. . . ." To accomplish the congressional

---

43. FTC, *Report on the Merger Movement: A Summary Report* 68 (1948) (noting that "all forms of economic activity have come under the domination of the Big Four, the Big Six, or in some cases, the leader").

44. *Brown Shoe Co. v. United States*, 370 U.S. 294, 311–18 (1962); *United States v. E.I. du Pont de Nemours & Co.*, 353 U.S. 586 (1957); *see also* Derek C. Bok, *Section 7 of the Clayton Act and the Merging of Law and Economics*, 74 Harv. L. Rev. 226, 233–38 (1960); Alan A. Fisher & Robert H. Lande, *Efficiency Considerations in Merger Enforcement*, 71 Calif. L. Rev. 1580 (1983); Herbert Hovenkamp, *Antitrust Policy After Chicago*, 84 Mich. L. Rev. 213, 249–50 (1985); Robert H. Lande, *Wealth Transfers as the Original and Primary Concern of Antitrust: The Efficiency Interpretation Challenged*, 34 Hastings L.J. 65 (1982).

45. *Brown Shoe Co.*, 370 U.S. at 311–18; *see also United States v. E.I. du Pont de Nemours & Co.*, 351 U.S. 377 (1956).

46. 353 U.S. 586 (1957).

47. 420 U.S. 223, 241 (1975). The first paragraph of 15 U.S.C. § 18 (2006) provides:

> No corporation engaged in commerce shall acquire, directly or indirectly, the whole or any part of the stock or other share capital and no corporation subject to the jurisdiction of the Federal Trade Commission shall acquire the whole or any part of the assets of another corporation engaged also in commerce, where in any line of commerce in any section of the country, the effect of such acquisition may be substantially to lessen competition, or to tend to create a monopoly.

> aim, the Government may proceed at any time that an acquisition may be said with reasonable probability to contain a threat that it may lead to a restraint of commerce or tend to create a monopoly of a line of commerce.[48]

Thus, there can be a violation at some time later even if there was clearly no violation—no realistic threat of restraint of commerce or creation of a monopoly—at the time of the initial acts of acquisition. Clearly, this result can obtain only because "acquisition" under § 7 is not a discrete transaction but a status which continues until the transaction is undone.[49]

[A] Vertical Integration Through Merger

A firm may expand business into new markets by new (*de novo*) entry or through acquisition of an existing firm. The latter is known as vertical integration through merger. It occurs when two firms stand in a buyer-seller relationship. In *United States v. Yellow Cab*,[50] the Supreme Court focused upon the intent of the acquiring firm as well as the anticompetitive effects of foreclosure. The Court held that a civil complaint charging monopolization under § 2 of the Sherman Act should not have been dismissed because defendants were charged with both the intent to restrain interstate commerce and with effectuating that intent. The Court rejected defendant's contention that their common ownership prevented application of the Sherman Act.

In *Yellow Cab*, Checker Cab, a manufacturer of cabs, had acquired several cab companies in several cities. The acquisitions resulted in control of a large portion of the taxicab services available in these cities, including 80% of the market in Chicago. The Court held that if anticompetitive intent could be shown, the acquisition violated the Sherman Act. "[A] conspiracy among those who are affiliated or integrated under common ownership"[51] may violate the Sherman Act if the underlying intent was to foreclose competition.

The acquisition of the cab companies by Checker Cab meant that the cab companies might be forced to purchase their cabs solely from Checker Cab. Competition would be unreasonably affected because other cab suppliers would be "foreclosed" from selling to those cab operators controlled by Checker. Cab companies may have to pay more for the cabs than they would in a competitive market. Higher costs to cab companies would result in higher prices to consumers. The Court concluded that:

---

48. 420 U.S. at 242 (quoting *Du Pont*, 353 U.S. at 597).

49. *Id.*

50. 332 U.S. 218 (1947).

51. *Id.* at 227. The complaint allegations in *Yellow Cab* were summarized by the Court in *United States v. Columbia Steel Co.* as follows: "there was a plan, an intent, to monopolize the cab business, from manufacture through operation in the four large cities, by acquiring cab operating companies or interests therein; tying those companies into a cab manufacturing company and requiring the operating companies to purchase their cabs from the manufacturer at a price above the prevailing market." 334 U.S. 495, 521 (1948).

> The fact that these restraints occur in . . . a vertically integrated enterprise does not necessarily remove the ban of the Sherman Act. . . . [A] restraint may result as readily from a conspiracy among those who are affiliated or integrated under common ownership as from a conspiracy among those who are otherwise independent. . . . [A]ny affiliation or integration flowing from an illegal conspiracy cannot insulate the conspirators from the sanctions which Congress has imposed.[52]

The Court's analysis has been challenged on the grounds that a vertically integrated firm cannot profit by selling to itself at an inflated price; the selling division's profits would be offset by the purchasing division's losses.[53] More likely is the result that the vertical integration will lead to a reduction of the costs of transacting in the market, thereby permitting cost savings to be passed on to the consumer.

Other market factors are relevant. If a manufacturer has a large captive source of sales, which provide sufficient profits, that manufacturer may not be inclined to spend the same amount of research and development money to improve cabs or lower the price. In the case of cab operating companies, the market was limited by local regulation.[54] With Checker Cab controlling so much of the market in major cities, there was little incentive for other cab manufacturers to spend money in research and development or to lower cab prices. Checker effectively became a price leader in the cab manufacturing market by controlling such a large share of the cab purchasing market. The foreclosure theory espoused in *Yellow Cab* has continued, but not without significant challenge.

In another case predating the 1950 amendments to the Clayton Act, the Court, in applying the Sherman Act, permitted a merger between a large steel supplier and a large steel fabricator. In *United States v. Columbia Steel Co.*,[55] the Court ruled that an asset merger of the purchaser, U.S. Steel, and supplier, Consolidated Steel, did not restrict the market opportunities of other steel suppliers. The *Columbia Steel* Court interpreted *Yellow Cab* as requiring a showing of an unlawful intent to monopolize or a substantial effect on the market in order to sustain a Sherman Act violation.

The Court implied that if a merger results in less than a monopoly it is lawful under the Sherman Act, absent illegal intent. It found that the government failed to make this showing. "A subsidiary will in all probability deal only with its parent for goods the parent can furnish. That fact, however, does not make the acquisition invalid. . . .[56]

---

52. 332 U.S. at 227. *But see Copperweld Corp. v. Independence Tube Corp.*, 467 U.S. 752 (1984) (holding that a parent and a wholly owned subsidiary are legally incapable of violating § 1 of the Sherman Act). *See* § 4.15[C].

53. Hovenkamp, *supra* note 12; Bork, *supra* note 14, at 195–201.

54. Edmund W. Kitch, Marc Isaacson & Daniel Kasper, *The Regulation of Taxicabs in Chicago*, 14 J.L. & Econ. 285, 327 (1971).

55. 334 U.S. 495 (1948). At the time *Yellow Cab* and *Columbia Steel* were decided, courts believed that § 7 of the Clayton Act did not apply to either vertical mergers or asset acquisitions.

56. *Id.* at 523.

The Court concluded that Consolidated's purchases of rolled steel products only accounted for 3% of the relevant product market. The merger produced one firm with a steel fabrication market share of 24% This did not foreclose a great enough percentage of the market to have a substantial effect on competition; 97% of the rolled steel products market was still available to other steel suppliers.

In *United States v. E.I. du Pont de Nemours & Co.*,[57] the Supreme Court returned to the "foreclosure theory" of *Yellow Cab* and found a violation under the Clayton Act. Du Pont's purchases of 23% of General Motors' stock prior to 1920 were sufficient to support the violation. It was the first time the Supreme Court applied § 7 of the Clayton Act to a vertical merger.

In *Du Pont*, the Court went much further than in *Yellow Cab*. No actual monopoly existed in *Du Pont*. As a matter of fact, General Motors still purchased paint and fabrics from other suppliers when those suppliers were the low bidder. Nonetheless, the Court concentrated on the percentage of the market affected by the purchase of Du Pont products by General Motors. The relevant product market was determined as automotive paint finishes and fabrics, despite a showing that other non-automotive finishes were interchangeable with automotive finishes.

In this limited market, Du Pont's sales to General Motors were seen as foreclosing other suppliers of automotive finishes. Du Pont supplied approximately 67% of General Motors paint finishes. Because General Motors controlled such a large share of the automotive market, approximately one-half, this foreclosed 33% of automotive finish sales from other suppliers.

In *Du Pont*, the Court noted that the two required elements of § 7 had been established: (1) The market affected was substantial, and (2) competition would be foreclosed in a substantial share of the relevant market. The automotive fabric and finish markets both were found to be substantial and were substantially affected by General Motors' and Du Pont's market shares. The resulting foreclosure, the Court concluded, also was substantial. The Court held that the standard under § 7 was whether, because of the acquisition, there was a reasonable probability of a substantial lessening of competition or the reasonable likelihood of foreclosure of a substantial share of the market. This "reasonable probability" standard connoted the liberal approach of § 7—to arrest restraints in their "incipiency."

The Court went even further in the first case decided under the 1950 amendments to the Clayton Act. In *Brown Shoe Co. v. United States*,[58] a vertical integration case, the Court invalidated an acquisition of a shoe retailer by a shoe manufacturer when the retailer controlled only 5% of its market and the manufacturer controlled only 1%. Even though the shoe market was unconcentrated and neither party to the merger controlled a substantial share, the Court noted a trend toward acquisitions of retailers by shoe manufacturers with certain manufacturers supplying increasingly large

57. 353 U.S. 586 (1957).
58. 370 U.S. 294 (1962).

percentages of the captive retailers' needs.[59] Other manufacturers were foreclosed from supplying these captive retailers, the Court opined. It relied upon the expressed intent of §7 to halt market concentration in the early stages and the absence of any business justification for the merger. The Court seemed most concerned with the fact that this was a merger between the fourth largest manufacturer and the eighth largest retailer. Said the Court: "Congress was desirous of preventing the formation of further oligopolies with their attendant adverse effects upon local control of industry and upon small business."[60]

Despite *Brown Shoe*, in the following decades, courts often approved vertical integration, largely on the theory that although vertical integration may hurt other competitors, its efficiency-enhancing potential will be a direct benefit to consumers through the pass-on of the cost-savings.[61] This trend continued in 2018 with the district court for the District of Columbia ruling against the Department of Justice in *United States v. AT&T Inc.*[62] AT&T, a content distributor, and Time Warner, a content creator, argued that a merger was necessary in order to remain competitive with already vertically integrated companies such as Netflix, Hulu, and Amazon.[63] "Watching vertically integrated, data-informed entities thrive as television subscriptions and advertising revenues declined," AT&T and Time Warner realized that neither would survive independently.[64]

The government acknowledged that the vertical merger could save AT&T customers hundreds of millions of dollars annually and that, "unlike in horizontal mergers, no competitor will be eliminated by the merger's proposed vertical integration."[65] Nonetheless, the government sought to enjoin the merger based on a fear the merger

---

59. Others have found contrary evidence. *See* John L. Peterman, *The Federal Trade Commission v. Brown Shoe Company*, 18 J.L. & Econ. 361 (1975). For a discussion of the possible similarities between the industry in *Brown Shoe* and assorted vertical mergers in the entertainment industry, see Patrick M. Cox, *What Goes Up Must Come Down: Grounding the Dizzying Height of Vertical Mergers in the Entertainment Industry*, 25 Hofstra L. Rev. 261 (1996). Cox opines that inquiries into the "real motivations behind the proposed mergers" and "concern regarding motivations and trends in the industry" are potentially successful lines of attack against some vertical mergers in the entertainment field. *Id.* at 309–10, 312.

60. 370 U.S. at 333; *see also Ford Motor Co. v. United States*, 405 U.S. 562 (1972) (condemning Ford's acquisition of a manufacturer of spark plugs).

61. *See, e.g., Paschall v. Kansas City Star Co.*, 727 F.2d 692 (8th Cir. 1984); *see also Port Dock & Stone Corp. v. Oldcastle Ne., Inc.*, 507 F.3d 117, 124 (2d Cir. 2007) ("[W]hen a monopolist has acquired its monopoly at one level of a product market, its vertical expansion . . . will ordinarily be for the purpose of increasing its efficiency, which is a prototypical valid business purpose [and therefore not a violation of section 2 of the Sherman Act]."). *But see Ash Grove Cement Co. v. FTC*, 577 F.2d 1368 (9th Cir. 1978). Some of the specific efficiencies associated with vertical mergers include design and production coordination and the internalization of incentives for each merger partner to help the other and forego free-riding opportunities. *See* Michael H. Riordan & Steven C. Salop, *Evaluating Vertical Mergers: A Post-Chicago Approach*, 63 Antitrust L.J. 513, 523–25 (1995).

62. 310 F. Supp. 3d 161 (D.D.C. 2018).

63. *Id.* at 164.

64. *Id.*

65. *Id.*

would lessen competition in the video programming and distribution market and lead to higher prices for Time Warner customers.[66]

The district court found the Government's claims that, once vertically integrated, AT&T and Time Warner would dominate their field to such an extent that competitors would be discouraged from entering to be "overly speculative."[67] After emphasizing that the government had the burden of proof to show "the merger was likely to lessen competition substantially," the court decided that none of the government's arguments met this burden.[68] Agreeing with the defendants that the potential benefits to consumers outweighed the potential harms, the court approved the merger.

The D. C. Circuit affirmed.[69] The appellate court noted that for vertical mergers, "unlike horizontal mergers, the government cannot use a shortcut to establish a presumption of anticompetitive effect through statistics about the change in market concentration, because vertical mergers produce no immediate change in the relevant market share."[70] Thus, there is no change in the HHI, which for horizonal mergers can signal that the merger would lead to an overly concentrated market. Consequently, "the government must make a 'fact-specific' showing that the proposed merger is 'likely to be anticompetitive.'"[71] If the government can make this showing, it has established its prima facie case, and "the burden shifts to the defendant to present evidence that the *prima facie* case 'inaccurately predicts the relevant transaction's probable effect on future competition,' or to 'sufficiently discredit' the evidence underlying the *prima facie* case."[72] The burden then shifts back to the government to produce "additional evidence of anticompetitive effects."[73] Under this burden-shifting framework, the D.C. Circuit held that the district court had not clearly erred when it found that the government failed to meet its burden of proof.

So, while some courts remain troubled by issues of entry barriers and foreclosure,[74] courts are most often focusing their analysis of vertical mergers on: (1) whether competitors of the supplier or the buyer will be foreclosed from the market; (2) whether there is a trend towards vertical integration in the market; (3) whether there is an intent to foreclose competition; and (4) whether barriers to entry are erected that foreclose equal access to markets.

66. *Id.*
67. *Id.* at 245.
68. *Id.* at 165.
69. *United States v. AT&T, Inc.*, 916 F.3d 1029, 1032 (D.C. Cir. 2019).
70. *Id.* at 1032.
71. *Id.*
72. *Id.* (citations omitted).
73. *Id.*
74. Information exchange and regulation evasion are also of concern. *See* Riordan & Salop, *supra* note 61.

[B] Horizontal Mergers

As noted previously, horizontal merger law first developed under the Sherman Act. Originally, in *Northern Securities Co. v. United States*, the Supreme Court implied that all mergers between competitors may violate § 1 when it stated that the Sherman "[A]ct is not limited to restraints of interstate and international trade or commerce that are unreasonable in their nature, but embraces *all* direct *restraints* imposed by any combination, conspiracy, or monopoly upon such trade or commerce."[75] Subsequent decisions limited the rule to railroad mergers.

In 1948 it became clear that the Supreme Court would only invalidate mergers under the Sherman Act if they verged upon a monopoly.[76] In *Columbia Steel*, the Court sanctioned a merger even though the steel industry was very concentrated, and even though the merger concentrated 24% of the market in one firm. The Court looked to other characteristics of the market, including the strength of competitors, the percent of the market controlled, and the intent of the merger.

But *Columbia Steel* is distinguishable in several respects from more modern cases under § 7. *Columbia Steel* was brought under the Sherman Act because U.S. Steel merely purchased the assets of Consolidated Steel; therefore, the Clayton Act did not apply at the time before the Celler-Kefauver Act. The Sherman Act requires a more substantial showing under the rule of reason test than does the amended Clayton Act. Also, evidence demonstrated that while the two firms both produced fabricated steel products, they were of different types and the two firms rarely bid on the same jobs. This last rationale was undercut by the elasticity of supply for steel products. This suggested the firms were not direct competitors in a relevant market.

The Court's horizontal merger decisions under the Clayton Act also have been somewhat inconsistent. After the 1950 Cellar-Kefauver Amendments to the Clayton Act, the Court began to respond to Congressional fears that larger, merging companies would destroy smaller businesses. In 1962, the Court gave its first response to Congressional concerns. In *Brown Shoe Co. v. United States*,[77] the Court held that the horizontal portion of the merger between Brown Shoe Co. (Brown) and Kinney Shoe Co. (Kinney) violated § 7 of the Clayton Act. In doing so, the Court listed some important factors in judging the validity of a merger in a deconcentrated market under the amended § 7: (1) market share data, (2) concentration percentages, (3) industry trends, and (4) entry barrier evidence.

The Court noted that Congress had plugged the loopholes in the Clayton Act and that § 7 now reached mergers involving acquisitions of assets, as well as stock acquisitions. The amended § 7 also reached vertical and conglomerate mergers, if their effects would tend to lessen competition in any line of commerce in any section of the country.

---

75. *N. Sec. Co. v. United States*, 193 U.S. 197, 331 (1904).
76. *United States v. Columbia Steel*, 334 U.S. 495 (1948).
77. 370 U.S. 294 (1962).

Most important, the Court noted that § 7 gave courts the authority to stop, in their incipiency, any trends toward a lessening competition. No longer did courts need to find that a substantial lessening of competition would occur as a direct result of the merger; the tendency to do so in the future was enough. Closely coupled to this was the fact that the amended § 7 allowed courts to stop mergers based on reasonable probabilities of anticompetitive effects, rather than certainties.

Brown Shoe, however, did not signal the demise of all mergers. The Court recognized that even under the amended § 7, some mergers were still legal or even commendable. A merger of "small companies . . . [with the purpose] to compete with larger corporations dominating the market" would be permitted, as would mergers involving a failing company that would otherwise be unable to have a viable competitive effect on the market.[78] In short, Congress intended in enacting § 7 to protect "competition, not competitors, and desire[d] to restrain mergers only to the extent that such combinations may tend to lessen competition."[79]

Brown Shoe involved a merger between a retailer and manufacturer of shoes. The merger had horizontal and vertical elements since each competed on two levels. The Court defined as the relative market every city with a population exceeding 10,000 and its surrounding territory in which both Brown and Kinney sold shoes at retail. Within that market, the combined share of Brown and Kinney sales exceeded 20% in most markets, and in some it ran as high as 50%. The Court noted that the merged market share was an important factor to be considered in determining the probable effects of a merger.

The Court, in invalidating the merger, gave effect to the Congressional desire to promote competition by protecting small, locally owned businesses, even if higher prices might occasionally result. In doing so, the Court relied heavily on the fact that the shoe industry had exhibited a trend toward concentration in the years preceding the merger, that a large national chain was involved in the merger, and that it believed that this merger would intensify the existing concentration. These factors resurfaced in significant ways in later decisions.

Brown Shoe established a broad, multifaceted analysis under § 7 for evaluating horizontal mergers. A plaintiff need not show monopoly power resulting from the merger or that there is an *actual* lessening of competition. *Brown Shoe* set an antimerger tone and signaled an inhospitality toward horizontal mergers. The Court feared industry concentration, believed that § 7 was designed to further deconcentration and the dispersion of economic power, and stressed the desirability of protecting small businesses from larger, perhaps more efficient, firms.

In 1963, the Court showed a greater willingness to condemn mergers in concentrated markets. In *United States v. Philadelphia Nat'l Bank*,[80] the Court invalidated a merger between two banks, though the merger would permit the banks to compete

78. *Id.* at 331.
79. *Id.* at 320.
80. 374 U.S. 321 (1963).

more effectively for loans with larger commercial banks outside the Philadelphia area. The Court reasoned that procompetitive effects in one market did not justify anticompetitive effects in another, and that beneficial economic consequences could not save mergers with anticompetitive tendencies.

The merger between the second and third largest banks in Philadelphia would have created the largest firm in the market, controlling 30% of the banking business in the relevant four county Philadelphia metropolitan area. With this large market share, in an already concentrated market, the Court presumed an inherently anticompetitive tendency that the banks were unable to rebut.[81]

In contrast to *Brown Shoe*'s analysis for mergers in deconcentrated markets, *Philadelphia Nat'l Bank* set the standard for mergers in concentrated markets. A presumption of illegality exists for horizontal mergers in concentrated markets when, as a result of the merger, the resulting firm controls an "undue market share" and market concentration significantly increases. Although the Court did not define "undue market share," the 30% challenged there served as the Court's benchmark for invoking the presumption of illegality. The Court noted that even a merger resulting in less than a 30% market share might raise an inference of illegality.

However, the presumption is rebuttable if the defense introduces evidence that the merger is not anticompetitive. The available defenses were not evident. To be sure, the Court seemed to reject as defenses enhanced efficiencies, ease of market entry, economies of scale, and increased competition in other markets. The "failing company" defense was approved, however, as an absolute defense. Note, even if the merger in a concentrated market is not illegal under *Philadelphia Nat'l Bank*, the merger may still be examined under the deconcentrated industry test of *Brown Shoe* where the economic effects will be weighed. The next case the Court decided seemed to further the rigidity of the presumption of illegality.

In *United States v. Von's Grocery*,[82] the Court invalidated a merger between the third and sixth largest grocery companies in Los Angeles, even though their combined sales only accounted for 7.5% of total sales in Los Angeles. The merger created the second

---

81. The District Court in the Northern District of Texas in *T&T Geotechnical, Inc. v. Union Pacific Resources Company*, 944 F. Supp. 1317 (N.D. Tex. 1996), denied an attempt to define the relevant market narrowly in accord with *Philadelphia National Bank.*

> In *Philadelphia National Bank*, the nature of the banking business at issue required proximity to customers, and the Court relied on this fact in concluding that the relevant market consisted of the immediate four-county area around the banks. In contrast, plaintiffs' business [geologic navigation for horizontal drilling] requires no proximity at all to their customers. Indeed, [one witness] testified that, for efficiency, T&T does all of its work in Fort Worth, communicating with clients by fax. [The witness] further testified that, given this means of operation, T&T could do business anywhere in the world that has good reliable telephone connections.

Id. at 1323–24.

Hence, the type and magnitude of plaintiff's business prevented the defendant from furthering a limited relevant geographic market claim based on the logic of *Philadelphia National Bank.*

82. 384 U.S. 270 (1966).

largest grocery chain in Los Angeles with annual sales over $170 million (in 1960s dollars). The Court again noted that the applicable product market showed signs of increased concentration. The total number of single store owners had dropped approximately 60%, and the number of chains with two or more stores had increased approximately 60%. "[T]he grocery business was being concentrated into the hands of fewer and fewer owners [and] the small companies were continually being absorbed by the larger firms through mergers."[83] Additionally, acquisitions and mergers in the retail grocery market had occurred rapidly in the Los Angeles area before the litigation began.

The Court felt that this increased concentration (i.e., a decrease in number of single-store retailers) was sufficient to prevent the merger of the third and sixth largest firms in the market. In addition, the Court was concerned that the merger disposed of a substantial competitor. The Court felt that preventing such a merger would further the intent expressed by Congress in its 1950 amendments: to arrest a trend toward increased concentration before that trend developed to the point where the market was left in the grip of a few large companies.[84]

After *Von's Grocery*, it seemed that the Supreme Court would invalidate any merger between high market share competitors whenever the relevant industry showed signs of concentration or where an aggressive competitor was acquired. Some critics worried that invalidating mergers such as those involved in *Brown Shoe* and *Von's Grocery* may actually prevent increased efficiencies that could result in lower prices to consumers.

In 1974, in *United States v. General Dynamics Corp.*,[85] the Supreme Court evaluated a merger between two of the top ten coal producers in the United States. The merging firms controlled approximately 23% (15% plus 8%) of coal sales in one defined geographic market and 11% (6.5% and 4.4%) in another relevant market. Evidence produced by the government showed a distinct trend toward increased concentration within the coal production industry. Noting that "[i]n prior decisions involving horizontal mergers between competitors, this Court has found *prima facie* violations of § 7 of the Clayton Act from aggregate statistics of the sort relied on by the United States in this case,"[86] the Court nevertheless permitted the merger.

The Court relied on a previously unquoted footnote from *Brown Shoe*, and "cautioned that statistics concerning market share and concentration, while of great significance, were not conclusive indicators of anticompetitive effects."[87] This indicated that the Court may require the plaintiff to show some actual anticompetitive effects from the merger, rather than relying solely upon statistical evidence of market shares and increasing concentration within the market. The Court concluded that in this

---

83. *Id.* at 273.

84. *Id.* at 277; *see also United States v. Pabst Brewing Co.*, 384 U.S. 546 (1966) (condemning a combined market share of 4.7%); *United States v. Aluminum Co. of America*, 377 U.S. 271 (1964); *Marathon Oil Co. v. Mobil Corp.*, 669 F.2d 378 (6th Cir. 1981); *RSR Corp. v. FTC*, 602 F.2d 1317 (9th Cir. 1979).

85. 415 U.S. 486 (1974).

86. *Id.* at 496.

87. *Id.* at 498 (*citing Brown Shoe Co. v. United States*, 370 U.S. 294, 322 n.38 (1962)).

market coal reserves, rather than market share, were a better indicator of future market power. Because defendant had weak reserves, the Court held that the merger did not portend a substantial lessening of competition.[88]

General Dynamics deemphasized market share and concentration ratios as determinative and instead held that such data could be rebutted by evidence that defendant was really an "unpromising or weak competitor." Conversely, such evidence presumably could be used to challenge a merger when the market share and concentration data are low but where the vital competitive factor is substantial. Thus, in *General Dynamics* the Court permitted the government's *prima facie* case to be rebutted by post-acquisition evidence that showed defendant lacked competitive strength and vitality. Accordingly, an analysis of market share data and concentration trends does not end the inquiry. These factors seem to be the primary index for measuring market power and, if left unrebutted, they can be the basis of a § 7 violation. But industry structural evidence must be an accurate measure of competitive ability; when it is not, nonstructural factors will be considered.[89]

A synthesis of the approaches used by the Supreme Court in horizontal mergers follows. *Brown Shoe, Von's Grocery* and *Philadelphia Nat'l Bank* show the likelihood of the Court invalidating mergers in markets where the plaintiff makes a statistical showing of increased concentration and a significant increase in market power

---

88. *See also Olin Corporation v. FTC*, 986 F.2d 1295, 1305–06 (9th Cir. 1993) (refusing to liken the pre-acquisition position of the plaintiff to that of the defendant in *General Dynamics* given the evidence suggesting that Olin's resources were not nearly as limited prior to the acquisition).

89. *See Kaiser Aluminum & Chem. Corp. v. FTC*, 652 F.2d 1324, 1335–37 (7th Cir. 1981). The Eleventh Circuit, in *FTC v. University Health, Inc.*, 938 F.2d 1206 (11th Cir. 1991), rejected an argument based on *General Dynamics*' weak competitor theory. The FTC challenged a proposed merger between two hospitals. The District Court had rejected the FTC's motion for a preliminary injunction, and, upon appeal, the Eleventh Circuit vacated and remanded the decision. The defendant attempted to rebut the FTC's clear evidence of anticompetitive effects by citing *General Dynamics* for the proposition that, because the acquired hospital was a "weak" and "not meaningful" competitor, the increased market share from the merger did not necessarily equal a lessening of competition. *Id.* at 1220. The Court of Appeals rejected the contention.

> We are not prepared, on the strength of [the] language [in *General Dynamics*], to hold that the acquisition of a "weak company" is absolutely immune from § 7 scrutiny. Rather, we view *General Dynamics* as standing for the unremarkable proposition that a defendant may rebut the government's *prima facie* case by showing that the government's market share statistics overstate the acquired firm's ability to compete in the future and that, discounting the acquired firm's market share to take this into account, the merger would not substantially lessen competition.... The acquired firm's weakness, then, is one of many possible factors that a defendant may introduce to rebut the government's *prima facie* case. It is, however, 'probably the weakest ground of all for justifying a merger.' Therefore, to ensure that competition and consumers are protected, we will credit such a defense only in rare cases, when the defendant makes a substantial showing that the acquired firm's weakness, which cannot be resolved by any competitive means, would cause that firm's market share to reduce to a level that would undermine the government's prima facie case.

Id. at 1221 (citations omitted).

The court determined that the defendant hospital had failed to make such a showing.

resulting from the merger. Although statistical evidence is significant under this approach, *General Dynamics* indicates that the importance of market share can be rebutted by showing that either the procompetitive effects outweigh anticompetitive consequences or that no anticompetitive effects exist because other factors indicate that defendant does not lack competitive vigor. A further distinction is that *Philadelphia Nat'l Bank* established only a *prima facie* test for a merger in a concentrated market, while *Brown Shoe* chartered a broader-based economic evaluation for mergers in deconcentrated markets. Even if a presumption of illegality exists, *Gen. Dynamics* teaches that it may be rebutted by nonstructural evidence of future market power or lack of it.[90] Under either standard, the Court will weigh the harms and benefits of the merger if rebuttal evidence is produced.

Lower federal courts, following *Gen. Dynamics*, have signaled that *Philadelphia Nat'l Bank's* presumptive test has been weakened, if not undercut. Consequently, market concentration becomes one of many factors for a court to assess. In particular, barriers to entry have become increasingly important in merger analysis. For example, in *United States v. Baker Hughes*,[91] the U.S. Court of Appeals for the District of Columbia Circuit approved a merger with a post-merger HHI over 4000. In support of its holding, the court noted that:

> a defendant seeking to rebut a presumption of anticompetitive effect must show that the *prima facie* case inaccurately predicts the relevant transaction's probable effect on future competition. The more compelling the *prima facie* case, the more evidence the defendant must present to rebut it successfully. A defendant can make the required showing by affirmatively showing why a given transaction is unlikely to substantially lessen competition, or by discrediting the data underlying the initial presumption in the government's favor.
>
> Imposing a heavy burden of production on a defendant would be particularly anomalous where, as here, it is easy to establish a *prima facie* case. The government, after all, can carry its initial burden of production simply by presenting market concentration statistics. To allow the government virtually to rest its case at that point, leaving the defendant to prove the core of the dispute, would grossly inflate the role of statistics in actions brought under section 7. The Herfindahl-Hirschman Index cannot guarantee litigation victories.[92]

---

90. For a good example of a successful rebuttal to a *prima facie* showing of illegality, see *FTC v. Butterworth Health Corp.*, 946 F. Supp. 1285 (W.D. Mich., 1996).

91. 908 F.2d 981 (D.C. Cir. 1990). Besides ease of entry, other factors to consider include: product durability, product differentiation, facilitating devices that promote collusion, and the extent of vertical integration in the industry. *See also Olin Corp. v. FTC*, 986 F.2d 1295 (9th Cir. 1993); *FTC v. University Health, Inc.*, 938 F.2d 1206 (11th Cir. 1991); *Nelson v. Monroe Reg'l Medical Center*, 925 F.2d 1555 (7th Cir. 1991).

92. *Id.* at 991–92.

There have been some criticisms of the functional approach, however.

> First, there are often problems with obtaining the necessary underlying data in a form that is of sufficient quality. . . . Second, assuming that the data are available and reliable, discussions with the agencies often turn into a battle of the applicable economic assumptions, econometric analysis, and computer simulation models. . . . Different answers to these and other technical questions may lead to predictions of either a de minimis or a significant price increase from a merger, so the government's analysis risks being fragile. . . . [I]f one can change the analysis substantially by making fair but different assumptions, or if the analysis is based on relatively small differences in statistical estimates, the government's approach is unlikely to be very useful. . . . Third, the methodology may be less predictable than traditional market definition analysis. . . . [F]aced with a client that wishes to merge with a competitor, a defense lawyer might be in a position of saying "it depends on the assumptions about the shape of the demand curve." A fourth drawback is that this new analysis can be time consuming and expensive, especially when the merging parties attempt to challenge the government's analysis or attempt to use these approaches to dissuade the agencies from challenging a merger. It can often cost hundreds of thousands of dollars to do a complete analysis in a particular case, and the analysis moves even more from existing case law to the realm of economists.[93]

Professors Lande and Langenfeld suggest that there needs to be a stricter standard delineating an acceptable maximum post-merger market share, regardless of the functional approach's deemphasis on market share.[94] The agencies also need to set out an acceptable post-merger price increase level, since the new models advanced by economists and antitrust scholars almost always predict some inflated price levels following any merger.[95]

Other commentators have suggested that it is the availability of close alternatives to the merged firm's products, regardless of relative market shares, that will affect prices post-merger.[96] Prices can rise substantially when the buyer is left with no choice but to buy from the merged firm because no other producer of the desired good exists. In some situations, "[t]he merged firm's negotiating leverage depend[s] upon the attractiveness of the buyer's next best alternative premerger, relative to the next best alternative after the merger, not upon concentration in the market as a whole."[97] Hence, although the determination of market shares (one part of the process of market

---

93. Robert H. Lande & James Langenfeld, *The Evolution of Federal Merger Policy*, 11 Antitrust 5, 7 (1997).

94. *Id.* at 8.

95. *Id.*

96. Jonathan B. Baker, *Unilateral Competitive Effects Theories in Merger Analysis*, 11 Antitrust 21, 25 (1997).

97. *Id.*

definition) is no longer as important as it once was,[98] identifying viable competitors (another part of the process) is still integral to merger analysis.[99]

Market definition was a critical inquiry in *United States v. H&R Block, Inc.*,[100] as the district court for the District of Columbia enjoined the proposed merger of H&R Block and 2SS Holdings, Inc. (TaxACT). The companies were the second and third largest providers of digital do-it-yourself tax preparation products ("DDIY"). The court found the merger would result in a duopoly with Intuit, the maker of "TurboTax." Regarding market definition, the court excluded assisted tax preparation because this would not constrain supracompetitive pricing of DDIY products. The court distinguished manual pen-and-paper tax preparation because this was not a product at all, and consumers would not switch to doing their taxes with pen and paper in response to a small but significant and nontransitory price increase (or SSNIP) in DDIY products.[101] Although all methods of preparation are conceivably in competition, the digital do-it-yourself method was set apart due to its "technology, price, convenience level, time investment, mental effort and type of interaction by the consumer."[102]

In the defined market for DDIY products, the merger would create a market dominated by two large players—H&R Block and Intuit—that together had 90 percent market share. Further, the merger would increase the HHI from 4,291 to 4,691, a significant increase in an already highly concentrated market. This was sufficient to shift the burden to the defendants. While defendants would ordinarily argue that there were little or no barriers to entry, the parties agreed that the proper focus for the DDIY product market was whether existing market participants would expand their production. The court found that the small firms in the market could not sufficiently expand to price discipline the dominant firms because of reputational constraints: consumers will only switch to a product that they trust, and it is expensive and time-consuming to build that trust. The court rejected the parties' efficiencies justifications for the merger on the grounds that they were neither merger specific nor sufficiently verifiable. The court ultimately agreed with the DOJ's argument that the merger would substantially reduce competition, risking both unilateral anticompetitive effects and concerted anticompetitive effects. Therefore, the court enjoined the merger, which was later abandoned.

Also in 2011, the Eighth Circuit affirmed a ruling permitting the acquisition of two heart medications, finding they were not part of the same relevant product market. In *FTC v. Lundbeck*,[103] the FTC, along with the Minnesota Attorney General, alleged anti-

98. *See also Re/Max International, Inc. v. Realty One, Inc.*, 924 F. Supp. 1474, 1489 (N.D. Ohio, 1996) (citing other factors besides market share, such as market competitiveness, trends, and number and viability of competitors, as significant factors in determining market power).

99. *Id.*

100. 833 F. Supp. 2d 36 (D.D.C. 2011).

101. See *infra* § 7.09[A] for a discussion of SSNIP.

102. 833 F. Supp. 2d at 37.

103. 650 F.3d 1236 (8th Cir. 2011).

trust violations arising out of Lundbeck's acquisition of the only two FDA-approved drugs to treat patent ductus arteriosus, a life-threatening heart condition that primarily affects babies with low birth weight. After the acquisition, Lundbeck increased the price of one drug 13-fold to align with the $1,522/treatment price of the other.[104]

Despite the alarming pricing increase, the FTC was unable to show cross-elasticity of demand between the drugs and therefore, according to the district court, could not establish the relevant market as FDA-approved drugs for the treatment of PDA. Pharmacists and other doctors had testified during the bench trial that their preference of one drug over the other was based on side effects and perceived safety concerns, as opposed to price differences.[105] The Eighth Circuit, subject to the clearly erroneous standard of review, affirmed the district court's factual finding that the drugs did not occupy the same product market. Judge Richard G. Kopf added a brief concurrence to voice his concern about relying on the doctor's testimony. In Judge Kopt's view, it was not appropriate to define "a product market based upon the actions of actors who eschew rational economic considerations," as the doctors who prescribed their preferred drugs were not ultimately responsible for paying for the drugs.[106] Therefore, the doctors may not be in the best economic position to react to price increases under a SSNIP analysis. Regardless, Judge Kopf concurred because the standard of review was so deferential.

Commentary regarding the *Lundbeck* market definition has been largely negative.[107] Rather than considering the reasonable interchangeability of use between the drugs in question, the district court in *Lundbeck* limited its analysis to their cross-elasticity of demand.[108] In agreement with Judge Kopf, criticism has focused on the court's reliance upon select doctors' testimony. Because several of the doctors testified that they found NeoProfen to be a safer drug than Indocin IV and based their purchasing decision on safety over price, the court determined cross-elasticity of demand did not exist. Ironically, the doctors' own testimony seems to suggest that the drugs could be used interchangeably. Critics have suggested that the testimony accepted represented only the views of average buyers and did not adequately account for the concerns of marginal, price-conscious consumers. The court has also taken criticism for its decision to rely on consumer testimony more heavily than post-acquisition price increases, which might have been sufficient evidence of cross-elasticity.[109]

Mergers may be condemned because they increase the risk of anticompetitive unilateral effects or anticompetitive coordinated effects. The concept of "unilateral

---

104. *Id.* at 1238.

105. *Id.* at 1240.

106. *Id.* at 1243.

107. *See* Christopher R. Leslie, *Antitrust Law as Public Interest Law*, 2 UC Irvine L. Rev. 885 (2012); Herbert Hovenkamp, *Response: Markets in IP and Antitrust*, 100 Geo. L.J. 2133, 2146–47 (2012); Herbert Hovenkamp, *Mergers, Market Dominance and the Lundbeck Case*, 12 CPI Antitrust Chronicle, Dec. 2011, at 1.

108. *See* Robert A. Skitol & Kenneth M. Vorrasi, *The Remarkable 50-Year Legacy of Brown Shoe Co. v. United States*, Antitrust 47, 51 (Spring 2012).

109. Hovenkamp, *Mergers, Market Dominance and the Lundbeck*, *supra* note 107, at 2.

effects" describes a situation in which the merged entity would have enough power to act like a monopolist. Coordinated effects can exist when the merged entity will not be the largest firm in the market but the merger will leave the market so concentrated that the remaining firms are likely to collude, either explicitly or tacitly. In *FTC v. H.J. Heinz Co.*,[110] the Commission challenged a proposed merger between Heinz and Beech-Nut, the second and third largest manufacturers of baby food, respectively. After the district court denied the FTC's motion for a preliminary injunction, the D.C. Circuit reversed. The FTC established its prima facie case by showing that the market was already highly concentrated, with an HHI of 4775, and that the merger would increase the HHI by 510 points. The FTC also showed that there were high barriers to entry. The defendants sought to rebut the commission's prima facie case by making three arguments: (1) Heinz and Beech-Nut did not compete at the retail level because stores stocked only one of them, along with Gerber's products; (2) the merger would increase efficiency; and (3) the merger would increase innovation by giving the combined entity sufficient shelf space to justify launching new products. The appellate court rejected each of these in turn. First, the court noted that antitrust law cares about competition at the wholesale level, not just retail competition. Second, the proffered efficiencies were not merger specific and were not overly persuasive given that Heinz (the largest baby food maker in the world, though third in the U.S. market) needed access to Beech-Nut's recipes. And third, the court faulted the firms' innovation arguments for lack of evidence. Ultimately, the court concluded that the merger increased the risk of collusion in this concentrated market, and it remanded the case to the district court with instructions to enter a preliminary injunction. The merger did not move forward.

[C] Conglomerate Mergers

[1] Mergers of Potential Competitors

The loss of a potential competitor has been the central issue in the attack on conglomerate mergers. In these mergers, parties do not compete in the same market before the merger; no direct anticompetitive effects result; and no change in market structure, market shares, or the level of concentration results. Conglomerate mergers do have secondary effects on competition and market structure. They can reduce future competition by eliminating a potential entrant and they may give the merged firm a decisive edge in financial resources that it can use to erect entry barriers or to engage in predatory conduct. Potential competitors can serve a function similar to that of substitute products—they can increase elasticity of demand facing existing sellers and they can serve as a restraining influence on price increases.[111]

---

110. 246 F.3d 708 (D.C. Cir. 2001).

111. Richard A. Posner, *Antitrust Policy and the Supreme Court: An Analysis of the Restricted Distribution, Horizontal Merger and Potential Competition Decisions*, 75 Colum. L. Rev. 282, 318 (1975).

In the first major case involving the merger of potential competitors, *United States v. Sidney W. Winslow*,[112] the Supreme Court permitted a product line extension merger among a firm producing 60% of all shoe lasting machines, a firm producing 70% of all shoe heeling machines, and a firm producing 80% of all shoe welt-sewing machines. These companies had patents for their machines and so entry into the markets was legally restricted. The Court, through Justice Holmes, concluded that the combined control of these companies after the merger was no different than that which existed before the merger. Since the companies did not compete against each other before the merger, the same proportions of control of each process existed after the merger as before. The Court reasoned that

> [o]n the face of it the combination was simply an effort after greater efficiency.... As... they did not compete with one another, it is hard to see why the collective business should be any worse than its component parts... [w]e can see no greater objection to one corporation manufacturing seventy percent of three noncompeting groups of patented machines collectively used for making a single product than to three corporations making the same proportion of one group each.[113]

The Court ignored, however, the fact each of the three firms may have served as a check or restraining force on the other two firms' pricing practices. If the three could enter each other's market easily, then the combination of three firms reduced potential entrants dramatically and substantially increased the combined firm's market power in each market. The firm producing heeling machines may have controlled 70% of the market but still could have not have any real market power because a slight increase in price would cause the lasting machine manufacturer to enter the market on a large scale. By eliminating this outside source of competition, the merger may have permitted the heeling machine manufacturer to use its full 70% share of market to control supply and prices. At bottom, the Court did not consider the cross-elasticity of supply and the restraining effect on price that a potential competitor can have sitting on the sidelines.

The Court went to the other extreme in 1964 and treated a merger involving potential competitors as if it were a horizontal merger. In *United States v. Continental Can Co.*,[114] the Court faced another product line extension merger between large firms in the can and bottle industries. The second largest maker of metal containers merged with the third largest maker of glass containers. The district court found that the bottle industry did not compete directly with the can industry except in the beer industry; only there did manufacturers use bottles and cans interchangeably.

The Court, however, noted that through extensive sales campaigns, industries using bottles could be tempted to switch to cans and vice-versa. This potential cross-elasticity of demand and supply caused the Court to lump bottles and cans together

112. 227 U.S. 202 (1913).
113. *Id.* at 217.
114. 378 U.S. 441 (1964).

in some product markets in what it termed "inter-industry competition." Once glass and metal containers were classified in the same product market, it followed that the merger was horizontal in nature. The merging firms were thus direct, actual competitors. If they were not grouped in the same market they were only potential competitors. Continental Can controlled 21.9% of industry (glass and metal) sales and Hazel-Atlas Glass controlled 3.1%. The Court concluded that a merger between competitors with such significant market shares would have a detrimental effect on competition. It also was concerned that approval of this merger might trigger a merger wave within the industry.

These two cases point out how firms are viewed as actual competitors, potential competitors, or even non-competitors; it depends on the definition of the relevant market. In turn that will depend on the elasticities of demand and supply. Continental Can and Hazel-Atlas did not compete as much as did the parties in *Brown Shoe*, but they were grouped into the same product market.

This categorization in *Continental Can* may not have been completely unfair, since a glass-using bottler facing a price increase could consider switching to cans and could probably do so at a reasonable price; cross-elasticity of demand would be much higher than in *Winslow*, where a user of shoe lasting machines could not possibly switch to a heeling machine to accomplish the same job. Complementary products, at issue in *Winslow*, are not substitute products as was the case in *Continental Can*.

The "potential competitor" theory first appeared in *United States v. El Paso Natural Gas Co.*[115] In *El Paso*, the Court invalidated a merger between El Paso and Pacific Northwest, two natural gas suppliers. El Paso was the sole out-of-state natural gas supplier in California; it sold a majority of the natural gas consumed in California. Pacific Northwest also was an out-of-state supplier of natural gas that never succeeded in selling in California, although it certainly tried. The Court noted that Pacific's attempts to sell to California consumers had resulted in El Paso lowering its price substantially. The Court viewed Pacific Northwest as a potential competitor whose presence on the sideline restrained El Paso's pricing. Actually, Pacific was a direct, if unsuccessful, competitor for sales of natural gas in California. The mistake in nomenclature had little effect on the result; the Court recognized that the merger would substantially reduce competition for California natural gas markets.

The Court faced a true potential competitor, in *FTC v. Procter & Gamble Co. (P&G).*[116] P&G sought to acquire Clorox, the leading manufacturer of bleach. Even though P&G did not manufacture bleach, its ability to do so may have restrained Clorox's pricing. The Court made little effort to analyze whether P&G's acquisition of Clorox would lead to unrestrained pricing or even whether it would result in collusion among bleach producers. Instead, the Court condemned the merger largely because Procter & Gamble had an advertising advantage that could injure bleach competitors

115. 376 U.S. 651 (1964). See the characterization of *El Paso*'s theory in *United States v. Marine Bancorporation, Inc.*, 418 U.S. 602, 623 n. 24 (1974).

116. 386 U.S. 568 (1967).

through advertising discounts. Because all bleaches were chemically the same, advertising played a key role in attempting to distinguish the products and hence in increasing their market share. The Court felt that the huge advertising advantages that would inure to the already dominant Clorox would erect entry barriers that would dissuade new entrants. The merger also would discourage price competition and production increases from existing bleach firms because they would fear retaliation from P&G.

In *P&G*, the Court also recognized that P&G's presence on the sidelines would restrain Clorox's pricing. *De novo* entry into the bleach market was possible for P&G and it was found to be a "likely prospective entrant."[117] Clorox probably felt that any use of its market power to increase prices made entry by P&G probable. "If Procter had actually entered, Clorox's dominant position would have been eroded and the concentration of the industry reduced. . . ."[118] The Court believed that no other potential competitor could exert this restraining influence once P&G had merged with Clorox.

That P&G's presence on the edge of the market would restrain Clorox's pricing is an application of the "perceived potential entrant" theory. Firms in the market fear outside entry and behave competitively. The Court in *P&G* accepted that theory as justifying invalidation of the merger between potential competitors. It also rejected the defenses of increased efficiency and economies of scale. "Possible economies cannot be used as a defense to illegality. Congress was aware that some mergers which lessen competition may also result in economies, but it struck the balance in favor of protecting competition."[119]

The Court has been more reluctant to accept the "actual potential entrant" theory.[120] This theory claims that a merger is illegal if the firm would have entered the market but for the merger and that entry through an alternative means would have been less anticompetitive. The Court has never used this theory to invalidate a merger.

In *United States v. Marine Bancorporation, Inc.*,[121] the Supreme Court refused to adopt the actual potential competitor theory. In *Marine Bancorporation*, a Seattle bank in a geographical market extension merger acquired a bank in Spokane at the opposite end of the state. The merger would have joined the second and ninth largest

---

117. *Id.* at 575.

118. *Id.*

119. *Id.* at 580 (*citing Brown Shoe Co. v. United States*, 370 U.S. 294, 344 (1962)). In part this was based on the Court expressed concern over the propensity of mergers to raise entry barriers. The acquisition also may have the tendency of raising the barriers to new entry. The major competitive weapon in the successful marketing of bleach is advertising. Clorox was limited in this area by its relatively small budget and its inability to obtain substantial discounts. By contrast, Procter's budget was much larger; and, although it would not devote its entire budget of advertising Clorox, it could divert a large portion to meet the short-term threat of a new entrant. Procter would be able to use its volume discounts to advantage in advertising Clorox. Thus, a new entrant would be much more reluctant to face the giant Procter than it would have been to face the smaller Clorox. 386 U.S. at 579–80.

120. *See United States v. Falstaff Brewing Corp.*, 410 U.S. 526 (1973).

121. 418 U.S. 602 (1974).

banks in Washington. The banks were not in direct competition, but the United States claimed that if the merger were prohibited, the Seattle bank would have found an alternative, less anticompetitive method to enter the Spokane market. Specifically, the government contended that the bank would have found a smaller existing firm, developed it through internal expansion, and made it competitive with both the existing banks and the acquired bank in the area.[122]

The Court held that at the very least, the government under the potential competition theory must show the merger is in a concentrated market, that the bank had other alternative means of entering the market and that those means offered a substantial likelihood of producing procompetitive effects. The government failed to carry this burden of proof. Whenever the government could show the existence of alternative methods of entry and a substantial likelihood of procompetitive effects, then the acquiring firm would be viewed as a perceived potential entrant and the case would be decided on those grounds. If the alternate method of entry and the procompetitive effects were so apparent, surely existing competitors in the market would see them and act accordingly.

But here the ease of entry on the part of the acquiring firm (the Seattle bank) was problematic. Given the entry restrictions on new banks under Washington state law that prohibited *de novo* branches, the Seattle bank could not enter the market without an acquisition of another bank. Thus it is unlikely that the Seattle bank could have been either an actual potential entrant or a perceived potential entrant (with a sideline or "wings" effect on price) since "[r]ational commercial bankers in Spokane . . . are aware of the regulatory barriers that render [the Seattle bank] an unlikely or an insignificant potential entrant except by merger with [the Spokane bank]."[123]

The Second Circuit has declined to apply the potential entrant theory and approved a merger between the leading manufacturer of automotive shock absorbers and a large manufacturer of auto parts, which did not manufacture shock absorbers. In *Tenneco, Inc. v. FTC*,[124] the court found that Tenneco had actually considered entry into the shock absorber market, but it had not considered *de novo* or toehold entry because the start up costs and the level at which economies of scale could be achieved were so high. The smallest, efficiently sized plant had to produce annually 6,000,000 shock absorbers. This produced barriers to entry so substantial that, the court held, Tenneco could not be considered an actual potential entrant. High entry barriers therefore may negate the theory that a firm is an actual potential competitor. The court held that to establish a § 7 violation under the actual potential competitor theory

> [the plaintiff] must show 1) that the relevant market is concentrated; 2) that [but for the acquisition the acquiring firm] would likely have entered the market in the near future either *de novo* or through toehold acquisition

---

122. *Id.* at 615.
123. *Id.* at 639.
124. 689 F.2d 346 (2d Cir. 1982).

> and 3) that such entry . . . carried a substantial likelihood of ultimately producing deconcentration of the market or other significant procompetitive effects.[125]

Although the court found that this merger occurred in a highly concentrated market, it declined to hold that Tenneco was likely to enter the market through other, less anticompetitive means because of the high entry barriers.

The court also rejected the perceived potential competition theory, because, although Tenneco was perceived by other competitors as a potential entrant, there was insufficient evidence to show that Tenneco had exercised a tempering impact on the conduct of existing firms. Thus, there was no "wings" effect—the second evidentiary requirement of the theory.[126]

Although the Fifth Circuit has approved the application of the "actual potential entrant" doctrine,[127] most circuits have not embraced the theory. For example, the Second Circuit has required a showing that a *de novo* or toehold entry must be proven to be "sufficiently probable and imminent."[128]

In *FTC v. Steris Corp.*,[129] the FTC challenged a merger between the second and third largest providers of sterilization for healthcare equipment. The Commission relied on the "actual potential entrant" doctrine because one firm was already competing in a particular technology market and the other firm had been planning to enter that market before the merger. The FTC argued that "the acquisition of an actual potential competitor violates Section 7 if (1) the relevant market is highly concentrated, (2) the competitor 'probably' would have entered the market, (3) its entry would have had pro-competitive effects, and (4) there are few other firms that can enter effectively."[130] Although the defendants argued that the actual potential entrant doctrine "has long been disfavored by numerous courts including the Supreme Court," the district court "assume[d] the validity of this doctrine" for purposes of evaluating the FTC motion for a preliminary injunction.[131] The court, however, concluded that the government failed to meet its burden with respect to the second element and denied the FTC's motion.

---

125. *Id.* at 352.

126. *Id.* at 355.

127. See *Mercantile Texas Corp. v. Board of Governors of the Federal Reserve System*, 638 F.2d 1255 (5th Cir. 1981), where the court approved the principle but remanded to determine the probable time of entry, the degree of competition within the market, and whether the potential competition offered was substantial.

128. *B.O.C. Int'l Ltd. v. FTC*, 557 F.2d 24, 29 (2d Cir. 1977); *see also* V Phillip Areeda & Donald F. Turner, *Antitrust Law* 69–161 (1980).

129. 133 F. Supp. 3d 962 (N.D. Ohio 2015).

130. *Id.* at 966.

131. *Id.*

[2] Potential Competition and Joint Ventures

The Supreme Court has applied the potential entrant doctrine to joint ventures under a § 7 challenge. In 1964, the Court applied this doctrine in *United States v. Penn-Olin Chemical Co.*[132] Pennsalt Chemicals and Olin-Mathieson Corp. had formed jointly Penn-Olin to build a plant to produce sodium chlorate in Kentucky, and to sell the product in the Southeast. Before the joint venture, two firms controlled 90% of the Southeastern market but neither Olin nor Pennsalt sold sodium chlorate in that market; both had considered and rejected the possibility of independently entering the market.

The district court upheld the joint venture on grounds that its effect was procompetitive. The court noted that the joint venture increased the number of competitors in the market by 50%, thus exerting more competitive influence on the market than either Pennsalt, Olin, or both would have done while waiting in the wings.

The Supreme Court disagreed, ruling that if, on remand, the Court found that one firm probably would have entered the market and the other would have remained a potential entrant, then the merger should be invalidated. To make this finding, the district court would have to first find that Pennsalt and Olin were potential competitors in the market, and second that one would enter the market while the other would still provide competitive restraint waiting in the wings. But the district court had found that both firms would not have entered the market and this finding was not disturbed by the Supreme Court. In light of this factual finding, the Court's remand order seemed futile since we know if one would have entered the market the other would not have, thus diminishing the probability that the nonentrant would be perceived as a potential entrant or that it would be in any position to exercise any sideline restraining effect. Nevertheless, *Penn-Olin* is important because the Court applied § 7 to joint ventures and because it set forth a test under the potential competitor theory that only requires a showing of "reasonable probability" of entry.

In sum, the cases teach that in order to strike down a merger under the actual potential competitor theory there must be a showing: (1) of reasonable probability that the acquiring firm, but for this merger, would have entered the market in the near future either through *de novo* entry or a toehold merger, (2) that the entry through other means would have resulted in a deconcentrated market or a procompetitive effect, and (3) that the market under review is concentrated. "Reasonable probability" is defined as to whether the defendant has both the capacity and incentive to enter. Capacity refers to the financial, technological, and legal means. On the other hand, in order to strike down a merger under the potential entrant theory, there must be a showing that: (1) the firm is perceived by competitors in the market as a potential entrant, (2) this perception creates a restraining effect on the competitors in the market, and (3) the market under review is concentrated.

---

132. 378 U.S. 158 (1964).

[D] Hart-Scott-Rodino Act

The Hart-Scott-Rodino Improvements Act (HSR) of 1976[133] has had a huge impact on the level and type of antitrust litigation following its passage. The HSR is broken down into three parts. Title I expands the precomplaint discovery abilities of antitrust enforcers in civil investigations of proposed mergers; Title II states the premerger notification requirements for some acquisitions of assets and voting securities, depending on the monetary values associated with the merger; and, Title III allows state attorneys general to bring parens patriae actions.[134] Title II generally has been the most heavily litigated and academically debated part of the Hart-Scott-Rodino Act since its passage.[135]

The notification requirement states that plans for "large mergers" must be presented to either the Department of Justice, the FTC, or both, under § 7(a) of the Clayton Act.[136] This allows the government to examine the proposed merger for possible anticompetitive effects. The notification requirement applies to mergers that result in an acquirer holding an aggregate total amount of the voting securities and assets of the acquired party in excess of $200 million.[137] A tiered filing fee structure is imposed for every notification transaction;[138] once the fee is paid, the standard 30-day waiting period begins to run. This waiting period may be extended by thirty days by either agency should they require more information, and any failure to comply with HSR requirements will lead to fines of as much as $51,000 per day, as of 2024.

The objective of the HSR is to give the government advanced warning of any exceptionally large mergers being planned, and to enjoin illegal mergers in their inception.[139] Because of the pervasive and sweeping nature of the legislation, its unavoidable consequence is to impede the progress of some harmless mergers in order to prevent the formation of those which violate the Clayton Act.[140] As such, the HSR has been subject to both praise and criticism by many antitrust scholars. Some antitrust lawyers feel that the HSR has helped to decrease the endless litigation associated with merger suits, bringing speedier relief to those potentially or actually harmed by the merger

---

133. 15 U.S.C. § 18a (2011). Subsection (a), the filing requirement section, reads as follows:

> (a) Filing
>
> Except as exempted pursuant to subsection (c) of this section, no person shall acquire, directly or indirectly, any voting securities or assets of any other person, unless both persons (or in the case of a tender offer, the acquiring person) file notification pursuant to rules under subsection (d)(1) of this section, and the waiting period described in subsection (b)(1) of this section has expired . . .

134. William Blumenthal, *Symposium: Twenty Years of Hart-Scott-Rodino Merger Enforcement—Introductory Note*, 65 Antitrust L.J. 813, 813 (1997).

135. *Id.*

136. 1995-2 Trade Reg. Rep. (CCH) ¶ 4231, 7927 (Nov. 14, 2001); *see also DOJ's Antitrust Division Unveils Merger Review Process Initiative*, Antitrust & Trade Reg. Daily (BNA) (October 15, 2001).

137. 15 U.S.C. § 18a.

138. http://www.ftc.gov/os/2007/07/P110014hsrreport.pdf.

139. William Blumenthal, *Symposium: Twenty Years of Hart-Scott-Rodino Merger Enforcement—Introductory Note*, 65 Antitrust L.J. 813, 814 (1997) (citation omitted).

140. *Id.* at 818.

and foregoing the often messy process of dismantling a fully functional merger by preventing its formation altogether.[141] Others criticize the HSR for replacing traditional litigation with far-reaching regulations, saying that the HSR is over-applied and overly costly in both monetary and nonmonetary terms.[142]

Still others have made suggestions for minor improvements in the statute. One proposal is that the government make a conscious effort to treat corporations and partnerships more equally under the HSR.[143] Another suggestion is taking steps toward simplifying the notification form and process.[144] Finally, some suggest extending the clearance review period until the merging parties have produced evidence of efficiency "ex post."[145] While it is apparent that many antitrust commentators have differing opinions about the HSR, it is also clear that the HSR is one of the most influential pieces of antitrust legislation in the United States.

§ 7.08 Failing Company Defense

Throughout the history of antitrust merger cases, the Court has implied that certain situations, such as acquisitions of undercapitalized or failing companies, may justify mergers that otherwise would be invalidated.[146] Although holding this doctrine out as a judicially created defense, the Court has limited its use. The defense will only save acquisitions that were the last resort for the acquired company.[147]

In *Citizen Publ'g Co. v. United States*,[148] the Court defined the limitations of the failing company defense. The case involved a merger through a stock acquisition of the *Star* and the *Citizen*, the only two newspapers in Tucson. The *Citizen* was losing

---

141. William J. Baer, *Reflections on Twenty Years of Merger Enforcement Under the Hart-Scott-Rodino Act*, 65 Antitrust L.J. 825, 826–31 (1997). *See generally* Sullivan, *supra* note 10.

142. Joe Sims & Deborah P. Herman, *The Effect of Twenty Years of Hart-Scott-Rodino on Merger Practice: A Case Study in the Law of Unintended Consequences Applied to Antitrust Legislation*, 65 Antitrust L.J. 865, 865–66, 877–78, 892 (1997). Much of the authors' criticism revolves around the premise that the HSR has reached proportions unintended by the Congress that passed it.

> Congress plainly did not intend to create a huge new merger regulatory scheme; it did not intend to give the antitrust agencies unilateral power to stop a transaction without ever going to court; and it did not intend to supplant discovery under the Federal Rules or the FTC Rules of Practice with "HSR discovery" or to impose burdensome information production requirements upon merging parties.

Id. at 878.

143. Malcolm R. Pfunder, *Some Reflections on, and Modest Proposals for Reform of, the Hart-Scott-Rodino Premerger Notification Program*, 65 Antitrust L.J. 905, 917 (1997).

144. *Id.* at 923.

145. Joseph F. Brodley, *Proof of Efficiencies in Mergers and Joint Ventures*, 64 Antitrust L.J. 575, 578 (1996).

146. For a good survey of the history and application of the failing company defense, see Edward O. Correia, *Re-examining the Failing Company Defense*, 64 Antitrust L.J. 683 (1996).

147. *See Dr. Pepper/Seven-Up Cos. v. FTC*, 991 F.2d 859, 865–66 (D.C. Cir. 1993).

148. 394 U.S. 131 (1969); *see also* Thomas J. Campbell, *The Efficiency of the Failing Company Defense*, 63 Tex. L. Rev. 251 (1984).

money and negotiated a joint operating agreement with the *Star*, which placed the management, production, and distribution of the two papers in the hands of a jointly held corporation (TNI) and which eliminated any business or commercial competition between the two papers. Relying on *International Shoe Co. v. FTC*,[149] the Court reasoned that the failing company defense would protect the merger only if one company "faced the grave probability of a business failure" and the acquiring company was the only available purchaser.

The Court held that in order to invoke this absolute defense to a § 7 charge, defendant would have to show (1) that the resources of one company were so depleted, and the prospects of rehabilitation were so remote, that it faced the grave probability of a business failure, and (2) that efforts were made before this merger to sell it to a noncompetitor or at least a less threatening competitor, such as a new entrant or a small competitor. Absent evidence on each of these requirements, the defense was unavailable.

The rationale underlying the defense was to protect the interest of the creditors, employees and stockholders, who, without the merger, would suffer substantial loss. From a competitive standpoint, if the acquired firm were going out of business anyway with no possibility of reorganization, the merger would not result in an adverse effect on competition since there would be no increase in concentration. In other words, the failing company's contribution to the market would have been lost without the acquisition.

Although recognizing the defense, the Court refused to apply it to the facts before it. There was evidence to support the fact that the *Citizen* was failing, but not that it was on the verge of going out of business or that the joint operating agreement was the only salvage prospect. Although the paper had been losing money, it had enough viability as a competitor that the *Star* was willing to share profits with the *Citizen*. Even if the *Citizen* was failing, there was no evidence that a market for its sale to a noncompetitor was not viable; the owners made no effort to sell the paper. The Court noted that even companies forced to reorganize under the Bankruptcy Act often emerged as strong competitive companies. The paper failed to show that no other buyer existed and that prospects of reorganization were nil.

In response to this judicially created failing company defense, Congress enacted the Newspaper Preservation Act in 1970,[150] which permits joint operating agreements between newspapers.[151] To qualify for the exemption, however, one of the papers

149. 280 U.S. 291 (1930).

150. 15 U.S.C. § 1801 (2011); *see also* John S. Martel & Victor J. Haydel, III, *Judicial Application of the Newspaper Preservation Act: Will Congressional Intent Be Relegated to the Back Pages*, 1984 BYU L. Rev. 123.

151. In particular, the "Act creates an exemption to the antitrust laws that permits a joint operating arrangement ('JOA') between two newspapers if the Attorney General determines that one of the papers is a 'failing newspaper' and that the arrangement 'will effectuate the policy and purpose' of the Act." *Mich. Citizens for an Indep. Press v. Thornburgh*, 868 F.2d 1285, 1287 (D.C. Cir. 1989) (affirming

must, in fact, be a failing newspaper. Under the Act, a "failing newspaper is defined as a newspaper publication which, regardless of its ownership or affiliations, is in probable danger of financial failure."[152] Provided this requisite is satisfied, a joint operating agreement may be appropriate.[153] Today, several large cities have daily newspapers operating under agreements similar to that in *Citizen Publ'g*.[154]

In *F.T.C. v. Arch Coal, Inc.*,[155] the court articulated the following legal test:

> A merger is not likely to create or enhance market power or facilitate its exercise if the following circumstances are met: 1) the allegedly failing firm would be unable to meet its financial obligations in the near future; 2) it would not be able to reorganize successfully under Chapter 11 of the Bankruptcy Act; 3) it has made unsuccessful good-faith efforts to elicit reasonable alternative offers of acquisition of the assets of the failing firm that would both keep its tangible and intangible assets in the relevant market and pose a less severe danger to competition than does the proposed merger; and 4) absent the acquisition, the assets of the failing firm would exit the relevant market.[156]

Even though the acquired firm's financial condition is not sufficiently weak to satisfy this test, the court nonetheless reasoned that "the financial condition of the prospective acquired company may reveal that its future competitive significance in the relevant market has been overstated." The court relied in part of the acquired firm's financial weakness to justify its decision to deny the FTC's motion for a preliminary injunction.

---

the Attorney General's approval of a joint operating arrangement between the Detroit Free Press and Detroit Newspapers).

152. 15 U.S.C. § 1802(5) (2006).

153. Joint operating agreements are appropriate for "printing, time, method and field of publication; allocation of production facilities; distribution; advertising solicitation; circulation solicitation; business department; establishment of advertising rates; establishment of circulation rates and revenue distribution; Provided . . ., that there is no merger, combination, or amalgamation of editorial or reportorial staffs, and that editorial policies can be independently determined." 15 U.S.C. § 1802(2). *See also Hawaii Newspaper Agency v. Bronster*, 103 F.3d 742, 749–50 (9th Cir. 1996) (holding that a Joint Operating Agreement between two Hawaiian newspapers was protected from state challenge by the Newspaper Preservation Act and the doctrine of preemption).

154. *See Mich. Citizens for an Indep. Press*, 868 F.2d 1285; *Comm. for an Indep. P-I v. Hearst Corp.*, 704 F.2d 467 (9th Cir. 1983); *see also Reilly v. The Hearst Corp.*, 107 F. Supp. 2d 1192 (N.D. Cal. 2000).

155. 329 F. Supp. 2d 109 (D.D.C. 2004), *case dismissed*, No. 04-5291, 2004 WL 2066879 (D.C. Cir. Sept. 15, 2004).

156. *Id.* at 154.

§ 7.09 Department of Justice and Federal Trade Commission *Merger Guidelines*

In 1968, 1982, and 1984, the Antitrust Division of the Department of Justice issued revised *Guidelines*.[157] In 1992, the Department of Justice and the Federal Trade Commission jointly issued the 1992 *Guidelines* concerning horizontal mergers and acquisitions. These *Guidelines* represent the first time that the Department and the Federal Trade Commission have issued jointly such *Guidelines*. Previously, both agencies issued separate *Guidelines* describing the analytical framework and standards used in evaluating a particular merger or acquisition and its effect on commerce.[158] Eighteen years later, the agencies produced another update to the review process in their 2010 *Guidelines*.[159] These *Guidelines*, however, only governed horizontal mergers. In 2023, the agencies issued new guidelines, the 2023 *Merger Guidelines*,[160] which address more than strictly horizontal mergers.

The *Guidelines* state the agencies' merger enforcement standards and interpretations, but they are without the force of law since they were not enacted by statute or formal rulemaking. The underlying theme of the *Guidelines* is that mergers should not be condemned unless they facilitate collusion, or increase or enhance market power to proportions of a monopoly or oligopoly—maintaining prices above competitive levels.[161] Accordingly, the *Guidelines* focus on the structure of the market and certain conduct occurring within markets. The *Guidelines* include exhaustive definitions of relevant markets and market power. They begin by defining market power as the ability to maintain price above competitive levels for a significant period of time.[162] Market power also is recognized as the ability of *buyers* to depress prices below competitive levels.

---

157. U.S. Dep't of Justice, *1984 Merger Guidelines*, 49 Fed. Reg. 26,823 (1984) [hereinafter *1984 Guidelines*]; *see also* Brunner, Krattenmaker, Skitol & Webster, *supra* note 2; Cohen & Sullivan, *supra* note 34, Eleanor M. Fox, *1982 Merger Guidelines: When Economists Are Kings?*, 71 Calif. L. Rev. 281 (1983); Steven C. Salop & Joseph J. Simons, *A Practical Guide To Merger Analysis*, 29 Antitrust Bull. 663 (1984).

158. The 1992 *Merger Guidelines* update the *Merger Guidelines* issued by the U.S. Department of Justice (DOJ) in 1984 and the Statement of the Federal Trade Commission Concerning Horizontal Mergers in 1982. U.S. Dep't of Justice & FTC, 1992 *Horizontal Merger Guidelines*, 57 Fed. Reg. 41,552 (1992) [hereinafter *1992 Guidelines*].

159. U.S. Dep't of Justice & Fed. Trade Comm'n, Horizontal Merger Guidelines (2010) [hereinafter *2010 Guidelines*].

160. U.S. Dep't of Justice & Fed. Trade Comm'n, Horizontal Merger Guidelines (2023) [hereinafter *2023 Guidelines* or *Merger Guidelines*], https://www.justice.gov/d9/2023-12/2023%20Merger%20Guidelines.pdf.

161. *1984 Guidelines, supra* note 157; *see also* U.S. Dep't of Justice, *1982 Merger Guidelines*, 47 Fed. Reg. 28,493 (1982) [hereinafter *1982 Guidelines*].

162. *1984 Guidelines, supra* note 157, § 2.

The *Guidelines* analyze market power in terms of the relevant product and geographic markets or service offered by each of the merging firms. For each of these products, the *Guidelines* require the Department of Justice to define the market in which firms could effectively exercise market power through collusion. That market is one in which a hypothetical firm could impose a "'small but significant and nontransitory increase in price' above current or future competitive levels."[163] The hypothesized price increase that the Department will use is generally 5%.

In analyzing whether a firm could exercise market power, the *Guidelines* evaluate both demand and supply elasticity. The hypothetical firm cannot effectively exercise market power if a price increase would cause (1) consumers to switch to other products,[164] or (2) consumers to switch to the same product manufactured by other firms in other areas,[165] or (3) producers of other products to shift and produce products in the relevant market,[166] either by modifying the use of present facilities, shifting the production of the present facility, or by constructing new facilities. The latter consideration, which affects producers, is known as elasticity of supply.

The 2023 Merger Guidelines are structured around eleven individual guidelines:

- Guideline 1: Mergers Raise a Presumption of Illegality When They Significantly Increase Concentration in a Highly Concentrated Market.
- Guideline 2: Mergers Can Violate the Law When They Eliminate Substantial Competition Between Firms.
- Guideline 3: Mergers Can Violate the Law When They Increase the Risk of Coordination.
- Guideline 4: Mergers Can Violate the Law When They Eliminate a Potential Entrant in a Concentrated Market.
- Guideline 5: Mergers Can Violate the Law When They Create a Firm That May Limit Access to Products or Services That Its Rivals Use to Compete.
- Guideline 6: Mergers Can Violate the Law When They Entrench or Extend a Dominant Position.
- Guideline 7: When an Industry Undergoes a Trend Toward Consolidation, the Agencies Consider Whether It Increases the Risk a Merger May Substantially Lessen Competition or Tend to Create a Monopoly.
- Guideline 8: When a Merger is Part of a Series of Multiple Acquisitions, the Agencies May Examine the Whole Series.
- Guideline 9: When a Merger Involves a Multi-Sided Platform, the Agencies Examine Competition Between Platforms, on a Platform, or to Displace a Platform.

---

163. *Id.*
164. *Id.* § 2.11.
165. *Id.* § 2.31.
166. *Id.* § 2.21.

- Guideline 10: When a Merger Involves Competing Buyers, the Agencies Examine Whether It May Substantially Lessen Competition for Workers, Creators, Suppliers, or Other Providers.
- Guideline 11: When an Acquisition Involves Partial Ownership or Minority Interests, the Agencies Examine Its Impact on Competition.

The first six guidelines lay out principles for determining whether a proposed merger is likely to substantially lessen competition and, therefore, violates antitrust law. The last five guidelines discuss how the agencies will apply these principles in particular situations. In looking for potential anticompetitive effects, the guidelines address how to define the relevant market, how to analyze market concentration, and how to rebut structural presumptions of illegality.

[A] Product Market[167]

The agencies determine the relevant product market by estimating the group of products that would be controlled by a monopolist in order to maximize profits by imposing a "small but significant and nontransitory" price increase. This is called a SSNIP test, and it was in previous iterations of the Merger Guidelines.[168] The agencies consider a five percent price increase to be small but significant. If a five percent increase in price for all of a product group would cause consumers to shift to substitutes, then the increase would not be profitable, and the product market is too narrowly defined. The agencies then add the next best substitute to the relevant product market and continues this process until there is no sufficiently attractive substitute to which consumers could shift. The 2023 Guidelines also invoke the SSNIP test, which refers to a small but significant and non-transitory increase in price or other worsening of terms. For example, with their newfound market power, the merging firms could be more likely to impose mandatory arbitration clauses on their customers and employees.[169]

When defining the product market, the agencies will look at the following evidence:

- "Direct evidence of substantial competition between the merging parties . . ."
- "Direct evidence of the exercise of market power . . ."
- "[E]vidence on observed market characteristics ('practical indicia'), such as industry or public recognition of the submarket as a separate economic entity, the product's peculiar characteristics and uses, unique production facilities, distinct customers, distinct prices, sensitivity to price changes, and specialized vendors."

---

167. *2023 Guidelines, supra* note 160, at 4.3; *2010 Guidelines, supra* note 159, § 4.1; *1992 Guidelines, supra* note 158, § 1.1; *1984 Guidelines, supra* note 157, § 2.1; *see also supra* § 7.05[A].

168. *1992 Guidelines, supra* note 158, § 1.0; *1984 Guidelines, supra* note 157, § 2.11.

169. Mark A. Lemley & Christopher R. Leslie, *Antitrust Arbitration and Merger Approval*, 110 Nw. U. L. Rev. 1 (2015). *See 2023 Merger Guidelines*, supra note 160, at § 4.3.

The 2023 Guidelines note that, like the courts, the agencies may also use the hypothetical monopolist test ("HMT") to define a relevant market. The HMT determines "whether a proposed market is too narrow by asking whether a hypothetical monopolist over this market could profitably worsen terms significantly, for example, by raising price."[170] In contrast to previous merger guidelines, the 2023 Guidelines refer to this as the Hypothetical Monopolist/Monopsonist Test, because it recognizes that antitrust law cares about monopsony power as well as monopoly power.

The agencies' definition of the relevant product market can make or break a merger, as was the case in *FTC v. Staples*.[171] The trial court upheld the FTC's challenge to the merger of two office superstore chains, Staples and Office Depot, who together accounted for only 5.5% of the total consumable office supply sales in North America.[172] The Commission had narrowed the definition of the relevant product market to "the sale of consumable office supplies through office superstores."[173] The defendants countered that the product market was the sale of office products overall. The court issued a preliminary injunction against the merger, finding that the Commission had established likelihood of success on the merits, using the narrower product market of the office superstores proposed by the Commission. The court noted that even before the merger, certain geographic markets were highly concentrated, with HHIs between 3597 and 6944. After the merger, Staples-Office Depot would have a dominant market share in 42 markets, with a 100% market share in 15 of those.[174] (This case illustrates the point that the relevant geographic market can actually be several smaller geographic markets.)

The court began its analysis by noting the difficulty of "overcom[ing] the first blush or initial gut reaction" that the relevant product market was only the sale of consumable office supplies through office superstores. The products in question—pens, paper, and sticky notes, as opposed to durables such as computers and fax machines—were "the same no matter who sold them."[175] Additionally, these products were sold not only by superstores, but also by other large retailers such as Wal-Mart and Target. However, the court asserted that the broad market definition the defendants advocated was illusory; even though any firm could be a competitor in the overall market, "for antitrust purposes" economically significant submarkets could exist.[176]

Both the Federal Trade Commission and the court in *Staples* relied in part on the concept of submarkets.[177] Specifically, the court relied on factors iterated in *Brown*

---

170. *2023 Merger Guidelines*, supra note 160, at § 4.3.

171. 970 F. Supp. 1066 (D.D.C. 1997).

172. *Id.* at 1073.

173. *Id.*

174. *Id.* at 1081.

175. *Id.* (citing *Brown Shoe Co. v. United States*, 370 U.S. 294 (1962).

176. *Id.*

177. The *Brown Shoe* "practical indica" for whether a submarket exists are "industry or public recognition of the submarket as a separate economic entity, the product's peculiar characteristics and uses, unique production facilities, distinct customers, distinct prices, sensitivity to price changes, and specialized vendors." *Brown Shoe*, 370 U.S. at 325–26.

Shoe to determine whether the Commission's market definition was correct.[178] It also relied on the Commission's evidence and its own qualitative judgments to assert that office superstores "are, in fact, very different [in terms of] appearance, physical size, format, the number and variety of [products] offered, and the type of customers targeted and served than other sellers of office supplies." Hard pricing evidence indicated that in markets where Staples was the only superstore, it was able to charge prices over 13% higher than where it competed with superstores Office Depot and Office Max, with no significant loss of sales. The court concluded from all of the above factors that there was a low cross-elasticity of demand between consumable office products sold by the superstores and the same products sold by non-superstore retailers. Thus, it was likely that the merger would lessen competition substantially in some geographic markets and create a monopoly in others.

In *Staples*, the court asserted that its analysis was guided by the *Brown Shoe* factors, but ultimately it concluded that the sale of office supplies through superstores was the relevant market because absent a superstore competitor, a superstore would be able to sustain a price increase at profitable levels.[179] The court averred that "[w]hatever term is used—market, submarket, relevant product market—the analysis is the same."[180]

In 2007, the FTC unsuccessfully challenged a proposed merger between two "premium natural and organic supermarkets [PNOS]."[181] The FTC argued that the relevant product market was restricted to only PNOSs, of which the merged firm would have a 100% market share in nearly all relevant geographic markets. The court disagreed and held that the relevant product market was at least all supermarkets, and that the merger was not likely to threaten competition in the broader market. The court cited as factors for its decision (1) increased and expanded offerings by conventional supermarkets of organic products, (2) frequent cross-shopping (comparing products and prices) between PNOSs and supermarkets, and (3) other competitive actions between PNOSs and supermarkets.[182] The D.C. Circuit, however, reversed, noting that a "core group of customers" strongly preferred PNOS and do not consider them interchangeable with conventional supermarkets.[183]

[B] Geographic Markets

When defining the relevant geographic market, the Guidelines note that "[a] market's geography depends on the limits that distance puts on some customers' willingness or ability to substitute to some products, or some suppliers' willingness or ability to serve some customers."[184] In order to determine how far consumers

---

178. *Staples*, 970 F. Supp. at 1080–81.
179. *Id.* at 1080.
180. *Id.* at 1080 n.11.
181. *F.T.C. v. Whole Foods Market, Inc.*, 502 F. Supp. 2d 1 (2007).
182. *Id.* at 35–36.
183. *FTC v. Whole Foods Mkt., Inc.*, 548 F.3d 1028, 1039 (D.C. Cir. 2008).
184. *2023 Guidelines, supra* note 160, at 4.3.D.2.

are willing to travel and how far suppliers are willing to transport their goods, the agencies will consider such factors as "transportation costs, language, regulation, tariff and non-tariff trade barriers, custom and familiarity, reputation, and local service availability."[185]

Overall, when performing market definition, the Guidelines note that "[r]elevant markets need not have precise metes and bounds."[186] Purported substitutes may be included or excluded based on how close or distant a substitute they are. The Guidelines provide that "[d]efining a relevant market sometimes requires a line-drawing exercise around product features, such as size, quality, distances, customer segment, or prices. There can be many places to draw that line and properly define a relevant market."[187]

[C] Measuring Market Concentration

After the relevant market is properly defined, the market shares of all firms in that market can be determined and the HHI can be calculated. As noted earlier, HHI refers to the Herfindahl-Hirschman Index (HHI). The index is calculated by squaring the percentage market share of each firm in the market and summing the squares. If a market has only four firms, each with 25% of the market, the HHI would be 2500 ($25^2 \times 4$). This index replaces the traditional four-firm concentration ratio previously used by the Department and by virtually all of the case law prior to 1982. The HHI is a measure of market concentration, which is important because the greater the concentration within the market, the more likely that firms can and will collude. Similarly, the greater percentage of the market controlled by a firm, the more likely that an output restriction is profitable.

The 2023 Guidelines provide two separate measures of market concentration to determine whether a proposed merger should be presumed to be illegal: (1) if the post-merger HHI is greater than 1,800 and the merger causes the HHI to increase by more than 100; or (2) if the merged firm's market share is greater than 30% and the merger causes the HHI to increase by more than 100. The Guidelines characterize a market with an HHI above 1,800 to be "highly concentrated."[188] The second presumption suggests that even if the market overall is not highly concentrated, if the merging parties have a combined market share that affords them market power, the merger should be presumed to substantially lessen competition if it meaningfully increases the HHI. These structural presumptions of illegality can be rebutted, but the greater

185. *2023 Guidelines*, *supra* note 160, at 4.3.D.2.

186. *2023 Guidelines*, *supra* note 160, at 4.3.

187. *2023 Guidelines*, *supra* note 160, at 4.3.

188. Previous iterations of the merger guidelines assigned significance to different HHI thresholds. For example, the 2010 Merger Guidelines divided market concentration into three categories: (1) unconcentrated (HHI below 1500); (2) moderately concentrated (HHI between 1500 and 2500); and highly concentrated (HHI above 2500). "Safe harbor" was created for unconcentrated markets.

the post-merger HHI and/or market share, "the stronger the evidence needed to rebut or disprove" the presumption.

[D] Anticompetitive Effects

In determining whether a merger increases the risk of coordination, the primary factors that the agencies will consider are: how concentrated the post-merger market would be; whether there had been actual or attempted prior efforts at price fixing or other coordination; whether the merger would eliminate a maverick, which is a so-called disruptive firm that is more likely to compete aggressively and not collude.[189] The 2023 Guidelines consider both "Actual Potential Competition" and "Perceived Potential Competition," in determining whether a proposed merger will substantially lessen competition.[190]

With respect to unilateral effects, the 2023 Merger Guidelines "consider whether a merger may entrench or extend an already dominant position."[191] This entails looking for direct evidence of market power or "market shares showing durable market power."[192] A proposed merger could entrench a dominant position if it raises barriers to entry, such as by increasing switching costs, interfering with the use of competitive alternatives, or depriving rivals of scale economies or network effects.[193] A merger could also entrench a dominant firm if it eliminates a nascent competitive threat from the market.[194]

[E] Defendants' Rebuttal

If the structural and other evidence establishes a presumption of illegality, the merging parties can rebut that presumption in several different ways.

First, the Guidelines recognize the failing firm defense, noting that under Supreme Court precedent, the defense has three requirements: (1) Evidence that the failing firm "face[s] the grave probability of a business failure"; (2) "The prospects of reorganization of [the failing firm are] dim or nonexistent"; and (3) "[T]he company

---

189. *2023 Merger Guidelines*, *supra* note 160, at 2.3. The Guidelines also list several "secondary factors": Market Concentration; Market Observability; Competitive Responses; Aligned Incentives; Profitability or Other Advantages of Coordination for Rivals; and Rebuttal Based on Structural Barriers to Coordination Unique to the Industry. On maverick firms, see Jonathan B. Baker, *Mavericks, Mergers, and Exclusion: Proving Coordinated Competitive Effects Under the Antitrust Laws*, 77 N.Y.U. L. Rev. 135 (2002).

190. *2023 Merger Guidelines*, *supra* note 160, at 2.3.

191. *Id.* at 2.6.

192. *Id.*

193. *Id.* at 2.6.A.

194. *Id.*

that acquires the failing [firm] or brings it under dominion is the only available purchaser."[195]

Second, the Guidelines recognize an entry and repositioning defense based on the argument that "the merger would induce entry or repositioning into the relevant market, preventing the merger from substantially lessening competition or tending to create a monopoly in the first place."[196] To successfully argue this defense, the merging parties need to show that the "entry induced by the merger would be 'timely, likely, and sufficient in its magnitude, character, and scope to deter or counteract the competitive effects of concern.'"[197] To show timeliness, the entry must be rapid enough to replace lost competition before anticompetitive effects are felt, and the entry must be durable. With respect to likelihood, the agencies will "analyze why the merger would induce entry that was not planned in pre-merger competitive conditions."[198] Finally, in order to be sufficient, the "[e]ntry must at least replicate the scale, strength, and durability of one of the merging parties to be considered sufficient."[199]

Third, the Guidelines recognize an efficiency defense. Consistent with the caselaw, the Guidelines lay out four considerations for an efficiency defense: (1) merger specificity, which means that the "substantial competitive benefits . . . could not be achieved without the merger under review"; (2) verifiability, meaning the benefits have been or can be verified using reliable methodology; (3) the efficiencies prevent a reduction in competition and do not merely benefit the merging parties; and (4) the benefits are not anticompetitive, meaning they "do not result from the anticompetitive worsening of terms for the merged firm's trading partners."[200]

[F] Remedies

In the fall of 2004, the Antitrust Division of the Department of Justice issued its Policy Guide to Merger Remedies,[201] which was updated in 2011.[202] The Antitrust Division issued a new Merger Remedies Manual in September 2020, but this was withdrawn in 2022.

---

195. *2023 Merger Guidelines, supra* note 160, at 3.1 (quoting *Citizen Publ'g Co. v. United States*, 394 U.S. 131 (1969)).

196. *2023 Merger Guidelines, supra* note 160, at 3.2.

197. *Id.* (quoting *FTC v. Sanford Health*, 926 F.3d 959, 965 (8th Cir. 2019)).

198. *Id.*

199. *Id.*

200. *Id.*

201. U.S. Dep't of Justice, *Policy Guide to Merger Remedies* (Oct. 2004) [hereinafter *2004 Merger Remedies*], *available at* http://www.usdoj.gov/atr/public/guidelines/205108.htm.

202. U.S. Dep't of Justice, *Antitrust Division Policy Guide to Merger Remedies* (June 2011), *available at* https://www.justice.gov/atr/page/file/1098656/dl.

§ 7.10 Private Enforcement of § 7

Congress provided for private enforcement of § 7. The Clayton Act is included in federal antitrust laws,[203] and § 4 of the Clayton Act creates a private cause of action for treble damages, plus attorney's fees, for injuries caused by anything forbidden in those antitrust laws.[204] Section 16[205] of the Clayton Act also permits private parties to bring an injunction action for violations of § 7.

Section 7 of the Clayton Act specifically provides that "no person engaged in commerce or in any activity affecting commerce shall acquire, directly or indirectly, the stock ... or ... assets ... of another [competitor], where the effect of such acquisition may be substantially to lessen competition, or tend to create a monopoly."[206] When a § 7 violation occurs, a private party may initiate either a treble damages action under § 4 of the Act[207] or seek injunctive relief under § 16.[208]

More specifically, § 16 enables private litigants to seek injunctive relief[209] for antitrust violations which "threaten loss or damage."[210] Provided that the alleged harm is "of the type the antitrust harms were designed to prevent and flows from that which makes the defendants' act(s) unlawful,"[211] a claimant may seek equitable relief in the form of: (1) a preliminary injunction, (2) a permanent injunction, or (3) divestiture.

---

203. 15 U.S.C. §§ 12, 15 (2011).

204. *See supra* §§ 3.01–3.02.

205. 15 U.S.C. § 26 (2011); *see supra* § 3.01. Nothing in the statutory scheme prevents a private plaintiff or state attorney general from challenging a merger or acquisition when the government, through either the Department of Justice or FTC, has approved it. *See generally Chrysler Corp. v. Gen. Motors Corp.*, 589 F. Supp. 1182 (D.D.C. 1984).

206. 15 U.S.C. § 18 (2011).

207. 15 U.S.C. § 15.

208. 15 U.S.C. § 26. "Any person, firm, corporation, or association shall be entitled to sue for and have injunctive relief ... against threatened loss or damage by a violation of the antitrust laws ... ." *Id.*; *see supra* § 3.01. Nothing in the statutory scheme prevents a private plaintiff or state attorney general from challenging a merger or acquisition when the government, through either the Department of Justice or the FTC, has previously approved it. *See generally Chrysler Corp. v. Gen. Motors Corp.*, 589 F. Supp. 1182 (D.D.C. 1984).

209. Essentially, an injunction represents an "*in personam* order, directing a party to act, or to refrain from acting in a specified way." Dan B. Dobbs, *Law of Remedies: Damages-Equity-Restitution*, § 2.11, at 249 (2d ed. 1993). Injunctions which direct a party to engage in specified conduct are deemed mandatory orders, whereas injunctions which forbid certain conduct are classified as prohibitory. *Id.*

210. *Zenith Radio Corp. v. Hazeltine Research, Inc.*, 395 U.S. 100, 130 (1969). The burden of proof requirements for injunctive relief under § 16 of the Clayton Act is lower than the actual injury to business or property requisites under § 4 of the Act. Consequently, a claimant may seek recovery for damages, even though no actual injury has transpired. Recovery, however, is dependent upon a claimant demonstrating "a significant threat of injury from an impending violation of the antitrust laws or from a contemporary violation likely to continue or recur." *Id.*

211. *Cargill Inc. v. Monfort of Colo., Inc.*, 479 U.S. 104, 113 (1986) (quoting *Brunswick Corp. v. Pueblo Bowl-O-Mat, Inc.*, 429 U.S. 477, 489 (1977)).

Whether an injunction or a realignment of a corporate structure will be ordered depends upon the district court's evaluation of "traditional equitable powers."[212]

In *California v. Am. Stores, Co.*,[213] the State of California alleged that a merger between American Stores, the fourth largest retail grocery chain in California, and Lucky Stores, the largest supermarket chain in the region, violated § 7 of the Clayton Act and consequently caused decreased competition and increased prices to consumers in sixty-two California cities.[214] The district court granted California's request for preliminary injunction.[215] On appeal, the Ninth Circuit reversed.[216] The Supreme Court granted California's writ of certiorari, to resolve a conflict between the First and Ninth Circuits.[217]

Based upon a review of the legislative history of § 16 and an analysis of each circuit court's reasoning, the Supreme Court declared that a district court is authorized to order divestiture under § 16 of the Clayton Act. Specifically, the Court held that the "statutory language of § 16 indicates Congress' intention that traditional principles of equity govern the grant of injunctive relief."[218] However, for a private litigant to effectively petition a court for such relief, the claimant must prove "threatened loss or damage to [personal] interests."[219] "This limitation [was] not designed to

---

212. *Zenith Radio Corp.*, 395 U.S. at 130. The Seventh Circuit has enunciated that "appellate review of an equitable award is based upon an abuse of discretion" standard. E. Thomas Sullivan & Herbert Hovenkamp, *Antitrust Law, Policy & Procedure* 917 (4th 1999). However, the Second Circuit has declared that a *de novo* review of the factual findings is warranted. *Id.* (citing *Norlin Corp. v. Rooney, Pace, Inc.*, 744 F.2d 255 (2d Cir. 1985)). *See generally* E. Thomas Sullivan, *The Jurisprudence of Antitrust Divestiture: The Path Less Traveled*, 86 Minn. L. Rev. 565 (2002).

213. 495 U.S. 271 (1990).

214. *Id.* at 274. This suit was commenced after the Federal Trade Commission authorized the merger, provided the merged firm divested itself of several designated supermarkets. *Id.* at 276.

In their complaint, the State of California sought a "preliminary injunction requiring American to operate the acquired stores separately until the case was decided, and then to divest itself of all of the acquired assets located in California." *Id.* at 274.

215. Noting that "Californians [would] be irreparably harmed if the proposed merger [were] completed," the district court concluded that the "State of California had proved a *prima facie* violation of Section 7 of the Clayton Act." *Id.* at 277.

216. The Ninth Circuit, relying on the "authority of its earlier decision in *International Telephone & Telegraph Corp. v. General Telephone & Electronics Corp.*, 518 F.2d 913 (9th Cir. 1975), set aside the injunction." *Id.* at 277–78. In particular, the Ninth Circuit "reasoned that divestiture was unavailable as a remedy in private actions under § 16 of the Clayton Act, and that § 16 did not permit indirect divestiture (an injunction which on its face does not order divestiture, but which has the same effect)." *Id.* at 278.

217. The First Circuit, in *Cia. Petrolera Caribe, Inc. v. Arco Caribbean, Inc.*, 754 F.2d 404 (1st Cir. 1985), held that divestiture was authorized under § 16 whereas the Ninth Circuit, in *International Telephone & Telegraph Corp. v. General Telephone & Electronics Corp.*, 518 F.2d 913 (9th Cir. 1975), held that the legislative history to § 16 did not indicate the framers' intent to authorize dissolution or divestiture as private party remedies. *Id.* at 278–79.

218. 495 U.S. at 281.

219. *Id.* at 296 (*citing Cargill, Inc. v. Monfort of Colo., Inc.*, 479 U.S. 104 (1986)). An alternative to bringing a private action is to make a third-party petition to the FTC or Department of Justice to support or instigate a government challenge to the merger. The "personal threat or injury" requirement

constrict the availability of injunctive remedies against violations that already have begun or occurred, but rather to expand their availability against harms that are as yet realized."[220] In particular, since "Congress endow[ed] the federal courts with equitable jurisdiction," absent an express or implicit statutory restriction, "the full scope of that jurisdiction will be recognized and applied."[221]

Consequently, the Court held that the "district court had the power to divest American of any part of its ownership interests in the acquired Lucky Stores, either by forbidding American to integrate operations of the two companies, or by requiring it to sell certain assets located in California." Although not applicable to this case, the Court also commented that equitable defenses are available to block injunctive relief in the form of divestiture. Said the Court, "equitable defenses such as laches or 'unclean hands' may protect consummated transactions from belated attacks by private parties when it would not be too late for the Government to vindicate the public interest."[222]

Even though the sweep of these statutes is broad in allowing private injuries to be redressed, the Supreme Court has created limitations on the application of private claims for relief. In both *Brunswick Corp. v. Pueblo Bowl-O-Mat, Inc.*,[223] and *Cargill, Inc. v. Monfort of Colorado, Inc.*,[224] the Court made clear that private plaintiffs, including competitors and targets of mergers, who bring claims under § 7 for either injunctive relief or monetary relief must show standing and antitrust injury—injury caused by a decrease in competition, the cause of which was in fact the merger.

---

may be forgone when the complaining party is not a direct participant in the suit or merger, but, rather, an interested third party. However, the government is more likely to take seriously third-party complaints if they come from a party directly or indirectly burdened from the proposed merger. *See* Lawrence R. Fullerton, *How Can I Stop that Merger? The Role of Third Parties in Agency Merger Reviews*, 9 Antitrust 37, 38 (1995). Also, third party complaints from customers may carry more weight than complaints from competitors in some instances. *Id.*

There are threats and possible downsides to this practice for the third party. Presentations can have the opposite of their intended effect, especially if made by competitors, leading the government to abandon challenges. *Id.* at 40. Second, materials submitted to the government by the challenging party may later be used against the third party itself should it attempt to engage in a merger in the future. *Id.* at 41. Finally, third party complainants run the risk of being publicly exposed through the Freedom of Information Act. *Id. See also* Tefft W. Smith & Hillard M. Sterling, *Challenging Competitor's Mergers: A Real Strategic Option*, 65 Antitrust L.J. 57 (1996).

220. 495 U.S. at 282 n.8 (*citing Zenith Radio Corp. v. Hazeltine Research, Inc.*, 395 U.S. 100, 130 (1969)).

221. *Id.* at 295.

222. 495 U.S. at 295.

223. 429 U.S. 477 (1977); *see supra* § 3.02[B].

224. 479 U.S. 104 (1986); *see supra* § 3.02[B].

§ 7.11 International Mergers and Acquisitions

Mergers between major firms have the potential for affecting not just United States commerce, but also competition on a multinational or global level.[225] Thus, just as the issue of extraterritorial enforcement of United States antitrust laws increasingly has become important in an integrated market,[226] so has international cooperation in merger review and enforcement. Dozens of countries have premerger notification requirements; a growing number, specifically the European Community (EC) and the United States, assert jurisdiction over a merger based on its competitive effect, and not the physical presence of the firms.[227] While most commentators agree that procedural convergence on standards for merger review is possible, substantive policy agreement on what constitutes a procompetitive or anticompetitive merger appears to be elusive.[228]

Transnational mergers present unique problems for those firms seeking to merge, both procedurally and substantively. Foreign acquirers seeking to merge with an American firm may be barred altogether from certain industries, or the acquisition may be subject to national security review.[229] With these exceptions, the United States antitrust laws are essentially neutral as to the nationalities of the firms. Transnational firms may merge after meeting the Hart-Scott-Rodino (HSR) filing requirements and passing the substantive merger review by either the Department of Justice or Federal Trade Commission.[230] The 1995 International Enforcement Guidelines delineated the special "foreign commerce" rules of the Hart-Scott Rodino Act; some transactions will be exempt entirely from reporting.[231] The subsequent substantive merger review is identical to that between two domestic firms: the agency will employ the 2010 *Merger Guidelines* to assess whether the merger will have the effect of substantially lessening competition in the United States.[232] However, market definition is com-

---

225. Daniel J. Gifford & E. Thomas Sullivan, *Can International Antitrust Be Saved for the Post-Boeing Merger World? A Proposal to Minimize International Conflict and to Rescue Antitrust from Misuse*, 35 Antitrust Bull. 55, 58 (2000).

226. *See supra* § 3.03[C].

227. Douglas H. Ginsburg & Scott H. Angstreich, *Multinational Merger Review: Lessons from Our Federalism*, 68 Antitrust L.J. 219, 220–21 (2000). *See generally*, E. Thomas Sullivan, *Harmonizing Global Merger Standards in the Political Economy of International Trade Law* 248–51 (2002).

228. *See, e.g.*, Ginsburg & Angstreich, *supra* note 227, 222–26; *see also* Daniel J. Gifford & Robert Kudrle, *Alternative Merger Standards and the Prospects for International Cooperation in the Political Economy of International Trade* 208–47 (2002).

229. *See* Spencer Weber Waller, *International Trade and U.S. Antitrust Law* § 8.01 (1992 & Supp. 2001).

230. *Id.*

231. U.S. Dep't of Justice & FTC, 1995 *Antitrust Enforcement Guidelines for International Operations* §§ 2.4, 4.22 (1995) [hereinafter *1995 Guidelines*].

232. See *2010 Guidelines, supra* note 159, at § 1.0.

plicated by inclusion of foreign production.[233] If foreign production is excluded, a prima facie violation of § 7 is likely to occur; if it is included, it may reduce the merged firm's market shares and concentration within the United States.[234] Additionally, the relevant geographic market may be narrowed to a few countries, or may be global in scope. While these factors are additional variables in the analysis, the structure of the merger evaluation is essentially the same.

The Department of Justice takes further guidance from the 1995 International Operations Guidelines.[235] The 1995 Guidelines analyze the jurisdictional issues that can arise with transnational mergers. If two foreign firms seeking to merge account for a large percentage of United States sales through direct imports, the agency will likely assert jurisdiction over the merger based on the effect on U.S. imports.[236] Conversely, if a proposed merger would effect U.S. export commerce, the agencies would also apply the "direct, substantial and reasonably foreseeable" effects test of the Foreign Trade Antitrust Improvements Act.[237] The 1995 Guidelines recognize that while the agency may assert "technical" jurisdiction over the merger, the principle of "positive comity" may require the DOJ to consult and cooperate with another country's antitrust authorities also reviewing the proposed merger.

Although the United States agency may ultimately approve a merger, the parallel enforcement agency of a foreign jurisdiction may consider it anticompetitive and thus signal its outright disapproval, effectively killing the merger. This was the case in 2001, when the European Commission quashed a merger between General Electric and Honeywell that the Department of Justice had approved.[238] Even if the parallel agency ultimately clears the merger, it may require the firms to make concessions and compromises in their lines of business. This was the case in 1997, when the EC cleared the McDonnell-Douglas-Boeing merger only after last-minute negotiations.

The McDonnell-Boeing merger threw into dramatic relief the differences in antitrust policy between the United States and the European Community. At issue was the European Commission's finding that the proposed merger, as evaluated under the European Union Merger Regulation, was unlawful.[239] The Federal Trade Commission had approved the merger. Prior to the merger, the market consisted only of three firms: McDonnell-Douglas, Boeing, and Airbus Industrie. The European Commission objected specifically to several exclusive supply contracts that Boeing had negotiated with U.S. airlines, stating that those contracts strengthened Boeing's dominant position. The exclusive supply contracts would have the effect of foreclosing Airbus from the U.S. customer base, and lowering Boeing's cost. When the Commission

233. Waller, *supra* note 229, at § 8.02.

234. *Id.*

235. *Id.* § 8.09.

236. *1995 Guidelines*, *supra* note 231, at § 3.14.

237. *Id.* § 3.14.

238. *EU Commission Bars Acquisition of Honeywell by General Electric*, 81 Antitrust & Trade Reg. Rep. 14 (BNA) (July 5, 2001).

239. Gifford & Sullivan, *supra* note 225, at 69.

withdrew its objection to the merger, it did so on the condition that Boeing would not enforce those contracts for ten years, nor seek to enter new exclusive supply contracts during that ten-year period. The reason was to maintain the interfirm rivalry between Boeing and its European counterpart, Airbus, and to protect Airbus from a perceived abuse of dominance by Boeing.[240]

In contrast, the FTC had approved the merger without objection, noting the efficiencies that would result. The conflict in the merger occurred despite the existence of a cooperation agreement between the United States and the EC. The United States and EC enforcement agencies simply differed in the goals each had for their respective antitrust law regimes: current United States merger review prioritizes the efficiencies that result from a merger; the EC advances a non-economic interest in protecting competitors.[241]

Currently, the European Community is reevaluating its competition policy, but the problems encountered with the McDonnell-Boeing merger are typical, if magnified by the size of the merged firms. As one commentator noted, "[w]hile we live in a global economy . . . we do not live a global state. There is no international antitrust code, nor are there international rules for resolving issues of jurisdiction and enforcement procedure."[242]

§ 7.12 Conclusion

Most merger cases decided under the antitrust laws arise either from the fear (1) that increased size and market power will harm smaller businesses, or (2) that increased concentration in markets will result in supracompetitive profits through higher prices that will harm consumers either by the resulting economic inefficiency or by redistributing wealth from consumers to producers. As a consequence, merger law has developed to prevent mergers and acquisitions from resulting in collusive pricing, monopoly power, exploitation of economies of scale, or oligopolistic interdependence. "Bigness" *per se* is no longer the target of § 7. Increased size and concentration also can result from economies of scale that can produce benefits to consumers as long as the savings are passed along. Although almost all antitrust observers agree that mergers that result in higher prices are the core target of § 7, many disagree on why higher prices are suspect. Some argue it is because higher prices are economically

---

240. *Id.*

241. Gifford & Sullivan, *supra* note 225; *see also* A. Douglas Melamed, *International Antitrust in an Age of International Deregulation*, 6 Geo. Mason L. Rev. 437, 444. *But see EU Commissioner Discusses Merger Remedies and Proposals*, 82 Antitrust & Trade Reg. Rep. 73 (BNA) (Jan. 25, 2002); Gifford & Kudrle, *supra* note 228.

242. Melamed, *supra* note 241, at 438; *see also* Sullivan, *supra* note 227. *See generally* E. Thomas Sullivan, *Comparing Antitrust Remedies in the U.S. and E.U.: Advancing a Standard of Proportionality* 48 Antitrust Bull. 377 (2003).

inefficient; others argue it is because they transfer wealth from consumers to producers with market power.

The trend away from presumptive illegality, based on statistical showings of increased concentration and market power, and toward a functional approach, based on a showing of actual anticompetitive practices or results, is likely to continue. This will result in increased importance for economic theory and place greater emphasis on understanding how individual markets are affected by certain market conduct, such as coordinated interaction and ease of entry. This is the essence of the *Guidelines*, with their focus on a detailed quantitative analysis rather than the general, qualitative approach of the case law. The result, under the *Guidelines*, yields fewer merger challenges, less court intervention, and more reliance on merger deregulation and market solutions. That resolution, of course, is driven by certain political and economic ideologies. As demonstrated in this chapter, a substantial tension exists between the case law, the present *Guidelines*, and certain economic theories.[243] But enforcement of the laws governing mergers has not been consistent[244] and rarely has there been unanimity in the enforcement of the merger laws.

Historically, the FTC's merger enforcement activity revealed a disparity between the thresholds stated in the *Guidelines* and the actual practice of the agency.[245] The petroleum industry is one exception, where government practice seems to follow the *Guidelines* more closely. Data released by the FTC showed that between 1996–2011, 71% of the agency's advanced investigations into oil sector mergers came in markets with an HHI below 2400.[246] Further, the oil sector accounted for all 90 challenges that the FTC brought during this period to markets with an HHI below 2000.[247] The pharmaceutical industry also comes under exceptionally heavy FTC scrutiny. Approximately 98% of advanced investigations into pharmaceutical mergers result in an enforcement action, while other sectors average 75%.[248] Regardless of sector, the FTC attempts to resolve most of its enforcement actions via negotiated settlements. Nine out of the 11 complaints filed by the FTC in district courts during fiscal year 2017 were accompanied by a proposed settlement.[249]

Perhaps as evidence of this relaxed attitude, in June of 2004 the FTC announced that it would not challenge the merger of R.J. Reynolds with Brown & Williamson Tobacco Co. The two firms were the second and third largest tobacco companies in

243. Cohen & Sullivan, *supra* note 34, at 505.

244. Sullivan, *supra* note 10, at 1000.

245. *See* FTC, *Merger Challenges Data, Fiscal Years 1999–2003, available at* www.ftc.gov.

246. Federal Trade Commission: Horizontal Merger Investigation Data, Fiscal Years 1996–2011, *available at*: https://www.ftc.gov/sites/default/files/documents/reports/horizontal-merger-investigation-data-fiscal-years-1996-2011/130104horizontalmergerreport.pdf.

247. FTC Report Shows That Oil Sector and Pharmaceutical Sector Mergers Are Under the Antitrust Spotlight, *available at*: https://www.lexology.com/library/detail.aspx?g=674d3352-9c1e-4248-9f2c-9d5fd0306149.

248. *Id.*

249. Federal Trade Commission and Department of Justice, Hart-Scott-Rodino Annual Report (2017).

the United States, in an industry where charges of price fixing have been frequent. Together, the market share of the two firms was approximately 32%, though that had been declining in recent years. The FTC stated its belief that the new firm, to be called Reynolds American, Inc., might be in a stronger position to compete against market leader Phillip Morris, USA.

Chapter 8

Price Discrimination

§ 8.01 Introduction

The Robinson-Patman Act prohibits certain instances of price discrimination, which occurs when a seller charges different prices to different buyers. This Depression-era Act was passed principally to protect small competitors.[1] Arguments based on economic theory suggest that it may actually cause prices to increase and output to decrease.[2] Consequently, the Act is viewed by many as misguided in the context of modern antitrust theory. Whatever strength the Act had by way of private enforcement has been diminished by a number of Supreme Court decisions.[3] On the other hand, although the interest of the Justice Department and the FTC in enforcing the Act has waned considerably over the years,[4] this could change with the political climate.

[A] The Clayton Act and Robinson-Patman Amendments

For antitrust purposes, the most relevant sections of the Robinson-Patman Act,[5] are §§ 2(a)–(f) which amend § 2 of the Clayton Act. Although both § 2 of the 1914 Clayton Act and the Robinson-Patman Act amendments of 1936 are nominally aimed at prohibiting price discrimination, a comparison of the two reveals the changing

1. *See* Hansen, *Robinson-Patman Law: A Review and Analysis,* Fordham L. Rev. 1113, 1120–24 (1983). *See generally* F. Rowe, *Price Discrimination Under the Robinson-Patman Act* (1962).

2. *See, e.g.*, R. Blair & D. Kaserman. *Antitrust Economics* (1985); R. Bork, *The Antitrust Paradox* (1978); R. Posner, *The Robinson-Patman Act: Federal Regulation of Price Differences* (1976); Schmalensee, *Output and Welfare Implications of Monopolistic Third-Degree Price Discrimination*, 71 Am. Econ. Rev. 242 (1981).

3. *See Brooke Group Ltd. v. Brown & Williamson Tobacco*, 509 U.S. 209 (1993); *J. Truett Payne Co. v. Chrysler Motors Corp.*, 451 U.S. 557 (1981).

4. *See* Hansen, *supra* note 1, at 1174–82.

5. The first section of the Robinson-Patman Act is an amendment to § 2 of the Clayton Act. Section 3 of the Robinson-Patman Act provides for criminal sanctions of up to $5,000, imprisonment not exceeding one year, or both if a person engages or assists in (1) general price discrimination, (2) geographical price discrimination, or (3) selling at unreasonably low prices to destroy competition or eliminate competitors. 15 U.S.C. § 13a. Private actions for treble damages are not available for

nature of the concerns of the drafters in 1914 and their 1936 counterparts. Language in the original version of the Clayton Act and subsequent interpretations indicate that the harm to be prevented was caused by firms, operating in multiple markets, who were thought to raise prices in markets in which they possessed market power in order to subsidize price cutting in markets in which they sought to gain power. Consequently, protection extended only to direct competitors of the discriminating firms. This left unprotected competitors of buyers that were able to elicit relatively favorable prices from their suppliers. In response, the 1936 amendments added language so that the Act currently prohibits discrimination:

> [i]n price between different purchasers of commodities of like grade and quality . . . where the effect of such discrimination may be substantially to lessen competition or tend to create a monopoly in any line of commerce, or to injure, destroy, or prevent competition with any person who either grants or knowingly receives the benefit of such discrimination, or with customers of either of them. . . .[6]

Today, Robinson-Patman Act violations are typically categorized as either "primary-line," "secondary-line," or "tertiary-line." Primary-line cases concern discrimination that may result in injury to the seller's competitors. Secondary-line cases, included by the Robinson-Patman amendments, involve discrimination that affects competition among customers of the discriminating seller. Tertiary-line cases involve injury further down the chain of distribution to the customers of the favored and disfavored purchasers.[7]

[B] Overview: The Components of the Robinson-Patman Act

[1] Price "Discrimination" and Price "Difference"

Section 2(a) of the Robinson-Patman Act makes it illegal for any person to "discriminate in price." As an economic matter, a seller discriminates when the difference in price charged to different customers does not reflect the difference in the marginal cost of selling to those customers.[8] Thus, even a seller charging the same price to different customers is engaged in price discrimination when the costs of serving those customers are different. Under the Robinson-Patman Act, however, "price

injuries caused by sales "at unreasonably low prices" but may be for injuries caused by "unlawful price discrimination." *Safeway Stores v. Vance*, 355 U.S. 389 (1958).

6. 15 U.S.C. § 13(a) (1976).

7. *See Feesers v. Michael Food, Inc.*, 498 F.3d 206 (3d Cir. 2007); *Perkins v. Standard Oil*, 395 U.S. 642 (1969). *See generally* F. Rowe, *supra* note 1, at 185–95; H. Shniderman, *Price Discrimination in Perspective* 39–41 (1977).

8. *See* Roger Blair & David Kaserman, *Antitrust Economics* (2d ed. 2008).

discrimination" generally has been held to mean "price difference."[9] Consequently, from the point of view of economic theory, the Act falls considerably short of being a complete bar to price discrimination. To a minor degree, this discrepancy between the Act's coverage and the economist's definition of "price discrimination" is cured by the Act's prohibition of "indirect" discrimination[10] and its provision for a "cost justification" defense for different prices.[11]

[2] Section 2(a) Components

In addition to the "price difference" requirement, § 2(a) contains a number of limiting elements. First, it applies only to *sales* of *commodities* of *like grade and quality*. Additionally, there must be at least two contemporaneous sales to different purchasers and at least one sale must result in the commodity crossing state lines.[12] The primary substantive requirement of the Act is that the discrimination must result in competitive injury. Finally, the Act not only prohibits sellers from discriminatory pricing, but § 2(f) prohibits buyers from inducing such discrimination.

[3] Defenses

Although their utility to the seller has been limited by judicial interpretation, there are two basic affirmative defenses to a price discrimination claim. First, the Act does not prohibit price differences that reflect "differences in the cost of manufacture, sale or delivery."[13] Second, no violation will be found if the price difference was the product of a good faith attempt to meet the "equally low price of a competitor."[14] An additional and seldomly used defense permits price differences that result from price changes from "time to time" in response to changing market conditions or the "marketability of the goods."[15] These defenses have diminished in importance, as liability under the Act, at least presently, is unlikely.

[4] Other Offenses

The Robinson-Patman Act prohibits three forms of discrimination beyond those called price discrimination. Section 2(c) makes it unlawful for a person "to pay or grant, or receive or accept" brokerage in any form except for "services rendered."[16] Sections 2(d) and (e) prohibit the granting of promotional allowances to the buyer

---

9. *FTC v. Anheuser-Busch, Inc.*, 363 U.S. 536, 549 (1960).
10. *See infra* § 8.03[B][3].
11. *See infra* § 8.05[A].
12. *Gulf Oil Corp. v. Copp Paving Co. Inc.*, 419 U.S. 186. 200 (1974).
13. 15 U.S.C. § 13(a) (1976).
14. *Id.* at § 13(b). For an example of conduct that goes beyond a "good faith" attempt and implicates § 1 of the Sherman Act, see *United States v. Gypsum Co.*, 438 U.S. 422 (1978).
15. *Id.* at § 13(a) (1976).
16. *Id.* at § 13(c).

by the seller in the form of payments or the provision of services or facilities unless allowances are available to all customers on "proportionally equal terms."[17]

[5] Coverage

Some of the more perplexing questions presented by the Robinson-Patman Act arise under § 2(a) and concern the determination of when discrimination occurs, when products are of like grade and quality, and what constitutes "competitive injury." These matters as well as defenses to a price discrimination charge and the elements of the Act are the focus of this Chapter. First, however, a discussion of the economic theory of price discrimination is essential for an understanding of the bases of modern criticism of the Act.

§ 8.02 The Economics of Price Discrimination

Economic theory suggests that the price and output effects of price discrimination cannot be confidently determined without examining demand and supply in the markets involved[18]—a difficult undertaking to say the least. The alarming implication for the Robinson-Patman Act is that price discrimination may, depending on a number of variables, result in lower prices and higher output—goals that the antitrust laws are designed to foster, not hinder.[19] Most of the contemporary criticism of the Act is fueled by uncertainty concerning its economic impact and the likelihood that any of the truly anticompetitive effects of discriminatory pricing can be responded to by enforcing other provisions of the antitrust laws.[20]

Economists generally categorize price discrimination as either first-degree, second-degree, or third-degree price discrimination. First-degree, or perfect, price discrimination means each individual consumer is charged the highest price they are willing to pay. This requires the seller to know each consumer's "willingness to pay" and charge personalized prices. Second-degree price discrimination entails a seller offering different versions of a good or service and having consumers sort themselves. For example, because airlines believe that business travelers are willing to pay more than leisure travelers, airlines charge a lower price for roundtrip tickets that straddle a weekend, figuring that leisure travelers are more likely to want to spend a weekend

---

17. *Id.* at §§ 13 (d) and (e).

18. *See generally* J. Robinson, *Economics of Imperfect Competition* (1933); Schmalensee, *supra* note 2.

19. *See* Schmalensee, *supra* note 2.

20. *See, e.g.*, R. Posner, *supra* note 2, at 52–53. Most of the contemporary economic analysis of the Robinson-Patman Act is derived from the analysis of A.C. Pigou, *The Economics of Welfare* (4th ed. 1938), and J. Robinson, *supra* note 18.

away than are business travelers. Third-degree price discrimination involves categorizing consumers into groups based on their perceived willingness to pay and charging consumers in the high-willingness-to-pay group a higher price than consumers in the low-willingness-to-pay group. Senior discounts and student discounts represent attempts at third-degree price discrimination because older people and students are generally perceived as having a lower willingness to pay. Each type of price discrimination is discussed at greater length below.

[A] First-Degree Price Discrimination

The fears of economists and antitrust scholars concerning the Robinson-Patman Act can be illustrated by reference to a theoretical construct called "first degree" or "perfect" price discrimination. The concept is best understood by reviewing profit maximizing price and output determination by a monopolist. In Figure 8-1—a reproduction of Figure 2-8—profit maximizing output is determined by the intersection of the marginal cost and marginal revenue curves. The profit maximizing price, Pm, is the highest price for which that quantity can be sold. Suppose that quantity Qm is 10. The monopolist would not sell an 11th unit because the marginal cost of that unit would exceed marginal revenue. This is not to say that the price for the 11th unit is not higher than the marginal cost of that unit. In fact, it would be. The problem for the monopolist is that in order to sell unit 11 the price of all units will have to be lowered. The marginal revenue from selling that unit is its selling price minus the revenue lost by lowering the price of all the other units sold. This is, of course, nothing more than an explanation of why the marginal revenue curve lies below the demand curve.

It would be a form of monopolist's heaven if the firm could somehow lower its price to sell additional units and not lower the prices for all units. This is, in fact, the test of the whether it makes sense for the monopolist to discriminate. It must be able to segregate its customers in order to sell to different customers at different prices. To the extent the monopolist can do this, its marginal revenue curve becomes the same as its demand curve. The most extreme example of this possibility holds true under first degree or perfect price discrimination. In this model, the monopolist is able to sell each unit to each customer at that customer's reservation price (the highest amount he or she would be willing to pay). In Figure 8-1, for example, unit 1 would be sold for P1, unit 2 for P2, and so on. Since the monopolist will sell as long as marginal revenue exceeds marginal cost and the demand curve is now the marginal revenue curve, the monopolist will sell a total of Qx units at a series of declining prices.

There are several things to note about this solution. First, the total output—where the demand curve and the marginal cost curves intersect—should look familiar. It's the same output one would expect under perfectly competitive market conditions. Second, the deadweight loss that was discussed as a product of monopoly pricing in Chapters 2 and 6 has also been eliminated. In short, price discrimination has resulted in higher output, lower prices for some (higher for others) and elimination of the deadweight loss.

Figure 8-1.

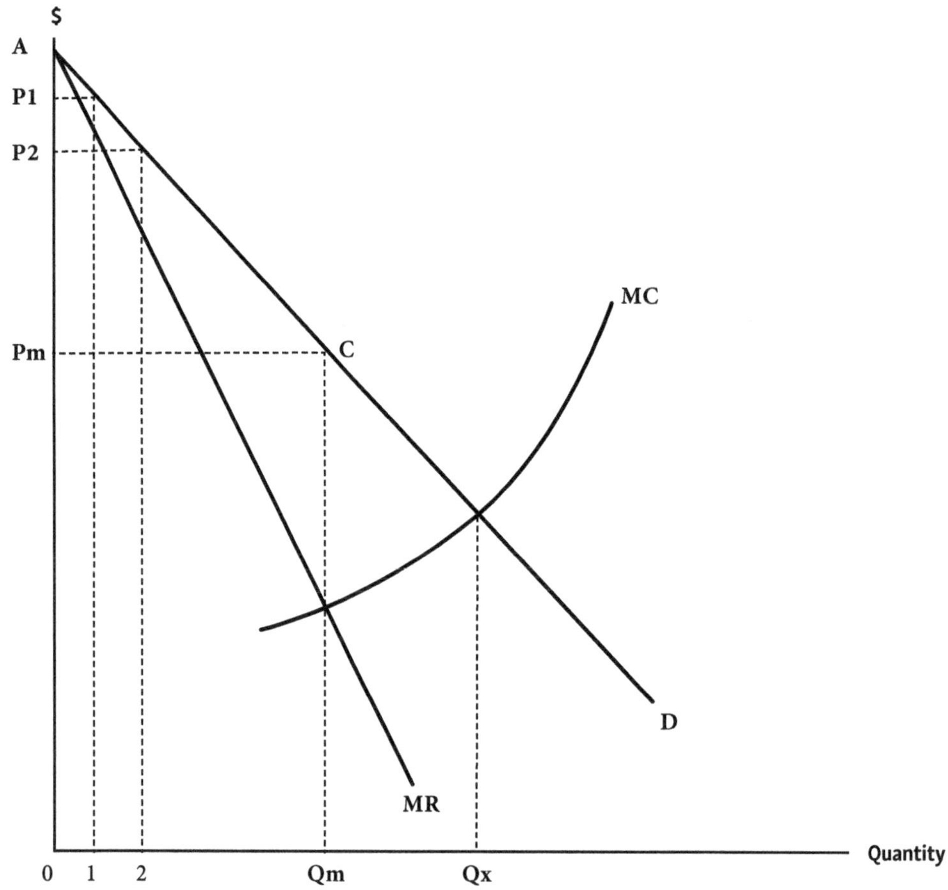

Other results under first degree discrimination may not be as encouraging. First, there is no longer any consumer surplus. Since the monopolist has sold to each customer at the highest price he or she is willing to pay, the monopolist has transferred all of the area which was consumer surplus (PmAC in Figure 8-1) to itself. One's reaction to this will depend upon whether they feel antitrust law should be concerned with distributive effects.

A second concern is probably less controversial. Obviously, the discriminating monopolist stands to gain a great deal. It must, however, isolate each buyer in order to sell at that buyer's reservation price without lowering the price to others and ensure that each low price buyer does not engage in arbitrage. Indeed, in theory, the attraction of perfect discrimination could be so strong that a monopolist may be tempted to invest a great deal in the buyer segregation effort. These expenditures, to the extent they are only designed to transfer the surplus created by the exchange from consumers to the seller, can be viewed as a new form of deadweight loss.[21]

---

21. R. Posner, *supra* note 2, at 7–10.

[B] Second-Degree Price Discrimination

Perfect or first degree price discrimination is really only a theoretical possibility. In fact, there is little likelihood that a monopolist would expend substantial effort in hopes of achieving perfect market segregation. It is not at all unlikely, however, that a monopolist might perceive an opportunity to segregate the market into two or more parts. This is "second degree" or "imperfect" price discrimination.[22] One possible result is illustrated in Figure 8-2. Here the monopolist has continued to sell to some buyers at Pm, the original profit maximizing price. It has also isolated a group of buyers who are willing and able to pay more, price Ph. In addition, if the monopolist is able to prevent them from reselling to those paying Ph or Pm, it will isolate a third group to which it will sell at price P1. In the graph five units will be sold at Ph, five will be sold at Pm and five will be sold at P1. Here again the monopolist has transferred some of what was consumer surplus to itself. On the other hand, it has increased output and is now selling to a third group that would not have purchased at the non-discriminatory price of Pm. Second degree price discrimination, like first degree, raises the possibility of a deadweight loss arising from efforts to classify buyers into their proper price group and segregate them. And, since second degree price discrimination is a more realistic possibility, the likelihood of experiencing such a loss is greater.

[C] Third-Degree Price Discrimination

Although second degree price discrimination is far more likely than first degree, it involves a simplification that causes it to deviate from what most monopolists are likely to encounter in the real world. Under second degree, the market was divisible so that all buyers willing to pay Ph or more, paid Ph. All buyers willing to pay an amount equal to Pm but less than Ph were charged Pm and only buyers unwilling to pay Pm, but willing to pay at least P1, were charged P1. This degree of market segregation is not likely.

In the more realistic model, "third degree" price discrimination, the problems of market segregation are recognized.[23] For example, by holding to price P1 in one market—say, one that is geographically separate—the seller will not charge as much as it could to those buyers in that market who are willing to pay Pm or Ph. Similarly, adhering to Pm in another market may exclude some individuals who are willing to pay only P1 and permit some buyers who are willing to pay Ph to buy for only Pm. Further complications arise because of the investment required to effectively segregate the market to prevent buyers in low price markets from reselling in competition with the monopolist in higher priced markets. Indeed, this investment may be so great that the monopolist may choose not to offer price P1 at all and output will not

22. *See* A.C. Pigou, *supra* note 20, at 275–79.

23. *Id. See also* L. Philips, *The Economics of Price Discrimination* 12–13 (1983).

Figure 8-2.

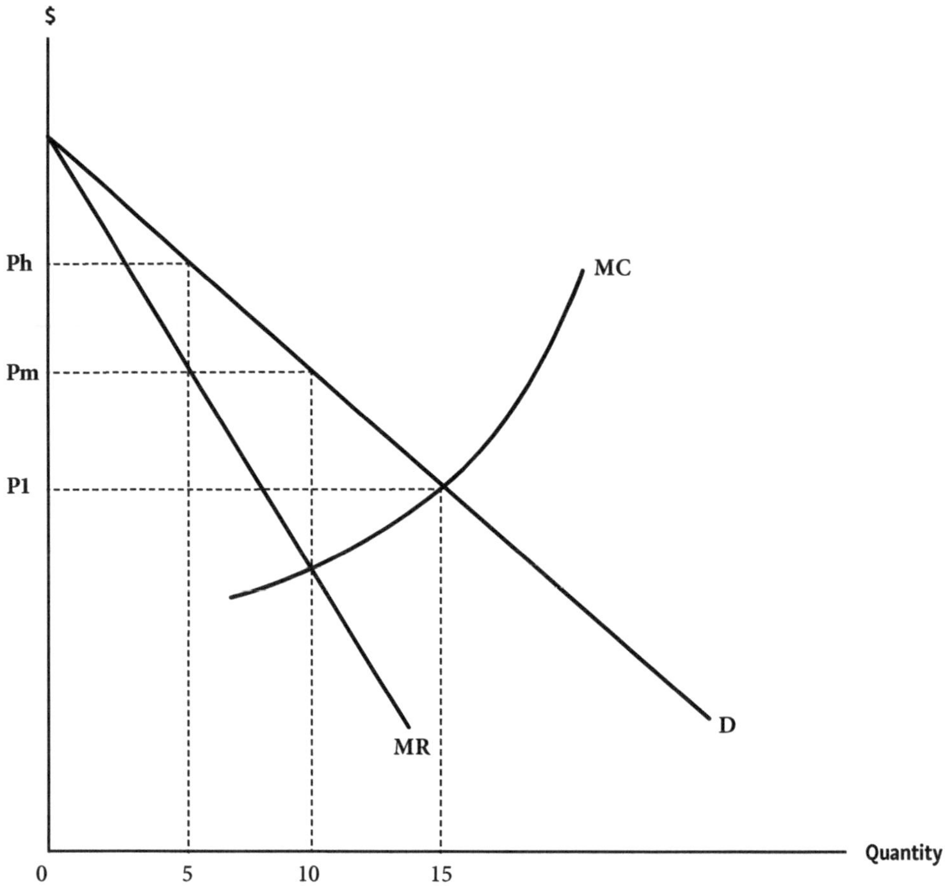

increase. If so, the only discrimination that would take place would be among those willing to pay at least Pm and output may actually fall.[24]

As a consequence of these more real world considerations, it is difficult to predict whether price discrimination will result in higher output and lower prices or not. The answer depends in large measure on the shape of the demand curves facing the seller.[25] What this means for the Robinson-Patman Act is fairly simple: Even if it were not difficult to interpret, and even if it were interpreted in a manner that was consistent with the economist's notion of price discrimination, there is no certainty concerning the benefits of its enforcement.

24. *See* J. Robinson, *supra* note 18, at 188–95.
25. *See id.*; Schmalensee, *supra* note 2.

§ 8.03 Definitional Issues

As noted earlier, the Robinson-Patman Act is directed at price differences, not price discrimination in a technical sense. The emphasis on price difference means that economic analysis is less important than it would be under a more economically based prohibition of price discrimination. Still, the plaintiff must present evidence that the defendant has made two sales of commodities of like grade and quality at two different prices to two different buyers. The issues of whether there is in fact a price difference and whether the goods are of like grade and quality are intriguing and can be quite complicated.

[A] Two Prices and Two Sales

The importance of the technical requirements of two prices and two sales is illustrated by *Lycon, Inc. v. Juneke*.[26] The plaintiff was a distributor that purchased equipment from the defendant. It then resold the equipment. The defendant also sold through its own retail stores. The retail prices were lower than the price available to the distributor. The court held that the plaintiff did not fall within the protection of the Act. First, the plaintiff was not a competitor of the supplier. Thus, there was no harm at the primary level. Second, although the plaintiff did compete with the retail sales the defendant did not make a sale to its own retail stores. Finally, even though the defendant did make retail sales these sales were to end users who did not resell in competition with the plaintiff.[27]

The different price issue was also addressed in *Liberty Lincoln-Mercury v. Ford Motor Co.*,[28] in which a Ford dealer used New Jersey law to force Ford to raise its reimbursement rate on parts installed under an automobile's warranty. Other dealers in New Jersey had not sought the same concessions. In reaction, Ford raised the wholesale price of vehicles in order to recoup the lower prices on parts. The court ruled that the plaintiff had failed to demonstrate a price difference. The court reasoned that the surcharge on vehicles actually had the effect of equalizing prices.[29]

---

26. 250 F.3d 285 (5th Cir. 2001) *See also Felder's Collision Parts, Inc. v. General Motors*, 960 F. Supp. 2d 617 (M.D. La. 2013).

27. 250 F.3d at 289.

28. 134 F.3d 557 (3d Cir. 1998).

29. *Id.* at 571. It is noteworthy that the court reasoned that even if there were a price difference it would not have an adverse competitive effect. *Id.* at 571.

[B] Price Differences

[1] Discounts

Suppose a seller publishes a price list in which the price per unit declines with the amount purchased. From one point of view, this means that buyers purchasing small quantities will pay a different price per unit than those who purchase larger quantities and § 2(a) would come into play. On the other hand, if the option of purchasing higher amounts for a lower price per unit is available to all, it seems inappropriate to regard the seller as having discriminated in any active fashion. A similar problem is presented when the seller quotes one price but offers a discount from that price for buyers who pay within a stipulated time period. Again, different buyers are charged different prices but the opportunity for the favorable price would seem to be available to all.

The Supreme Court provided the test for determining whether such discounts are discriminatory in *F.T.C. v. Morton Salt*,[30] perhaps the leading price discrimination case. Morton Salt offered substantial discounts to customers who purchased salt in greater than carload lots. Its defense was that the discounts were available to all purchasers on an equal basis. As a factual matter only five large purchasers qualified for the lowest discount. In finding that the discount amounted to the type of discrimination forbidden by the Robinson-Patman Act, the Supreme Court noted that "[t]heoretically, these discounts are available to all, but functionally they are not."[31]

A further requirement is illustrated by *Mueller v. FTC*[32] in which a manufacturer offered different discounts to jobbers depending upon whether items purchased were shipped directly to end users or warehoused.[33] The manufacturer contended that the higher discount was available to all jobbers willing to carry an inventory of the items. The Seventh Circuit Court of Appeals sided with the FTC and rejected the argument, noting the lack of *objective* standards to indicate how a jobber became eligible for the more favorable discount.[34]

In *Smith Wholesale Co. v. Phillip Morris USA, Inc.*,[35] plaintiffs, distributors of cigarettes to retail outlets, complained of a market share based discount. Under the plan, plaintiffs were afforded discounts based on the percentage of their total sales that were of defendant's brands. The defendant's brands tended to be relatively expensive and the plaintiffs argued that because their customers sold in rural "low-end" markets in which consumers tended to purchase less expensive cigarettes they were unable to obtain the discounts. In effect, they argued that the discounts were not functionally available to them because of the nature of the demand faced by their customers.

---

30. 334 U.S. 37 (1948).
31. *Id.* at 42.
32. 323 F.2d 44 (7th Cir. 1963). *See also FLM Collision Parts v. Ford Motor Co.*, 543 F.2d 1019 (2d Cir. 1976).
33. This so-called "functional discount" is discussed in § 8.04[B][1], *infra*.
34. 323 F.2d at 46.
35. 477 F.3d 854 (6th Cir. 2007).

Moreover, it put them in an untenable position. They could achieve the discounts only by reducing sales of less expensive cigarettes, thereby raising the percentage of sale of the Phillip Morris brand.

The Sixth Circuit Court of Appeals affirmed the lower court's grant of summary judgment for the defendant. It held that the discount was functionally available to all. It reasoned that the price differences experienced by plaintiffs were the result of choices related to marketing strategy and brand prioritization.[36]

[2] Base Point Pricing

A potentially troublesome problem in the determination of whether price discrimination exists surfaces when a seller makes use of a uniform delivered price or a basing point pricing system. As noted in the discussion of horizontal restraints in Chapter 4, the use of delivered pricing means that the prices charged to different buyers may deviate in different degrees from the cost of actually serving them. For example, in a uniform delivered price scheme, the marginal cost of serving distant buyers will not be fully reflected in the price. Similarly, in a basing point system, although the delivered prices will vary depending upon the buyer's distance from the seller's basing point, the actual delivered charge will not reflect the seller's costs unless the basing point and point of origin are the same.

The question becomes whether the relevant price for § 2(a) purposes is the delivered price or the "mill-net" return. Certainly the "mill-net" approach would mean that enforcement of the Act would parallel the economist's definition of price discrimination. And, for a period after passage of the Act, the Supreme Court, despite legislative history suggesting the contrary,[37] seemed receptive to a "mill-net" approach and held that basing point pricing violated the Act.[38] Primarily as a result of FTC's enforcement policy,[39] the relevant price has shifted to the delivered price or the price "laid down" by the buyer.[40] The reasoning is that the actual price paid is the relevant one in determining the buyer's ability to compete with other buyers in the resale market.[41]

Thus a system of uniform delivered prices probably no longer falls within the purview of § 2(a).[42] On the other hand, a basing point pricing system would result in the

---

36. *Id.* at 881.

37. *See generally* F. Rowe, *supra* note 1, at 87–89.

38. *See Corn Products Ref. Co. v. FTC*, 324 U.S. 726 (1945); *FTC v. A.E. Staley Mfg. Co.*, 324 U.S. 746 (1945); *FTC v. Cement Institute*, 333 U.S. 683 (1948). *See generally* P. Areeda, *Antitrust Analysis* 1095–97 (3d ed. 1981); F. Rowe, *supra* note 1, at 88–90.

39. *See* L. Sullivan, *Antitrust*, 688 (1977), *citing* National Lead Co., 497 F.T.C. 791 (1953), *modified sub. nom., National Lead Co. v. FTC*, 227 F.2d 825 (7th Cir. 1955), *original order aff'd*, 352 U.S. 419.

40. *See, e.g., Rose Confections Inc. v. Ambrosia Chocolate Co.*, 52 A & T.R.R. 768 (April 13, 1987). *See generally* P. Areeda, *Antitrust Analysis* 1095–97 (1981); F. Rowe, *supra* note 1, at 92–108. *But see Chicago Spring Prods. Co. v. United States Steel Corp.*, 254 F. Supp. 83 (N.D. Ill. 1965), *aff'd. per curiam*, 371 F.2d 428 (7th Cir. 1966).

41. *See Report of the Attorney General's National Committee to Study the Antitrust Laws* 58 (1955), at 217.

42. *See, e.g., Clay Prods. Ass'n.*, 47 F.T.C. 1256 (1951); *National Lead Co.*, 49 F.T.C. 791 (1953).

requisite price difference.[43] If the basing point were the point of shipment, however, the difference may be excused by the cost justification defense.[44] When the basing point is not the point of actual shipment there exists both the required price difference and the lack of a cost justification defense. Even here, however, one can argue that freight absorption is a form of meeting competition, another defense found in the Act, and the occurrence of phantom freight is simply profit maximizing pricing and not prohibited by the Act.[45]

[3] Indirect Price Discrimination

The Robinson-Patman Act also forbids "indirect" price discrimination.[46] Applied literally, the concept of "indirect" price discrimination could be broad enough to bring the economist's definition of discrimination into the scope of the Robinson-Patman Act. This has not, however, been the course taken. Indirect discrimination has been reserved for instances in which buyers pay the same nominal price, but some are favored by the seller in terms of ancillary services.[47]

For example, in *Corn Products Refining Co. v. FTC*,[48] sellers would announce price increases and then permit buyers a "grace" period during which orders would be filled at the previous price. Some buyers were, however, given a longer period of time during which they could take advantage of the earlier price. The petitioner argued that this was not price discrimination but discrimination in the "terms and condition" of sale.[49] The argument found support in the legislative history of the Act which indicated that Congress specifically had rejected listing discriminatory "terms of sale" as violating the Act.[50] The Court relied on an examination of the "practical effect"[51] of the difference in treatment in order to distinguish differences in "terms of sale" that would constitute an indirect form of price discrimination[52] from those that would not. It held that the petitioner's practice amounted to indirect price discrimination.

[4] Indirect Purchasers

Both the express terms of § 2(a) and any coherent interpretation of the concept of price discrimination require that the different prices be charged to different purchasers. A definitional issue in this regard can arise when a buyer who is unable to

---

43. *See* P. Areeda, *supra* note 38, at 1095.

44. *Id.*

45. This is suggested by Areeda, *supra* note 38, at 1096.

46. 15 U.S.C. § 13(a) (1976).

47. *See* F. Rowe, *supra* note 1, at 104–05 *citing Corn Products Refining Co. v. FTC*, 324 U.S. 726 (1945); *National Nut Co. v. Kelling Nut Co.*, 61 F. Supp. 76 (N.D. Ill. 1945); *General Foods Corp.*, 50 F.T.C. 885 (1954). *See also* Hansen, *supra* note 1, at 1127 n. 82.

48. 324 U.S. 726 (1945).

49. *Id.* at 740.

50. *Id.* (citing H. Rep. No. 2951, 74th Cong. 2nd sess., p. 5).

51. *Id.* at 739.

52. *Id.* at 740.

purchase directly from the manufacturer, purchases from a middleman to whom the manufacturer has sold. Obviously the resale to this indirect purchaser is likely to be made at a higher price than that paid by those who have purchased directly from the manufacturer.[53] The question is whether the manufacturer is merely exercising its right not to sell to potential purchasers or whether the use of the middleman is a method of practicing price discrimination while attempting to avoid the different purchaser requirement of the Act.[54] Lower court decisions suggest that the dual purchaser requirement of § 2(a) is met when the manufacturer is closely affiliated with or controls the middleman or the manufacturer bargains directly with the eventual indirect purchasers.[55]

Although *FTC v. Fred Meyer, Inc.* reveals an inclination to protect indirect purchasers,[56] the issue must be viewed in light of the notable leeway permitted a seller under the Act. For instance, the Act does not require a manufacturer to sell to anyone who is willing to pay for the product. Hence, a manufacturer can refuse to sell its products to certain buyers.[57] Moreover, the Act does not require sales at different levels in the chain of distribution to be made at the same price.[58] Finally, the Act permits different discounts to middleman purchasers depending upon the customers to whom the commodity is resold as long as the discount is functionally available to all purchasers at that level of distribution.[59]

[C] "Commodities" of "Like Grade and Quality"

The proscription of § 2(a) of the Robinson-Patman Act is applicable only if the commodities sold and they are of "like grade and quality." The commodity issue has not been the subject of a great deal of discussion, but the issue has come to the forefront when the commodity is actually little more than a mechanism for allowing access to intellectual property. For example, a CD containing a software program may be worth a few pennies. In these cases, the usual approach is to assess the dominant nature of the transaction.[60] This test is carried over from contract law and, in particular, decisions concerning whether Article 2 of the Uniform Commercial Code applies.

---

53. This example is suggested by P. Areeda, *supra* note 38, at 1057.

54. *See, e.g., George Haug Co. v. Rolls Royce Motor Cars*, 148 F.3d 136 (2d Cir. 1998).

55. *See, e.g., Security Tire & Rubber Co. v. Gates Rubber Co.*, 598 F.2d 962, 965–66 (5th Cir. 1979); *B.B. Walker Co. v. Ashland Chem. Co.*, 474 F. Supp. 651 (M.D.N.C 1979); *Snyder v. Howard Johnson's Motor Lodges*, 412 F. Supp. 724, 730–31 (S.D. Ill. 1976).

56. 390 U.S. 341 (1968).

57. This raises other antitrust issues. See Chapter 6 (discussing when unilateral refusals to deal violate § 2 of the Sherman Act) and Chapter 4 (discussing when concerted refusals to deal violate § 1 of the Sherman Act).

58. *See Texaco, Inc. v. Hasbrouck*, 496 U.S. 543 (1990).

59. *FLM Collision Parts v. Ford Motor Co.*, 543 F.2d. 1019, 1021 (2d Cir. 1976).

60. *First Comics, Inc. v. World Color Press, Inc.*, 884 F.2d 1033 (7th Cir. 1989).

In *Innomed Labs. LLC v. Alza Corp.*,[61] the Second Circuit considered a more complex issue. The sale involved a semi-exclusive right to distribute a patented pharmaceutical product. The Second Circuit rejected a district court jury instruction that the issue of whether commodities were involved depended on the "the dominant nature of the transaction." The cases applying the dominant nature test, according to the court, applied only when the items were fused together. In cases involving exclusive distribution rights, the two components are not fused and the fact that exclusivity is involved does not change the fact that a commodity is sold.

A difficult problem is presented when two commodities are similar but not the same. The courts have held that a slight physical difference is not enough to escape the coverage of § 2(a) as long as the commodity offers "substantially identical performance."[62]

A related issue arises when the commodities are physically identical but may be perceived by the public to be different due to variations in brand names and labeling. The leading case addressing the problem is *FTC v. Borden Co.*[63] in which the Borden Company sold chemically identical brand name and private label evaporated milk at different prices. The Fifth Circuit held that different products were involved and set aside a Commission order prohibiting the price difference.[64] The Supreme Court reversed the Fifth Circuit, holding held that a pronounced public preference for a particular name brand, which results in a willingness to pay a higher price for that name brand, does not establish a difference between the products that would render § 2(a) inapplicable.[65] The Supreme Court reasoned that the impact of consumer preference should be considered under the competitive injury and cost justification provisions of the Act.[66] Ironically, on remand, the Fifth Circuit found the competitive injury to be insubstantial and once again sanctioned Borden's price differential.[67]

§ 8.04 Injury to Competition

The Clayton Act's pre-1936 ban on price discrimination was intended to prevent injury to competitors of the seller. As indicated earlier, the theory supporting such concerns was that large national firms could eliminate smaller competitors in one market by charging low prices that were subsidized by supracompetitive prices charged by the firm in markets in which it enjoyed significant market power. This is now referred to as primary-line injury. The Robinson-Patman Act amendments to the

61. 368 F.3d 148 (2d Cir. 2004).

62. *Bruce's Juices v. American Can Co.*, 87 F. Supp. 985 (S.D. Fla. 1949), *modified*, 190 F.2d 73 (5th Cir. 1951).

63. 383 U.S. 637 (1966).

64. 339 F.2d 133 (5th Cir. 1964).

65. 383 U.S. 637, 640 (1966).

66. *Id.* at 645–47.

67. *Id.*

Clayton Act expanded the protection to "any person."[68] Most importantly, it increased the coverage of the Clayton Act to "secondary-line" cases or the customers of the discriminating firm. In either case, the substantive question is whether the effect of the discrimination "may be to substantially lessen competition or tend to create a monopoly . . . or to injure, destroy or prevent competition."[69]

[A] Primary-Line Price Discrimination: Reconciling the Robinson-Patman Act with General Antitrust Goals

[1] Utah Pie v. Continental Baking

The most dramatic example of an inconsistency between the Robinson-Patman Act and modern approaches to antitrust policy overall can be found in the 1967 case, *Utah Pie v. Continental Baking.*[70] The case arose when Utah Pie, a local producer and seller of frozen desert pies with a dominant share of the relevant market, began to experience stiff price competition from national firms. Utah Pie's market share declined from to 66% to 45%. At the same time, though, its total sales increased and it continued to earn a profit.[71] The competitors of Utah Pie were, in fact, selling in the Utah market at prices that were lower than those charged in their other markets. There was some evidence of below cost pricing in Utah. In a suit by Utah Pie against the national producers, a jury found the national producers guilty of violating § 2(a) of the Robinson-Patman Act. The verdict was overturned by the Tenth Circuit Court of Appeals which reasoned that there was insufficient evidence to support a finding of competitive injury.[72]

The Supreme Court reversed, holding that there was sufficient evidence from which a jury could find the necessary injury to competition.[73] The Court explained that the Robinson-Patman Act was not designed to insure that a competitor would survive the forces of price competition but simply that certain rules were observed, one of which was not selling at different prices in different markets. Moreover, it suggested that it was not necessary to find consistent price undercutting or "blatant predatory . . . discrimination."[74] In a decision that could be regarded as discouraging rather than encouraging competition,[75] the Court found it compelling that there had been a "deteriorating price structure"[76] in the market during the period of competition.

---

68. 15 U.S.C. § 13(a) (1976).
69. 15 U.S.C. § 13(a) (1976).
70. 386 U.S. 685 (1967).
71. *Id.* at 689.
72. *Continental Baking Co. v. Utah Pie*, 349 F.2d 122 (10th Cir. 1965).
73. 386 U.S. at 700–01.
74. *Id.* at 702.
75. *See generally* Bowman, *Restraint of Trade by the Supreme Court: The Utah Pie Case*, 77 Yale L.J. 70 (1967); *see also* R. Blair & D. Kaserman *supra* note 2, at 275–76.
76. 386 U.S. at 701.

The opinion came very close to saying that price differences and resulting increases in competitive pressure in a market are sufficient to satisfy the requirements of § 2(a). The net result is that competitors in the position of the national firms in *Utah Pie* seemed to be faced with the prospect of having to lower prices in all markets in order to engage in competition in any one market. This prospect would be acceptable if it actually occurred. A more likely prospect, however, is that lower prices in all markets would be too high a penalty for the national firm to pay in order to gain a share of a local market and it would opt to leave the market to a local monopolist. The *Utah Pie* decision has been widely criticized by a broad range of antitrust scholars.[77]

[2] Brooke Group Ltd. v. Brown & Williamson Tobacco

The inconsistency between *Utah Pie* and modern antitrust policy can be boiled down to the issue of whether the antitrust laws are designed to protect competition or competitors. In a 1993 decision, *Brooke Group Ltd. v. Brown and Williamson Tobacco*,[78] the Supreme Court adopted the view that the Robinson-Patman Act was to be interpreted in a manner that protected competition, not necessarily individual competitors,[79] and linked the Robinson-Patman Act to § 2 of the Sherman Act.

Brooke Group arose as the result of a price war between cigarette manufacturers that were attempting to boost sagging sales through the introduction of generic cigarettes. Ligget, the plaintiff, claimed that Brown & Williamson had engaged in a strategy of offering discriminatory volume rebates to wholesalers. Some of the rebates meant that prices were below cost. Ligget claimed that the purpose of the strategy was to force it to raise the price of its generic cigarettes to levels closer to those of branded cigarettes.[80] The Court distinguished *Utah Pie* by noting that since that decision it had become evident that the injury in primary-line cases "is of the same general character as the injury inflicted by predatory pricing actionable under § 2 of the Sherman Act."[81] The Court noted that the standard in an attempt to monopolize claim under § 2 of the Sherman Act was that the activity create or be accompanied by a dangerous probability of success and that under the Robinson-Patman Act the standard was whether there was "'a reasonable possibility' of substantial injury to competition." It sought to resolve this distinction by observing that "whatever additional flexibility the Robinson-Patman Act standard may imply, the essence of the claim under either statute is the same...."[82]

Having provided the link between the Robinson-Patman Act and the Sherman Act, the Court then announced a rigorous two-part test for those employing a predatory

77. *See, e.g.*, Christopher R. Leslie, *False Analogies to Predatory Pricing*, 172 U. Pa. L. Rev. 329, 397 (2024); D. Daniel Sokol, *Antitrust's "Curse of Bigness" Problem*, 118 Mich. L. Rev. 1259, 1279 (2020); Robert H. Bork, *The Antitrust Paradox* 210 (1978)

78. 509 U.S. 209 (1993).

79. *Id.* at 222.

80. *Id.* at 217.

81. *Id.* at 221.

82. *Id.* at 222.

pricing theory in an attempt to monopolize case and for those claiming primary-line injury under the Robinson-Patman Act. Plaintiffs would be required to show that the defendants had charged prices below an appropriate measure of cost (which the Court did not define) and that they had a reasonable prospect, under the Robinson-Patman Act, or a dangerous probability, under § 2 of the Sherman Act, of "recouping its investment in below-cost prices."[83]

The Court applied its standard to the case at hand by noting that the cigarette industry was a highly concentrated oligopoly. This meant that any efforts by a firm engaged in predatory pricing to recoup its investment was risky. In order to be successful, not only would the price-cutting firm be required to raise its prices to supra-competitive levels, all the firms in the industry would also have to charge recoupment level prices. The Court did not rule out this theory of liability as a matter of law. It did, however, hold that Ligget had not produced sufficient evidence that Brown & Williamson would be able to achieve the market power necessary to raise prices or that coordination among manufacturers was likely to do so.[84]

[B] Secondary-Line Discrimination

[1] The Inference of Injury

The victims of secondary-line price discrimination are the customers of the defendant rather than the defendant's competitors. Injury, but not damages, at this level may be inferred from evidence of loss of sales by the disfavored buyer[85] or from substantial price differences. The leading case with respect to the latter possibility is *FTC v. Morton Salt*[86] in which the Supreme Court held evidence of a system of substantial quantity discounts was sufficient to establish a *prima facie* violation of § 2(a). According to the Court, "in a case involving competitive injury between a seller's customers, the Commission need only prove that a seller charged one purchaser a higher price for like goods than he had charged one or more of the purchaser's competitors."[87] The Court thus flatly ruled out the need to show actual injury. Indeed, the inference of injury has been permitted even when the disfavored seller did not raise prices above those charged by favored buyers.[88]

Initially, the Supreme Court seemed to affirm its unwillingness to require a detailed analysis of actual effect in order to prevail in a § 2(a) case.[89] Of particular interest is

---

83. *Id.* at 224.

84. *Id.* at 234.

85. *See, e.g., Curtiss Candy*, 44 F.T.C. 237 (1944); *Standard Oil*, 41 F.T.C. 263 (1945), *aff'd.*, 173 F.2d 270 (7th Cir. 1949), *rev'd on other grounds*, 355 U.S. 396 (1958).

86. 334 U.S. 37 (1948).

87. *Id.* at 45.

88. *See, e.g., Standard Motor Products, Inc. v. FTC*, 265 F.2d 674 (2d Cir. 1959); *P. & D. Manufacturing Co. v. FTC*, 245 F.2d 281 (7th Cir. 1957).

89. *See, e.g., J. Truett Payne Co. v. Chrysler Motors Corp.*, 451 U.S. 557. 562 (1981).

the language of the Court in *Falls City Industries v. Vanco Beverages*[90] in response to the suggestion that narrower primary-line standards should be extended to secondary line cases:

> [Petitioner] does not, however, suggest any economic reasons why *Morton Salt*'s "self-evident" inference should not apply when the favored competitor is not extraordinarily large. Although concerns about the excessive market power of large purchasers were primarily responsible for passage of the Robinson-Patman Act . . . , the Act "is of general applicability and prohibits discrimination generally," . . . The determination whether to alter the scope of the act must be made by Congress, not this Court. . . .[91]

Although the *Morton Salt* inference is broad, it is important to note that the opinion stressed that the discount was substantial.[92] Indeed, even though the *Falls City* Court seems to stand firm on the *Morton Salt* inference, it, too, emphasized the importance of the *Morton Salt* factual context by characterizing *Morton Salt* as permitting the inference of injury to competition when there is "proof of substantial price discrimination between competing purchasers over time. . . ."[93] Moreover, the *Falls City* Court expressly recognized the possibility that the inference may be rebutted by "evidence breaking the causal connection between price difference and lost sales and profits."[94] This *dicta* reflects the outcomes in some lower court decisions in which the inference of competitive injury was not permitted because the facts were not sufficiently similar to *Morton Salt*.[95]

The *Morton Salt* inference does not apply automatically when a seller makes a good available to buyers at different prices depending in their position in the chain of distribution. For example, one may take the view that a wholesaler buying from a manufacturer and supplying storage and transportation services in entitled to a lower price than a retailer to whom the manufacturer sells directly. This so-called "functional discount" is a result of the fact that the buyers differ in the marketing functions they provide.

According to the Supreme Court in *Texaco v. Hasbrouck*,[96] the presumption of competitive harm is not warranted when the discount does no more than provide "due recognition and reimbursement for actual marketing functions."[97] One of the issues created by *Morton Salt* is whether defendants in a secondary-line case may

---

90. 460 U.S. 428 (1983).

91. *Id.* at 436.

92. *Id.* at 437.

93. *Id.* at 435.

94. *Id.*

95. *See, e.g., Minneapolis-Honeywell Regulator Co. v. FTC*, 191 F.2d 786 (7th Cir. 1951).

96. 496 U.S. 543 (1990). The Court seemed to view the discount as raising a "tertiary-line" issue since the impact was at the retail level and the favored buyers were distributors that purchased from Texaco and sold to retailers.

97. *Id.* at 562. Interestingly, the defendant, Texaco, was unable to establish the necessary connection between the discounts offered to distributors and the services those distributors provided.

overcome the inference of competitive harm by demonstrating that the market itself has not become less competitive. The issue is fundamental to antitrust and requires a response to the age-old question of whether the antitrust laws protect competitors or competition. In the case of the Robinson-Patman Act there seems to be little debate that the purpose of the Act was to protect small competitors. Still, in an effort to reconcile secondary-line cases with the rest of antitrust, some courts have indicated that defendants may escape liability by showing that the market did not become less competitive[98] while others have rejected this view.[99]

After *Brown & Williamson Tobacco*, pressures grew to bring price discrimination law into line with the rest of antitrust law. Nevertheless, a number of courts rejected this extension of *Brown & Williams Tobacco*[100] by relying on the fact that the *Brown & Williams Tobacco* Court was only faced with the issue of primary-line price discrimination. These courts noted the distinct rationale for the passage of the Robinson-Patman Act. Thus, "the Robinson-Patman Act's amendments to the Clayton Act stemmed from dissatisfaction with the original Clayton Act's inability to prevent large retail chains from obtaining volume discounts from suppliers, at the disadvantage of small retailers who competed with chains."[101] The Supreme Court resolved this tension between the original purposes of the Act and more general antitrust policy in 2006, as discussed next.

[2] In Competition

Although the Robinson Patman Act does not use the precise phrase "in competition" in order for secondary line injury to occur, the favored and disfavored buyers must compete with each other. In *Volvo Trucks of North American, Inc. v. Reeder-Simco, GMS, Inc.*,[102] the Supreme Court responded to the question of "whether a manufacturer offering its dealers different wholesale prices may be held liable for price discrimination proscribed by Robinson-Patman, absent a showing that the manufacturer discriminated between dealers contemporaneously competing to resell to the same retail customer." The Court's answer was "no" but perhaps more surprising was the Court's effort to interpret the Act's prohibition of secondary line price discrimination in a manner that was consistent with the remainder of antitrust law.

In *Volvo Trucks*, the plaintiff was a distributor of Volvo Trucks. This dealer, along with others, would make fleet sales through a bidding process. They did not carry inventory and based their bids on the prices Volvo quoted to them. The plaintiff

98. *See, e.g., Boise Cascade Corp. v. FTC*, 837 F.2d 1127 (D.C. Cir. 1987).

99. *See, e.g., J.F. Feeser v. Serv-A-Portion, Inc.*, 909 F.2d 1524 (3d Cir. 1990); *George Haug Co. v. Rolls Royce Motors Co.*, 148 F.3d 136 (2d Cir. 1998).

100. *See, e.g., Coastal Fuels of Puerto Rico v. Caribbean Petroleum Corp.*, 79 F.3d 182 (1st Cir. 1996); *Chroma Lighting v. GTE Products Corp.*, 111 F.3d 653 (9th Cir. 1997); *Allied Sales and Service, Inc., v. Global Industrial Technologies*, 2000 U.S. Dist. LEXIS 7774 (S.D. Ala. May 1, 2000). *But see Bob Nicholson Appliance, Inc. v. Maytag Co.*, 883 F. Supp. 321 (S.D. Ind. 1994).

101. *Coastal Fuels*, 79 F.3d at 192.

102. 546 U.S. 164 (2006).

claimed that other dealers were given more favorable prices than it was. It was unable to show, however, that it was treated less favorably when it was in head-to-head competition with other Volvo dealers. In other words, even though there was evidence that dealers in the same geographic market were charged different prices and that this was a product of a policy to limit the number of dealers, the plaintiff did not compete on a transaction-by-transaction basis and there could be no competitive harm.

More than any other case, *Volvo Trucks* illustrates the conflict between the prohibition of secondary-line price competition and post *Sylvania*[103] antitrust policy. According to the majority:

> Interbrand competition, our opinions affirm, is the "primary concern of antitrust law." *Continental T. V., Inc. v. GTE Sylvania, Inc.*, 433 U.S. 36. The Robinson-Patman Act signals no large departure from that concern. Even if the Act's text could be construed in the manner urged by Reeder and embraced by the Court of *Appeals*, we would resist interpretation geared more to the protection of existing *competitors* than to the stimulation of *competition*. . . . By declining to extend Robinson-Patman's governance to such cases, we continue to construe the Act "consistently with broader policies of the antitrust laws."[104]

Without regard for whether the Court adhered to the intent of the Robinson-Patman Act in this specific factual context, there can be little doubt that the Court signaled a powerful inclination to bring secondary-line cases in line with its post-*Sylvania* philosophy more generally. This view is expressed by Justice Steven (joined by Justice Thomas) in dissent:

> I cannot avoid, however, identifying the irony in a decision refusing to adhere to the text of the Act in a case in which the jury credited evidence that discriminatory prices were employed as means of escaping contractual commitments and eliminating specifically targeted firms from a competitive market. The exceptional quality of this case provides strong reason to enforce the Act's prohibition against discrimination even if Judge Bork's evaluation (with which I happen to agree) is completely accurate.[105]

The "in competition" issue arose in *Feesers, Inc. v. Michael Foods, Inc.*[106] There, the plaintiff sold food products to food service facilities. Another party, Sodexho, operated facilities and sold food products. In effect, a food service facility could self-operate and purchase from Feesers or agree to have Sodexho operate and supply food. Feesers purchased food from Michael Foods and resold it. The food sold by Sodexho also came from Michael Foods but somewhat less directly. The final price paid by Sodexho for the food was lower than that paid by Feesers. The lower court held that

103. *See* Chapter 5.
104. 546 U.S. at 180–81.
105. 546 U.S. at 187. Justice Stevens refers to Robert Bork, *The Antitrust Paradox* 382 (1978).
106. 498 F.3d 206 (3d Cir. 2007).

Feesers did not establish that it was in competition with Sodexho. It required Feesers to demonstrate that it had actually lost customers as a result of the difference in food prices as opposed to the fact that Sodexho offered management services. It reasoned that the two firms were not in competition because they operated at different functional levels—Feesers sold food to be prepared by others and Sodexho sold prepared food. The Court of Appeals for the Third Circuit reversed. It held that a plaintiff was only required to prove that it competed with a favored purchaser and that price discrimination existed over time.[107] The issue of "competition" could be assessed by examining whether, as an economic matter, the firms competed for the same group of customers. Here, according to the court, there was evidence that customers could switch from self operation to operation by Sodexho.[108] The dissent argued that to be consistent with *Volvo Trucks* the Robinson-Patman Act should be narrowly construed. In this case, according to the dissent, the parties should be regarded as operating in different markets.

The case was remanded and at the trial court level, Feesers prevailed in a rare victory for a plaintiff under the Robinson-Patman Act.[109] On appeal, though, the Third Circuit reversed again and seemed to have changed its interpretation of *Volvo Trucks*.[110] The court started with the premise that, "[i]n a bid market, if the competition between the favored and disfavored purchaser occurs before the purchase of the goods from the seller, then the disfavored purchaser cannot show that it and the favored purchaser were competing purchasers."[111] According to the court, it is necessary to apply this rule to avoid "unprincipled application" of the Act.[112] In an unusual concession, the court noted that it might be placing "form over substance" but felt this was required by *Volvo Trucks*.[113] Nevertheless, in a bidding context, two sales at different prices do not take place and the formal requirements of the Robinson-Patman Act are not met.

[3] Showing Actual Harm

Although *Falls City* and *Hasbrouck* suggest limitations on the *Morton Salt* inference and *Volvo Trucks* indicates a willingness to reinterpret the Robinson-Patman Act, the Court's 1981 decision in *J. Truett Payne Co. v. Chrysler Motor Corp.*[114] may be the most influential in limiting the reach of the Act. In *Truett Payne*, the Court, relying primarily on *Brunswick Corp. v. Pueblo Bowl-O-Mat, Inc.*,[115] distinguished the applicable substantive statute, § 2(a) of the Robinson-Patman Act, from § 4 of the Clayton Act, which is the relevant remedial statute when a private plaintiff seeks treble

107. *Id.* at 213.
108. *Id.* at 214.
109. At this point, it was five years after litigation initially started.
110. *Feesers v. Michael Foods, Inc.*, 591 F.3d 191 (3d Cir. 2010).
111. *Id.* at 198
112. *Id.* 199.
113. *Id.*
114. 451 U.S. 557 (1981).
115. 429 U.S. 477 (1977).

damages. According to the Court, the *Morton Salt* inference is sufficient to establish a *prima facie* substantive violation or that an injury may result. In order to recover treble damages under § 4, though, "a plaintiff must make some showing of actual injury attributable to something the antitrust laws were designed to prevent."[116] Since the antitrust laws protect competition, not competitors,[117] it follows that the private plaintiff must demonstrate that the damages were associated with an actual decline in competition.[118]

The Court specifically rejected the argument that plaintiff was entitled to "automatic damages" calculated by multiplying the amount of "overcharge" times the number of units purchased.[119] *Truett Payne* is consistent with other Supreme Court decisions that restrict "private" attorney general enforcement of the antitrust laws.[120] In its wake, *Morton Salt* lost much of its clout. If the plaintiff can meet the requirements of § 4 of the Clayton Act by showing actual harm flowing from a less competitive market, there is far less need to rely on the *Morton Salt* inference of harm. For now, *Morton Salt* appears to be a standard only available to the FTC or Justice Department if they were inclined to enforce § 2(a).

[4] The Combined Effect of "In Competition" and "Antitrust Injury"

The full impact of the Supreme Court's decision to blend the Robinson-Patman Act into more general modern antitrust policy is illustrated by *Drug Mart Pharmacy Corp. v. American Home Products Corp.*[121] Plaintiffs were owners of independent pharmacies which were unable to buy drugs from the major drug manufacturers as the same discounted prices enjoyed by mail order pharmacies and other large buyers. The court applied a two-step test and required plaintiffs to demonstrate that they had suffered a competitive injury and antitrust injury. Plaintiffs failed the first test, even though the shift in market *share* to favored purchasers was documented, because plaintiffs were unable to identify a substantial number of *individual* customers who had shifted their purchases from the independent pharmacies to the favored pharmacies. The court permitted plaintiffs to rely on the *Morton Salt* inference but found it had been rebutted.[122]

The court relied on the same reasoning—the failure to trace the whereabouts of lost customers—it had applied to its competitive harm analysis to the analysis of antitrust injury. In effect, if plaintiffs were unable to establish competitive harm under

116. 451 U.S. at 562.

117. *Brown Shoe v. U.S.*, 370 U.S. 294, 320 (1962).

118. *See* Chapter 3, § 3.02[B]. *See generally* Blair and Harrison, *Rethinking Antitrust Injury*, 42 Vand. L. Rev. 1540 (1989).

119. 451 U.S. at 561.

120. *See Brunswick Corp. v. Pueblo Bowl-O-Mat Corp.*, 429 U.S. 477 (1977); *Cargill, Inc. v. Monfort of Colorado*, 479 U.S. 104 (1986).

121. 2012 U.S. Dist. LEXIS 115882 (E.D.N.Y. Aug. 16, 2012).

122. *Id.* at *40.

the court's very demanding standard, they would also be unable to establish antitrust injury. This proposition seems obvious—a firm suffering no harm has not suffered antitrust injury. The reasoning of the court, though, is not obvious. According to the court, even if plaintiffs *had* established competitive harm, presumably through the tracing process, they would not have demonstrated antitrust injury. Rather than explain what would be necessary under that hypothetical situation, the court simply repeated the inability to trace as the rationale for finding no antitrust injury. In 2012, the Second Circuit Court of Appeals affirmed the lower court decision in *Drug Mart,*[123] noting that it was necessary for plaintiffs to actually identify which customers were lost to the favored purchasers.[124]

In *U.S. Wholesale Outlet & Distribution, Inc. v. Innovation Ventures, LLC*, defendant Living Essentials, LLC, sold its 5-hour Energy, a caffeinated drink, to two sets of purchasers—Costco Wholesale Corp., which resold 5-hour Energy at its Costco Business Centers, and other traditional wholesalers ("the Wholesalers"), which resold 5-hour Energy to convenience stores and grocery stores.[125] The Wholesalers sued Living Essentials for violating § 2(a) of the Robinson-Patman Act by offering them less favorable pricing, discounts, and reimbursements than it offered Costco. The plaintiffs also argued that they were entitled to injunctive relief under § 2(d) of the Robinson-Patman Act. Following trial, the jury ruled in favor of the defendant,

On appeal, the Ninth Circuit first explained that

> To establish secondary-line discrimination [under § 2(a)], a plaintiff must show that (1) the challenged sales were made in interstate commerce; (2) the items sold were of like grade and quality; (3) the seller discriminated in price between the disfavored and the favored buyer; and (4) "'the effect of such discrimination may be . . . to injure, destroy, or prevent competition' to the advantage of a favored purchaser." *Volvo*, 546 U.S. at 176–77 (quoting 15 U.S.C. § 13(a)). The fourth component of that test, the element at issue in this case, ensures that section 2(a) "does not ban all price differences," but rather "proscribes 'price discrimination only to the extent that it threatens to injure competition.'" *Id.* at 176 (quoting *Brooke Group Ltd. v. Brown & Williamson Tobacco Corp.*, 509 U.S. 209, 220 (1993)).[126]

The trial focused on the fourth element—whether the Wholesalers and Costco were in competition—because the district court had ruled on summary judgment that "the Wholesalers had proved the first three elements of their section 2(a) claim—that the products were distributed in interstate commerce, of like grade and quality, and sold at different prices to Costco and to the Wholesalers."[127]

123. *Cash & Henderson Drugs, Inc. v. Johnson & Johnson*, 799 F.3d 202 (2d Cir. 2012).
124. *Id.* at 210–11.
125. 89 F.4th 1126, 1133 (9th Cir. 2023).
126. *Id.* at 1134.
127. *Id.* 1134–35.

At trial, the district court instructed the jury that the sales had to be "reasonably contemporaneous" and that "the Wholesalers had to prove that any difference in prices could not be justified as 'functional discounts.'"[128] The Ninth Circuit held that the district court did not abuse its discretion in issuing these jury instructions.

Turning to the § 2(d) issue and regarding the question of whether Costco and the Wholesalers were in actual competition, however, the Ninth Circuit held that the district court abused its discretion in finding that Costco and the Wholesalers operated at different functional levels with respect to resales of 5-hour Energy and therefore competed for different customers of that product. First, the Ninth Circuit criticized the district court for assuming that the jury must have found that Costco and the Wholesalers were not in competition because they ruled for the defendant on the § 2(a) claim. But the Ninth Circuit noted that § 2(a) requires a showing that the two buyers "were in competition with each other, *and* that discriminatory price concessions or discounts caused a potential injury to competition."[129] Thus, the jury could have found that the Wholesalers and Costco were in competition but the § 2(a) claim nevertheless failed because the plaintiff did not show a potential harm to competition. Second, as a factual matter, both Costco and the Wholesalers sold to retailers. Thus, the Ninth Circuit reversed the district court's decision regarding the plaintiffs' § 2(d) claim.

§ 8.05 Seller's Affirmative Defenses

The Robinson-Patman Act provides two basic defenses. The "cost justification" defense is included as a proviso to § 2(a) and is, therefore, applicable to price differences alone. The "meeting competition defense," on the other hand, is found in § 2(b) and by its terms applies to differences in price, services or facilities. A third defense worth noting, but infrequently invoked, permits price differences associated with "price changes . . . in response to changing conditions affecting the market for or the marketability of the goods concerned. . . ."[130]

[A] Cost Justification

[1] The Basic Defense

The cost justification defense permits a seller who has charged different prices to escape liability by showing that the prices reflect "due allowance for cost of manufacture, sale or delivery . . . resulting from the differing methods or quantities in which

128. *Id.* at 1135.

129. *Id.* at 1145 (emphasis added).

130. 15 U.S.C. § 13(a) (1976). *See, e.g., Bargain Car Wash. Inc. v. Standard Oil Co. (Ind.)*, 466 F.2d 1163 (7th Cir. 1972).

such commodities are . . . sold or delivered."[131] In theory, the application of a cost-based defense could bring enforcement of the Act into conformity with the economist's definition of price discrimination. This has not occurred and the defense, for the most part, has not been of great value to defendants.[132] The problem lies in the fact that the matching of costs and prices required to successfully employ the defense is not always likely to be gleaned from ordinary accounting records.[133] Thus, potentially costly and extensive cost accounting procedures must be developed in anticipation of a possible Robinson-Patman Act charge. Moreover, although the FTC and the courts have permitted the grouping of sales and the use of averages to simplify the defense, a problem arises when members of a classification do not share common characteristics.[134]

[2] United States v. Borden

The most important judicial review of the cost justification defense occurred in 1962 in *United States v. Borden*.[135] Two Chicago dairies, Borden and Bowman, were charged with violating the Robinson-Patman Act by granting grocery-store chains discounts in excess of discounts available to independent stores. Buyers were given percentage discounts that increased with volume to a maximum level. The grocery store chains, however, were granted a flat rate discount that was more favorable than the maximum discount available to others and which was not dependent on volume.[136]

Both dairies introduced cost studies to justify the differential. Borden's cost justification study was based on a comparison of its average cost per $100 of sales to the chains with the average cost per $100 of sales to the independents. Bowman based its study on differences in volume and delivery methods. In particular, it noted that deliverymen spent a substantial amount of time on services that benefitted only the independents.[137]

The Court analyzed how accurately the price differences reflected the costs of serving individual buyers. Borden's study was rejected because in many instances buyers were not classified in accordance with the costs of serving them. For example, although the distinction between chains and large independents was based essentially

---

131. 15 U.S.C. § 13(a) (1976). Professor Areeda notes that a policy of marginal cost pricing probably would not satisfy this requirement. P. Areeda, *supra* note 38, at 1104.

132. *See Automatic Canteen Co. of Am. v. FTC*, 346 U.S. 61, 79 (1953); *Sylvania Elec. Prods.*, 51 F.T.C. 282, 290 (1954). *See generally* H. Shniderman, *supra* note 7, at 95–123; Hansen, *supra* note 1, at 1142–45.

133. *See* F. Rowe, *supra* note 1, at 303–06; Freer, *Accounting Problems Under the Robinson-Patman Act*, 65 J. Acct. 480 (1938).

134. *See Master Lock Co.*, 27 F.T.C. 982 (1938); *International Salt Co. & E. Salt Co.*, 49 F.T.C. 138 (1952); *American Motors Corp. v. FTC*, 384 F.2d 247 (6th Cir. 1967); *Curtiss Candy Co.*, 44 F.T.C. 237 (1947); *see generally* Standridge, *An Analysis of the Cost Justification Defense Under Section 2(a) of the Robinson-Patman Act*, 9 Rut. Cam. L.J. 219, 230–33 (1978).

135. 370 U.S. 460 (1962).

136. *Id.* at 463.

137. *Id.* at 470.

on differences in average volume, there were independents with volumes higher than some chains. In addition, all independents were assigned costs associated with cash collections but not all independents paid cash.[138] Bowman's customer classification scheme was found to suffer from similar arbitrary divisions and cost assignments.[139]

[3] The "Cost Justification" Standard

In applying its somewhat exacting requirements, the Court announced the standard for reviewing cost classifications:

> A balance is struck by the use of classes for cost justification which are composed of members of such selfsameness as to make the averaging of the cost of dealing with the group a valid and reasonable indicium of the cost of dealing with any specific group member. High on the list of "musts" in the use of the average cost of customer groupings under the proviso of [section] 2(a) is a close resemblance of the individual members of each group on the essential point or points which determine the costs considered.[140]

The general test, as articulated in *Borden*, offers little in the way of certainty with respect to the degree of "selfsameness" required. Nor does the test take into consideration the fact that different sellers may face very different obstacles in determining the costs to be attributed to a particular buyer or group of buyers.[141] Although there are occasional cases that reflect a more receptive attitude toward the cost justification defense, no clear trend has been established.[142]

[B] Meeting Competition

The "meeting competition" defense permits a seller to escape liability by showing that a difference in price, or the availability of services or facilities, was the result of a "good faith" attempt to meet an "equally low price of a competitor, or the services or facilities furnished by a competitor." The defense is limited to attempts to meet, not beat, competition. Although there has been some division of authority on the issue, it now appears that the defense is available whether the action was designed to retain old customers or gain new ones.[143] The defense is available only when the seller is responding to a direct competitor.[144] Discrimination designed to assist a customer

---

138. *Id.*

139. *Id.*

140. *Id.* at 469.

141. *See generally* Standridge, *supra* note 134.

142. *See, e.g., FTC v. Standard Motor Products*, 371 F.2d 613 (2d Cir. 1967); *American Motors Corp. v. FTC*, 384 F.2d 247 (6th Cir. 1967). *See generally* F. Rowe, *supra* note 1, at 276–94; H. Shniderman, *supra* note 7, at 15–23.

143. *See Falls City Indus., Inc. v. Vanco Beverages, Inc.*, 460 U.S. 428 (1983).

144. *See FTC v. Sun Oil Co.*, 371 U.S. 505 (1963); *see also Exxon Corp. v. Governor of Maryland*, 437 U.S. 117 (1978).

in competition with one of its own competitors has been regarded as falling outside the defense.[145] Although it was initially interpreted rather narrowly, the "meeting competition" defense has always offered greater hope to defendants than the "cost justification" defense.[146]

The "meeting competition" defense is available only to sellers who act in "good faith" when attempting to equal the terms of competitors. This is important because a "good faith" effort that overshoots its goal and actually undercuts competitors still falls within the defense. The issue of what constitutes good faith, however, has been an area of considerable uncertainty and can arise in two contexts.

[1] Good Faith: Verification and Information Exchange

A pivotal issue in the "meeting competition" defense is whether the seller's price differential is based on sufficient information about actions of competitors to be regarded as a good faith response. In *FTC v. A.E. Staley Manufacturing Co.*, the Supreme Court announced that the defendant must show "the existence of facts which would lead a reasonably prudent person to believe"[147] that the discrimination was necessary to meet the offers of competitors. In applying the standard, the Court upheld the Commission's finding that responding to "verbal information received from salesmen, brokers or intending purchasers," in the absence of independent efforts to "investigate or verify" did not satisfy the good faith standard.[148]

The issue of verification can leave defendant in a quandary. On one hand, steps taken to verify the prices charged by competitors may violate § 1 of the Sherman Act because competitors sharing price information can increase price levels.[149] On the other hand, different treatment that is not based on sufficient evidence may leave the seller unable to successfully invoke the "meeting competition" defense. The Supreme Court addressed this dilemma in *U.S. v. United States Gypsum*,[150] in which defendants charged with a violation of § 1 of the Sherman Act attempted to justify their price information exchanges as necessary to comply with the terms of the meeting competition defense.[151] The Court noted the dangers inherent in exchanges and the limited reliability of exchanges as a means of verifying prices. It indicated that the "meeting competition" defense did not require direct discussions between competitors.[152] The Court did not go so far as to suggest that the defense was available to a seller who

145. 324 U.S. 746, 759 (1945).

146. *See, e.g., Falls City Indus., Inc. v. Vanco Beverage, Inc.*, 460 U.S. 428 (1983).

147. 324 U.S. at 759.

148. *Id.* at 758.

149. *United States v. Container Corp. of America*, 393 U.S. 333 (1969); *United States v. United States Gypsum*, 438 U.S. 422 (1978). *See* Joseph Harrington, Jr. & Christopher R. Leslie, *Horizontal Price Exchanges*, 44 Cardozo L. Rev. 2301 (2023).

150. 438 U.S. 422 (1978).

151. *Id.* at 448.

152. *Id.* at 457.

casually relied on "uncorroborated reports of buyers."[153] It listed, however, independent factors that a seller could rely upon, short of inter-seller verification, to develop a good faith belief that a concession was necessary. These included reports from customers other than those granted the favorable terms, threats of termination, and examination of general market data. It now seems clear that this list includes reports from established customers.[154]

[2] Good Faith: Breadth of Response

The issue of good faith also has arisen when sellers have responded to competitors with a pricing system or area-wide price cuts as opposed to customer-by-customer concessions. The issue is one that had divided the circuits.[155] The difference between circuits can be traced to *Staley* which rejected the "meeting competition" defense offered for a discriminatory pricing system apparently because the system was not designed to respond to "individual competitive situations."[156] Significantly, the pricing system at issue in *Staley*, a basing point system, was instituted in order to match an illegal basing point system of the defendant's competitor. Thus, the case could stand for the proposition that meeting competition must be on a consumer-specific basis. Alternatively, it suggests that one may not discriminate in order to meet the competition of a rival whose pricing scheme violates the Robinson-Patman Act. *Falls City Industry, Inc. v. Vanco Beverage, Inc.* clarified the issue, indicating that "good faith" did not require consumer-specific pricing. The standard adopted was whether the discriminating seller's area-wide scheme reflected a reasonable belief "that the lower price he charged was generally available from his competitors throughout the territory and throughout the period in which he made the lower price available."[157]

§ 8.06 Other Offenses

[A] Section 2(c): Unlawful Brokerage Payments

Three components of the Robinson-Patman Act—§§ 2(c), (d) and (e)—do not require a showing of competitive harm as does § 2(a). Consequently, it is wise to attempt to reframe a price discrimination case as one involving the practices covered in these sections. Section 2(c) is designed to eliminate price concessions disguised as payments or discounts for brokerage services "except for services rendered. . . ."

153. *Id.* at 453.

154. *See, e.g., Great Atlantic & Pacific Tea Co. v. FTC*, 440 U.S. 69 (1970).

155. *See, e.g., Exquisite Form Brassiere, Inc. v. FTC*, 360 F.2d 492 (D.C. Cir. 1965) (individual customer response required); *William Inglis & Sons Baking Co. v. ITT Continental Baking Co.*, 668 F.2d 1014 (9th Cir. 1981) (market-wide response permissible if reasonable belief of equally low offers available).

156. 324 U.S. at 753.

157. 460 U.S. at 451.

Until 1960, three aspects of § 2(c) seemed fairly clear. First, it appeared to cover only payments or discounts that were linked to a claim that the buyer had performed brokerage-type services.[158] Second, the section was distinct from § 2(a) because it did not require more than one transaction. The final area of relative certainty arose from a narrow interpretation of the exception in § 2(c) for instances in which services were actually rendered by the buyer for the benefit of the seller. Courts decided early that any services rendered by the buyer were really for the buyer.[159] Thus, the section worked as a absolute prohibition of payments or discounts based on the brokerage services provided by the buyer.

All three areas of certainty were upset by the Supreme Court's 1960 decision in *FTC v. Henry Broch & Co.*[160] In *Broch*, an independent broker, working on behalf of the seller, lowered his commission from 5% to 3% in order to bring the price of the commodity down to the level acceptable to the buyer. The buyer made no demand for a brokerage allowance and did not know of the agent's agreement to lower his commission. The Court, in a five to four decision, held that the concession violated § 2(c). The rationale of the Court was that the allowance was ultimately the result of the buying power of the buyer and there was no difference between "the seller's broker splitting his brokerage commission with the buyer and his yielding part of the brokerage to the seller to be passed on to the buyer in the form of a lower price."[161]

According to the Court, the primary problem with the defendant's concession was that it was not part of an overall price decrease but was made for the purpose of obtaining a particular sale. Thus, it was discriminatory. Indeed, the Court observed that, "[a] price reduction based upon savings in brokerage expenses is an 'allowance in lieu of brokerage' when given only to favored customers."[162] The key, therefore, was not simply the allowance but the discriminatory result. Although the majority argued otherwise, it seems inescapable that it had somehow combined § 2(a) with § 2(c) or at least blurred the already thin line separating § 2(a) discrimination from § 2(c) "allowances in lieu of brokerage."[163]

A final element of the *Broch* decision is the Court's language concerning the exception for "services rendered." In *dicta* the Court indicated that if there had been a question of whether the buyer had rendered some service to the seller or to the broker, "[w]e would have quite a different case."[164] This statement has had the effect of reviving the dormant "services rendered" exception.[165]

---

158. *See generally* F. Rowe, *supra* note 1, at 330; L. Sullivan, *supra* note 39, at 69; Hansen, *supra* note 1, at 1155.

159. *See* L. Sullivan, *supra* note 39, at 698.

160. 363 U.S. 166 (1960).

161. *Id.* at 174 (notes omitted).

162. *Id.* at 176.

163. *See, e.g., Thomasville Chair Co. v. FTC*, 306 F.2d 541 (5th Cir. 1962). *See generally* F. Rowe, *supra* note 1, at 343–46.

164. 363 U.S. at 173.

165. *See, e.g., Thomasville Chair Co. v. FTC*, 306 F.2d 541 (5th Cir. 1962); *Central Retailer-Owned Groceries, Inc. v. FTC*, 319 F.2d 410 (7th Cir. 1963).

Although § 2(c) generally has been viewed as complementing § 2(a) in the sense of protecting small competitors, it also has been applied to prohibit certain forms of commercial bribery. There is support for this view in a footnote in *Broch.*[166] In general, the connection to the more typical offense is obvious in that a buyer (or seller) who bribes a broker who represents a seller (or buyer) is typically asking for more favorable treatment that a competitor. Moreover, since § 2(c) does not require competitive harm, the section can and has been interpreted broadly to prohibit bribes as long as payment passes ultimately from the buyer to the seller or vice-versa[167] and somewhere in the process there is "corruption of and agency or employment relationship."[168]

The difficulty of defining exactly what is required by this second step is illustrated by *Bridges v. MacLean-Stevens Studios, Inc*,[169] in which parents of students sued a photography studio that the school had selected to take school photos. The school agreed to make the studio the exclusive supplier in return for a twenty percent commission. The parents argued that the commission amounted to a bribe and that the school had an obligation to act on their behalf. The court held that section 2(c) did not apply because the parents were not required to buy the photos at all. Because the school had no control over the parents' ultimate decision, the court found that an agency relationship was lacking.[170]

[B] Promotional Allowances

Under § 2(d) payments by a seller to a buyer for services or facilities used by the buyer in "processing, handling, sale or offering for sale" must be available on a "proportionally equal" basis to all customers. Section 2(e) includes the same prohibition with respect to supplying services or facilities. Like § 2(c), §§ 2(d) and 2(e) are designed to prohibit disguised forms of discrimination. Similarly, competitive impact is not at issue.[171] Unlike § 2(c), both sections clearly require more than one transaction. Additionally, the language of the sections suggests substantial differences between §§ (d) and (e) but they have been interpreted in parallel fashion.[172] For example, since the meeting competition defense of § 2(b) expressly applies to discrimination in price or services, that defense would seem to apply to § 2(e), but not to § 2(d). In fact, the meeting competition defense has been held to apply to both §§ 2 (d) and (e).[173]

---

166. 363 U.S. at 166–167, n.6. *See also Motor Transport Co. v. Trucking Unlimited*, 404 U.S. 508, 513 (1972).

167. *See Seaboard Supply Co. v. Congeleum*, 770 F.2d 367 (3d Cir. 1985); *Environmental Tectonics v. W.S. Kirkpatrick, Inc.*, 847 F.2d 1052 (3d Cir. 1988).

168. *Stephen Jay Photography, Ltd. v. Olan Mills, Inc.*, 903 F.2d 988, 993 (1st Cir. 1990).

169. 201 F.3d 6 (1st Cir. 2000).

170. *Id.* at 11.

171. *See FTC v. Simplicity Pattern Co.*, 360 U.S. 55 (1959).

172. *See, e.g., Zwicker v. J.I. Case Co.*, 596 F.2d 305 (8th Cir. 1979); *Kirby v. P.R. Mallory & Co.*, 489 F.2d 904 (7th Cir. 1973); *Vanity Fair Paper Mills, Inc. v. FTC*, 311 F.2d 480 (2d Cir. 1962).

173. *See, e.g., Allen Pen Co v. Springfield Photo Mount Co.*, 653 F.2d 17 (1st Cir. 1981); *Shulton Inc. v. FTC*, 305 F.2d 36 (7th Cir. 1962).

Another issue is whether the payment or service is properly characterized as an indirect price discrimination under § 2(a) or as an allowance under either § 2(d) or § 2(e). The distinction is crucial because § 2(a) requires proof of competitive injury. The trend that has emerged is to classify assistance that takes place at the original sale as indirect price discrimination. The seller's assistance with his customer's resale, on the other hand, is likely to be examined under §§ 2(d) or 2(e).[174]

Both §§ 2(d) and 2(e) require that allowances be available to all customers or purchasers[175] on proportionally equal terms. In *FTC v. Fred Meyer, Inc.*,[176] suppliers provided allowances to a retail grocery chain. Comparable allowances were not available to wholesalers or to the retailers to whom those wholesalers sold and who ultimately competed with the grocery chain. The action was defended as falling outside the purview of the "any customer" language of § 2(d) because the disfavored wholesalers were not competing with the grocery chain. Moreover, the "disfavored" retailers were not direct customers of the suppliers.[177] The Court, reasoning that a narrower definition of "customer" would frustrate the purposes of the Act, held that the indirect retailers were within the protected class.[178]

The requirement of proportionally equal terms has been defined primarily by the FTC. According to the Commission, "[n]o single way to proportionalize is prescribed by law."[179] On the other hand, it suggests that allowances be available on a dollar volume or quantity of goods purchased basis.[180] In addition, the seller has an affirmative obligation to insure that all competing customers are aware of the allowances.[181]

Determining what constitutes an allowance is not always a simple task. In *Freightliner of Knoxville, Inc. v. DaimlerChrysler Vans LLC*,[182] a purchaser and reseller of vans complained that a competing seller was afforded more favorable treatment because that competitor received an allocation of other vehicles in a related product line and customers of the competitor were entered into a program that gave them priority as far as vehicle service. The first "allowance" was rejected since it was not clear what the connection was between the defendant and the actual allocation of the related vehicles. In addition, the court questioned whether the practice would be regarded as a form of discrimination covered by the Act.[183] Finally, the allocation related to the initial sale from supplier to reseller and was not an effort to assist at the resale level.

---

174. *See generally* F. Rowe, *supra* note 1, at 381–85.
175. 15 U.S.C. §§ 13(d), (e) (1976).
176. 390 U.S. 341 (1968).
177. *Id.* at 348–49.
178. *Id.* at 354.
179. FTC, *Guides for Advertising Allowances and Other Merchandising Payments and Services*, 16 C.F.R. § 240.7 (1987).
180. *Id.*
181. 16 C.F.R. § 240.8 (1987).
182. 484 F.3d 865 (2007).
183. *Id.* at 873.

The court did, however, rule that a program that resulted in different service opportunities for customers could violate the promotional allowance standards.[184]

Woodman's Food Market, Inc. v. Clorox Co.,[185] a case that would seem to fit the category of price discrimination, was recast as one involving promotional allowances. The defendant there sold its products in large size containers to discount warehouses but did not make the same packaging available to the smaller plaintiff. The court found that the larger packaging amounted to a price discount and, thus, actually fell under § 2(a).[186] Plaintiffs also argued that the size difference was discriminatory, because it affected consumer convenience. That argument failed, as the court ruled that "[s]ize alone is not enough to constitute a promotional service or facility for purposes of subsection 13(e); any discount that goes along with size must be analyzed under subsection 13(a); and the convenience of the larger size is not a promotional service or facility."[187] The court acknowledged, however, that it is possible "under different facts to imagine package size or design as part of a 'service or facility' when combined with other promotional content."[188]

§ 8.07 Buyer Liability

[A] Generally

The Robinson-Patman amendments to the Clayton Act were primarily aimed at the secondary-line competitive injury resulting from large chain stores obtaining more favorable treatment from suppliers than their independent competitors. In this context the buyer's monopsony power is the likely cause of the discrimination. Buyer liability is, therefore, an important component of the regulatory scheme. Section 2(f) imposes liability on buyers that "knowingly . . . induce or receive a discrimination in price."[189] This is, however, a misleadingly narrow account of the buyer's potential liability under the Act in its entirety. For example, buyer liability is also expressly included in the § 2(c) brokerage allowance provisions. Furthermore, although the promotional allowance sections do not seem to extend to buyer liability and do not constitute "discriminations in price," courts have been receptive to the FTC's labeling of buyers' inducement of allowances as an "unfair method of competition" under § 5 of the Federal Trade Commission Act.[190] In addition, allowances in excess of the

184. *Id.*
185. 833 F.3d 743 (7th Cir. 2016).
186. *Id.* at 748.
187. *Id.* at 750.
188. *Id.*
189. 15 U.S.C. § 13(f) (1976). For a discussion of monopsony power, see Chapter 6.
190. *See, e.g.*, *Grand Union Co. v. FTC*, 300 F.2d 92 (2d Cir. 1962); *R.H. Macy & Co. v. FTC*, 326 F.2d 445 (2d Cir. 1964).

actual cost of the services provided may be viewed as a form of indirect price discrimination under § 2(a).[191]

Fred Meyer is illustrative of the various routes to buyer liability.[192] It involved both price discrimination and promotional allowances. The buyer was liable under § 2(f) for inducing the seller to discriminate in terms of price and was found to have engaged in an unfair method of competition by inducing the granting of favorable promotional allowances.[193] The substantive analysis of the Court on the latter issue was, however, devoted entirely to § 2(d) of the Robinson-Patman Act.

[B] The Plaintiff's § 2(f) Case

Because § 2(f) refers to "discrimination . . . prohibited by [the Act]," there is no § 2(f) violation unless there is a price difference that is injurious to competition and not excused by any of the defenses in the Act. According to *American Canteen Co. v. FTC*,[194] the leading § 2(f) case, there can be no violation by a buyer "if the lower prices he induces are either within one of the seller's defenses . . . or not known by him not to be within one of those defenses."[195] The plaintiff's burden of establishing a *prima facie* § 2(f) case includes producing evidence of the discrimination and the lack of a reasonable belief by the buyer that a defense was available.[196] This burden is slightly less onerous than it might initially appear due to the inferences courts have permitted regarding reasonable beliefs on behalf of the defendant.[197]

[C] The "Meeting Competition" Defense

American Canteen specifically concerned a cost justification defense. The Court equivocated on where the burden would lie if a meeting competition defense were raised.[198] This question was settled in 1979 by *Great Atlantic & Pacific Tea Co. v. FTC*,[199] a case which produces an interesting twist in the relationship of § 2(f) to buyer's defenses. A & P was charged with violating section 2(f) when, in negotiations with Borden over the sale of "private-brand" milk, it induced Borden to lower its price. Borden's price turned out not simply to meet but actually beat competing sellers.[200] A & P

---

191. *American Booksellers Ass'n, Inc., v. Barnes & Noble, Inc.*, 135 F. Supp. 2d 1031 (N.D. Cal. 2001).

192. 390 U.S. 341 (1968).

193. *Id.* at 345–46.

194. 346 U.S. 61 (1953).

195. *Id.* at 74.

196. *Id.* at 62.

197. *See, e.g., American Canteen Co. of America v. FTC*, 346 U.S. 61 (1953); *American Motors Specialties v. FTC*, 278 F.2d 225 (2d Cir. 1960). *See generally* F. Rowe, *supra* note 1, at 442–46.

198. 346 U.S. at 78.

199. 440 U.S. 69 (1979).

200. *Id.* at 73.

argued that if Borden had a meeting competition defense, then there was no violation of the Act and it had not violated § 2(f). The Commission's position was that the meeting competition defense should be applied from the point of view of the buyer.[201] In this case, even though the seller might have a good faith belief that it had simply met competition, the buyer knew that, in fact, the seller's price exceeded that standard.

The Court held for the buyer relying on a broad view of the derivative nature of § 2 (f).[202] In essence, if the seller would have had a meeting competition defense[203] there can be no § 2(f) violation even if the buyer induces the lower price and knows that the seller, in response to that inducement, has gone further than necessary to meet competition. The Court stopped short of saying that the same standard would apply to a buyer who deliberately misled a seller.[204] On the other hand, it did not adopt Justice Marshall's view, in dissent, that sellers charged with violating § 2(f) should be held to the same standard of good faith as buyers who invoke § 2(b).[205]

201. *Id.* at 74–75 n.5.
202. *Id.* at 81–82.
203. *Id.*
204. *Id.*
205. *Id.* at 89.

Appendix

Selected Antitrust Statutes

Sherman Act

Section 1. Every contract, combination in the form of trust or otherwise, or conspiracy, in restraint of trade or commerce among the several States, or with foreign nations, is declared to be illegal. Every person who shall make any contract or engage in any combination or conspiracy hereby declared to be illegal shall be deemed guilty of a felony, and, on conviction thereof, shall be punished by fine not exceeding $10,000,000 if a corporation, or, if any other person, $350,000, or by imprisonment not exceeding three years, or by both said punishments, in the discretion of the court. [15 U.S.C. § 1.]

Section 2. Every person who shall monopolize, or attempt to monopolize, or combine or conspire with any other person or persons, to monopolize any part of the trade or commerce among the several States, or with foreign nations, shall be deemed guilty of a felony, and, on conviction thereof, shall be punished by fine not exceeding $10,000,000 if a corporation, or, if any other person, $350,000, or by imprisonment not exceeding three years, or by both said punishments, in the discretion of the court. [15 U.S.C. § 2.]

Section 3. Every contract, combination in form of trust or otherwise, or conspiracy, in restraint of trade or commerce in any Territory of the United States or of the District of Columbia, or in restraint of trade or commerce between any such Territory and another, or between any such Territory or Territories and any State or States or the District of Columbia, or with foreign nations, or between the District of Columbia and any State or States or foreign nations, is declared illegal. Every person who shall make any such contract or engage in any such combination or conspiracy, shall be deemed guilty of a felony, and, on conviction thereof, shall be punished by fine not exceeding $10,000,000 if a corporation, or, if any other person, $350,000, or by imprisonment not exceeding three years, or both said punishments, in the discretion of the court. [15 U.S.C. § 3.]

Section 4. The several district courts of the United States are invested with jurisdiction to prevent and restrain violations of sections 1 to 7 of this title; and it shall be the duty of the several United States attorneys, in their respective districts, under the direction of the Attorney General, to institute proceedings in equity to prevent and restrain such violations. Such proceedings may be by way of petition setting forth the case and praying that such violation shall be enjoined or otherwise prohibited. When the parties complained of shall have been duly notified of such petition the court shall proceed, as soon as may be, to the hearing and determination of the case; and pending such petition and before final decree, the court may at any time make such temporary restraining order or prohibition as shall be deemed just in the premises. [15 U.S.C. § 4.]

Section 5. Whenever it shall appear to the court before which any proceeding under section 4 of this title may be pending, that the ends of justice require that other parties should be brought before the court, the court may cause them to be summoned, whether they reside in the district in which the court is held or not; and subpoenas to that end may be served in any district by the marshal thereof. [15 U.S.C. § 5.]

Section 6. Any property owned under any contract or by any combination, or pursuant to any conspiracy (and being the subject thereof) mentioned in section 1 of this title, and being in the course of transportation from one State to another, or to a foreign country, shall be forfeited to the United States, and may be seized and condemned by like proceedings as those provided by law for the forfeiture, seizure, and condemnation of property imported into the United States contrary to law. [15 U.S.C. § 6.]

Section 6a. [This Act] shall not apply to conduct involving trade or commerce (other than import trade or import commerce) with foreign nations unless—

(1) such conduct has a direct, substantial, and reasonably foreseeable effect—

(A) on trade or commerce which is not trade or commerce with foreign nations, or on import trade or import commerce with foreign nations; or

(B) on export trade or export commerce with foreign nations, of a person engaged in such trade or commerce in the United States; and

(2) such effect gives rise to a claim under the provisions of this Act, other than this section.

If [this Act] applies to such conduct only because of the operation of paragraph (1) (B), then [this Act] shall apply to such conduct only for injury to export business in the United States.

[15 U.S.C. § 6a; added by Foreign Trade Antitrust Improvements Act of 1982, Pub. L. No. 97–290, § 402 96 Stat. 1246.]

Section 7. The word "person," or "persons," wherever used in sections 1 to 7 of this title shall be deemed to include corporations and associations existing under or authorized by the laws of either the United States, the laws of any of the Territories, the laws of any State, or the laws of any foreign country.

[15 U.S.C. § 7.]

Clayton Act

Section 1. (a) "Antitrust laws," as used herein, includes the Act entitled "An Act to protect trade and commerce against unlawful restraints and monopolies," approved July second, eighteen hundred and ninety; sections seventy-three to seventy-seven, inclusive, of an Act entitled "An Act to reduce taxation, to provide revenue for the Government, and for other purposes," of August twenty-seventh, eighteen hundred and ninety-four; an Act entitled "An Act to amend sections seventy-three and seventy-six of the Act of August twenty-seventh, eighteen hundred and ninety-four, entitled 'An Act to reduce taxation, to provide revenue for the Government, and for other purposes,'" approved February twelfth, nineteen hundred and thirteen; and also this Act.

"Commerce," as used herein, means trade or commerce among the several States and with foreign nation, or between the District of Columbia or any Territory of the United States and any State, Territory, or foreign nation, or between any insular possessions or other places under the jurisdiction of the United States, or between any such possession or place and any State or Territory of the United States or the District of Columbia or any foreign nation, or within the District of Columbia or any Territory or any insular possession or other place under the jurisdiction of the United States; *Provided*, That nothing in this Act contained shall apply to the Philippine Islands.

The word "person" or "persons" wherever used in this Act shall be deemed to include corporations and associations existing under or authorized by the laws of either the United States, the laws of any of the Territories, the laws of any State, or the laws of any foreign country.

(b) This Act may be cited as the "Clayton Act".

[15 U.S.C. § 12.]

Section 2.

[Amended by the Robinson-Patman Act, reprinted *infra*.]

Section 3. It shall be unlawful for any person engaged in commerce, in the course of such commerce, to lease or make a sale or contract for sale of goods, wares, merchandise, machinery, supplies, or other commodities, whether patented or unpatented, for use, consumption, or resale within the United States or any Territory thereof or the District of Columbia or any insular possession or other place under the jurisdiction of the United States, or fix a price charged therefor, or discount from, or rebate upon, such price, on the condition, agreement, or understanding that the lessee or purchaser thereof shall not use or deal in the goods, wares, merchandise, machinery, supplies, or other commodities of a competitor or competitors of the lessor or seller, where the effect of such lease, sale, or contract for sale or such condition, agreement, or understanding may be to substantially lessen competition or tend to create a monopoly in any line of commerce.

[15 U.S.C. § 14.]

Section 4. (a) Except as provided in subsection (b), any person who shall be injured in his business or property by reason of anything forbidden in the antitrust laws may sue therefor in any district court of the United States in the district in which the defendant resides or is found or has an agent, without respect to the amount in controversy, and shall recover threefold the damages by him sustained, and the cost of suit, including a reasonable attorney's fee. The court may award under this section, pursuant to a motion by such person promptly made, simple interest on actual damages for the period beginning on the date of service of such person's pleading setting forth a claim under the antitrust laws and ending on the date of judgment, or for any shorter period therein, if the court finds that the award of such interest for such period is just in the circumstances. In determining whether an award of interest under this section for any period is just in the circumstances, the court shall consider only—

(1) whether such person or the opposing party, or either party's representative, made motions or asserted claims or defenses so lacking in merit as to show that such party or representative acted intentionally for delay, or otherwise acted in bad faith;

(2) whether, in the course of the action involved, such person or the opposing party, or either party's representative, violated any applicable rule, status, or court order providing for sanctions for dilatory behavior or otherwise providing for expeditious proceedings; and

(3) whether such person or the opposing party, or either party's representative, engaged in conduct primarily for the purpose of delaying the litigation or increasing the cost thereof.

(b) (1) Except as provided in paragraph (2), any person who is a foreign state may not recover under subsection (a) an amount in excess of the actual damages sustained by it and the cost of suit, including a reasonable attorney's fee

(2) Paragraph (1) shall not apply to a foreign state if—

(A) such foreign state would be denied, under section 1605(a)(2) of title 28 of the United States Code, immunity in a case in which the action is based upon a commercial activity, or an act, that is the subject matter of its claim under this section;

(B) such foreign state waives all defenses based upon or arising out of its status as a foreign state, to any claims brought against it in the same action;

(C) such foreign state engages primarily in commercial activities; and

(D) such foreign state does not function, with respect to the commercial activity, or the act, that is the subject matter of its claim under this section as a procurement entity for itself or for another foreign state.

(c) For purposes of this section—

(1) the term "commercial activity" shall have the meaning given it in section 1603(d) of title 28, United States Code, and

(2) the term "foreign state" shall have the meaning given it in section 1603(a) of title 28, United States Code.

[15 U.S.C. § 15.]

Section 4A. Whenever the United States is hereafter injured in its business or property by reason of anything forbidden in the antitrust laws it may sue therefor in the United States district court for the district in which the defendant resides or is found or has an agent, without respect to the amount in controversy, and shall recover threefold the damages by it sustained and the cost of suit. The court may award under this section, pursuant to a motion by the United States promptly made, simple interest on actual damages for the period beginning on the date of service of the pleading of the United States setting forth a claim under the antitrust laws and ending on the date of judgment, or for any shorter period therein, if the court finds that the award of such interest for such period is just in the circumstances. In determining whether an award of interest under this section for any period is just in the circumstances, the court shall consider only—

(1) whether the United States or the opposing party, or either party's representative, made motions or asserted claims or defenses so lacking in merit as to show that such party or representative acted intentionally for delay or otherwise acted in bad faith;

(2) whether, in the course of the action involved, the United States or the opposing party, or either party's representatives, violated any applicable rule, statute, or court order providing for sanctions for dilatory behavior or otherwise providing for expeditious proceedings;

(3) whether the United States or the opposing party, or either party's representative, engaged in conduct primarily for the purpose of delaying the litigation or increasing the cost thereof; and

(4) whether the award of such interest is necessary to compensate the United States adequately for the injury sustained by the United States.

[15 U.S.C. § 15a.]

Section 4B. Any action to enforce any cause of action under sections 15, 15a, or 15c of this title shall be forever barred unless commenced within four years after the cause of action accrued. No cause of action barred under existing law on the effective date of this Act shall be revived by this Act.

[15 U.S.C. § 15b.]

Section 4C. (a) (1) Any attorney general of a State may bring a civil action in the name of such State, as parens patriae on behalf of natural persons residing in such State, in any district court of the United States having jurisdiction of the defendant, to secure monetary relief as provided in this section for injury sustained by such natural persons to their property by reason of any violation of sections 1 to 7 of this title. The court shall exclude from the amount of monetary relief awarded in such action any amount of monetary relief (A) which duplicates amounts which have been awarded for the same injury, or (B) which is properly allocable to (i) natural persons who have excluded their claims pursuant to subsection (b)(2) of this section, and (ii) any business entity.

(2) The court shall award the State as monetary relief threefold the total damage sustained as described in paragraph (1) of this subsection, and the cost of suit, including a reasonable attorney's fee. The court may award under this paragraph, pursuant to a motion by such State promptly made, simple interest on the total damage for the period beginning on the date of service of such State's pleading setting forth a claim under the antitrust laws and ending on the date of judgment, or for any shorter period therein, if the court finds that the award of such interest for such period is just in the circumstances. In determining whether an award of interest under this paragraph for any period is just in the circumstances, the court shall consider only—

(A) whether such State or the opposing party, or either party's representative, made motions or asserted claims or defenses so lacking in merit as to show that such party or representative acted intentionally for delay or otherwise acted in bad faith;

(B) whether, in the course of the action involved, such State or the opposing party, or either party's representative, violated any applicable rule, statute, or court order providing for sanctions for dilatory behavior or otherwise providing for expeditious proceedings; and

(C) whether such State or the opposing party, or either party's representative, engaged in conduct primarily for the purpose of delaying the litigation or increasing the cost thereof.

(b) (1) In any action brought under subsection (a)(1) of this section, the State attorney general shall, at such times, in such manner, and with such content as the court may direct, cause notice thereof to be given by publication. If the court finds that notice given solely by publication would deny due process of law to any person or persons, the court may direct further notice to such person or persons according to the circumstances of the case.

(2) Any person on whose behalf an action is brought under subsection (a)(1) of this section may elect to exclude from adjudication the portion of the State claim for monetary relief attributable to him by filing notice of such election with the court within such time as specified in the notice given pursuant to paragraph (1) of this subsection.

(3) The final judgment in an action under subsection (a)(1) of this section shall be res judicata as to any claim under section 15 of this title by any person on behalf of whom such action was brought and who fails to give such notice within the period specified in the notice given pursuant to paragraph (1) of this subsection.

(c) An action under subsection (a)(1) of this section shall not be dismissed or compromised without the approval of the court, and notice of any proposed dismissal or compromise shall be given in such manner as the court directs.

(d) In any action under subsection (a) of this section—

(1) the amount of the plaintiffs' attorney's fee, if any, shall be determined by the court; and

(2) the court may, in its discretion, award a reasonable attorney's fee to a prevailing defendant upon a finding that the State attorney general has acted in bad faith, vexatiously, wantonly, or for oppressive reasons.

[15 U.S.C. § 15c.]

Section 4D. In any action under section 15c(a)(1) of this title, in which there has been a determination that a defendant agreed to fix prices in violation of sections 1 to 7 of this title, damages may be proved and assessed in the aggregate by statistical or sampling methods, by the computation of illegal overcharges, or by such other reasonable system of estimating aggregate damages as the court in its discretion may permit without the necessity of separately proving the individual claim of, or amount of damage to, persons on whose behalf the suit was brought.

[15 U.S.C. § 15d.]

Section 4E. Monetary relief recovered in an action under section 15c(a)(1) of this title shall—

(1) be distributed in such manner as the district court in its discretion may authorize; or

(2) be deemed a civil penalty by the court and deposited with the State as general revenues;

subject in either case to the requirement that any distribution procedure adopted afford each person a reasonable opportunity to secure his appropriate portion of the net monetary relief.

[15 U.S.C. § 15e.]

Section 4F.

(a) Whenever the Attorney General of the United States has brought an action under the antitrust laws, and he has reason to believe that any State attorney general would be entitled to bring an action under this Act based substantially on the same alleged violation of the antitrust laws, he shall promptly give written notification thereof to such State attorney general.

(b) To assist a State attorney general in evaluating the notice or in bringing any action under this Act, the Attorney General of the United States shall, upon request by such State attorney general, make available to him, to the extent permitted by law, any investigative files or other materials which are or may be relevant or material to the actual or potential cause of action under this Act.

[15 U.S.C. § 15f.]

Section 4G. For the purposes of sections 15c, 15d, 15e, and 15f of this title:

(1) The term "State attorney general" means the chief legal officer of a State, or any other person authorized by State law to bring actions under section 15c of this title, and includes the Corporation Counsel of the District of Columbia, except that such term does not include any person employed or retained on—

(A) a contingency fee based on a percentage of the monetary relief awarded under this section; or

(B) any other contingency fee basis, unless the amount of the award of a reasonable attorney's fee to a prevailing plaintiff is determined by the court under section 15c(d)(1) of this title.

(2) The term "State" means a State, the District of Columbia, the Commonwealth of Puerto Rico, and any other territory or possession of the United States.

(3) The term "natural persons" does not include proprietorships or partnerships.

[15 U.S.C. § 15g.]

Section 4H. Sections 15c, 15d, 15e, 15f, and 15g of this title shall apply in any State, unless such State provides by law for its nonapplicability in such State.

[15 U.S.C. § 15h.]

Section 5. (a) A final judgment or decree heretofore or hereafter rendered in any civil or criminal proceeding brought by or on behalf of the United States under the antitrust laws to the effect that a defendant has violated said laws shall be prima facie evidence against such defendant in any action or proceeding brought by any other party against such defendant under said laws as to all matters respecting which said judgment or decree would be an estoppel as between the parties thereto: *Provided*, That this section shall not apply to consent judgments or decrees entered before any testimony has been taken. Nothing contained in this section shall be construed to impose any limitation on the application of collateral estoppel, except that, in any action or proceeding brought under the antitrust laws, collateral estoppel effect shall not be given to any finding made by the Federal Trade Commission under the antitrust laws or under section 45 of this title which could give rise to a claim for relief under the antitrust laws.

[15 U.S.C. § 16(a).]

Section 6. The labor of a human being is not a commodity or article of commerce. Nothing contained in the antitrust laws shall be construed to forbid the existence and operation of labor, agricultural, or horticultural organizations, instituted for the purposes of mutual help, and having capital stock or conducted for profit, or to forbid or restrain individual members of such organizations from lawfully carrying out the legitimate objects thereof; nor shall such organizations, or the members thereof, be held or construed to be illegal combinations or conspiracies in restraint of trade, under the antitrust laws.

[15 U.S.C. § 17.]

Section 7. No person engaged in commerce or in any activity affecting commerce shall acquire, directly or indirectly, the whole or any part of the stock or other share capital and no person subject to the jurisdiction of the Federal Trade Commission shall acquire the whole or any part of the assets of another person engaged also in commerce or in any activity affecting commerce, where in any line of commerce or in any activity affecting commerce in any section of the country, the effect of such acquisition may be substantially to lessen competition, or to tend to create a monopoly.

No person shall acquire, directly or indirectly, the whole or any part of the stock or other share capital and no person subject to the jurisdiction of the Federal Trade Commission shall acquire the whole or any part of the assets of one or more persons engaged in commerce or in any activity affecting commerce, where in any line of commerce or in any activity affecting commerce in any section of the country, the effect of such acquisition, of such stocks or assets, or of the use of such stock by the voting or granting of proxies or otherwise, may be substantially to lessen competition, or to tend to create a monopoly.

This section shall not apply to persons purchasing such stock solely for investment and not using the same by voting or otherwise to bring about, or in attempting to bring about, the substantial lessening of competition. Nor shall anything contained in this section prevent a corporation engaged in commerce or in any activity affecting commerce from causing the formation of subsidiary corporations for the actual carrying on of their immediate lawful business, or the natural and legitimate branches or extensions thereof, or from owning and holding all or a part of the stock of such subsidiary corporations, when the effect of such formation is not to substantially lessen competition.

Nor shall anything herein contained be construed to prohibit any common carrier subject to the laws to regulate commerce from aiding in the construction of branches or short lines so located so as to become feeders to the main line of the company so aiding in such construction or from acquiring or owning all or any part of the stock of such branch lines, nor to prevent any such common carrier from acquiring and owning all or any part of the stock of a branch or short line constructed by an independent company where there is no substantial competition between the company owning the branch line so constructed and the company owning the main line acquiring the property or an interest therein, nor to prevent such common carrier from extending any of its lines through the medium of the acquisition of stock or otherwise of any other common carrier where there is no substantial competition between the company whose stock, property, or an interest therein is so acquired.

Nothing contained in this section shall be held to affect or impair any right heretofore legally acquired: *Provided*, That nothing in this section shall be held or construed to authorize or make lawful anything heretofore prohibited or made illegal by the antitrust laws, nor to exempt any person from the penal provisions thereof or the civil remedies therein provided.

Nothing contained in this section shall apply to transactions duly consummated pursuant to authority given by the Secretary of Transportation, Federal Power Commission, Surface Transportation Board, the Securities and Exchange Commission in the exercise of its jurisdiction under section 79j of this title, the United States Maritime Commission, or the Secretary of Agriculture under any statutory provision vesting such power in such Commission, Board, or Secretary.

[15 U.S.C. § 18.]

Section 7A. (a) Except as exempted pursuant to subsection (c) of this section, no person shall acquire, directly or indirectly, any voting securities or assets of any other person, unless both persons (or in the case of a tender offer, the acquiring person) file notification pursuant to rules under subsection (d)(1) of this section and the waiting period described in subsection (b)(1) of this section has expired, if—

(1) the acquiring person, or the person whose voting securities or assets are being acquired, is engaged in commerce or in any activity affecting commerce;

(2) (A) any voting securities or assets of a person engaged in manufacturing which has annual net sales or total assets of $10,000,000 or more are being acquired by any person which has total assets or annual net sales of $100,000,000 or more;

(B) any voting securities or assets of a person not engaged in manufacturing which has total assets of $10,000,000 or more are being acquired by any person which has total assets or annual net sales of $100,000,000 or more; or

(C) any voting securities or assets of a person with annual net sales or total assets of $100,000,000 or more are being acquired by any person with total assets or annual net sales of $10,000,000 or more; and

(3) as a result of such acquisition, the acquiring person would hold—

(A) 15 per centum or more of the voting securities or assets of the acquired person, or

(B) an aggregate total amount of the voting securities and assets of the acquired person in excess of $15,000,000.

(b) (1) The waiting period required under subsection (a) of this section shall—

(A) begin on the date of the receipt by the Federal Trade Commission and the Assistant Attorney General in charge of the Antitrust Division of the Department of Justice (hereinafter referred to in this section as the "Assistant Attorney General") of—

(i) the completed notification required under subsection (a) of this section, or

(ii) if such notification is not completed, the notification to the extent completed and a statement of the reasons for such noncompliance, from both persons, or, in the case of a tender offer, the acquiring person; and

(B) end of the thirtieth day after the date of such receipt (or in the case of a cash tender offer, the fifteenth day), or on such later date as may be set under subsection (e)(2) or (g)(2) of this section.

(2) The Federal Trade Commission and the Assistant Attorney General may, in individual cases, terminate the waiting period specified in paragraph (1) and allow any person to proceed with any acquisition subject to this section, and promptly shall cause to be published in the Federal Register a notice that neither intends to take any action within such period with respect to such acquisition.

(3) As used in this section—

(A) The term "voting securities" means any securities which at present or upon conversion entitle the owner or holder thereof to vote for the election of directors of the issuer or, with respect to unincorporated issuers, persons exercising similar functions.

(B) The amount or percentage of voting securities or assets of a person which are acquired or held by another person shall be determined by aggregating the amount or percentage of such voting securities or assets held or acquired by such other person and each affiliate thereof.

(c) The following classes of transactions are exempt from the requirements of this section—

(1) acquisitions of goods or realty transferred in the ordinary course of business;

(2) acquisitions of bonds, mortgages, deeds of trust, or other obligations which are not voting securities;

(3) acquisitions of voting securities of an issuer at least 50 per centum of the voting securities of which are owned by the acquiring person prior to such acquisition;

(4) transfers to or from a Federal agency or a State or political subdivision thereof;

(5) transactions specifically exempted from the antitrust laws by Federal statute;

(6) transactions specifically exempted from the antitrust laws by Federal statute if approved by a Federal agency, if copies of all information and documentary material filed with such agency are contemporaneously filed with the Federal Trade Commission and the Assistant Attorney General;

(7) transactions which require agency approval under section 1467a(e) of Title 12, section 1828(c) of Title 12, or section 1842 of Title 12;

(8) transactions which require agency approval under section 1843 of title 12 or section 1464 of title 12, if copies of all information and documentary material filed with any such agency are contemporaneously filed with the Federal Trade Commission and the Assistant Attorney General at least 30 days prior to consummation of the proposed transaction;

(9) acquisitions, solely for the purpose of investment, of voting securities, if, as a result of such acquisition, the securities acquired or held do not exceed 10 per centum of the outstanding voting securities of the issuer;

(10) acquisitions of voting securities, if, as a result of such acquisition, the voting securities acquired do not increase, directly or indirectly, the acquiring person's per centum share of outstanding voting securities of the issuer;

(11) acquisitions, solely for the purpose of investment, by any bank, banking association, trust company, investment company, or insurance company, of (A) voting securities pursuant to a plan of reorganization or dissolution; or (B) assets in the ordinary course of its business; and

(12) such other acquisitions, transfers or transactions, as may be exempted under subsection (d)(2)(B) of this section.

(d) The Federal Trade Commission, with the concurrence of the Assistant Attorney General and by rule in accordance with section 553 of title 5, consistent with the purposes of this section—

(1) shall require that the notification required under subsection (a) of this section be in such form and contain such documentary material and information relevant to a proposed acquisition as is necessary and appropriate to enable the Federal Trade Commission and the Assistant Attorney General to determine whether such acquisition may, if consummated, violate the antitrust laws; and

(2) may—

(A) define the terms used in this section;

(B) exempt, from the requirements of this section, classes of persons, acquisitions, transfers, or transactions which are not likely to violate the antitrust laws; and

(C) prescribe such other rules as may be necessary and appropriate to carry out the purposes of this section.

(e) (1) The Federal Trade Commission or the Assistant Attorney General may, prior to the expiration of the 30-day waiting period (or in the case of a cash tender offer, the 15-day waiting period) specified in subsection (b)(1) of this section, require the submission of additional information or documentary material relevant to the proposed acquisition, from a person required to file notification with respect to such acquisition under subsection (a) of this section prior to the expiration of the waiting period specified in subsection (b)(1) of this section, or from any officer, director, partner, agent, or employee of such person.

(2) The Federal Trade Commission or the Assistant Attorney General, in its or his discretion, may extend the 30-day waiting period (or in the case of a cash tender offer, the 15-day waiting period) specified in subsection (b)(1) of this section for an additional period of not more than 20 days (or in the case of a cash tender offer, 10 days) after the date on which the Federal Trade Commission or the Assistant Attorney General, as the case may be, receives from any person to whom a request is made under paragraph (1), or in the case of tender offers, the acquiring person, (A) all the information and documentary material required to be submitted pursuant to such a request, or (B) if such request is not fully complied with, the information and documentary material submitted and a statement of the reasons for such noncompliance. Such additional period may be further extended only by the United States district court, upon an application by the Federal Trade Commission or the Assistant Attorney General pursuant to subsection (g)(2) of this section.

(f) If a proceeding is instituted or an action is filed by the Federal Trade Commission, alleging that a proposed acquisition violates section 18 of this title, or section 45 of this title, or an action is filed by the United States, alleging that a proposed acquisition violates such section 18 of this title, or section 1 or 2 of this title, and the Federal Trade Commission or the Assistant Attorney General (1) files a motion for a preliminary injunction against consummation of such acquisition pendente lite, and (2) certifies to the United States district court for the judicial district within which the respondent resides or carries on business, or in which the action is brought, that it or he believes that the public interest requires relief pendente lite pursuant to this subsection, then upon the filing of such motion and certification, the chief judge of such district court shall immediately notify the chief judge of the United States court of appeals for the circuit in which such district court is located, who shall designate a United States district judge to whom such action shall be assigned for all purposes.

(g) (1) Any person, or any officer, director, or partner thereof, who fails to comply with any provision of this section shall be liable to the United States for a civil penalty of not more than $10,000 for each day during which such person is in violation of this section. Such penalty may be recovered in a civil action brought by the United States.

[15 U.S.C. § 18a(a)–(g)(1).]

Section 8. (a) (1) No person shall, at the same time, serve as a director or officer in any two corporations (other than banks, banking associations, and trust companies) that are—

(A) engaged in whole or in part in commerce; and

(B) by virtue of their business and location of operation, competitors, so that the elimination of competition by agreement between them would constitute a violation of any of the antitrust laws;

if each of the corporations has capital, surplus, and undivided profits aggregating more than $10,000,000 as adjusted pursuant to paragraph (5) of this subsection.

(2) Notwithstanding the provisions of paragraph (1), simultaneous service as a director or officer in any two corporations shall not be prohibited by this section if—

(A) the competitive sales of either corporation are less than $1,000,000, as adjusted pursuant to paragraph (5) of this subsection;

(B) the competitive sales of either corporation are less than 2 per centum of that corporation's total sales; or

(C) the competitive sales of each corporation are less than 4 per centum of that corporation's total sales.

For purposes of this paragraph, "competitive sales" means the gross revenues for all products and services sold by one corporation in competition with the other, determined on the basis of annual gross revenues for such products and services in that corporation's last completed fiscal year. For the purposes of this paragraph, "total sales" means the gross revenues for all products and services sold by one corporation over that corporation's last completed fiscal year.

(3) The eligibility of a director or officer under the provisions of paragraph (1) shall be determined by the capital, surplus, and undivided profits, exclusive of dividends declared but not paid to stockholders, of each corporation at the end of that corporation's last completed fiscal year.

(4) For purposes of this section, the term "officer" means an officer elected or chosen by the Board of Directors.

(5) For each fiscal year commencing after September 30, 1990, the $10,000,000 and $1,000,000 thresholds in this subsection shall be increased (or decreased) as of October 1 each year by an amount equal to the percentage increase (or decrease) in the gross national product, as determined by the Department of Commerce or its successor, for the year then ended over the level so established for the year ending September 30, 1989. As soon as practicable, but not later than January 31 of each year, the Federal Trade Commission shall publish the adjusted amounts required by this paragraph.

(b) When any person elected or chosen as a director or officer of any corporation subject to the provisions hereof is eligible at the time of his election or selection to act for such corporation in such capacity, his eligibility to act in such capacity shall not be affected by any of the provisions hereof by reason of any change in the capital, surplus, and undivided profits, or affairs of such corporation from whatever cause, until the expiration of one year from the date on which the event causing ineligibility occurred.

[15 U.S.C. § 19.]

Section 12. Any suit, action, or proceeding under the antitrust laws against a corporation may be brought not only in the judicial district whereof it is an inhabitant, but also in any district wherein it may be found or transacts business; and all process in such cases may be served in the district of which it is an inhabitant, or wherever it may be found.

[15 U.S.C. § 22.]

Section 13. In any suit, action, or proceeding brought by or on behalf of the United States subpoenas for witnesses who are required to attend a court of the United States in any judicial district in any case, civil or criminal, arising under the antitrust laws may run into any other district: *Provided*, That in civil cases no writ of subpoena shall issue for witnesses living out of the district in which the court is held at a greater distance than one hundred miles from the place of holding the same without the permission of the trial court being first had upon proper application and cause shown.

[15 U.S.C. § 23.]

Section 14. Whenever a corporation shall violate any of the penal provisions of the antitrust laws, such violation shall be deemed to be also that of the individual directors, officers, or agents of such corporation who shall have authorized, ordered, or done any of the acts constituting in whole or in part such violation, and such violation shall be deemed a misdemeanor, and upon conviction therefor of any such director, officer, or agent he shall be punished by a fine of not exceeding $5,000 or by imprisonment for not exceeding one year, or by both, in the discretion of the court.

[15 U.S.C. § 24.]

Section 15. The several district courts of the United States are invested with jurisdiction to prevent and restrain violations of this Act, and it shall be the duty of the several United States attorneys, in their respective districts, under the direction of the Attorney General, to institute proceedings in equity to prevent and restrain such violations. Such proceedings may be by way of petition setting forth the case and praying that such violation shall be enjoined or otherwise prohibited. When the parties complained of shall have been duly notified of such petition, the court shall proceed, as soon as may be, to the hearing and determination of the case; and pending such petition, and before final decree, the court may at any time make such temporary restraining order or prohibition as shall be deemed just in the premises. Whenever it shall appear to the court before which any such proceeding may be pending that the ends of justice require that other parties should be brought before the court, the court may cause them to be summoned whether they reside in the district in which the court is held or not, and subpoenas to that end may be served in any district by the marshal thereof.

[15 U.S.C. § 25.]

Section 16. Any person, firm, corporation, or association shall be entitled to sue for and have injunctive relief, in any court of the United States having jurisdiction over the parties, against threatened loss or damage by a violation of the antitrust laws, including sections 13, 14, 18, and 19 of this title, when and under the same conditions and principles as injunctive relief against threatened conduct that will cause loss or damage is granted by courts of equity, under the rules governing such proceedings, and upon the execution of proper bond against damages for an injunction improvidently granted and a showing that the danger of irreparable loss or damage is immediate, a preliminary injunction may issue: *Provided*, That nothing herein contained shall be construed to entitle any person, firm, corporation, or association, except the United States, to bring suit for injunctive relief against any common carrier subject to the jurisdiction of the Surface Transportation Board under subtitle IV of Title 49. In any action under this section in which the plaintiff substantially prevails, the court shall award the cost of suit, including a reasonable attorney's fee, to such plaintiff.

[15 U.S.C. § 26.]

Robinson-Patman Act

Section 1. (a) It shall be unlawful for any person engaged in commerce, in the course of such commerce, either directly or indirectly, to discriminate in price between different purchasers of commodities of like grade and quality, where either or any of the purchases involved in such discrimination are in commerce, where such commodities are sold for use, consumption, or resale within the United States or any Territory thereof or the District of Columbia or any insular possession or other place under the jurisdiction of the United States, and where the effect of such discrimination may be substantially to lessen competition or tend to create a monopoly in any line of commerce, or to injure, destroy, or prevent competition with any person who either grants or knowingly receives the benefit of such discrimination, or with customers of either of them: *Provided,* That nothing herein contained shall prevent differentials which make only due allowance for differences in the cost of manufacture, sale, or delivery resulting from the differing methods or quantities in which such commodities are to such purchasers sold or delivered: *Provided, however,* That the Federal Trade Commission may, after due investigation and hearing to all interested parties, fix and establish quantity limits, and revise the same as it finds necessary, as to particular commodities or classes of commodities, where it finds that available purchasers in greater quantities are so few as to render differentials on account thereof unjustly discriminatory or promotive of monopoly in any line of commerce; and the foregoing shall then not be construed to permit differentials based on differences in quantities greater than those so fixed and established: *And provided further,* That nothing herein contained shall prevent persons engaged in selling goods, wares, or merchandise in commerce from selecting their own customers in bona fide transactions and not in restraint of trade: *And provided further,* That nothing herein contained shall prevent price changes from time to time where in response to changing conditions affecting the market for or the marketability of the goods concerned, such as but not limited to actual or imminent deterioration of perishable goods, obsolescence of seasonal goods, distress sales under court process, or sales in good faith in discontinuance of business in the goods concerned.

(b) Upon proof being made, at any hearing on a complaint under this section, that there has been discrimination in price or services or facilities furnished, the burden of rebutting the prima-facie case thus made by showing justification shall be upon the person charged with a violation of this section, and unless justification shall be affirmatively shown, the Commission is authorized to issue an order terminating the discrimination: *Provided, however,* That nothing herein contained shall prevent a seller rebutting the prima-facie case thus made by showing that his lower price or the furnishing of services or facilities to any purchaser or purchasers was made in good faith to meet an equally low price of a competitor, or the services or facilities furnished by a competitor.

(c) It shall be unlawful for any person engaged in commerce, in the course of such commerce, to pay or grant, or to receive or accept, anything of value as a commission, brokerage, or other compensation, or any allowance or discount in lieu thereof, except for services rendered in connection with the sale or purchase of goods, wares, or merchandise, either to the other party to such transaction or to an agent, representative, or other intermediary therein where such intermediary is acting in fact for or in behalf, or is subject to the direct or indirect control, of any party to such transaction other than the person by whom such compensation is so granted or paid.

(d) It shall be unlawful for any person engaged in commerce to pay or contact for the payment of anything of value to or for the benefit of a customer of such person in the course of such commerce as compensation or in consideration for any services or facilities furnished by or through such customer in connection with the processing, handling, sale, or offering for sale of any products or commodities manufactured, sold, or offered for sale by such person, unless such payment or consideration is available on proportionally equal terms to all other customers competing in the distribution of such products or commodities.

(e) It shall be unlawful for any person to discriminate in favor of one purchaser against another purchaser or purchasers of a commodity bought for resale, with or without processing, by contracting to furnish or furnishing, or by contributing to the furnishing of, any services or facilities connected with the processing, handling, sale, or offering for sale of such commodity so purchased upon terms not accorded to all purchasers on proportionally equal terms.

(f) It shall be unlawful for any person engaged in commerce, in the course of such commerce, knowingly to induce or receive a discrimination in price which is prohibited by this section.

[15 U.S.C. § 13.]

Section 2. [Rights of action prior to June 19, 1936 (15 U.S.C. § 21a); not reproduced.]

Section 3. It shall be unlawful for any person engaged in commerce, in the course of such commerce, to be a party to, or assist in any transaction of sale, or contract to sell, which discriminates to his knowledge against competitors of the purchaser, in that, any discount, rebate, allowance, or advertising service charge is granted to the purchaser over and above any discount, rebate, allowance, or advertising service charge available at the time of such transaction to said competitors in respect of a sale of goods of like grade, quality, and quantity; to sell, or contract to sell, goods in any part of the United States at prices lower than those exacted by said person elsewhere in the United States for the purpose of destroying competition, or eliminating a competitor in such part of the United States; or, to sell, or contract to sell, goods at unreasonably low prices for the purpose of destroying competition or eliminating a competitor.

Any person violating any of the provisions of this section shall, upon conviction thereof, be fined not more than $5,000 or imprisoned not more than one year, or both.

[15 U.S.C. § 13a.]

Section 4. Nothing in this Act shall prevent a cooperative association from returning to its members, producers, or consumers the whole, or any part of, the net earnings or surplus resulting from its trading operations, in proportion to their purchases or sales from, to, or through the association.

[15 U.S.C. § 13b.]

Federal Trade Commission Act

§§ 1, 5

Section 1. A commission is created and established, to be known as the Federal Trade Commission (hereinafter referred to as the Commission), which shall be composed of five Commissioners, who shall be appointed by the President, by and with the advice and consent of the Senate. Not more than three of the Commissioners shall be members of the same political party. The first Commissioners appointed shall continue in office for terms of three, four, five, six, and seven years, respectively, from September 26, 1914, the term of each to be designated by the President, but their successors shall be appointed for terms of seven years, except that any person chosen to fill a vacancy shall be appointed only for the unexpired term of the Commissioner whom he shall succeed: *Provided, however,* That upon the expiration of his term of office a Commissioner shall continue to serve until his successor shall have been appointed and shall have qualified. The President shall choose a chairman from the Commission's membership. No Commissioner shall engage in any other business, vocation, or employment. Any Commissioner may be removed by the President for inefficiency, neglect of duty, or malfeasance in office. A vacancy in the Commission shall not impair the right of the remaining Commissioners to exercise all the powers of the Commission.

The Commission shall have an official seal, which shall be judicially noticed.

[15 U.S.C. § 41.]

[15 U.S.C. § 13b.]

Section 5. (a) (1) Unfair methods of competition in or affecting commerce, and unfair or deceptive acts or practices in or affecting commerce, are hereby declared unlawful.

(2) The Commission is empowered and directed to prevent persons, partnerships, or corporations, except banks, savings and loan institutions described in section 18(f)(3) of this title, Federal credit unions described in section 18(f)(4) of this title, common carriers subject to the Acts to regulate commerce, air carriers and foreign air carriers subject to part A of subtitle VII of Title 49, and persons, partnerships, or corporations insofar as they are subject to the Packers and Stockyards Act, 1921, as amended [7 U.S.C. § 181 *et. seq.*], except as provided in section 406(b) of said Act [7 U.S.C. § 227(b)], from using unfair methods of competition in or affecting commerce and unfair or deceptive acts or practices in or affecting commerce.

(3) This subsection shall not apply to unfair methods of competition involving commerce with foreign nations (other than import commerce) unless—

(A) such methods of competition have a direct, substantial, and reasonably foreseeable effect—

(i) on commerce which is not commerce with foreign nations, or on import commerce with foreign nations; or

(ii) on export commerce with foreign nations, of a person engaged in such commerce in the United States; and

(B) such effect gives rise to a claim under the provisions of this subsection, other than this paragraph.

If this subsection applies to such methods of competition only because of the operation of subparagraph (A)(ii), this subsection shall apply to such conduct only for injury to export business in the United States. [Added by Foreign Antitrust Improvements Act of 1982, Pub. L. No. 97–290, § 403.]

(b) Whenever the Commission shall have reason to believe that any such person, partnership, or corporation has been or is using any unfair method of competition or unfair or deceptive act or practice in or affecting commerce, and if it shall appear to the Commission that a proceeding by it in respect thereof would be to the interest of the public, it shall issue and serve upon such person, partnership, or corporation a complaint stating its charges in that respect and containing a notice of a hearing upon a day and at a place therein fixed at least thirty days after the service of said complaint. The person, partnership, or corporation so complained of shall have the right to appear at the place and time so fixed and show cause why an order should not be entered by the Commission requiring such person, partnership, or corporation to cease and desist from the violation of the law so charged in said complaint. Any person, partnership, or corporation may make application, and upon good cause shown may be allowed by the Commission to intervene and appear in said proceeding by counsel or in person. The testimony in any such proceeding shall be reduced to writing and filed in the office of the Commission. If upon such hearing the Commission shall be of the opinion that the method of competition or the act or practice in question is prohibited by this Act, it shall make a report in writing in which it shall state its findings as to the facts and shall issue and cause to be served on such person, partnership, or corporation an order requiring such person, partnership, or corporation to cease and desist from using such method of competition or such act or practice. Until the expiration of the time allowed for filing a petition for review, if no such petition has been duly filed within such time, or, if a petition for review has been filed within such time then until the record in the proceeding has been filed in a court of appeals of the United States, as hereinafter provided, the Commission may at any time, upon such notice and in such manner as it shall deem proper, modify or set aside, in whole or in part, any report or any order made or issued by it under this section. After the expiration of the time allowed for filing a petition for review, if no such petition has been duly filed within such time, the Commission may at any time, after notice and opportunity for hearing, reopen and alter, modify, or set aside, in whole or in part, any report or order made or issued by it under this section, whenever in the opinion of the Commission conditions of fact or of law have so changed as to require such action or if the public interest shall so require, except that (1) the said person, partnership, or corporation may, within sixty days after service upon him or it of said report or order entered after such a reopening, obtain a review thereof in the appropriate court of appeals of the United States, in the manner provided in subsection (c) of this section; and (2) in the case of an order, the Commission shall reopen any such order to consider whether such order (including any affirmative relief provision contained in such order) should be altered, modified, or set aside, in whole or in part, if the person, partnership, or corporation involved files a request with the Commission which makes a satisfactory showing that changed conditions of law or fact require such order to be altered, modified, or set aside, in whole or in part. The Commission shall determine whether to alter, modify, or set aside any order of the Commission in response to a request made by a person, partnership, or corporation under paragraph (2) not later than 120 days after the date of the filing of such request.

(c) Any person, partnership, or corporation required by an order of the Commission to cease and desist from using any method of competition or act or practice may obtain a review of such order in the court of appeals of the United States, within any circuit where the method of competition or the act or practice in question was used or where such person, partnership, or corporation resides or carries on business, by filing in the court, within sixty days from the date of the service of such order, a written petition praying that the order of the Commission be set aside. A copy of such petition shall be forthwith transmitted by the clerk of the court to the Commission, and thereupon the Commission shall file in the court the record in the proceeding, as provided in section 2112 of title 28, United States Code. Upon such filing of the petition the court shall have jurisdiction of the proceeding and of the question determined therein concurrently with the Commission until the filing of the record and shall have power to make and enter a decree affirming, modifying, or setting aside the order of the Commission, and enforcing the same to the extent that such order is affirmed and to issue such writs as are ancillary to its jurisdiction or are necessary in its judgment to prevent injury to the public or to competitors pendente lite. The findings of the Commission as to the facts, if supported by evidence, shall be conclusive. To the extent that the order of the Commission is affirmed, the court shall thereupon issue its own order commanding obedience to the terms of such order of the Commission. If either party shall apply to the court for leave to adduce additional evidence, and shall show to the satisfaction of the court that such additional evidence is material and that there were reasonable grounds for the failure to adduce such evidence in the proceeding before the Commission, the court may order such additional evidence to be taken before the Commission and to be adduced upon the hearing in such manner and upon such terms and conditions as to the court may seem proper. The Commission may modify its findings as to the facts, or make new findings, by reason of the additional evidence so taken, and it shall file such modified or new findings, which, if supported by evidence, shall be conclusive, and its recommendation, if any, for the modification or setting aside of its original order, with the return of such additional evidence. The judgment and decree of the court shall be final, except that the same shall be subject to review by the Supreme Court upon certiorari, as provided in section 1254 of Title 28, United States Code.

(d) Upon the filing of the record with it the jurisdiction of the court of appeals of the United States to affirm, enforce, modify, or set aside orders of the Commission shall be exclusive.

(e) No order of the Commission or judgment of court to enforce the same shall in anywise relieve or absolve any person, partnership, or corporation from any liability under the antitrust acts.

(f) Complaints, orders, and other processes of the Commission under this section may be served by anyone duly authorized by the Commission, either (a) by delivering a copy thereof to the person to be served, or to a member of the partnership to be served, or the president, secretary, or other executive officer or a director of the corporation to be served; or (b) by leaving a copy thereof at the residence or the principal office or place of business of such person, partnership, or corporation; or (c) by mailing a copy thereof by registered mail or by certified mail addressed to such person, partnership, or corporation at his or its residence or principal office or place of business. The verified return by the person so serving said complaint, order, or other process setting forth the manner of said service shall be proof of the same, and the return post office receipt for said complaint, order, or other process mailed by registered mail or by certified mail as aforesaid shall be proof of the service of the same.

(g) An order of the Commission to cease and desist shall become final—

(1) Upon the expiration of the time allowed for filing a petition for review, if no such petition has been duly filed within such time; but the Commission may thereafter modify or set aside its order to the extent provided in the last sentence of subsection (b) of this section.

(2) Except as to any order provision subject to paragraph (4), upon the sixtieth day after such order is served, if a petition for review has been duly filed; except that any such order may be stayed, in whole or in part and subject to such conditions as may be appropriate, by—

(A) the Commission;

(B) an appropriate court of appeals of the United States, if (i) a petition for review of such order is pending in such court, and (ii) an application for such a stay was previously submitted to the Commission and the Commission, within the 30-day period beginning on the date the application was received by the Commission, either denied the application or did not grant or deny the application; or

(C) the Supreme Court, if an applicable petition for certiorari is pending.

(3) For purposes of subsection (m)(1)(B) of this section and 57b(a)(2) of this title, if a petition for review of the order of the Commission has been filed—

(A) upon the expiration of the time allowed for filing a petition for certiorari, if the order of the Commission has been affirmed or the petition for review has been dismissed by the court of appeals and no petition for certiorari has been duly filed;

(B) upon the denial of a petition for certiorari, if the order of the Commission has been affirmed or the petition for review has been dismissed by the court of appeals; or

(C) upon the expiration of 30 days from the date of issuance of a mandate of the Supreme Court directing that the order of the Commission be affirmed or the petition for review be dismissed.

(4) In the case of an order provision requiring a person, partnership, or corporation to divest itself of stock, other share capital, or assets, if a petition for review of such order of the Commission has been filed—

(A) upon the expiration of the time allowed for filing a petition for certiorari, if the order of the Commission has been affirmed or the petition for review has been dismissed by the court of appeals and no petition for certiorari has been duly filed;

(B) upon the denial of a petition for certiorari, if the order of the Commission has been affirmed or the petition for review has been dismissed by the court of appeals; or

(C) upon the expiration of 30 days from the date of issuance of a mandate of the Supreme Court directing that the order of the Commission be affirmed or the petition for review be dismissed.

(h) If the Supreme Court directs that the order of the Commission be modified or set aside, the order of the Commission rendered in accordance with the mandate of the Supreme Court shall become final upon the expiration of thirty days from the time it was rendered, unless within such thirty days either party has instituted proceedings to have such order corrected to accord with the mandate, in which event the order of the Commission shall become final when so corrected.

(i) If the order of the Commission is modified or set aside by the court of appeals, and if (1) the time allowed for filing a petition for certiorari has expired and no such petition has been duly filed, or (2) the petition for certiorari has been denied, or (3) the decision of the court has been affirmed by the Supreme Court, then the order of the Commission rendered in accordance with the mandate of the court of appeals shall become final on the expiration of thirty days from the time such order of the Commission was rendered, unless within such thirty days either party has instituted proceedings to have such order corrected so that it will accord with the mandate, in which event the order of the Commission shall become final when so corrected.

(j) If the Supreme Court orders a rehearing; or if the case is remanded by the court of appeals to the Commission for a rehearing, and if (1) the time allowed for filing a petition for certiorari has expired, and no such petition has been duly filed, or (2) the petition for certiorari has been denied, or (3) the decision of the court has been affirmed by the Supreme Court, then the order of the Commission rendered upon such rehearing shall become final in the same manner as though no prior order of the Commission had been rendered.

(k) As used in this section the term "mandate," in case a mandate has been recalled prior to the expiration of thirty days from the date of issuance thereof, means the final mandate.

(l) Any person, partnership, or corporation who violates an order of the Commission after it has become final, and while such order is in effect, shall forfeit and pay to the United States a civil penalty of not more than $10,000 for each violation, which shall accrue to the United States and may be recovered in a civil action brought by the Attorney General of the United States. Each separate violation of such an order shall be a separate offense, except that in the case of a violation through continuing failure to obey or neglect to obey a final order of the Commission, each day of continuance of such failure or neglect shall be deemed a separate offense. In such actions, the United States district courts are empowered to grant mandatory injunctions and such other and further equitable relief as they deem appropriate in the enforcement of such final orders of the Commission.

(m) (1) (A) The Commission may commence a civil action to recover a civil penalty in a district court of the United States against any person, partnership, or corporation which violates any rule under this Act respecting unfair or deceptive acts or practices (other than an interpretive rule or a rule violation of which the Commission has provided is not an unfair or deceptive act or practice in violation of subsection (a)(1)) with actual knowledge fairly implied on the basis of objective circumstances that such act is unfair or deceptive and is prohibited by such rule. In such action, such person, partnership, or corporation shall be liable for a civil penalty of not more than $10,000 for each violation.

(B) If the Commission determines in a proceeding under subsection (b) of this section that any act or practice is unfair or deceptive, and issues a final cease and desist order, other than a consent order, with respect to such act or practice, then the Commission may commence a civil action to obtain a civil penalty in a district court of the United States against any person, partnership, or corporation which engages in such an act or practice—

(i) after such cease and desist order becomes final (whether or not such person, partnership, or corporation was subject to such cease and desist order), and

(ii) with actual knowledge that such act or practice is unfair or deceptive and is unlawful under subsection (a)(1) of this section.

In such action, such person, partnership, or corporation shall be liable for a civil penalty of not more than $10,000 for each violation.

(C) In the case of a violation through continuing failure to comply with a rule or with section 5(a)(1), each day of continuance of such failure shall be treated as a separate violation, for purposes of subparagraphs (A) and (B). In determining the amount of such civil penalty, the court shall take into account the degree of culpability, any history of prior such conduct, ability to pay, effect on ability to continue to do business, and such other matters as justice may require.

(2) If the cease and desist order establishing that the act or practice is unfair or deceptive was not issued against the defendant in a civil penalty action under paragraph (1)(B) the issues of fact in such action against such defendant shall be tried de novo. Upon request of any party to such an action against such defendant, the court shall also review the determination of law made by the Commission in the proceeding under subsection (b) of this section that the act or practice which was the subject of such proceeding constituted an unfair or deceptive act or practice in violation of subsection (a) of this section.

(3) The Commission may compromise or settle any action for a civil penalty if such compromise or settlement is accompanied by a public statement of its reasons and is approved by the court.

(n) The Commission shall have no authority under this section or section 18 of this act to declare unlawful an act or practice on the grounds that such act or practice is unfair unless the act or practice causes or is likely to cause substantial injury to consumers which is not reasonably avoidable by consumers themselves and not outweighed by countervailing benefits to consumers or competition. In determining whether an act or practice is unfair, the Commission may consider established public policies as evidence to be considered with all other evidence. Such public policy considerations may not serve as primary basis for such determination.

[15 U.S.C. § 45.]

Table of Cases

Index

[References are to sections.]